MW01196058

BUSINESS LAW FOR THE ENTREPRENEUR AND MANAGER

Fourth Edition

Frank J. Cavico
Bahaudin G. Mujtaba

ILEAD Academy, LLC
Davie, Florida. United States of America
www.ileadacademy.com

Frank J. Cavico and Bahaudin G. Mujtaba, 2020. *Business Law for the Entrepreneur and Manager, 4th Edition.*

Cover Photo Design by: Cagri Tanyar

ISBN-10: 1-936237-17-2

ISBN-13: 978-1-936237-17-3

Subject Code:
BUS010000: Business & Economics-Business Law
LAW000000: Law-General
LAW022000: Law-Corporate

Dedication

This book is dedicated to legal, ethical, moral, and socially and environmentally responsible entrepreneurs, managers, and leaders!

ACKNOWLEDGEMENTS

First, we would like to thank the following colleagues for their contributions and guidance in preparing this book:

1) A. George Petrie
2) Belay Seyoum
3) Cagri Tanyar
4) Daniel Dawes
5) Don Ariail
6) Don Valeri
7) Hatasakdi Na Pombejra
8) John Wayne Falbey
9) Joseph Durden
10) Josephine Sosa-Fey
11) Laura Yanez
12) Marissa Samuels
13) Miguel A. Orta
14) Miguel Valdez
15) Nicolas-Michel Polito
16) Nile M. Khanfar
17) Norman D. Glick
18) Shakila Faqeeri
19) Silvano Ferrari
20) Stephanie Ferrari
21) Stephen C. Muffler
22) Steven V. Cates
23) Thomas M. Tworoger
24) William Freeman

The authors in particular want to thank their Huizenga College colleagues for the able, thorough, and diligent editing of the revised edition.

Second, we would like to thank all those who have helped us get to this point.

Third, we thank you for reading this material. For suggestions and questions, you can contact us (cavico@nova.edu or mujtaba@nova.edu) at any time.

Frank and Bahaudin

TABLE OF CONTENTS

PREFACE to the 4th Edition

All entrepreneurs, managers, and their employees are impacted by law each day; and almost all human activity is affected by the law. In the business world, when contemplating a business transaction or decision, an entrepreneur or manager not only must consider the physical, financial, personnel, and managerial aspects, but also the legal ramifications. Moreover, as the business and entrepreneurial "world" is now a truly diverse workplace, an entrepreneur or manager must be cognizant of laws impacting his/her employees, suppliers, and customers. The main purpose of this book, therefore, is to introduce the reader to fundamental principles of the laws regulating business as well as their practical application in the United States. The first chapter begins by discussing law and the basic legal principles impacting entrepreneurs and managers; the last chapter concludes with some basic business laws that current and aspiring entrepreneurs and managers must become aware of and understand. The chapters in-between expand on other important legal concepts that will be beneficial to entrepreneurs and managers. The authors want the discerning reader to be conscious of the scope and complexity of laws affecting business. The authors accordingly intend to help the reader recognize legal situations in business as well as everyday life; and the authors especially want to impart an awareness of potential legal problems, and how to avoid them.

Have you ever wondered why some firms are "Incorporated or Inc.," some are "Limited Liability Company, or LLC," while others are "limited partnership" and so on? Do you know which is appropriate for an aspiring entrepreneur who wants to open his/her own business? Did you know that you can protect your business plan as a legally protected trade secret? Well, if you are not totally familiar with these terms and concepts, there is no need to worry. This book is designed to help you become familiar with such concepts so you can make appropriate decisions about your company's status. Entrepreneurs and managers deal with "laws of the land" every day, and consequently must be aware of its nuances and complexities in order to successfully and interdependently work with others in the community, industry, and country. Thus, entrepreneurs and managers should become aware of the fundamental aspects of the legal system so they avoid legal problems and can seek the help of experts when dealing with complex issues. *Business Law for the Entrepreneur and Manager,* now in this 4th edition, is designed to provide the foundational aspects of the "American" legal system, as practiced in the United States, for current and aspiring entrepreneurs and managers. By reading and becoming familiar with the various topics presented, you will be better prepared to more effectively deal with legal challenges.

The 4th edition of *Business Law for the Entrepreneur and Manager* introduces the reader to fundamental principles of the laws regulating business as well as their practical application in the United States. The various chapters cover such topics as the law and the basic legal principles impacting entrepreneurs and managers, the foundational business laws that entrepreneurs and managers in the United States must become aware of and understand, as well as other important legal topics such as constitutional law, administrative law, torts, products liability, crimes, contract law, sales and agency laws, commercial paper, various forms of business organizations, and debtors and creditors laws. The study of this legal material will be very beneficial to entrepreneurs, managers, and human resources professionals.

The material presented in this book is more comprehensively covered, with a global perspective, as well as more government regulations of business law, and managerial strategies, in our other book entitled *Legal Challenges for the Global Manager and Entrepreneur* (by Kendall-Hunt). Academicians, managers, and entrepreneurs who want a full and academic global coverage of legal challenges should find it very helpful. Requests for an examination copy of that book and its supplementary instructor's resources should be sent to Kendall-Hunt at the company's website. This book is designed to be used academically for foundational business law courses, as well as practically, as a guide and an enlightening learning tool that the hard-working and on-the-go manager or entrepreneur will find useful. This book covers some of the most important and foundational laws that aspiring entrepreneurs and managers must understand and obey. A student or manager in the U.S. will find the explication of U.S. laws very important, particularly the emphasis on the moral "gaps" in U.S. law. The book is neither a bulky legal tome nor merely a "popular" legal offering; but rather an attempt to cover the laws governing business with a substantive, understandable, and pragmatic approach.

This edition to this book seeks to make the reader more legally knowledgeable and astute. The book attempts to identify as many legal challenges as possible in establishing, operating, and managing a business in today's very competitive global business environment. The book recommends strategies and tactics to overcome these challenges and to achieve a successful business in a lawful and moral manner. Yet overcoming business law challenges is not the only goal of this book. The authors naturally want the reader to be able to more clearly foresee legal problems so as to avoid them; but the authors also want the reader to learn how to use the law and the legal system to more effectively establish, manage, and develop the business. Accordingly, an important objective of this edition of this book is to focus on "preventative law," that is, making the business person aware of the law, its applicability to business, and the legal consequences of business decision-making. The goal is to proactively avoid legal problems before they materialize, as opposed to the "trials and tribulations" (and "trials" perhaps literally) of reactively dealing with them when they occur. One major purpose of this book, therefore, is to help business people recognize legal risks and thus avoid legal liability.

The new edition to the book, moreover, has materially expanded the constitutional law section of the first chapter by discussing recent very important Supreme Court decisions, particularly regarding online gambling and the religious freedom of business people. Also, the book has expanded the examination of bribery in international business, especially pursuant to the U.S. federal statute, the Foreign Corrupt Practices Act, as well as the Organization of Economic Development's Convention against bribery. Particularly noteworthy and important to the 4th edition is the inclusion of an expanded and very substantive chapter – *Business Ethics and Corporate Social Responsibility* - dealing with philosophy, ethics, morality, business ethics, applied business ethics, corporate social responsibility, corporate governance, and business sustainability, that is, environmental responsibility. The authors strive to show what ethics is, how ethics can be used to make moral determinations in business, and why business should act not "merely" legally but also in a moral manner. Moreover, the authors discuss what the concept of "social responsibility" means for business today, how the value of social responsibility is distinguished from the law and from ethics, and why a business should be concerned with being a "socially responsible" one. A major objective of the new chapter is not "just" to teach ethics, but also "to do" ethics; that is, the authors' purposes for the new chapter are not merely to deliver moral information in a didactic, sermonizing, or "preachy" way, but also to stimulate and assist the student and reader to do better, clearer, and more well-reasoned ethical thinking about moral questions; and as such to impart the analytical skills needed to apply ethical concepts to business decision-making. Similarly, the authors want the student and reader to be cognizant of the concept of "social responsibility," how that term is applied to business, especially to corporations, what it means to be a socially responsible firm, and why a firm should be a socially responsible one today. Furthermore, the authors want the students to be aware of the concept of "sustainability" as applied to business, which characteristically means the environmental responsibility of business. The chapter also includes a discussion of codes of ethics, which shows how corporate codes are related to the law, ethics, and social responsibility. The chapter concludes with some case studies on current and controversial topics that can be used for analytical and discussion purposes. Before the conclusion section, we have added a new chapter on the IRS, Tax Court, and court procedures which are important for entrepreneurs and managers who do business in the United States of America. The 4th edition also includes an expanded Definition of Terms section as well as the addition of Case Problems dealing with constitutional law. Moreover, the authors have developed a text-based website with further cases, case studies, case problems (beyond those provided in the text), and other supplemental materials, including author videos, to help the reader comprehend the legal, ethical, and social responsibility concepts and principles, and particularly how they are applied in a modern business environment. Additional case studies, case problems, and other resource materials, such as relevant videos by the authors, can be accessed at the following link: http://www.business.nova.edu/course-materials/business-law/

The 4th edition in addition to the expanded chapters and materials as noted above includes the following: practical discussions on current legal controversies, such as the liability for "hacking" automobiles, the advertising of legal marijuana, social media and lending, and the JP Morgan fraudulent account scandal and the VW deceptive emissions scandal; an expanded discussion of securities law, including recent federal cases on the liability of tippers and tippees for trading on inside information as well as the new SEC rules on corporate pay; an expanded discussion of intellectual property law, including a recent Supreme Court trademark case as well as a discussion on how to protect your intellectual property by means of solicitation and non-disclosure agreements and during interviews; several recent case studies on legal and ethical controversies, for example, the legal liability of autonomous cars, along with discussion questions; and an Appendices with a sample "three value" term paper assignment guideline for legal, ethical, and social responsibility/sustainability analyses as well as a "success" document with the authors' thoughts and advice for personal, business, and professional success.

The authors are most grateful for all the support and encouragement to publish the 4th edition and particularly for the many most helpful suggestions for improving the book from colleagues, managers, human resources professionals, students, friends, and readers from across the globe. Furthermore, by using this book, you are contributing to the *Business Ethics and Global Social Responsibility Scholarship*, which has been established at the Huizenga School of Business and Entrepreneurship at Nova Southeastern University to support scholarly research and coursework by students, which will advance the fields of business ethics and global social responsibility. This scholarship was conceived and created by the authors of this book, and Huizenga Business College professors, Dr. Frank J. Cavico, J.D., LL.M., Professor Emeritus of Business Law and Ethics, and Dr. Bahaudin G. Mujtaba, M.B.A. / D.B.A., Professor of Management and Human Resources. Professors Cavico and Mujtaba are co-funded this academic scholarship initiative with the support of the H. Wayne Huizenga College of Business and Entrepreneurship and Nova Southeastern University. Thank you for exploring and leading discussions, and advancing knowledge on legality, morality and ethics, as well as social responsibility, in the world of management, entrepreneurship, and leadership!

There two quotes from William Shakespeare's *The Merchant of Venice* that are relevant to this book: "Now, what news on the Rialto?" "There is no power in Venice can alter a decree established. 'Twill be recorded for a precedent, and many an error by the same example will rush into the state. It cannot be" (William Shakespeare, Merchant of Venice, Act III, Sc. 1 and Act IV, Sc. 1). They underscore the importance of global trade, commerce, and business to the success and fame of Venice, as well as the critical need to conduct business in a principled-based, legal, ethical, and socially responsible environment. Remember that it was the Venetians who first used the term "communally controlled capitalism," that is, capitalism, and very successfully capitalism, yet tempered by law, ethics, and social responsibility; and it was also the Venetians who "coined" the concept of commercial paper (as explicated in a chapter in this book). Also, recall the motto of the Venetian Republic – "For the honor and profit of Venice." So, like the Venetians of "olden days," the authors want the readers to do well in business, but to do well honorably, and thereby act in a legal, ethical, moral, socially responsible, and sustainable manner.

Overall, we sincerely hope that, as with the previous editions of this book, you also enjoy this newest edition; and that you find it similarly useful and beneficial–academically and practically – as well as intellectually stimulating, thought-provoking, and challenging; and the authors sincerely hope too that all the stated aforementioned objectives are attained in an efficacious and enjoyable manner; and as a result the knowledge of the reader is increased, the mental acuity of the reader is enhanced, and the mental discipline of the reader is strengthened. The authors thus want you to be very successful; and your success brings us great happiness and satisfaction.

Frank and Bahaudin

1 – INTRODUCTION TO LAW AND THE LEGAL SYSTEM

Entrepreneurs and aspiring managers deal with laws of the land every day and thus must be aware of its nuances and complexities in order for them to successfully and interdependently work with others in the community, industry, and country. Entrepreneurs and managers cannot be successful in the long-term if they are not aware of the laws impacting them as well as their employees, suppliers, vendors, and customers. As such, entrepreneurs and managers should become aware of the fundamental aspects of the legal system, so they can avoid legal problems and seek the help of experts when dealing with complex issues. This book is designed to provide the foundational aspects of the "American" legal system, as practiced in the United States, for current and aspiring entrepreneurs and managers. By reading and understanding the various chapters of this book, not only will business professionals become aware of the complexities of the legal system, but entrepreneurs and managers will also be better prepared to seek help from the right experts when they need assistance.

The book seeks to make the reader more legally knowledgeable and astute. The book also attempts to identify as many legal challenges as possible in establishing, operating, and managing a business in today's very competitive global environment. The book recommends strategies and tactics to overcome these challenges and to achieve a successful business. Yet overcoming challenges is not the only goal of this book. The authors naturally want the reader to be able to more clearly foresee legal problems so as to avoid them, but the authors also want the reader to learn how to use the law and the legal system to more effectively establish, manage, and develop the business.

There are three parts to this initial chapter: Part I provides foundational information on the nature of law and the legal system; Part II explains the nature of alternative dispute resolution; and Part III examines constitutional law and how the U.S. Constitution is applied to and governs business.

PART I – LAW AND LEGAL SYSTEM

The "law" is complex, and it has many definitions. Fundamentally, the *law* is the entire body of principles that govern conduct and which can be enforced by the courts or other government tribunals. If there were no society-made laws, many people would still act in a "proper" manner based on societal norms, moral beliefs, conscience, or religion. However, not all people would act in such a "good" manner. Therefore, a basic purpose of the law is to provide a degree of order and control to human activities. The law thus serves as an instrumentality of control by means of substantive legal rules, legal procedures, and mechanisms of legal promulgation, adjudication, implementation, and enforcement.

Sources of the Law

When most people think of the term, the "law," they usually are thinking of a statute enacted by a legislative body, such as the United States Congress or a state legislature. *Statutory law* encompasses in addition the legislative ordinances enacted by constituent government elements of states in the United States, that is, ordinances and codes promulgated by counties and municipalities. Law also includes constitutional law, such as in the United States the federal, that is, national, constitution as well as state constitutions. Constitutional law in the U.S. as in most legal systems is supreme. Law further includes regulatory law, that is, the laws, in the forms of rules and regulations promulgated by administrative agencies, which have been delegated sovereign law-making powers by the legislative bodies. In the United States, a good part of the law that regulates business stems from government administrative agencies on not only the federal level but also the state and local level. Law consists, moreover, of *case law*, called the "common law" in the Anglo-American judicial tradition, which is the law expressed by judges in court decisions. Treaties are another source of the law. As a matter of fact, in the United States, the federal constitution explicitly gives the President the power with the advice and consent of the Senate to enter into treaties with foreign governments. Executive orders, finally, are yet one more source of the law. These are orders from the executive branch of government, for example in the U.S. by the President or the governor of a state. The authority to issue executive orders is either expressly granted to chief executive officers or implied from the federal or state constitutions.

Classification of the Law

There are many different classifications to the law. Generally, law can be divided into "public" law and "private" law. *Public law* impacts the "people" as a whole who are directly involved with the law; the aim of public law is to serve the societal interest as well as to seek to achieve justice; and "the people's" interests are represented by government agencies and officers. Prime examples are constitutional law, administrative law, and criminal law. Whereas *"private" law* deals with the legal problems, relations, and interests among private individuals; society and "the people" are not involved as a whole. Prominent illustrations of private law are the laws of contracts, torts, and property. Related to public and private law, though narrower in focus, are the criminal law and the civil law. The *criminal law* deals with legal wrongs committed ultimately against society, since society cannot function unless people and their property are protected. Criminal infractions are punished by society, particularly by the sanction of imprisonment; and in so doing the wrongdoer makes amends to society. Whereas the *civil law* deals with legal wrongs committed by one private party against another private party, for example, a lawsuit for breach of contract or for the tort of negligence, and the payment of money is the usual means of redress. The term "civil law," however, has another meaning. In many legal systems, the sole or primary source of the law is found in detailed statutes, called codes. Court decisions have a secondary importance, and, as a matter of fact, in some legal systems do not even have the force of law. The civil law in this sense is premised on the Napoleonic Code, but harkens back even further to the Roman law. Today, most European countries and all Latin American countries have "civil law" systems, as well as, to some extent, the state of Louisiana in the United States due to its Spanish and French origins and former rule. Civil law, moreover, must be differentiated from the "common law," which is a system of law which relies substantially on judicial-made case law for the law. Great Britain and the United States are two examples of common law systems. In a common law system, there of course will be statutory law too; and accordingly the function of the courts will be to not only make law but also to interpret statutory law and to review statutory law. One final important classification to the law is the distinction between *substantive law* and procedural law. The former defines the legal relation of people with other people or people with the state, and sets forth their respective rights and duties; whereas *procedural law* is the legal method, means, or process by which the substantive law is administered and the parties' and society's rights and duties are enforced.

The Common Law v. Statutory Law

In the Anglo-American legal tradition, it is necessary to explicate the meaning of the core legal concept – the "common law" – as well as to explore the relationship between the common law and statutory law. In early English days, the kings and their royal representatives officiating as courts made up the law on a case-by-case basis; yet not from a subjective starting point, but rather rooted in the customs and prevailing mores in the community. Over time, as more and more cases were decided, discrete bodies of law were developed. Moreover, after time, courts looked to earlier cases to see what legal principles were enunciated; and then, most significantly, followed these prior legal principles in deciding present cases. Following these foundational legal principles became the heart of the common law of England. The English common law was of course adopted by courts in the United States.

In common law systems, two concepts are critical: one is a "precedent," and the other and related one is the doctrine of "stare decisis." A *precedent* is an earlier case with the same or similar facts which has enunciated certain legal rules; and the system of "*stare decisis*" means that a court will follow established precedents in resolving the case "at bar." If a similar case is found, a court will stick to same rule in settling the present case. The strength of "stare decisis" is that the system brings order, uniformity, certainty, and predictability to the law. When a rule is applied to more and more cases with the same or similar issues, the greater the likelihood that the rule will be followed in the future; and thus an attorney will be better able to advise his or her client of how a court will decide in the client's potential case. Nevertheless, there are some problems with precedents and the system of "stare decisis." First, the more dissimilar the issues and factual patterns between the precedent case and the current legal controversy, the more the uncertainty as to legal result ensues; and consequently the present court now has some flexibility in resolving the dispute. Second, if there are no cases or very few cases with the same or similar issues and facts, then a court similarly will possess more latitude in determining what rule of law to apply. Third, if there are no cases on point anywhere, then a court is free to decide the dispute, yet again based on prevailing customs or if none on what is just. The next "precedent" problem arises when there is a "bad" or "unfair" rule that is "stuck" in the system and as a result is applied again and again. Fortunately, this happenstance has not been a regular occurrence, and there have not been that many "bad" laws; and of course a court is not bound to keep to precedent slavishly but rather ultimately to do justice. Finally, the original reason behind a precedent may no longer exist, but the courts may keep on applying the rule; yet again this has not been a widespread problem, as courts are cognizant of changed conditions. As an example of the latter situation, in the old common law, hospitals were regarded as charities and thus were "cloaked" with charitable immunity, meaning that a hospital was not legally responsible for the wrongs committed by its employees. Now, obviously, hospitals are responsible due to heightened public policy concerns as well as the fact that hospitals have become "big business" and business protected by insurance too.

Despite the primacy of case law in common law systems, statutes are important, particularly in the United States. Today, many branches of the law are based on legislatively and formally made enactments, for example, corporation law in the U.S. which is based predominantly on state corporate codes. However, there are still many branches of the law, such as contracts, agency, and torts, that are governed by the common law. In examining statutory law, three main areas need to be addressed: 1) the process by which statutory law is created; 2) the differences between statutory law and the common law; and 3) statutory interpretation.

The term "*statutory process*" connotes the power that legislative bodies have in enacting statutes. There are, however, limitations to this power, specifically 1) subject matter limitations imposed by the constitutions; 2) procedural requirements; and 3) a requirement that statutes be reasonably definite and not vague. Regarding the first limitation, in the United States, the federal constitution sets forth the legal parameters for legislation by the federal, that is, national, legislature and the state legislatures. The U.S. Constitution grants specific powers to the federal government, called enumerated powers, for example, the power to declare war, to maintain a postal system, and to make uniform bankruptcy laws. All other powers are reserved to the states. The federal legislature thus must point to an express power or a power implied from a select power, such as the power to create a draft and impose a selective service requirement, in order to legislate. Whereas the states, the original sovereign entities in the United States, have full power to legislate based on their "*police power*," which certainly is more than a law enforcement tool, but rather the authority to pass any legislation that the state legislature deems necessary to promote or protect the health, safety, and welfare of the citizens and people residing in the state. The second limitation in the U.S. is based on the federal constitution, as well as the state constitutions, which sets forth procedural requirements for promulgating statutes. For example, in the U.S. Constitution, all revenue bills must originate in the House of Representatives, and at the state level the subject of every bill must be in the title, and there can be only one subject per law. Finally, laws must be reasonably certain and definite. Consequently, if a statute is worded so that persons of ordinary intelligence cannot comprehend its meaning, the statute is invalid and illegal.

There are two major differences between the common law and the statutory law: 1) the process of creation; and 2) the form after each becomes operative. The process for legislative enactments is that a statute becomes a law only after passing through formal steps, for example, in the U.S. at the federal level by a bill passing through both houses of Congress and then approved by the President. Common law rules, to compare, emanate from the judicial branch of government, and are legal rules created by judges to settle cases and controversies. A statute is found in an official text, which typically is quite specific, and becomes part of a code; whereas common law decisions are published in casebooks, called "reporters" in the U.S., and which are more general in content. There are, moreover, other differences between statutes and the common law. Social and political forces have more impact on the formation of statutory law; whereas judges are more insulated from such pressures. Legislatures, moreover, have an option to make laws; legislators can refrain from acting; whereas judges must settle controversies that are presented in their courts. Courts can make law only in deciding cases that come before them. The legislative power, especially at the state level in the United States, is very broad. A legislature can enact statutes where case law is non-existent. In addition, and most significantly, legislative bodies can pass laws which can expressly overrule the common law. The legislative body, elected by the people, is "closest" to the people, and accordingly legislative laws will supersede the common law.

The courts, however, do have a role in the statutory process. The legislative bodies, as noted, do have broad power to enact statutes, but the courts also have a corresponding power. That is, the scope and meaning of a statute will not be known until a statute is construed by the courts in settling actual concrete disputes under the statute. This search for legislative intent, called *statutory interpretation*, is a major source of the law, and one performed by courts. In interpreting a statute, courts will adhere to the "plain meaning" rule, which holds that if the language of the statute is so clear, that only one result is logically indicated, the court will not consider any other factors, and give deference to the will of the legislative body. Nonetheless, the "plain meaning" rule may not be appropriate to evaluate many statutes because the statutes may be drafted with imprecise language. There are very few words that are subject to just one evident meaning. Moreover, the legislative body may have acted intentionally by being a bit imprecise so as to have some flexibility in the statute's application. Courts then have more interpretative power; but courts will look at the statute as a whole to determine its intent, as well as examine the problem that prompted the statute's enactment, and refer to the legislative history of the statute to look for clues as to legislative intent.

Legal Reasoning

Legal reasoning is the process of critical legal analysis that judges use to resolve a case. Attorneys and law students also use this process to analyze or "brief" a case. The first step is to summarize the facts of the case, paying very close attention to the key or "operative" facts in the case, that is, the facts that will be crucial in the ultimate resolution of the case. The second step is to ascertain the issues in the case. The issues are the legal questions that the court will be asked to resolve. Characteristically, courts start out by addressing general legal issues and then move on to narrower component issues. The third step is to state the rules of law that will be used to decide the case. It is important to note that these rules have precedent quality, that is, they can be used to resolve the case at bar and other cases with the same or similar facts. The fourth step is to apply these rules of law to the unique facts of the case and thereby to render a decision as to who prevails and who does not prevail in the case. Frequently, this decision is designated as a "holding." The final step is to provide the reasoning for the decision. The reasoning typically is based on the law and the application of the law to the concrete facts of a particular case, but the reasoning can extend to the rationale behind the rules of law themselves. Usually at the appellate, or review, level in the United States legal system, these decisions are framed as judicial "opinions." Ascertaining the issues is the crucial step, since how can one know what to answer if one does not know the questions?

Entrepreneurs and managers should become aware of laws, respect them and make sure their employees enforce them with all workers that work in this country. As the law continues to serve its purposes through means of legal regulations, procedures, and mechanisms of legal promulgation, adjudication, implementation, and enforcement, managers and entrepreneurs should be fully prepared to embrace them with dignity and respect. It is especially vital for managers and entrepreneurs to understand how legal issues, including laws, affect business practices and performances in various countries, as this knowledge can only help with the achievement of their goals. From the sources of law, classification of the law, to the legal reasoning, and diverse legal perspectives, management is oftentimes faced with the challenges of establishing successful strategies to help their employees, as well as themselves to embrace local and global cultures, laws, policies, and most importantly business practices, while at the same time respecting the laws and the company's regulations.

The United States Court System

The United States court system goes beyond the early colonial times and extends to present day. The Founding Fathers of the United States established a justified legal system that allowed for individual states to comprise their own laws in accordance to their beliefs and ideas. Yet, the legal system varied during the separation of the Northern and Southern states as slavery was a major factor during the 1700s, culminating in the U.S. Civil War. However, after President Lincoln's leadership role, slavery was abolished, and the court system came to be what seemed to be more liberal, justified, and democratic. Today, the legal system continues in accordance to the United States' Constitution, which was written to allow for flexibility. The powers are separated throughout three areas, including the judicial, executive, and legislative branches. The powers are then narrowed down to the state and local offices, where officials and representatives are elected by the citizens of the United States. The differences and similarities between the state and federal court systems in the United States will be examined, along with the conflicts of laws, equity, and court procedures at the federal, state, and local levels.

The courts in the United States are endowed by the federal and state constitutions with the judicial power. The federal Constitution and its application to business will be discussed in the U.S. Constitutional Law and business sections. The *judicial power* encompasses three powers: 1) adjudication, that is, the application of legal and rules to factual disputes in order to settle cases and controversies; 2) judicial review, that is, the power to evaluate statutes and other actions by the two other branches of government to ensure that they are constitutional; and 3) statutory interpretation, that is, the power to construe and clarify legislation for exact meaning. As noted, the United States is a federal system of government, with two distinct levels of government, the national/federal government and the state governments, and thus there are two separate court systems. Although the fifty state court systems have their differences, any detailed explication is beyond the scope of this book; rather, this book will look at the common elements in the state court systems and compare this general state model to the federal court system.

State v. Federal Court Systems in the United States

At the apex of the state court system is the highest court in the state, typically called the state supreme court. A state supreme court possesses appellate jurisdiction, that is, the power to hear and decide judgments of the lower courts of the state. A state supreme court decision is final in all cases not involving federal Constitutional law or statutory law or treaties. Below the *state supreme court*, the intermediate courts form the next level in the state court system. These courts also possess appellate jurisdiction, and hear cases from the "inferior" courts in the state system. These intermediate courts typically are called *district courts of appeal*; and in larger and more populated states, there will be several courts of appeal established in geographic regions throughout the state. Below the courts of appeal is the level of original jurisdiction courts. These courts possess both civil and criminal jurisdiction, and thus they are usually the first courts to hear and resolve disputes between private parties as well as criminal offenses against the state. Typically, these original jurisdiction courts are referred to as *circuit courts*. Inferior courts also include the county courts, which hear minor civil and criminal matters, but which also possess the original jurisdiction to decide real estate cases within their jurisdiction. Finally, state inferior courts also include small claims courts, at times called summary procedure tribunals, as well as traffic courts.

At the apex of the federal court system is the *U.S. Supreme Court*, which is the only federal court expressly created by the Constitution. It is the highest court in the United States. The U.S. Supreme Court possesses both original and appellate jurisdiction. The former extends to cases concerning ambassadors and public ministers as well as cases in which two states are parties; whereas the court's appellate jurisdiction extends to all cases brought into the federal court system, as well as the appellate jurisdiction of certain cases decided by the state supreme courts.

The intermediate level in the federal system is composed of the *U.S. Courts of Appeal*. The United States is divided into eleven judicial circuits and each circuit has a designated court of appeals. These courts have appellate jurisdiction only, and thus review the final decisions of the courts of original jurisdiction in the federal system. The *District Courts* are the courts of original jurisdiction in almost all cases maintained in the federal court system. They are the trial courts for federal, civil, and criminal matters. Finally, there are *specialized federal courts* created by Congress to determine specialized matters, such as the Patent Court and the Tax Court.

Courts and Jurisdiction

Legal rights are meaningless unless they are enforceable. Accordingly, one major function of government is to provide a system where the rights of parties under the law can be determined and enforced. The instrumentality of government so empowered is known in the Anglo-American system as a "court." *A court* is a tribunal established by government to hear and decide cases and controversies properly brought before it, to grant redress to aggrieved parties, to deter wrongdoing, and to enforce punishment against wrongdoers. This legal process ordinarily is called a "lawsuit" for civil cases and a "prosecution" for criminal cases. However, it should be noted here that other instrumentalities of government, for example, administrative agencies, have been created to enforce certain distinct areas of law and to thereby determine rights and obligations.

Jurisdiction is the power each court has to try cases and to decide certain types of controversies. As mentioned, original jurisdiction is the power a court has to hear a case when it is first brought into the legal system; whereas appellate jurisdiction is the authority a court has to review a judgment of a lower court or an administrative agency. The term "jurisdiction," however, should not be confused with the term "venue." *Jurisdiction* deals with the original authority of a court to hear a case; but once a court has jurisdiction, venue rules will govern where geographically the case will be heard. The *venue* of a lawsuit usually is the location of the court nearest to where the defendant to the lawsuit resides or where the incident or transaction at issue occurred. Venue assumes that a court has jurisdiction, and "merely" determines where within the court's jurisdiction the case will be heard.

There are two indispensable prerequisites for a court to obtain original jurisdiction: first, the court must have *jurisdiction over the subject matter* of the lawsuit; that is, a case must fall within a court's general, special, limited, or monetary jurisdiction; and second, the court must have jurisdiction over the person against whom the lawsuit is being brought. As a general rule, if a court lacks either requirement, and enters a judgment, the judgment is void and thus has no legal effect. Regarding subject matter jurisdiction in a federal system such as the U.S., the general rule is that cases begin in the state courts; but two very important exceptions hold that if a case is a "federal question" case or if there is "diversity of citizenship" between the litigants, the federal courts properly will assume jurisdiction. A *federal question* case is any case where the person bringing the lawsuit is basing his or her case on the federal constitution, a federal statute or administrative regulation, or a U.S. treaty. *Diversity of citizenship* case is where the person bringing the suit, usually called the plaintiff in such a context, and the defendant, the person being sued, are citizens of different states. Significantly, there is no federal question requirement for a "diversity" lawsuit; but there is a requirement that the amount in controversy in the lawsuit be over $75,000.

In examining the original jurisdiction of a court, an action *in personam* must be differentiated from an action *in rem*. An *action in personam* is an action where the plaintiff is seeking to hold the defendant liable on a personal obligation. To illustrate, the plaintiff is suing the defendant to recover money damages for an alleged breach of contract by the defendant; the plaintiff is suing the defendant to recover a debt allegedly owed by the defendant to the plaintiff; or the plaintiff is suing to recover damages for personal injuries that the defendant purportedly negligently inflicted upon the plaintiff. When the plaintiff brings an action in personam, the court must have jurisdiction over the person of the defendant. A court can acquire in personam jurisdiction in a variety of ways. The first method arises when the defendant resides within the territorial jurisdiction of the court, and the defendant is "served" with a summons and copy of the plaintiff's complaint, or the sheriff or other designated court officer leaves the summons and complaint with an adult at the place of the defendant's residence or work. The second method of securing personal jurisdiction occurs when the defendant resides elsewhere, but is personally served by the sheriff with a summons and complaint when the defendant is within the court's territorial jurisdiction. An *action in rem* is one in which the plaintiff is seeking to enforce a right against certain property owned by the defendant. The suit must be brought in the court where the property, the "res," is located. There ordinarily is no need for personal service, but there is a service by "publication," that is, the publishing of a notice of the lawsuit in a newspaper which circulates in the geographic area. One example would be a mortgage foreclosure action against real estate, which must be brought in the county court where the property is located. Another example would be a divorce lawsuit, since a marriage is considered by the law to be a "res," and thus publication usually will be sufficient service for a court to obtain jurisdiction of even an out-of-state spouse.

Finally, there are two types of state statutes that directly impact on the courts' jurisdiction: Long Arm statutes and Motorist Implied Consent statutes. A state *Long Arm statute* permits a cause of action to be instituted against an out-of-state resident defendant in the plaintiff's home state if the defendant does business in the state and thereby impliedly gives his or her consent to be sued on a claim arising out of that business. The plaintiff typically serves the Secretary of State for that state and thereby acquires jurisdiction over the out-of-state defendant. However, the U.S. Supreme Court has ruled that in order for an out-of-state defendant to be subject to the jurisdiction of a state court, the state must have "minimum contacts" with the defendant. Of course, doing business and having business operations in the state will satisfy that standard; but a problem exists today with the advent of the Internet since there is not yet a definitive legal answer as to what type and level of Internet activities will satisfy the "minimum contacts" standard. Finally, a *Motorist Implied Consent statute* is a state statute that maintains that when a non-resident operates a motor vehicle within the borders of the state, he or she impliedly consents to appoint the state's Secretary of State as an agent for accepting service if the non-resident is involved in a motor vehicle accident within the state.

Conflict of Laws

A problem arises in a legal system composed of sovereign legal entities, states in the U.S., when a legal situation occurs with acts or transactions that have contact with more than one state and/or parties from different states. Which state's laws will be applicable in such a multiple state case? For example, if the plaintiff, a citizen of Florida, makes a contract in Georgia with the defendant, a citizen of New York, with performance to be rendered in New Jersey; and the defendant refuses to carry out the contract; and then is sued in federal court in New York (to satisfy personal and diversity jurisdiction, assuming the requisite amount in controversy). What state law should the federal court apply? In answering this question, the courts will apply *Conflict of Laws rules*. There are three main ones: 1) if the case is a contract case, as above, and if the issue is the validity of the contract, then the law of the state in which the contract was made will govern the case; but if the issue is the performance of the contract, then the law of the state where performance took place or is to take place will govern; 2) if the case is a tort case, the law applicable is the law of the state where the injury occurred; and 3) in all other cases, the law of the state with the "most significant relationship" to the lawsuit will apply to the case. One way that the parties to a contract can eliminate "conflicts" uncertainties as well as jurisdictional disputes is to have in their contracts "forum selection" clauses which will designate the court to hear a potential controversy as well as "choice of law" clauses which will designate the law of a particular jurisdiction as the controlling law of any possible breach of contract lawsuit.

As a fundamental principle of contract law, the contract should specify where disputes are to be adjudicated and which jurisdiction's law will be applied to any dispute. The contract thus should expressly and clearly state that all the parties to the contract agree to submit to the jurisdiction of the courts in the designated locale. However, it must be pointed out that a court may refuse to enforce a choice of law provision in a contract if the law selected contravenes a fundamental public policy of the state where the court that is deciding the dispute is located.

Law v. Equity

In Anglo-American legal history, after the Norman Conquest of England in 1066, the early English kings established a nationwide system of courts; and the kings designated individuals as their personal representatives to settle disputes, originally based on the prevailing customs in the community. These controversies were decided on a case-by-case basis and over time a body of decisions on a variety of subjects was created. These decisions, as noted, became precedents, and formed the foundation of the common law.

However, even early on in English jurisprudence, problems with the common law-precedent system developed. There was a tendency for too many cases to be decided the same; and the common law system became rigid. Moreover, since the primary relief that the common law could grant was the payment of money damages, there were certain wrongs for which no adequate remedy existed at common law for a court to enforce. Consequently, the parties began to petition the early English kings for particular types of relief that were not available from the ordinary courts of law which were bound by the common law. The king, of course, was not bound by recognized legal principles, but had the power as well as the duty to decide cases based on conscience, fairness, and justice. Gradually, there were so many of these special appeals to the king that the king turned over these cases to his Chancellor and ordered him to decide these cases in the king's name in an equitable manner. When deciding these disputes became too demanding for the Chancellor, he appointed legal representatives to act in his and the king's name and to decide these cases in an equitable manner. Thus eventually there evolved in England an additional and different system of law, called Courts of the Chancery and later Courts of Equity, which were empowered to provide relief when there was no adequate remedy at law.

Several equitable remedies were created to do justice, but the two most important ones were the decree of injunction and the decree of specific performance. They are still today very important legal remedies. The *injunction* originated when a plaintiff asked a common law court of law to stop the defendant from doing a particular act, such as trespassing on the plaintiff's land or committing a nuisance hindering the plaintiff's enjoyment of his or her property. The court of law had to deny that request as the only type of relief such a court could grant was money damages for past injury; the court did not have the power to prevent future trespass or nuisance. As a result, the plaintiff asked the king for relief; and if the king or Chancellor or his representative deemed the request to be justified, an order in the king's name commanding the defendant to stop doing the wrongful act was issued; and this order, called an injunction, was enforced by the king's inherent power to do justice and to maintain law and order, specifically by the king's *"contempt" power*, which included fines and imprisonment for refusing an order of the king. *Specific performance* started as a request by a plaintiff for an order commanding a defendant to live up to the terms of a contract made with the plaintiff. However, a court of law once again could only order the defendant to pay money damages for the loss caused by the defendant's breach of contract. So a *Court of Equity* was asked to issue such a decree; and would do so if money damages were inadequate to fully compensate the plaintiff, for example, when the subject matter of the valid and breached contract was a rare heirloom. Today in Anglo-American jurisprudence, there has been a fusion of courts of law and courts of equity, and as a result today the same court administers both legal and equitable remedies, though in the latter case, it must be noted, there is no right to a jury trial. The injunction and the decree of specific performance, as well as other equitable remedies, will be covered throughout this book in a modern-day business context.

Court Personnel, Organization, and Procedure

The most important personnel of the courts are the judge, clerk, and jury. The *judge* is primary court officer, who is either appointed or elected, and whose function is to preside over and manage trials, maintain the order and dignity of the proceedings, to decide questions of law, and to instruct the jury on the applicable law of the case. Each court has the power to make rules to transact legal business before the court as well as to preserve order. As mentioned, a violation of an order from a judge, as well a violation of the court's rules, or an affront to the dignity of the court, will result in a party being held in "contempt of court," which can be punished by fine or imprisonment. The *clerk* of the court is the court officer whose function it is to keep accurate records of cases and to enter cases on the court calendar. The *jury* is the body of citizens sworn by the courts to decide questions of fact, to apply the law to the facts, and thereby to render a verdict, which the court will convert to a legally enforceable judgment.

Court procedure is a very consequential area of the law, since what good are substantive rights if one does not know how to enforce them procedurally. Yet procedure is a very detailed and complex legal matter. There are many precise and specific procedural rules as to how, when, and where a lawsuit may be brought to the courts and how it is to be maintained in the courts. As noted, in a federal system such as the U.S., there are procedural rules for the federal courts as well as the state courts. Moreover, on the state level, there is no uniform judicial procedure, as the laws of each state differ. Thus, an explication of procedural law is way beyond the purposes of this book; but nonetheless the authors would like to make some basic and general observations regarding court procedure, using the civil "side" of the courts as the illustration.

A *civil lawsuit* must be commenced by a party through instituting a cause of action. A court can only settle disputes between individuals when one of the parties formally requests the court to do so. A civil suit begins when one party files a written request, called a complaint or a petition. As noted, the plaintiff is the person who initiates the action; and the defendant is the person being sued. A person who is contemplating filing a lawsuit must be very careful about the applicable Statute of Limitations. This type of statute establishes the time period within which a lawsuit must be brought. Statutes of Limitation begin to "run" when the occurrence or transaction first transpired. For example, generally, in a negligence lawsuit, the injured party has two years to bring the lawsuit; in a breach of contract case, the aggrieved party has four years; and in a fraud lawsuit, the victim has six years. If the time period to bring the suit has expired, the Statute of Limitations is said to "toll," and the plaintiff's lawsuit will be dismissed.

The ordinary order of civil court events is as follows: 1) The plaintiff files a *complaint* with the clerk of the court, which sets forth the nature of the claim and the remedy sought). 2) The next step is service of process, whereby the clerk issues a summons with a copy of the complaint attached which must be served on the defendant. This "service" gives the defendant notice that a cause of action is being brought, and subjects the defendant to the power of the court. 3) In response, the defendant can file a motion to dismiss the lawsuit, for example, for failing to state a legally recognizable cause of action, or due a lack of subject matter or due to lack of personal jurisdiction. 4) If the defendant's motion to dismiss is overruled, or if the defendant did not file one, then the defendant must respond to the complaint. The defendant's response is called the "*answer*," wherein the defendant either admits or denies the plaintiff's allegations. If the defendant fails to answer within the prescribed time limits, the defendant is said to "default," resulting in a default judgment being rendered against the defendant, and as a result the plaintiff wins the case by default. The complaint and the answer are usually called the "pleadings," which are distinguished from "motions," which are "merely" requests to the court for an order.

If the pleadings indicate that the only questions involved in the lawsuit are questions of law, the judge can decide the case on the pleadings alone. One party actually can request the judge to decide the case as a matter of law if there are no genuine factual issues to be resolved. This type of request is called a motion for *summary judgment*. However, if there are factual issues to be decided, then the case must be turned over to a jury for the jury to determine the facts. An example of a "pure" law question is the issue: When does an offer to enter into a contract with no time period stated expire? The judge will instruct the jury that the law holds that such an offer expires at the expiration of a "reasonable" period of time. Yet what is "reasonable"? The "reasonableness" issue, in contract law and throughout Anglo-American jurisprudence, is a question of fact for the jury to resolve. Of course, if all the parties agree, the case may be tried by the judge alone, without a jury, and thus the judge will decide both questions of law and questions of fact.

If the lawsuit is not resolved on summary judgment motion, the next stage is called the "*discovery*" process. Discovery encompasses the parties asking for and receiving pertinent factual information regarding the case, for example, by means of asking official questions to the other side, called interrogatories, asking for admissions, deposing the parties and witnesses under oath, and requesting physical exams, photos, and documents. The purposes of discovery are to be sure that each side is fully aware of the facts and to encourage settlements. After discovery, a jury must be selected. The jury selection process is known as "*voir dire*," which entails the parties and the judge asking prospective jurors questions to ascertain their qualifications, abilities, and biases. The parties typically can challenge jurors for cause, which obviously requires a reason for a juror's dismissal, but without any numerical limitation as to the challenges; and a party can also assert "peremptory" challenges to automatically dismiss a juror even in most cases without a reason, though the number of peremptory challenges is limited, usually to three.

The basis for the jury's factual determination is the evidence. Evidence is presented by both parties in conformity with substantive and procedural evidentiary rules. The "trier of fact," usually the jury, can only decide questions of fact on the basis of the evidence presented. Evidence consists of testimony, that is, answers by persons to questions in court, and "real" evidence, that is, papers, books, records, and tangible things, for example. As a general rule, evidence in order to be admissible must be relevant, material, and unbiased. For example, evidence that one of the parties to a breach of contract dispute was previously divorced would be inadmissible for irrelevancy. A "witness" is a person who testifies in court; and who has direct contact with the facts in the case. That is, the witness saw events occur, or heard one of the parties say something. Otherwise, the evidence will be deemed to be "hearsay" and is excludable. A person can be subpoenaed and thus compelled to appear in court as a witness. The party initiating the lawsuit has certain legal "burdens," the burden of persuasion and the burden of proof. The former refers to the obligation to introduce sufficient evidence to keep the lawsuit going; and the latter refers to the obligation of a party to convince a jury of an issue. For example, in a criminal case, the state has the burden of proof to prove its case "beyond a reasonable doubt," that is, to a moral certainty; whereas in a civil case, the usual standard is a "*preponderance of the evidence*," that is, there is greater evidentiary weight for than against a particular issue. In some civil cases, for example, fraud, there is an intermediate standard for the burden of proof – "clear and convincing" evidence.

It is also instructive to briefly outline the ordinary trial procedure, again taking a civil case perspective. The attorney for the plaintiff commences the legal proceeding by making an opening statement to the jury, discussing the nature of the plaintiff's cause of action and what the plaintiff expects to prove. The defendant's attorney then makes a rebuttal statement and also states what the defendant expects to prove. The next step is the direct examination when the plaintiff's attorney presents his or her witnesses and asks questions. Next is the *cross-examination* stage where the defendant's attorney asks the same witnesses other questions in an effort to disprove prior answers. Then the defendant is allowed the same cross-examination process. After all the witnesses are examined and cross-examined, the following step is called the summation, where the attorneys for each side summarize the evidence, argue legal and factual points, and suggest to the jury the particular verdict that the attorneys feel is proper and just. At this stage, the parties can make a motion for a "*directed verdict*" to the judge. Such a motion argues that one of the parties failed to introduce evidence or that the evidence is so weak that the case should not go to the jury, and rather that the judge should direct a verdict for a particular party. Assuming no directed verdict motion or its denial, the judge at that time will "*charge*" *the jury*; that is, the judge will instruct the jury as to the rules of law governing the particular case. These points of law are called the jury's "instructions." After receiving their "instructions," the jury will deliberate on the weight and sufficiency of the evidence, decide the facts of the case, apply the law to the facts, and thereby render a decision, called a "verdict." The judge then will enter a judgment in accordance with the jury's verdict. A party who is dissatisfied with the verdict and judgment can appeal the case to the proper appellate court. However, an appellate court will not retry the case and will not hear witnesses. Rather, the appellate court will perform two functions: first, it will examine the whole record to see if the lower court judge made an error of law; and second, the appellate court will determine whether the jury's verdict was supported by substantial evidence. If there is an error in the law or if there is insufficient evidence to support the verdict, the appellate court will set the verdict aside, and the case will have to be retried. Assuming no appeal or an unsuccessful appeal, the losing party must comply with the judgment of the court; and if not, the prevailing party can take steps to carry out the judgment, typically called "execution," such as asking the court to compel the sale of the defendant's property. Once the legal matter is decided, it is regarded as "res judicata," meaning the case is final and cannot be relitigated. Finally, the "full faith and credit" clause of the U.S. Constitution requires that the court judgments in one state be given complete legal effect in "sister" states.

Expert legal counsel is strongly advised for the entrepreneur as the law is very extensive and very complex, and mistakes and omissions can be quite costly. Moreover, a lawyer will be able to discern issues and foresee potential problems that a lay business person might not have even thought of. As such, bringing a lawyer into the process in the beginning will save the entrepreneur time, effort, and money in the long-term. Should the entrepreneur opt for a large or a small law firm? One advantage of a large firm is that it typically would have legal experts in several specialty areas, such as securities law and intellectual property, which may be important to the entrepreneur. Yet large law firms typically charge more per hour, but may be able to accommodate an extended payment schedule. Also, large firms may be more bureaucratic in nature and involve many lawyers and legal assistants and administrative assistants so that dealing with all these personnel, especially less experienced ones, may translate into more time, effort, and money spent by the entrepreneur. Small firms characteristically contain generalist attorneys. An attorney in a small firm usually will charge less and there will be more personal contact. If the entrepreneur initially is seeking advice on what type of business entity to form and to achieve the formation, then a business law attorney at a small firm should suffice. Of course, if the entrepreneur asks his or her generalist attorney to act in specialized legal areas, the entrepreneur should be aware that he or she may wind up "paying" for that education. How does the entrepreneur find an attorney? There are many lawyer referral services and law directories, such as state and local bar associations, but usually these are impersonal and uncorroborated sources, and thus generally not sufficient. A better way is to seek a referral from family, friends, work colleagues, and other business people and entrepreneurs in the locality. Accountants, financial advisors, and real estate agents and brokers are also good sources for referrals as they regularly work with attorneys. Local universities are another good source of referrals. For example, the professors who teach legal subjects are attorneys, and though most do not practice, they certainly can make recommendations. Also, many universities use adjunct professors, and many of these professors who teach law subjects as adjunct professors are practicing attorneys in the community. Local attorneys often serve as guest speakers at universities and for the local chamber of commerce and local community groups.

Whether the attorney works in a large or small firm, the entrepreneur must determine the firm's billing procedure. Will the work be billed on an hourly basis or by the project? Charging by the hour is fine if the attorney can efficiently and effectively complete the legal task; yet billing per hour could end up quite costly if there is an educational component for the attorney. Hourly prices can range from $125 to several hundred dollars for each billable hour. If the work is done by the project, the amount asked, for example, to form a limited liability company, would be a "flat fee" and one that can be compared to other attorneys and law firms. It is incumbent on the entrepreneur to ascertain exactly what legal services are included in the flat fee as well as for the billable hour. For example, the entrepreneur must determine how and to what extent travel time, time spent answering emails and phone calls, research and writing of legal memos and documents, and consulting with legal assistants and other attorneys are handled in the fee structure. The entrepreneur should not be shy! That is, ask for price estimates, maximum price limits, and sample bills; ask how long the task is expected to take; ask that administrative and clerical type actions performed by the attorney be billed at a lower rate; ask that telephone calls under a certain number and time not be billed; and review carefully any invoices, and challenge any expenditures that the entrepreneur feels are unauthorized, improper, or unreasonable.

Of course, as a matter of common sense as well as "good business," the more educated, prepared, organized, and proactive the entrepreneur is when dealing with attorneys, the more efficiently, economically, and effectively will the entrepreneur be able to use the attorney's services. Have the necessary documents readily at hand; explain what is intended and what the situation is clearly and succinctly. "Time is money," thus the advice to the entrepreneur is: "Do not waste the attorney's time, and your money"! Finally, the entrepreneur must be aware of the attorney-client privilege, which protects as confidential communications between a lawyer and his or her client who is seeking legal advice. If the client is a corporation, the privilege still exists and protects communications between the company's lawyer and company personnel, so long as the nature of the communication relates to the employer's duties and the relationship with the lawyer is directed by the employee's manager or a corporate officer. Note, though, that the privilege belongs to the corporation and not the employee, and thus the employee cannot claim it if his or her corporation brings a lawsuit against the employee.

Summary of Part I
The variations among the state and federal court systems in the United States, conflicts of laws, equity, and court procedures at all levels were determined to help illustrate a clear view of the U.S. legal system. Due to the instability in the political, social, and economic environments, managers and entrepreneurs are at times forced to overcome challenges that conflict with the goals of their companies. Therefore, legal systems have been established to help managers and entrepreneurs resolve such problems. The United States legal system was created in order to provide for a fair and equal opportunity for all citizens, including domestic and international businesses. The court system varies at the local, state, and federal levels, where elections are held for the people to elect representative officials. In addition, the levels of legal systems also differ based on their rules; therefore, managers and entrepreneurs must also learn to abide by laws of their national country, as well as the local, state, and federal laws governing the United States when doing business in the United States. As an alternative to traditional courts and legal procedures, many businesses today are utilizing alternative dispute resolution mechanisms to decide disputes.

PART II - ALTERNATIVE DISPUTE RESOLUTION
The two foremost types of alternative dispute resolution (ADR) are mediation and arbitration. Mediation is a process by which a neutral third party acts as a conciliator and assists the parties to the controversy in reaching a compromise solution. Arbitration is a process whereby the parties to a controversy submit the dispute for a final and binding decision to a neutral third party who is not a traditional court judge. Litigation by means of traditional judicial procedures is not the only method of resolving business disputes. Litigation is viewed as too expensive, too time-consuming, and especially in the United States with the prevalent use of a lay jury to decide the facts of a case, too unpredictable. Therefore, there has been a major trend globally to the use of alternative dispute resolution (ADR) mechanisms as a substitute for traditional court procedures. This section accordingly will examine the main types of alternative dispute resolution, pointing out the advantages and disadvantages of ADR, especially the problems of appealing an arbitrator's decision.

Mediation

Mediation seeks to bring about a compromise solution to the dispute that is satisfactory to all the parties. It is absolutely fundamental to note that a mediator does not impose a binding solution on the parties; he or she is not a decision-maker, though the mediator does enter the decision-making process. In essence, the mediator, who is a neutral, disinterested, and objective third party, acts as a conciliator and facilitator. The mediator schedules and oversees negotiation sessions, opens up lines of communications, points out the strengths and weaknesses of each party's position, transmits proposals, and proposes compromise solutions. Only the disputing parties can adopt any particular resolution.

Three important legal issues involving mediation are: 1) the confidentiality of the mediation process, 2) legally requiring mediation, and 3) the conduct of the mediator. First, regarding confidentiality, characteristically most mediations are conducted in a confidential manner and thus the parties thereto have an expectation that the communications made during the mediation will not be disclosed to others or used in court proceedings. Although in the United States there is no common law basis for the confidentiality of the mediator-client relationship, some states now have statutes providing for such confidentiality, in particular protecting settlement negotiations by deeming them inadmissible evidence. The Federal Rules of Evidence in the U.S. also make statements made in the course of settlement negotiations inadmissible in legal proceedings. It is important to note that the federal law just protects settlement negotiation statements and not other communications, such as assertion of legal claims and defenses, such as fraud, and statements of fact, and also just deals with evidence inadmissibility and not ultimate disclosures. What complicates matters, of course, is that the mediator has in fact two clients who typically will possess conflicting interests and objectives. Consequently, one client's desire to maintain confidentiality may be opposed by another. Furthermore, even if both clients want to waive confidentiality, the mediator may not be willing to do so since the mediator may fear that the whole mediation process could be harmed and that the mediator could be brought into a court case and compelled to testify. Statutes typically do allow confidentiality to be waived but only if the participants and mediator consent. Also, statutes will provide exceptions to confidentiality if there are allegations of malfeasance or malpractice on the part of the mediator, if there is an allegation that fraud or duress occurred during the mediation, if there is evidence of a crime, or if there is an allegation that a party refused to mediate in good faith. The second mediation legal issue arises when there is an attempt to legally mandate that a party mediate. Mediation is supposed to be a voluntary alternative dispute mechanism, so the question of coercing a party to mediate is certainly a problematic one. In order to resolve this problem, it is essential to distinguish purely private and voluntary mediation, where the parties are merely trying to get professional help to solve a dispute that they cannot solve on their own, from court required mediation. In the first situation, there can be no coercion as the process is voluntary and private. However, the parties may have contracted to submit a dispute to mediation, and, if so, the failure to do so could result in a lawsuit for breach of contract for the failure to mediate or the failure to mediate in good faith, for example, by not listening, not making proposals, not making counter-proposals, and not negotiating. Of course, a contract to mediate will be enforced to the same degree as any other contract, which means that the standard contract defenses, such as fraud, can be used to contest the mediation contract. In a court situation, a judge may offer and suggest that the parties attempt mediation as an alternative to litigation. However, a court may have the authority to require some degree of mediation, and then the mediation will have a coercive element because the court may be able to impose sanctions, such as contempt of court, the payment of attorneys' fees, and preventing a party from proceeding in court, until the mediation has been conducted. Moreover, in some situations, not only is mediation ordered by the court, but the judge is bound to take cognizance of the mediator's evaluation of the case and, in some cases, to take cognizance of the mediator's recommendation. The third mediator issue deals with the conduct of the mediator. Mediators are bound to be neutral, impartial, and fair. The mediator thus cannot be perceived as favoring one party or one result over another. Obviously, if a mediator cannot be trusted by the parties to be fair and objective then the entire mediation process will collapse. Clearly, then, if the mediator has any financial interest in a particular outcome, or bias for or against a party, or had a prior relationship with a party, such as a legal one, then the mediator will be seen as not fair and impartial. Furthermore, if the mediator is unfair, biased, or incompetent, these circumstances can be used as defenses in a lawsuit to enforce a contract for mediation. Related to the conduct issue is the issue of the qualifications of the mediator. However, for private mediators, there are few uniform and consistent standards for mediators in jurisdictions in the U.S. and for different types of disputes. However, in the business and commercial arenas, these mediators are usually legal business law experts who have a great deal of knowledge and experience in certain fields. If a mediator is connected to, and referred by, a court, the mediator typically will have to meet that jurisdiction's requirements for a mediator, for example, that the mediator have a college degree, possess mediation training or experience, and be monitored. For private as well as court connected mediators, there are professional organizations, such as the Association for Conflict Resolution and the American Arbitration Association, which provide mediation courses and training and grant certificates as to the mediator's professional qualifications.

Arbitration

Arbitration is a process whereby a neutral third party is granted the power by the parties to a controversy to determine a binding solution to a dispute. Such a decision characteristically involves the determination of the rights and liabilities of the parties and the rendering of a "win-lose" resolution. Moreover, typically, the parties will contractually agree that the arbitrator's decision be legally binding; and in such a situation, the arbitrator is at times referred to as a "private judge," and in fact the arbitrator very well may be a retired judge. Moreover, in the United States, most union contracts include arbitration agreements; but these are negotiated by the union with employers, rather than imposed as a condition of employment. In the United States, the use of arbitration has spread from business and employment to other sectors, for example, to agreements between business and consumers, such as in contracts for credit cards, communications, cable, and cell phone services, other financial services, retail sales, health clubs, travel agencies, and summer camps. The use of arbitration in the U.S. has risen dramatically since a very important Supreme Court decision upheld the use of arbitration in an employment discrimination context.

The U.S. Federal Arbitration Act and the Uniform Arbitration Act

The right to arbitrate arises from a contract between the parties. The contract can be a preexisting one in which the parties have agreed to submit all or certain issues for arbitration, or the parties can enter into a present contract arbitrate an existing disputes. Since arbitration is contract based, the parties are legally obligated to arbitrate only those issues which they agreed to arbitrate in their contract. If a party refuses to arbitrate, the aggrieved party can petition a traditional court for an order directing the arbitration to be carried out. If a party refuses to carry out the terms of the arbitrator's decision, the aggrieved party can seek a court order directing that the arbitrator's decision be carried out. The key statute in the United States is the Federal Arbitration Act of 1925 which allows arbitration and makes arbitrators' decisions enforceable in the federal courts. Most states also have statutes under which arbitration agreements will be enforced, premised on the Uniform Arbitration Act, which seeks to promote arbitration on a consistent basis on the state level as well as the enforceability of arbitration awards.

Advantages and Disadvantages of Arbitration

The advantages of arbitration are many. Arbitration certainly is less expensive and less time-consuming than the traditional judicial manner of resolving disputes. Arbitration also allows the use of subject matter experts for very complex cases; whereas most traditional court judges are "generalists." Arbitration is also less formal than traditional court adjudication, for example, by not following as strictly the rules of evidence, such as the "hearsay rule." Arbitration is usually private too, which businesses and employers like as they are spared any potential bad publicity, and also there is no public record. There is no traditional jury in an arbitration proceeding. Juries are very risky, especially for large corporations, and especially when it comes to damages. Class action suits pose even a greater risk to a company. Arbitration, finally, is voluntary (presumably) since it is based on contractual agreement and thus consent. However, arbitration at times is criticized as "second-hand," "second-rate," or "second class" justice because arbitration deprives an aggrieved party of his or her "day in court." Moreover, an arbitrator does not have to follow the law, including existing federal and state law, and legal procedures and evidentiary rules as strictly as a traditional judge. Fact-finding plainly can be more restricted by an arbitrator than a traditional judge. Damages are often "capped"; appeals are very limited, as will be seen; and arbitration itself can be costly, especially for an aggrieved employee or consumer. Many employees and consumers may not even realize that they have agreed to arbitration, as the clauses are commonly placed as one of many provisions in a larger contract. Another problem is that the law does not spell out what rights, obligations, and remedies the arbitration process must include. In addition, arbitration usually is one-sided; that is, arbitration is mandatory for a business and employer and not an employee and consumer. The business or employer usually can pursue a traditional court remedy. Furthermore, since arbitration usually is a confidential process, arbitration could keep private matters of societal concern which should perhaps be made public, for example issues regarding product safety and anti-competitive practices.

The Arbitration Process

Arbitration commences with a formal arbitration "submission"; that is, the parties refer certain issues to the arbitrator for resolution. Virtually any business, commercial, or contract matter can be submitted to arbitration. The submitted issues can be factual, legal, or both, and can also encompass questions regarding the arbitration agreement and the interpretation thereof. When a dispute arises, the parties can agree to submit the dispute to arbitration. However, typically, disputes are arbitrated because of an arbitration clause in a contract entered into before the dispute arose. Usually such a clause will state that any dispute arising under the contract will be resolved by means of arbitration. The basic arbitration procedures consist of the following: the parties being given notice of the time and place of the arbitration hearing; a hearing being held where open statements are made, testimony is taken (without any formal pleadings or motions and without the strict rules of evidence being followed), evidence is presented, witnesses are examined, and closing arguments are made; the arbitrator establishes the rules, which again are less formal than a traditional court; and the arbitrator deliberates and renders his or her decision. Often, the decision is made orally and without explanation. The decision of the arbitrator is called the "award," and it is binding on all parties to the dispute on all issues submitted.

If a party to an arbitration procedure is dissatisfied with the arbitrator's decision, he or she has the right to appeal it to a traditional court, and also may ask the court to render an order compelling the other party to comply with the arbitration award; but in the United States, the scope of judicial review of an arbitration award is very, very limited; and in the U.S. the scope of judicial review is much more restricted than an appellate court's review of a trial court decision. A judge will examine the award to see if it covered matters that were beyond the issues submitted. If the arbitrator exceeded his or her conferred powers in deciding the dispute, his or her decision can be overturned by a court. A judge also will always seek to ascertain if there was any fraud, corruption, bribery, conflict of interest, bias, or other misconduct in the rendering of the award. Consequently, an award may be set aside by a court if there is sufficient evidence of an arbitrator's bad faith or misconduct. The refusal or failure of the arbitrator to hear relevant evidence will also be grounds for the reversal of an award. All these types of arbitrator misconduct cases are rare. However, a traditional court in the U.S. will not review the merits of the decision, whether there was sufficient evidence to support the decision, or even if the award was contrary to the evidence presented. Judges, of course, just may be a bit biased towards arbitration since it keeps disputes off crowded court dockets. However, a court may have to get involved initially if there is a dispute as to whether a particular matter is one that must be resolved by arbitration. Such a problem is commonly called an "arbitrability" issue, and very well could be a traditional legal one. Arbitration, in essence, provides a viable alternative to the traditional legal system in resolving disputes; yet the prudent business person should be well advised to take heed of the advantages, but also the disadvantages of arbitration, as an alternative dispute resolution procedure.

A key arbitration legal issue that must be resolved prior to the arbitration is whether a dispute should in fact be arbitrated. Typically this problem arises when a contract has an arbitration clause and one of the contract parties refuses to arbitrate. Then, the legal issue becomes a breach of contract and contract enforceability issue for the courts. As noted, the Federal Arbitration Act (FAA) in the United States decrees that arbitration agreements are enforceable just like any other contract. The courts, moreover, have ruled consistently that a dispute is considered to be appropriate for arbitration unless a statute clearly disallows arbitration. The FAA also provides procedural mechanisms for enforcing arbitration agreements in federal court. Assuming the contract containing the arbitration agreement is not vitiated by fraud or some other legal doctrine, the courts have uniformly held that these arbitration agreements in contracts are legal and enforceable, even when they are imposed on consumers and employees on a "take-it-or-leave-it" basis by large and powerful businesses and employers, and even if the arbitration agreement may adversely affect statutory rights under consumer protection and Civil Rights statutes. In order for an arbitration agreement to not be enforced against a consumer or employee, it would have to be manifestly and grossly unfair and one-sided, for example, if the arbitration agreement allows an employer, but not the employee, to institute legal proceedings in a traditional court. The arbitration award, moreover, can be enforced by traditional judicial remedies for enforcing monetary judgments, such as attachment, seizure, and sale of property and garnishment of funds and wages. Furthermore, since the FAA is a federal statute, the courts have ruled that the FAA and court decisions interpreting and implementing the FAA preempt any conflicting state laws. Accordingly, there evidently is a federal legal policy favoring arbitration of disputes.

Regarding the confidentiality of arbitration, it is interesting and important to note that under the common law and under most states' law and federal law, arbitration is not deemed confidential, though it is private, as opposed to a traditional court trial which the public usually can freely enter. Consequently, as a general rule, arbitration proceedings are discoverable in a court case and can also be admitted into evidence. One must investigate a particular jurisdiction to see if the state has any confidentiality laws protecting arbitration proceedings. Of course, the parties to the arbitration proceeding can, and actually may have very good reasons to, provide that the arbitration proceedings be kept confidential.

Another important legal area regarding arbitration occurs after the arbitration is completed and one of the parties wants to challenge the arbitration decision in a traditional court. As a very firm general rule, rising to the level of a legal presumption, the rule of law holds that arbitration decisions are not appealable to the courts. The rationale is that the parties have freely (presumably) chosen arbitration to resolve their dispute, which includes a non-appealable decision element. However, the FAA does provide some limited circumstances, where an arbitration decision can be appealed and overturned by the courts, for example, where there is evidence of fraud or corruption, misconduct or bias by the arbitrator, or where the arbitrator has exceeded his or her authority granted by the arbitration agreement, for example, by deciding an issue that was clearly not one subject to arbitration. However, unlike a traditional court decision, an arbitrator's decision cannot be overturned by a court if the arbitrator has made a mistake as to the law, for example, in the existence, interpretation, or application of the law. Perhaps if there is evidence that the arbitrator manifestly disregarded the applicable law, a party may be successful in getting a court to vacate the award. Yet arbitration awards can be corrected or modified by the courts if there are clerical or mathematical mistakes. Finally, a traditional court always has the authority, as it does with any type of contract case, to strike down the arbitration award for contravening the public policy of the jurisdiction.

Another important legal area in arbitration involves the choice of law for the arbitration proceeding. That is, what jurisdiction's law should apply to the dispute if the parties are from different legal jurisdictions or if the dispute or transaction is multi-jurisdictional or international? The answer to this question is simple. That is, the parties in their arbitration agreement can specify what jurisdiction's law will apply to the dispute. If the parties fail to do so, they are "asking for trouble" since it is possible that many different sources of law could apply to the transaction, for example, the place where the arbitration agreement was formed, the place where the dispute arose, the place with the most significant relationship to the dispute, or perhaps a statute or treaty which specifies the choice of law. Generally, in the United States, if the dispute arises in the U.S., the choice of law is made by referring to the FAA. The situation is more complicated in international transactions, where there are wide and at times divergent legal systems and bodies of laws. Thus in order to avoid confusion and unintended consequences, the parties should choose the forum for arbitration, that is, the country where any arbitration will be held, as well as the choice of law for the arbitration. In the international context, of course, reference must be made to international treaties governing arbitration.

Arbitration and Employment
In 2018, the U.S. Supreme Court once again ruled in favor of upholding arbitration clauses in employment contracts. The court ruled in the case of *Epic Systems v. Lewis* that an arbitration clause requiring workplace disputes to be settled by arbitration would prohibit employees from joining together in a class-action lawsuit against their employer. Employees, moreover, also could not bring joint arbitration claims. The case dealt with a pay dispute by company employees who contended the company had underpaid its workers. The employees' employment contract contained a clause that workplace disputes be resolved by arbitration rather than litigation, and, moreover, that each employee must file his or her claims individually, that is, one-by-one, whether in court or by means of arbitration. The decision is important in not just upholding the validity and enforceability of arbitration agreements, but also for the court's giving supremacy to arbitration pursuant to the 1925 Federal Arbitration Act as opposed to the collective rights of non-unionized employees pursuant to the National Labor Relations Act which otherwise protects collective actions by employees. However, unionized employees covered by a collective bargaining agreement with their employer could still assert rights jointly pursuant to that agreement or rights granted by federal labor law.

Online Dispute Resolution
Arbitration and mediation now can be conducted online where the parties can communicate "virtually" with each other and the arbitrator or mediator. There exist

today several entities, such as Cybersettle, ClickNSettle, and Settlement Online, which provide online dispute resolution services. However, before engaging in alternative dispute resolution, or for that matter even negotiation, whether on ground or online, the business person should require an agreement that any statements or offers of settlement made during the course of these processes will not be admissible in a court of law (if these alternative processes fail to solve the dispute and the parties end up in litigation).

PART III – CONSTITUTIONAL LAW

Foundational United States Constitutional Concepts

The *United States Constitution* is the supreme law in the United States. Neither the U.S. Congress nor any state may promulgate a law that conflicts with the U.S. Constitution. The Constitution is the source of lawmaking authority for the vast amount of laws that govern business in the United States. This section examines fundamental constitutional concepts and provisions, paying particular attention to their ramifications for business.

The Constitution serves two general purposes in the United States. First, it establishes the structure of government, and allocates power among the various branches of government. Second, it prevents the very government it established from taking certain actions that may infringe the liberties of the people it governs, in particular actions that restrict their individual rights.

Of course, through U.S. history, there have been many changes in the Constitution caused by the way the Supreme Court has interpreted the Constitution. As a result, many Constitutional provisions now have different practical meanings when they were first enacted. The result is that in the U.S. constitutional law is an evolving field of law. The reason for the Constitution's flexibility is that it is a relatively short document, with certain key provisions quite vaguely stated, such as "due process" of law and "equal protection" of law. There also has been a perceived need to adapt the Constitution to changing social conditions. Regarding the latter rationale, the hoary maxim in the U.S. is that the "Supreme Court follows the election returns." Even if overstated, it is a fact that the Supreme Court's decisions do at times reflect the social conditions of the country in which the court then operates.

There is an explicit amendment process to the U.S. Constitution. In theory, constitutional change can be accomplished through the formal amendment process; yet the amendment process is difficult to use, and consequently amendments to the Constitution are relatively infrequent. Accordingly, the result is that the Supreme Court is the Constitution's main "amender." Thus, the Court has the final authority to determine the Constitution's meaning. In particular, as aforementioned, the U.S. Supreme Court has the power of judicial review, which means the Court can declare actions of other government bodies unconstitutional, thereby affording the Justices of the Supreme Court policy-making powers in the U.S. governmental system. However, there are certain limits on the Supreme Court's power to shape the Constitution. First, the Constitution's language is not completely "open-ended"; actually, some provisions are quite clear. Second, based on the old common law precedent system, past constitutional decisions bind the Court to some degree. Third, the Supreme Court is dependent on the other branches of government to make its decisions effective. Finally, the Court ultimately is dependent on the public's belief in the Court's fairness, integrity, and fidelity to the rule of law.

One of the most fundamental Constitutional concepts is the doctrine of *federalism*. The United States, like many other countries, such as Mexico, is a federal system of government. Federalism is recognized in the Constitution as the premise for the structure of government in the United States as well as the basis for the relations between the national government, called the "federal" government, and the constituent government entities, called "states" in the United States, and called "provinces" in other federal systems. In the United States, the states formed the union; but power is divided by the Constitution between the national government and its constituent states. The Constitution grants certain specific powers to the national government, most notably in Article I of the Constitution which grants powers to Congress. The states, as the original sovereign entities, retain the powers not granted to the national government. As a matter of fact, the 10th Amendment to the U.S. Constitution explicitly states that the powers not given to the national government nor denied to the states are reserved to the states or the people. The rationale for federalism is that society is best served by a distribution of powers and functions among a central government, constituent government entities, the states, and local government components of the states, such as counties and municipalities. Clearly, particular levels of government are better equipped to deal with certain problems, such as the national government's ability to wage war.

Closely related to notion of federalism is the doctrine of *delegated powers*. Historically in the United States, the states as the original sovereign entities delegated, or transferred, certain enumerated powers to the national government, and reserved all other powers to the states. The very significant consequence is that in the United States the national government possesses no powers apart from those delegated to it by the states. Accordingly, the national government can only exercise those enumerated powers expressly granted to it. However, these enumerated powers are very broad; and furthermore the national government can exercise power "*necessary and proper*" to carrying out its enumerated powers. Since there are two main levels of government in the United States, the principle of federal supremacy is of monumental consequence. The *Supremacy Clause* of Article IV of the Constitution holds that the Constitution and laws and treaties of the United States, that is, the national government, supersede state law. As a result, if there is a conflict between federal and state law, the federal law will invalidate an inconsistent state law, even a state constitutional provision.

Another critical constitutional concept is the *separation of powers* doctrine. The U.S. Constitution divides the federal government into three branches – the legislative, executive, and judicial branches. Article I establishes the legislative branch, called a Congress, which is composed of a Senate and a House of Representatives. The legislative branch is accorded the sole power to make laws on the federal level. Section 8 of Article I describes the specific areas in which Congress can legislate, for example, commerce and taxation. Article I also sets forth rules for the promulgation of legislation. Article II establishes the executive branch of government and places the executive power in the President. The President is empowered by the Constitution to "take care that the laws be faithfully executed." Accordingly, the President has the power to enforce the laws passed by Congress. The President is also designated as the commander-in-chief in Article II. Finally, Article II sets forth the procedure for electing the President. Article III of the Constitution grants the judicial power to the Supreme Court and other federal courts that later were established by Congress. Article III defines the scope of the federal judicial power. Each branch of government, therefore, performs a separate function; and no branch may exercise the authority of another branch.

Closely allied to the separation of powers doctrine is the system of *checks and balances*. That is, in addition to separating the government into three distinct branches, the Constitution creates a system of checks and balances among Congress, the President, and the courts. Each branch of government has certain power to limit the actions of the other branches. For example, Congress can declare war, but the President is the commander-in-chief; Congress can make laws, the President can veto laws, and Congress can override a Presidential veto; the President makes appointments to the Supreme Court, but the Senate must confirm such appointments; and the Supreme Court has the power to declare actions of the other two branches unconstitutional. The objective of a system of checks and balances is to ensure that no one branch of government accumulates too much power.

Powers of the Federal Government and the States

Federal Legislative Powers

The *legislative power* on the federal level, as mentioned, is vested in Congress. The legislative power encompasses not only the power to make laws, but also the power to investigate, to hold hearings, and to consider matters upon which legislation my be enacted. The source of this power is Article I, Section 1, which states that "All legislative powers...shall be vested in a Congress." The scope of the federal legislative power is based, one recalls, on the enumerated powers specifically granted to Congress; the powers not delegated to Congress are reserved to the states by virtue of the 10th amendment. However, in addition to the enumerated powers, Congress has implied powers. Implied powers stem from the *"necessary and proper"* clause found in Section 8, Clause 18, of Article I. This momentous provision holds that in addition to the enumerated powers, Congress shall have the power to make all laws which shall be necessary and proper for carrying into execution the enumerated powers and all other powers vested by the Constitution in the government of the United States. As a result, Congress can legislate by any appropriate "means," such as a draft, to accomplish "ends," such as declaring war and raising an army, specified in its enumerated powers. Consequently, as will be seen, certain broad federal powers have been implied from the "necessary and proper" clause.

The commerce power is the preeminent and authoritative power of Congress under Article I, Section 8, Clause 3, to regulate commerce with foreign nations and among the several states. This all important power will be discussed in detail in the next major section of this chapter. The taxing power of Congress stems from Article I, Section 8, Clause 1, which states that Congress has the power to lay and collect taxes, duties, imposts, and excises. The main purpose of this power is, of course, to raise revenues for the federal government. Yet taxation also has been employed by Congress as a regulatory device since the act of taxation can encourage or discourage certain activities. Such taxation schemes, moreover, have been upheld by the courts even though their primary purpose is regulatory as opposed to revenue-raising. Due to the broad scope of the taxation power in conjunction with the equally broad power of Congress to regulate commerce, the taxing power of Congress has few limits. The spending power of Congress also comes from Clause 1 of Article 8, which states that Congress has the power to pay debts, provide for the common defense and the general welfare of the United States. It is also a broad power since it is based on any subject matter or activity that Congress can legislate or regulate. By such spending, Congress disposes of revenues accumulated from its taxing power. However, there are some limitations on the spending power of Congress. Spending first must be for the "general welfare," that is, a truly public purpose, though that determination is left up to Congress. Naturally, exercising this spending power involves policy choices and political issues, which are beyond the scope of this book to discuss. Finally, another limitation to spending is that Congress cannot exercise this power in derogation of any other independent Constitutional right, such as conditioning the receipt of money on censoring certain content to speech.

As mentioned, Congress is granted the power in Article I to declare war as well as to raise and support armies and navies. Congress is also empowered in Article I to make uniform laws regarding naturalization and citizenship, which encompasses the power to make rules for the exclusion, admission, and deportation of aliens, as well as the power to make uniform bankruptcy laws, to coin money, and to establish post offices.

Federal Executive Powers

The source of the *executive power* of the U.S. government is found in Section 1 of Article II of the Constitution, which confers the entire executive power to the President. The essence of the President's executive power comes from the aforementioned "take care" clause, where the President is empowered to "take care that the laws be faithfully executed," as well as from the President's designation as "commander-in-chief." The President, moreover, has certain other specific powers, for example, the appointment power, the pardon power, the veto power, and the treaty power. Regarding the status of the latter, it is important to note that pursuant to the Supremacy Clause of Section 2 of Article VI, treaties confirmed by the Senate are regarded as the "supreme law of the land." It is also noteworthy to relate that the President does not possess an express right to executive privilege, but one has been recognized by the courts in order to protect the confidentiality of certain presidential communications.

Federal Judicial Powers

The source of the federal *judicial power* is Article III of the Constitution. Specifically, in Section 1 of that Article, the federal judicial power is vested in a Supreme Court and in such "inferior" federal courts as Congress deems to establish. Section 2 of Article III deals with the scope of the federal judicial power and limits the jurisdiction of the federal courts to four types of cases: 1) cases arising under the Constitution, an act of Congress, or a federal treaty, usually called "*federal question*" cases; 2) cases in which the United States is a party; 3) cases in which a state and citizens of another state are litigants; and 4) cases in which the parties are citizens of different states, usually called "*diversity*" *cases*. There is, however, an important limitation on the scope of the federal judicial power, and that is the 11th Amendment to the U.S. Constitution. As interpreted by the courts, this amendment holds that a citizen of one state cannot sue another state in federal court without that state's consent. Moreover, this amendment has been construed as preventing suits in federal courts by citizens of the states being sued. Yet there are permissible federal lawsuits despite the 11th Amendment, for example, suits against the political subdivisions of a state, such as a county, or states against state officials for violating constitutionally protected rights.

The U.S. Supreme Court according to the Constitution has both original, that is, trial, jurisdiction, and appellate jurisdiction. The Court's original jurisdiction extends to cases involving ambassadors and consuls, as well as legal controversies between two or more states; whereas the Court's appellate jurisdiction is based on the Court's power of "judicial review," that is, the Court's power to declare acts by the other branches of government, as well as state statutes and court decisions, unconstitutional. There are, however, certain limitations on the jurisdiction of the federal courts. First, the federal courts' jurisdiction extends to a "case or controversy," that is, a legal matter must be definite and concrete; the litigants must have adverse legal interests; and these interests must be factual, adverse, and substantial. As such, the federal courts will not issue "advisory," that is, hypothetical, opinions. There are no "moot" cases before the federal courts; all matters must be real, and must be resolved. Moreover, in order for the federal courts to assume jurisdiction, the parties before the court must have "standing," that is, they must be personally, imminently, and directly harmed by the action or law being challenged. Parties are not allowed to litigate in the abstract; they must be injured in fact. The full meaning of the "standing" doctrine is comprehensively covered in the authors' *Legal Challenges for the Global Manager and Entrepreneur* book (2008 by Kendall Hunt Publishing). The federal courts, as noted, will resolve "federal questions," that is, a case with a substantial federal constitutional or statutory question; but the courts will not entertain mere "political questions," that is, questions of foreign relations and military affairs, which the courts deem more appropriately left to the other "political" branches of the government to resolve, such as the "burning" issue in the U.S. in the 1970s as to the legality of the "undeclared" war in Vietnam.

Federal v. State Powers

The Constitution of the United States, as previously mentioned, forms a federal system of government. The 10th amendment to the Constitution reserves to the states all powers not delegated by the Constitution to the federal government. However, in the realm of exclusive federal powers, state action is prohibited due to the express provisions in the Constitution. For example, due to Article 1, Section 10, and the powers given expressly to the federal government, no state can form a treaty or coin money. However, there are powers known as "*concurrent*" *powers*, that is, powers that can be exercised by both the federal and state governments, for example, the power to regulate commerce. The states, moreover, possess what are known as "police powers"; yet this term is a misnomer since the power of the states to enact laws is considerably more extensive than the criminal law connotation to "police." Rather, the states have the inherent sovereign power to enact any law that furthers the health, safety, and welfare of the citizens and residents of the state. Yet due to the Supremacy Clause, if the federal government has expressly "spoken" on a matter, any inconsistent state law will be deemed unconstitutional and prohibited. Moreover, if Congress has been deemed to *"preempt"* a field, usually by the existence of detailed and pervasive federal regulation, no state legislation at all will be allowed, for example, in the area of airline safety regulations.

Regulation of Commerce and Taxation
The rule pertaining to the regulation of foreign commerce is simple and straightforward to state, and that is, that such an area is exclusively a federal power. However, the issue of regulation of interstate commerce is a considerably more problematic matter indeed. The regulation of interstate commerce is construed as a concurrent power; that is, the federal power to regulate interstate commerce is deemed to be concurrent with the states' power to regulate transactions that occur within the states. The source of the federal power stems from Article I, Section 8, Clause 3, of the Constitution, which states that Congress has the power to regulate commerce among the states. This power encompasses the power of Congress to regulate the channels and facilities of interstate commerce, such as common carriers, highways, and communication transmission facilities, as well as activities that affect interstate commerce, such as activities, commercial or non-commercial, that have national economic effect, and even if such activities are wholly intrastate in origin. Moreover, the fact that a single business or individual sought to be regulated has only a small impact on interstate commerce is immaterial. The legal test for the exercise of federal power is whether there is an aggregate effect on other states by the class of activities regulated. The critical legal issue is not how much commerce is involved, but how does the activity affect interstate commerce. In one classic "commerce" and Civil Rights case, the Supreme Court upheld the Civil Rights Act over the objections of a local motel owner who discriminated against African-American travelers. The motel owner argued that his business was strictly intrastate and local, and thus beyond the reach of the Civil Rights Act, enacted by virtue of the Commerce Clause. The Court explained that since the motel was accessible to interstate traffic, was advertised nationally, and that a majority of its guests were from other states, the motel was engaged in interstate commerce and thus subject to the Civil Rights Act and its non-discrimination public accommodations provisions.

The legal result of the Commerce Clause is to grant to Congress almost unlimited power to regulate commerce, since virtually every business engages in some activity that affects more than one state. Actually, one is hard-pressed to find in modern times a business activity that does not have a sufficient "national" economic effect for Congress not to regulate. One "exceptional" and leading Commerce case occurred in 1995 when the Supreme Court in *United States v. Lopez* ruled that Congress exceeded its regulatory power under the Commerce Clause when Congress attempted to ban the possession of guns near schools. The Court struck down the Gun-Free School Zones Act as unconstitutional since the attempted area of regulation had an insufficient connection with interstate commerce. However, in a counterbalancing commerce clause case, the Supreme Court in 2005 in *Gonzales v. Reich* deemed that the federal government could regulate predominantly non-commercial activities that took place entirely within a state's border. The case dealt with California's medical marijuana law, which is a law that many states have today, though with differing requirements. Even though marijuana is legal in these states for medicinal purposes, the drug is still illegal under the federal Controlled Substances Act. The law was challenged by two women in California, who were using medical marijuana pursuant to their doctors' advice, and who contended that the federal government could not regulate an activity that was legal in a state; and thus the Controlled Substances Act was unconstitutional. The Supreme Court, however, disagreed, ruling that Congress has the power to prohibit the possession and non-commercial cultivation of marijuana even if wholly within a state as part of a larger regulatory drug scheme as represented by the statute. Consequently, even though legal in a state, medical marijuana users nonetheless can be prosecuted by the federal government. What is even more interesting is that today, as of the writing of this updated edition, two states, Colorado and Washington, have legalized the recreational use of marijuana, yet which cultivation, sale, or use is still presumably a federal offense (though likely a low criminal priority for the Obama Administration).

A momentous and most interesting Commerce Clause as well as taxation power case, dealt with the constitutional validity of President Obama's health care program. The case was decided in 2012 by the Supreme Court. The Court, in a 5-4 decision, upheld President Obama's healthcare law, the Affordable Care Act, also popularly known as "Obama Care," which was the most significant legislative achievement in the President's first term. The decision means that Obama Care will be fully implemented in 2014, with provisions extending coverage to more of the uninsured, providing coverage for pre-existing medical conditions, and, significantly, imposing new taxes to finance the health care expansion. The Supreme Court, in upholding Obama Care, said that Congress acted properly and constitutionally based on its power to tax when it mandated that people buy health insurance or pay a penalty (interpreted as a tax). Chief Justice John Roberts, who wrote the majority opinion, said it was reasonable to construe what Congress has done as increasing taxes on people who choose not to buy health insurance; and Congress clearly has the constitutional power to tax. Roberts reasoned that the financial penalty for not having insurance possessed the essential feature of a tax, which is to produce revenue for the government. Furthermore, Justice Roberts stated that the label of a "penalty" in the law as well as the fact that the law was intended to influence behavior did not matter. Roberts reasoned that the penalty functioned like a tax, just like other taxes, such as on cigarettes, which were enacted principally to create incentives for behavior rather than to raise revenue. Therefore, it seemed that the Chief Justice was seeking to uphold the law, but under the most narrow legal interpretation possible. The use of the Commerce Clause of the Constitution to sustain the law was denied by Roberts and the Court's four "conservative" justices, Justices Antonin Scalia, Samuel Alito, Clarence Thomas, and Anthony Kennedy. The Commerce Clause gives Congress the power to regulate commerce "among the several states." However, Roberts stated that Congress has never attempted to rely on the Commerce power to force people not engaged in commerce to purchase a product they did not want. Rather, Roberts relied on the power of Congress to "lay and collect taxes" to save the insurance mandate and thus to save Obama Care. The Supreme Court decision, therefore, in the long-run may set a new limit on Congress' power under the Commerce Clause to regulate interstate commerce. However, the dissent authored by Justice Ruth Bader Ginsburg, and joined by Justices Stephen Breyer, Sonia Sotomayor, and Elena Kagan, the "liberal" wing of the Court, said the Commerce Clause was sufficient to justify upholding Obama Care, principally because it addresses a significant interstate problem, that is, access to health care.

In addition to the power of the federal government, the states do possess the concurrent power to regulate interstate commerce. The federal power, although potentially all-pervasive, is not exclusive. Accordingly, an issue exists as to the extent to which the states can regulate commerce. Congress, of course, can expressly authorize the states to regulate interstate commerce; conversely, Congress may prohibit state regulations that otherwise might be permissible. Yet if there is no express Congressional authorization or prohibition of state laws, the aforementioned "preemption" doctrine is used to resolve the regulatory question. The "preemption" doctrine in essence asks that when there is relevant federal legislation, but no express prohibition of state law, is the federal intent, as divined by the Supreme Court, to forbid any state legislation. If the federal courts, and ultimately the Supreme Court, feel that the federal government has preempted, or occupied, the entire regulatory field, no state legislation will be allowed, even if there is no direct conflict with federal law. The idea is that once Congress is said to have "preempted" a field, only uniform national regulation will be permitted. The critical "preemption" decision will be left up to the federal courts, but the more complete the federal regulatory scheme is, and the more the subject matter has been historically regarded as a matter of federal concern as opposed to local concern, such as licensing of nuclear reactors compared to highway safety, the more likely the courts will say that Congress has expressed its intent to occupy the entire field. To illustrate, in 2008 in *Riegel v. Medtronic, Inc.*, the Supreme Court ruled that the Medical Device Amendments Act of 1976, which included a preemption provision for medical devices, which passed the Food and Drug Administration's strict pre-market approval process, preempted the civil law action, based on the common law torts of negligence and strict liability, by a party who claimed he was injured by a defective medical device. Yet an important, and differing, Supreme Court preemption decision occurred in 2011 regarding the always controversial subject of immigration, when the Supreme Court ruled in *Chamber of Commerce of the United States v. Whiting* that an Arizona law that mandated that the courts in that state revoke the business licenses and corporate charters of in-state employers who knowingly or intentionally employ unauthorized immigrants was not preempted by the federal Immigration Reform and Control Act.

If there is no preemption, no prohibition, and no direct conflict, the states are allowed to regulate local transactions and activities, even though they may affect interstate commerce. There are certain requirements, however. First, there can be no discrimination against interstate commerce. Thus, a state regulation that discriminates against interstate commerce will be struck down as invalid. "Discrimination" in this legal context means that a state is singling out interstate commerce for regulation and/or imposing more burdensome regulations on interstate commerce, for example, by excluding incoming trade, requiring a higher price for incoming trade, requiring the performance of business operations locally, or restricting outgoing trade, even if the state's purpose is meritorious in that it seeks to protect local business or to protect local natural resources and preserve the local environment. For example, a state statute prohibiting the importation into the state of waste material in order to conserve the state's remaining landfill space and to reduce pollution was deemed unconstitutional as impermissibly discriminating against interstate commerce. However, if the state regulation does not discriminate against interstate commerce, the regulation may be valid if it passes the "balancing" test. That is, the federal courts will balance the burden on interstate commerce imposed by the state regulation, for example, by weighing the difficulties and costs of compliance, against the strength of the state interest in order to determine if the state regulation imposes an unreasonable burden on interstate commerce. One key factor for the courts is whether the state regulation furthers local health, safety, and welfare interests, as opposed to merely protecting local economic interests. Yet even a health and safety state regulation will be deemed invalid if it substantially, and thus unreasonably, burdens interstate commerce. For example, state laws regulating the length of trucks on state highways as well as the type of mudguards on trucks have been struck down because of their substantial inconvenience to interstate commerce and their minimal local safety benefit.

Regarding the power of the states to tax interstate commerce, there are two basic rules. First, premised on the Supremacy clause and the Interstate Commerce clause, Congress has the complete power to authorize to forbid state taxation that affects interstate commerce. Second, when Congress has not "spoken," the states may be able to tax interstate commerce if, in order to satisfy the Interstate Commerce clause, the tax is not discriminatory and not an unreasonable burden on interstate commerce, and, in order to satisfy the Due Process clause, there is a sufficient connection, or "nexus," between the taxing state and the subject matter or activity being taxed. Interstate commerce must "pay its way," and is not immune from state taxation; but such taxation must be fair, and thus there must be a just apportionment of the tax to the "contacts" or physical presence that the interstate commerce has with the "tax situs," that is, the taxing state, and the benefits and protection that the interstate commerce receives from the taxing state.

Privileges and Immunities

The *privileges and immunities* afforded by the Constitution are divided into two main categories – privileges and immunities of national citizenship and those of state citizenship. Concerning the first type, the 14th amendment holds that no state shall enact a law which shall abridge the privileges and immunities of citizens of the United States. For example, state laws that would restrict the right of the people of the U.S. to move and pass freely from state to state or owning property or to commencing a business in a state would be struck down as unconstitutional. However, as construed by the Supreme Court, the rights in the Bill of Rights are not privileges and immunities of national citizenship, and thus, the 14th amendment Due Process and Equal Protection clauses must be used to provide protection of individual rights from state action. Concerning the privileges and immunities of state citizenship, Article IV, Section 2, of the Constitution holds that the citizens of each state are entitled to all the privileges and immunities of citizens of the several states. As a result, a state cannot discriminate against non-citizens and non-residents unless the state regulation is very closely related to a substantial state interest. For example, state laws requiring hiring preferences have been struck down, but state laws charging higher state university tuition for out-of-state students as well as higher fees for hunting and fishing licenses for out-of-state residents have been upheld as reasonable and not unduly burdensome regulations. Mention also must be made of the Full Faith and Credit Clause of Article IV, Section 1, of the U.S. Constitution, which holds that the states must give "Full Faith and Credit" to the public acts and judicial proceedings of every other state.

The Bill of Rights, Constitutional Guarantees, and Business
The first ten amendments to the Constitution are known as the *Bill of Rights*. Of course, in addition to the Bill of Rights, other amendments have been added to the Constitution. The purpose of the Bill of Rights is to protect the citizens of the United States from the very government created by the Constitution. Accordingly, the Bill of Rights embodies a series of protections for the individual against various types of infringement by the federal government; and thus the Bill of Rights serves as a limitation against government power. The 1st Amendment protects freedom of speech, association, religion, and assembly. The 2nd Amendment holds that the right of the people to "keep and bear arms" shall not be infringed. The 4th Amendment contains provisions regarding warrants and searches and seizures. The 5th Amendment contains provisions regarding the privilege against self-incrimination, as well as a prohibition against "double jeopardy," that is, being subject to the same offense twice. The 6th Amendment provides for a speedy and public trial, the rights to counsel, confrontation of witnesses, and cross-examination in criminal cases. The 7th Amendment provides for the right to a jury trial in certain cases. The 8th Amendment forbids the infliction of "cruel and unusual" punishment and also forbids excessive bail. The Bill of Rights originally was a limitation only on the federal power, and thus only protected against actions by the federal government, and not by the states. However, by means of the Due Process clause of the 14th Amendment, which protects against state action, and a process called the "incorporation" doctrine, almost all the protections of the Bill of Rights now have been deemed applicable to the states as well. These rights, moreover, protect not only natural people but also, though to a lesser degree, artificial legal "persons," such as the corporation and other business entities, as will be seen in the Business Organizations chapter.

These rights, as well as other constitutional rights, it must be underscored, are not absolute. The Supreme Court, as final interpreter of the Constitution, gives meaning to these rights and determines the boundaries of these freedoms. For example, freedom of speech, although extremely important in the U.S. legal and political system, is not absolute; and consequently speech can be restrained and even punished when it becomes fraudulent, defamatory, or obscene. One does not have the freedom "to yell 'fire' in a crowded theatre," as the famous old saying holds.

"State Action"

The language of the 5th and 14th Amendments as well as the Bill of Rights is applicable only to *"state action"*; that is, these core federal constitutional provisions only protect against and restrict government action, and not the acts of "mere" private parties and businesses. *"State action"* encompasses the actions of the legislative, executive, and judicial branches as well as administrative agencies on the federal, state, and local government levels, the subdivisions thereof. One can assert Constitutional rights against government entities, and not private sector entities. Even if a private entity is substantially funded by the government, even if it is very heavily regulated by the government, and even if it is a government granted monopoly, it characteristically will be deemed mere private. Thus, for example, a government employee may be able to argue that his or her discharge from public sector employment was unconstitutional since the discharge was premised on an impermissible restriction of free speech or association, a wrongful infringement on privacy, or an unreasonable search and seizure; however, a private sector employee cannot ordinarily utilize these constitutional concepts against his or her private sector employer. There is a monumental difference between a government employee criticizing his or her "boss," and a private sector employee so doing, as the former may be able to sustain a literal "federal case" to protect his or her job, whereas the private sector employee may find oneself summarily discharged with no legal recourse. However, it should be noted that some state constitutions afford constitutional rights to employees in the private sector, for example, the California state constitution which provides for a right to privacy for all employees in the state.

Regulating offensive and hateful speech on the Internet has emerged as another difficult issue – legally and morally. As emphasized, the U.S. Constitution as well as state constitutions protect against government interference with a person's rights. Consequently, in 2017 when Internet service providers and domain name registrars, such as Google and GoDaddy, began to refuse service to extreme right-wing groups, Neo-Nazis, the Klan, and other racist organizations the freedom of speech issue arose as to the propriety of these organizations "policing" the Internet to prevent "hate speech." As emphasized, since these are private companies and not government restricting speech there is no constitutional First Amendment involved. As such, the question became whether it is ethical for these private entities, large and very powerful ones, to be censoring speech, even reprehensible and repulsive speech, on these online forums since the speech is legally protected. Public debate is certainly limited; and censorship, even if done to prevent further societal polarization and harm, can get way out of hand since who really is to decide between "good" speech and "bad" speech. This contentious practice, therefore, though legal, calls for a Utilitarian and Kantian analysis to ascertain its morality.

Due Process and Equal Protection

The 5th and 14th Amendments protect against government deprivation of life, liberty, or property without *due process of law*. These amendments are most often used to provide procedural safeguards, notably adequate notice and a fair hearing, before government can take any action against a person or a business. It is critical to note that a corporation is considered a "person" for due process protections. In addition to procedural due process, there is a body of law called "substantive due process," which the courts theoretically can use to review the substance of legislation, but the modern legal approach of the courts has been to defer to the legislative branches of government, and thus to presume that legislation of an economic or social nature, especially government regulation of business, is valid so long as the legislation rationally relates to a legitimate government purpose. However, if government legislation infringes a "fundamental right," such as the voting, interstate travel, marriage, family, and/or First Amendment rights, then substantive due process would require that government have a "compelling government interest" to infringe on such rights. Yet in modern times most situations involving fundamental rights have been handled by the courts using the Equal Protection clause.

Procedural due process is an extremely important legal concept which protects "life," "liberty," and "property" interests from being impaired by the government. Due process in essence means that the process which the government uses to deprive a person (including a corporate "person") of life, liberty, or property (for example, in the latter corporate situation, to fine the business for violating a regulatory law), must be a fair process. Fairness entails the government giving adequate notice to a person that it is going to take some adverse action and then providing a person with a fair hearing before an objective decision-maker. At the hearing the government must demonstrate that it has sufficient reasons – constitutionally, legally, and factually – to deprive a person of a liberty or property interest. The Due Process clause, moreover, has also been interpreted by the courts to require that statutes be reasonably definite and precise and not vague or overbroad. The Due Process clause, finally, has been interpreted to put limits on punitive damage awards (designed to punish and deter wrongdoing, such as an intentional tort or deceit). To illustrate, in one case, *BMW of North America v. Gore* (1996), the Supreme Court overturned a $4 million dollar punitive damage, premised on a $4,000 compensatory award judgment, in a civil case for the fraudulent repainting of a car due to some minor pre-delivery damage. Later, the Supreme Court provided some guidance as to what Due Process permits for punitive damage awards. In the case of *State Farm v. Campbell* (2003), the Court indicated that a 4 to 1 ratio between punitive and compensatory damages, though not "binding," was nonetheless "instructive" for Due Process limitations.

The 14th Amendment to the Constitutional also holds that no state can deny a person *equal protection of the laws*. "Person" for equal protection purposes also includes the artificial legal person, that is, the corporation. Initially, it must be pointed out that the Equal Protection clause in the 14th amendment only limits the actions of the states; there surprisingly is no similar provision in the U.S. Constitution applicable to the federal government. However, the Due Process clause in the 5th Amendment, which does apply to the federal government, has been interpreted by the courts as including an "equal protection" guarantee from federal government interference.

All statutes and regulations to some degree classify people and businesses, for example, in the tax code there are different rates for different incomes. To classify is to discriminate, though in a more euphemistic sense. However, in order to pass the equal protection test, these classifications must be legally permissible. For most laws that regulate business, the courts use a "rational basis" standard to determine the constitutionality of a regulatory law. That is, a government classification need only have a reasonable and rational relationship to the achievement of a legitimate and proper government interest or purpose in order to pass equal protection assessment. For certain other classifications, such as gender, age, and legitimacy, there is an intermediate standard of review, and thus these types of classifications will be upheld if they are substantially related to important government interests. However, certain other government classifications involving "suspect categories," such as classifications based on race, color, or national origin, or those that burden "fundamental rights," such as freedom of speech and the right to privacy, must pass a much more rigid legal test, called "strict scrutiny." Pursuant to this demanding legal test, such a government classification will violate the equal protection guarantee unless the classification is found to be necessary to a compelling government interest.

In 2013, the Supreme Court enunciated two major decisions dealing with gay marriage. In the first, *United States v. Windsor* (2013), the Court struck down on 5th Amendment Due Process and Equal Protection grounds the key provision in the federal Defense of Marriage Act (DOMA) which recognized marriage as solely between a man and a woman and consequently denied federal benefits to married gay couples who were validly married in states which recognize gay marriage (12 states as of the writing of this edition). Justice Anthony Kennedy, writing for a 5-4 majority, stated that DOMA infringed on gay married couples' "liberty" interest protected by the Due Process clause as well as disparaged, demeaned, and harmed them for no legitimate purpose in contravention of the Equal Protection clause. The decision means that as far as federal rights and benefits (for example, tax, social security, and immigration) are concerned, federal law must treat same-sex marriages the same as traditional marriages, assuming, of course, a gay couple has a valid marriage in a state that recognizes gay marriage. The case was a major victory for gay rights. However, the second Supreme Court holding, in *Hollingsworth v. Perry* (2013), was a much more narrow one, decided on procedural grounds; and was not the sweeping decision outlawing bans on gay marriage that gay rights advocates had wanted and hoped for. In the case, the Supreme Court dismissed an appeal on technical "standing" grounds challenging a lower federal court decision that invalidated on constitutional grounds a California law, in the form of a voter referendum, which banned gay marriage in the state. By dismissing the appeal, the Court let stand the decision of the federal district court which struck down the law. The result means that gay couples can now be legally married in California; but the Court decision just affected that one state. The decision did not adversely affect bans on gay marriage in other states; and thus the result will be to expect more challenges on federal constitutional grounds to other states' bans on gay marriage.

Equal Protection and Affirmative Action
The term "affirmative action" represents a wide variety of programs, from one extreme of setting rigid, fixed job quotas that must be filled by women and minority group members, to the other most "mild" extreme of taking special proactive efforts to ensure that women and minority group members are included in the pool of applicants for hiring or promotion. Almost everyone morally condemns the former and morally approves the latter. In the middle, however, is the type of affirmative

action plan that takes race, ethnic heritage, or sex into account when selecting among qualified candidates and that gives such individuals a preference over equally or more qualified white men. Such a preference plan raises a loud emotional outcry, from those who praise it as just redress for past discrimination and stereotyping, to those who condemn it as immoral "reverse discrimination."

The United States Supreme Court, in a very significant affirmative action decision in 2003, permitted the use of race as a preference factor in the college admissions process; but the court also issued a stern warning that colleges cannot use rigid affirmative action systems that resemble quotas, and that they also must adopt race neutral policies as soon as practicable. Justice Sandra Day O'Connor, writing for a 5-4 court majority, stated that the University of Michigan Law School did not violate the "equal protection" guarantee of the 14th Amendment to the Constitution. Significantly, Justice Sandra Day O'Connor stated that the goal of creating a diverse student body was a sufficiently "compelling government interest" to justify the law school's consideration of race as a "beneficial" admissions factor. She added, however, that race-conscious admissions policies should not go on forever. Twenty-five years from now, Justice O'Connor stated, the court would expect that racial preferences will no longer be necessary.

The University of Michigan's undergraduate admissions policy – a point system that quantified the importance of race – did not survive the Court's scrutiny in another companion case. In that case, Chief Justice William Rehnquist, writing for a 6-3 majority, stated the numerical policy made race the decisive factor in admissions decisions, and thus was unconstitutional. Justice Clarence Thomas, the court's only black member, issued a bitter condemnation of affirmative action as a well-intended but patronizing and ultimately discriminatory attempt by whites to help African Americans. Thomas' dissent began with a quote from an address by Frederick Douglas criticizing abolitionists in 1865 for interfering with blacks' efforts to help themselves. Thomas stated that he believes that blacks can achieve success "without the meddling of university administrators." He declared that a state's use of racial discrimination in higher education admissions is categorically prohibited by the Equal Protection Clause of the Constitution.

In the majority opinion in the law school case, Justice O'Connor rejected the argument of the Bush administration that race-neutral alternatives could be as effective in creating diversity as affirmative action. The Constitution, said Justice O'Connor, does not prevent the law school's "narrowly tailored" use of race in admission decisions in order to achieve a compelling interest in obtaining educational benefits that are produced from a diverse student body. The Michigan law school uses race as a potential "plus" factor to promote diversity, stated Justice O'Connor. The goal of the law school's affirmative action policy was to produce a "critical mass" of minority students on campus. She supported the decision by citing studies showing that diversity promotes learning outcomes and better prepares students for an increasingly diverse workforce, for society, and for the legal professions. Diversity is necessary, she maintained, for developing leaders with "legitimacy" in the judgment of the people. Moreover, she stated that effective participation by members of all racial and ethnic groups in the civic life of the nation is critical if the U.S. truly will achieve the goal of being one "indivisible" nation. She emphasized, in addition, that businesses have made it clear that the skills and knowledge essential in today's increasingly global marketplace can only be created through contact and experience with widely diverse peoples, cultures, ideas, and views.

U.S. Solicitor General Theodore Olsen, however, condemned the Michigan policies as a "thinly disguised quota." Some critics contended that the decisions mean that universities can still racially discriminate so long as they are not obvious about it. Civil rights advocates, however, hailed the decision as a major victory and claimed it not only strengthened affirmative action in a college setting, but also gives added impetus to the use of race in pursuit of diversity elsewhere, especially in employment. The University of Michigan's president, Mary Sue Coleman, said she was delighted by the decision because the principle of diversity was upheld, and she stated the school would fix its undergraduate policy so that it is not construed as a mechanical quota-based system. Unlike the law school, the undergraduate school awards a specific, predetermined number of points to applicants whose ethnicity or race is underrepresented on campus, specifically a 20-point bonus on a 150-point scale where 100 points guaranteed an admission. The majority of the Court found that this resembled a quota system, a practice previously struck down as unconstitutional. The undergraduate decision also could cause employers to rethink their reliance on quantitative evaluations of job applicants and employees. While the law school decision does allow colleges to consider race as a preferential factor in making decisions, the court made clear that diversity should not be defined solely in terms of race and ethnicity. Universities, therefore, will have to look more broadly at socio-economic factors, special talents and life circumstances, such as family background and income and education levels, in searching for a diverse student body. Justice O'Connor required that universities now must give applicants a personal "holistic" look. The Supreme Court's University of Michigan affirmative action cases in 2003, therefore, emerge as landmark decisions with wide-ranging implications not only for education but also for business and for society as a whole, especially so because the use of race has been upheld legally as a permissible component to an affirmative action preference plan.

The very difficult and contentious issue of affirmative action again reached the U.S. Supreme Court, and also once again in the context of education. In 2006, the Supreme Court heard arguments in a secondary school desegregation case in which two school boards, one in Seattle, Washington, and the other in Louisville, Kentucky, were attempting to preserve voluntarily imposed race-based integration plans. The school board plans were controversial because race was used as a factor to assign students to schools in order to achieve more racially diverse schools. The school districts contended that racial integration is an essential component to a public school education; and that such an objective is a compelling government interest so as to justify a limited use of race in implementing policies that produce integrated schools. The parents that challenged the race-based school assignment plans contended that the Equal Protection clause of the 14th Amendment to the U.S. Constitution as interpreted by the Court forbids any consideration of race in school enrollment decisions. However, proponents of the plan said that the limited use of race is necessary to redress the legacy of racism and school segregation in the United States. Moreover, proponents argued that there are positive benefits for the students and ultimately for society as a whole for students to attend racially diverse schools. Achieving a diverse student body, one recalls, was deemed to be a sufficiently "compelling" interest for the Court to uphold the University of Michigan's law school's affirmative action policy in which race was allowed to be used as one "plus" factor in an otherwise "holistic" evaluation of a candidate for admission. In the Seattle case, involving a city, it is important to note, which never imposed official segregation, students are allowed to enroll in any of ten high schools. However, if a particular high school has more applicants than seats, school official are empowered to use several tie-breaking factors, including race, in order to achieve an enrollment that approximately reflects the city-wide student population. In Seattle, whites account for 40% of the population, with blacks, Hispanics, Asians, and Native Americans accounting for the other 60%. In the Louisville case, the city once had a legally imposed dual, "separate but equal," school system, in which certain schools were reserved for whites and others for blacks. As a result of civil rights litigation, a federal court in 1975 imposed the remedy of mandatory busing in order to achieve integration of the schools. However, in 2000, a federal judge dissolved the desegregation order, finding that the schools had been successfully integrated. In order to maintain integrated schools, school officials in Louisville decided to continue the desegregation policy, which seeks to keep black enrollment in each school between 15% and 50%. A parent whose child was denied admission to neighborhood schools because the child's enrollment would have an adverse effect on desegregation sued because her child was assigned to a school impermissibly due to the child's race.

Even the initial questions and comments by the Justices of the Supreme Court reflected the conservative-liberal dichotomy to the Court. For example, the "liberal" members talked in terms of the benefits of diversity and emphasized the need and desirability of local school officials to develop policies that use race to achieve diversity in school composition. Whereas the "conservative" members asserted that despite the laudable benefits of integration and diversity, the means used to attain these "good" ends must be race neutral, non-discriminatory, and thus moral ones. Of course, the key vote in, as well as author of, the Michigan law school, 5-4, decision, Justice Sandra Day O'Connor, was no longer on the Court. The key vote, according to legal experts, was Justice Anthony Kennedy, who appears to be very reticent about using race as the classifying factor in admissions decisions. Although it is always difficult to predict the Court, many legal experts nonetheless expected that the Court would enunciate a "split decision" as in the precedent Michigan case. That is, the Court would most likely strike down the Louisville plan since race is the sole factor in assigning students; but uphold the Seattle plan where race is used as "merely" one factor, granted a potential "tipping" one, among a variety of criteria employed to determine school assignments. However, in 2007, the Supreme Court, in a surprising, momentous, landmark, and very close 5-4 decision, struck down *both* the Louisville and Seattle affirmative plans as unconstitutional. Chief Justice John G. Roberts, Jr., writing for the majority, declared that the two school districts had failed to meet their "heavy burden" of justifying the "extreme means" the districts had chosen to classify children by means of their race when making school assignments. Chief Justice Roberts very succinctly explained the Court's reasoning: "The way to stop discrimination on the basis of race is to stop discriminating on the basis of race."

Yet the decision may not entirely eliminate the use of race as a factor in making educational decisions. Justice Kennedy, joining the majority, but also writing a concurring opinion, opined that there might be some "narrow circumstances" that would allow the use of race as a criterion in education. Justice Kennedy also declared that "This nation has a moral and ethical obligation to fulfill its historic commitment to creating an integrated society that ensures equal opportunity for all of its children." Nevertheless, the decision very likely will force educational institutions to devise race-neutral criteria, such as socio-economic factors, in designing affirmative policies and plans. As a matter of fact, in the majority opinion, Chief Justice Roberts stated that other means aside from race should be used to promote diversity in schools. Everyone seems to agree that classroom diversity is a very important educational objective, but how to achieve it fairly and constitutionally is emerging as a daunting challenge – legally, morally, and practically.

In 2013, the Supreme Court again tackled the difficult and contentious issue of affirmative action – and again in the context of education. The case, *Fisher v. University of Texas* (2013), dealt with the Texas affirmative action policy of offering admission to the "flagship" Austin campus of the University of Texas to any high school graduate in the top ten percent of his or her high school graduating class in the state. One high school student, a white female, who was not in the top ten percent in her school, was denied admission to the University of Texas at Austin. She claimed that she had higher SAT and GRE scores than black students admitted pursuant to the "ten percent" rule, and thus she contended that she had been discriminated against because of her race in violation of the 14th Amendment to the United States Constitution. The Supreme Court was expected to enunciate a "sweeping" decision, either upholding or striking down affirmative action. However, the Court enunciated a compromise decision. The Court in a 7-1 decision did not invalidate affirmative action. But the Court, with Justice Anthony Kennedy writing for the majority, made it much more difficult for a university (and other entities) to legally sustain an affirmative action program. The Court held that affirmative action programs that have a race component must undergo the rigid legal test of "strict scrutiny." Strict scrutiny, in essence, in the context of affirmative action in education, has three main components: first, the university must demonstrate that having a diverse student body is a "compelling government interest" for an affirmative action admissions program with a race factor; second, the university must show that its admissions program is tailored narrowly to obtain the educational benefits of diversity; and third, the university must show that there is no other practical race-neutral alternative that would produce the same educational benefits of diversity. The Supreme Court then sent the case back to the lower federal courts to determine if the University of Texas "passed" this "strict scrutiny" test. Supporters of affirmative action in education and other areas were naturally pleased the Supreme Court did not totally invalidate affirmative action, but were concerned that the practical result of such a demanding legal standard would jeopardize affirmative action programs. One thing is sure, though, and that is to expect more affirmative action lawsuits in education and other areas.

Freedom of Speech, Press, and Association

The 1st Amendment to the U.S. Constitution states that "Congress shall make no law...abridging the freedom of speech, or of the press, or of the right of the people to peaceably to assemble, and to petition the government for a redress of grievances." The 1st Amendment has been interpreted to encompass the freedom to associate, and not to associate, and also to protect the privacy of one's associations. Actions, gestures, expressions, as well as articles of apparel, taken or used to communicate an idea, which are designated as "symbolic conduct" or "symbolic speech," are also afforded protection under the 1st Amendment, including the burning of the U.S. flag. Moreover, even offensive, vile, and hateful speech is protected. To illustrate, the Supreme Court ruled in 2011 in *Synder v. Phelps* that a Baptist church had the free speech right to picket and protest against homosexuality and other American "sins," including displaying posters that stated "Thank God for dead soldiers" and "God hates fags," at the funeral of a soldier killed in the Iraq war. It is important to point out that the Court underscored that the protest addressed matters of public concern, the protest was peaceful, and the protest occurred in a public place, on a public street, at a distance from the funeral (approximately 1000 feet as specified by the police). Moreover, the protest did not interfere with the funeral; and the fact that the content of the message was very distressing and caused emotional distress was irrelevant – at least for 1st Amendment purposes. The *Synder* case also illustrates the critical distinction the courts make between the "content" versus the "context" of speech. As emphasized, the content can be hateful; but the government cannot punish people for what they say; yet the government can control in the interests of public safety and welfare the "context" of speech, that is, where, when, and how people exercise their free speech rights.

Free speech rights, in addition, have been extended to the Internet by the federal courts. To illustrate, in the case of *Mukasey v. ACLU* (2009), the Supreme Court refused to review a federal appellate decision which ruled that the federal Child Online Protection Act was an unconstitutional violation of the 1st amendment right to free speech since the statute was overbroad, infringed on expression of content, and also that other means, such as software filters, were available to protect children from inappropriate material online. To compare, the Supreme Court in the case of *United States v. American Library Association* (2003) upheld the constitutionality of the Children's Internet Protection Act, which required schools and libraries to install software filters on computers to prevent children from accessing adult content. The Court explained that the federal statute did not violate the 1st Amendment since the filtering system was flexible, for example, a library could disable it for an adult patron, and thus the law did not unduly burden free speech.

Furthermore, any government restrictions on speech must be narrowly tailored so as not to suppress protected speech or expression. To illustrate, in the Supreme Court case of *United States v. Stevens* (2010), the Court struck down as unconstitutionally overbroad a federal statute that made it a crime to create, possess, or sell depictions of animal cruelty in interstate commerce. The case involved a person who created and sold videos of pit-bull dog fights and dogs attacking wild boars. The Court reasoned that the statute was overbroad and thus violated the 1st amendment because the law legitimately could be applied to legal activities, such as pictures or filming of hunting or depictions of the inhumane treatment of animals.

These First Amendment rights, one recalls, also are applicable to the states by means of the 14th Amendment Due Process clause. Yet these 1st amendment freedoms are not absolute. As a general rule, the government may prohibit and punish speech that produces such negative consequences for society as to outweigh the value of the speech, for example, obscene speech, child pornography, "fighting words" (that is, speech likely to incite violence), or defamatory speech. Regarding the latter, when the "victim" of the defamation is a public official and the defamation regards his or her public duties or official conduct, the courts require as part of "free speech" protections that a showing of "malice" be made. That is, the public official suing for defamation is required to show by clear and convincing evidence that the defendant published the defamatory statement knowing it to be false or with reckless disregard of its truth or falsity. This burdensome "malice" requirement also applies to "public figures," that is, famous people in the community, who also seek to sue for defamation. The courts, therefore, are very protective of speech and plainly recognize the importance of free speech rights in a democracy such as the United States. Nonetheless, if the government interest in restricting speech is sufficiently strong, and the restriction on speech is narrowly tailored so as not to "chill" permissible speech, the courts will uphold the infringement on speech.

A developing as well as problematic area of the law is the conflict between constitutionally protected hateful speech and the concept of a "hate crime" pursuant to the federal Hate Crimes Prevention Act. According to this statute it is illegal and a crime to physically harm a person based on his or her race, religion, national origin, gender, sexual orientation as well as other protected categories. However, what if the "hate" is manifested "merely" in speech? Speech, as we know, is protected by the First Amendment, and speech of a political nature, even if offensive, vile, and reprehensible, is generally protected. Yet there is a developing body of law that maintains that certain speech, and the words alone, can amount to a hate crime punishable by the government. The Supreme Court and the federal courts have ruled that general comments, even if highly offensive are permissible legally. However, if the words convey an intent to harm a person or persons, contain an expression of violence, convey a sense of immediacy and imminence to the threats, and are specifically directed to a particular person or individuals then there may be a hate crime violation. So, for example, in one case, saying that one hates Muslims and wishes them harm is not a hate crime, but one saying the aforementioned words and adding that one intends to bomb an Islamic Center at a particular place and time would rise to the level of a hate crime merely based on the speech without the violent and hateful act being perpetrated.

Corporate Free Speech

The U.S. Supreme Court made a very significant decision regarding free speech, politics, and business in the case of *Citizens United v. Federal Election Commission* (2010). The court, in a 5-4 determination, substantially overturned campaign finance laws to the benefit of corporations. The ruling reverses a long-standing limitation on corporate money going into federal elections by allowing businesses as well as labor unions to spend money – and as much as they want – directly to support a candidate or to oppose a candidate on television or by means of other media or literature, so long as the contribution is independent of the candidate and the campaign. That is, the decision, though broad in scope, leaves in place the prohibition on direct contributions to candidates from corporations and unions. A corporation long has been considered a "person" under the law for many rights, including most constitutional rights; but there had been restrictions on a corporations' exercise of political free speech rights. Supporters of the decision long have argued that the prohibitions were an unconstitutional infringement on free speech; and accordingly they now claim the court's decision is a major victory for First Amendment free speech rights. The decision even allows union and corporation political advertisements in the closing days of an election. Critics countered by saying the decision will give "big business" too much power and influence in political campaigns. Justice Anthony M. Kennedy, writing for the majority, stated that the 1st Amendment prohibits Congress from punishing citizens or associations of citizens from engaging in political speech. The decision could result in millions of dollars flowing into elections now in the United States from corporations and labor unions, especially for television advertising. Candidates also will not be able to stop corporations and unions from running ads. Yet, a candidate who is short on money may appreciate corporate or union support. Corporations and unions now can spend as much as they want to advance or defeat political candidates, and they can do so by name, in advertising, commercials, and literature; but there can be no coordination with the candidates or their campaigns. One thing is for sure, and that is that voters will now be getting a lot more information about candidates on which to base a voting decision. The "marketplace for ideas" created and sustained by the 1st Amendment has certainly been broadened and increased. Of course, more campaign ads also may mean more "negative ads" as well as a greater potential for more "voter burn-out" over ads. Regardless, the media, especially television and radio stations, should see substantial financial gains as a result of the court's decision. Furthermore, shareholders of corporations as well as members of labor unions should now pay much closer attention as to how these entities spend their money on political campaigns and candidates.

Freedom of Speech – Political Speech v. Commercial Speech
The 1st amendment grants the most extensive protection to "political speech," that is, speech regarding politics, political candidates, elections, and public affairs issues, such as immigration reform. For example, one federal court of appeals ruled that doctors have the 1st amendment right to recommend marijuana to sick patients, and the patients have the equivalent right to receive such information; and thus the federal government's attempt to revoke the doctors' prescription licenses was unconstitutional. Moreover, even if hateful and false, political speech is protected. This type of speech is regarded as a fundamental right, and as such can only be restricted or punished if the government has a compelling government interest, for example, to prevent an imminent riot or violence. The "antidote" for false political speech is true political speech; and thus emerges the "battle of ideas" in a democracy such as the United States where rational and free debate on the issues serves the public interest. The motivation behind political speech thus is to advance a particular

political or public affairs agenda. Even if the political speech is advocated by a corporation, which although an artificial legal person is a constitutional "person" nonetheless, the political corporate speech is fully protected.

The motivation behind *"commercial speech,"* however, is "merely" monetary and economic. Commercial speech consists of business marketing and advertising activities. The primary objective of commercial speech is to propose and consummate a commercial transaction. Yet commercial speech is speech, and accordingly is also protected by the 1st Amendment. The public does have a "right to know." Consumers do have a legitimate interest in the free flow of commercial information which is deemed to be necessary for the consumer to make a well-informed economic decision. For example, statutes prohibiting licensed pharmacists from advertising, preventing attorneys from advertising (even for lawsuits), and prohibiting ads for birth control and abortion have all been struck down as violating free "commercial" speech rights. Even local prohibitions on "for sale" signs on property in residential areas have been struck down. Accordingly, the Supreme Court has given a very high degree of protection to safeguarding "mere" commercial speech. The line between political speech and commercial speech, however, is at times very difficult to discern. In one recent case, Nike Corporation was sued under a California consumer protection statute for its allegedly deceptive advertising. In defending itself against accusations of exploiting its workers in Asia, the company's representatives were not entirely accurate as to the benefits the company provided to its workers. The consumer group thus sued the company for its misleading defense which it claimed violated the state truth-in-advertising law. Nike defended itself by contending that its speech was "political," as it dealt with a topic of global business concern, and thus its speech did not have to be entirely accurate, and for that matter could be outright false. The California consumer group argued, however, that the speech was "only" commercial speech, since the motivation behind Nike's defensive commentary was economic. The case went to the California supreme court, which ruled in a split 4-3 decision, that Nike's efforts to defend itself before critics of its labor practices overseas amounted to commercial speech; and thus the company could be sued under the California law for its deceptive advertising, since in order to be constitutionally protected, commercial speech must be true and non-deceptive. The case was appealed by Nike to the U.S. Supreme Court, which granted a hearing, and then, while oral arguments were in process, unexpectedly and very surprisingly decided not to decide the case. The decision of the state court was thus left standing; and as a result Nike eventually settled with the consumer group for $1.5 million. Many people in the legal and business communities were very disappointed in the Supreme Court's action, as the court was expected to use the case to more clearly define the line between political and commercial speech.

Nevertheless, once "commercial" speech is established, it plainly can be regulated more extensively than "pure" political speech. There are two basic requirements in order for commercial speech to be constitutionally protected: first, the speech must concern a legal transaction and legal subject matter; and second, the speech cannot be false, deceptive, or misleading. However, even if lawful and true, commercial speech can still be regulated by government if: 1) government has a rational and substantial government interest to restrict the speech; 2) the restriction directly advances the government interest; and 3) the restriction is narrowly tailored and thus is not more extensive than necessary to serve the government's interest. The key component to the preceding legal tests is what constitutes a "substantial" government interest. An important federal law case dealt with commercial speech in the context of telemarketing; and well-illustrated the "substantial interest" test. Pursuant to the Do-Not-Call Implementation Act passed by Congress in 2003, the Federal Trade Commission created a Do-Not-Call List, which is a registry of names of persons not wanting to receive telemarketing calls. Companies cannot make unsolicited phone calls to consumers who place their names on the registry unless the companies have done business with the consumer in the recent past. This law was challenged on constitutional grounds as an infringement of the companies' 1st amendment commercial speech rights. However, the federal courts have ruled that the FTC's regulations were not unconstitutional restrictions on commercial speech because they furthered substantial government interests by protecting personal privacy and reducing the amount of telemarketing abuse.

There is a very interesting and important series of Supreme Court cases dealing with the commercial speech rights of providers of "vice" products and services. In the past, the Supreme Court had upheld a Puerto Rican law prohibiting any advertising of casino gambling aimed at residents, as opposed to tourists, due to a substantial (and paternalistic) government interest in protecting the residents of the Commonwealth from the "evils" and "vice" of gambling. However, the U.S. Supreme Court in a series of recent commercial speech cases has abandoned its paternalistic approach to formulating a substantial government interest, and thereby has greatly increased the type and content of "mere" commercial speech protected by the 1st amendment.

The leading Supreme Court commercial speech case was the seminal 1996 unanimous decision of *44 Liquormart, Inc. v. Rhode Island*. This decision severely curtailed the government's power to restrict truthful and non-deceptive advertising and marketing. In the *Liquormart* case, the Court struck down a state ban on advertising the prices for liquor and alcoholic beverages. The rationale of the Rhode Island legislature was a paternalistic and benevolent one of protecting the "good people" of the state of Rhode Island from the "evils" of "demon rum." The idea was that price advertising would lead to competitive price "wars," thereby lowering the price of liquor and alcoholic beverages, and thus making them more affordable and "drinkable" to the citizens and residents of that state. This rationale is called the "vice" doctrine, and had been an adequate rationale in the Puerto Rican gambling case; but not in the case of the Rhode Island liquor price advertising ban. Now, according to the U.S. Supreme Court, government no longer has the broad discretion to suppress truthful and non-deceptive commercial speech, even for paternalistic purposes. Adults now must have the ability to receive information on legal products and services, even if traditionally they are branded as "vices" and have a high potential for abuse. Today, "thanks" to the Court, one can "find one's way to heaven, or one can find one's way to hell." Government is no longer the consumer's "mother," "father," or "big brother." Restricting speech is thus viewed as more dangerous than restricting the vice activity. Obviously, it is now much more difficult for the government to set limits on how business markets, promotes, and advertises its products. The *44 Liquormart* case was definitely a precedent, because soon thereafter in 1999, the U.S. Supreme Court ruled in a unanimous decision, *Greater New Orleans Broadcasting Association v. United States*, that private casinos now are legally entitled to advertise gambling activities on television and radio. Such advertising of the lawful service of gambling, or "gaming" to its supporters, is constitutionally protected commercial speech, declared the court, even if it too is regarded by many as a vice. Both Supreme Court, commercial speech, "vice" decisions have enormous implications for the regulation of tobacco, a legal product which is even more controversial than consuming liquor and gambling.

Another important commercial speech case decided by the Supreme Court dealt with violent video games. Violent video games have given rise to a major legal and ethical controversy between supporters of First Amendment rights to free speech and free expression and government efforts to protect young people from the alleged harmful effects of violent video games. Critics of violent video games contend that they appeal to the deviant interests of children, but the key legal question is whether these games are protected by the 1st amendment to the Constitution. In California, in 2005, the legislature promulgated a law that banned people under the age of 18 from buying or renting violent video games that appeal to "a deviant or morbid interest in minors." The California legislature based the law on findings that violent video games stimulate "feelings of aggression" and promote "anti-social or aggressive behavior." Yet, in 2011, the U.S. Supreme Court in a 7-2 decision, in the case of *Brown v. Entertainment Merchants Association,* struck down the California law as an unconstitutional infringement on the 1st Amendment to the U.S. Constitution. Justice Scalia, who wrote the majority opinion, stated that even when the objective of government is to protect children, the protections of the First Amendment still are applicable. He explained that the viewing of videogames is essentially the same as reading books or viewing plays and movies. Games, he said, like books, communicate ideas and social messages, and they have many familiar literary devices, such as characters, dialogue, plot, and music, in addition to features that are distinct to the game medium, such as the player's interaction with the "virtual" world. Justice Scalia also added that depictions of violence have never been subject to government regulation. He mentioned Grimm's fairy tales and Saturday morning cartoons as examples of violence depicted in the media. The Supreme Court, as well as other federal courts, have not treated violent content the same as sexual material, which government can restrict or punish notwithstanding the First Amendment if the material is obscene. Justice Scalia explicitly stated that speech about violence is not obscene.

Nonetheless, despite the wider scope the Court has granted to the meaning of commercial speech, it must be emphasized that if the marketing of an adult "vice" product or activity is aimed at children, then government legitimately can assert that it can, and should be, the "parent" and protect children from these adult activities and products. Protecting the child thus emerges as a substantial government interest, which will allow government to prohibit and punish certain types of commercial speech, which is why the "Joe Camel," cartoon-like, cigarette advertising campaign is now advertising "history." However, the once voluntary advertising ban of liquor on television is also "history" due to the *44 Liquormart* case. Of course, it remains to be seen what will happen, commercially as well as legally, to such new, and novel, products as "sweet cigarettes," beer-flavored ice cream, and beer-flavored popsicles. Moreover, today, a very controversial product has emerged to test the parameters of "free" commercial speech, and that is the legalization of marijuana and not only for medical purposes but for recreational uses. How does one go about advertising and marketing one's marijuana business? The answer, not to be "flip," is carefully! Although marijuana is now legal today in many states for both purposes, it is still illegal pursuant to federal law and actually is classified in the same category as heroin. Moreover, the current Administration is making pronouncements indicating more rigorous enforcement of federal laws. So, a major problem is now confronting marijuana businesses – medical and especially recreational – which want to market and advertise their products and services. As emphasized, marketing and advertising are considered to be "speech," even though the motivation is "merely" more sales or money as opposed to politics or public affairs, and thus protected by the "commercial speech" doctrine under the First Amendment. However, to be protected as commercial speech the product or service advertised must be legal, which obviously marijuana is not under federal laws. Thus, there is a major hindrance to the marketing and advertising of marijuana. And because of the product's illegality, such social media giants as Facebook and Google do not allow marijuana ads, even in those states where the product is legal under state law.

Freedom of Religion
In the 1st Amendment, there actually are two separate and distinct religion clauses. One is called the Establishment Clause, which prevents the government from establishing a "state" religion or from preferring one religion over another. The second one is called the Free Exercise Clause, which prevents the government from interfering with the free exercise of religion. Government in the United States is supposed to be neutral to religion, though there are many ways that government can indirectly, and thus legally, support religion, such as providing health tests and vaccinations to parochial school children. Awarding monetary vouchers to the parents of a child to be used for tuition in any local school, including religious schools, is another matter, as that contentious issue is still a matter of legal controversy, though there is a leading Supreme Court decision upholding a city voucher program for inner-city residents. The explication of the "establishment" legal area, however, is beyond the purposes of this book. Finally, as with "free" speech, freedom of religion is not an absolute right; and consequently, to illustrate, the Mormons in Utah cannot legally practice polygamy even if sanctioned by their religious beliefs, though the Cuban people in Miami legally can sacrifice chicken and goats as part of their Afro-Caribbean Santeria religion.

Freedom of religion also emerges as an important and at times perplexing legal issue in an employment setting, since an employer legally cannot discriminate against an employee based on the employee's religion, but also must make a reasonable accommodation to the employee's religious beliefs. This significant legal area to business is based not on the federal constitution, however, but rather on the federal Civil Rights Act, specifically Title VII regarding employment, which prohibits discrimination based on religion in all the "terms and conditions" of employment, and which also requires employers to make a reasonable accommodation to their employees' religious beliefs, observances, and practices.

The Supreme Court in recent years has enunciated two important decisions regarding religious freedom and business. The first was a 2014 case which dealt with the Affordable Care Act and closely-held corporations. The U.S. Supreme Court ruled that closely-held corporations have the freedom of religious beliefs to avoid covering certain contraceptive drugs and devices in employee health plans, although the drugs and devices are mandated by the Affordable Care Act (aka, "Obama Care"). The Court's decision was a 5-4, and one that has emerged as a significant decision in extending the religious protections enjoyed by people and religious organizations to certain employers. The closely-held companies that challenged the Obama Care mandate were Hobby Lobby Stores, Mardel, and Conestoga Wood Specialties Corp. They objected to the coverage of certain contraceptive drugs and birth-control devices in their health plans. Obama Care requires employers to cover all forms of contraception approved by the government without charging employees a copayment. The three companies objected to the "morning-after pill" and certain intrauterine devices because they consider them the same as an abortion, which they object to on religious grounds. Hobby Lobby Sores, Inc. is an Oklahoma City arts-and-craft chain owned by an evangelical Christian family; and Conestoga is a Pennsylvania cabinet-making company owned by a Mennonite family. Justice Samuel Alito, who wrote the majority decision, stated that the ruling protects the free exercise of religious rights of people who own and control these closely-held for-profit companies. The law in question before the Court was the 1993 Religious Freedom Restoration Act, which President Clinton signed into law, and which allows people to seek exceptions from federal laws that "substantially burden" their religious expression unless the laws further a "compelling government interest" which could not be achieved by less restrictive means. Justice Alito stated that the 1993 Act did not exclude for-profit corporations from its protections. The Act sets a very high standard for lawful interference with, or restriction of, religious beliefs and expression. The government could not meet the aforementioned "compelling" standard; and thus the government could not force the owners of these businesses to cover certain birth-control methods under the contraceptive-mandate of Obama Care, since to do so would violate their religious beliefs. The decision has broadened the Court's view of religious freedom, thereby making it easier for other companies as well as individuals to seek additional exemptions from federal laws that they believe unduly restrict their religious beliefs and free exercise of religion. The decision, though, is a narrow one since it applies only to closely-held corporations whose owners have sincere religious beliefs and run their businesses according to religious principles. It is also important to note that the decision does not apply to publicly-traded corporations, which typically have many shareholders as owners; rather the Supreme Court decision just applies to closely-held corporations, which are typically family-owned and managed and have few

The Supreme Court's decision, it must be emphasized, only exempts closely-held corporations from covering contraceptives in employee health plans. Closely-held corporations are typically small, family-owned and managed corporations, whose shares are not publicly traded. The three companies in the case – Hobby Lobby, Mardel, and Conestoga Wood Specialties Corp. – are owned and controlled by members of a single family. Closely-held corporations also can be composed of a small number of people who usually personally know one another. Some states have special closely-held corporation statutes that allow these corporations to be exempt from traditional corporate formalities, for example, having a board of directors, and thereby to allow the closely-held corporation to be operated much like a partnership. Moreover, there typically are restrictions on the sale or transfer of the shares of closely-held corporations to outside purchasers. However, there is no limit to the number of employees a closely-held corporation can have. The Internal Revenue Service (IRS) defines a closely-held corporation as one where more than half the value of the outstanding shares is owned by five or fewer individuals. By limiting the decision to closely-held for-profit corporations the Supreme Court essentially referred future decisions mainly to state corporation law.

The second case was a 2018 Supreme Court decision dealing with a clash between religious freedom and gay rights. The court, in the case of *Masterpiece Cakeshop v. Colorado Civil Rights Commission*, made a ruling in a case where a Colorado baker refused to bake a wedding cake for a gay couple due to the baker's religious beliefs against gay marriage. The baker lost at the state level at the Colorado Civil Rights Commission as well as the Colorado court of appeals; however, the Supreme Court ruled in favor of the baker. The case was expected to be a major decision on First Amendment religious freedom rights as opposed to the rights of gay people to be free from discrimination. Yet the Court in a 7-2 decision, in a majority opinion written by Justice Anthony M. Kennedy, ruled in favor of the baker on very narrow grounds, stating that the baker was not given a fair hearing by the state civil rights commission regarding the sincerity and extent of his religious beliefs. The Court also stated that comments made by certain members of the commission were inappropriate and dismissive and indicated an animus against and hostility to religion and to the baker's religious beliefs. The hearing consequently was neither fair, neutral, nor respectful, and thus the civil rights commission's determination had to be overturned. As such, as noted, the decision was a narrow one based on unique facts, and thus should not serve as a precedent; nonetheless some gay groups feared the decision would provide an opportunity for certain groups and people to discriminate based on religious grounds.

The Second Amendment and the Right to Bear Arms

The 2nd Amendment to the Constitution guarantees the right to bear arms. However, the specific wording of the amendment has caused controversy as to whether this right is an individual or collective right. The 2nd amendment specifically says: "A well-regulated Militia, being necessary to the security of a free State, the right of the people to keep and bear Arms, shall not be infringed." A "liberal" reading of this language would construe the right to bear arms as a collective one, that is, done through and by means of a government created and controlled militia. However, a "conservative" reading of the 2nd Amendment would construe the right as an individual one, that is, every individual American has the fundamental right to own a gun. To date, in a recent series of cases, the U.S. Supreme Court has tended to the conservative interpretation. In the 2008 case of *District of Columbia v. Dick Anthony Heller*, the Court struck down a Washington, D.C. gun ban that effectively prohibited handgun possession, ruling that individuals have a constitutional right to keep loaded arms for their self-defense, at least in their homes; and then in the 2010 case of *McDonald v. Chicago*, the Court extended its ruling to all states and municipalities. However, in the *Heller* case the Court also said that "reasonable" gun regulations could be constitutionally permissible, that is, regulations designed to prohibit the possession of firearms by felons or the mentally ill, as well as laws forbidding the carrying of firearms in sensitive places, such as schools and government buildings, and regulations imposing conditions and qualifications on the commercial sale of guns, for example, expanded background checks which the U.S. Congress is debating at the writing of this book. The Supreme Court is also expected to decide whether to take up another important 2nd Amendment case in 2013, dealing with the right to carry arms beyond the home. New York and other states have laws that impose stringent conditions on obtaining licenses to carry concealed weapons in public. The New York law, for example, requires people who want a permit to carry a gun in public to show that they have a special need for self-protection. The high court in New York has upheld the state law; and New York gun owners have appealed to the U.S. Supreme Court. Similarly, Maryland will not issue concealed-carry permits unless a person can show a "good or substantial reason" why he or she needs to carry a gun in public. These laws are being challenged as contravening the 2nd amendment. Consequently; and if the Court decides to take the New York case, the Supreme Court's decision will emerge as another landmark 2nd Amendment decision since the Court would rule on how far the constitutional right to gun possession extends beyond one's home.

The Fourth Amendment and Business Searches

The 4th Amendment in the Bill of Rights prohibits "unreasonable searches and seizures" by government; and also requires that for a valid search a warrant must be issued based on "probable cause." For example, in 2013 the Supreme Court ruled that the 4th Amendment requires that the police in most circumstances must obtain a warrant before requiring a suspected drunken driver to have blood drawn by means of needle stick. Related to the 4th Amendment is the judicially created *"exclusionary rule,"* which holds that as a matter of due process of law any evidence obtained in violation of the 4th amendment cannot be used against a criminal defendant at trial. As a general rule, a search warrant, issued by a neutral judge or magistrate and not by the police or law enforcement officials, is required in order to have a lawful search by the police; and this warrant must be based on a probable cause, supported by an oath or affirmation. Probable cause means that the law enforcement authorities have sufficient reliable evidence that a reasonable person would be persuaded that a search is justified. The warrant also must be specific, that is, describe in particular what is to be searched and/or seized; and the search cannot extend beyond the parameters of the warrant, though items in "plain view" can be seized. Whenever a person has a reasonable expectation of privacy as to a place, a warrant will be required. Clearly, searches of homes are protected by the 4th amendment; but what about businesses?

The courts have held that the protections of the 4th amendment also protect places of business from warrantless searches; but also the courts have ruled that the standards for government regulators to inspect a business, for example, to comply with pollution, workplace safety, and zoning laws, are much less stringent than the typical criminal law search warrant that a police or other law enforcement officer needs. The rationale for a lesser standard for business is that government has legitimate regulatory functions to enforce a variety of health, safety, and welfare laws and regulations. To do so means that government regulators need information; and information can be obtained by inspections of businesses among other ways. These agency inspections are governed by the 4th amendment. However, the requirements for obtaining an agency warrant to inspect under the 4th amendment are lenient compared to the criminal law standards. The agency inspector still must get a warrant to inspect a business, but the inspector does not have to point to evidence of a violation or even cite specific reasons. "Probable cause" need not be demonstrated; not even a "reasonable suspicion" of a violation need be shown. All the government agency has to demonstrate is that its inspections of businesses pertain to the agency's regulatory functions, are necessary to protect the public health, safety, welfare, or morals, and that a period of time has lapsed since the agency's last inspection. Thus, typically, the agency must proceed with a warrant, but the warrant is an administrative law warrant, at times called a "*blanket warrant*," under which, for example, certain neighborhoods can be inspected for zoning code violations, or certain types of business can be inspected for worker safety violations. It is thus important to note that people's homes can be inspected by government inspectors, but the purpose is not a criminal law one, but "merely" a regulatory one. There are also exceptional cases where an agency is allowed to inspect without a warrant, such as in the case of a health emergency, or if a business is a "pervasively regulated" one, such as a liquor store, auto reclamation center, gun dealer, or mining business.

The Fifth Amendment and Eminent Domain

The 5th Amendment to the U.S. Constitution states that private property cannot be taken for public use without just compensation. This legal protection applies to the states by means of the 14th amendment and the "incorporation" doctrine. "Property" is broadly defined as including real or personal property as well as tangible or intangible property. The precise definition of "public use," however, has been a problem area in the law; and very recently the Supreme Court has enunciated a decision which markedly expands the definition of "public use." One point is evident, though, and that is the "taking" must be for a "public use." If property is not taken for such a use, it cannot constitutionally be appropriated by the government, even if "just compensation" is paid. A use is "public" if it is rationally related to some conceivable public purpose; that is, the "taking" serves some social, economic, health, safety, welfare, moral, or aesthetic ends. Another problem under eminent domain law is to ascertain whether a government action is a "taking" for which compensation must be paid, or "merely" a "regulation" pursuant to the state's "police power," for which compensation does not have to be paid. Obviously, if there is a physical appropriation of the property, for example, by means of a formal "condemnation" proceeding, or a permanent physical invasion, for example, by imposing a right-of-way easement on private property to benefit the public, then typically there will be a "taking."

Yet if there is "only" a regulation of the property, for example, an environmental regulation that forbids any more development of private property by wetlands, but one that has an adverse economic impact on the value of the property to its owner, has there been a "taking"? A reduction in economic value of property is inherent in any government regulatory scheme, for example, zoning ordinances which typically are upheld. Yet if the government regulation has an unduly harsh burden on an individual property owner, frustrating his or her reasonable investment expectations for the property, leaving a person with no realistic economic alternatives, and without corresponding widespread public benefit, the courts may say that a "taking" has occurred, at times called a "regulatory taking." Of course, government can still achieve its regulatory aims, but it will now have to pay for them. And pay what? "Just compensation" must be paid if there is a "taking," and "just" means the "fair market value" of the property, without considering any unique value of the property to its owner. Due Process, naturally, requires adequate notice, a fair hearing, a decision, and an opportunity to appeal that decision when the power of eminent domain is exercised by government.

In 2005, a divided U.S. Supreme Court, in a very significant property rights decision, ruled that local governments can take private property by the Constitutional power of eminent domain and turn the property over to private developers for economic development, thereby increasing the tax base and/or creating jobs. The case considerably expanded the scope of the 5th Amendment, which grants government the power through eminent domain to seize property for "public use." The decision, though predicated on a Connecticut municipal seizure, has nationwide implications. Specifically, the Fifth Amendment states that private property shall not be taken for *public use* without just compensation. The case is significant because historically it used the power of eminent domain for projects that were clearly "public," such as roads, schools, and airports. All state constitutions also have a "public use" requirement for eminent domain. The public use requirement had been thought to restrict eminent domain to the government taking private property only to create things directly owned or primarily used by the general public, such as bridges, parks, and public buildings. Presently, however, many state and local governments have been using the eminent domain power to take property that was "blighted" or in a blighted area that local government wanted to redevelop. The decision is especially important for areas in which there is little vacant land and where local governments are seeking to redevelop urban areas. In the specific case, *Kelo v. City of New London, Connecticut*, Susette Kelo and several other homeowners in a working class, but not blighted, neighborhood of New London, decided to fight eviction from their homes, filed suit after city officials announced plans to raze their homes for a river front hotel, condominiums, health club, and offices, as well as a pedestrian riverwalk, to be developed by a private entity, called the New London Development Corporation. City officials contended that the private developer's plans served a public purpose by increasing economic development, and that the economic growth outweighed the homeowners' private property rights, even though the area to be condemned was not a slum. The Court, however, emphasized that the states, either judges or legislatures, can provide as much protection to property owners as they choose, and thus put tighter restrictions on politicians who seek to transfer private property from one owner to another. For example, the Michigan Supreme Court recently decided that economic development is not a valid reason to take property from owners who do not want to sell. One point is clear, and that is that the decision now will further embolden local governments and private developers to take property for economic development.

In order to avoid such perceived abuses of private property rights that the Supreme Court may have unleashed in the very significant *Kelo* decision, many state legislatures have taken the initiative to protect private property rights. For example, in 2006 the Florida legislature passed a bill as well as a constitutional amendment that effectively would prohibit government agencies from using eminent domain to transfer private property from one individual to another private individual (that is, to private developers). A 3/5s majority vote in both the state Senate and House of Representatives would be required to grant an exemption to this law. The bill also would make it illegal for government agencies to condemn property merely because it is blighted or slum-ridden. Florida, actually, is one of more than a dozen states that so far have reformed eminent domain laws as a result of the Supreme Court's momentous decision. In another state restriction on the expanded local government power of eminent domain, the Ohio Supreme Court ruled unanimously in July of 2006 that a Cincinnati suburb could not constitutionally take private property for a large redevelopment project. The state court's opinion, based on the state constitution, was diametrically opposed to the federal Supreme Court's decision, which was permissible since the federal high court stated that state constitutions could set different (and higher) standards for property rights. The Ohio case involved a city called Norwood, which wanted to seize about 70 homes for a $125 million redevelopment project to build offices, shops, and restaurants in a neighborhood that was regarded as "deteriorating." Though the state court did say that economic factors could be taken into consideration in determining whether a seizure of private property was legal, the economic benefit to government as well as the local community could not be the only factors to be used to justify the use of eminent domain. Furthermore, the court found that the critical term "deteriorating" was unconstitutionally vague.

Impairment of Contractual Obligations

Article I, Section 10, of the U.S. Constitution, called the Contract Clause, provides that no state shall pass any law impairing the obligation of contracts. "Impairment" means any termination or limitation on the rights and duties to the parties to the contract. It must be emphasized, that this "impairment" provision is only applicable to state legislation and not decisions by the state courts. Consequently, a state court's overruling of a decision by an earlier state court is permissible even though there may be an adverse effect on either public or private contracts. Moreover, the courts have allowed the modification of contracts by legislation if to do so is in the public interest and the impairment is reasonable. As to the federal government, the Contract Clause does not apply at the federal level, and thus Congress may enact legislation which adjusts economic interests, including contracts, and may do so retroactively, so long as Congress has a rational public purpose to do so.

Privacy Rights

Significantly, there is no specific guarantee to a right of privacy in the U.S. Constitution. However, such a right is found in several state constitutions, for example, the California constitution. Nonetheless on the federal level, a right to privacy has been found by the federal courts derived from the guarantees of principally the 1st, 4th, 5th, and 9th amendments to the U.S. Constitution. For example, the U.S. Supreme Court in seminal privacy decision invalidated a Connecticut state law that in essence prohibited the use of contraceptives. As previously emphasized, the privacy protection in the federal constitution protects against incursions of privacy by the government only, including government as an employer, but not incursions by the private sector, including private sector employers.

Pursuant to the Do-Not-Call Implementation Act passed by Congress in 2003, the Federal Trade Commission created a Do-Not-Call List which is a registry of names of persons not wanting to receive telemarketing calls. Companies cannot make unsolicited phone calls to consumers who place their names on the registry unless the companies have done business with the consumer in the recent past. This law was challenged on constitutional grounds as an infringement of the companies' First Amendment commercial speech rights. However, the federal courts have ruled that the FTC's regulations were not unconstitutional restrictions on commercial speech because they furthered substantial government interests by protecting personal privacy and reducing the amount of telemarketing abuse.

Summary

This chapter focused on the definition and nature of law, the delineation of the legal system in the U.S., and impact of the United States Constitutional Law on businesses. It focused on specific areas that can affect businesses, such as the regulation of commerce and taxation. Additionally, the first ten amendments to the Constitution, known as the Bill of Rights, has a strong influence on business practices in that it serves as a limitation against government power, especially when government attempts to restrict speech, including commercial speech. These laws are imperative to business entrepreneurs, managers, and leaders, as neglecting them can lead to serious penalties and consequences. Some of the rights which were covered in-depth are Equal Protection, Freedom of Speech, Press and Association, Freedom of Speech-Political Speech v. Commercial Speech, and the Fifth Amendment and Eminent Domain. This chapter also examined arbitration and mediation as alternatives to the traditional judicial system in resolving disputes.

Discussion Questions

1. In common law systems such as the United States, why are the legal concepts of "*precedent*" and "*stare decisis*" critical? Provide business examples with brief explanations thereof.
2. What are the differences between case law and statutory law in the United States? What takes precedence and why? Provide examples and brief explanations thereof.
3. What are the steps that an attorney would use to analyze a legal situation? Why are they important analytical tools to the manager or entrepreneur? Apply the steps to a business controversy.
4. Common law legal systems have very general statutes and very great reliance on case law and the concept of precedent, whereas civil law legal systems have very detailed statutes and do not rigidly adhere to the concept

of precedent. Which system is superior? Which system would you as a global business manager or entrepreneur prefer to do business in? Why?

5. What is the concept of federalism, such as in the United States, and why does federalism have such significant legal and practical ramifications for the manager and entrepreneur? Provide business examples with brief explanations thereof.

6. What is the difference between an action "at law" and one "at equity"? Provide an example of a legal and equitable remedy together with a brief explanation of each.

7. What is the concept of "jurisdiction" and why is it so very important in the U.S. or for that matter any legal system? Provide examples with brief explanations thereof.

8. How does jurisdiction differ from venue? Provide an example of each with a brief explanation thereof.

9. What is the distinction between jurisdiction *in personam* and *in rem*? Why is this differentiation critical in the law? Provide an example of each with a brief explanation thereof.

10. What are state Long Arm statutes and why are they very important in the obtaining of jurisdiction? Provide an example along with a brief explanation thereof.

11. What is meant by the term "conflicts of laws"? Why is this legal doctrine of potential extreme importance to the success or failure of a lawsuit? Provide a business example with a brief explanation thereof.

12. Explain and illustrate how the U.S. Constitution separates and divides power so as to protect the people of the U.S. from abuse by government and government tyranny.

13. Why is the constitutional concept of "interstate commerce" so critical in the U.S. government and regulatory system? Provide business examples with brief explanations thereof.

14. When and under what circumstances can a state in the U.S. regulate interstate commerce? Provide an example with a brief explanation thereof.

15. What are some of the fundamental provisions in the Bill of Rights that affect business? Provide examples with brief explanations thereof.

16. How does the "equal protection" clause affect the debate about affirmative action preference plans in education and in employment? Provide examples along with brief explanations thereof.

17. What are the "rational basis" and "compelling interest" standards in equal protection law? Illustrate how they operate. Why are they absolutely critical to legal analysis of government programs that classify people?

18. What is the distinction between "political speech" and "commercial speech" in the United States? Why does that distinction have very important ramifications for U.S. businesses? Provide examples with brief explanations thereof.

19. What is the power of eminent domain pursuant to U.S. law? How has that power been materially expanded by the U.S. Supreme Court? Provide business examples with brief explanations thereof.

20. What are the definitions of and distinctions between arbitration and mediation? Provide an example of how each could be used in a business context along with a brief explanation thereof.

2 – TORTS AND BUSINESS

In United States law, *a tort* is a wrongful act against a person or property for which a legal cause of action may be brought for the harm sustained. The term "tort" is a very old one, harkening back to the early common law in England, and even before that to the Norman-French conquest of England. A tort is a private wrong, the violation of private duty created by the law, and the violation of which results in a private injury. To compare, a crime is a public wrong, the violation of a publicly created duty, and the violation of which results in harm to the "state." Yet it is important to note initially that the same act may constitute both a tort and a crime, for example, an assault and battery, which the state can prosecute as a crime and the victim can also sue for intentional tort damages. A breach of contract is a private wrong too, resulting in a private injury, but the breach arises from the violation of a duty created consensually by the parties. Torts can be personal torts, arising from an injury to a person's body, feelings, or reputation, for example; and torts can be property torts, arising from harm to land, real estate, or personal property, for example. The purposes of tort law are to provide protection to certain legally recognizable interests, to afford a remedy if these interests are wrongfully harmed, and to allocate the risk and cost of injury on a just basis. Speaking very generally, people are free to act as they please in the United States so long as their actions do not infringe on or invade the interests of others.

Intentional Torts in the United States

The three major categories of torts in the United States are intentional torts, the tort of negligence, and the doctrine of strict tort liability. In a civilized society, a person cannot intentionally injure another person or harm his or her property. Each person in society is entitled to have certain interests, such as freedom from bodily injury, protected. If another person intentionally invades such a protected interest, the perpetrator violates a legal duty to the injured person who as a result has the legal right to sue for damages for the intentional wrong. Moreover, in a civilized society, everyone is held to a legal duty to exercise reasonable care when one acts. Thus, the victim of one who acts in a careless manner can bring a law suit for damages to compensate for the injury caused by the violation of the duty to exercise reasonable care. Such a lawsuit is premised on the tort of negligence. Finally, society by means of the legal system may create doctrines that impose liability without fault for types of activities that the law brands as "ultra-hazardous." In such a case, the person so acting is held accountable, even without any intentional wrongdoing or even negligent conduct, for any resultant harm. This type of tort liability without fault is called "strict liability" and is premised on utilitarian rationales.

Introduction and Elements
Intentional torts provide a legal remedy for those people whose protected personal or property interests are purposefully invaded or harmed by another. The required elements, or components, to an intentional tort law suit generally are: 1) a wrongful act by another, 2) requisite intent, 3) causation, and 4) damages. The victim as the plaintiff must establish all these elements to the tort in order to have a prima facie, or initial, case against the defendant actor.

A purposeful act that is committed volitionally, that is, voluntarily, by the defendant is first required. Thus, if one strikes another during the throes of a medical seizure, or if one is pushed by a wrongdoer into a third party who suffers harm, one has not committed a volitional act. This act, of course, must intentionally invade a legally protected interest and consequently be a wrongful act. The requisite intent can be specific or general. Specific intent exists when a person's objective is to cause a certain result or consequences; whereas general intent exists when a person does not have a specific goal or result, but acts knowing with substantial certainty that certain consequences will ensue. An example of the latter intent would occur when a person does intend to push another person, who falls and injures himself or herself. The actor may not have intended that specific harm, but is liable nonetheless due to the substantial certainty of the victim falling and injuring himself or herself. An interesting old common law doctrine concerning intent and intentional torts is called the "transferred intent" doctrine, usually found in assault and battery cases. Transferred intent is a legal device that is used when a defendant intends to cause harm to one person, but actually injures another person. The defendant's intent to commit the wrongful act is transferred from the intended "target" to the actual victim, who then can sue for the appropriate intentional tort. The causation requirement means that the harmful result giving rise to liability must have been caused by the defendant's wrongful act. The causation test will be met when the conduct of the defendant is a substantial factor in bringing about the plaintiff's injury. Finally, there must be some type of injury or harm, which can be minor, but nevertheless will support an award of damages, including punitive damages.

Intentional Torts against the Person
The first intentional tort to the person is a *"battery."* A battery is a purposeful, intentional act by the defendant that causes a harmful or offensive contact to the person of the plaintiff. "Harmful" or "offensive" conduct is measured by the standard of a reasonably prudent person, that is, a person of ordinary sensibilities and not an

overly sensitive person. The "person" of the plaintiff refers to not only the physical body of the plaintiff, but his or her clothes, or a purse or laptop suspended from the body. It is noteworthy to point out that there is no apprehension requirement for a battery; and thus a plaintiff may recover for a battery even though he or she was not even conscious of the harmful or offensive conduct. There is no requirement of an actual injury; and the plaintiff can recover nominal damages even though there are no material damages sustained by the plaintiff. Moreover, nominal damages can serve in many jurisdictions as a predicate for a punitive damage recovery. For example, a male co-worker deliberately patting a female colleague on the rear may not cause her actual physical harm, but it certainly is "offensive" conduct by any ordinary standard of reasonableness, and thus grounds for a battery, as well as being the basis for a sexual harassment lawsuit.

Closely related to a battery is its "cousin," the "*assault*." An assault is an act by a defendant which causes a reasonable apprehension of fear in the victim of an immediate harmful or offensive contact to the victim's person, that is, the fear of a battery. "Apprehension" is measured by the "reasonableness" test; and as such the fear of harm must be a reasonable expectation and not an exaggerated one. Moreover, as opposed to a battery, in order to have this fearful apprehension or expectation, the plaintiff must have been aware of the defendant's act. However, a person may be placed in a situation of reasonable apprehension of immediate harmful or offensive conduct, even though the defendant is not actually capable of committing a battery on the plaintiff. This circumstance is called the "apparent ability" doctrine; and the classic example arises when the wrongdoer points an unloaded gun at the victim who does not know that the gun is unloaded. Legally, it is sufficient if the defendant has the apparent ability to bring about the contact. Words alone, as a general rule, no matter how violent, do not constitute an assault; rather some overt act is necessary, such as raising one's arm as if to strike or making a fist. Words, however, may form the basis of another independent intentional tort. Finally, with assault there is a requirement of immediacy. That is, the apprehension must be of immediate harmful or offensive conduct; and consequently neither the threat of future harmful contact nor a conditional threat is sufficient for an assault.

The next intentional tort to the person is "*false imprisonment*." This tort occurs when a defendant acts or fails to act and thereby confines or restrains the plaintiff to a bounded area. Confinement or restraint can be effectuated by physical barriers or by physical force directed at the plaintiff or a member of his or her family as well as physical force being directed at the plaintiff's property. Threats of physical force to oneself or one's family or one's property will be sufficient, as will be the failure to provide a means of escape or egress, even when the plaintiff originally has come under the defendant's control. Generally, moral pressures and conditional threats will be insufficient means of confinement or restraint. There is, however, no need to resist the physical force used to confine or restrain the plaintiff. Moreover, the time of confinement and restraint is immaterial for the cause of action, though material as to the amount of damages. Moreover, there is no requirement that the plaintiff be aware of the confinement. Finally, for an area to be "bounded," the plaintiff's freedom of movement must be limited in all directions. Merely blocking one of many exits is insufficient; and thus if there is a reasonable means of escape, which the plaintiff was aware of, the area is not bounded, and there is no tort liability. One important business ramification of the false imprisonment tort occurs in shoplifting cases where a merchant suspects a person of shoplifting and detains that person to make an investigation. What exactly is the merchant's liability for false imprisonment? Under the common law as well as pursuant to several state statutes, merchants have been accorded a "privilege" to detain a suspected shoplifter for an investigation. There typically are three basic elements to this merchant's "privilege": 1) the merchant must have a reasonable belief as to the occurrence of a theft; 2) the detention must be conducted in a reasonable manner, and concomitantly only non-deadly force can be used; and 3) the detention must be for a reasonable period of time and only for the purposes of making an investigation as to the suspected theft. Under the common law, this privilege was referred to as the merchant's "shoplifter detention" privilege, but today pursuant to modern state statutes, the privilege is more euphemistically referred to as a "merchant's protection" privilege.

The tort of *intentional infliction of emotional distress* arises when the defendant purposefully acts in an extreme, outrageous, and atrocious manner and thereby causes the plaintiff to suffer severe emotional distress. The wrongful conduct must be conduct that goes beyond all bounds of decency tolerated by a civilized society. Such conduct is again measured by a "reasonableness" test. Mere indignities and annoyances are insufficient. However, if the defendant knows that the victim is more sensitive and thus more susceptible to emotional distress than an ordinary person, then the defendant's conduct will be measured by that "sensitivity" standard. Children and the elderly would be examples of usually more sensitive people. Although business examples of this intentional tort are rare, they do occur, usually in a situation where an employee is discharged in an abusive, threatening, humiliating, mocking, and disrespectful manner in full view of his or her co-workers. Although the employer may have the legal right to discharge, especially if the employee is an employee at-will, the outrageous manner of the discharge may give rise to a separate independent tort.

A major intentional tort with widespread business ramifications is *defamation*. The elements to a cause of action for defamation that the plaintiff must prove are as follows: 1) false and defamatory language by the defendant; 2) "of or concerning" the plaintiff, that is, identifying the plaintiff to a reasonable reader, listener, or viewer; 3) "publication" of the defamatory language to a third party; and 4) resulting injury to the reputation of the plaintiff. As a basic component to the tort, the false statements must be defamatory; that is, the defendant's language must adversely affect the victim's reputation in the community; one's honesty, integrity, or virtue must be impugned or assailed. Declaring to a discharged employee that he or she is a criminal, a thief, a cheat, and a liar would suffice. The "of or concerning" the plaintiff requirement means that a reasonably prudent person would understand that the defamatory statement referred to the plaintiff. The "publication" requirement mandates the defamatory statement must be communicated to a third party who understands it as such. So, for example, if the employer in the preceding example did make such defamatory accusations of criminality and immorality but only to the employee, with no one else present, then publication is lacking. Similarly, if the defamatory statement is made in a letter, memo, or email which only the employee sees, then there is no publication. Conversely, if the employer makes the false accusations of employee criminality publicly, on a loudspeaker, employee bulletin board or "virtual" discussion board, or in a "global" email, then there is publication. Regarding the intent requirement, defamation is at times called a "quasi-intentional tort" because even though intent is required, it is merely the intent to publish, and not the intent to defame. As such, once a purposeful publication is established, it is no defense that the defendant did not know that the statements were defamatory; and also it is no defense that the defendant did not intend to defame the plaintiff. Moreover, one who repeats or republishes defamatory material is liable just the same as the original publisher. This rule is called the "repetition" rule and holds that each repetition is a separate publication for which the victim can recover damages.

The "injury to the reputation" requirement of defamation presents a problem, since now one must carefully distinguish between two types of defamation – libel and slander – because the plaintiff's burden of proof as to damage to the plaintiff's reputation may differ on the nature of the defamation. *Libel* is a defamatory statement recorded in writing or some other permanent form, such as a picture, statue, movie, television, or radio. There are two important kinds of libel. The first is called "libel per se." Libel per se occurs when a statement is defamatory and libelous on its face, without the need for any extrinsic facts or explanation. The rule of law is that in such a case damage to the plaintiff's reputation is presumed by the law, and accordingly the plaintiff can recover damages without the necessity of proving damages. The second kind of libel is called "libel per quod." This form of libel is not defamatory on its face, and as a result requires reference to additional facts to establish its defamatory nature. In such a case, most courts will not presume damage to the plaintiff's reputation, and thus the plaintiff will be required as a general rule to plead and prove special damages, for example, that the defamation caused the loss of employment or a business opportunity.

Slander is spoken defamation; it is oral and heard; it is in less permanent and less broad areas of dissemination. As a general rule, damage to the plaintiff's reputation is not presumed, and thus the plaintiff has to plead and prove special damages. However, there are four categories of slander that are considered so harmful they are called "slander per se." The legal consequence of uttering a slander per se is that damage to the plaintiff's reputation is presumed. The four slander per se categories involve defamatory statements that: 1) a person is guilty of a serious crime of moral turpitude (and not a minor offense); 2) adversely affect a person's profession, business, or trade; 3) impute a loathsome disease to a person; and 4) historically impute that an unmarried woman is unchaste.

There are four chief defenses to defamation: 1) consent, 2) truth, 3) absolute privilege, and 4) qualified or conditional privilege. Consent by the plaintiff to the publication of the defamatory statement will be a defense. Consent will be discussed in a forthcoming section of this chapter in conjunction with other intentional torts. Truth is a total defense to a lawsuit for defamation; no matter how defamatory the statement is, if it is true, the truth will be a complete defense to a cause of action for defamation, though not necessarily for other intentional torts. An absolute privilege to defame arises in court trials and other government hearings proceedings, and protects litigants, witnesses, attorneys, judges, and other government personnel. A qualified or conditional privilege will operate as a complete defense; but it may be forfeited by the presence of malice, in the sense of spite or ill-will, or abuse; that is, the publishing of the defamatory statement occurred with an improper motive or for an improper purpose. The qualified privilege can be used to protect not only the public interest, but also the private interest, for example, to protect a statement by a former employer to a prospective employer regarding a job applicant. In the absence of malice or abuse, the qualified privilege will even protect defamatory and false statements by the former employer concerning the former employee. However, regardless of the existence of such a common law privilege to defame, which some states have formalized in statutory form, most employers are very fearful of being sued for defamation by former employees and thus are very reticent to be expressive, let alone expansive, in communications regarding former employees.

When defamation occurs on the Internet, unique problems emerge, especially with the "repetition" rule and the liability of re-publishers of defamatory statements. In particular, the legal issue arose as to whether an Internet service provider (ISP) could be construed as a "re-publisher" and thus potentially liable for defamatory statements made by users of their online services. This perplexing question was resolved by a federal statute in the United States, The Communications Decency Act of 1996, which holds that the provider as well as the user of an "interactive" computer service shall not be liable as a publisher or speaker for information provided by another content supplier. Moreover, the courts have ruled that even when an Internet service provider becomes aware of the defamatory statements on its online system, and fails to promptly remove them, the ISP is still not legally liable, though one would assume that ethically the ISP would feel duty-bound to remove the offensive material as soon as possible.

Defamation can also occur against one's property, and at times this tort is called "disparagement of property," which can include a variety of legal wrongs, such as slander of quality, trade libel, or slander of title. The essence of this type of defamation is that the defendant makes an intentional, false, accusation impugning the quality or ownership of another's goods or property. Ordinarily, the standard defamation rules apply to this variant of the tort, but with one major exception. In the "property" form of defamation, in order to recover damages, the aggrieved party will not have any damages presumed; rather, the plaintiff will have to prove that the disparagement to his or her property or ownership rights caused an actual property loss.

The intentional tort of *invasion of privacy* protects the right to maintain one's private life free from unwanted intrusion and unwarranted publicity. Invasion of privacy is a broad legal doctrine as it consists of not one, but rather four distinct invasions of a person's privacy and personality. The four "privacy" torts succinctly stated are: 1) appropriation, 2) intrusion, 3) "false light," and 4) public disclosure.

The "appropriation" tort occurs when the defendant appropriates without permission the plaintiff's name or picture for the defendant's commercial advantage, typically for the advertisement, marketing, and promotion of the defendant's products or services. "Intrusion" occurs when the defendant intrudes on the plaintiff's private life, private affairs, or seclusion. It is absolutely essential for "intrusion" tort liability that the intrusion invades a person's private domain, and not a public domain. For example, taking a picture of a celebrity in a public place is not legally actionable. Moreover, the aggrieved party is held to a reasonableness standard; that is, only a reasonable expectation of privacy is protected by the tort. In an employment setting, an employer must be careful when conducting surveillance of employees, monitoring employees, and searching employees, even in the workplace as the employee is still entitled to some "private space" therein. Moreover, when conducting surveillance off-the-job, for example, to enforce an employer's policies of no-dating of co-workers or no-smoking at all, the employer must be extremely careful not to contravene the employee's privacy rights protected by the "intrusion" tort. Of course, an astute employer will give the employee notice that certain types of surveillance, monitoring, and searches will be conducted, since it will be more difficult for an employee to claim a reasonable expectation of privacy if he or she is informed that an intrusion therein, for example, for drug-testing, will be conducted under certain circumstances.

Another emerging employment issue with privacy concerns and Smart Phones, particularly when employers require employees to install GPS or other tracking type devices on their Smart Phones and/or other technology so that the employers can monitor their communications and movements while on- and off-duty, especially when employees spend a great deal of time on-the-road. Many companies sending employees out on service calls track their movements using mobile applications. Tracking movements can help employers plot better delivery routes and thus save on fuel costs, as well as helping employers to know when employees are "goofing off." But some employees are tracking employees on a continual basis, thus triggering privacy concerns – legal and ethical. Under the common law tort of invasion of privacy, employees are entitled to a reasonable expectation of privacy on- and off-duty. Moreover, the invasion of privacy must be outrageous, say the courts. Of course, if an employer has a legitimate business reason for monitoring employees and tells the employee that he or she will be monitored, and why, it will be a challenge indeed to prevail on an invasion of privacy lawsuit. Some states, such as California, have in their state constitutions privacy protections that protect private sector employees from having their private life intruded on by their employers; but the employer's conduct must be an unreasonable invasion of privacy. The problem emerging is that today technology has blurred the lines, both legally and morally, between what is on- and off-duty work and also what is in one's work life as opposed to what is in one's personal and private life.

Finally, as will be discussed in the Internet Law chapter, a U.S. federal statute allows the employer to monitor the employee's use of the employer's email system. Also actionable as a privacy tort is the publication of facts by the defendant which places the plaintiff in a "false light." "False light" means the public disclosure attributing to a person a view or opinion which he or she does not possess or actions which he or she did not take. Finally, public disclosure of private facts about the plaintiff by the defendant is actionable as a privacy tort. Of course, the facts must be private and not in the public record. It must be emphasized that even if the facts about a person are true, the tort may still lie.

The legal wrong of fraud is also a very broad formulation under the common law. Fraud is covered in detail in the chapter on Contract Law. However, to underscore certain fundament points now, one must be cognizant that the most serious type of fraud is intentional fraud, also known as intentional misrepresentation, and known in the old common law days as "deceit." Deceit, as will be shown, provides a defense to a breach of contract suit, a legal means to rescind or cancel a contract, and most importantly for the purposes of this chapter, the grounds for an intentional tort lawsuit. There are, however, as also will be seen, many difficult hurdles in pleading and proving a "deceit" lawsuit, in particular the necessity of showing that the defendant knowingly and purposefully lied and intended to lie in order to induce the victim to do or not do a particular act or transaction.

The next intentional tort, which also has significant business ramifications, is the tort of *intentional interference with contractual or business relations*. This tort requires the presence of a contact, a business relationship, or the expectancy of a business relationship, which the defendant is aware of and which the defendant interferes with by improper means in order to advance its own business interests. An example would arise when one competing company wrongfully induces a key employee at another firm to break one's contract with his or her employer and to work for the competitor. Intent is required, of course, and in the sense that the evidence is necessary that the defendant intentionally induced the former employee to break his or her contract with the former employer, not merely that the employee breached it, and then went to work for the defendant competitor. This tort, therefore, is a very complicated one, whose full explication is beyond the purposes of this type of book. Yet, one other major problem with this tort is that the laws governing wrongful interference tort are not clear as to what are legitimate and proper competitive actions in seeking new personnel and new business as opposed to wrongful "pirating," predatory, abusive, and malicious tactics. The line between illegal predatory and abusive competition and "merely" aggressive, "tough," "hard-hitting," and legal competition is not an easy one to draw, not only for this intentional tort, but also under antitrust law, particularly for monopolization analysis, as are often seen in the discussion of antitrust laws.

Solicitation of one's co-workers to leave their employment and work for a new firm, especially one to be established by a fellow employee, is a very problematical area legally. In particular, the tort of intentional interference of contract can arise when an employee of a firm plans to leave and start his or her own business and then commences to solicit key employees of the employer during or after employment. If such solicitation occurs during current employment, particularly when the employee has an employment contract for a certain term, the prospective entrepreneur risks a lawsuit based on the old common law's duty of loyalty to one's employer. And in either case, the entrepreneur risks a tort lawsuit for the intentional interference of contract. Both can result in an injunction and the latter can result in tort damages. So, to be safe, the entrepreneurial employee should merely tell his or her co-workers that he or she is leaving or has left, and then if the employees ask why, the entrepreneur can state that he or she plans to, or has started, a new business, and give them a phone number and email where the entrepreneur can be reached. Telling one's co-workers about one's future plans is permissible, but "raiding" them may be a violation of tort and contract law (if there is an "anti-piracy" clause in a contract).

The final intentional tort to the person is the wrongful institution of legal proceedings, often called "malicious prosecution." This tort is based on a private defendant (and not a government prosecutor) wrongfully instituting criminal (and not civil) proceedings against a party, which terminate in that party's innocence, and which the defendant lacked probable cause to prosecute and possessed an improper motive for instituting the criminal action. The next major category of intentional torts deals with intentional torts to one's property.

Intentional Torts against Property

The law recognizes that there are protected interests regarding not only one's person but also one's property. Accordingly, there are four main types of intentional torts to property: 1) trespass to land, 2) trespass to chattels, 3) conversion, and 4) defamation to property. The latter tort was previously covered in the defamation section.

A *trespass to land* happens when a person purposefully and physically invades another's land or real property. The interest protected by this tort is the interest of exclusive possession of real property. Some physical invasion of the land is required, though it is not necessary that the defendant actually come on the premises. For example, a defendant can be liable for a trespass by intentionally causing objects or third parties to come upon the plaintiff's land. A trespass can exist, moreover, when a defendant remains on a plaintiff's land after the defendant's original lawful right of entry has ended. However, if no physical object or person enters the land, then there is no "invasion" and thus no trespass; however, the defendant may still be liable under nuisance law if the plaintiff's use and enjoyment of the premises is materially and unreasonably impeded, for example, by noise or odors. There is one caveat regarding the intent requirement to trespass to land. That is, although intent is required, the intent to trespass is not required; rather, only the intent to do the act that constitutes the trespass is sufficient. A mistake, therefore, as to the lawfulness of the defendant's entry on the land is not a defense. Finally, there is no requirement of actual damages in order to have a cause of action in trespass; that is, actual injury to the land or real estate is not required; damages, at least nominal damages, are presumed. In addition, if the trespass continues, it may evoke a lawsuit in equity by the landowner for an injunction.

The next type of intentional tort to property is *trespass to chattels* or, in more modern parlance, trespass to personal property (as opposed to real property). This tort requires a purposeful act by the defendant which interferes with the plaintiff's right of, and interest in, possession of a chattel (or thing). This type of trespass can arise by intermeddling, that is, conduct which directly damages the personal property, such as intentionally "keying" another's automobile, or by dispossession, that is, by temporarily depriving a person of his or her right to possession of a chattel, such as "borrowing" another's bicycle for a ride. As with trespass to land, mistake is not defense; however, contrary to the "land" tort, trespass to chattels requires some actual damage to the property or a dispossession for an appreciable length of time; nominal damages are not presumed for a trespass to chattels. Note that if the interference with, or dispossession of, the chattel is so serious or so long, the tort may be "upgraded" to the intentional property tort of conversion, which may require the defendant to pay the full value of the property as damages. Conversion will be covered in the next subsection.

Yet before that important property tort can be examined, one problem area in the law, caused by the advent of the Internet, must be addressed, and that is whether "spam" and "spamming" can be conceived as a trespass to property. Spam, of course, is bulk, unsolicited, and "mass" email. Because of the burden in time, effort, and money that "spamming" may inflict on an online user or an Internet service provider, some courts in the United States have stated a willingness to accept "spam as trespass" lawsuits. The courts, though, typically will require a showing of material economic harm produced by voluminous spamming, and not mere annoyance, before imposing tort damage liability under a trespass to chattels theory or issuing an injunction. Moreover, due to the uncertainty of tort law as well as the many, and at times conflicting, state statutes regulating spam, the U.S. Congress in 2003 enacted the *CAN-SPAM Act*, fully known as the Controlling the Assault of Non-Solicited Pornography and Marketing Act, which went into effect on January 1 of 2004. This federal statute applies to any electronic and commercial mail messages; and it also preempts any state anti-spam laws (except state laws prohibiting false and deceptive email practices). The CAN-SPAM Act, it is essential to underscore initially, does not prohibit spam; rather, the federal law prohibits certain types of spamming practices, such as not having a return address or having a false return address on the email, "harvesting" email addresses from others' Web sites, as well as sending mass emails to randomly generated email addresses. The Act also requires an "opt-out" provision, thereby enabling a recipient to block further emails from the same source, as well as the appropriate labeling of any sexually oriented materials appearing in the email message. While the federal statute certainly will preempt conflicting state anti-spam statutes, it remains to be seen whether CAN-SPAM will also override the old common law of torts, especially the "virtual" use of the trespass to chattels intentional tort doctrine. It also should be mentioned that another anti-spamming statute was promulgated in 2006, the U.S. Safe Web Act (also known as the Undertaking Spam, Spyware, and Fraud Enforcement with Enforcers Beyond Borders Act), which is designed to prevent spam originating from servers in other countries. The U.S. Safe Web Act enables the U.S. Federal Trade Commission to share information and cooperate with foreign government agencies to investigate and eventually prosecute spamming, spyware, and other instances of fraud and deception on the Internet.

The intentional tort "cousin" to trespass to chattels is the tort of *conversion*. The essence of conversion is a purposeful act by the defendant which amounts to an exercise of dominion and control over a chattel of the plaintiff's, which is so long or serious in nature that the defendant must pay the full value of the chattel as damages. Conversion may be effectuated by a variety of methods: 1) wrongfully acquiring the property (for example, by theft or embezzlement, which also makes the civil wrong of conversion a crime); 2) wrongfully transferring the property, such as by selling or mis-delivering it; 3) wrongfully detaining the property, such as refusing to return it to its rightful owner; 4) substantially changing the property; 5) destroying or severely damaging the property; or 6) misusing the property. The property, of course, converted must be tangible personal property, and not land or real property. Recall also that conversion is an intentional tort; and thus "merely" causing accidental damage to or loss of the property is not sufficient for the tort of conversion, though, as will be seen in this chapter, it may be grounds for the tort of negligence. At times, it is difficult to draw the line between "mere" trespass to chattels and the more serious legal wrong of conversion. The more serious the damage to the property is, the longer the time that the defendant holds the property, and the more extensively the defendant uses the property, the more likely that a jury will find that the conversion tort has been committed. Assuming a conversion, the aggrieved party gets as damages the fair market value of the property at the time and place of conversion. This means of redress can in essence be a "forced sale" even if the defendant offers to return the property, as a plaintiff is not obligated to take an item back. Finally, the plaintiff, if he or she does want the item back, can seek a writ of "replevin" from the court, ordering the defendant to return the item.

Defenses
Although the discussion of the intentional torts to persona and property in this chapter has touched on several defenses germane to specific torts, mention should be made of three general categories of defenses: 1) consent, 2) self-defense, and 3) defense of property.

The *consent* defense holds that as a general rule, a defendant is not liable for a wrongful act if the plaintiff has consented to that act. Consent may be given expressly or impliedly. Implied consent is often referred to as "apparent consent," that is, the consent that a reasonably prudent person would give in such circumstances, for example, when engaging in a bodily contact sport, or shopping on "sale day" in a crowded shopping mall. Consent, moreover, will also be implied by the law, for example, in an emergency situation where some type of action, such as medical care, is necessary to save an unconscious person's life. Similarly, pursuant to many states' Good Samaritan statutes, a rescuer who voluntarily assists at the scene of an emergency may be absolved from intentional tort liability by statute, though typically the rescuer is still obligated to effectuate the rescue or render aid in a careful and non-negligent manner.

Self-defense is an ancient legal doctrine, and one that still affords a viable defense to intentional tort liability. When a person possesses reasonable grounds to believe that he or she is being attacked, or about to be attacked, that person may use such force as reasonably necessary to protect against the potential harm. This defense is available when one has a reasonable belief as to another party's hostile actions. The "apparent necessity" of defending oneself is all that is required, not actual necessity; and therefore a reasonable mistake as to the existence of the danger does not negate the defense, with the "classic" example being the "unloaded gun" case. Moreover, under the old common law, though with some differences among the states today, there is no duty to retreat. Thus, most courts would hold that there is no duty to try to escape; rather, a person may "stand ground," and thereby defend oneself. Yet how much force can be used in this self-defense? As a general rule, only that force which reasonably appears necessary to prevent the harm will be authorized; consequently, one may not use force likely to cause death or serious bodily injury unless one reasonably believes that he or she is in danger of serious bodily injury. If more force than necessary is employed, the actor will lose his or her legal right to self-defense. As a result, he or she become the potentially tortious aggressor. Finally, it is important to note that if properly used, the right to self-defense extends to third party injuries. That is, if in the course of reasonably defending oneself, one accidentally injures a bystander, the actor is still protected by the defense.

The common law right to self-defense encompasses one's right to defend his or her property. Accordingly, one may use reasonable force to prevent the commission of a tort against his or her property. There are material limitations, however. First, a request to desist must precede the use of force, unless it appears futile or dangerous to do so. Second, this type of defense is limited to preventing the commission of a tort against the property; and as such, once the tort is complete or the plaintiff is permanently dispossessed of his or her property, he or she may not use force to recapture or avenge the tort. Yet there is a "hot pursuit" exception, which arises when a person is in "hot pursuit" of someone who wrongfully dispossessed him or her of the property. Once again, only reasonable force can be used, but for defending property "reasonable" does not include force which will cause death or serious bodily injury.

These common law intentional torts protect against intentional infringements of legally protected interests. When injury to a person or harm to property occurs not through intentional or purposeful conduct, but rather by means of unintentional and careless conduct, another vital area of the law is brought forth – the tort of negligence.

The Tort of Negligence in the United States

The legal wrong of *negligence* is an unintentional tort. The actor does not want to bring about the injurious consequences of his or her act, but the conduct creates a risk of harmful consequences. This tort derives from the very old common law, with recorded decisions dating back to the 1300s in England; but the tort is even older than that time period. The purpose of this body of the law is to protect a person's interest in being free from harm carelessly caused by another party's conduct. As one "price" for living in a civilized "kingdom," a person is held to a fundamental duty; that is, when one decides to affirmatively act, regardless of the activity, one owes an obligation to others to act in a reasonable, prudent, and careful manner. The failure to exercise this requisite degree of care will subject the careless actor to legal liability for the tort of negligence.

The term "negligence," moreover, is a legal term that is used in two ways. First, it is the name given to the civil wrong tort lawsuit for acting unreasonably; and second, it is a type of wrongful conduct which is itself a component of the tort cause of action. In the latter sense, negligence is the conduct that falls below the standard of care imposed by the law for the protection of others from the risk of harm. Intent is not an issue in a negligence case. Even though an actor does not intend a harmful outcome, even though he or she may be morally blameless, nonetheless he or she may be liable civilly for committing a legal wrong. The common law will not allow a person to defend his or her behavior on the ground that his or her subjective person or frame of mind was to act in a non-negligent manner. The ultimate issue, therefore, is not the reasonableness of the defendant's state of mind, but the reasonableness of his or her conduct. Negligence, however, is not absolute liability or even liability without fault. In every case, it must be demonstrated that the defendant was at fault by failing to comply with the legal duty to conduct himself or herself in a reasonably prudent manner under the circumstances. Intent is immaterial; conduct is critical. The duty of due care, and thus potential negligence liability, applies to anyone who acts, whether driving a car, operating as a surgeon (in which negligence is treated as malpractice doctrine with certain specialized rules as will be seen), manufacturing or selling goods, providing services, or hiring, retaining, supervising, disciplining, and discharging employees.

Elements of the Negligence Cause of Action
In order to prevail in a negligence lawsuit, a plaintiff must establish the four key elements to the cause of action: 1) duty of care, 2) breach of duty, 3) causation, and 4) damages. The first component of negligence is the *"duty of care."* The plaintiff must show the existence of a duty, recognized by the law, requiring the defendant to conform his or her conduct to a legally established standard in order to protect the plaintiff from an unreasonable risk of harm. When a person engages in an activity, he or she is held to a duty of due care to act as a reasonably prudent person. As such, the "actor" must take precautions against creating unreasonable risks of injury to other people or their property. However, there is no legal duty imposed upon a person to take precautions against events which cannot be reasonably foreseen. This standard of care from the old common law days has been characterized as the "reasonably prudent man" (and now in modern times called the "reasonably prudent person" standard). This "mythical" legal person is an average person in the community acting under circumstances surrounding the defendant. It is important to note that the defendant's individual characteristics are not considered, for example, whether the defendant is stupid or excitable; rather, the defendant's conduct is measured against this "reasonable prudent person." In the case of a manufacturer of goods, generally, a manufacturer will be held to a standard of care to see that a consumer is not harmed by the goods. Consequently, there may be liability imposed against the manufacturer for failing to inspect and/or test the goods and to maintain suitable quality control, for failing to disclose and to warn of known defects in the goods, and the failure to use due care in the design, manufacture, and sale of the goods. This duty of due care extends to all people who might foreseeably be injured by the goods, and not just the buyer of the goods. Also, it is important to point out that there are particular standards of conduct for some people that are different from the normal reasonable person standard. For example, members of a profession, such as doctors and lawyers, are deemed to hold and to exercise the knowledge and skills of a typical member of that profession. Such a specialized standard of care brings the negligence doctrine into the realm of malpractice law, which essentially is based on common law negligence principles, but which usually requires expert witnesses to educate the jury as to the particular standard of care in the profession. For example, in a nursing malpractice case against a nurse who is accused of conduct falling below the professional standard of care for "blindly" following and not questioning a doctor's orders, an expert witness will have to testify before the jury to state and explain what the nurse's duty

of care is in such a situation, which obligation is beyond the common knowledge of a lay jury.

The second element to a lawsuit for negligence is the breach of the duty of due care. *Breach of duty* occurs when the defendant's conduct fails to conform to the required standard of care. That is, when the defendant's conduct falls below the level required by the applicable standard of care owed to the plaintiff, the defendant has breached his or her duty. This breach can be triggered by an act or by a failure to act when the law imposes an affirmative obligation to act. This key negligence question is regarded as a "question of fact," and thus for the jury to decide, although guided by expert witnesses, most notably present in malpractice cases. That is, in a malpractice case the jury will decide if a nurse acted not as a reasonably prudent person but as a reasonably prudent professional nurse based on the standards and scope of practice of the nursing profession.

The third requirement to a negligence cause of action is *causation*. The law requires a sufficient causal connection between the defendant's careless conduct and the resulting harm. The causation element is satisfied by a showing of two elements: 1) the existence of actual causation, called "cause in fact," and 2) the presence of legal causation, called "proximate cause." It is very important to note that the common law naturally not only requires causation, but also that the common law makes a critical distinction between the two types of causation. Causation in fact is really a matter of physics. That is, it is a series or chain of events, with one event leading to another and ultimately producing a final conclusion. Before legal liability can be imposed on a defendant, there must be sufficient evidence that the defendant's careless action was a cause in fact of the plaintiff's injuries. The standard legal test for establishing causation in fact is called the "but for" test. This legal test holds that an act is the cause in fact of an eventual consequence if the latter would not have occurred "but for" the first act. However, when there are several forces that combine and bring about the plaintiff's injuries, and any one of them would have been sufficient to cause the plaintiff's injuries, a special causation test is used, called the "substantial factor" test. This test holds that causation in fact is established in a multiple causation situation when the defendant's conduct was a substantial factor in causing the plaintiff's injuries. In addition to demonstrating causation in fact, the plaintiff also must show as part of his or her negligence lawsuit that the defendant's careless conduct was also a proximate cause of the plaintiff's injury. Whereas causation in fact is a matter of physics, the doctrine of proximate cause is more a question of policy. *Proximate cause* is a most interesting common law formulation, because it is a doctrine that protects careless people! Even if one acts carelessly, the doctrine of proximate cause maintains that not all a plaintiff's injuries and harms in fact caused by a carelessly acting defendant will be proximately caused. Rather, the doctrine holds that a careless defendant is not legally responsible for the unforeseeable, remote, or unusual consequences of his or her careless act. Accordingly, proximate cause serves as a limitation on the defendant's liability. It is the function of the jury in a common law system to determine whether proximate cause and also causation in fact are present. For example, in a case being litigated as of this writing, there is a negligence lawsuit being asserted by the District of Columbia, that is, Washington, D.C., against certain gun manufacturers, contending that they carelessly "over-supplied" guns to the state of Virginia, which has liberal gun laws, and that these guns have been purchased legally in Virginia, and then illegally brought into the District, where they have been used illegally to commit crimes and to harm people, and these injured District residents, who for the most part have no health insurance, have been treated and cared for by District public hospitals, thereby costing the District a great deal of money for health care expenditures. Assuming that the District can adequately establish the duty and breach of duty elements with its novel "over-supply" theory, is it provable that these guns in fact caused the injuries, and then is it foreseeable that the guns would end up in the District and be used criminally to create harm and injury? All these questions are for the jury to resolve. How should one decide if one was on such a District jury?

The fourth and final element to a cause of action for negligence is the requirement of damages; that is, the plaintiff must prove some type of actual loss or damage. Damages are not assumed in a negligence case; nominal damages are not awarded; rather, some type of actual harm or injury to a legally protected interest is necessary. The objective of damages is compensatory; that is, to restore the plaintiff insofar as possible to his or her condition before the injury or harm occurred. Damages include special damages, such as economic losses, lost wages, medical expenses, business profits, and future expenses, Moreover, additional damages for "pain and suffering" or emotional distress are recoverable, as are damages for disability and disfigurement. Finally, if the defendant's careless conduct is grossly negligent or reckless in nature, then the plaintiff can recover an extra award of damages, called punitive damages, at the discretion of the jury to punish the defendant and to deter others from engaging in such grossly negligent behavior. It is necessary to point out that several states in the United States have by statute curtailed the jury's power to award unlimited punitive damages, for example, by requiring that punitive damages not exceed five times the amount of the compensatory award. It is also necessary to point out that the United States Supreme Court has ruled that punitive damages cannot be extreme or excessive, that is, they must bear some reasonable relationship to the harm done, or otherwise they will be unconstitutional as violating the Due Process clause of the Constitution.

Generally speaking, damage liability for the tort of negligence is deemed by the common law to be "*joint and several.*" That is, when there are more than one defendant who have caused the plaintiff's damages, they are all equally responsible for paying the judgment, regardless of the percentage of fault attributed to them. As such, for example, a defendant who is accorded only 20% of the fault may nonetheless have to pay 100% of the damages if the other and more culpable defendant cannot pay. The first defendant is the proverbial "deep pocket" defendant who ends up paying. The policy behind this old common law rule is that it is preferable for a party who is at least partially at fault to pay all as opposed to the innocent and injured plaintiff only receiving partial compensation; and the "deep pocket" defendant can always proceed, at least theoretically, against his or her co-defendants. However, it must be noted that several states in the United States have now by statute changed this common law rule, and as a result hold that a defendant only has to pay his/her apportioned share of the damages regardless of the ability of his or her co-defendants to pay the plaintiff fully.

Negligent Hiring

The negligence doctrine certainly can be applied to the employer's hiring of employees; and consequently the employer can be deemed negligent if it does not use due care in the hiring of its employees, for example, choosing the wrong person for a specific job. The rationale is that the employer has a duty to customers, clients, and the general public to act with due care and as a reasonably prudent employer when it comes to hiring the employees to staff its business. For example, if the employer is contemplating hiring a person for a position that requires driving a vehicle, the prudent employer would ask about driving accidents, tickets, driver license status, and any license suspensions, as well as drug or alcohol use; and the employer also should check with the Department of Motor Vehicles for the pertinent jurisdiction. If the employer breaches this duty, and harm is caused to customer or other third party, he or she can sue the employer for negligence. This lawsuit, it should be noted, is one directly against the employer for its own negligence; it is not a vicarious or imputed liability lawsuit (though there may be such a lawsuit if the carelessly selected employee carelessly injures a third party in the course of employment).

Negligent hiring typically is based on the employer failing to investigate or failing to do a careful investigation on the background – work, professional, personality – of the employee, and a proper investigation would have discovered some troublesome or problematic fact about the employee. Recall, however, that the employer, as does any person or business that acts, does not have to act perfectly. Negligence law does not require that a party be, in effect, an insurer against harm. The fundamental legal duty is "merely" to act carefully. So, regarding hiring, if the employer does conduct an investigation, and it is a reasonable one, the employer would not be directly liable even if a more thorough or different type of investigation would have discovered a problem regarding the employee.

Negligence and Landowners

The principles of negligence have long been applied to the owners of land ascertain the duties of landowners to those people who come upon their land. This area of law is also called "*premises liability*." The fundamental principle is that an owner of land owes a duty to exercise reasonable care to safeguard people who come upon the land. This duty extends to land owners who are also landlords and thus have a legal duty to exercise reasonable care to safeguard their tenants and their tenants' guests in the common areas of the leasehold, such as entrance ways, parking areas, laundry rooms, pools, and clubhouses. Under the common law, the basic duty of the landowner was more precisely defined by the status of the person who came upon his or her land. The first category is called "business invitees." These are people who are invited to come upon the land for the benefit of the landowner. The landowner has a duty to protect invitees from dangers that the landowner knew of or should have known by means of a reasonable inspection. That is, for a business invitee there is an affirmative duty to discover and remedy or at least warn of any hidden dangers that might harm the business invitee. So, a supermarket is continually inspecting its premises for wet spots on the floor or banana peels or broken glass or any other hazardous conditions that could cause injury. The supermarket would put up warning signs, cones, or tape until the dangerous condition is corrected. The second category of people that can come upon the land is called "guests." These are people who come upon the land with the owner's permission for the primary benefit of themselves and not the landowner. Examples would include social guests of the landowner as well as sales people who solicit the landowner on their own motivation. The landowner owes a duty to warn guests of dangers that the landowner is aware of or should be aware of, but there is no affirmative duty to inspect for hazards. Finally, the third category is "trespassers." These are people who come on the land without the landowner's knowledge and/or consent. In most states, based on the old common law, the landowner does not owe the trespasser any duty except not to intentionally harm the trespasser, for example, by means of hidden devices or traps, such as "spring guns." However, in some states, even the trespasser has the right to be warned of hidden or latent dangers which could not be readily seen on the surface. However, if a risk or hazard is so obvious, such as a pond or big pit or construction site on the property, then the landowner need not as a general rule warn of the dangerous condition (though the landowner may have liability to children injured based on the "attractive nuisance" theory).

Special Negligence Doctrines
There are a variety of special negligence doctrines, each with its own peculiar rules, but with far-reaching consequences, that must be briefly addressed. The first is called the *doctrine of res ipsa loquitur*, from the Latin meaning "the thing speaks for itself." This doctrine may emerge as a very critical one for a plaintiff seeking to establish the breach of duty element to negligence. In essence, *res ipsa loquitur* maintains that the fact that a particular injury occurred may in and of itself establish a breach of the duty owed to the plaintiff. This doctrine is a legal device that a plaintiff may be able to use to permit a jury to consider the issue as to whether the defendant was negligent where the facts of the case indicate that the plaintiff's injuries resulted from the defendant's negligence, the jury may be able to infer the defendant's liability. There are two critical components that a plaintiff must be able to demonstrate in order to take advantage of the *res ipsa loquitur* doctrine: 1) the accident causing the plaintiff's injury is not the type that ordinarily would occur unless someone was negligent, for example, when an auto abruptly swerves off the road in "good" driving conditions, or a bottle or can of soda sitting on a supermarket shelf suddenly explodes; 2) evidence exists showing that the instrumentality that caused the injury was in the sole control of the defendant, such as the defendant driving the erratic car, or the defendant had the power and opportunity to exercise control, such as the exploding bottle case. If these two requirements are present, the legal effect of the doctrine is that the plaintiff has thereby established an initial case for negligence, and accordingly the judge will send the case to the jury, presuming the causation and damages elements are present, of course. However, if the defendant can submit evidence of due care, the jury has the power to reject the plaintiff's *res ipsa loquitur* inference of negligence, and as such ultimately find for the defendant. The rationale behind the doctrine, which is a very old common law one, is that it may be very difficult in certain circumstances for a plaintiff to acquire sufficient evidence to show a breach of the duty of due care, for example, when the plaintiff is injured by a poorly made product but the plaintiff

cannot show the careless situation that existed at the defendant's manufacturing facility.

The second is called the *"negligence per se" doctrine*. At times, the standard of care in a negligence case by proving that statute which provides for a criminal penalty applies to a particular case. The legal result is that the duty enumerated in the statute will replace the more general common law duty of due care. In such a case, the plaintiff must prove that the plaintiff is in a class intended to be protected by the statute and that the purpose of the statute was to prevent the type of harm that the plaintiff suffered. That is, generally speaking, the statute must pertain to the plaintiff's injury, for example, when a consumer is injured by an inadequate warning label on a drug when a statute or regulation sets forth the warning, or when an auto driver is injured by another driver who has violated traffic control laws. The notable effect of establishing the violation of a statute is the occurrence of "negligence per se." That is, the plaintiff will have established a conclusive presumption of the duty and breach of duty elements to a negligence lawsuit. Of course, the plaintiff still has to plead and prove the remaining elements of the cause of action.

The next special negligence area is the doctrine of *negligent infliction of emotional distress*. When can a victimized plaintiff recover mental anguish damages? That is always a key negligence issue. There are four key precepts to this legal doctrine. First, if there is a physical injury, then damages for the attendant emotional distress are recoverable as part of the physical injury. This rule is the traditional "pain and suffering" rule. Second, if there is a physical impact to the plaintiff, which in itself causes no actual physical injury, but which is accompanied or followed by emotional distress, then damages are permitted for such emotional distress. An example would be when a defendant negligently drives his or her car into the plaintiff, who is not physically injured in any way but who does suffer fright and shock. This rule typically is designated as the "impact rule." Third, the more modern rule that even if there is no physical impact, but the plaintiff nonetheless suffers physical disorders, such as shock to the nervous system, then damages are permissible for the emotional and mental suffering. Finally, if there is no impact, and the plaintiff does not suffer any physical disorders, but the plaintiff does suffer emotional distress, then there is no recovery permitted. An example of the last rule would arise when the defendant negligently "sideswipes" the plaintiff's auto, and the plaintiff is very frightened and upset, but does not suffer any physical disorder or illness, which means the plaintiff has no cause of action. As noted, the rule is different for the intentional infliction of emotional distress, where no "impact" at all is necessary, though the wrongful conduct must be severe and cause actual and severe emotional distress.

There is, finally, a distinction of great consequence that the common law makes between nonfeasance and misfeasance. *Nonfeasance* means not acting; and most significantly as a general rule there is no legal duty imposed on a person to affirmatively act to aid, rescue, or benefit another person. As a result, as a general rule, nonfeasance, that is, not acting is not legally actionable as the tort of negligence. The "classic" case is the drowning example, where the expert swimmer in a boat with a rope and life preserver does nothing and watches the victim drown. The old English precedents dealt with drowning cases; and as such so long as one did not cause the risk of drowning, for example, by pushing another person into the water, there is no legal liability for not rescuing a drowning person. Sad-to-say, one does not have to go back to the old English common law for precedents because in Ft. Lauderdale, Florida in the summer of 2018 occurred a horrendous case. Apparently, a person with disability fell into a pond and was struggling to survive. Five young men, between the ages of 14 and 16, not only did not help the victim or call for help but mocked and ridiculed him as he struggled. Moreover, and it is hard to believe that this happened in a civilized society; the teenagers actually videotaped him on a cell phone while watching him drown and die. The young men, moreover, showed no remorse. The local prosecutor condemned their actions and inaction as "callous" (which seems to mild a word); but stated there would be no prosecution since there was no duty to rescue based on the nonfeasance doctrine. A civil lawsuit would be precluded based on the same rationale. As a general rule, the state of Florida as well as other states, based on the doctrine of non-feasance, do not have laws obligating citizens and residents to render aid, help anyone in distress, or even call for help. Therefore, legally, there is no liability; morally, however, is another question (and the subject of a moral duty to help or rescue will be covered in the Business Ethics and Corporate Social Responsibility chapter of this book.).

However, there are many exceptions to nonfeasance. Even if one does not have a duty to act, once one decides to act and affirmatively undertakes to do so for the assistance or benefit of another, one then has a duty to act carefully. Consequently, if the careless "rescuing" causes injury then tort liability for negligence may exist. Similarly, if the defendant's own negligence places another in danger, the defendant is now under an obligation to use reasonable care to aid or rescue that person. Another example stems from the old common law whereby common carriers and innkeepers are under an affirmative legal duty to warn and to aid and assist passengers and guests and to prevent injuries to them and to third parties. Finally, members of a profession may be obligated not by the law, but by the codes of ethics of their profession, to affirmatively act to aid people, for example, a registered nurse who is morally bound by the code of ethics of the nursing profession and the Florence Nightingale Oath to provide medical assistance.

Defenses

There are three main defenses to a lawsuit for negligence: 1) contributory negligence, 2) comparative negligence, and 3) assumption of the risk. Contributory negligence is careless conduct on the plaintiff's part that is a contributing cause to his or her own injury. Contributory negligence is a very harsh common law doctrine because it acts as a complete bar to recovery regardless of how slight the plaintiff's own negligence. However, in most states in the United States today, by statute the defense of contributory negligence has been abolished and replaced by the doctrine of *comparative negligence*. Comparative negligence is not a complete defense; rather, the plaintiff's damages are determined, the jury makes a finding on each party's fault, and the plaintiff's damages are accordingly reduced by the proportion the plaintiff's own fault bears to the total amount of the plaintiff's harm. *Assumption of the risk* arises when the plaintiff encounters a known risk voluntarily, for example, by going on stairs that are visibly being repaired. When the plaintiff thereby in essence consents to assuming the risk of injury from a particular hazard, this "assumption" is a complete defense for the defendant. The traditional example of assumption of the risk doctrine would occur when one goes to a baseball game. That is, the baseball fan is knowingly and voluntarily taking a known risk, which is, being hit by a baseball. Yet what about being hit by a hot dog thrown by a vendor? There actually is a precedent in that the Missouri Supreme Court has ruled that a fan hit and injured by a flying hot dog does not assume a risk that is tied to an essential character of watching a baseball game. Accordingly, the injured fan could sue the ball park for negligence but of course would have to sustain that cause of action. Regardless, there now is precedent that a ball park will have to train its vendors on how to properly transmit hot dogs to the fans in the stands.

The Doctrine of Strict Tort Liability in the United States

Strict liability, or liability without fault, is a special type of liability imposed by the common law. Although an actor not only did not intend any harm, and even though he or she acted in a careful and prudent manner, the actor is nevertheless legally responsible for any injuries caused by his or her conduct. Strict liability is imposed in three types of situations. One instance involves activities that the law regards as "ultra-hazardous," such as construction blasting, crop "dusting," fumigation, and reservoirs and dam construction and maintenance. These activities and conditions are potentially so highly dangerous and threaten substantial injury to the public, regardless of how much care is exercised, that the duty of safety is an absolute one. Insurance is the only "answer" in such a case. Another category of strict liability case deals with the liability of the owners and possessors of dangerous animals, which as a topic is interesting but beyond the purposes of this book. The final category of strict liability is the highly significant and consequential business law and consumer protection doctrine of strict tort liability for the manufacturers and sellers of defective products, which will be covered in the Products Liability chapter of this book.

Summary

This chapter described the tort law of the United States, including several subcategories associated with it. The law itself was originally created to protect victims faced with physical harm, as well as to prevent future unjust cases. Its purpose continues to serve today; and it is also expanding into several areas, including the manufacturing business. Countries around the world have followed in the "footsteps" of the United States by developing product liability laws, tort laws, etc. in order to protect consumers. In addition, the laws are also created to protect businesses and manufacturers from consumers that are willing to take advantage of products and the laws. It is for this reason that managers and entrepreneurs are often forced to develop strategies to avoid legal problems with tort law. Firms should provide thorough training programs for their staff, including management, with the proper training and examination of all laws, specifically those pertaining to their type of business. This should be done to not only protect the image of the firm, but also the consumers. In essence, entrepreneurs and managers are obligated to acknowledge, understand, and abide by the various tort laws that exist in countries around the world in order to achieve their goals.

Discussion Questions

1. What is an intentional tort? Explain and illustrate how an intentional tort to the person could be committed in a business context. Explain and illustrate how an intentional tort to property could be committed in a business context.

2. What is the intentional tort of defamation? How can the intentional tort of defamation arise in a business context? Provide an example and a brief explanation thereof.

3. What is the tort of negligence? Explain and illustrate how the tort of negligence could be committed in a business context.

4. How is the standard of care and its contravention ascertained in the U.S. legal system? Provide business examples with brief explanations thereof.

5. Describe and illustrate the types of damages that are available in intentional tort and negligence cases.

6. What is the doctrine of *res ipsa loquitur* in U.S. negligence law? Why is it a potentially very valuable legal doctrine to a consumer injured by a product? Provide an example with a brief explanation thereof.

7. What is the doctrine of proximate cause? Why has it been called the careless person's (or business') "best friend"? Provide an example with a brief explanation thereof.

8. What is the distinction between misfeasance and nonfeasance in U.S. law? Why is that distinction very important in the U.S. legal system? Provide examples with brief explanations thereof. Can one have a moral duty to rescue and come to another's aid even if one does not have a legal obligation to do so? Why or why not? Provide an example, preferably a business-related one, with a brief explanation thereof.

9. How might an employer commit tort violations in discharging an employee that the employer has the legal right to terminate? Provide examples along with brief explanations thereof.

CHAPTER
THREE

3 – PRODUCTS LIABILITY

Product safety emerges as a very important legal challenge for the manager of a manufacturing, distribution, and sales company. What is the extent of a company's legal obligation to consumer safety? What is a firm's legal responsibility for the products it produces, distributes, and/or sells? Should a company legally guarantee the safety of those who buy and use its products? This chapter examines various views regarding the legal duties of business to consumers; and seeks to ascertain the legal responsibilities of various entities on the product manufacturing and marketing chain toward the consumer. The corpus of law dealing with products safety typically is designated as "products liability" law. There are a variety of product liability legal theories in U.S. law. Where does a company's duty to protect consumers begin, and where does it end – legally and in a global marketing and legal environment? This chapter seeks to answer these important questions.

U.S. Legal Doctrines

Several legal theories in the U.S. impact on product safety, to wit, contract law, the tort of negligence, the tort of fraud, warranty law based on the Uniform Commercial Code and federal statute, and a relatively new and very significant legal doctrine – strict liability in tort. Some of these theories are common law based and others are statutory in nature. There are also federal and state agencies that deal with product safety, particularly the federal Consumer Products Safety Commission.

Contract Law

Contract law will be covered extensively later, but it is important to note now that there may be a contractual relationship between the consumer and the seller of the product; and if so, the seller will be obligated by virtue of contract law to fulfill the duties and promises created by the contract as to the nature, characteristic, and quality of the product.

Tort Law – Negligence and Fraud

The tort of fraud, in its old, common law, intentional "deceit" formulation, which was covered in the previous chapter, requires, in addition to an express purposeful misrepresentation about a product by the wrongdoer and reasonable reliance by the deceived and aggrieved party on the misrepresentation, a finding supported by sufficient evidence that the wrongdoer made the misrepresentation intentionally and with "*scienter*," that is, an "evil mind" intent on purposefully causing and inducing the innocent party to make an erroneous conclusion. That old, Anglo-American, common law "intent" requirement makes the utilization of the tort of intentional fraud a very problematic one in a products liability case. Lying about the quality or characteristics of a product, or for that matter anything, is not automatically illegal; but fraudulently and deceitfully lying is!

The tort of negligence, also covered in the previous chapter, requires that the manufacturer, wholesaler, distributor, and retailer of the product exercise reasonable and ordinary care in the manufacture, distribution, and sale of the product. These entities on the marketing chain all have a duty to exercise due care not to harm the consumer or user of the product. The failure to comply with this legally imposed duty of due care may subject an entity on the marketing chain to legal liability based on the Anglo-American common law of negligence. For example, if a product has a warning thereon that it can cause burns, a prudent retailer will store and display it on an upper shelf where young children cannot get their hands on it; but the prudent manufacturer should also have a child-proof cap thereon.

One point regarding negligence is critical to make; and that is that negligence law definitely is not a scheme of insurance or guaranty law. That is, if a party, say the manufacturer, acted carefully in the production of the product, took all reasonable steps to protect the consumer, and informed the consumer of any "irremovable" risks, then the manufacturer acted reasonably and carefully and thereby fulfilled its legal obligation pursuant to negligence law. The fact that the consumer was still injured is an unfortunate "accident," and a non-compensable one, at least under negligence principles. Again, negligence is not an insurance scheme, and consequently a manufacturer is not acting illegally if a consumer was harmed by an unavoidable risk or one that could not have reasonably been foreseen or prevented.

Warranty Law

Warranty law, based predominantly in the United States on the Uniform Commercial Code (UCC), will require that the seller of the product "live up to" the claims that are expressly made about the product as well as to comply with any warranties that are implied in the transaction and are imposed by the law. Warranty law will be covered in detail in the chapter discussing Sales Law and the Uniform Commercial Code. However, it is important to note for the purposes of this chapter that the injured consumer may confront certain major obstacles when pursuing legal rights under UCC warranty law. First, there is no legal obligation that the manufacturer or seller makes any express warranties at all. Yet some warranties, as will be seen in Chapter 5, are implied by the law, and thus automatically imposed on certain manufacturers and sellers of goods. Nonetheless, these implied may be legally disclaimed by the manufacturer and seller, thereby rendering the implied warranties legally moot.

Moreover, as also will be seen, there are notice and common law privity requirements in attempting to hold certain parties on the marketing chain liable for breach of warranty. Therefore, establishing warranty liability emerges as a difficult task for the injured consumer.

There also is a body of warranty law in the United States based on a federal statute, the Magnuson-Moss Warranty Act, promulgated by Congress in 1975. Yet it is appropriate to point out here that there are two major problems with the Act as far as an aggrieved product consumer is concerned. First, the Act does not require a manufacturer or seller to make any express warranties at all; and second, the Act does not create any implied warranties for the consumer. However, if a manufacturer or seller does make an express warranty, the Act requires that it be labeled as a "full warranty," which guarantees the repair or replacement of the defective product, or a "limited" warranty, which limits the scope of the full warranty in some manner.

Strict Liability in Tort

Strict liability in tort is a relatively new, at least compared to negligence and fraud tort law, legal cause of action for the aggrieved consumer. Strict liability is a very important and far-reaching legal doctrine, one created to promote consumer safety and to protect the consumer; and thus strict liability is a doctrine that is very frequently asserted by the consumers harmed by products. The doctrine is a common law formulation; it was first promulgated by the Supreme Court of California in 1963, in the seminal case of *Greenman v. Yuba Power Products, Inc.*; and for an additional time frame point of reference, the doctrine was adopted in Florida by that state's Supreme Court in 1976. All states in the U.S. now have adopted strict liability, though in varying formulations.

The doctrine was first enunciated in the Restatement (Second) of Torts, a compendium of existing law as well as recommendations of what the law should be, drafted by legal experts, and published by the American Law Institute. Restatements of the Law are not law per se, but they are very persuasive legal authority. The Restatement formulation for strict liability now has been adopted in varying forms by virtually all the states in the United States. Strict liability in tort holds that one who sells any product in a defective condition unreasonably dangerous to the user, the consumer, or his or her property is liable to the ultimate user or consumer if: 1) the seller is engaged in the business of selling such a product, that is, the seller is an entity of the marketing chain; and 2) the product is expected to, and in fact does, reach the user or consumer without substantial change in the condition in which it was sold. Moreover, the doctrine of strict liability in tort applies although: 1) the seller has exercised all possible care in the preparation, distribution, and sale of the product, thereby clearly distinguishing strict liability from the tort of negligence; and 2) the user or consumer has not purchased the product from, or entered into any contractual relationship with, the seller of the product, thereby obviating the old contract "privity" requirement. Strict liability regarding products has been applied to manufacturers, wholesalers and distributors, retailers, as well as commercial *lessors* of products. Damage to property is a recoverable element of damages in a strict liability lawsuit, but not, however, purely economic losses, that is, lost income, at least in the majority of states.

One procedural legal problem will arise when a U.S. consumer seeks to bring a products liability action against a manufacturer in a foreign country. While a substantive legal discussion of obtaining jurisdiction over a foreign manufacturing is beyond the purposes of this book, the authors must point out that the U.S. consumer harmed by the foreign-product will have to satisfy state or federal jurisdictional requirements in securing jurisdiction as well as to satisfy the Due Process requirements of the U.S. Constitution, which require, according to the U.S. Supreme Court, a showing of "minimum contacts" between the foreign manufacturer and the United States. If the foreign manufacturer regularly sells, markets, advertises, services, or directly or indirectly distributes goods in the U.S., even though a U.S. distributor (which the foreign manufacturer plainly cannot hide behind), that type of presence will demonstrate a sufficient connection to the U.S. consumer market for the aggrieved consumer to not only sue the foreign manufacturer, but to sue it in the U.S. courts.

The essence of strict liability in tort for products is the finding of a "*defect*" in the product. In most jurisdictions, if a product is defective, it is presumed also to be "unreasonably dangerous" to the user or consumer. Products can be deemed "defective" in three ways: 1) the product contains a "flaw," 2) the product lacks a warning, or 3) the product is defectively designed.

First, regarding *flawed products*, the main consideration is to measure the product in its manufactured state with the manufacturer's own specifications and standards for that type of product; and then if the product does not even meet the manufacturer's own "specs," the product is legally flawed, defective, unreasonably dangerous, and the manufacturer (as well as distributors and retailers of the flawed product) is strictly liable in tort for the flawed product when it causes harm. It is important to note that evidence of how the product became flawed is not an issue in a strict liability "defect" lawsuit. Strict liability is not a negligence lawsuit. Consequently, the fact that the manufacturer demonstrated that it had even an elaborate inspection, testing, and quality control scheme (which obviously failed!) is irrelevant in a strict liability lawsuit (though such evidence would be critical to the disposition of a negligence lawsuit). In the U.S., the term "flaw" is used as one of the criterion for "defectiveness"; but in Germany, the term "run-a-away" product is commonly employed, and that latter term more accurately "captures" the usual situation; that is, the manufacturer, though truly striving for that "zero defect" objective (and award!) somehow allowed the product to "run-a-away" from all the manufacturer's quality control and safety checks. Finally, it is interesting to note that one ordinarily does not see "flaw" cases reported in the law reports since typically the cases are settled before an official and recorded legal disposition. What real defense does the manufacturer have if the evidence indicates that its product which caused harm does not even conform to the manufacturer's own product standards?

Second, a product can be deemed defective because it lacks a warning or the warning is inadequate. To be legally sufficient, the warning must address the nature and severity of the risk, how the consumer should handle the risk, as well as indicate any reasonable alternatives. The warnings, as well as labels and instructions, must clearly, simply, and prominently warn the consumer of the dangers involved in using the product. Yet, the manufacturer is not supposed to warn of risks that the reasonable and rational person should be aware of; yet nevertheless after such "classic" lawsuits as the McDonald's hot coffee case, in which the product was construed as defective due to the lack of a warning that the coffee was hot (actually, very, very hot!), manufacturers now "err on the side of caution" and warn of risks that one might think a reasonable person should be cognizant of. For example, warnings not to use a snow-blower on the roof, not to use a CD rack as a ladder, not to allow children to play in a dishwasher, and not to fold a baby carriage with the baby in it, seem "pretty" obvious, and one would think would be within the purview of common sense and rationality, but nonetheless the nature of a warning "defect" under strict liability motivates manufacturers to issue such warnings. An example of an obvious risk that a manufacturer would not have to warn could be in the case of a cigarette lighter which typically would ignite and cause a fire when applied to flammable material. Another would be a knife or an axe which might strike one's hand when cutting or chopping. Yet there is one recent legal precedent that does clearly state that the risk of harm from a product can be so evident that the product does not require a warning. The case was a New Jersey state one in which a college student who fell off a loft bed sued and recovered a $170,000 award from a local jury. The student claimed that his fall and injuries, mainly a dislocated shoulder, were caused by the lack of a warning label on the loft bed, which was about six feet off the floor. However, in August of 2006, a three judge panel of the state court of appeals unanimously overturned the ruling, stating that the obviousness of the danger was an absolute defense. The appeals court explained that warnings would lose their efficacy and meaning if they were placed on every product that is known to be dangerous, such as a knife or scissors, glass, a bat or ball, or bicycle, that would pose a generally known risk of injury if abused, misused, dropped, or fallen from. Nonetheless, the injured student's attorney stated that the case would be appealed to the New Jersey Supreme Court. So, the definitive legal pronouncement as to obviousness of the risk and the concomitant need for a warning, at least in New Jersey, still has to be determined. A general warning will not protect a manufacturer from liability for a defectively designed or manufactured product. For example, an automobile manufacturer will not be able to obviate its liability under strict liability law for defectively designed or flawed brakes merely by stating that the brakes may fail under certain conditions. Note, though, that the obverse is not true; that is, an injured consumer can proceed with a failure to warn strict liability lawsuit even if there was neither a design nor manufacturing defect.

Third, a product can be defective because it is *defectively designed*. Yet, is that not a tautology? That is, that a product is defective because it is defective! Such a legal standard brings U.S. products liability law closer to the "old" socialist, European, insurance scheme; that is, product-causation-harm equals manufacturer-pay. However, as first enunciated by the California Supreme Court, there is a test, though an imprecise one, for determining whether a product is defectively designed. There are three parts to the test, all of which must be applied to the product to ascertain if it is defectively designed: First, does the product meet the "state-of-the-art"? That is, going back in time to when the product was made (and not at present time perhaps many years later during a lawsuit), and given the level of science, engineering, and technology at that time, could anything more have been done to make the product safer? If so, the next part to the test is to factor in two constraints –

practicality of use and economic feasibilities. That is, could the product have been made safer and still have the product function as a product of that type? For example, a knife can be designed to be perfectly safe, but then it would not cut. Similarly, a car could be designed to be totally safe to its occupants, but it would look like a tank. As to the economic variable, a similar question is posed: Could the product be designed to be safer, and still be affordable? Once again, how much does a tank cost, what is its fuel mileage? Yet, not to be facetious, because the technology does exist to put "crash" air bags throughout a vehicle, but then how much would that safety feature add to the cost of a car, especially an "economy" one? If the product is rendered unaffordable by the additional safety feature, the manufacturer is not legally obligated to adopt it. However, the test for a "design defect," one must underscore, is a very vague one; and, moreover, the application and ultimate decision regarding this legal theory is typically in the U.S. in the hands of a lay jury – a jury guided by experts, of course, but who knows what a jury will do in a given situation, especially when faced with an injured, and perhaps very sympathetic, plaintiff. It is also important to note that the Restatement of Torts was again amended, and in 1997 the Restatement (Third) of Torts was approved. Regarding design defects, the new Restatement continues the emphasis on an alternative design that was available, reasonable, and practical, but was not incorporated into the product, as the essence of "defectiveness."

The "classic" design defect case was the series of Ford Pinto cases commencing in the late 1970s, where the costs of incorporating the available design improvement (structural alteration of the car) were minimal ($11.00 per vehicle) compared to the risks (ruptured fuel tanks and car fires at collisions over twenty-five miles per hour); and consequently Ford was found to be legally liable on strict liability as well as negligence grounds (and was subject to considerable punitive damage liability too). The amount that Ford had to pay in damages and settlements exceeded $50 million, which was more than double what the alternative design implementation would have cost the company. In another automobile design defect cases, Daimler-Chrysler in 1999 was ordered to pay a $60 million judgment in a class action suit in which a jury in Pennsylvania determined that the air bags in certain of its vehicles were defectively designed because they could burn a driver's hands or wrists when deployed due to the venting of hot gasses used to inflate the bags. The jury determined that the air bag was defective because it could have been designed differently and more safely by incorporating "smart" air bag technology, such as the use of sensors, which can reduce the force at which air bags are deployed. In another case, General Motors in 1999 was ordered by a California jury to pay $4.9 billion to six people who were severely burned when their Chevrolet Malibu exploded in flames in a rear end collision. The tanks were mounted 11 inches from the rear bumper. The jury determined the vehicle to be defective in design because the gas tank was placed too close to the rear bumper; and an alternative design would have placed it over the axle or incorporated a shield. The cost of changing the placement of the tank was $8.59 per vehicle.

Today, an interesting products liability dilemma – legally and scientifically – is emerging – the "hacking" of cars, particularly whether a "hacked" car is a defective product pursuant to strict liability, as well as the concomitant need for cyber-security for cars and other vehicles. The fear, of course, is that hackers might be able to hack into a car's engine and brakes remotely from a laptop and perhaps even to commandeer the vehicle. The concern is that hackers might be able to take over a vehicle while one is driving it, especially at highway speeds. Lawmakers, government regulators, car manufacturers, and consumers naturally are concerned. The Jeep demonstration and other tests have demonstrated the vulnerabilities of cars to hacking. Consequently, the apparent inability of a car to withstand a cyber-attack raises the legal issue of whether there is a safety defect in the car. If the National Highway Traffic and Safety Administration (NHTSA) deems a car to have a defect the agency can demand a recall of that vehicle line, which obviously is costly to a manufacturer's reputation and pocketbook. However, auto manufacturers contend that a cyber-attack on a car is not a legal "defect"; rather, they say that hacking into a car is an intentional wrongful act by a bad person, comparable to someone slashing a car's tires. The proliferation of driverless features in cars, such as automatic braking and increased wireless communication, has heightened security concerns. A major problem is that the main federal law dealing with safety, defects, and recalls of autos was promulgated in 1966, long before sophisticated (and perhaps hack-prone) technology existed. Accordingly, government regulators have focused on more traditional aspects of vehicles, such as seat-belts, brakes, air bags, as well as how well vehicles can withstand crashes. In addition to the aforementioned regulatory law administered by the NHTSA there are two bodies of common law that could apply to the hacked car controversy, and which could result in lawsuits by private parties against auto manufacturers and sellers. The first is negligence law, based on the old English common law. Pursuant to negligence law, a car manufacturer has a legal duty to act as a "reasonably prudent" car manufacturer and to exercise due care in the design and production of its vehicles. The failure to do so subjects the manufacturer to civil damages for the tort, or civil wrong, of negligence, including "pain and suffering" damages as well as additional punitive damages if the negligence is gross, for harms caused by its negligent actions. The duty of due care requires that the manufacturer guard against and warn of risks that the manufacturer knew of or should have known of and which are reasonably foreseeable. The second area of law, also based on the common law but of modern vintage, is products liability law, specifically the doctrine of strict liability in tort. Strict liability imposes civil tort liability and tort damages on anyone on the marketing chain (manufacturer-wholesaler/distributor-retailer) who produces and/or sells a "defective" product. There is no need for an injured party to prove negligence; the liability is "strict," that is, without fault. However, it is indispensable that the product be adjudged to be a "defective" one. One important objective of strict liability law, particularly the design defect doctrine, is to advance product safety. Yet how these common law theories will be applied to the hacked car controversy will only be determined when there are actual lawsuits instituted and judges and juries render decisions.

The manufacturer or seller of a product is allowed to assume the product will be used in a normal fashion. Accordingly, the manufacturer or seller generally will not be held liable for harm or injuries resulting from the abnormal use of the product. There is an exception, however, that may arise when the abnormal or unusual use of the product is deemed to be foreseeable. For example, using a lawnmower with the grass bag removed could be deemed to be a foreseeable misuse of the product, thereby resulting in the manufacturer's or seller's liability when a bystander is injured by a projectile that is shot through the unguarded lawnmower.

There are decided advantages to the consumer with the strict liability doctrine. Strict liability in tort for products is not negligence law; thus evidence of a lack of due care is not required. Strict liability is not warranty law; thus disclaimers as well as notice and privity requirements are not operational. The injured consumer or user only must establish that the product was defective when it left the seller's hands and that the defect caused the injury. There are, however, some defenses that a defendant manufacturer (or wholesaler or retailer) can interpose, to wit: 1) assumption of the risk, that is, the user of the product assumed the risk of its use by being aware of the defect or danger and nonetheless used the goods anyway; 2) misuse or abuse of the product; or 3) disregarding the manufacturer's instructions as to proper and safe use.

The justification for the doctrine of strict liability in tort is asserted, originally by the California Supreme Court, as a consumer safety one. Accordingly, the doctrine is supported on Utilitarian "greater good" grounds that it will not only maintain consumer safety but also advance consumer safety since a manufacturer now will be legally obligated to "keep up" with the "state-of-the-art." There is also a "risk distribution" rationale behind strict liability law. That is, the costs of injuries for defective products should be borne by the manufacturer or seller who placed the product on the market rather than the injured consumer; and then the manufacturer in essence can "spread" the risk by factoring it into the price of the product. Moreover, the manufacturer as well as other entities on the marketing chain can obtain insurance to protect themselves, and then once again, the additional cost of the coverage can be factored into the price of the product.

Products liability litigation in the United States also has dealt with tobacco, guns, and "fast food," and particularly the relationship of these products to the design defect component to the strict tort liability doctrine. The tobacco cases are most interesting because they reveal the uncertainties and risks of the U.S. jury system to the litigants. Examine and reflect on the two Florida cases, for example. In one, in 1999, a jury in Miami-Dade County found in a class action suit against several tobacco companies that the cigarettes they manufactured and sold to Florida smokers were defective and unreasonably dangerous and caused a variety of fatal illnesses. Yet earlier, in 1997, another Florida jury, this time in Jacksonville, found that R.J. Reynolds, the maker of Salem cigarettes that the plaintiff smoked, was neither negligent in the plaintiff smoker's death nor did the tobacco company, ruled the jury, make an unreasonably dangerous and defective product. Why the disparity in outcomes? The Florida tobacco cases reveal the distinction between the roles of the judge and the jury in the United States. The judge determines questions of law and instructs the jury as to the law and the meaning of the law, for example, the design defect test part of the strict liability doctrine, but then the jury, as the "trier of fact" applies the law to the facts of the cases and renders a verdict. The design defect test, as are many legal precepts in a common law system such as the U.S., is not a precise formulation, which consequently accords the jury a great deal of discretion. Cigarettes certainly are not technically flawed, but are the warnings adequate? Moreover, most importantly, can a plaintiff sustain his or her burden of proof in convincing a jury that a tobacco company can make a safer cigarette, and also do so in a practical, feasible, and economic manner? Those are difficult burdens to overcome, though not insurmountable ones.

The strict liability doctrine also has spawned a series of gun suits, in which injured plaintiffs argue that guns are defective products. The lawsuits typically are not based on the contention that guns are flawed products (and actually they seem to work very well, and therein lies the problem!), or even the assertion that warnings are inadequate (since ordinarily there are many warnings as to the proper transportation, use, cleaning, and storing of guns). Rather, the products liability lawsuits involving guns are based on the premise that guns are defectively designed products, and specifically the charge is made that the design of guns should incorporate modern "smart gun" technology designed to prevent unauthorized users from firing the guns. One example of "smart gun" technology would be a feature, such as a fingerprint code or some type of sensor on the handle or trigger, which would recognize the unique characteristics of someone's grip. The gun industry, in defending product liability suits, argues that such "smart gun" technology is still in the developmental stage, and had not reached the scientific, as well as legally binding, level of state-of-the-art technology. Other issues involve the practicality of adopting such technology, and still having a gun that can be used efficaciously for legitimate purposes such as target shooting, hunting, and especially self-defense. There is also the economic feasibility issue of incorporating such safety features into a gun and still having the gun remain as an affordable product of that type. One very noteworthy, tragic, and very revealing gun products liability case, called the Grunow case, occurred in Florida in 2002. In that case, the widow of a teacher, who was slain in 2000 by one of his students, an irate thirteen year old forbidden by the teacher from seeing his girlfriend in class, and who used his grandfather's pistol to kill the teacher, sued the distributor of the weapon, (since the manufacturer was bankrupt) claiming that the weapon was defective in design because it did not have better safety features, such as an internal locking system. The jury in West Palm Beach awarded the widow $1.2 million but also stated on the verdict form that the gun was not defective. The judge, of course, was obligated to throw out the jury's verdict, since the jury, apparently very sympathetic to the widow, nonetheless found for the defendant distributor on the critical design defect question. It is also interesting to note that in 2002 former New Jersey Governor McGreevy signed into law the first "smart gun" law that mandates that all new handguns that are sold in that state be equipped with safety features that would allow only the owner of the weapon to fire it. New Jersey was the first state to enact such legislation. However, the law does not specify what "smart gun" technology must be; rather only that it must recognize the owner as well as be commercially available and feasible.

The emerging area of products liability lawsuits in the U.S. deals with food, specifically "fast food" and soda, and the allegation that such food and drink cause obesity and related health problems. Several lawsuits alleging that "fast food" violates the strict liability doctrine have been filed; but none as of this writing have been successful. Yet perhaps as a result, many companies now are placing calorie and nutritional information prominently on the food labels or cartons as well as displaying such information in the restaurants at the food-counters. Such meritorious behavior is certainly "socially responsible" conduct, but also activity that will go a long way to complying with the "warning" element to strict liability. The much more interesting, as well as perplexing question, is whether "fast food" is defectively designed. Could a cheeseburger, large fries, and Coke be made safer, and still taste the appetizing same? Are there alternatives to certain ingredients of the food or the substances or manner in which it is cooked that emerge as reasonable alternatives? Are these alternatives presently available, and are they practical and feasible? These are issues that will have to be addressed and answered in this growing new field of products liability litigation.

Two other legal doctrines that impact strict liability law are *market share liability* and *statutes of repose*. The former benefits plaintiffs and the latter benefits defendants. Normally, an injured plaintiff has to demonstrate that the defective product that caused the plaintiff harm was produced by a particular defendant manufacturer. However, in some instances, it may be very difficult if not impossible for a defendant to pinpoint which manufacturer out of the many that produced the product, or perhaps which one of the many distributors of the product, made or supplied it to the plaintiff. Accordingly, in some states a court may interpose the doctrine of *market share liability*. This legal principle holds that manufacturers who sold a defective product, or distributors who supplied it, such as lead-based paint, will be compelled to share to burden of damages based on the percentage each holds of the pertinent product or distribution market. A *statute of repose* is similar to a statute of limitations. A statute of repose is a state statute (and most states have such a statute) that holds that the manufacturer or seller of a product cannot be sued for producing or selling a product that caused harm unless the lawsuit is brought within 10 or 12 years, depending on the state statute, from the date the product was made of sold.

The Consumer Products Safety Commission

The Consumer Products Safety Commission (CPSC) is a U.S., federal, independent, regulatory agency, created by Congress in the Consumer Product Safety Act (CPSA) in 1972. However, it is important to note for the purposes of this products liability chapter that the CPSA does not create an additional private lawsuit for damages for consumers injured by dangerous products; rather the CPSA affords the consumer as a private party the right to sue for an injunction to prevent violations of the Act or rules and regulations promulgated by the CPSC.

Summary

The use of any product involves some degree of risk; and accordingly a key legal question under U.S. common law, statutory law, as well as regulatory principles, is to ascertain the acceptable level of known risk. No one reasonably expects a manufacturer to make a product completely safe or to reduce the risk of harm to zero. Generally speaking, a product will be legally safe if it complies with the applicable legal standards for product safety; and if there are still risks attendant to the use of the product it nevertheless will be deemed legally safe if the risks are known and judged acceptable and reasonable to a rational person in view of the benefits to be derived from the use of such a "risky" product.

Products are made for the purposes of engaging and fulfilling consumers' needs, as well as creating profits for businesses. However, the liability that comes with the development of new products can be very high, depending upon the product itself. Therefore, businesses are forced to seek ways of developing harmless products, as they are likely to face major lawsuits should their products cause harm to the consumers. In the previous chapter, torts and businesses were discussed, where the term tort was defined as a wrongful act against a person which may cause a legal action. The term itself is applicable to the production of products, as they too can be harmful, even if used in the correct manner. Therefore, tort laws were initially established in the products field to help consumers attain justice due to the caused harm. They were also developed in order to create pressure on manufacturers to develop safe products. In essence, the tort laws, products liability laws, lawsuits, and other legal mechanisms have allowed manufacturing firms to create efficient and effective products that are beneficial to all, while protecting consumers from products that cause harm.

Discussion Questions

1. How can the legal doctrines of negligence, fraud, and warranty be used by an injured consumer in a products liability lawsuit? Provide examples of each with a brief explanation thereof.
2. What is the doctrine of strict tort liability in the United States? What makes a product defective pursuant to this doctrine? Provide examples with brief explanations thereof.
3. What is the warning component to the "defect" test to strict liability? Why do you think that manufacturers now "err on the side of caution" and warn of risks that a reasonable person would be aware of? Provide examples with brief explanations thereof.
4. What are some of the emerging areas in strict liability design defect law? Why? Provide examples with brief explanations thereof.
5. Is it morally fair to hold a retailer liable under strict liability for selling a defectively designed product when the product came to the retailer from the manufacturer in a sealed package which the retailer was not allowed to open? Provide an example with a brief explanation thereof.
6. Is it morally fair to hold a manufacturer legally liable for harms caused by a product that has complied with all federal and state regulatory safety, operational, warning, and design standards? Why or why not? Provide an example with a brief discussion thereof.

4 – CONTRACT LAW

A *contract* is an agreement between two or more persons that is enforceable at law. Business transactions are based on such agreements, wherein each party to the agreement obtains certain rights and assumes certain obligations. When an agreement between the parties meets all the requirements of a contract, the law makes the agreement binding on the parties thereto. As a result, if one party fails or refuses to perform (that is, breaches the contract), the other aggrieved party now has a legal action for damages or enforcement of performance. Contracts, accordingly, are the foundation of all business, because business – locally, nationally, and globally – consists of making and performing contracts. Business people thus can rely on agreements and the promises therein being fulfilled, because they are legally binding obligations. Contracts formed online can also be legally binding agreements. The concept of an electronic or "e-contract" is covered in the Internet Law chapter of this book.

Contract Law in the United States
It is very important to note that a contract is an agreement, but an agreement is not necessarily a contract. A "mere" agreement arises when two or more persons' minds meet on any subject, regardless of how trivial; yet a contract emerges only when the parties intend to be legally bound by the terms of their agreement. The purpose of this chapter, therefore, is to ascertain when agreements rise to the level of legally enforceable agreements, that is, contracts, pursuant to U.S. law. In the U.S., contract law is based primarily on the common law, that is, judge-made law stemming from old English roots. However, the common law of contracts has been modified significantly in the U.S. by the promulgation of statutory law of contracts, called Sales law based on the Uniform Commercial Code, and which subject matter is covered in the next chapter. Moreover, with the advent of the Internet, several federal statutes have been passed in order to bring the old common law of contracts into conformity with modern technology.

Classification of Contracts

The initial order of business is to define the types of contracts among are possible under Anglo-American common law. The first classification is between express and implied and quasi-contract contracts. An *express contract* is one based on words – oral or written – in which the parties signify their intention to enter into a contract as well as the terms of the contract by words expressed at the time of the agreement. An *implied contract*, however, is one in which the duties and obligations the parties assume are not done so expressly, but rather are implied by their acts and conduct or deduced from the circumstances. That is, the parties indicate by their conduct what their intentions are. A very basic though typical example would occur when one person asks another to perform a service, and nothing is said by either party as to compensation; and in such a case, the law will imply a promise to pay a reasonable compensation, presuming naturally that the expectation of compensation is itself reasonable. Another classic example will occur when a bidder raises his or her hand at an auction, thereby indicating an acceptance, a contract, and a sale. The *quasi-contract* is a very unique feature of the old common law, as it is not a "real" contract as the express and implied ones. Rather, a quasi-contract is a legal fiction created by the law in order to prevent the unjust enrichment of one person at the expense of another. In essence, the courts "pretend" that a contract has been formed, and thereby impose an obligation on a person receiving a benefit or service, even though that person had no intention of entering into a contract, but the objective of this fictitious legal device is to prevent this person from being unfairly and unjustly enriched. The classic common law example would occur when a doctor renders emergency services to a victim lying unconscious on the street, and, when the person recovers, he or she may be liable for the reasonable value of the doctor's services. There is one major limitation on the quasi-contract doctrine, however, and that is the benefit conferred cannot have been granted unnecessarily, negligently, or through misconduct, or otherwise the contact will not be imposed by the law. Quasi-contract (also called *Quantum Meruit*) is used to recover the value of products or services that were provided in good faith in the absence of any contract in circumstances where the products and services were plainly necessary, but the party receiving them could not contractually agree to purchase them. For example, a person who is unconscious on the side of the road and who is taken care of by paramedics, doctors, and a hospital, will be obligated by virtue of the quasi-contract doctrine to pay for the reasonable values of these services, even though he/she did not ask for them and did not agree to pay for them.

The next classification of contracts examines the distinction among valid, void, voidable, and unenforceable contracts. A valid contract is one that is enforceable by the courts and contains the following elements, all of which will be addressed in detail in this chapter:

1) mutual agreement between the parties to do or not do a certain thing, which must be a genuine agreement;
2) the parties must be competent to contract;
3) the promises and obligations of each party to the contract must be supported by the common law requirement of "consideration";
4) the subject matter and purposes of the contract must be legal and lawful; and

5)   in some cases, the contract must be evidenced by a writing.

A *void contract* is a legal nullity; it has no legal effect; and is not enforceable in court. The usual example of a void contract is an agreement between two parties to commit an illegal act. A *voidable contract* is an enforceable contract; but one party thereto has the choice to perform or reject the contract and withdraw without liability. However, until that one party decides to avoid the contract and does so, the contract remains in full force. Two classic examples are a contract between an adult and a minor, which is voidable at the option of the minor though enforceable against the adult, and an agreement induced by fraud, which is voidable at the option of the defrauded party. Finally, an *unenforceable contract* is a valid contract, but the courts will not enforce it because a party has an affirmative and superseding defense, such as the "running" of the Statute of Limitations (the legally prescribed time within to bring a lawsuit) or the Statute of Frauds (which may require a writing for a contract to be enforceable).

As can be surmised from the preceding discussion, contracts can be oral or written. Some types of contracts, such as a contract to sell real property, must be evidenced by a writing in order to be enforceable pursuant to Anglo-American law. However, there is nothing inherently wrong with an oral contract, which is enforceable as a general rule, though certainly not advisable as a written contract due to the likely disputes as to the oral agreement's exact terms.

Contracts also can be executory and executed. *An executed contract* is one whose terms have been fully performed by all the contract parties; whereas an *executory contract* is one in which the terms of the contract have not yet been fully carried out by all the contract parties. Thus, if one purchases merchandise, pays for it, and receives it, that contract is now executed; but if one agrees to work for another for a year and the other party promises to pay a monthly salary, that contract is executory as both parties still owe performance, to wit, the work performance and the pay performance.

The final classification of contracts in the common law system is the important differentiation between unilateral and bilateral contracts. In a *unilateral contract*, an act is done in consideration of a promise; that is, an agreed upon exchange for one party's promise is not another party's return promise, but rather the performance of some act by the other party. For example, when a homeowner says to a roofer, "If you repair my roof, I promise to pay you $1000," a unilateral contract is contemplated. The critical as well as problematical point for contract law is that a unilateral contract can only be accepted by the actual full performance of the requested act. In a bilateral contract situation, there is a mutual exchange of promises to perform some future act; that is, one promise is made in consideration for the promise of the other contract promise. In a *bilateral contract*, one party wants, not the immediate performance of an act, but the making of a return promise. For example, one party promises to sell his/her vehicle to another party for a price and the other party in return promises to purchase the vehicle at that price. The most efficacious way to spot a bilateral contract is to look for the parties exchanging promises; a promise for a promise is bilateral. The unilateral v. bilateral distinction is a significant one under the common law, because in a bilateral situation, if either party refuses to perform the promise, there is liability for breach of contract; but in a unilateral situation, there is no promise made by one party to the contract, and thus that party is not liable for breach of contract if he or she fails to perform. Yet when he or she does perform the requested act, that party can enforce the contract. The promise is thus only binding on one contract party.

Remedies for Breach of Contract

Assuming that a contract is a valid one, what are the remedies to the aggrieved party when the other contract party fails to live up to his or her part of the bargain, that is, has breached the contract. The basic types of relief are damages, rescission, specific performance, an injunction, and reformation.

Damages are regarded as a legal remedy, that is, a remedy at law as opposed to one based in equity. There are several types of damages that may be awarded for a breach of contract. First, damages may be nominal. In such a case, the plaintiff can prove that the defendant did breach the contract, but the plaintiff is unable to establish any loss. Nevertheless, the court can award a nominal sum to the plaintiff, which may be sufficient to impose the court costs as well as perhaps attorneys' fees on the defendant. *Nominal damages* also may serve in some jurisdictions a predicate for punitive damages. Finally, the fact that the plaintiff went through the time, effort, and expense of suing the defendant even though the plaintiff did not sustain any real loss, certainly indicates to the community, particularly the business community, that the plaintiff is not a person to be trifled with and that the plaintiff will insist on contractual obligations being fulfilled. Second, damages may be compensatory. *Compensatory damages* arise when the plaintiff can prove a breach of contract and also can prove an actual injury. In such a case, the plaintiff is entitled to monetary compensation for the exact amount of his or her loss. The objective is to place the aggrieved party in the financial position he or she would have occupied if there had been no contract breach by the defendant. In a breach of an employment contract situation, the wrongfully discharged and vindicated employee would be entitled to reinstatement as well as a back pay award and also reinstatement of seniority and other benefits. However, there is an important principle that constrains the conferring of compensatory damages, called the *Mitigation Rule*. This is a rule of contract law that benefits defendants who wrongfully breach contracts. Pursuant to the Mitigation Rule, even if the defendant purposefully breaches the contract, the plaintiff, although the injured party, has a legal duty to make a reasonable and good faith effort to minimize his or her damages. So, in the employment scenario where the employer has breached the contract, the employee is under a legal duty to make a reasonable and good faith effort to find suitable alternative employment. A plaintiff pursuant to the Mitigation Rule will not be allowed to let his or her losses mount up when they could be reasonably avoided. Compensatory damages for breach of contract also encompass expectation damages and reliance damages. *Expectation damages* are those which compensate the aggrieved contract party for the amount lost as a result of the other contract party's breach of contract; that is, the damages are the amount required to place the aggrieved party in the position he or she would have been in if the contract had been performed. This form of compensatory damages is also called the "benefit of the bargain" standard for damages. *Reliance damages* compensate the aggrieved party for any expenditure made in reliance on a contract that was subsequently breached. The purpose is to return the aggrieved party to the position he or she was in before the contract was formed. When is the aggrieved party entitled to receive consequential damages based on lost future profits? The rule of law holds that lost future profit damages can be obtained only if the non-breaching party can show with some certainly the profit that would have been earned if the other party had not breached the contract. Otherwise the damages will be deemed as "speculative" and the aggrieved party will not be able to recover any lost profits. Consequently, this limitation on contract damages can emerge as a problem for entrepreneurs who attempt to recover lost profits for a business enterprise that never commenced or was operated for only a short period of time. Third, related to compensatory damages are *consequential damages*. Consequential damages are damages above and beyond compensatory damages which resulted from the breach of contract and which the parties to the contract should have foreseen as likely at the time the contract was made. It is imperative to note that in order to recover consequential damages, there must be a showing that the breaching party was aware, or should have been aware, of the special circumstances at the time of contracting. The speculative damage limitation on consequential damages may pose a problem for an entrepreneur seeking lost future profit damages. Since an aggrieved contract party must show the profit that he or she would have received if the other party had not breached the contract, it could be very difficult for an entrepreneur to recover lost future profits if the business never started or has just commenced or has been in operation for merely a short period of time. A generalized knowledge of the other party's business affairs ordinarily will not be sufficient. The preeminent illustrations of *consequential damages* are loss of profits and loss of good stemming from the original breach of contract. There is, however, a limitation on consequential damages, called the *Speculative Damage* rule. This restraining precept holds that in order to recover consequential damages, the plaintiff's loss must be reasonably certain of computation; and if not the damages may be deemed "speculative" and consequently not recoverable. A typical "speculative" example would be a plaintiff who is seeking lost profits from a new business that never had any profits! The fourth type of damages is called *liquidated damages*. Liquidated damages arise when the parties to a contract include an explicit provision in the contract that fixes the amount of damages to be recovered if one party breaches the contract. It must be emphasized that the liquidated damage clause in the contract will govern the award of damages, and therefore will be the only recoverable damages, even if the actual loss is more, or the obverse, if there is no actual loss. The courts usually will require that the liquidated damage amount be reasonable and also that the actual damages would have been difficult to ascertain before the courts will enforce such a provision. If the liquidated damage amount is construed to be unreasonable or excessive, it will be deemed a "penalty" and stricken from the contract, and the plaintiff will get actual damages only. Finally, theoretically, a breach of contract plaintiff can recover damages for emotional distress as well as punitive damages for a breach of contract, but such awards are rare in breach of contract cases, as they require some element of a very personal subject matter to the contract in the case of emotional distress, or some evidence of bad faith, recklessness, maliciousness, or fraudulent conduct in the case of punitive damages.

Other types of relief in a contract law setting are termed "equitable" remedies, as opposed to the "legal" relief of monetary damages, since these remedies originated in Anglo-American law in Courts of Equity. The main equitable remedies are: rescission, specific performance, the injunction, and reformation. A *rescission* is an order from a court that cancels contract and releases the injured party from all contractual obligations. For example, if a party is fraudulently induced into entering into a contract, that victimized party can immediately bring suit requesting rescission, instead of waiting to be sued by the other party to enforce the contract. Yet if neither damages nor rescission are adequate remedies, a court may compel the defendant contract party to carry out the terms of the contract. This remedy, however, is limited. It is available for the breach of real estate contract or a contract where the subject matter is deemed unique personal property, or perhaps pursuant to the Uniform Commercial Code when goods though not unique are in very short supply. It must be underscored that the remedy of *specific performance* cannot be utilized to enforce an employment contract or a contract for personal services, due to U.S. Constitutional constraints as well as very serious practical ramifications. An *injunction* is a court order forbidding a defendant from doing a particular act. Injunctions are granted when there is a showing by the aggrieved of the inadequacy of money damages as a remedy as well as a demonstration of irreparable harm if the injunctive relief is not granted. A typical use of an injunction would arise in an employment situation where the employee quits the employer's employment and then in violation of the terms of a legal covenant-not-to-compete seeks to work for a competitor of his or her former employer. In such a case, especially if the former employee had access to confidential and proprietary information, the former employer can seek an injunction and a court order mandating that the former employee not work for the new employer and obey the terms of the non-competition clause in the contract. Violations of injunctions are punished by a court's contempt powers. The final major equitable remedy is *reformation*, which is an order by a court in essence rewriting the terms of an agreement to conform to the actual intent of the parties which was not reflected in the contract due to some type of error or mistake.

The Requirements of a Valid Contract

In order to attain the legal status of a binding and enforceable contract under Anglo-American common law principles, five requirements ordinarily must be present: mutual agreement, which must be genuine, as well as consideration, capacity, legality, and in some instances a writing. It is of great consequence to relate that under the common law, these requirements are measured by an objective test; that is, whether the requirements for a contract are present are determined by a "reasonable person" standard, and not by the subjective intentions of the parties. Determining "reasonableness" is ordinarily regarded as a question of fact for the jury to resolve under an Anglo-American legal scheme.

1. Mutual Agreement

a. The Offer

The first element to a valid contract is the presence of *mutual agreement* between the parties. Mutual agreement can be broken down into two essential components – an offer and an acceptance. Accordingly, the initial question one asks to determine if a contract exists is whether an offer has been made and was this offer followed by an acceptance. The *offer* is the legally recognized beginning to the contract; it is the proposal to enter into a contact. The offeror is the person who makes the offer; and the offeree is the person to whom the offer is made. The offer is the proposal made by the offeror to the offeree indicating what the offeror will give in return for a specified return promise or act by the offeree. There are several requirements to have a valid offer. First, the offer must manifest a definite intent on the offeror's part to enter into a contract. Consequently, communications by one person where the language therein is merely tentative, exploratory, as well as where the language requests additional information, is not "offer" language. Such language does not manifest a sufficient intent to enter into a contract; rather such language is merely preliminary negotiations language. The fact that a statement looks toward a contract in the future does not make the statement an offer if it merely shows the intent to begin negotiations. For example, phrases suggesting only preliminary negotiations include: "Are you interested...," "I would like to get...," or "Would you give...."

Similarly, if a person's language is construed as merely an *"invitation to make an offer,"* then there will not be an offer made. Invitations to make offers may look like offers, but in actuality there are invitations to the public to make offers at certain times and places. The classic examples of mere "invitations" are advertisements, catalogs, price lists, and window displays. They are merely invitations to the public to make offers to merchants which the merchants can either accept or reject. The "invitation to make an offer" doctrine thus illustrates the protection that the old common law gave to merchants; that is, if invitations were construed as offers, a merchant might find itself over-accepted when the merchant's stock of goods is oversold; and then the over-accepted merchant would be subject to lawsuits for breach of contract. There are, however, two exceptions to the "invitation" rule. The first arises when the "invitation" is clearly phrased as an offer, invites those to whom it has been addressed to take a specific action, and, most importantly, limits the quantities involved so as to protect the merchant from being over-accepted. The second exception involves "rewards," that is, announcements to the public that a reward will be paid for the return of lost property or the capture of a criminal.

The second element for a valid offer is that it must be reasonably definite, which is measured by an objective, reasonable person test. The offer and the material terms therein must be reasonably definite; but the omission of minor terms should not affect the offer's validity. Accordingly, pursuant to the common law, the offer must make clear the subject matter of the proposed contract, the quantity, the time of performance, and the price, as well as other material terms. As will be seen later in the next chapter, the Uniform Commercial Code (UCC) makes some important modifications as to the necessary ingredients to an offer, especially pertaining to the price term.

The third element for a valid offer is that it be seriously intended. Accordingly, an "offer" made in jest, in a joking manner, in fear, or anger or spite, is not a valid offer. However since the test for determining the validity of a contract is a "reasonableness" one, there may be times when an offer is not seriously intended by the offeror, but the offeree had no way of knowing the secret thoughts and feelings of the offeror. Accordingly, if the offeree is reasonably certain that the offer was made in earnest and accepts, there very well may be a binding contract, even though the offeror did not intend that the offer was a serious one. Again, and this fact cannot be emphasized enough, the test for a contract under the common law is an objective one and not a subjective one.

The fourth and final requirement for a valid offer is that the offer be communicated to the offeree. The rule of law is that an offer cannot be accepted by the offeree until the offeror has communicated it to the offeree; and an offer will not be legally "communicated" until the offeree has knowledge of it. Consequently, if the offeror's offer falls into the hands of the offeree without the knowledge and consent of the offeror, it cannot be accepted. Similarly, if an offer is directed to a specific individual or business, it cannot be accepted by anyone else. There is one exception to this rule, at least in some states in the United States, based on public policy rationales, and that exception pertains to reward offers which may be "accepted" even if the person doing the requested act was not even aware of the reward offer.

Once a legally recognized offer has been made, the next area to examine is termination of offers. Regarding termination, it is critical to distinguish between revocation and rejection of offers. *Revocation* is the retraction or withdrawal of the offer by the offeror; and such a revocation ends the offer and terminates the offeree's power of acceptance. There are several important common law rules that apply to revocation. First, an offeror may revoke the offer at any time prior to the acceptance. Second, the revocation is effective when it is actually received by the offeree. Revocation can also be implied, for example, when the offeror sells the subject matter of the offer to another, and the offeree knows of this. Finally, a revocation of an offer to the public must be accomplished in substantially the same manner as its announcement; and the fact that the offeree did not hear or read of the withdrawal is irrelevant. It is also important to differentiate "firm offers" from options. A *firm offer* is an offer that includes a statement that it will be held open for a particular period of time. Under the common law, even a firm offer can be revoked prior to the expiration of the stated term; but this rule has been changed under the UCC, as will be seen later in the next chapter when the subject of a UCC merchant's firm offer is discussed. What is an option or an option contract? Very simply, an *option* is a firm offer in which the offeror has received something of value from the offeree in order to keep the offer open. When a firm offer rises to the level of an option, it neither can be revoked during its specified period of time nor can it be terminated by the purported rejection of the option by the offeree, at least in some states, since the offeree has "paid" for the right to change his or her mind as to accepting the option during the time period. Offers can also be revoked due to a lapse of time. The basic rule of law is that the offer is revoked by the lapse of time specified in the offer. Yet what if the offer does not state a time period? If no time is specified, then the offer is revoked by the passage of a reasonable period of time. "Reasonable," of course, depends on the facts and circumstances of a particular case, and is thus for the jury to decide. Key factors would be the presence of language by the offeror asking for an immediate reply, the means of communication used, whether the subject matter of the offer fluctuates in price, or whether the subject matter of the offer is perishable goods. As opposed to revocation, a *rejection* of the offer is a statement by the offeree to the offeror that the offeree does not accept the offer. The basis rule of law is that a rejection terminates the offer, even though the offer may not have otherwise elapsed. Rejections are effective only when they are actually received by the offeror. Offers, finally, can be terminated by operation of the law, that is, automatically when the offeror dies or goes insane, the subject matter is destroyed, or there is intervening illegality of the subject matter of the offer or some aspect of the intended contract. This automatic termination occurs even if the offeree was not aware of the changed circumstances at the time that he or she "accepts."

b. The Acceptance

An offer can become a contract only if it is accepted by the offeree. The *acceptance* is the expression of assent by the offeree to the terms of the offer, by which the offeree exercises the power conferred upon him/her by the offeror to create a legally binding agreement. There are five requirements to have a valid acceptance: 1) the offeree must know of the offer; 2) the offeree must manifest an intention to accept; 3) the acceptance must be unqualified and unconditional; 4) the acceptance must be made in a manner requested or authorized by the offeror; and 5) the acceptance must be communicated to the offeror.

There are four major problems inherent in the common law's acceptance doctrine. First is the effect of silence. The general rule of law is that silence by the offeree does not constitute an acceptance. That is, the offeror can not state in the offer that if the offeror does not hear from the offeree within a period of time, the offeror will conclude that the offeree had accepted. The exception to this rule, though, occurs if the offeree has led the offeror to believe that the offeree's silence will constitute an acceptance. So, if the offeree responds to the offeror by stating that if the offeror does not hear from the offeree within a stated period of time, then acceptance will be effectuated, is a permissible and legal means of "silence" as an acceptance. Similarly, if the parties in their past dealings have used silence as a means of acceptance, then the offeree's silence may be construed as an acceptance, at least for the transaction presently under contention.

The second problem area deals with the legal concept of a *counteroffer*. The conventional, Anglo-American, common law precept holds that an offer must be accepted without any deviation in the terms of the offer. As a result, if the purported acceptance varies, qualifies, conditions, adds to or subtracts from the offer, the communication is viewed as a counteroffer. Moreover, the effect of a counteroffer pursuant to the common law is to serve as a rejection of the offeror's offer, which ends the offeror's offer forever, even if the offeree also states that he or she is "accepting" the offer. This old common law is at times called the "*Mirror Image*" rule, by which the acceptance must be a "mirror image" of the offer. Counteroffers, however, must be distinguished from mere inquiries, in which the offeree is not rejecting the offer, but is merely seeking more information about the offer. If the inquiry, for example, about lowering the price of the offered goods, is answered in the negative by the offeror, the original offer still can be accepted, presuming it is not revoked. How does one differentiate a counteroffer/rejection from a mere inquiry? The test is a reasonableness one, ultimately for a jury to resolve as a question of fact, and asks whether a reasonable person in the "shoes" of the offeror would have construed the communication from the offeree as an offer itself, as opposed to just a request for more information. It is very important to note that material changes in the old common law counteroffer rules have been made in contracts for the sale of goods under the Uniform Commercial Code, which will be seen later in the next chapter, as well as when a party attempts a counteroffer against an electronic offeror on the Web due to The Uniform Computer Information Transactions Act, as is examined in the chapter on Internet Regulation.

The third problem area regarding acceptance deals with the legally required means that the offeree must use to communicate the acceptance to the offeror. The initial common law rule holds that when the offeror clearly states the medium of communication that the offeree must use, then that method must in fact be used or else the offeree's intended "acceptance" will be construed as a counteroffer. Presuming that a particular means of acceptance has not been demanded by the offeror, the prevailing and newer common law rule is that an acceptance can be communicated by any means reasonable under the circumstances. What is "reasonable"? If the offeree uses in accepting the same means of communication that the offeror used in making the offer, such means will be deemed reasonable ordinarily. Custom in the industry or trade as well as the past practices of the parties themselves are important "reasonableness" factors. Such a "reasonable" acceptance as a general rule will be legally effective on dispatch, though one exception pertains to acceptances by FAX, which are only effective on receipt. It is important to note that the offeror can negate the rule holding that an acceptance is effective on dispatch merely by stating in his or her offer that the acceptance of the offer will be effective only on receipt by the offeror.

The final problem with acceptance deals with the acceptance of unilateral offers. In a unilateral offer situation, the offer, which calls for the performance of an act, can only be accepted by the performance of the act – full and complete performance. Thus, the offeror technically, but legally, can revoke his or her unilateral offer before full performance, even though the offeree has started to perform, and perhaps substantially so. How does the law protect the partially performing offeree in such a situation? There is always the quasi-contract doctrine. In some jurisdictions, the offeror's right to revoke is suspended for a reasonable period of time so as to give the partially performing offeree an opportunity to complete performance and thus accept the unilateral offer and turn it into a legally binding contract. In other jurisdictions, as well as under the Uniform Commercial Code, the beginning of performance by the offeree is construed as an acceptance, thereby turning the performance of the unilateral action into an implied bilateral promise to complete performance.

2. *Consideration*

The term "*consideration*" in its Anglo-American, common law, contract meaning may not be familiar to many business people. Yet this contract requirement is indispensable to the formation of a legally binding contract. The general rule of law maintains that a contract will not be enforced unless it is supported by "consideration." If there is no consideration present, then ordinarily an agreement is not enforceable even if the promises thereto are in writing. For example, if an employer promises an employee a bonus, and the employee of course agrees, the employee nonetheless is well advised to ensure that the employer's promise is supported by consideration. Similarly, if the employee promises the employer that the employee will not compete against the employer upon leaving the employer's employ, the employer is well counseled to ensure that the employee's promise is supported by consideration. Promises not supported by consideration are generally not legally binding, and thus it is quite legal to break them, though usually not ethical to do so.

In determining exactly what consideration is, the first step is to define the two crucial parties in the contact scenario. The "*promisor*" is the party who makes a promise; and the "*promisee*" is the party to whom the promise is made. Consideration is viewed as whatever the promisor demands in return for his or her promise. The test for consideration under Anglo-American common law is called the "*legal detriment*" test. The first step in applying this step is to focus on the promisee, the person to whom the promise is made, and to ask oneself the following question: Has the promisee incurred a legal detriment under the contract? If so, then consideration is present, and accordingly the promisor's promise is enforceable. What exactly is legal detriment on the part of the promisee? Detriment can be based on the promisee doing any one of four actions as a result of the promisor's promise: 1) the promisee can make a return promise to do something which he or she is not otherwise legally obligated to do; 2) the promisee can make a return promise not to do something which he or she has a legal right to do (called "forebearance"); 3) the promisee can do something that he or she is not otherwise legally obligated to do; or 4) the promisee can refrain from doing something that he or she has a legal right to do (again, called "forebearance"). It is important to note that for a promise or an act to refrain from doing something to be deemed "detriment" and consideration, the activity the promisee is promising to give up or giving up must be a lawful one.

There are several problem areas with the old common law construct of consideration. The first involves the mutuality requirement. Pursuant to the *mutuality of obligation rule*, in order for a promise to be construed as detriment, it must impose a real obligation on a party. If a party's promise does not do so, it will be branded as fake or illusory and thus cannot serve as consideration. For example, if there is in a contract a cancellation clause in which one party reserves an unlimited and unrestricted right to cancel, then that party has a "free" way out of the contract and the promises that he or she made therein are merely fake or illusory ones. However, if the cancellation clause is somehow limited, for example, by requiring that the contract be in effect for a stipulated period of time before any cancellation thereof, or basing cancellation on a specified event, or having a notice requirement followed by a time period, then the promises in the contract will be real, and thus will be able to serve as detriment and consideration.

The second problem area under consideration deals with the adequacy of consideration. Pursuant to the common law precept, the law is not concerned with the adequacy or sufficiency of consideration, merely the presence of consideration, that is, the presence of technical legal detriment. Thus, as a general rule, the adequacy of consideration, that is, the relative value or worth of the two promises or the promise for the act, is irrelevant. The common law does not prohibit "bad" bargains; and a common law court will not "police," fix, and readjust the monetary values of the respective promises and acts. However, when a judge is asked to issue an equitable remedy, such as a specific performance, or when the contract is deemed an "unconscionable" one under the Uniform Commercial Code, then a judge will consider the adequacy of consideration.

The third problem area of consideration, which already has been alluded to, deals with insufficient consideration. The general rule of law is that performing or promising to perform an action that one is already legally obligated to do is insufficient consideration. One can be under a pre-existing public duty to do an act, and as a result if one's performance falls within the scope of one's public duties, neither one's promise to perform or actual performance will serve as legal detriment. For example, if in return for a promise of money, a police officer promises to watch one's business, or a witness promises to tell the truth, or an employee promises to perform his or her job carefully, all those promises are insufficient consideration to support the promisor's promise of a money payment because the parties are already legally obligated to do those duties. The same situation arises when the pre-existing duties are contract-based ones. If one party is already obligated by a prior contract to perform an act for another party, then neither a new promise to perform the same act, typically for more money, nor the actual performance of the act, will be consideration for the promisor's promise to pay more money. This common law can be succinctly stated as follows: Modification of a contract requires new consideration. So, for example, if a repairperson demands more money from a homeowner for doing the same repair work that was originally contracted for, the homeowner's promise to pay more is not enforceable since the repairperson "suffered" no real detriment in doing the already contractually obligated action. However, as will be seen later in this chapter, the Uniform Commercial Code makes a material change to this modification rule. Even under the old common law, there are exceptions to the "modification" rule. So, if there is an agreed upon subsequent promise of different performance than originally contacted for, even if slightly different, then there will be sufficient consideration to support a promise to pay more money for even substantially the same act. Similarly, if there are unforeseen and extreme difficulties in the performance of the contract, then a new promise to pay more money for the same act is enforceable, presuming agreement between the parties, of course. Finally, there is nothing to prevent the parties from mutually rescinding their first contract, thereby canceling it, and then substituting a brand new contract for the same act for more money. These common law rules are very important when it comes to the payment of debts. For example, the common law holds that the partial payment of a past-due debt is insufficient to support the creditor's promise to cancel the remainder of the obligation. The reason is that the creditor is already entitled to the part payment, and thus the debtor is not promising anything new or different to the creditor. Even, in most states in the United States, if the creditor accepts a partial payment in the form of a check from the debtor which is indorsed "payment in full," and which is then cashed or deposited by the creditor. Yet if the debtor pays the debt early or performs some service, in addition to paying the lesser sum, then the creditor's promise to discharge the debt will be enforceable. Moreover, if a debt is legitimately deemed an "unliquidated" one, that is, genuinely in dispute as to the existence of the amount of the debt, then the cancellation of the honestly disputed debt for a lesser amount than the creditor initially claimed will be enforceable. In essence, both the creditor and the debtor undergo detriment by forgoing their right to institute a lawsuit to get a court to rule on the existence or amount of the obligation.

The next problem area pertaining to consideration deals with past performance. That is, a contract party is motivated by a past event to make a promise to pay. Characteristically, the past event was some transaction between the parties in which one party benefited, and now that party feels morally obligated to the other. Yet, under the common law, past performance or moral consideration is not consideration and consequently any promises based thereon are unenforceable. Sometimes this "past performance" rule is phrased as the "bargained for exchange" requirement of consideration. That is, the promise must cause the detriment; and the detriment cannot come first and then motivate a "moral" promise.

The final problem area regarding consideration concerns the exceptions to consideration. For example, the promise to pay a debt barred by the *Statute of Limitations* (which sets forth time periods in which to institute a lawsuit), is ordinarily enforceable even without new consideration, though a writing may be required. Promises to charities also are enforceable without consideration based on grounds of public policy. Lastly, the doctrine of "*promissory estoppel*" may serve as a substitute for consideration. This common law doctrine maintains that even if there is no technical legal detriment present, if one party makes a promise to another, and the person to whom it has been made reasonably relies on it, and then acts on it and in so doing substantially changes his or her position or suffers great inconvenience, the original promising party will be estopped (that is, legally prevented) from even raising the issue of a lack of consideration.

3. Capacity

The third requirement for a valid contract is the element of contract capacity. Capacity means that the parties must be fully legally competent to contract; but it does not mean that a party must be intellectually competent to contract. One can make under the common law all the "stupid" contracts one is capable of doing! If a party totally lacks the legal capacity to contract, for example, a person adjudged insane, the resulting contract is void, that is, a legal nullity. One, however, can have partial capacity to contract, for example, minors, and in such a case the contract is deemed to be voidable and can be disaffirmed (that is, set aside) by the party with partial capacity. Yet until that party disaffirms, the contract is valid and binding on both parties.

Minors, that is, those people under the state's age of majority (usually age 18) for contracting, are the best example of contract parties with partial contract capacity. The general rule in the United States is that all minors' contracts are voidable at their option. To disaffirm, the minor must merely indicate to the other party his or her intention not to be bound. *Disaffirmance* can be expressed by words or implied by actions. This right to disaffirmance continues until the minor reaches the age of majority as well as until a reasonable time thereafter. It is important to note that this right to disaffirm is one-sided, as it inures only to the benefit of the minor.

Even if a contract is executed, that is, fully performed, by the minor and adult, the minor can still disaffirm. The minor thus receives his or her consideration back, and the minor's only obligation is to return the consideration he or she received back to the adult, if the minor is able. As a result of this rule, which is the majority rule in the United States, the minor is not liable for any damage, depreciation, or use of the property. The rationale for this rule is to protect minors from mistakes of their youth and lack of judgment, regardless of any hardship to the adult contracting parties. So, in order to avoid the potential problems of contracting with minors, an adult, for example, a merchant, may not want to deal with them, or contract with the minor's parents, or have the minor certify in writing that he or she is 18 years of age.

There are three exceptions to the general rule of the voidability of minors' contracts. One exception involves a significant canon in the common law, called the doctrine of *ratification*. In the context of minors' contracts, the ratification doctrine maintains that once a minor reaches 18 years of age, he or she can ratify contracts made earlier. Ratification occurs when the minor indicates to the other party his or her intent to be bound by the earlier contract. Ratification can be express, for example, when the minor upon reaching 18 years promises to abide by the agreement; or ratification can be implied, for example, when the minor reaches 18 years and continues to use goods or services, for more than a reasonable time, that the minor received and is receiving under an earlier contract. The second exception concerns the minor's liability on the contract when subject matter of the contract is deemed to be a "necessity," such as food, clothing, shelter, or medical care. If the contract to purchase a necessity is still executory, then the minor is still allowed to disaffirm; however, if the contract is executed, then the minor will be liable on the contract, but not necessarily for the contract price of the necessity, but the reasonable value therefore as set by a court. The final exception governs those situations where the minor misrepresents his or her age. Again, if the contract is executory, the minor can still disaffirm, even if he or she lied. However, if the contract is executed, the minor will only be permitted to disaffirm if there is no loss to the other party; and as a result, the minor in such a case must restore the consideration received as well as account for any loss, damage, depreciation, or use. Clearly, the minor who lies will receive less legal protection from the law.

4. Legality

Legality is a required element to a valid contract; and accordingly the contract's purpose, subject matter, and means of performance must be legal. The contract cannot be for the attainment of an objective that is prohibited by any law. A contract contrary to a statute or regulation is illegal and void. For example, many counties in the state of Florida, in the aftermath of hurricanes, enacted laws that prohibit "price-gouging," specifically by prohibiting the sale of essential commodities at "unconscionable" prices during the time of a declared emergency. Moreover, a contract which is contrary to the public policy of a particular jurisdiction, that is, a contract determined by the high court in that jurisdiction to be adverse to public health, safety, and welfare, is illegal and void.

Contracts contrary to statute are illegal, for example, gambling contracts in most U.S. jurisdictions. Such a contract is illegal and void; and the court system will leave the parties where it finds them; and thus neither party to the illegal agreement can use the court system to sue the other for the breach of the gambling debt. However, the advent of Internet gambling has created major problems – legal as well as practical – for U.S. government authorities, primarily due to the fact that the locations where the Internet gambling companies are located do in fact legalize that type of Web gaming; and thus when the consumer-gambler located in the U.S. makes a wager, he or she is engaging in a lawful activity. Of course, if and when the U.S. consumer does not pay his or her gambling obligations, and the foreign firm attempts to sue in the U.S. courts, the U.S. consumer very well might interpose a defense of illegality. Another problem that has arisen with the advent of online gambling is whether online poker is a game predominated by chance, that is, illegal (in most states) gambling, as opposed to a game predominated by skill, which would be legal. A game of pure skill would be chess; whereas a game of pure chance would be slot machine playing. A game of more skill than chance would be bridge; whereas a game of more chance than skill would be sports betting (because one's knowledge and skill regarding sports does not affect the game play). Poker is somewhere in between, it seems; but a definite answer would be critical to contractual liability between the parties playing. One recalls that a contract with an illegal subject matter is a void contract, a nullity, and thus a court will leave the parties where it finds them (which means "good luck" in getting your poker winnings if you are "gambling"). The rulings by the state courts are mixed on the issue; but there is a federal case saying that poker is more of a skill game and thus not illegal gambling. Nevertheless, players and particularly Internet poker companies continue to operate in a rather "gray area" legally at least until there are more court precedents or state legislation. Today, the states of Nevada and New Jersey, as well as Great Britain, allow and regulate online poker playing.

Another problem area concerning legality of contracts arises when a licensing statute is contained in the contracting. In the United States, at all levels of government, there are laws, primarily in statute form, that make it illegal to operate certain types of businesses, trades, or professions without a license. Accordingly, the issue arises as to whether an unlicensed person or business can recover for services rendered under a contract. The critical point for contract analysis is to distinguish between two types of licensing statutes: regulatory and revenue-raising. The former is a statute designed to protect the public from incompetent and/or unethical people or businesses. Therefore, if the applicable licensing statute is a regulatory one, then the rule of law is that the unlicensed person or business cannot recover as the contract is illegal and void. An example would be a contract by a lawyer not licensed to practice law in that particular jurisdiction. Of course, the lawyer as well as any unlicensed person under a regulatory scheme could confront very serious criminal sanctions for not having a license. However, if the licensing statute is "merely" a revenue-raising one, that is, one designed primarily to raise money from licensing fees, then the contract by the unlicensed business or person is valid and he or she can recover; yet that person or business might be subject to civil or even criminal punishment for violating the law. An example would be a corporation that fails to pay its charter fees or annual license fees. Its contracts would nonetheless be valid, though it might lose its charter if the licensee fees are not pay. Another similar revenue-raising example would be an occupational license that a municipality typically requires for a person or a business to do business in that local jurisdiction.

Usury is an ancient term, but one that nevertheless has meaning for modern day contract law. In some states in the United States, there will be statutes that establish the maximum rate of interest that can be charged on ordinary (that is, non-corporate) loans. The typical usury interest rates are 15-18% per year for obligations up to $500,000, and rates up to 25% for obligations over $500,000. Charging interest in excess of the state's permitted interest rates is deemed to be usury, and is illegal. The result of usury is that the lender is prohibited from collecting the excess interest, but the lender still can recover the principal and the interest at the lawful rate, though in some jurisdictions the lender cannot recover any interest at all.

Regarding contracts that are illegal because they are against *public policy*, two chief business contract circumstances will be examined. One involves contracts with *covenants-not-to-compete*; and the other concerns contracts with exculpatory clauses. First and foremost, a fundamental general rule of law is that a contract in restraint of trade or commerce is illegal and void. Consequently, if a person contracts and thereby agrees not to engage in a particular business, trade, or profession, that contract is illegal and void as against public policy. However, if that promise not to do business is in the form of a non-compete agreement which is an ancillary part of a larger contract, for example, the contract for the sale of a business or an employment contract, then that non-compete promise may be enforceable. In order to resolve the legality of non-competition agreements, it is initially necessary to ask whether the non-competition agreement appears in a contract for the sale of a business or an employment contract. In the contract for the sale of a business, the covenant must be reasonable in time, that is, duration, and place, that is, geographic trade territory. If the covenant is reasonable in both time and place, the seller of the business will be prohibited from entering the designated business area for the specified period of time. Even though there is some restraint on trade and competition, the covenant is justified as a reasonable means to prevent the seller of a business from in essence "retaking" the asset of goodwill by engaging in the same or similar business again in the same area and thereby seeking his or her old customers to patronize. Covenants not to compete also arise in employment contracts, whereby typically the employee promises not to work for a competitor of the employer or to engage in a similar business for a specified period of time. In most U.S. jurisdictions, such a covenant is legal and enforceable, regardless if it produces a harsh effect on the employee, if the covenant is reasonable as to time and place and the employer can demonstrate a legitimate business interest to justify the covenant. One final covenant point has to be covered, and that is what happens when the covenant is unreasonable. The majority rule is that if a covenant is unreasonable in any one of its core legal requirements, then the whole covenant is illegal and void and stricken from the contract, which is otherwise valid. In such a case, the buyer of the business or the former employer gets no legal protection against competition. The minority rule is that a judge will reform a covenant to make it reasonable and enforceable.

A contract with an *exculpatory clause* is one in which one of the parties to the contract agrees to free the other party of all liability for physical injury or monetary harm negligently caused by the other party. This type of clause is usually found on valet parking and dry cleaning tickets. As a general rule, the courts will strike down an exculpatory clause as illegal and void, though some courts may want a showing that the clause affected a large segment of the public and involved a quasi-public business, such as a communications company, or where the party inserting the exculpatory clause had superior bargaining power over the other party, such as an auto dealership.

The final area to examine under the legality requirement to contracts is the effect of illegal contracts. As noted, illegal contracts are void and unenforceable, and consequently neither party to the illegal agreement can be assisted by courts in any way, regardless of the consequences to the parties. There are two exceptions, however. The first is called the "protected parties" exception. The exception arises when there is a statute designed to protect a certain class of people. Accordingly, any contract made in violation of the statute is enforceable by persons within that class, despite the technical illegality of the agreement. For example, a member of the public can sue an unlicensed member of a profession, such as the legal profession, for breach of contract as well as for legal malpractice since the purpose of the statute licensing attorneys is to protect the public from incompetent and/or unethical lawyers. The second exception to the general effect of illegality is called the "divisibility" or "severability" doctrine. The rule of law is that if a contract is severable into separate agreements, and the parts which are legal can be performed separately, the contract is enforceable as to the legal parts. Yet if the contract is indivisible, that is, the promises therein are so interdependent that the contract can only be performed as a single entity, the illegality in any one part will "contaminate" the entire contact and render the whole contract illegal and unenforceable. For example, as mentioned, a contract with an illegal covenant-not-to-compete will generally be upheld, though the illegal covenant component will be stricken from the contract. To compare, a contract in which a landlord's rental payment is derived from the legal sale of food and beverages and the illegal proceeds from gambling most likely will be struck down in its entirely.

5. *Writing*

As a general rule, oral contracts are just as enforceable as written contracts, yet only if the terms can be proven in court. However, there are certain classes of contracts that will not be enforced unless their terms are evidenced by a writing. This rule is commonly known in Anglo-American law as the *Statute of Frauds*. The reason for the Statute of Frauds, not to be confused with the separate and distinct legal wrong of fraud, is to prevent the use of perjury and false testimony in proving the existence and terms of an oral contract. Accordingly, if a writing is required and not present, then the contract is deemed unenforceable, though the defendant has an affirmative obligation to assert the Statute of Frauds as an affirmative defense or else see it waived. It is also very important to underscore that the Statute of Frauds only applies to executory contracts. As such, if the parties enter into an oral agreement that should have been written, but both parties have fully performed, the law will not allow the transaction to be set aside due to the lack of a writing.

Pursuant to the Statute of Frauds, there are six categories of contracts that must be evidenced by a writing. The first is a contract to sell land, including structures permanently attached to the land, or any interest in land, such as a mortgage or easement. Of course, in the usual situation there will be a formal written contract to expressly reflect the parties' agreement. This real estate contract is different from the deed, which is the legal instrument later executed by the seller to transfer legal title of the real estate to the buyer, as will be seen in the chapter on Real Property Law. There are two exceptions to this first rule. One pertains to real estate leases for a year or less, which ordinarily are enforceable even if oral, though certainly not advisable. The second exception is called the doctrine of Part Performance, which holds that an oral contract for the sale of land is enforceable if the buyer has paid part of the purchase price, taken possession of the property, and made substantial improvements to the property.

The second category of contracts that must be evidenced by a writing deals with executory bilateral contracts that are by their own terms incapable of being performed within a year from the date in which the contract was formed. The reason for the rule is that disputes over the provisions of an oral contract are even more likely to occur when the oral contract is a long-term one. Moreover, witnesses die, and their memories fade. So, for example, a contract to manage a business for five years, or a three year employment contract, must be evidenced by a writing in order to be enforceable. There is, however, one interesting, though perhaps a bit convoluted, exception to this rule. The exception holds that if there is any possibility, regardless of how remote and unlikely, under the terms of the contract, for the contract to be fully performed within one year from the time the contract was made, then no writing is required, even though actual performance actually took longer than one year. For example, an agreement by a caretaker to take care of a person for his or her life can be oral since there is a possibility that the person cared for will die within the year of contract formation.

The third category of contracts that must be evidenced by a writing is a contract of *guaranty*. The first and foremost point is to distinguish *guaranty contracts* from *suretyship contracts*. A suretyship contract involves a promise made by a party, called a surety, to a third person, typically a creditor or merchant, to be responsible for the debts or obligations of a third person. The contract is between the surety and the creditor or merchant. The surety is primarily liable for the debt; and the creditor can demand payment directly from the surety the moment the debt is due. The creditor does not have to exhaust any legal remedies against the debtor first. In layperson terms, the surety is regarded as a "co-signer" on the original obligation, and thereby becomes jointly liable for the payment thereof together with the original debtor. Surety agreements do not have to be in writing, it must be emphasized. To compare, a guaranty contract is one in which a party, the guarantor, makes a secondary (or at times called a *"collateral"*) promise to pay the debt or obligation of another. The guarantor is secondarily liable on the obligation; and thus the guarantor can be legally required to pay the obligation only after the principal and primary debtor defaults and after the creditor has made a good faith attempt to collect from the debtor. The Statute of Frauds requires these secondary guarantee promises to be in writing to be enforceable. There is an exception, however, called the "Benefit to the Promisor" exception, which holds that if the promisor's main purpose in guaranteeing the debt or obligation of another was to gain some advantage or benefit for himself or herself, then the oral guarantee promise will be enforceable. One point should be very clear, and that is when one is "backing" or co-signing an obligation, one should be absolutely certain if one is a surety or "merely" a guarantor.

The fourth category of contracts that must be evidenced by a writing is an agreement by an executor, administrator, or personal representative to pay the debts of an estate from his or her own personal funds. The fifth category involves contracts made in consideration of marriage, such as pre-nuptial agreements, which must be evidenced by a writing. The last category of contracts that must be evidenced by a writing is a contract under the Uniform Commercial Code (UCC) for the sale of goods for $500 or more. The UCC's Statute of Frauds will be covered later in the next chapter.

Now that one is cognizant of the classes of contracts that must be evidenced by a writing, the next issue to examine is the type of writing required. The Statute of Frauds, it is important to note, does not require a formal written contract prepared by an attorney, though such a practice is surely advisable in the business realm. Rather, all that is required is some type of note, memo, letter, paper, sales slip, invoice, or even check, which in written form, contains the essential terms of the agreement, and which also is signed by at least one key party, the "party to be charged," that is, the party against whom the claim for breach of agreement is made. It is significant legally to relate that the memo need not be in existence at the time the agreement was made; rather, it need only be in existence when the lawsuit is brought. In addition, there is no requirement that the person who ultimately signs the memo do so with the intention of binding himself or herself. Lastly, it is important to mention that a statute governing Internet transactions, the *Uniform Electronic Transactions Act* (UETA), holds that an electronic signature is equal to a written signature on a paper contract, and that an electronic record satisfies the writing requirement for a contract pursuant to the Statute of Frauds. UETA will be covered in detail in the Internet Regulation chapter.

The final area to cover in the general area of the "writing" requirement is a rule, called the *Parol Evidence rule*, which is an evidentiary principle as well as a contract law precept. The Parol Evidence rule maintains that when the agreement between the parties is reduced to a writing which is intended as the complete and final expression of the parties' agreement, then no modification or contradiction of that agreement will be allowed by oral testimony or by other writings made prior to or at the same time as the parties' "final" agreement. This rule does not apply to subsequent transactions; and the parties can later modify, or for that matter, completely rescind their prior agreement. In addition, the parties are allowed to use other oral or written evidence to help explain or interpret their agreement as well as to show that the assent to the agreement is not genuine. It must be emphasized that the Parol Evidence rule only applies when the parties intend their written agreement to be final and complete; and that is one reason why in business contracts one characteristically sees an "integration" clause which explicitly states that all prior written and oral agreements have been incorporated into the "final and complete" contract.

Genuineness of the Agreement

Although a contract may appear to be genuine and valid in all respects, it nevertheless may be unenforceable because the consent of one of both parties thereto was lacking. There are four major doctrines in Anglo-American law which render the consent to the agreement invalid: mistake, fraud, duress, and undue influence. A contract obtained under these circumstances is voidable and can be set aside at the option of the innocent and aggrieved party.

It is critical when examining the mistake doctrine to first differentiate two types of mistake – unilateral mistakes and mutual (or bilateral) mistakes. A *unilateral mistake* is made by one party to the contract without the knowledge of the other party. The unilateral mistake rule maintains that such a mistake has no effect on the validity of a contract. There is as a general rule no relief for the mistaken party and he or she must perform the contract or be sued for breach. Unilateral mistakes ordinarily arise in four ways: 1) errors in computation, such as in a bid, where one's party offer is mistakenly low; 2) mistakes in word processing or transcription; 3) errors in transmission by an intermediary, such as an interpreter, translator, or telegraph service; and 4) mistakes in judgment as to the value, quality, or worth of the subject matter of the contract. In all the aforementioned cases, the contract is binding regardless of the mistake by one of the contract parties. The reason for this common law is that the parties to a contract deal at "arm's length," and unless there is affirmative fraud or a duty to disclose, a unilateral error is not defense to performance. So, one should be very careful in putting together construction bids, for example, and similarly when selling "junk" or a "cheap" stone that turns out to be a priceless antique or precious jewel. Yet there is an exception to the general common law rule of no relief for unilateral mistake. This exception is called the "palpable mistake" rule; and it holds that if the mistake is so obvious and patent that the non-mistaken party is, or should have been, aware of the mistake, then the contract is voidable by the mistaken party. The reasoning for the exception is that it would be very unfair for the non-mistaken party to in effect "snap up" the contract with the obvious mistake therein.

The *mutual mistake* rules are different. The general rule is that if a mistake is made by both parties to the contract, then the contract is voidable by the party adversely affected, though either party can technically rescind the agreement. For example, mutual mistakes as to the existence, nature, character, or identity of the subject matter of the contract, the quantity thereof, or the means of performance, will provide relief to performance of the contract. The rationale for the rule is that the parties' minds never truly meet and thus any "agreement" is not genuine. There is, however, an interesting exception to the general mutual mistake rule; and this exception holds that when both parties know the identity and nature of the subject matter, but are mistaken as to the future value of the subject matter, then there is no relief for the party adversely affected, and the contract must be performed.

Duress is the forcing of a person to enter into a contract by means of threats to the person, his or her family, or property. Such compulsion in essence "robs" a person of free will, thereby invalidating consent, rendering the contract voidable at the option of the aggrieved party. One distinction that the law draws is important for the duress doctrine, and that is the difference between threatening someone with a criminal action or regulatory proceeding and merely threatening a civil suit. The former threat is regarded as duress and will invalidate the consent to any contract secured by such a threat; whereas the latter threat, presuming it is made in good faith, is not duress, even if one is mistaken as to his or her right to sue. Finally, one should be aware of the concepts of *economic duress or business compulsion*, whereby one party in an inferior bargaining position is the victim of a wrongful threat by a party in a superior bargaining position to cause financial ruin or to put someone out of business, and as a result the victim "agrees" to enter into a contract with very unfavorable terms. Such economic duress will render the contract voidable and thus will serve as a contract defense; and, moreover, in some jurisdictions, economic duress will give rise to a separate tort cause of action for money damages and other tort relief.

The last area to address concerning the genuineness of the agreement is the significant doctrine of *fraud*. Yet "fraud" is a very general legal formulation which covers a wide variety of legal wrongs based on misrepresenting facts. The first important point is to recognize that if fraud is committed in the contract inducement or performance, that legal wrong can be used in four main ways: 1) the victim of the fraud can interpose the fraud as an affirmative defense in a breach of contract lawsuit for non-performance; 2) the victim of fraud, instead of waiting to be sued for breach of contract, can proceed to a court and ask the court to rescind the contract on grounds of fraud; 3) if the contract is executed, the victim can sue at law to recover money or goods turned over to the wrongdoer as well as to sue for contract damages; and 4) the fraud may rise to the level of the legally actionable tort of fraud and the victim thereof can sue the perpetrator of the fraud for the intentional tort of fraud. The second important point is to recognize that there are three types of misrepresentation wrongs: 1) fraud in the old common law sense of deceit; 2) negligent misrepresentation; and 3) innocent misrepresentation. Fraud in the sense of *deceit*, to be accurate, is called *intentional fraudulent misrepresentation*, and, as will be seen, requires evidence of an intent to deceive. The remedies for deceit encompass the full range of contract remedies and defenses, equitable rescission, and tort relief and tort damages, including punitive damages. Fraud in the sense of *negligent misrepresentation* is premised on a misrepresentation made not intentionally but by carelessness. The party making the misrepresentation does so not purposefully, but because of a failure to exercise reasonable care before making the misrepresentation, for example, by not uncovering crucial underlying facts. Negligent misrepresentation provides contract remedies and rescission and also tort damages, but not punitive damages. The last generic "fraud" category is called "*innocent misrepresentation*," and it is a most interesting legal notion indeed. In this situation, a party does make a misrepresentation, but the party honestly believes that the statement is true and there is no negligence in making the misstatement. In such a case, the aggrieved party can rescind the contract and receive restitution, but there is no damage recovery.

The fraud legal wrong of greatest consequence is fraud in the sense of an intentional misrepresentation, that is, deceit. This type of fraud is in essence lying; but legally recognized lying, as not every lie is illegal in the "eyes" of the law, just fraudulent lying! Fraud thus can be defined as knowingly and purposefully inducing a person to enter into a contract as a result of an intentionally or recklessly made false statement of material fact. Fraud makes the resulting contract voidable; and affords the victim restitutionary and damage remedies, and also serves as the basis for a weighty intentional tort lawsuit. However, there are many elements to the legal wrong of fraud-deceit-lying that must be satisfied before the aggrieved party can interpose or sue on the doctrine.

Fraud is premised on a false statement of material fact; that is, any words or conduct that likely would cause an innocent party to reach an erroneous conclusion. Actively concealing material facts and thereby preventing the other party from discovering the truth is treated as fraud, even though there are no express misrepresentations. It is, however, critical to note that the misrepresentation must concern "fact," that is, actual, historical events, circumstances, or occurrences, and not mere opinions or predictions, which are not legally actionable, unless perhaps made by an "expert." The person making the false statement must know that it was false at the time made, or made the statement in reckless disregard of its truth or falsity. Deceit is an intentional legal wrong and accordingly there must be evidence that the wrongdoer possessed an "evil mind," called the *scienter* requirement. That is, there must be evidence of a purposeful intent or design to deceive and to induce the innocent party to act. Even if these requirements are met, there still must be a showing that the aggrieved party reasonably relied on the misrepresentation. Consequently, if the party making the misrepresentation can show that the other party knew of the true facts before taking the action, for example entering into a contract, then there is no reasonable reliance present and thus no deceit. Similarly, if a buyer is given an opportunity to view and inspect goods, the buyer is presumed to know about any obvious or patent defects; and as a result the buyer cannot accept "blindly" whatever the seller misrepresents. Moreover, a non-lawyer misrepresenting the law is as a general rule not grounds for fraud. The perhaps a bit "twisted" logic for this rule is that since "ignorance of the law is no excuse," everyone is presumed to know the law, and thus reliance on a lie about the law is not reasonable. Finally, if the person bringing the fraud lawsuit seeks to recover monetary damages based on the fraud, he or she must show some type of financial harm or physical injury as a result of the misrepresentation.

One major problem with fraud is the general rule that silence is not fraud. The rationale for this old common law rule goes back even further to Roman times and the Roman saying Caveat Emptor, that is, "Let the buyer beware." Consequently, refraining from disclosing pertinent facts unknown to the other party is not fraud. Under the common law, there is no duty to volunteer information. Another reason given for this rule is that the essence of fraud is the affirmative misleading of one person by another. For example, there is no duty for a seller of a pre-owned car to tell a prospective buyer that the car was previously in an accident. There are, however, many exceptions to this rule. One common law one arises if one is deemed to be a *fiduciary*, that is, one is in a relationship of trust and confidence with another party, such as the attorney-client relationship, or between partners, or the principal-agent relationship. In such a case, there is a duty to speak and silence will equate to fraud. In addition, several states by statutes have modified the old common law and now hold, for example, that the seller of real property has an affirmative duty to disclose latent and hidden defects which a basic inspection would not disclose, such as subsoil conditions, or termite infestation. There are also federal statutes, for example pertaining to securities fraud, as will be seen in the Securities Regulation section, in which the old common law "silence" rule has been changed by legislative pronouncement and thus where silence can be fraud.

Third Party Rights and Obligations in Contracts

A contract creates both rights and obligations. As a general rule, a person not a party to the contract neither has any right to the benefits derived from the contract nor any obligation to discharge the duties therein. There are, however, three chief exceptions to this rule: 1) third party beneficiary contracts, where the parties to the contract intend that a third party will benefit from the contract; 2) assignments of contract rights, where one contract party transfers his or her contract rights to a third party; and 3) delegation of contract duties, where one contract party delegates his or her contract duties to a third party. These three exceptions will be briefly addressed and compared and contrasted.

The essential *third party beneficiary* rule is that the parties to a contract may contract to have a performance or benefit rendered to a third party. The third party's rights are created at the time the contract was made; and, moreover, this third party who is to be benefited by the contract can sue to enforce it; but only if the third party is a "donee" or "creditor" beneficiary, and not merely an *"incidental" beneficiary*. The former two categories of third parties are regarded as intended beneficiaries; whereas the latter is a beneficiary who is only incidentally or indirectly affected by the contract; and as a consequence, the incidental beneficiary cannot sue to enforce the agreement. An example would be a home supply "superstore" which would be only incidentally benefited by all the home improvement contracts between homeowners and contractors in the local community. Another example involved an actual case against Wal-Mart, which was sued by the employees of its overseas suppliers because of the poor labor conditions and overtime at the suppliers' factories. The workers sued as third party beneficiaries to Wal-Mart's contracts with the suppliers; but a federal judge dismissed the lawsuit. In a creditor beneficiary situation, the creditor is a creditor of one of the original contract parties, and that contract party's intent is to discharge a debt owed to the creditor. Typically the original contract party performs some service for the other contract party who in turn pays off the debt to the performing party's creditor. In a donee beneficiary situation, the original contract party does not owe any duty or obligation, but wants to make a gift to the third party. The classic donee example is a life insurance contract, wherein the insured designates a beneficiary, who is regarded by the law as a donee beneficiary, who accordingly can enforce the contract against the life insurance company.

An *assignment* arises in the law when one of the original contract parties later transfers his or her contract rights to a third party who was not a party to the original contract. An assignment extinguishes the contract rights (but not duties) in the transferring party, and sets those rights up in the third party. No special formalities are necessary for an assignment; any words that show an intent to transfer will suffice. The assignment can be oral unless the original contract or the subject matter of the assignment is governed by the Statute of Frauds or the original contract requires any assignment to be written. Consideration is not required either; and thus even a "gratuitous" transferee of contact rights can enforce those rights. However, if there is no consideration, the assignment can be rescinded by the original contract party at any time before the contract has been performed.

Three key "players" emerge in this assignment "drama": 1) the *assignor*, who is the original contract party who is transferring his or her rights; 2) the *assignee*, the new third party to whom the rights are transferred: and 3) the *obligor*, the other original contract party who now owes performance to the assignee. As a general rule, all contract rights are assignable, as the law favors the free transfer of contract rights as being "good" for business transactions. Nonetheless, there are four situations where an assignment would be deemed impermissible: 1) when the assigned right is the right to receive unique personal services, such as an executive administrative assistant; 2) where the assignment would materially affect the duties of the obligor, for example, when the obligor's duty to deliver goods would be significantly expanded; 3) when there is a prohibition against assignment in the original contract, which the courts will enforce unless the assigned right is the right to receive money, which can be freely assigned despite a purported restriction in the original contract; or 4) where a federal or state statute prohibits the assignment, such as a wage assignment. As noted, the effect of the assignment is to set up the assignee as the "real party in interest," which means that the assignee can sue directly on the contract, and in his or her own name, and as a result without the assignor being joined as a party. The rights transferred to the assignee by the assignment are not lost or modified by the assignment. However, and this next rule is critical, the non-assigning party, that is, the obligor, retains all defenses as though there was no assignment; and consequently the obligor can interpose any defense, such as fraud or failure of consideration, that the obligor had against the assignor against the assignee. This contract law assignment defense situation is very different from the transfer of rights under commercial paper law, where the party obligated to pay on the paper, such as a negotiable promissory note, may not be able to interpose certain contract defenses if the paper is negotiated to a Holder in Due Course, who is an elevated and special person in the "eyes" of the law. One last problem area regarding assignments is whether notice of the assignment is required. The technical legal rule is that no such notice to the other original contract party, that is, the obligor, is required. However, as a matter of the utmost practicality, the assignee should promptly notify the obligor of the assignment, because absent notice, the obligor has the right to assume that the contracts rights have not been assigned; and consequently if the obligor performs those rights for the assignor and not the assignee, the obligor is not liable to the assignee.

The final third party area to examine is the *delegation of duties* doctrine, which is comparable to assignment law, except that in a delegation situation, one of the original contract parties, called the *delegator*, is transferring his or her contract duties and obligations to a new third party, called the *delegatee*, who is now responsible for performing those duties for the other original contract party, called the obligee. As a general rule, all contract duties are delgable, unless performance by the delegatee would vary materially from that of the delegator, or where the duties involved are personal ones, such as legal representation; but if the duties are merely standard, routine, and non-personal ones, such as in the typical general contractor-sub-contractor scenario, the transfer of the duties will be upheld, even over the objections of the obligee. Consideration is not required for a delegation; yet in the "real world" one party would not agree to assume contract duties without being paid therefore. There is another important difference between assignment and delegation. A delegation does not excuse the duty of the original contract party, the delegator, to perform; rather with a delegation the primary duty to perform is placed on the delegatee, but the delegator is still secondarily liable for performance of the contract duties. Whereas in an assignment, as one recalls, the assignment extinguishes all rights in the assignor and sets up the rights entirely in the assignee. Finally, a delegation must be distinguished from a novation, which will be covered in the next section of this chapter, where the original contract party transfers duties to a new party and then that original contract party is completely released from the contract by the other original contract party, who also agrees to accept the new third party as a substitute contract party.

Performance and Discharge of Contracts

The fundamental contract law concept of "*discharge*" basically means that contract obligations have come to an end; and as such the duties of the parties have been terminated. Discharge can occur in an assortment of ways. The most prevalent method of contract discharge is for the contract to be performed by the parties. That is, each party completely fulfills his or her promises and all terms of the contract are carried out; and therefore the contract is discharged by performance. There naturally are no legal problems in such a situation, which is how the vast majority of contracts come to an end. The other side of the spectrum will be a discharge resulting from one party's breach of the contract. That is, one party refuses or fails to perform contract duties to a minimum required by the law. In such a case, there is a breach of contract, triggering a potential lawsuit, of course, but also discharging the other party's duties and thereby terminating the contract. A contract also can be anticipatorily breached; that is, one party, prior to the time set for performance, clearly and unambiguously announces his or her intention not to perform; and in such an anticipatory breach situation, the innocent party can sue immediately for breach of contract.

There are, however, three major potential troublesome areas with a party's performance: 1) the time of performance; 2) satisfactory performance; and 3) substantial performance. First, regarding *time of performance*, the general common law rule maintains that if a contract does not provide the time by which performance is to be completed, each party has a reasonable time to perform. Moreover, even if the contract does state when performance is to be rendered, performance ordinarily must occur on that date or a reasonable time thereafter. So, what if a party wants to ensure performance on a certain date? Under the common law, a party can make performance on an exact date mandatory by inserting in the contract an express "*time is of the essence*" clause, requiring performance on a set date; and with such a clause, performance must occur on that exact date, or otherwise there is a breach of contract. There is, moreover, a related "essence" rule which maintains that "time is of the essence" may be implied from the subject matter of the contract, for example, the purchase of fireworks for a Chinese New Year's celebration. Second, the question of a *satisfactory performance* may arise in a contract where there is a clause stating that a party's performance must be "satisfactory" to the other party. Such a clause will be upheld; however, the performance must be such to satisfy a "reasonable" person, and not the subjective desires of the other contract party. Yet if the satisfaction clause in the contract involves the personal taste of one party, such as in a contract to paint one's picture, then a party can reject on grounds of personal dissatisfaction, even if not reasonable, so long as that party is acting honestly and in good faith. The final performance problem area concerns the *substantial performance* doctrine. The problem arises, especially in construction contracts, where the promisor's performance is to some degree defective or deviates from the terms of the contract. What are the rights of the substantially performing party? The modern common law rule is that the substantially performing party may demand his or her rights under the contract and can recover the contract price but minus the amount necessary to correct the defect or deviation in performance. Significantly, the substantially but not fully performing party has not breached the contract. However, there are two requirements for a party to take advantage of the substantial performance doctrine. First, there must be, in fact, substantial performance; that is, the performance must be near complete and the missing or defective part must be minor and not material; and second, the defects and deviations could not have been intentionally or willfully caused or the result of bad faith, though carelessness is permissible. If either of these two requirements is missing, then the performing party cannot rely on the substantial performance doctrine, and, moreover, will be in breach of contract.

    Contracts can be discharged by the occurrence or failure of a "condition" in a contract. A condition typically is an express "conditional" clause in a contract that states that some event must occur before one party has a duty to perform or refrain from performing. There are two main types of condition clauses – condition precedent and condition subsequent. In a *condition precedent* situation the duty of performance of a promise in a contract will not become operative until a specified act or event takes place. The contract formed is a valid one, but if the event does not occur, the condition is said to have "failed," and the contract is discharged, and consequently the obligations of the parties come to an end. Examples would be a contract with a promise to purchase real property, "subject to," "on condition," or "provided" that financing can be obtained and/or zoning approval can be secured. The result with a condition subsequent can be the same, that is, the discharge of the contract. In a *condition "subsequent"* situation, there is a contract, and usually some performance, but there is a clause in the contract that states that if a specified future event occurs, the contract is cancelled, inoperative, or void. Any remaining contract duties are thereby discharged by the occurrence of the specified condition, and the contract comes to an end. An example would be a long-term lease to rent property for a "fast food" restaurant located near a school with a provision in the contract that if the school is permanently closed, the contract becomes void. An example of a condition precedent would be a clause stating that the approval of loan application by bank is the procurement of insurance by the borrower. There is, however, a restriction on conditions, that is, the condition of a party's obligation cannot be made conditional on some occurrence or event exclusively within the control of that party (otherwise, that party's obligation would not be a real one, and the conditional promise would be fake or illusory one).

The next area of discharge of contracts deals with the doctrine of discharge caused by *impossibility of performance*. The general rule is that a party's duty to perform is discharged where, after the contract is made, the promised performance has become, without that party's fault, impossible to perform. "Impossibility" can be present when either the subject matter of the contract, the source of supply, or the means of performance is destroyed, though in the latter two cases, there should be an express designation of the intended supply source or performance means. A contract also will be discharged by impossibility when after the contract is made, new laws make the contract illegal. Finally, in a personal services or employment contract, the death or physical incapacity of the performing party discharges the contract.

The impossibility of performance doctrine must be compared and contrasted with two related doctrines – the common law's *frustration of purpose* doctrine and the Uniform Commercial Code's "commercial impracticality" rule. The former doctrine, which one must note is a minority view in the United States, holds that if the purpose or value of the contract has been destroyed, then the contract is discharged, even though technical performance is still possible. The courts will insist that the purpose of the contract be known and recognized by both contract parties, and that the party must not have assumed the risk of the contract becoming worthless. An example would be a contract by an auto dealer with a contractor to build a showroom for the new Chinese car imports, but the U.S. government in effect bans the importation of such cars by putting extremely high tariffs thereon. Pursuant to the Uniform Commercial Code (UCC), a seller's duty to deliver goods pursuant to a UCC sales contract will be discharged when performance becomes commercially impractical, even though performance is still technically possible, if the seller promptly notifies the buyer of the problem. "Classic" illustrations of "impracticality" would be severe shortages of supplies or raw materials or a drastic increase in prices caused by unforeseen circumstances, such as a war or embargo or local crop failure. A "mere" increase in cost to the seller or change in market price will ordinarily be inadequate for a seller to take advantage of this UCC precept.

Discharge, finally, can be caused by the agreement of the parties. The parties may mutually agree to rescind, that is, cancel, their contract, thereby terminating it and discharging both parties' obligations. Contracts also can be discharged by an accord and satisfaction as well as a novation, which are similar though not identical legal doctrines. In an *accord and satisfaction*, the contract parties agree that one contract party will accept and the other will render a performance different from the original contract. This agreement is called the "accord"; and when this accord is performed the original contract is discharged along with the accord agreement. In a novation, the contract party who is entitled to receive performance under the contract agrees to release the party bound to perform, and also to substitute another party to perform in the original contract party's place. A *novation* is more than a delegation of duties situation because the released party is completely discharged, and the new party alone is responsible for performance.

Each individual country as well as each state within the United States has its own body of contract law that will be used to determine if a contract is valid, if it has been breached, and what the remedies for breach of contract are. These laws may be dissimilar; yet the choice of one country's or one state's laws may be dispositive of the contractual dispute. Therefore, a contract should also include a *choice-of-law* provision that states which country's law or state's law will govern the contract. Closely related to the choice-of-law provision is the "*forum selection*" provision. By means of a forum selection the parties promise to litigate any disputes in a specifically designated jurisdiction pursuant to that jurisdiction's law. Otherwise, if there are no such provisions and the laws are dissimilar, a "*conflicts of law*" situation will emerge, and a legal determination will first have to be made to determine which jurisdiction's body of law applies to the contract, even before any substantive contractual issues can be raised. Typically, the country or state with the most significant relationship to the contract will have its body of law applied to the controversy. Although the two types of contract provisions are closely related, the "choice-of-law" provision may be more specific and will be most useful if there is uncertainty about the exact nature of the law in a specific jurisdiction. For example, an employment contract may state in a forum selection clause that the law of the employer's state will apply, which state law recognizes the validity of covenants not to compete; yet if the covenant is arguably breached in a state, such as California, that does not recognize the validity of non-competition agreements, then an argument can be made that the contract dispute is a performance one, and thus the state where the breach occurred, that is, California, has the most significant relationship with the contract. In the latter case, the employee would prevail. So, to be safe, the employer should stipulate a "choice of law" clause in the contract specifying that its state's law, which recognizes covenants not to compete, will apply to any contract dispute.

When contract negotiations have been lengthy and complicated, the parties can avoid disputes about what they finally agreed to in the contract by including a clause, called an *integration or merger clause,* which states that the contractual agreement embodies the entire agreement of the parties and prevails over all prior as well as contemporaneous agreements, promises, and/or representations of the parties. Furthermore, the contract parties can reduce disputes by including a *non-reliance clause* in the contract, which states that the parties attest that they have not relied on any representations or promises that may have been made during the course of contract negotiations and drafting that are not explicitly set forth in the written contract. Such a clause should help to ward off claims by one party that he or she was fraudulently or negligently induced to enter into the contract.

Recent Fraud Cases
In recent years two major fraud scandals have emerged to tarnish the reputations of two gigantic corporations and engulf them in a "story sea" of civil and criminal lawsuits. The two scandals are the Wells Fargo Bank fake accounts scandal and the Volkswagen Deceptive Emissions scandal. In 2016 the gigantic bank, Wells Fargo, which is headquartered in San Francisco, and which has over 100,000 employees in 6000 branches, was engulfed in a massive legal and ethical scandal. The bank was accused of extensive fraudulent sales practices. The bank's employees, in order to meet very aggressive sales targets, opened up bank and credit card accounts, transferred money between those accounts, and created fake email addresses for online banking accounts in order to fraudulently sign up customers for the bank's accounts. All this activity was done without the customers' knowledge and consent

and thus was unauthorized and illegal. Moreover, debit cards were issued and activated, and PIN numbers created, again without the customers' authorization. Millions of fake accounts were opened for customers over a five-year period. Multiple accounts are profitable in of themselves, of course, for the fees they generate, but banks also have discovered that the more accounts a customer has the less likely the customer is to move to another bank. The U.S. Consumer Financial Protection Bureau deemed the bank's sales tactics to be widespread and illegal practice. Consequently, the federal government and the state of California settled with Wells Fargo with the bank paying a $185 million fine over the bank's sales practices. The bank also refunded $2.6 million to its customers. Also, in 2018 the bank agreed to pay $480 million to settle shareholder suits. Moreover, in 2018 the bank was fined $1 billion by the Consumer Financial Protection Bureau and the Office of the Comptroller of Currency, which is the largest fine ever levied on a banking institution. In addition, a class action suit was filed in U.S. District Court in Utah by bank customers, alleging fraud, negligence, invasion of privacy, and breach of contract. The plaintiffs are asking for damages for the aforementioned legal wrongs, including identity theft, as well as for anxiety and emotional distress, and legal fees. The scandal plainly has had a harmful effect on the bank's customer base. With consumer checking account openings down and applications for credit cards down too. The scandal, moreover, has caused the bank's stock to fall. Moreover, the bank has lost its position of being the largest U.S. bank by market value (as now J.P. Morgan Chase & Co. has assumed that number one position). In October of 2016, the CEO of Wells Fargo since 2007, John Stumpf, "retired" as a result of the scandal over the bank's fraudulent sales practices. He had been known as a proponent of a business strategy called "cross-selling," where account holders were pressured to open new accounts with the bank, which was, in the short term at least, a very successful strategy as the bank's stock rose 30% during his tenure. Stumpf, who had been with the bank for 34 years, gave up his role as chairman of the board. Stumpf, where he had earned $19.3 million in 2015; he also forfeited $41 million in stock awards. However, his retirement compensation package totaled $134 million (including salary, stock options, and other forms of compensation). No criminal charges have yet to be filed in the scandal. However, in 2018, the bank was still undergoing legal problems as the Federal Reserve ordered the bank to remove four directors from its board and the Federal Reserve also said it was freezing the bank's growth from 2017 until it could demonstrate that it improved internal controls and business practices and to stop and to prevent what the Federal Reserve stated were "widespread consumer abuses." The result of the scandal, in addition to the adverse legal and financial consequences, is that the reputation of the bank as an ethical institution has been severely harmed. A short-term, misguided, and immoral policy of setting unrealistic sales goals that the employees could not meet unduly pressured the employees to overly influence the customers to open accounts and obtain services they did not want or need; but then, even worse, the bank's employees simply opened the unauthorized and fraudulent accounts, thereby acting in an illegal as well as unethical manner. Wells Fargo's chief operating officer, Tim Sloan, 50 years old, who had been with the bank for 29 years, succeeded Stumpf as CEO; and he also joined the board as a member. He intends to improve the bank's reputation by focusing on addressing customers' needs and concerns. Sloan, of course, will have to deal with all the ongoing government investigations and legal actions as well as consumer lawsuits deals. The bank has now terminated product-sales targets for employees. The bank is working on an entirely new incentive plan that will stress consumer service. The bank is also conducting internal investigations, hiring new compliance personnel, reaching out to harmed customers, and revamping the bank's compensation plan so as to remove incentives for illegal behavior. Wells Fargo also initiated an advertising campaign, called "Moving forward to make things right." The bank stated in its promotional materials that it will put its customers' interests and financial needs first by eliminating sales goals for retail banking, it will communicate with customers when new accounts are opened, it will enable customers to fully see all their accounts by means of online banking, and that the bank will provide full refunds to customers for any fees or costs associated with the opening of unauthorized accounts. The bank also established a hotline for customer concerns and complaints. The bank also now has a very impressive Social Responsibility and Sustainability website where it extolls its many charitable, civic- and community-minded, and environmentally responsible programs and activities. Yet can the bank get its reputation for morality and ethics back? One recalls the old maxim: "Once a reputation for integrity is lost it is very difficult to get it back."

Also, in 2016, the U.S. government on filed a criminal lawsuit against Volkswagen AG (VW) alleging violations of the Clean Air Act. Violating this statute can lead to civil as well as criminal penalties. The U.S. government also filed a civil lawsuit on behalf of the Environmental Protection Agency. The lawsuits emerged from the diesel emissions scandal, one of the biggest scandals in corporate auto history, or even generally for business. The government's lawsuit alleged that VW illegally installed software, called "defeat-devices," to make its diesel engines pass U.S. emissions standards, particularly strict ones in California set by the California Air Resources Board, during laboratory testing. The essence of the complaint was that the company obstructed efforts by the government to learn the truth about the excess emissions as well as making material omissions and providing misleading information. The effect of the deceptive software was to boost the vehicles' performance; but the fraudulent devices also resulted in the emission of green-house gasses up to 40 times more than current U.S. environmental standards. The cheating software had been installed in VW diesel vehicles – cars and SUVs – sold since the 2009 model year, thereby potentially affecting 11 million vehicles. The decision to defraud regulators was made about a decade ago when VW began a major effort to sell diesels in the United States. However, at the time, the company's technology was inadequate for the vehicles to comply with the increasingly more stringent emissions standards, particularly in the U.S., to prevent smog-forming pollutants. In 2017, VW pled guilty to violating the Clean Air Act and paid a fine to the U.S. government of almost $3 billion. However, individual VW executives "pleaded ignorance" of the fraud and have blamed only a small number of lower level software developers and engineers for the creation and use of the computer software used to trick emission tests and regulators. So far, the U.S. government and the German government have initiated criminal prosecutions of two VW engineers. In addition to the criminal prosecutions, VW has paid billions of dollars in civil fines. Moreover, VW is facing many lawsuits from consumers, dealers, and state regulators, as well as international investigations. Individual consumers, the owners of the diesel vehicles, have paid up to $6000 more for what they thought was a "green" diesel compared to a gasoline-fueled model. They can receive compensation from the company in the form of $1000 rebates, retrofits, as well as the option to trade in their vehicles. So far, the compensation to VW consumers is also in the billions of dollars. Moreover, in a major development in 2018 the U.S. government indicted former VW CEO Martin Winterkorn on criminal charge stemming from the emissions scandal. The main charges deal with conspiring with other company officials to violate the U.S. Clean Air Act. Yet, aside from all the legal complications and expense as well as possible imprisonment of company executives a key question for VW, similarly for Wells Fargo, will be how does the company get its reputation for integrity back? Can the company, in effect, "buy" it back?

Summary
This chapter provides an in-depth analysis of contract law and its associated elements, including legal definitions, classifications, remedies for breach of contract, the requirements of a valid contract, and rights and obligations of all parties. The popular use of contracts is mostly seen in the international business arena, specifically by "westernized" nations, such as the United States. However, as industrialized nations continue to work with developing countries in terms of exporting and importing, and manufacturing of goods, contracts are highly recommended. The vitality of contract law has become a significant factor for all global industries. Thus, managers, entrepreneurs, and employees are now encouraged and expected to understand the variations in laws that exist among different countries when entering into an agreement. As the world continues to turn global, managers, entrepreneurs, employees, as well as organizations and countries, are depending on contracts in order to ensure successful business negotiations and relationships.

Discussion Questions
1. What are the requirements that convert a mere promise into a legally binding one, that is, a contract? Provide a business example with a brief explanation thereof.
2. What are the distinctions among valid, void, and voidable contracts under the common law of contracts? Why are those differentiations very important to contract law analysis? Provide examples along with brief explanations thereof.
3. What are the types of damages that an aggrieved party may be able to obtain for a breach of contract? Provide business examples with a brief explanation thereof.
4. What is the "mitigation" rule? Explain and illustrate how it would operate in a breach of contract for the sale of goods and a breach of an employment contract.
5. What is the "offer" and how are offers terminated? Provide business examples along with brief explanations thereof.

6. What is an "acceptance" and how may it be legally effectuated? Provide business examples along with brief explanations thereof.

7. What is the old common law contract "mirror image" rule? Why is it still a very important legal doctrine today? Provide a business example with a brief explanation thereof.

8. What is the old common law concept of "consideration" and why is it still a very important contract law rule? Provide a business example with a brief explanation thereof.

9. What is the "legal detriment to the promisee" test in consideration law? Why is it so important? Provide an example with a brief explanation of such legal "detriment."

10. How do consideration rules operate in the area of repayment of debts? Provide examples along with brief explanations thereof.

11. What are some of the major exceptions to consideration? Provide examples with brief explanations thereof.

12. Why is the type of licensing statute involved in a transaction a critical factor in determining the legality of a contract by an unlicensed business or person? Provide examples with a brief explanation thereof.

13. What are some of the types of contracts that must be evidenced by a writing to be enforceable? Provide examples with a brief explanation thereof.

14. Why is it critical to distinguish between the two types of mistakes in contract law? Provide business examples of each with a brief explanation thereof.

15. Define, explain, and illustrate the major exception to the unilateral mistake doctrine.

16. What are the elements of a lawsuit for fraud (in the form of deceit or intentional misrepresentation)? Provide a business example with a brief explanation. Why is it so difficult to establish a legal cause of action for fraud/deceit?

17. What is the difference between assignment and delegation? Provide business examples of each with a brief explanation thereof. Why do these two legal doctrines typically go "hand-in-hand" in the "real world" of business?

18. What contract duties cannot be assigned? Conversely, what contract duties cannot be delegated? Provide examples with brief explanations for both categories.

19. What is the doctrine of "substantial performance"? Provide a business example with a brief explanation thereof. Why is this doctrine informally known as the contractor's "best friend"?

20. Compare and contrast "conditions subsequent" and "conditions precedent." Provide a business example of each with a brief explanation. How can they be used contractually by the shrewd business person to protect himself or herself from potentially harmful contingencies. Provide examples.

21. Compare and contrast the three main types of "impossibility" doctrines; and provide a business example of each with a brief explanation thereof.

5 – SALES LAW AND THE UNIFORM COMMERCIAL CODE

In addition to being aware of the common law of contracts, a business manager or entrepreneur doing business in the United States must be aware of a new and relatively recent body of law governing contracts – the *Uniform Commercial Code* (UCC) which governs contracts for the sale of goods and which makes some major changes in the old common law of contracts. The UCC is designed to change the common law to reflect modern commercial practices, particularly the mass distribution of goods to consumers. The UCC was first introduced in 1951 as a proposed uniform sales law by a group of legal and commercial experts; offered to the state legislatures; and now has been adopted by virtually every state in the United States. However, although the Code is supposed to be consistent and uniform among the states, which the UCC usually is, there may be differences, and material ones, that have been made to the Code upon its adoption by a particular state. Thus, the prudent business person is well-advised to carefully check his or her state's version of the UCC, which is found in the state's commercial statutes, and not definitely rely on the generic version of the UCC or for that matter this book or any book treating the UCC.

The Uniform Commercial Code has several major sections, called Articles, which seek to extensively regulate commercial transactions. For example, Article 3 deals with commercial paper transactions; and Article 4 deals with banking transactions. An examination of the entire UCC is beyond the scope of this book; rather, the authors will concentrate on Article 2, which deals with the sales of good, and especially those sections of Article 2 which make material changes in the common law of contracts. It also should be mentioned initially that the UCC's Article 2A applies to the commercial lease of goods, which in fact will be very important when examining UCC warranty law later in this chapter.

The UCC's Article 2 "just" applies to the sale of goods. Accordingly, the old common law still governs service contracts, including employment agreements, as well as real estate sales contracts. Accordingly, first and foremost, it is critical to define the UCC's indispensable term - "*good*." A "good" is moveable, tangible, personal property, that is, a thing. Land, structures and buildings attached to the land, as well as fixtures, that is, things which are so attached to the real estate that their removal would cause material harm to the real estate, are not goods, as they are not "personal" but "real" property. "Tangible" means a physical existence is required in order to be a "good"; thus patents, copyrights, trademarks, investment securities, and contract rights are not "goods."

As mentioned, the UCC applies to sales of goods, and not services. Yet a major problem arises when there is a mixed transaction, that is, the same transaction involves the sale of goods and also the provision of some services. By legislative or judicial decree, some of these "mixed" cases have been settled. For example, anything specially manufactured for a buyer is a good, as is computer software. Similarly, a meal in a restaurant is deemed to be the sale of a good, and not a service; but a blood transfusion usually is regarded as a service and not a sale of the blood. The test the courts will apply to determine the nature of the subject matter of the contract is called the *"predominant feature"* test, in which the major aspect of the contract will determine its nature as a sale of goods or service contract. For example, in a construction contract, the predominant feature is the building and not the purchase of the building supplies, and as such the common law will govern the contract. This distinction between sales and service is crucial to the law of contracts since the UCC makes some very significant changes to the old common law of contracts, and, in addition, the UCC's body of warranty law applies only to the sale of goods (and the commercial lease of goods). For example, the courts have ruled in the case of combined medical sales of goods and service contracts that the implantation of medical devices, as well as the transfusion of blood, are predominantly medical services and not sales of goods; consequently, a patient will not be able to sue a hospital for breach of the UCC's implied warranty of merchantability since the patient is predominantly purchasing implantation and transfusion services and not purchasing goods in the form of devices or blood. The patient, of course, can still sue for any negligence in the performance of the service, but the plaintiff patient will have to prove the elements of the tort of negligence.

It is also necessary to define another key term in the UCC – *"merchant."* However, it must be underscored right away that the UCC's Article 2 applies to the sale of goods by anyone; but there are some special provisions of the UCC, and with some unique harsh effects, that apply only to merchants. So, who is a "merchant"? A merchant is a person or business that regularly deals in goods of a particular kind, that is, as a retailer, wholesaler, distributor, or manufacturer. A merchant also can be a person who holds himself or herself out as having knowledge and/or skill peculiar to the goods and commercial practices involved in the transaction. There obviously can be an overlap between the first and second categories. Finally, one can be deemed a merchant by employing a merchant for a particular transaction, for example, as an agent or broker.

Lastly, it is of great consequence that the UCC states that implied in every UCC contract is a *covenant of good faith and fair dealing*, in which the parties are deemed to promise not to do anything to hinder, impair, frustrate, or destroy the reasonable expectations and legitimate rights of the other contract party to enjoy the "fruits" of the contract.

Formation of the Sales Contract

As previously mentioned as well as emphasized, certain UCC provisions make some very material changes in the old common law of contracts when the contract is for the sale of goods. Moreover, many of these UCC changes have "relaxed" the old common law rules pertaining to the formation of a binding contract; and thus the UCC reflects a rationale to make it easier to enter into commercial contracts, especially for merchants.

The first UCC alteration rule deals with the offer, specifically the irrevocability of the offer. The common law is that an offer to make a contract can be revoked by the offeror at any time before acceptance. Even a "firm offer," that is, one with a promise not to revoke it attached, is nevertheless still revocable by the offeror under the common law. Also, the offeree paying the offeror something of value to keep the offer open, that is, consideration, converts the offer into an irrevocable one, that is, an "option." The UCC has a unique option dealing with the revocability of offers, called a "merchant's firm offer." If a UCC offer is made by a merchant, is written and signed by the merchant, and explicitly states that it is a "firm offer" or at the least that it will be held open, then the merchant's firm offer will be irrevocable, even without consideration. The merchant's firm offer will be irrevocable for the time specified therein, and if no time is stated for a "reasonable" time, but in no event longer than three months.

The second area in the formation of the sales contract deals with the definiteness of the agreement. Generally speaking, as opposed to a common law contract, a sales contract will be enforceable even if one or more terms is left open, presuming a court feels that the parties intended to make a binding contract. Of course, the larger the number of undecided terms, the less likely a court will find that the parties intended to be legally bound.

The first contract term to examine is the price provision. Under the common law, the courts ordinarily would refuse to enforce a contract without a fixed price term, as the agreement would be branded as too indefinite. The UCC rule is totally the opposite. A fixed price is not essential to a valid UCC sales contract. The purchase price can of course be specified, but most significantly it can be completed omitted or left open. The UCC contract is thereby valid, but what is the price of the goods? The UCC holds that if the contract is silent as to the price, the courts should assume that the price is a "reasonable" price at the time and place of delivery of the goods. Also permissible in UCC contracts are "agreements to agree" by the parties to set the price of the goods in the future, agreements to refer the pricing of the goods to a third party, and even a contract provision in which one of the contract parties reserves to himself or herself the right to fix the price in the future, though the party with the reserved right must do so in good faith.

The quantity provision in a contract is one term that both the common law and the UCC concur. That is, both bodies of law require that there be a quantity term, and that the quantity of the subject matter is set forth explicitly, specifically, and definitely; otherwise the contract will be deemed invalid and void for indefiniteness. There is one exception in the UCC for requirements and output contracts, that is, contracts where a buyer promises to buy all of his/her requirements from a seller, and/or where a seller promises to sell all of its output to a buyer. These types of contracts, so critical to commerce, usually have been upheld as valid contracts, despite "charges" of an absence of definitiveness as well as a lack of consideration.

The UCC modifies the time provision for performance of a contract to a degree. If no time for performance is stated in the UCC contract, then the rule is the same as the common law; that is, one can perform the contact within a reasonable time period. However, if the UCC contract does specify a time for performance, then the UCC contract must be performed on that date; and no "time is of the essence" clause is required. This UCC alteration of the common law is based on the UCC's "perfect tender" rule, which will be discussed later in this chapter.

It is also quite permissible under the UCC, and perhaps the common law too, to have a valid contract with an open delivery provision. In the case of the UCC, if no place for delivery is specified in the contract, then the place of delivery is deemed to be the seller's place of business, or if none, then the seller's residence. However, if both parties know that the goods are at another location other than the seller's business or residence, then that place where the goods are located is the place of delivery.

Similar to the offer component to mutual agreement, the UCC makes some major changes regarding the offeree's acceptance. Two principal alterations will be addressed – acceptance by shipment and an acceptance with additional terms, popularly known as the "*battle of the forms*" since a great deal of modern business is conducted by standard forms prepared by commercial buyers and sellers of goods. Concerning the first topic, acceptance by shipment, the problem arises when a buyer offers to purchase goods from a seller for "prompt" or "immediate" shipment. The question is what exactly must the seller do to form a binding contract? Under the common law, this type of offer was regarded as an offer to form a unilateral contract, and as a result the actual and complete shipment by the seller was the only way to accept. However, pursuant to the UCC, a seller can accept by either promptly shipping the goods or also by promising to ship the goods, thereby blurring the distinction the common law drew between unilateral and bilateral contracts. Another related and perplexing issue emerges if the seller promptly and immediately ships non-conforming goods. Under the common law, such a shipment would most likely be construed as a counteroffer, but pursuant to the UCC, the shipment of conforming goods by the seller is both an acceptance of the contract as well as a breach of the contract. However, the UCC does allow the seller to ship the non-conforming goods to the buyer as merely an "*accommodation*," which the Code construes as a counteroffer, presuming the seller promptly notifies the buyer in writing that the seller is shipping as a courtesy and is not accepting the offer.

The second UCC acceptance alteration to relate is one of great consequence. The change deals with purported acceptances which contain additional terms than in the original offer. Recall the common law's "mirror image" rule, whereby the offeree's acceptance must be identical to the offeror's offer; and consequently any additions or variations in the "acceptance" will render it a counteroffer, and thereby a rejection of the original offer. The UCC makes a very dramatic change to the common law counteroffer rule. Yet first it is necessary to point out that even under the UCC if the offeree clearly states that there can be no contract formed unless the offeree's exact set of terms is accepted by the original offeror, then the offeree's response is treated as a counteroffer. In essence, the offeree is saying "take-it-or-leave-it" on the offeree's terms. However, when the offeree "merely" sets forth additional terms in the acceptance than contained in the offeror's offer, the UCC holds that a contract nonetheless exists. However, the next issue to resolve is what happens to the additional terms. The general rule is that the additional terms are only construed as proposals for additions to the contract which the parties can negotiate over. Yet if the dealings are between two merchants, then the additional terms automatically become part of the contract unless either: 1) the offeror's original offer expressly limited acceptance to the offered terms (that is, the offeror has in essence said "take-it-or-leave-it"); 2) the additional terms are regarded as "material" alterations to the contract, such as an arbitration clause or a disclaimer of warranties; or 3) the original offeror within a reasonable time notifies the offeree who is proposing the additional terms that the offeror objects to them.

The UCC also makes a very big change in the old common law consideration requirement when a UCC contract is modified. Under the common law, as one recalls, modification of a contract requires new or different consideration; but pursuant to the UCC, modification of a sales contract is valid even without new or different consideration, presuming, of course, that the parties have mutually agreed to the rescission. So, an agreement between the parties to extend the time of delivery of the goods, or for the buyer to pay more money for the same goods, is enforceable. Also, even though consideration is not required, a writing may be necessary if the original contract is within the UCC's Statute of Frauds, the modification brings the contract within the scope of the Statute of Frauds, or the original contract requires any modification to be in writing.

The UCC's Statute of Frauds becomes operative when the price for the goods is $500 or more; and thus in such a contract a sufficient writing will be necessary to have a valid contract. Yet the lack of a writing does not make a UCC contract void, but merely unenforceable, which means the lack of a writing must be plead as an affirmative defense and also means that one may waive the writing requirement by making an admission in one's pleading or testimony as to the existence of the sales contract. There are four chief exceptions to the UCC's Statute of Frauds writing requirement. The first is called a "written confirmation" by a merchant doctrine. When both parties to the transaction are merchants, and one merchant receives in writing a confirmation of an oral sales agreement, and the writing is adequate to bind the sender merchant, then the writing will also bind the recipient merchant unless he or she objects in writing within 10 days. This rule is a very novel UCC proposition since the recipient merchant is bound even though he or she did not sign anything. The second exception deals with partial acceptance of goods, and holds that a UCC oral agreement is enforceable by the receipt and acceptance of goods, but only to the extent of the goods received and accepted. Similarly, the third exception deals with the partial payment of goods, and maintains that an oral agreement is enforceable with respect to goods for which payment has been received and accepted. The final exception governs the situation where goods are specially manufactured by the seller for the buyer. Specially manufactured goods are defined as goods not suitable for resale to others in the ordinary course of the seller's business. In such a circumstance, an oral agreement is enforceable against the buyer if the seller has made a substantial beginning on the manufacturer of the goods or has made commitments for the procurement of raw materials.

The last UCC doctrine that brings about a material change in the old common law of contracts is the UCC's *"unconscionability" doctrine*. One recalls the common law precept that a court will not be concerned with the adequacy of consideration, that is, the relative worth of the promises and/or acts in the contract, only the presence of consideration. Yet the UCC brings into the law of sales the equitable concept of fairness in the guise of "unconscionability." Accordingly, a court will not enforce a UCC contract if it is unconscionable. The UCC, however, deliberately refrains from defining what constitutes an "unconscionable" contract. The courts, nevertheless, have attempted to define this central term, for example, by saying it means a contract that is so unfair it "shocks the conscience" of the courts, or a contract that has terms extremely and unreasonably favorable to one party and unfavorable to the other party. While the meanings are not clear, one fact is, and that is the courts will not be receptive to "unconscionability" allegations by one merchant against another or claims of unfairness by a sophisticated business person against the other contract party.

Title and Risk of Loss

The ultimate goal of a sale of goods contract is to transfer the ownership of the goods and all rights and responsibilities thereto from the seller to the buyer. One major problem arises if there is a passage of time after the formation of the sales contract and the eventual transfer of ownership to the buyer. Events can occur during this lapse of time, for example, the goods can be damaged, destroyed, lost, or stolen. Thus, the key legal issue arises as to which contract party bears the responsibilities for the goods. Prior to the UCC, this question was resolved by ascertaining who had title to the goods. Although title is still important for taxation issues, the UCC has abandoned the concept of title as the determining factor of who is responsible for the goods. Rather, the UCC has established specific rules, called risk of loss rules, to determine responsibilities for the goods.

The UCC's *risk of loss* rules determine which party, the buyer or the seller, bears the loss when, without the fault of either party, some harm comes to the goods prior to or during their delivery to the buyer. The UCC rules specify exactly when the risk of loss passes from the seller to the buyer. There are several UCC risk of loss rules but there are three important general ones. First, if there is a risk of loss provision in the sales contract which specifies at what point the risk of loss shifts from the seller to the buyer, the provision controls the risk question. Second, presuming no such contract provision, if the goods are shipped by a carrier from the seller to a buyer, it is essential to determine the type of carrier contract. If the carrier contract is a shipment contract, which requires the seller to place the goods in the hands of the carrier and not to deliver them to a particular destination, the risk of loss passes to the buyer upon delivery of the goods by the seller to the carrier; but if the carrier contract is a destination contract, which requires the seller to deliver the goods to a particular destination, the risk passes to the buyer only when the goods arrive at the destination and the buyer is so notified. It also should be noted that in the sale and delivery of goods, there are a variety of specialized destination and shipment contracts, each with its own unique risk of loss provisions. It is beyond the scope of this book to examine all the specialized provisions in railroad, trucking, airplane, and ship carrier contracts. Third, in most other risk of loss situations, the key factor is whether or not the seller is a merchant. If the seller is a merchant, the risk passes to the buyer only when the buyer actually receives the goods; but if the seller is not a merchant, the risk passes to the buyer when the seller has placed the goods at the buyer's disposal and so notified the buyer.

Warranties

In making a sale of goods, the seller often warrants or guarantees the title to the goods or that the goods conform to a certain standard or operate in a certain way. By making such a guarantee, the seller thereby agrees to redress any loss or damages that the buyer may suffer if the title to the goods or the goods themselves are not as represented. Warranties can concern the title to goods or the quality of the goods. Warranties can be express, that is, created by the words or actions of the seller, or implied, that is, imposed automatically by the law.

Regarding the title to goods, two important warranties must be mentioned. Both are implied warranties. One is the *implied warranty of good title*, where the seller is deemed to guarantee the good title to the goods and that the transfer is rightful. Note that the seller does not have to be a merchant to have this warranty imposed; and also that ignorance of a defect in the title is no excuse. The second implied title warranty is a warranty that the goods are free from any liens or encumbrances of which the buyer at the time of sale had no knowledge thereof.

Regarding the quality of the goods, it is necessary to differentiate express warranties of quality from implied warranties of quality. Express warranties of quality come from the express words or actions of the seller. The seller need not use the exact words "warranty" or "guaranty"; and the buyer need not demonstrate that the seller intended to make such a warranty. There are three types of express warranties: 1) affirmation of fact or promise, 2) conformity to description, and 3) conformity to model or sample. First, an *express warranty by affirmation of fact or promise* occurs when the seller makes a statement of fact or promise to the buyer in the course of negotiations, which relates to the goods, and which is part of the *"basis of the bargain."* The factual statement or promise creates an express warranty that the goods conform to the statement or promise made about them. No technical words are necessary to create an express warranty, which may be oral or written. "Basis of the bargain" means that the buyer has in part relied on the warranty in making his or her decision to buy the goods. Comparable to fraud law, warranty law holds that mere opinions or predictions cannot form the basis of an express warranty unless perhaps made by an expert. There is a major distinction between saying that the car is a "great car" and a "good buy" and that the car has a "200 horsepower engine" and "only 75,000 miles," as the latter are factual statements and the former are merely opinionated utterances. An example of "puffing" would be "this car is a top-notch car," whereas the statement "this car gets 28 miles per gallon" would be a factual statement and the basis of an express warranty. The second type of express warranty, conformity to description, is similar to and overlaps the first one. Accordingly, any description of the goods by the seller that is part of the basis of the bargain creates an express warranty that the goods conform to the description. A description can encompass any descriptive name or words, such as "seedless grapes," "pitted prunes," or "boneless chicken," or a trade term, such as "Post-It" notes or "Granny Smith" apples. Finally, the third type of express warranty arises when a model or sample is used to sell the goods, and in such a case the goods must conform to the model of sample. A sample is a part of the actual goods taken from the whole whereas a model is a scale representation of the goods but is not taken therefrom. One last express warranty issue to address is to determine who on the marketing chain is legally responsible for an express warranty. A manufacturer or wholesaler is only liable for the warranties made by the retailer at the time of sale if the retailer had the legal authority to make such warranties. However, a retailer will be held to adopt any express warranties made by the manufacturer or wholesaler, and will be equally liable thereon.

In addition to the express warranties which are explicitly made by the seller of goods, the UCC implies certain other warranties simply because a sale of goods is made in a certain manner. These implied warranties are imposed regardless of the seller's intentions and despite the fact that the seller has made no statements or promises regarding the goods. Unless these warranties are expressly disclaimed by the seller, which will be seen shortly, the implied warranties arise by operation of law in every sale of goods, used as well as new, although some states by statute have curtailed implied warranty liability for certain very old used goods.

There are three very important implied warranties created by the UCC – merchantability, fitness for a particular purpose, and wholesomeness. The first to examine is the implied warranty of merchantability. The rule of law is that in every merchant's contract of sale, the UCC will imply a warranty that the goods are of "*merchantable*" quality. It is critical to point out that only a seller who is a merchant (with respect to the type of goods sold by the merchant) is deemed to make this warranty. Neither a sale by a private individual nor an occasional sale by a merchant who regularly deals in other goods will trigger the warranty. What does the key term "merchantability" mean? The standard for merchantability includes several criteria: 1) the goods must be fit for the ordinary purposes for which the goods are used; 2) the goods must meet normal commercial standards for goods of that type; 3) the goods must do their ordinary job safely; 4) the goods must be around the middle range of quality (and not the highest); and 5) the goods must be adequately packaged and labeled. For example, a shoe should have its heel well enough attached so that it does not break off during normal walking, as opposed to mountain climbing. Similarly, a refrigerator that keeps food cold but then shorts out and causes a fire is not doing its ordinary job safely. The second implied warranty is called the *fitness for a particular purpose warranty*. If a seller is aware of a particular use of goods by a buyer and the buyer has relied on the seller's judgment to select suitable goods, an implied warranty of fitness for that particular use is thereby created by the law. It is essential that the seller have knowledge of the buyer's intended use. That is, the seller should know what the buyer's special requirements are and that the buyer is relying on the seller to fulfill those special requirements. For example, when a buyer goes to a sporting goods and camping store and asks the seller for hiking shoes capable of hiking on a mountain trail, a "fitness" warranty likely will be imposed. It must be underscored that this implied warranty applies to both merchants and non-merchants, so long as the knowledge and reliance factors are present, whereas the merchantability warranty just applies to merchants. The third and final type of implied warranty is *wholesomeness*. When the goods sold are food or beverages, a warranty automatically arises that the goods be fit for human consumption. A retailer grocer, it is important to note, is deemed to make this warranty regardless of whether the grocer or the customer selects the goods, and notwithstanding that the goods came to the grocer prepackaged and in sealed containers. Restaurants are also deemed to make this warranty since they sell goods primarily and service secondarily and regardless of whether the food is sold in or off the premises. There is one troubling issue with the wholesomeness warranty. That is, just how "wholesome" does the food have to be? How fit must the food be for human consumption? Obviously, if the food is contaminated it is unfit. Likewise, if there is a foreign object in the food, such as metal, glass, or a rodent, the food is contaminated. The problem occurs when there is a natural object in the food, such as a chicken or fish bone in a can of tuna or chicken. In most states in the United States, the food is not unwholesome, and thus the implied warranty is not breached, since the object in the food is merely natural. Yet some states, instead of the "foreign v. natural" test, use a "reasonable expectation" test and thus would ask whether a reasonable person would expect a fish bone in a can of tuna as opposed to a fresh grilled grouper sandwich in the Florida Keys.

Although warranty law can provide the consumer a great deal of legal protection, there is one very serious problem with warranties, especially implied ones, and that is that they can be in certain circumstances disclaimed by the seller, and thereby excluded from the sales transaction. Moreover, they also can be waived by the buyer. In the typical waiver situation, the buyer has inspected the goods prior to the sale, and consequently the buyer is not allowed to bring a lawsuit for breach of warranty as to any obvious or patent defect or any defects which a reasonable inspection ought to have revealed. In addition, if the seller insists on or demands an inspection, and the buyer refuses, the buyer is not permitted to bring a breach of warranty claim for defects in the goods which a reasonable inspection should have revealed.

As to the *disclaimer* of warranties, as a general rule the seller can disclaim and exclude warranties; but any disclaimer must be "conspicuous," that is, a reasonable person should be aware of the disclaimer; and thus "fine-print" disclaimers will not be effective. Also, a disclaimer protects only the person or business that inserts it, and not any other seller in the marketing chain. The first disclaimer area to examine is the disclaimer of express warranties. Now, the disclaimer of an express warranty is theoretically possible, but the UCC also states that any such disclaimer will be "disregarded" if it is unreasonable. The courts have construed this UCC provision by maintaining that if an express warranty formed part of the basis of the bargain, any attempted disclaimer thereof is unreasonable, thereby in effect meaning that express warranties as a practical matter can rarely be disclaimed. Sellers, however, have much greater freedom under the UCC to disclaim implied warranties. The first method is by a "catch-all" disclaimer, such as a buyer buys the goods "as is," "with all faults," "as they stand," or "in their present condition." Such language if conspicuous ordinarily will exclude all implied warranties of quality. The second way pertains to disclaiming the implied warranty of merchantability. The rule is that the merchantability warranty can be disclaimed, and the disclaimer can even be oral, but the word "merchantability" must be specifically mentioned. The third way concerns disclaiming the "fitness" warranty; and the rule is that this warranty can be disclaimed, and the word "fitness" need not be mentioned, but this disclaimer must be in writing. Finally, in some jurisdictions, a seller can effectively disclaim the merchantability and fitness warranties by limiting the seller's liability solely to the "repair or replacement of defective parts."

In order to prove a breach of warranty, a plaintiff must show the following: 1) a sale of goods; 2) a warranty was made and not disclaimed; 3) the goods did not conform to the warranty; 4) the plaintiff was injured; and 5) that the plaintiff's injuries were factually and proximately caused by the non-conforming goods. If the plaintiff can do so, he or she may be able to recover damages as the following: 1) any loss of value in the goods or the fair market value of the goods; 2) consequential damages, such as loss of goodwill and lost profits; 3) property damages; 4) personal injury damages; and 5) incidental damages, such as storage and inspection fees and return freight charges. There are, however, two serious obstacles to a plaintiff's recovery for breach of warranty. One is the old common law "privity" doctrine, which meant that there had to be a contractual relationship between the parties in order for one to maintain a lawsuit against the other. Thus, only the actual buyer of the goods could sue for breach of warranty, and he or she could only sue his or her immediate party in the marketing chain, usually the retailer. The UCC has liberalized the old common law privity rule to a degree by allowing lawsuits not only by the immediate buyer but also by the buyer's family, household, and guests. However, these parties still only could sue their immediate party in the marketing chain. In some jurisdictions, the privity rule has been abolished for breach of warranty lawsuits and anyone who could have reasonably be expected to use, consume, or be affected by the goods could sue, and could sue anyone on the marketing chain. An example of the latter point of view would be a lawsuit against a manufacturer by an innocent bystander who was injured by a homeowner's use of a not "merchantable" lawnmower produced by the manufacturer. Finally, another problem with a breach of warranty lawsuit is notice requirement. The rule of law is that in order to recover for breach of warranty, the buyer must give notice of the breach within a reasonable time after the breach is discovered. The notice can be oral or written, and should attempt to identify the breach or at the least indicate that there is a problem with the goods. If there is no notice, the buyer's cause of action is totally barred. The breach of warranty law provided by the UCC, therefore, does afford some legal redress to the consumer, but there are, as has been seen, many difficulties with a breach of warranty lawsuit.

Performance and Remedies

The final two and related areas to cover in the law of sales are the performance of the sales contract, that is, the obligations of both the seller and buyer that are necessary to fulfill their agreement, and the remedies available to the buyer or the seller if either party fails to live up to the sales contract obligations.

Performance of the sales contract can be divided into two basic areas: first, the seller's obligation, which is to deliver conforming goods; and second, the buyer's obligation, which is to accept and pay for the goods. Taking the seller's obligation first, how does a seller deliver goods? The rule of law is that a seller fully performs his or her delivery obligation by making a *"tender" of delivery*. That is, the seller is required to place and hold conforming goods at the buyer's disposition and also give the buyer notification necessary to take delivery. The seller, in addition, must keep the goods available for a reasonable period of time, and must make the "tender" at a reasonable hour. Of great consequence to the parties is the UCC's "perfect tender" rule, which holds that if the goods or the tender of delivery fail in any respect to conform to the contract, the buyer is not obligated to accept them. That is, the goods and their tender must conform in every detail to the terms of the contract. The old common law "substantial performance" doctrine, therefore, does not apply to UCC contracts, which represents a noteworthy change the Code makes to the common law. The *"perfect tender" rule* may seem harsh; but there are some exceptions to the doctrine. The first is called the *Cure Doctrine*. If the seller makes a tender of delivery which is deficient, but where the time of performance has not yet expired, the seller can cure any defects by promptly notifying the buyer of his or her intention to cure and then making a conforming delivery before expiration of the time for performance. The second exception deals with installment contracts and holds that when goods are required or authorized to be delivered in separate lots, the buyer can reject a particular installment only if the defect substantially impairs the value of the installment. Moreover, the defect in a particular installment is a breach of the sales contract only if it impairs the value of the whole contract. Thus, the UCC applies the doctrine of substantial performance to installment goods contracts. The third exception is the aforementioned doctrine of commercial impracticality which not only may discharge performance but also may excuse a delay in performance. Finally, if the seller makes improper shipping arrangements, the buyer can reject delivery only if material loss or delay results.

The buyer's fundamental obligations under the sales contract are to provide facilities to receive the goods and then to accept the goods. Note, however, that before acceptance, the buyer is permitted to inspect the goods. Acceptance means that the buyer takes the goods as his or her own and then pays for the goods. Acceptance can occur in three ways: 1) the buyer expressly indicates acceptance by words; 2) the buyer has had a reasonable opportunity to accept the goods and fails to reject them in a reasonable time; or 3) the buyer performs any act inconsistent with the seller's ownership of the goods, such as using, consuming, or reselling the goods. The buyer is also allowed to make a partial acceptance; that is, when part of the goods is defective, the buyer can accept the conforming part and reject the non-conforming part. The buyer is allowed to pay for the goods with a check, but the seller can demand payment in legal tender, that is, currency, but then the seller must afford the buyer a reasonable time to secure the currency.

The Uniform Commercial Code provides corresponding remedies for the breach of the sales contract. The buyer's remedies are divided into two categories: when the seller fails to deliver the goods and where the seller delivers non-conforming goods. In the first instance, the buyer can cancel the contract, recover any prepayments made, and *"cover."* Cover entails the buyer purchasing goods elsewhere in a commercially reasonable manner and receiving damages, measured as the difference between the cover price and the contract price. However, if the buyer does not wish to cover, the buyer can obtain the difference between the market price and the contract price. Where the seller delivers non-conforming goods, the buyer can cancel the contract, recover any prepayments made, and pursuant to the "perfect tender" rule reject the delivery, which must be done within a reasonable time and with notification to the seller. However, if the buyer has already accepted the goods, it is generally too late for the buyer to reject; rather the buyer must revoke his or her acceptance. It is very important to emphasize that a revocation of an acceptance must be premised on a defect in the goods that substantially impairs the value of the goods; significantly, the "perfect tender" rule applies only to buyers' rejections and not to revocations. A revocation, moreover, must occur within a reasonable time after the buyer discovers the defect in the goods and before any substantial change in the condition of the goods. The effect of a rejection or revocation is that the buyer does not have to pay for the goods; the seller has the responsibility of taking the goods back; and the buyer can cover and receive damages. The buyer can also accept the goods despite the non-conformity and recover damages, the measure of which is the difference between the actual value of the goods and the value if the goods had conformed to the contract.

The seller's remedies for breach of the sales contract are likewise divided into two categories: when the buyer breaches before receiving the goods, and where the buyer breaches after receiving the goods. In the first case, the seller can cancel the contract, withhold or stop delivery of the goods, or resell the goods in a commercially reasonable manner and recover damages, the measure of which is the difference between the contract price and the resale price. However, if the seller chooses not to resell the goods, the measure of damages is the difference between the contract price and the market value of the goods. When the buyer breaches after receiving the goods, the seller can recover the purchase price as damages. Damages also can encompass consequential damages, for example, lost profits and damage to goodwill and business reputation, as well as incidental damages, for example, inspection and storage fees and return freight charges.

The UN Convention on Contracts for the International Sale of Goods[1]

Whenever a contract dispute arises from doing business with two or more countries, there is no worldwide court to resolve the disagreement. The United Nations Convention on Contracts for the International Sale of Goods (CISG) creates a mechanism to solve this problem. As of 2006, thirty seven nations have ratified this treaty which provides a uniform text of law for international sales of goods. The CISG establishes uniform legal rules to govern the formation of international sales contracts and the rights and obligations of the buyer and seller. The CISG is given automatic application to all contracts for the sale of goods between traders from all countries that have adopted the CISG.

The CISG only applies to international commercial sales of goods. Each of these elements constitutes an important limitation on the scope of the CISG applicability. First, the sale must be international in character. A sale is considered international if it involves parties whose places of business are in different nations.

---

[1] Contributed by Miguel Orta, Nova Southeastern University.

Second, the CISG covers the sale of goods, and may not apply to contracts that include services. Where a contract includes both goods and services elements, the CISG will apply unless the preponderant part of the obligations of the party who furnishes the goods consists in the supply of labor or other services. Finally, the CISG only applies to commercial transactions, and does not apply to sales of goods that are bought for personal, family, or household use, unless the seller, at any time before or at the conclusion of the contract, neither knew nor ought to have known that the goods involved were bought for such use. Additionally, the CISG does not apply to the following types of sales: by auction; on execution or otherwise by authority of law; of stocks, shares, investment securities, negotiable instruments or money; of ships, vessels, hovercraft or aircraft; or of electricity.

The CISG's rules closely follow Article 2 of the Uniform Commercial Code (UCC), which is fully in force in 49 of the 50 United States. Under the CISG, a proposal to create a contract is not sufficiently definite as an offer unless it indicates the goods and expressly or implicitly fixes or makes provision for determining the quantity and the price. By contrast, the UCC is more flexible in contract formation and will find an agreement valid, despite missing terms including performance and price, if the parties intended to be bound by the agreement, and a reasonably certain basis exists for granting a remedy.

Under the CISG, an offer becomes irrevocable if it indicates through a fixed time for acceptance or otherwise that it is irrevocable, or if the offeree reasonably relies on the offer as being irrevocable, and acts in reliance on it. Under the UCC, an irrevocable offer must be in a signed writing that by its terms assures that the offer will be held open. Contract acceptance occurs upon receipt thereof by the offeror under the CISG. Many UCC jurisdictions hold that acceptance occurs when it is mailed, dispatched, or transmitted by the offeree to the offeror. The CISG does not require that a sales contract be reduced to a writing. Under the UCC's Statute of Frauds, oral contracts selling goods for a price of $500.00 or more are generally not enforceable, unless, for example, the existence of a contract is conceded to, or payment or delivery and acceptance have occurred. The CISG generally leaves questions relating to the validity of a contract, and the effect that the contract may have on the goods sold, to be determined by applicable domestic law.

Summary

This chapter emphasized that business managers and entrepreneurs doing business in the United States must be aware of a new and relatively recent body of law governing contracts – the Uniform Commercial Code (UCC) which governs contracts for the sale of goods and which makes some major changes in the old common law of contracts. The UCC is designed to change the common law to reflect modern commercial practices, particularly the mass distribution of goods to consumers. The Uniform Commercial Code has several major sections, called Articles, which seek to extensively regulate commercial transactions. For example, UCC's Article 2 "just" applies to the sale of goods. Accordingly, the old common law still governs service contracts, including employment agreements, as well as real estate sales contracts.

Contract laws, as discussed in this and previous chapters, illustrate the major elements associated with agreements and contracts. As discussed in this chapter, sales contract law and its vital components, including title and risk of loss, warranties, as well as performance and remedies, are all to be conducted in accordance to the guidelines provided by the UCC. The UCC is an important tool for managers to understand, specifically when designing contracts with their business associates and customers. Therefore, it becomes important for all managers, firms, and employees to fully understand the laws, regulations, and concepts associated with contracts.

Discussion Questions

1. Why is the concept of a "good" critical to UCC law? Provide an example with a brief explanation thereof. What body of law governs "mixed" contracts? Provide an example of the latter along with a brief explanation thereof.

2. What are some of the major changes the UCC makes in the common law of contracts regarding the offer? Provide examples with brief explanations thereof.

3. What are some of the major changes the UCC makes in the common law of contracts regarding the acceptance? Provide examples with brief explanations thereof.

4. What is the UCC's Statute of Frauds rule and what are some of the major exceptions thereto? Provide examples with brief explanations thereof.

5. What are the three major types of implied warranties pursuant to the UCC? Provide an example of each with a brief explanation thereof. Why is the legal concept of a "disclaimer" critical in warranty law? Provide an example of a disclaimer with a brief explanation thereof.

6. What is the UCC's "perfect tender" rule and how does it drastically change the old common law of contracts regarding performance? Provide an example with a brief explanation thereof. What is the "cure" exception? Again, provide an example with a brief explanation of the latter.

7. Describe, explain, and illustrate some of the major UCC "risk of loss" rules.

8. What are some of the major terms of sale in contracts that affect the risk of loss for damage or loss of goods in transit? Provide examples with brief explanations thereof.

9. Define, explain, and illustrate the UCC's "commercial impracticality" doctrine.

10. What are some of the fundamental rights and duties of the buyer and seller regarding the delivery and acceptance of goods? Provide examples together with brief explanations thereof.

6 – AGENCY AND EMPLOYMENT LAW

Agency and employment laws are very important commercial law subject matters since a great deal of the world's work is performed by agents. For example, the essence of agency law is to accomplish legally binding results by utilizing the services of others. The term "agency," however, is a very broad one, which concerns the rights and liabilities created in one person by the acts of another. Agency law encompasses three fundamental and distinct legal fields: 1) contract rights and liabilities of third persons created by parties who use agents and employees; 2) tort liability of persons for the wrongful acts of their agents and employees; and 3) contract and tort duties which the parties to an agency relationship owe to one another.

Agency is one of the most common, basic, and pervasive legal relationships in global business. Nearly everyone will come into contact with the agency relationship, usually in the form of a sales agent or employee. The usefulness to business everywhere is obvious, since no single person can perform all of the actions required to conduct a business. Moreover, the business owner can conduct multiple business operations simultaneously and on a worldwide basis by means of agency. The corporate entity, furthermore, as an artificial, though legal, "person," only can act through agents and employees and consequently only can enter into contracts by means of agents and employees. This section accordingly will examine agency and employment laws in the United States.

Part I – Agency Law

Definition of Key Terms
There are three critical and foundational classifications made in agency law: 1) the employer-employee relationship, called "master and servant" in the old common law; 2) the principal-agent relationship; and 3) the employer-independent contractor relationship. It must be emphasized that these legal categories are not mutually

exclusive ones, and thus one person, for example, a sales person, can be both an agent and employee.

The first classification is the *employer-employee* one. An *employee* is a person who is employed to render services of any type and who remains under the control of another in performing these services. The essential characteristic of the employer-employee relationship is the power and right to control. The employer, that is, the "master," must at all times control or have the right to control the physical conduct of the employee, that is, the "servant," in the performance of his or her duties. There is no or very little discretion in the sense of independent thought and judgment exercised by one regarded as a conventional "employee."

The second relationship is the *principal-agent relationship*. An *"agent"* is a person who works for another, called the *"principal,"* but who also acts for and in the place of the principal in order to effectuate legal relations with third parties. The essence of the principal-agent relationship is that the agent transacts business for the principal, represents and negotiates for the principal, and, most significantly, enters into contracts on the principal's behalf. The agent, moreover, can bind the principal to contracts with third parties. An employee "merely" works for another; whereas the agent represents another and thus ordinarily possesses a great deal of discretion in carrying out the purposes of the agency. An agent can be a "special agent," that is, authorized to bring about a particular undertaking for the principal, or the agent can be a "general agent," that is, authorized to represent the principal in any and all authorized dealings.

Finally, an *independent contractor* is a person who renders services in the course of an independent occupation. The independent contractor contracts with the employer only as to results, not how the work is to be done. Thus, the primary feature of this relationship is that the employer has no right of control as to how the work is done. As noted, a person may fulfill both roles, for example, an architect who is also empowered to make certain contracts on behalf of a property owner. Determining if a person working for an employer or an independent contractor is a crucial legal decision since many bodies of law, such as tort liability principles, as well as federal and state employment, tax, safety, and Workers' Compensation laws, will apply to "employees" but not to independent contractors.

From the employer's perspective, it may be financially advantageous to classify a worker as an independent contractor as opposed to an employee. There are several advantages to the employer for using independent contractors as opposed to employees, to wit: the employer is generally not liable for the torts committed by the independent contract in performing the employer's work; the employer does not have to hold and pay Social Security and Medicare taxes; the independent contractor is not entitled to unemployment compensation and usually, depending on the state, not entitled to worker's compensation; the independent contractor is not entitled to minimum wage and overtime pay requirements of federal and state labor law; the employer need not withhold income tax from the pay of the independent contract (but may have to file an informational return with the IRS or other tax agency); and the employer will not be providing such employment benefits as health insurance (though if the employer has over 50 employees the employer must be careful of the Obama Care 30 hour a week rule mandating health insurance or the payment of a "fine"), and life insurance, paid holidays and vacations, and retirement plans. From the employer's perspective, therefore, it may be financially advantageous to classify a worker as an independent contractor as opposed to an employee.

What steps can an employer take to ensure that a worker is classified as an independent contractor as opposed to an employee? First, a written contract explicitly designating the worker's status as an independent contractor and spelling out his or her services and the conditions of employment is critical. However, merely calling an employment relationship an "independent" one is certainly evidentiary, but not dispositive of the issue. Other factors, which should be spelled out in the contract, include the responsibilities of the contractor, the time frame for their performance, that payment will be in a lump or divided sum for the performance of those services, and that the contractor will supply all the necessary tools, supplies, and equipment. If any other workers are to be hired, the responsibility to do so, as well as any insurance (liability and workers' compensation), benefits, and taxes must be the responsibility of the contractor.

However, even if an employer calls and names a party doing work for the employer as an "independent contractor," merely using that label is not dispositive of the issue of the status of the party. Rather, the courts will examine the actual working relationship between the parties to determine if the party is truly an independent contractor or really is an employee. Of course, though not controlling on the issue of status, the fact that a party is called an independent contractor certainly is evidence of that status.

Creation of the Agency Relationship

The agency relationship can be created in four ways: 1) agreement of the parties; 2) ratification; 3) estoppel; and 4) operation of the law. An agency relationship is consensual in nature and thus the relationship usually arises by an agreement between the parties. Accordingly, contract law principles form an important component to agency law. Thus, a manifestation of mutual agreement by the parties is required; that is, the principal indicates that he or she consents to having the agent act in his or her behalf, and conversely that the agent indicates his or her consent to so acting for the principal. This mutual agreement can be expressed, by oral or written words, or implied by conduct. In order to be principal, one must have the legal capacity to enter into a contract. That is, only a person having contract capacity can appoint another as his or her agent. Yet any person may be an agent, regardless of contract capacity, such as a minor being designated as an agent. Consideration is not a requirement to the agency relationship, and thus one can be a "gratuitous agent." Regarding the purposes of an agency relationship, any legal purposes that do not contravene public policy are permitted. For example, appointing someone as one's agent to vote in a public election will be deemed contrary to public policy and thus prohibited.

As to other formalities, there generally are none, yet with one notable exception. If the Statute of Frauds requires the contract that the agent makes with a third party to be in writing, then concomitantly the agent's original authority from the principal must be in writing. This requirement is called the "*Equal Dignity*" rule. For example, if one intends to appoint another as his or her agent to sell real estate, two writings will be required: the real estate contract the agent enters into to sell the property to a third party, and also the agent's authority from the principal to act as his or her agent. What if there is a failure to comply with the Equal Dignity rule? If the agent's original authority is not in writing, any contracts governed by the Statute of Frauds and executed by the agent will not be enforceable against the principal. Rather, the contract, even though in writing, will be deemed voidable by the principal. The term *"power of attorney"* frequently is used to designate an express agency relationship. A power of attorney is an express written instrument that confers authority on an agent. Powers can be "special," that is, authorizing the agent to do certain acts only, or "general," that is, authorizing the agent to do all business for the principal. Both should be witnessed and acknowledged by a notary public. In either case, the agent is at times called an "attorney in fact," which appellation should not be confused with an "attorney at law," as the latter is an attorney admitted to state Bar Associations and thus licensed to practice law in certain jurisdictions.

The second method in which the agency relationship can come into existence is by means of the *"ratification"* doctrine. Ratification occurs when a person who is not an agent or an agent who exceeds his or her authority makes a contract for a purported "principal." However, the principal then accepts the benefits of the unauthorized contract or affirms the conduct of his or her alleged "agent." In such a case, the principal is bound to the agreement by his or her ratification thereof, even though there may never have been an agency agreement. Ratification can be express, that is, by the principal giving his or her express approval, or implied, by accepting the benefits or gaining some advantage from the unauthorized agreement. There are two important limitations on the ratification doctrine. First, there can be no partial ratification; that is, the principal cannot ratify the beneficial aspects of the agent's unauthorized behavior and refuse to affirm the rest. Second, before ratification by the principal, the third party can rescind the unauthorized transaction. Ratification will be discussed further in the section dealing with liability of the parties.

An *agency by estoppel* arises when a "principal" either intentionally or carelessly creates an appearance of an agency relationship. That is, the principal, by his or her conduct, has misled a third party to reasonably believe that he or she is dealing with a real agent of the principal, thereby relying on the "agent" and consummating some transaction with the "principal." In such a case, the principal will be estopped, that is, prevented, from denying the existence of the agency relationship. Agency by estoppel typically arises when a merchant-employer by words or conduct directed to a third party customer leads the customer to believe that a mere sales employee is an agent who is empowered to do more business than merely sell items at a certain price. That is, the "principal" has "cloaked" a person with the attributes of agency. It must be underscored that two critical requirements of such an estoppel are that the words and conduct come from the principal and not the agent, and that the third party reasonably relied on the manifestations of agency.

Finally, the agency relationship can take place by operation of the law. The law will impose an agency relationship even in the absence of a formal agreement, for example, family situations where one spouse purchases necessities and charges the other spouse's account. In such a case, the latter spouse is liable as a principal on public policy grounds.

Duties of the Principal and Agent

This area of agency law can be logically divided into two categories: 1) the principal's duties to the agent, and 2) the agent's duties to the principal. In both cases, these obligations can arise by the agency agreement or automatically by the operation of the law.

The principal owes three basic duties to the agent: 1) compensation, 2) reimbursement, and 3) cooperation. The principal, as the party employing the agent, must pay the agent the agreed upon value for the agent's services, unless of course the agent's services are to be rendered gratuitously. The principal also must reimburse the agent for all expenses and losses reasonably incurred by the agent in discharging his or her duties for the principal. Finally, the principal must assist the agent and cooperate with the agent and do nothing to hinder the agent's performance of his or her duties. For example, if a sales agent is given an exclusive territory, the principal is not allowed to "invade" the territory and make sales; and if so, the agent can recover the profits that he or she would have made.

The agent owes four basic duties to the principal: 1) obedience, 2) due care, 3) accounting, and 4) the *fiduciary duty*. The agent's first duty is to obey the clear and legal instructions of his or her principal. If the instructions are ambiguous, the agent is obligated to interpret them in a reasonable manner. Of course, if there is an emergency, the agent can deviate from the instructions in order to protect the principal's property and to effectuate the purposes of the agency. The agent is under a duty to use reasonable care in performing the work of the agency. If the agent fails to perform at all, the agent is liable for breach of contract. If the agent performs but performs carelessly, the agent is liable also for the tort of negligence. Even if an agency is a gratuitous one, the agent nonetheless owes the principal this duty of due care. The agent, in addition, has a duty to render an accounting to the principal. That is, the agent must keep and make available to the principal an accounting of all property and money received and paid out for the principal. The agent cannot mix his or her property and money with that of the principal; and if an agent does commingle property and money, and the distinct ownership thereof cannot be ascertained, the principal can legally claim all the property and money. Finally, and most importantly, the agent owes the principal the duties of a fiduciary. The agency relationship is one of those special and lofty legal relationships that the law deems to be fiduciary in character; that is, the parties to the fiduciary relationship are in a relationship of trust and confidence and accordingly owe each other the duties of loyalty, faithfulness, honesty, integrity, and full disclosure. The agent, therefore, is under a duty of faithful service. Moreover, the agent is obligated to notify the principal of all matters that come to the agent's attention and which might affect the subject matter or purposes of the agency. Furthermore, an agent cannot directly compete nor act for persons who compete with the agent's principal, nor can the agent acquire an interest in a business that competes with the principal, unless the principal consents, of course. For that matter, an agent is not allowed to take a position adverse to his or her principal absent consent. Thus, any secret profits, rebates, commissions, advantages, or benefits that an agent obtains by virtue of his or her employment rightfully belong to the principal. Specifically, if an agent is a purchasing agent authorized to purchase certain property for the principal, the agent cannot without permission purchase that property for himself or herself. Similarly, if an agent is a sales agent, authorized to sell property for the principal, he or she cannot buy the property for himself or herself, even if the price paid is a fair one. A dual agency, that is, an agent acting for more than one principal, is not permitted, unless, of course, both principals are fully informed and give their consent. An agent who acts in such a dual capacity, for example, representing both a selling and a buying principal, cannot recover any commissions even if the transaction is a fair one. An agent, in addition, including a former agent, cannot disclose confidential or proprietary information, including customer lists and trade secrets, of his or her principal. When the agent violates his or her fiduciary duty, the principal can sue for breach of contract. However, since under the common law, the breach of a fiduciary relationship is considered to be a most serious one, the principal is allowed to sue for the intentional tort of fraud, which includes the possibility of a punitive damage recovery. Moreover, any transaction of the agent who breached the fiduciary duty is considered to be voidable at option of the principal. Finally, any profits or advantages gained by the wrongfully acting agent are deemed to be held in a constructive trust for the benefit of the principal.

Termination of the Agent's Authority

Agency relationships come to an end, thereby terminating the agent's authority, in two main ways: 1) termination by the acts of the parties themselves, and 2) termination automatically by operation of the law. An agency relationship can be terminated by the acts of the parties in any one of five ways: 1) lapse of time, 2) accomplishment of the purposes of the agency, 3) occurrence of a condition, 4) mutual agreement, and 5) by the act of only one party. Regarding the "time" method, if an agency is created for a specific period of time, it terminates at the expiration of that period of time. If no time period is stated, the agency expires upon the passage of a reasonable period of time. If the purpose of the agency is accomplished, even if by the efforts of another agent or the principal, the agency is terminated, presuming of course that the agent has knowledge of this key fact. Moreover, the occurrence of a specified event or condition will terminate the agency, presuming of course that the principal and agent had agreed to the condition. Mutual agreement can cancel an agency, just as it can cancel a contract. The principal and agent can always agree to cancel their agency, regardless of a previously existing contract or specified time period. The problem in agency law, however, arises when one party unilaterally seeks to end the agency relationship.

The common law rule is that because an agency relationship is a consensual one, it is terminated whenever either party acts to end the relationship. Even though such a termination contravenes a binding agency agreement, a party can nonetheless cancel it, as the parties have the "power" to do so, though not necessarily the "right." When the agent terminates, that action is called "*renunciation*"; and when the principal terminates, the action is called "*revocation*." It is critical to observe that if either the renunciation or revocation breaches a valid agency agreement, the parties can be sued for breach of the agreement and may have to pay money damages as a result thereof; but the agency relationship still comes to an end. There is one important exception, however, constraining the principal's power to revoke, called the "*agency coupled with an interest*" rule. Pursuant to this precept, if an agency is created for the benefit of the agent, and the agent has been given some type of legal interest in the subject matter of the agency, the principal is not allowed to revoke the agency. The classic example of "interest" agency is when a debtor borrows money from a creditor, and as security turns over title to certain property to the creditor, who is then appointed by the debtor/principal as the creditor/agent with the power to sell the property if the debtor defaults on the obligation. Note that the mere expectancy of an agent to make commissions, profits, or fees is not sufficient to create an "agency coupled with an interest."

Agencies are also terminated by the operation of the law. First, if either the principal or agent dies or goes insane, there is automatic termination of the agency relationship. This termination does not depend on either the agent or a third party acquiring knowledge of the principal's death. Thus, any transaction by an "agent" after his or her principal's death is not binding on the principal's estate. Yet again the exception is an "agency coupled with an interest." Second, the loss or destruction of the subject matter of the agency may result in the relationship's termination. If the destruction or loss is total, the agent's authority is terminated; but if the loss is partial, the rule is that the agency relationship is terminated if further actions by the agent will not be in the best interests of the principal. Third, a change in circumstances affecting the value of the subject matter of the agency may result in its termination. Specifically, if there are unforeseen and substantial changes which materially affect the value of the subject matter of the agency, and it is reasonable to assume that the principal would not want the agent to proceed, then the agency is terminated. An example would be when an agent is authorized to sell "scrub land," and then oil is surprisingly discovered thereon. Fourth, bankruptcy of the parties may result in a termination by operation of the law. If the agent goes bankrupt, there is a termination when the agent's ability to act for the principal is impaired, for example, when the agent is the principal's investment broker. If the principal goes bankrupt, the agency relationship is terminated when there is a reasonable presumption that the principal would not want the agent to act. Finally, a change in the law, which makes the subject matter or the performance of the agency illegal, renders the agency terminated.

Liability of the Parties

The major categories of agency liability are 1) the liability of the principal to third parties, and 2) the liability of the agent. Regarding the liability of the principal, the key initial consideration is to ascertain if the agent was authorized and was acting within the scope of his or her authority when making a contract with a third party. It is a fundamental rule of agency law that a principal is only legally responsible when his or her agent is authorized to act for the principal. Accordingly, it is critical to determine the source of the agent's authority. There are two general sources of agent authority – actual authority and apparent authority. Moreover, actual authority includes four types of authority – express, implied, incidental, or emergency.

Actual authority is the power to carry out whatever the principal has expressly or impliedly granted to the agent to accomplish the purposes of the agency as well as to accomplish any authority incidental thereto including emergency authority. Express authority is the authority specifically and explicitly accorded to the agent by the words, oral or written, of the principal. Implied authority is the authority impliedly granted by the principal to the agent by the conduct of the principal manifested to the agent. Implied authority also encompasses the types of authority that an agent in a similar position reasonably would possess. Incidental authority is that authority granted to the agent that is necessary to accomplish the purposes of the agency. Finally, if there is an emergency or some unforeseen contingency, and the agent cannot contact the principal for further instructions, the agent is deemed to have the authority to do those acts necessary to protect and to preserve the property, rights, and interests of the principal.

Actual authority must be differentiated clearly from the next important type of agent authority – *apparent authority*. Apparent authority arises when the principal, by his or her own words or conduct manifested to third parties, has reasonably misled third persons to believe that an "agent" has authority to act on a "principal's" behalf. The critical distinction between the two types of authority is that "actual" is based on an expression of authority made by the principal directly to the agent; whereas "apparent" authority is premised on the "principal's" expression of authority to third parties. As the old common law maxim states, "an agent cannot create his own apparent authority." One important factor in determining the existence of apparent authority is whether the third party reasonably believes and relies on the principal's assertions. The principal's manifestation of agency authority can be express by words, for example, by saying that a "mere" clerk employee is "my sales agent," or by conduct, for example, by cloaking the "agent" with possession and thus apparent ownership of goods.

As mentioned briefly earlier in the chapter, the ratification doctrine is a method by which authority can be created in an agent. *Ratification* in essence is the affirming by the principal of a prior act supposedly done on the principal's behalf, but which was not authorized. The legal result is that the prior unauthorized act is now treated as if it had been authorized by the principal from the outset. Ratification can be express, by the principal notifying the agent or the third party that the principal wishes to be bound, or implied, by conduct of the principal, such as retaining the benefits of an unauthorized transaction, or bringing suit to enforce an unauthorized agreement made by the agent, or by failing to act when a reasonable principal would have objected to the agent's unauthorized course of conduct so as not to cause a third party unnecessary effort or expense. There are several other requirements to ratification. First, an act must be capable of ratification; that is, a principal can only ratify acts which the principal could have authorized at the time the act was done. Second, the "agent" must have indicated to the third party that the agent was acting for a principal and not only for the agent. Consequently, an undisclosed principal cannot ratify. Third, in order to ratify, the principal must be aware of all material facts, or have reason to know, pertaining to the transaction. When the principal does learn of the material facts, such as the discovery of valuable minerals on land the principal's unauthorized agent sold to a third party and which transaction the principal ratified, the principal can rescind his or her ratification. However, if the principal is ignorant of material facts, but this ignorance stems from the principal's failure to investigate or make inquiry, when the "reasonable person" would do so, then the ratification will be ineffective. Fourth, the ratification must occur within a reasonable time after the principal learned of the transaction. Fifth, the whole transaction must be ratified; the principal cannot just ratify the beneficial parts. Finally, the formalities for the ratification must be the same as necessary for the original transaction. Thus, if the original transaction must have been in writing, then the ratification also must be in writing. The key legal effect of the ratification is aptly described by the "relation back" rule, which holds that once the "agent's" act is ratified, it is treated as authorized from the outset. However, until the principal does ratify, the third party can treat the contract with the unauthorized "agent" as an offer, which, until ratification, the third party can revoke. Moreover, if there has been a change of circumstances and as a result it would be unfair to the third party for the principal to ratify, then ratification will be ineffective, for example, when the principal attempts to ratify an unauthorized contract by the "agent" to sell property, which subsequently has been damaged or destroyed, to the third party.

One very important consequence of the principal-agent relationship is the notion of *imputed knowledge and notice*. As a result of the agency relationship, the principal may be charged with the knowledge of facts that have been disclosed to the principal's agent. The rule of law is that notice to an agent equals notice to the principal when the receipt of notice is within the scope of the agent's actual or apparent authority.

What is the liability of the agent in agent-principal-third party relationship? The first and foremost rule of law is that when an agent acts properly for his or her principal, there is no personal liability on the agent's part. However, when the agent acts without authority or exceeds his or her authority, the agent is personally liable to the third party unless the principal ratifies the transaction. There are three major problem areas when attempting to ascertain the liability of the agent when the agent acts for: 1) *non-existent principals*, 2) *undisclosed principals*, and 3) *partially disclosed principals*. The first situation is handled legally in a straightforward manner in that an agent who purports to act for a non-existent principal is personally liable for the transaction. As will be seen in the Business Organizations chapter, a corporate promoter who negotiates and then contracts on behalf of a corporation which has not yet received its corporate charter, and thus legal existence, from the state, takes upon himself or herself a very great legal risk. The undisclosed principal case is most interesting. The agent deals with the third party, but makes no statement regarding the agency or the name of the principal, and the agent's name alone appears on the contract. There are several legal rules that govern the legal rights and duties among the agent, the principal, and the third party. First, the agent is personally liable on the contract. However, if the agent is held liable to the third party, the agent, presuming he or she was acting within the scope of his or her authority, may have an indemnification action against the principal. Second, once the principal's identity is made known, the principal is also liable on the transaction, again assuming the agent's acts were authorized. In such a case, the third party can either elect to sue the principal or the agent, but of course is only entitled to one recovery. Third, and most importantly, the principal is allowed to enforce the contract against the third party even though the third party thought that he or she was only dealing with the "agent." However, if the agent had fraudulently misrepresented to the third party that he or she was acting alone and in a non-representational capacity, then the third party is permitted to rescind the contract. Fourth, where the performance by the principal would impose a greater burden on the third party than performance by the agent, such as in a requirements contract, or where the performance involved a personal element, such as a services contract, the third party similarly will be allowed to rescind. Finally, once the third party has paid or performed for the agent and before the third party has become aware of the principal's identity, the third party can rescind. Yet once the third party becomes aware that the agent has been acting for a principal, then the third party must perform for the principal. Regarding the most interesting partially disclosed principal situation, in such a case the third party knows the agent is acting as an agent, but does not know the identity of the principal. Typically, the agent will sign the contract in his or her own name, but also will indicate that he or she is signing as an agent. There are three concise rules that govern this situation. First, the agent is still personally liable on the contract. Second, the principal is liable. Third, the principal is entitled to all the rights and benefits of the contract, but with the same limitations as the undisclosed principal scenario.

When goods or services are purchased on credit through a sales agent, the seller-principal may afford itself some flexibility by including in the contract a conditional clause, specifically an approval clause stating that the buyer's sales order, although signed by the principal's agent and normally binding on the seller-principal, nonetheless is not a valid contract unless and until it has been approved by the seller-principal. Using such a conditional contract clause will enable the sales agent to take orders, embody them in a contract, yet not without unknowingly binding the seller-principal to an unauthorized buyer or order.

Agent's Authority for Contracts for Business Entities
When a contract is entered into with a business entity, whether corporation, partnership, or limited liability company (LLC), it is critical to ensure that the person signing the contract on behalf of the entity has the legal authority to do so. Typically, any general partner in a partnership or the managing member of an LLC will have such authority to bind the business. However, for an LLC as well as a partnership situation, it is important to be aware of the fact that state LLC and partnership statutes may require that some major transactions have to be approved by all the LLC members or all the partners in the partnership. Regarding the corporation, the contract with the corporation must be signed by an appropriate corporate officer. The CEO thus generally has the authority to enter into most contracts on behalf of the corporation. However, pursuant to state corporation laws, some types of contracts must be first authorized by the board of directors, such as agreements for the issuance of stock or to sell most of the corporation's assets. Consequently, the prudent person will first seek evidence, characteristically in the form of a board resolution, or perhaps a provision in the corporation's articles of incorporation or bylaws, that specifies that the corporate officer in fact has the appropriate contract authority.

Because agents are fiduciaries in a relationship of trust and confidence with their principals and since they "stand in the shoes" of their principals, the business officer, manager, and entrepreneur must be very careful in selecting agents. Agents can bind the business contractually as well as adversely affect it by means of tort law by their actions or inactions; and thus agents can affect the finances and reputation of the business – for good and for bad.

Tort Liability for the Acts of Others

The first category of relationships to examine in order to ascertain tort liability is the "master-servant" (to use the old common law term) relationship, which is now called the employer-employee relationship. The key issue is to determine the legal liability of the master/employer for the torts of his or her or its servant/employee. The governing rule, which goes back to Roman times, is called the doctrine of *respondeat superior*, which in essence means "let the master answer" for the wrongs of his or her servant. This seminal legal doctrine thus holds that the master/employer is legally liable for all torts committed by the servant/employee acting within the scope of employment. As a result, a third party injured by an employee's tort can proceed against both the employee and the employer. The employee is of course directly liable, and the employer is "merely" vicariously liable. The nature of the employer's *vicarious liability* is "strict"; that is, the employer is responsible even though the employer has exercised due care in the hiring and the supervising of the employee. This liability is also "joint and several," which means the employer can be sued alone or together with the employee. The employer, however, has the right, at least theoretically, of indemnification from the wrongdoing employee. In order for the doctrines of *respondeat superior* and vicarious liability to apply, two essential elements must be established: first, was there a master-servant relationship, as opposed to a principal-agent or employer-independent contractor one; and second, was the servant's wrongful act committed within the course or scope of his or her employment. In order to have a master-servant relationship, the employer must have the power and right to control the physical manner in which the employee performs his or her job. In neither the principal-agent nor the employer-independent contractor relationship is this physical control element present. It must be noted, however, that there is a legal doctrine, called "employment by estoppel," which is created when one person intentionally or carelessly creates the appearance that another person is in his or her employ, and a third party reasonably relies on that "appearance" to his or her detriment. In such an "estoppel" situation, the "employer" is now legally prevented (or "estopped") from denying the employment relationship and is thus liable to the third person as if a "master." For example, if a health club advertises that it employs skilled "trainers," who wear the logo of the health club on their exercise clothes, and relying on the advertising and name recognition, a person engages the services of such a trainer, and is thereby negligently injured, the defendant health club may be estopped from denying that the trainer is its "servant."

One of the most difficult questions in agency law is to determine the status of a person employed as either a servant/employee or an independent contractor. Answering this question is crucial not only for tort liability but also for tax and Workers' Compensation liability, though the latter two fields are beyond the scope of this book. Regarding tort liability, one recalls the seminal doctrine of *respondeat superior*, which is limited to wrongful acts committed only by a servant/employee, and not by an independent contractor. As a consequence of this doctrine, vicarious liability does not apply when the tortious acts are committed by a person's independent contractor. Therefore, as a general rule, the employer is not liable for injuries and harms caused by the employer's independent contractor, even though the independent contractor was acting for the employer's benefit. As previously mentioned, the key test in determining whether a person is an employee or an independent contractor is the "right to control." That is, does the employer have the right to control the employing party's conduct in the actual performance of the work? In the master-servant relationship, the master has the right to control; whereas in the employer-independent contractor relationship, the employer is only bargaining for results, and retains no control. The classic and clear case is when a home owner hires an electrician or plumber to do repairs; accordingly, the home owner is hiring an independent contractor. However, if the nature of the relationship is not clear, there are several pertinent factors that the law will apply: 1) the actual extent of control over the details of the work; 2) whether the person employed has an occupation or business of his or her own which is distinct from the employer; 3) whether the type of work done is usually done under direction or independently by a specialist; 4) whether the employer provides the place of work and supplies the instrumentalities and tools for the work; 5) the method of payment, that is, whether by time or by completed project; and 6) the level of skill, knowledge, and expertise required for the work. Making this critical determination is regarded as a question of fact for the jury in a common law system to decide. However, some typical examples of independent contractors would be legal and accounting professionals hired by an employer, as well as medical professionals, the employer retains to treat its employees. Also, general building contractors that a property owner hires to do work, and the sub-contractors retained by the general contractor, usually will be regarded as independent contractors since they own their own businesses and are not controlled by the property owner. There are, however, exceptional situations, based on grounds of public policy and utility, when an employer will be liable for the torts of his or her independent contractor. One exception arises when the nature of the work is highly dangerous or ultra-hazardous. The other concerns non-delegable duties; that is, where an employer is under a duty by law or public policy which is not delegable, and thus where the employer will be liable for the wrongful conduct of its independent contractor. Examples of non-delegable duties are: an employer's duty to provide and maintain a safe place of employment for its employees; a landlord's duty to provide and maintain safe rental premises and to make proper repairs; and the duty of an owner of a business open to the public to keep the premises safe for the public.

Once the nature of the person employed has been established as a servant/employee, the second critical issue to resolve before imposing vicarious liability on the employer is the *scope of employment* question. That is, did the employee commit the wrongful act within the course or scope of his or her employment? In answering this question, which again is viewed by the common law as a question of fact for the jury to decide, several rules of law must be addressed. First, in order to be within the scope of employment, express authorization by the master is not necessary; that is, it is not a requirement to show that the master explicitly authorized or permitted the particular act, so long as the act occurred within the normal course of the employee's duties. For example, if the employee is hired to make deliveries using the employer's vehicles, but instead the employee uses his or her own vehicle, and negligently causes an accident, the employer is nonetheless still liable, even though the act was not authorized, because it was still within the scope of the employee's duties. Moreover, even if certain acts are specifically forbidden by the employer, the acts nevertheless still may be within the scope of employment. For example, even though the owner/employer of an automobile service franchise tells an employee not to do certain types of precision mechanical work, but the employee nonetheless does so, and thereby causes harm, the employer may still be liable if that type of mechanical work is within the scope of employment for the employee. The rationale for this rule is that otherwise merely by instructing one's employees never to do certain activities, the employer could unfairly absolve itself of vicarious liability. The doctrine of *respondeat superior* also can apply to intentional torts committed by the servant/employee. The rule of law holds that if the intentional tort occurs within the scope of the employee's employment and is intended to further the employer's business interests, then the employer is liable. However, if the employee in committing the intentional tort is motivated to further his or her own personal interests, then the employer is not vicariously liable. Therefore, there is a major difference legally between a "bouncer" in a bar who ejects a loud and abusive patron with excessive force, thereby committing a battery, and a delivery employee who upon delivering a package to a person, recognizes this person as a "long lost enemy" and strikes this person, thereby committing a battery, since the employer in the first case will be vicariously liable for the intentional tort, but not the employer in the second scenario.

One important intersection of agency law and vicariously liability law deals with a principal's tort liability for his or her agent's misrepresentations. The essence of the agency relationship, one recalls, is representational; that is, the agent "stands in the shoes" of the principal, negotiates for, and enters into contracts on the principal's behalf. Obviously, therefore, the agent will be making representations to a third party on behalf of the principal; and accordingly, the principal is exposed to tort liability when the third party enters into a contract and thereby sustains a loss due to the agent's misrepresentations. Again, the essential vicarious liability requirements have to be shown: Was the agent actually or apparently authorized to make representations? If so, was the alleged misrepresentation made within the scope of the agent's authority? If these requirements are present, the principal will be liable for the agent's misrepresentations, even intentionally fraudulent ones. The rationale for holding the principal liable for such an intentional tort is that the principal by using and empowering an agent has thereby placed the agent in a position to make representations and by so doing has given an aggrieved third party the impression that the agent has such authority.

The doctrine of *respondeat superior* generally is a rule imposing civil liability; and thus is not applicable to the criminal law. Therefore, ordinarily, a master is not criminally liable for the acts of his or her servant. Yet, there are exceptions, for example, pursuant to regulatory laws governing the sale of alcohol and tobacco to minors, as well as the sale of adulterated drugs and impure food. Also, the corporate entity, as "master," can be deemed vicariously liable for the criminal acts of its officers, agents, and employees, as will be seen in the chapter on Business Organizations.

The "scope of employment" requirement to vicarious liability also presents some interesting legal and factual questions. One concerns the employee's use of the employer's vehicle or equipment outside the scope of employment. The general rule of law is that the mere fact the employer allowed the employee to use its vehicle or equipment is not sufficient to impose liability on the employer if the use is outside the scope of employment. The employer only will be deemed liable when the vehicle or equipment is used for advancing the employer's own business rather than furthering the employee's personal interests. So, in the classic example, the employee who uses the employer's vehicle and who also has permission to take the employer's vehicle home, uses the vehicle for the employee's own recreational use, and thereby negligently causes an injury; and as such, the employer will not be deemed vicariously liable. Another "scope" issue concerns employees who commute to and from work. In such a traveling to and from work situation, the employee will be deemed to be outside the scope of employment, unless, of course, the employee in addition to his or her standard commute will also be doing a special errand for his or her employer. Traveling salespersons, furthermore, are always deemed to be within the scope while traveling, even while not technically working. The departure by an employee from authorized activity has always presented a problem to the common law. The problem arises when the employee temporarily departs from his or her instructed duties and undertakes some personal business. Under the old common law, this situation was called, most quaintly though quite accurately, "*detour and frolic*." The classic case occurs when the employee, while delivering goods for the employer, goes out of his or her way to visit a "friend," and while so doing, injures a third party. The deciding legal issue, of course, is whether the employee was acting within the scope of his or her employment when the harm occurred. There are two main rules governing "detour and frolic": First, only a substantial departure will take the employee outside the scope of his or her employment. That is, if the deviation from the direct route is only a minor one, to do an incidental personal chore or act, causing just a slight delay, and the employee's principal purpose is still to serve the employer's business, then the employee is still within the scope. Second, presuming a substantial departure, when is there sufficient re-entry into the "scope" for there to be vicarious liability for the employer? For there to be a sufficient "scope" re-entry, the common law requires that the employee resume the intent to further the employer's business, physically turn back to the departure point, and come reasonably close to the departure point. All these key issues are deemed to be questions of fact for a jury to decide in a common law system. Also related to the "scope" issue is the unauthorized guest problem; that is, when the employee without authority invites third persons to join the employee in the employer's vehicle, and the third party is injured due to the employee's negligence. The majority rule under the common law is that the employer is not liable because such an invitation is construed to be outside the scope of employment, even when the employee's conduct which in fact caused the harm is within the scope; but it should be noted that there is a distinct minority view that would hold the employer vicariously liable in the latter case.

Finally, vicarious liability pursuant to the doctrine of *respondeat superior* must be distinguished from the employer's liability based on the employer's own personal breach of a legal duty. That is, the employer will be liable for tortious acts or a person in the employer's employ when the employer is directly and personally at fault, even if the harm itself is caused through an employee. For example, if the employer directed or authorized the wrongful act, the employer will be liable as if the employer itself had committed the legal wrong. Similarly, if the employer knows that his or her employee is acting in a reckless or careless manner, and allows the employee to continue performing, then the employer, together with the employee, will be liable for careless retention and supervision. Finally, initially, the employer could be negligent in hiring the employee, if the employer or a "reasonable, prudent person" knew that the employee was not qualified or capable of doing the work in a careful manner. In such a case, the employer also may be liable for acts normally outside the scope of employment. These aforementioned types of liability are regarded as "direct" as opposed to vicarious.

Part II – Employment Law
Today's employment and labor laws can be very complex and challenging for most professionals. Despite the complexity of employment laws, managers and entrepreneurs are expected to become familiar with "the basics." Managers and entrepreneurs, at a minimum, should be familiar with the legal, moral, and ethical mores and expectations of each country where they are operating. This part to the chapter discusses employment laws in the United States.

The Employment at-Will Doctrine in the United States
The starting-off point for any discussion of the employment law and practice in the United States is the employment at-will doctrine. This doctrine, originally adopted from English law, is a mainstay of the law of the United States, being the general rule of employment in virtually all the states in the United States. What is interesting, of course, is that the doctrine now has been abrogated in England; but it is still very vital in the United States today and emerges as the traditional legal principle governing employee terminations.

The *employment at-will* doctrine holds that where an employee is hired for an indefinite period and there is no contract or no contract provision limiting the circumstances by which the employment relationship can be terminated, then the employee can be discharged at any time, with no warning, notice, or explanation, for no reason or cause, for no good reason or cause, or even, according to the old (and still precedent) cases, for a morally wrong reason or cause. The employee, however, also can terminate the employment relationship under the same circumstances. So, theoretically either party can sever the employment relationship, but in the "real world" it is the employer that possesses the greater economic and bargaining power and thus the party who can inflict the more severe abuse due to the "lawless" nature of this rule. The vast majority of employees today are surely not quitting their jobs for arbitrary and capricious reasons, and telling their bosses, in the words of the famous old Country Western song, to "take this job and shove it"!

There are many examples of the employment at-will doctrine in operation. There are also concomitant illustrations of employees' attempts to circumvent the doctrine and thereby to convert their discharges into "wrongful discharges." In one Florida case, a woman employee of the Florida Marlins baseball franchise was fired allegedly for taking her daughter to work on "Take Your Child To Work Day" in violation of company policy and when her employer specifically told her that it did not participate in that program. Assuming the employee was an employee at-will, she could legally be discharged, though whether such a discharge was a moral one is another question. However, the employee is also asserting that a male employee who took his son to work that day was not disciplined at all; and thus the woman employee's "losing" employment at-will case could readily be converted into a "winning" Civil Rights sex discrimination case.

The objective for the terminated employee at-will is to convert his or her discharge into a "wrongful discharge." That often used, general term refers to any civil action instituted by an employee against his or her employer for unlawful termination of the employment relationship. There is no single theory of wrongful discharge in the United States; rather there exists a wide variety of statutory and common law theories that an employee can try to use to challenge his or her discharge.

Statutory Exceptions

Due to the potential for abuse engendered by the traditional employment at-will doctrine, many legislative enactments have been promulgated in the U.S. at the federal and state level to delimit the scope of an employer's legal license to terminate an employee. Three major statutes are state whistleblower protection laws, the federal Civil Rights Act, and the federal National Labor Relations Act. These three important statutes are covered extensively in the authors' book, *Legal Challenges for the Global Manager and Entrepreneur.*

Many states in the U.S. now have whistleblower protection statutes that protect employees in that state, including most significantly private sector employees, who disclose wrongdoing by their employer or fellow employees. Discharging an employee for "blowing the whistle" or threatening to do so is a violation of these statutes, thereby granting the terminated employee, even an at-will one, a legal cause of action against his or her employer. Although it is beyond the scope of this type of book to examine in detail the several state whistleblower protection statutes, certain general observations can be made. First, in order to be protected, the statutes uniformly require that the employee disclose some type of legal wrongdoing, that is, a violation by the employer or fellow employees of an actual "legal" law, rule, or regulation. Moreover, the statutes are consistent in requiring that the employee report this legal violation to some type of governmental regulatory or law enforcement agency and not to the media or even a public interest group. Similarly, the statutes are fairly consistent in holding that the wrongfully discharged employee receive as legal redress the usual employment remedy of "reinstatement and back pay" and neither damages for "pain and suffering" nor punitive damages. However, the state statutes do diverge in two major respects. Some will allow the whistleblowing employee to report the wrongdoing directly to an appropriate government agency; whereas others will mandate that the employee first bring his or her concerns to the immediate supervisor and then up through the management hierarchy. Second, some statutes, such as Florida's, will require as a legal predicate an actual violation of the law; whereas others, such as New Jersey's, will protect the good faith whistleblower who makes a report of wrongdoing but who ultimately is erroneous in his or her assertion of illegality. Thus, some states will protect whistleblowing based on an employee's reasonable suspicions of illegal wrongdoing.

One of the major tenets of the National Labor Relations Act (NLRA) states that an employer cannot terminate an employee to discourage or encourage union activity. To do so would be an illegal "unfair legal practice." Of course, an employee must make an initial case that his or her discharge was motivated by the employee's pro-union support or activity. If the employee does make such an initial showing, the employee does not automatically prevail; rather, in order to defend itself from a charge of an unfair labor practice pursuant to the NLRA the employer now has to demonstrate a legitimate job-related reason for the employee's discharge. As such, the employee is no longer in the terminable at-will category. The NLRA also protects employees who engage in "concerted protected activity" for their mutual aid and protection. Such activity would of course involve the employees advocating, supporting, or joining unions. Moreover, such activity has been deemed by the National Labor Relations Board, the federal agency which enforces the NLRA, to encompass online communication between and among employees on social media if the employees are acting together to seek to change and improve conditions at work. Accordingly, these employees even if only at-will cannot be discharged since they are engaging in conduct protected by the NLRA. Note that an employee merely acting alone on social media to complain about work is insufficient due to the "concerted" requirement. Moreover, employees communicating on social media merely to "vent" or complain about their boss or employer, especially if vile and intemperate language is used, is also insufficient for legal protection, as there must be some evidence that the employees are acting to better working conditions. Thus, in order to utilize the NLRA, the affected employees must come under the Act's coverage. Finally, it is important to point out that managers and supervisors as well as independent contractors and agents are excluded from the NLRA's coverage; rather only "employees" recovered.

Title VII of the Civil Rights Act prohibits a discriminatory discharge based on certain protected categories, to wit: race, color, sex, national origin, and religion. These protected categories have been expanded by the Americans with Disabilities Act to protect employees with disabilities and to protect older employees from age discrimination by virtue of the Age Discrimination in Employment Act (ADEA). These statutes are also extensively covered in the authors' book, *Legal Challenges for the Global Manager and Entrepreneur*; and the ADEA is also covered in the authors' book, *The Aging Workforce: Challenges and Opportunities for Human Resource Professionals*. As such, similar to the NLRA, if an employee makes an initial case that his or her discharge was an impermissible discriminatory one then the employer now is compelled to defend itself against discrimination charges by offering a legitimate, job-related reason for the discharge. Once again, the adversely affected employee is "taken out" of the employment at-will doctrine. The Civil Rights Act also includes a non-retaliatory provision, forbidding the employer from discharging the employee for exercising rights under the Act. As with the NLRA, not all employees are covered by the Civil Rights Act; and not all discriminatory discharges are prohibited, only those based on certain "protected" categories. For example, the federal Civil Rights Act in Title VII protects against sex discrimination in employment, but the courts have not yet construed the gender category to encompass protection based on the employee's sexual orientation (as gay or lesbian) and/or "gender identity," that is, in the latter case, more extensive protection for employees who are gay, lesbian, bisexual, sexually transitioning, or transgenders. However, as noted in the first chapter, the U.S. is a federal system of government; and thus it is permissible for a state to have in its civil rights laws more protections (but certainly not less) than the federal government affords by means of national law. So, today, many states now have protections against job discrimination based on sexual orientation and/or gender identity. In addition to federal and state statutory exceptions to the employment at-will doctrine, there is a large amalgam of common law theories and causes of action that can be used by a purportedly wrongfully discharged employee.

Common Law Exceptions

There are three general common law legal theories that can be used by the discharged employee to convert his or her case into a wrongful discharge case: 1) contract-based theories, 2) tort-based theories, and 3) the "public policy" doctrine, which can be either a contract- or a tort-based theory depending on the jurisdiction. Tort theories can be premised on intentional torts as well as the tort of negligence. The premise is that when the terminated employee sues the employer for the independent tort, the employer in defending itself against the tort lawsuit must demonstrate a legitimate reason for the employee's discharge.

Contract-based theories consist of express contracts, implied contracts, and the covenant of good faith and fair dealing as applied to terminations. One initial and very fundamental point to make is that if the employee has a contract with the employer and the contract includes a provision that terminations will be based only for "good cause," then the employee clearly is not an employee at-will. An example would be a college professor at a private university who has "tenure," which is at times misconstrued as being lifetime employment but rather is "only" continued employment subject to a termination for good cause. Whether a private sector business employee in a global and very fluid economy can negotiate such a contract is another matter indeed. However, in addition to being express, contracts, as noted in the Contract Law chapter, can be implied. So, even though there is no express contractual provision regarding termination, the courts may construe the employment relationship and setting, past personnel practices of the employer, and especially the statements, actions, and policies of the employer, to require good cause for a discharge. The courts will particularly focus on any express codes of ethics or conduct or handbooks or manuals to see if there is language regarding notice and warnings, disciplinary procedures, and rehabilitation steps, or even for language that the employees will be treated fairly and with respect. For example, if there are statements, oral or written, by the employer that the employee's employment is permanent, that there will be no arbitrary discharges, that the employee will be employed so long as he or she satisfactorily does the job, or that the employee will only be terminated for a good reason, these statements may be enough for a court to say that there is an implied contract that the employee be discharged only on a showing of good cause.

The implied contract theory may be used to protect an employee at-will by limiting the employer's right to discharge without just, good, or reasonable cause, even in the absence of an express written employment contract. Some key factors to establish an implied contract case are: (1) the employee was a long-term employee; (2) the employee received raises, promotions, and bonuses throughout his or her career; (3) the employee was given assurances that he or she would remain in the employer's employ if the employee did a good job; (4) the employer had stated that it would not terminate employees unless the employer had good cause; (5) the employee had not been formally counseled, criticized, or warned about his or her performance; and (6) the employer had employment manuals or codes of conduct that gave assurances of discharge for cause only.

Employment At-Will and Disclaimers

Assuming the employer wants to preserve the at-will employment status of its employees, the employer should insert disclaimers in its handbooks and codes of conduct for its employees. The disclaimer should state that nothing in the handbook and code should be construed to create an express or implied employment contract, that the employee's status with the company is as an employee at-will, that nothing can change the at-will employment status of the employee except an express written contract signed by the CEO or high level executive of the firm, and that the employer reserves the right to change, modify, revise, add to, subtract from, suspend, or discontinue employment policies and practices at any time. However, for certain employees, the employer may want to consider binding these employees contractually to the firm. Such employees would be very qualified and capable ones who would be difficult to replace, especially in a "tight" job market, such as highly trained employees, particularly when the employer has invested the time and effort in the training, or the employees have access to confidential information and trade secrets.

Tort-based Limitations on Employment At-Will

Tort-based theories include intentional torts and the tort of negligence. Accordingly, intentional torts as well as the tort of negligence, which are separate and distinct from the at-will employment relationship, but which occur as part of the discharge, can convert the at-will employee's termination into a wrongful discharge action. Torts were covered in the Torts and Business chapter, but, for example, the intentional torts of assault and battery, defamation, fraud, and invasion of privacy can be used as the predicate for a wrongful discharge suit, presuming the employee possesses sufficient evidence to sustain the tort lawsuit. So can the tort of negligence, for example, caused by a negligent job evaluation of an employee or negligently not warning the employee of a poor evaluation. Yet there are problems with using these theories in an at-will employment context. For example, regarding the tort of intentional interference with contractual relations, the courts may take a narrow view of the tort and say that the employee at-will has no valid contract to be interfered with at all. Moreover, it is a basic premise of the interference tort that a contract party cannot interfere with his or her own contract, but only breach it; rather, the interference must be done by a third party. Similarly, regarding the tort of intentional infliction of emotional distress, one recalls that the requisite conduct must be atrocious and outrageous; and consequently "merely" firing an at-will employee will be insufficient to trigger tort liability unless there is some attendant outrageous conduct in implementing the discharge. However, in one case the terminated employee, a social work manager at a hospital, recovered

$105,000 from a jury for being discharged in an abusive manner that caused her emotional distress. The employee was forced to leave her belongings in a plastic bag and was escorted out the door by security guards in full view of gaping coworkers. Moreover, a supervisor told her that she would be arrested for trespassing if she returned, even though there were no allegations of criminal wrongdoing or any indication of disloyalty. As one management seminar speaker underscored, not to be flippant, but do not laugh at fired workers!

The "public policy" doctrine is a tort-based, common law doctrine which is adhered to, though in varying degrees, by all the states in the United States. The "public policy" doctrine maintains that an employee, even an at-will employee, cannot be discharged for engaging in an activity that public policy encourages, or conversely for not engaging in an activity that public policy discourages, such as illegal and immoral conduct. The definition of "public policy" is not clear, but generally it concludes activities that promote the health, safety, and welfare of the citizens and residents of a state as well as activities that encourage lawful and ethical conduct. Ultimately, the high court of each state, the state supreme court, will determine what "public policy" means on a case-by-case basis, though the courts are guided by the state's constitution, statutes, and prior judicial decisions. So, for example, firing an at will employee for serving on a jury or grand jury, for filing a Worker's Compensation claim, or for filing a safety report with state regulators are all violations of public policy since the law favors all those activities. Similarly, firing an employee for refusing to violate a statute or to participate in illegal activity will typically trigger the "public policy" doctrine. Moreover, whistleblowing, that is, disclosing wrongdoing by the employer or fellow employees, even if not protected by a state whistleblower protection statute, may afford the whistleblowing employee at-will the legal recourse to challenge a discharge. In one interesting public policy case, an employer fired an armored truck driver who left his vehicle unguarded while he attempted to rescue a woman from a knife-wielding robber. The supreme court of the state of Washington, however, ruled that the defendant company wrongfully terminated the plaintiff employee for violating the company's work rule, which prohibited armored truck drivers from leaving their vehicles unattended. The state supreme court decided that a discharge for saving a woman from a life-threatening situation violated public policy, which encourages such "heroic" conduct. The court emphasized that society values and thus should encourage voluntary rescues in life-threatening circumstances. In another more mundane U.S. case, though not to the terminated employee, the employee was fired from his grocery store job for wearing a Green Bay Packers football T-shirt to work, which does not seem that dramatic, except the store was located in Dallas, and the employee wore the shirt during the weekend of the National Football Conference championship game when the "home team," the Dallas Cowboys, was playing Green Bay. There is no civil rights act to the authors' knowledge that protects Green Bay Packers football fans from discrimination! In another oft-cited and notorious case, an at-will employee, an engineer in a defense and technology company, was encouraged to "speak his mind" in company employee forums, called Dialog, All-Hands, and Straight-Talk. The company even provided a "facilitator" to encourage employees to speak up. The employee did in fact speak up, criticizing his employer's upper-level managers for receiving "enormous" bonuses at a time of poor economic performance, layoffs, and budget reductions, and without regard to the fate of lower level company employees, the interests of shareholders and the public good. The employee was discharged and sued for a violation of public policy, contending that he was commenting on important public issues; but the court ruled that the expression of his opinion of his company's management was merely "a matter between him and his employer" and thus not a public policy violation. Yet, a public policy claim, if successful, in most states, is a violation of the "public policy" doctrine and a tort violation, which means that the wrongfully discharged employee has a tort lawsuit against his or her employer for tort damages, including damages for "pain and suffering" and punitive damages. For example, in one noteworthy case, an employee, a gastro-intestinal research scientist, was fired by his pharmaceutical company employer for protesting the company's alleged failure to disclose the adverse side-effects of an anti-ulcer drug it was developing. The employee complained to the Food and Drug Administration. A California jury found that the scientist had been discharged in violation of the fundamental public policy of the state of California and awarded him $2.5 million for economic loss and emotional distress as well as $15 million in punitive damages.

The covenant of good faith and fair dealing is implied in all contracts, including employment contracts. Most courts would say that the covenant will not automatically require good cause for all terminations, as such a construction is viewed as too unwarranted an interference with the legitimate exercise of managerial discretion. However, a court may construe this covenant to prohibit an employer from discharging an employee in bad faith or for a bad cause. Factors that a court will use to imply the covenant are the length of time of employment, not giving an employee a sufficient time to adapt to new performance standards, any assurances about future employment, any promotions and commendations, and most importantly if the discharge was motivated to deprive the employee from obtaining commissions or benefits. The violation of this covenant, in addition to providing contract remedies, may be deemed by the courts to be a tort violation, thus affording the employee tort remedies. Yet it should be mentioned that most courts in the U.S. have been very reticent in using the covenant in an employment discharge situation.

Summary

"Commerciality" has become a well-known concept in the business industry, and it is for this purpose that governments, specifically the U.S. government, have established commercial and agency laws. Agency law, its development, duties of agents and principals, termination of an agent's authority, liability of parties, and torts, are all elements that pertain to agency law, which have been thoroughly discussed in this chapter. As firms continue to conduct business practices with their partners, they are obliged to abide by the local and federal laws. Therefore, the agent and principal relationship is a vital tool for firms as well as managers and entrepreneurs who are focused on successful results.

The goal of employment law in the United States has been to achieve a proper balance between the employer's right to hire, manage, and fire employees, and the employee's right to be treated fairly and to maintain his or her job. Considering the "lawless" nature of the employment at-will doctrine, this objective has been a difficult one to attain, necessitating government intervention by means of major federal Civil Rights and labor law statutes. Moreover, not only the legislative branch of government, but also the judicial branch, has questioned the conventional adherence to the employment at-will doctrine, a legal precept that can legally legitimize an immoral (but legal!) discharge. Courts, accordingly, have increasingly recognized further common law exceptions to the employment at-will doctrine and thereby have provided more "wrongful discharge" remedies for the unfairly terminated employee. Nevertheless, the employment at-will doctrine is still today in the U.S. *the* key legal doctrine governing the employment relationship, especially in a non-unionized setting.

Discussion Questions

1. Why is it critical to differentiate between employees and independent contractors under agency law? Provide examples of each with a brief explanation thereof.
2. What are the exceptional circumstances under which an employer may be liable for the legal wrongs of its independent contractor? Provide examples with brief explanations thereof.
3. Explain and illustrate how and why the principal-agent relationship is an indispensable one for business today.
4. How is the principal-agent relationship created? Provide examples with brief explanations thereof.
5. Explain and illustrate the doctrines of "apparent agency" and "ostensible employment." How can they be a "trap for the unwary"?
6. What are the duties that a principal and agent owe to one another? Provide examples along with brief explanations thereof.
7. What are the doctrines of *respondeat superior* and vicarious liability? Provide examples of each with a brief explanation thereof. Are these doctrines morally fair to an employer? Why or why not?
8. Why is the concept of "course or scope of employment" a crucial factor in vicarious liability law? Provide an example with a brief explanation thereof.
9. What is the employment at-will doctrine? Why is it possible to have a legal but immoral discharge pursuant to this doctrine? Provide an example of the latter along with a brief discussion thereof.
10. What is the public policy exception to the employment at-will doctrine? Why is it such a potentially expansive legal doctrine? Provide an example of a discharge that violates public policy along with a brief explanation thereof.

7 – BUSINESS ORGANIZATIONS

The establishment of a business can be complex and requires understanding national and local laws. Entrepreneurs that want to establish a business must become aware of the laws that apply to each type of business prior to deciding whether to have a sole proprietorship, a partnership, a corporation, a limited liability company, a franchise, or a joint venture with another national or international organization. This chapter outlines some of the information that business owners, academic scholars, and entrepreneurs need to know about the various types of business organizations in the United States. The chapter outlines some of the risks and benefits associated with each type of organization so the entrepreneur can decide which format best fits his or her purposes for the business.

The main consideration in choosing a business form to do business will be the extent to which the entrepreneur's personal assets will be protected from the obligations and liabilities of the business. Other factors typically will be the type of tax treatment for the business, particularly avoiding double taxation, as well as converting ordinary income into lower long-term capital gains, the attractiveness of the entity to potential investors and lenders, the potential for attractive incentives for employees, and the costs and effort to start, form, and maintain the business.

Business Organizations in the United States

Sole Proprietorship
The *sole proprietorship* is the most basic form of business organization, as the owner of the business is in essence *the* business. Any person who does business individually without utilizing any of the other forms of business organization is doing business as a sole proprietorship. The advantages and disadvantages of this way of doing business as well as the other forms of doing business to be examined in this section will be discussed later in the chapter.

Partnership

Partnership law in the United States was originally by the common law, that is, case law, but to a lack of legal consistency among the several states, a proposed statute, called the Uniform Partnership Act (UPA), was drafted in 1914, inspired by, and borrowing from, the English Partnership Act of 1890. Pennsylvania was the first state to adopt the UPA in 1915; and today virtually all of the states in the U.S. have adopted the UPA. The UPA is a fairly comprehensive statute, but it does not cover every conceivable case or prescribe every rule of law; and therefore it may be necessary to examine other bodies of law, in particular contract and agency law, in order to resolve partnership disputes. It is important to point out initially that in the U.S. there is no federal partnership law per se, but rather a series of state partnership statutes based on, though not necessarily identical to, the UPA. Partnership law in the U.S. is consistent to a degree, but it is not absolutely uniform, despite the title to the UPA, so the prudent business person is well-advised to check the individual state version of the UPA where he or she is contemplating doing business as a partnership. The basic scheme of the UPA is to regulate with great precision the rights of the partners as against third parties, but to permit great flexibility among the partners in their relations to one another. For example, Section 18 of the UPA states that the rights and duties of partners are determined by the rules in the UPA, but *subject* to any agreement between or among them. Therefore, the UPA rules apply in the absence of contrary agreement; yet with one important exception regarding the fiduciary duties of the partners which cannot be varied or delimited by the partnership agreement.

The core definitions of partnership law and practice are found in Section 6 of the UPA. A *partnership* is an association of two or more persons to carry on as co-owners a business for profit. "Business" includes every trade, occupation, or profession; and thus the object of a partnership can literally be any and all business transactions. Moreover, "person" includes individuals, partnerships, corporations, and other associations. The name of a partnership can be any name, even if distinct from the persons composing the partnership, or no name. However, states in the U.S. all have "fictitious name" statutes for businesses that require the filing of a fictitious name with a state or local government entity and also usually publishing the fictitious name in a newspaper in general circulation where the partnership does business. The penalty for non-compliance is that the partnership will not be allowed to bring a lawsuit or to defend itself from a lawsuit. The duration can be for a fixed term, or the completion of an objective or set of objectives. Furthermore, a partnership need not have a fixed term, in which case it is called a "partnership at will," which means that it can be dissolved at any time by any partner without violating the partnership agreement.

The ownership element to a partnership is critical. Ownership entails the power of ultimate control and the concomitant right to make management decisions. "Control" is thus a very important factor in determining whether a partnership exists. A problem arises if partnership management is centralized in one partner, the classic "managing partner," but co-ownership and thus a partnership can still be found if the other partners have a right to control. Another problem in partnership is to determine if a partnership is a legal entity separate and distinct from its members, such as a corporation or a limited liability company, or "merely" an aggregate or association of individuals. Generally, the UPA follows the *"aggregate"* view of the partnership. For example, partners have unlimited personal liability for partnership debts, contracts, and torts. As such, the partnership is not a legal entity shielding the partners from personal liability like a corporation. Also, for U.S. federal income tax purposes, a partnership does not pay taxes; rather it files an "information return"; and partnership income and losses are taxed to the individual partners. Yet, a partnership is treated as an entity for some purposes. For example, the partnership can acquire real and personal property in its own name. Also, a partnership can sue or be sued in its own name. However, a judgment against a partnership can only be enforced against partnership assets, and not against the personal assets of the partners (so obviously in a lawsuit the plaintiff will name and serve the individual partners too). Finally, federal bankruptcy law in the U.S. treats the partnership as an entity.

The concept of a *"partnership by estoppel"* is an important one in the UPA. Section 16 of the UPA states that one, who by words or conduct, represents himself or herself as a partner, or consents to another person representing him or her as a partner, may be deemed liable as a partner, regardless of intent, because that "partner" is estopped (that is, prevented) from even raising the issue of lack of technical partner status. Section 16 is designed to be used by third parties who have extended credit to the partnership or who have entered into contracts with the partnership based on a good faith and reasonable reliance on representations of partnership status.

Typically, though, a partnership is based on contract, and thus is a consensual relationship. The general rule is that a partnership is formed by an agreement; and thus the consent of the parties and their intention to become partners are indispensable elements to the formation of a partnership. However, it is not necessary that the agreement and consent be manifested by an express contract; rather, they may be implied from the representations and conduct of the parties. As to the formalities of any partnership agreement, there really are none, and, in addition, the agreement as a general rule does not have to be in writing. However, there are two important "writing" exceptions: first, if the partnership is for an express period of more than a year, a written agreement is necessary; and second, similarly, a writing may be required for the partnership agreement, depending on the particular state exercising jurisdiction, if the main purpose of the partnership is to buy and sell and invest in real estate. Regardless, a writing spelling out the rights and duties of the partners is always strongly advisable in any and every case.

Together with the "intention" and "control" factors, the sharing of profits and losses of a business is an essential element of every partnership. The sharing of profits and losses indicates that there is a "community of interest" between or among the partners as co-owners of a business. It is important to note that profits and losses need not be shared equally; rather, the division may be left to the parties in their agreement. Section 7(4) of the UPA contains a significant provision pertaining to profits and losses. It states that the receipt by one person of the share of profits of a business makes a *prima facie* case (that is, presumed to be true unless contradicted by other evidence) that a person is a partner in a business. However, Section 7(4) continues by stating that no such inference of a partnership may be drawn if the profits are received in payment of a debt, as wages for an employee or agent, as rent to a landlord, as an annuity to a surviving spouse of a deceased partner, on interest on a loan, or as consideration for the sale of goodwill or a business or other property. Furthermore, Section 7(3) of the UPA holds that merely sharing the gross receipts of a business does not of itself establish a partnership. Finally, joint ownership of property does not of itself establish a partnership, as a business enterprise is required for a partnership.

Partnership property can consist of any property – real or personal, tangible or intangible – that be privately owned. At times, it is necessary to clearly differentiate between partnership property, the partner's interest in the partnership, and the property of individual partners, as there may be different creditors, tax considerations, and inheritance ramifications. Section 8(1) of the UPA defines partnership property as all property originally brought into the partnership or subsequently acquired by the partnership by purchase or otherwise on account of the partnership. The problem of determining the exact ownership of property can be a problem when property is used in the partnership business but the title to the property resides in an individual partner. The controlling factor in ascertaining the ownership of property is the intent of the partners, as manifested by their partnership agreement, records, and "books." However, if that intent is not clear, the courts will apply certain criteria to determine ownership. If the property was acquired with partnership funds or assets, Section 8(2) of the UPA states that such property is partnership property unless a contrary intention appears. This section will create a presumption, though a rebuttable one, that the property so acquired belongs to the partnership even if the title to the property is in a partner's name or even several or all of the partners' names. Yet the fact that property was purchased with the personal funds of an individual partner is merely evidence that the property belongs to the partner, since it may be that the partner contributed that property to the partnership or purchased the property for the partnership. However, if the property was purchased with the personal funds of an individual partner, and the title to the property resides in that partner, and the property is real estate, the courts very likely will demand a clear showing of intent for the real estate to be treated as partnership property. Other criteria for determining ownership of property include whether the property was used for partnership purposes, whether the partnership paid for repairs and improvements to the property, whether the partnership paid insurance premiums on the property, and whether the partnership paid taxes on the property. The preceding factors, however, are not conclusive, but are merely evidentiary factors in determining intent.

In addition to the right to manage the business, the property rights of a partner are designated in Section 24 of the UPA as rights in specific partnership property and the partner's interest in the partnership. Section 25 of the UPA explains the partner's rights in specific partnership property. The partner is treated as a co-owner with his or her other partners of specific partnership property, holding such property as "tenants in partnership." "Tenants in partnership" means that a partner has the equal right to possess specific partnership property for partnership purposes, subject to the agreement, of course. Moreover, no partner has the right to possess partnership property for any other purpose without the consent of the other partners. As to the nature of the individual partner's interest in the partnership, Section 26 of the UPA states that such an interest is the partner's share of partnership profits and any surplus after a final settlement of all accounts. Also, most significantly, this interest is deemed to be personal property. Consequently, even if the partnership holds real estate and also is in the real estate business, the partner's interest in the partnership is personal, and not real, property, which means that for inheritance purposes the property passes to the personal property beneficiaries in the deceased partner's Will and Testament. Section 27 of the UPA states that a partner can assign his or her interest in the partnership, but that such an assignment does not make the assignee a partner, but rather the assignee is entitled to receive the share of any profits the assigning partner would have received. Finally, regarding property, Section 28 of the UPA deals with the rights of creditors of the individual partners. These creditors do not have the right to attach, seize, or execute on partnership property; rather, the creditor of an individual partner must obtain a judgment against the partner, and then secure a "charging order" against the partner-debtor's interest in the partnership. The effect of such an order will be that the creditor will be entitled to receive all profits and any surplus that would have gone to the partner-debtor until the debt is satisfied.

The contract of partnership usually (and most advisedly) will specify the rights, duties, and liabilities of the parties between or among themselves; and thus any questions pertaining to the governance of the partnership should be able to be resolved by reference to the terms of the agreement. Section 18 of the UPA does provide important rules for determining rights and duties of the partners, but that section also states that the UPA rules are subject to any partnership agreement. As a result, the partners are free to vary many aspects of the relationship between or among themselves. Yet, there is one significant exception; that is, the partners cannot by their agreement vitiate the fiduciary nature of the partnership relationship. Also, any limitations on the authority of a partner or partners to bind the partnership legally on contracts and other obligations, although effective between or among the partners themselves, may not be effective to bind third parties who have no knowledge of these limitations. The basic principles for managing the partnership business are found in Section 18(e) of the UPA. This section states that all partners have equal rights in the management of the partnership and the conduct of partnership business. If there is a disagreement, a majority vote rules. However, the following actions require the unanimous consent of the partners: 1) deciding extraordinary matters; 2) determining fundamental changes in the partnership business; 3) admitting new partner(s); 4) deciding to do acts in contravention of the partnership agreement; and 5) doing acts enumerated in Section 9(3), such as disposing partnership good will, submitting a partnership claim or liability to arbitrations, confessing a judgment against the partnership, assigning partnership property in trust for creditors, or doing any act that would make it impossible to carry on partnership business, such as selling all assets or an essential asset of the partnership. Voting by majority rule is, of course, just one option; and thus the partners in their agreement can specify other voting arrangements, such as voting by a partner's interest in profits or other schemes for weighted voting, or by having high voting requirements for defined types of actions, such as a 3/4s vote for expelling a partner.

The UPA certainly allows one partner to be the "managing partner." Actually, it is quite common in partnership practice to concentrate all management authority in one partner or a small committee. This is more efficient, but it surely increases the workload as well as intensifies the fiduciary duty of the managing partner. Section 18(f) of the UPA deals with the compensation of partners. This section holds that a partner is not entitled to remuneration for acting in the partnership's business; rather the partner is only entitled to his or her share of the profits. This rule holds even if one partner has greater skill and knowledge, one partner is the managing partner, one partner devotes more time and effort to the partnership, and even if the creation of the profits can be attributed to one partner's efforts. The courts will not rewrite the partners' agreement for them. Accordingly, if the partners desire that a salary be paid to a partner, typically the managing partner, all the partners must agree; and an explicit salary provision in the initial partnership agreement would most surely be advisable. Not even the illness or disability of a partner will be grounds to impose salaries or to adjust salaries or the share of profits, so again this unfortunate contingency should be provided for expressly in the agreement. Furthermore, there is no duty for a partner to work at all for the partnership, since some partners will only contribute capital, and others services. There is also no restriction on a partner having other business interests or taking other employment, so long as there is no competition with the partnership. Once again, the partnership agreement should expressly treat all these issues.

The sharing of profits and losses in the partnership is governed by UPA Section 18(a). Section 18(a) has three important rules: first, each partner must be repaid his or her contributions to the partnership, whether by way of capital or advances; second, then the partners share equally in the profits and surplus remaining after all liabilities, including to the partners, are satisfied; and third, if there are losses, each partner must contribute to those losses, whether capital, advances, or otherwise, according to the partner's share of the profits. The mere fact the partners' capital contributions are unequal, or the one partner has put in all capital and the others have contributed only services and skills does not change the UPA rule on equal sharing. Of course, the partnership agreement can specify how profits are to be divided if other than equally. Such an agreement will also bind the partners as to the sharing of losses in the absence of a special agreement. Related to Section 18(a) is Section 18(b), dealing with indemnity and contribution. Section 18(b) states that the partnership must indemnify every partner in respect to payments made and personal liabilities reasonably incurred in the order and proper course of partnership business or for the preservation of partnership property. If the partnership does not have sufficient funds to indemnify a partner, he or she is entitled to ratable contributions from co-partners. Sections 18(c) and (d) deal with the interest a partner is entitled to for making a loan, advance, or capital contribution to the partnership.

Section 21 of the UPA is a very important section because it firmly establishes the fiduciary nature of the partnership relationship. The relationship of the partners to each other and to the partnership is a fiduciary one, just like the relationship between principals and agents, as was discussed in the Agency Law chapter; that is, the relationship is one of trust and confidence, good faith, loyalty, full disclosure, and fairness. Competing against the partnership, for example, making secret profits or commissions, or personally taking advantage of a business opportunity that is within the scope of the partnership's business, would be illustrations of a breach of the fiduciary duty. One recalls from the Torts and Business chapter that the violation of a fiduciary relationship is the equivalent of fraud. Section 22 grants each partner the right to a formal accounting of all partnership affairs when there is a violation of the fiduciary duty, as well as when the partner is wrongfully excluded from partnership business or the possession of partnership property and also under other circumstance when it is just and reasonable to have a formal accounting. Section 19 requires that the partnership books be kept at the principal place of business, and that every partner has access thereto for inspection and copying. Section 20 states that a partner must render on demand true and full information on all matters relating to the partnership to an inquiring partner or his or her legal representative.

The tort liability of the partnership and partners is addressed in the UPA in Sections 13 and 15. Section 13 deals with the liability of the partnership. It holds that the partnership is bound by any wrongful act or omission of any partner acting in the ordinary course of business of the partnership which causes injury or loss to a third party. This liability encompasses liability for negligent acts, willful and malicious acts, and intentional torts, such as fraud, assuming that they are committed with the scope of partnership business. Section 15, specifically 15(a), deals with the nature of the individual partner's liability. This section maintains that the partners are jointly and severally liable for everything chargeable to the partnership under Section 13. The effect of these two sections is that the UPA dictates that a partner assumes liability for the torts of his or her co-partners. The effect of "joint and several" liability, as noted in the Torts and Business chapter, is that a cause of action can be legally instituted against a single partner without joining the others. Moreover, a judgment against a single partner does not definitely dispose of the liability of the other partners in lawsuits against them. The matter is not "*res judicata*" since the liability is "several." Also, based on agency and vicarious liability principles as discussed in the Agency Law chapter, the partnership and partners are liable as principals for the acts of their agents as well as employers for the acts of their employees, presuming that the agents and employees were acting within the scope of their authority. The UPA does not deal specifically with the criminal liability of the partnership. Yet based on old common law principles, the partnership ordinarily is not recognized as a separate and distinct entity for criminal law purposes, as a corporation is. The result is that technically a partnership cannot commit a crime. However, the individual members of the partnership may be criminally responsible as individuals for unlawful acts committed by the partnership. However, if a crime requires specific intent, only the partner who possesses such intent may be charged criminally. Yet there are some criminal statutes, such as selling alcohol or tobacco to minors, that impose absolute liability, including criminal liability, on the partners, and even if the unlawful act was done without the knowledge or consent of the other partner(s).

The contract liability of the partnership and partners is governed by Section 9 of the UPA. First, Section 9(1) affirms the old common law rule that a partner is considered to be an agent of the partnership for the purpose of partnership business. The result of this section is that the principles of agency law regarding an agent's authority to contractually bind his or her principal are incorporated into partnership law. There is, however, also an express "*apparent authority*" doctrine in Section 9(1). This section holds that an act of a partner for apparently carrying on in the usual way the business of the partnership binds the partnership, unless the partner has no authority and the third party who dealt with the partner had knowledge of the lack of the partner's authority. This section means that the right of a partner to contractually bind the partnership can be restricted by the partnership agreement. However, any secret limitations by the partners as to one or more partner's limited contract authority will not be binding on the third party who lacked knowledge of the limitations. Of course, the partner who exceeds his or her limited authority has committed a violation of the partnership agreement; but that fact is moot to the third party who lacks knowledge. Section 9(2) further elaborates on the "apparent authority" doctrine by holding that an act of a partner not apparently for carrying on the business of the partnership in the usual manner does not bind the partnership unless the act is authorized by all the other partners. As to the nature of a partner's contract liability, Section 15(b) states that the partners are only "jointly" liable for the contract obligations as well as debts of the partnership. Thus, a contract claimant or creditor must sue all the partners. If a lawsuit is brought against less than all, any subsequent legal action will not be able to be maintained against a partner who was not joined as an original defendant. Moreover, the release of one "joint" partner releases all. Significantly, "joint" liability means that each partner is still liable for the whole amount of the contract obligation or debt. Finally, a partnership can be sued in its firm alone, without the necessity of joining the other partners; but in such a case a judgment against the partnership is only binding on partnership property and not the individual property of the partners; thus, plainly, a plaintiff will sue and serve not only the partnership but also the individual partners. A plaintiff who does so and recovers a judgment will then be able to "execute" the judgment against either partnership property or the individual personal property of the partner, though in some states, a judgment creditor will have to proceed against partnership property first.

The final area of partnership law, and a complex and at times confusing one, to cover is the dissolution and termination of the partnership. There are four key concepts that must be learned. The first is "*dissolution*" which is a technical UPA term defined in Section 29 as the change in the relation of the partners caused by any partner ceasing to be associated in carrying on the business of the firm. That is, dissolution is the point of time when the partners cease to carry on business together as partners. Yet, dissolution may not necessarily cause the termination of the partnership. Thus, the second concept is a dissolution which leads to the continuation of the business in an altered form. Conversely, the third concept is a dissolution which leads to the "*winding up*," that is, the *liquidation*, of the partnership when all partnership affairs are settled, and which ultimately leads to its termination, which is the fourth concept. There are two general categories of dissolution: 1) dissolution caused by certain events that automatically dissolve the partnership by the operation of the law (but which may not necessarily result in the partnership's termination); and 2) situations in which a court, upon application, may decree dissolution. Moreover, the first category of dissolutions can be further subdivided into dissolutions caused without any violation of the partnership agreement, and dissolutions in contravention of the partnership agreement. Section 31 of the UPA enumerates the causes for automatic dissolution. Section 31(1) states that dissolution can be caused without any violation of the agreement between the partners by the expiration of the term or the particular undertaking of the partnership, or when there is no definite term or undertaking, by the express will of any partner, merely by an expression of an intent to dissolve. In the latter case, a partner can dissolve even though dissolving the partnership results in losses to the other partners. However, since partners are fiduciaries, the right to dissolve cannot be exercised in bad faith, for example, by a partner dissolving to arrogate to himself or herself a profitable partnership business opportunity. A partnership can also be dissolved without violating any partnership agreement when a partner is expelled from the partnership pursuant to an expulsion provision in the partnership agreement. In such a case, the remaining partners are allowed to carry on the business; and the expelled partner cannot compel a liquidation and termination of the partnership, though the expelled partner is entitled to be paid the net amount due from the partnership and to be discharged from all partnership liabilities. Section 31(2) of the UPA states when a partnership can be dissolved in contravention of the partnership agreement. The rule is that any partner at any time may effectuate a dissolution of the partnership by merely expressing his or her will, even though such dissolution is in contravention of the agreement. The rationale of the UPA is that a partner has the power, though not necessarily the right, to dissolve the partnership, which is emphasized as a consensual relationship. However, the wrongfully dissolving partner may be liable for breach of the partnership agreement and thus for damages; and the remaining partners are allowed to continue the business. Section 31(4) deals with the death of a partner. The rule of law is that the death of any partner results in a dissolution of the partnership, unless otherwise stated in the partnership agreement. Moreover, absent an agreement, the personal representative of the deceased partner can force a liquidation and termination of the partnership, or can agree with the remaining partners to continue the business. Section 32 of the UPA deals with judicial dissolution of the partnership, and specifies those events that may lead to a dissolution provided there is an appropriate judicial declaration. For example, the death or disability of a partner, misconduct, gross negligence or neglect, or breach of the partnership agreement by a partner, as well as the fact that the business can only be carried on with substantial losses, are all grounds for judicial dissolution upon proper application to a court. Note that mere quarrels, disagreements, minor differences, and friction, as well as ordinary or developmental business losses, ordinarily will not be grounds for judicial dissolution. Accordingly, the astute reader can see that a partnership is a very fragile way of doing business since so many things can cause its dissolution. For example the withdrawal, retirement, or admission of a new partner is a very common event in the life of a partnership, but none of these contingencies are mentioned in the UPA. Consequently, unless there is an explicit provision in the partnership agreement, any of these events will cause a dissolution of the partnership. Dissolution, however, does not automatically terminate the partnership, as it may continue in an altered form. However, dissolution may lead to the next stage of the partnership – the winding up or liquidation stage, where the business continues but only so far as to conclude preexisting partnership affairs. Neither existing contracts are discharged, nor are creditors' rights impaired. The partnership continues to have legal existence for the purpose of fulfilling outstanding agreements, settling accounts, and converting assets into cash. The partners are still liable for existing partnership debts. Section 41 holds that if the dissolved partnership is continued instead of being liquidated, the new partnership remains liable for the debts of the previous partnership, and as such the creditors of the first or dissolved partnership become creditors of the partnership continuing business. Whether a dissolved partnership is continued or liquidated and terminated depends primarily on the terms of the agreement; and thus it is imperative to have a well and thoroughly drafted partnership agreement, specifying causes for dissolution, and then clearly stating that such a dissolution will result in the continuation of the business in an altered form and not the liquidation and termination of the business. Section 40 of the UPA provides the rules for distribution of partnership assets upon a dissolution which has led to a liquidation and winding up of the partnership. There are four categories of liability, ranked in order of payment, specifically liabilities owing to: 1) creditors other than partners, 2) partners other than for capital and profits (for example, loans or advances by partners), 3) partners with respect for capital contributions, and 4) partners with respect to profits. If there are losses, that is, the partnership liabilities exceed assets, each partner must contribute to making good the losses in accordance with his or her share of the profits. If a partner is insolvent or refuses to contribute his or her share, the remaining partners must make up that share proportionately to their share of the profits.

One major advantage to the partnership way of doing business is that the partnership pays no income taxes. It is not considered an entity for tax-paying (as opposed to tax-reporting) purposes. Accordingly, in a partnership the partnership's income or losses "flow through" to each individual partner and thus are reported on the partner's individual tax return. There is, moreover, more flexibility in a partnership, as opposed to a corporation, when it comes to allocating income and losses. For example, in a partnership where one partner contributes services and the other capital, the tax losses generated from the expenditure of the capital contributed by the "cash partner" can be allocated to that partner. A disadvantage of a partnership is the tax treatment of foreigners (that is, persons who are not citizens or permanent residents of the United States). Investing in a partnership usually would equate to a foreigner being engaged in a trade or business in the U.S., thereby allowing the U.S. to tax the foreign partner's income generated from the partnership. A foreign partner would also have to file a tax return. However, with a corporate investment in stock or bonds, a foreigner usually would not pay any income tax on the income from a U.S. corporation which the foreigner invests.

Assuming business people are contemplating doing business as a partnership, it is strongly advised that the prospective partners consult with an attorney and have drafted a detailed and specific partnership agreement. As noted, in the absence of an agreement, state partnership law in form of the Uniform Partnership Act (UPA) will govern the relations of the parties, and perhaps not in ways that some of the partners intended. To illustrate, the UPA requires partners to share profits and losses equally regardless of the partners' individual initial capital contributions. The partner contributing a larger capital contribution may want and expect a larger share of the profits. If so, it is incumbent on this partner to have an appropriate partnership provision so as to supersede the UPA sharing equally rule. Another example deals with the paying of salaries to partners. Again, in the absence of an agreement the UPA controls; and the UPA provides no salaries for partners regardless of the time and effort a partner may spend in managing, and making successful, the business. As such, the prospective managing partner should insist on a salary provision in the partnership agreement so as to override the UPA. Of course, drafting a detailed and specific partnership agreement will make the partnership way of doing business more difficult and expensive to form, but nonetheless the formulation of a partnership agreement is essential to regulating the relation of the partners to one another and thus the smooth functioning of the partnership. Finally, there are standard partnership legal forms that one can purchase, and such forms can give the prospective partners an idea as to the provisions they may want, but since a partnership is typically a unique type of business relationship as well as a very personal one, an attorney should be consulted to draft an agreement unique to the incipient partnership.

Joint Venture

A *joint venture* is a type of business relationship where two or more persons combine their knowledge, labor, and property to achieve a single undertaking. A joint venture is very similar to a partnership, for example, in absence of an agreement to the contrary, members to the joint venture share profits and losses equally. The major difference, of course, between the joint venture and the partnership is that the former is for a single transaction or undertaking, whereas a partnership is for a continuing business relationship. The precise point of division between a partnership and a joint venture is very blurred, however. Yet in most states, the courts will apply the UPA to resolve joint venture disputes. Today, the joint venture is primarily used in transnational business alliances in order to achieve some specific purpose. An interesting and very socially responsible use of the joint venture method of doing business is manifested by the U.S. ex-basketball star, Ervin "Magic" Johnson, who is "teaming up" with major travel businesses to bring more minorities into the rapidly growing business of selling travel "packages" from home. The name of the joint venture is the Magic Johnson Travel Group, which will supply the computer software and training to sell cruises from home. "Partners" in the joint venture include Royal Caribbean Cruises and GoGo Worldwide Vacations. As a matter of fact, Johnson, a leading advocate of developing urban areas, has formed joint ventures with several businesses, including Burger King, Starbucks, and AMC Theatres, to develop inner-city locations. Another example of a joint venture, in the international arena, is the venture formed by the U.S. Carnival Cruise Corporation's Italian cruise company Costa Crociere and the European firm Marinvest to build and operate a cruise terminal north of Rome. The European Union's antitrust regulator, the European Commission in Brussels, approved the project in 2006.

Limited Partnership

The *limited partnership* is a business entity that did not exist at common law; it was created by statute, specifically the Uniform Limited Partnership Act (ULPA) which most states in the United States have adopted. The goals of the ULPA were to allow small businesses to compete for capital and to afford investors to obtain a commercial interest in a business but without the personal liability of partners. The ULPA follows the pattern and rules of a general partnership in many respects, but imposes extensive formalities as well as restrictions of the activities of certain partners in return for their release from personal liability. A limited partnership is defined by the Act as one formed by two or more persons, and having as its members one or more general partners and one or more limited partners. The general partner undertakes the management and assumes the personal liability of the business; whereas the limited partners make a financial or property contribution to the business and thereby obtains a property interest therein. The limited partner is precluded from undertaking any management responsibilities. The formation of a limited partnership is patterned after the ULPA, but with one important exception; that is, the limited partnership requires the filing of a detailed registration statement, called a certificate, containing many formalities, with the appropriate state authority. There are two major drawbacks to a limited partnership: first, there are many, complicated, and very rigid formalities to its creation; and second, it was not clear how much review, advisory, or veto power a limited partner could exercise before he or she was deemed to participate in management and thus suffer the very harsh penalty of forfeiting the protection from personal liability. Because of these difficulties, the limited partnership was never developed to the extent initially predicted, especially now with the creation and growth of the Limited Liability Company. Yet the limited partnership still exists, but as a very specialized business structure used in the tax fields as a tax shelter. This use of the limited partnership is beyond the scope of this book.

It should be noted that in 1976 the ULPA was revised by the Revised Uniform Limited Partnership Act (RULPA) in an attempt to further encourage its use as a business form. The RULPA allows greater participation by a limited partner and tries to establish some clear and permissible boundaries for limited partners to get involved in the business. A limited partner exercising "control" over the business is still prohibited. However, the RULPA enumerates certain "safe acts" that a limited partner can do, such as consulting or advising the general partner, approving or disapproving amendments, being an agent or employee of the business, acting as a surety of the business, as well as voting on certain matters (including dissolution, removing the general partner, selling all the assets of the business, incurring extraordinary indebtedness, and changing the nature of the business), without being deemed to "control" the business. Yet this revision of the ULPA has not increased the use of the limited partnership, which basically except for the aforementioned specialized uses, has been superseded by the Limited Liability Company method of doing business.

Limited Liability Partnership

In yet another new form of doing business, *limited liability partnerships* (LLPs) have come into being pursuant to state statutory law. Many states have enacted similar legislation to permit the creation of LLPs. LLPs today are designed primarily to be used by attorneys, accountants, and other professionals as a way of doing business; and thus any detailed explication of the LLP form is beyond the scope of this book. However, some fundamental LLP points must be made. One key aspect to the LLP way of doing business is that this form does not have to have a general partner who is personally liable for the debts and obligations of the partnership. Instead, all partners are limited partners; and thus can lose only their capital contribution should the partnership fail or be sued. There is, most significantly, no personal liability beyond the partner's capital contribution. The tax benefits of the LLP form are obvious; that is, LLPs enjoy "flow-through" tax advantages as do the other types of partnership. No tax thus is paid at the partnership level; and all profits and losses are reported on the individual partners' income tax returns. The LLP is created formally by the filing of an "articles of partnership" with the relevant state's Secretary of State's office. This is naturally a public document. Note that a "domestic" LLP is one formed in the state of organization. Such an LLP may do business in other states, but must register as a "foreign" LLP.

There are two important points regarding LLP law: 1) In most states, LLPs are restricted to certain types of professionals, such as accountants and lawyers; and 2) Most states require LLPs to carry a minimum of $1 million in liability insurance to cover negligence, wrongful acts, and misconduct by partners or employees of the LLP. The rationale, of course, is that third parties will have a compensation source to recover for their injuries. In some states, *any* partnership may register with the Secretary of State's office as an LLP. The registration fee initially was $100 for each partner who is a state resident. Usually, an LLP must maintain $100,000 per partner in liability insurance coverage. These are the amounts in the original statute, and one can expect them to increase, of course. The name of a registered limited liability partnership must contain the words "limited liability" or the designation "LLP." A partner in an LLP is not individually liable for the obligations or liabilities of the partnership, whether in tort or contract, arising from errors, omissions, negligence, malpractice or wrongful acts committed by another partner or by an employee or agent of the partnership. Each partner remains, however, liable, individually and jointly and severally, for all other debts and obligations of the partnership, including his or her own errors, omissions, negligence, malpractice, or wrongful acts, as well as those committed by any person under his or her direct supervision or control. Partnership assets, of course, are subject to all partnership liabilities, including malpractice claims.

Corporation
The corporate form of doing business in the United States is a creation of the states. The corporate charter is granted by the state, and no one can conduct business as a *corporation* without such a grant from the state. The states can regulate the incorporation of a business as well as the activities of the corporation. State statutes, as the discerning reader is aware, can vary; there is no federal or uniform corporate statute, though there is a "model" act that has been offered to the states for official legislative enactment, called the Revised Model Business Corporation Act. In most states, a corporation is formed by the filing of an appropriate document with the appropriate state official, usually the Secretary of State of the state, who is charged with the primary responsibility of administering corporate laws, and the paying of a specified fee. Corporate existence begins on the date of filing as indorsed on the charter. Most states have four types of corporate statutes: 1) general business corporate statutes, which will be the focus of this book; 2) non-profit corporation statutes; and 3) professional corporation statutes designed for attorneys, physicians, and accountants; and 4) small, "close," or "closely held" corporation statutes, though

the latter for all practical purposes has now been superseded by the Limited Liability Company form of doing business, as will be seen.

A corporation is defined as an artificial legal entity, independent of its owners-investors, created by the state, pursuant to a corporate charter, with powers conferred upon it by the state. A "domestic" corporation is one formed under the laws of the particular state; and a "foreign" corporation refers to all other corporations, either from "sister" states or international jurisdictions. State corporate laws have special provisions to enable a foreign corporation to transact intrastate business. A distinction is at times made between "publicly held" corporations and "closely held" corporations. The former are corporations whose outstanding shares are held by a large number of people, whose shares are traded on national or international security exchanges, whose stock prices are published, or whose activities are regulated by the Securities and Exchange Commission (SEC). A *"closely held" corporation*, however, is one with relatively few shareholders, usually less than 35, where all or most of the shareholders participate in management. There is no real outside market for shares, and such corporations are not regulated by the SEC. Some states have special statutes or special statutory provisions for "close" corporations. One characteristic provision is that the free transferability of shares of the close corporation may be restricted.

The corporation, it must be underscored, is a separate legal entity, distinct from its shareholders; that is, it is an artificial legal person. The corporation is owned by its shareholders and managed by a board of directors chosen by the shareholders. The corporation as a "person" can conduct business in its own name, much in the same way a "real" person can. So, business can be done, assets acquired, contracts entered into, and liabilities incurred, and all in the name of the corporation. Moreover, the corporation can sue or be sued as if a person, pay taxes, obtain business licenses and permits, and own bank accounts. Of course, as an artificial person, the corporate entity acts exclusively by and through officers, employees, and agents. For Constitutional law purposes in the U.S., the corporation is treated as a "person" for "due process" and "equal protection" purposes, as well as for the 4th and 1st amendments, but not for the 5th amendment privilege against self-incrimination. There are certain distinct advantages to the corporate form of doing business. First and foremost is limited liability. Corporate obligations and debts are separate and distinct from those of the shareholders, even if one shareholder owns all the shares. The corporation, of course, is unlimitedly liable, but the shareholders are not personally liable for the debts of the corporation. The shareholder's liability is limited to the amount of his or her investment. Another positive feature of the corporation is centralized management in a board of directors and officers selected by the board. Directors and officers may be shareholders, but it is not technically required that they have any ownership interest in the corporation. Continuity of existence is another advantage. Theoretically, corporate existence can be perpetual. As opposed to a partnership, which is a very fragile way to do business, as has been seen, the existence of a corporation is not dependent on who its owners and investors as well as directors and officers are at a particular time. If a shareholder or director dies, or if a shareholder sells or transfers his or her shares, the corporation continues to exist as a separate entity. Furthermore, if it is necessary to raise additional capital, new shareholders may be brought in without changing or disturbing the corporate form.

Other advantages of the corporate form are transferability of ownership, as shares are freely transferable, access to capital markets, by means of issuance of stock and bonds to the public, and the attractiveness of the corporate form of doing business to investors. The major disadvantage of the corporation in the U.S. is double taxation. The corporation is taxed as a separate entity with its own tax rates for corporate earnings; but then if the corporation pays these now diminished earnings as dividends to the shareholders the dividends are treated as income to the shareholders and taxed again. In a partnership, one recalls, total income is taxed only once, directly to the partners. However, there is a specialized corporate form, called a "sub-chapter S" (S) corporation from the pertinent section in the Internal Revenue Code, whereby the corporation can be taxed as a partnership. There thus will be only a single tax on corporate income at the shareholder level. Corporate income is not taxed separately; and if the S corporation has losses, a shareholder can use the losses to offset other income. Yet there are numerous requirements for an S corporation. The most notable ones are as follows: only a domestic corporation with 100 or less shareholders can be an S corporation; the S corporation can only have one class of stock; resident aliens cannot be shareholders; and there are limits to the amount of money that can be placed in pension funds.

Corporate Formation
The formation of a corporation is a fairly straightforward process. A state of incorporation will have to be selected, of course. A small corporation that intends to do business in one jurisdiction will obviously choose that state to incorporate. If a corporation plans to do business in other states, the corporation will need a certificate of authority, which usually is a formality, but the states will naturally require a fee as well as an official registered corporate agent in the state. As to the "mechanics" of filing, one must check (or rather have one's attorney check) the specific state statute as to details. The filing of a document with the appropriate state official, usually the Secretary of State of the state, is mandatory along with the payment of a filing fee. The document must be notarized in some states. The document is most typically called an "*articles of incorporation*," though in some states it is called a "certificate of incorporation" or a charter. Also, some states may require local filing of the document too, and others also may require newspaper notice of the filing. If the document conforms to the laws of the state, it is approved, and corporate existence is deemed to begin at the date and time of filing as determined by the Secretary of State. *Incorporators* are the person(s) who execute and sign the articles of incorporation. Three is the traditional number required, but today many states will require only one. Generally, incorporators must be over 18 years of age if the incorporators are natural people, as opposed to another corporation or a partnership, which can be incorporators too. Moreover, there are no citizenship or residency requirements. The functions of the incorporator(s) are to execute and deliver the articles to the Secretary of State, then receive the charter back from the Secretary of State, and finally call the first meeting of the initial Board of Directors (which is named in the articles) where the organization of the corporation is completed. Since the role of the incorporators is merely a ministerial one, with ceremonial overtones, serving as an incorporator generally will not give rise to any personal liability on the incorporator's part. An

incorporator should not be confused with a "subscriber," who is a person who agrees to buy shares in the corporation, and upon so doing becomes an investor and participant.

The "articles of incorporation" is an agreement among the incorporators concerning the organizational details of the corporation. It is also deemed to be an agreement between the corporation and the state, the corporation and the shareholders, and an agreement among the shareholders themselves. The exact requirements for the document of course are ascertained by reference to a particular state's corporate law; but generally speaking there are just a few uniform requirements for a valid "articles of incorporation." First, it must be in writing.

Second, it must name the corporation. Most states will require that the name be distinct or distinguishable from all other corporate names, or not be the same or deceptively or confusingly similar. The Secretary of State of the state will have a registry of corporate names, and the states have procedures to check names as well as to register for a brief, usually six month period, a prospective corporate name for a nominal fee while the corporate papers are being prepared for filing. In addition, the name must have attached to it some words indicating "corporateness," such as "Incorporated," "Inc.," "Company," or "Co." There also may be a requirement for the corporation to comply with a local "fictitious name" statute, which would apply to any business form, whereby the principals behind the fictitiously named business must register with the state. The entrepreneur contemplating forming a corporation (or an LLC, that is, a Limited Liability Company) should first conduct a name search in order to ascertain if the desired name (and website) is available. There are state and local registries for fictitious names as well as domain name registries and federal and state trademark and service-mark registries. The entrepreneur should register not only the company name and website but also the trademark and service-mark. Note that many state corporation statutes allow a person to reserve a name for a fee for a certain time period, for example, six months, while the entity is being formed with that name.

The duration of the corporation can be perpetual. In some states, the articles must state the time period for duration, which can be perpetual; whereas others just presume that the existence will be perpetual unless a shorter period is stated. Usually a provision for the purposes of the corporation must be included, but a "general purposes" provision is fine, whereby the corporation seeks to do "any and all lawful business." Of course, specific purposes can be stated, but then if the corporation wants to do business beyond these limited purposes, it must amend its articles. As to corporate powers, it ordinarily is not necessary to state them, as most states either have very long and broad lists of corporate powers which every corporation automatically possesses, or simply state that a corporation has all the powers a natural person has for the carrying on of business. Thus, it is not necessary to recite powers in the articles. However, the articles can preclude the corporation from exercising certain powers, such as making loans to directors or officers. Most states will also require a capitalization provision in the articles. An act beyond the powers or purposes of the corporation is known as an *ultra vires* act, which can be enjoined by the state or by a shareholder lawsuit, and also which can be the basis of a corporate action to recover damages against the directors and/or officers who committed the *ultra vires* act. In most states, the *ultra vires* doctrine has been abolished as a defense against or by third parties; that is, no executed act of the corporation with a third party can be deemed invalid as *ultra vires*.

Concerning capitalization, usually information as to the type, number, and price of shares the corporation is authorized to issue must be stated. However, there is no requirement that any shares authorized actually be issued. Also, some states may have minimum capital requirements, for example, that the corporation receives $500 or $1000 before commencing business; and if so, usually an affidavit to that effect will be sufficient to satisfy the appropriate state official. Directors are required for a corporation and must be named in the articles. Some states require three, unless there are only one or two shareholders; but in most states a corporation need only have one director. The function of the initial board (or sole director) named in the articles is to complete the organization of the corporation; the initial board serves until the first annual meeting of shareholders, when the shareholders elect the board. There are often residency and shareholder requirements to be a director. Every corporation is also required to have a registered office and a registered agent at that office. The registered office characteristically is the corporate attorney's office, and that attorney is designated as the registered agent. Of course, the registered office can be the corporation's business office, and the registered agent can be a corporate employee so designated. The purpose of the registered office and agent is to provide a place and a person to receive service of process, tax notices, and other official communications from the state or otherwise. The articles must have the names and address of the incorporators. Finally, the articles can include any other provisions for the regulation of business, such as preemptive rights and cumulative voting, which will be explained in due course, as well as changing quorums, for example, from 1/3 to 3/4, or having larger voting proportions for some actions. The "articles of incorporation" must be distinguished from the *bylaws*. The latter are the private rules and regulations for governing and managing the internal affairs of the corporation. The bylaws are not filed; they are not part of the public record. The bylaws may have to be approved by all the original incorporators prior to the election of directors, or may have to be approved by the board of directors, or by the shareholders, or by a combination thereof depending on the particular state statute. Any very important internal provision or perhaps a very unusual one should be in the articles and not the bylaws. A corporate seal is no longer required in most states; though it is desirable to have such a seal since it differentiates corporate transactions from the transactions of its individual members. The organizational meeting previously mentioned is the meeting of the initial board of directors. The purposes of such a meeting are to accept share subscriptions, accept contracts, leases, and loans, issue shares of stock and set the consideration for shares, select officers, and adopt bylaws. Even if a corporation is a very small or "closely held" one, such a meeting should occur, though it could be informally conducted, and there should be minutes kept for the meeting.

The bylaws of a corporation can focus on a variety of subject matters dealing with corporate governance. For example, the bylaws can include provisions dealing with the number of directors (though note that some state laws may require the number to be stated in the articles of incorporation), the calling of board of directors meetings, the voting rights of directors, how board vacancy are to be filled, the removal of directors, and the term for the directors are to serve. Bylaws can also have provisions for restricting the transferability of shares as well as for granting a "right of first refusal" for the corporation or its assignees to purchase shares at the time of a transfer by a third party. These latter bylaw provisions can be very important to a new, small, and closely-held corporation since it is critical that the stock be owned by the people who commenced the business and who are directly and substantially involved with its success.

A potential problem area in corporate law and practice concerns pre-incorporation transactions. A *pre-incorporation transaction* is one on behalf of the corporation or in the corporation's name which occurs before the articles are filed, and thus before there is any official corporate status. There are two main types of pre-incorporation transactions: 1) subscriptions for shares and 2) contracts by promoters. A *share subscription* is an offer to purchase and pay for a specified number of un-issued shares of the corporation. In a pre-incorporation subscription, the corporation is legally not yet formed (and thus a contract offeree does not technically exist!). A post-incorporation subscription is a subscription for un-issued shares of an already existing corporation. Corporate statutes in most states typically make pre-incorporation subscriptions enforceable by the corporation for a limited period (usually six months) after the formation of the corporation. In such a case, the subscription is irrevocable by the subscriber and consideration is irrelevant. Of course the person who subscribes does not become a shareholder until the subscription price is fully paid. A *promoter* is a person who develops and organizes a corporation. That is, he or she procures the capital, assets, personnel, and facilities, and secures the subscriptions for shares. Then, usually as a last step, the promoter arranges for the corporation to be formed. The objective of the promoter is to take these actions in only the corporation's name, though a third person, especially a creditor, may want the personal liability of the promoter. The critical question concerns whether the promoter is personally liable for contracts made on behalf of the corporation. In a majority of states, the answer is "yes," even if the promoter signs the contract in the corporation's name and signs in a representative capacity. The promoter is construed in the majority of cases as an agent for a non-existent principal, that is, the corporation that has not yet been legally formed, and thus is personally liable. In order to avoid liability, the promoter is advised to obtain a continuing offer or an option on behalf of the corporation. After the corporation is formed, it is not automatically bound on pre-incorporation contracts entered into on its behalf because, once again, it did not exist and thus the promoter was not its agent. A corporation, however, may become liable for a promoter's contract by expressly or impliedly adopting them, or by accepting the continuing offer or option which the promoter made on the corporation's behalf. Promoters, it must be emphasized, are also regarded as fiduciaries and owe duties of trust, confidence, good faith, full disclosure, fairness, and honesty to the corporation and its shareholders (prospective as well as present). For example, if the promoter sells property to the corporation, the promoter must make full disclosure to the board of directors and to the shareholders and the contract for sale must be a fair one. The promoter, however, is not automatically entitled to reimbursement for expenses incurred in promoting or for any salary during the pre-incorporation period. Moreover, if there is a failure to incorporate, the promoter must return all money back to the subscribers and cannot deduct anything for expenses or salary.

Another major problem area in corporate law and practice concerns the defective formation of a corporation. That is, there are mistakes and delays in the filing of the articles. The mistakes can be minor, such as having an incorrect address, or major, such as an attorney preparing but then forgetting to file the articles. Delays naturally can result, for example, because the state's Secretary of State may decline to accept the first filing because of the minor defect that has to be, and which is, corrected. The problem is that in the meantime the "corporation" has commenced business. The overriding issue, at least for the "shareholders," is what is their liability for the obligations of this "corporation"? There are three legal doctrines that apply to this "defective" situation: 1) *de jure* corporate status, 2) *de facto* corporate status, and 3) corporation by estoppel. First, a *de jure corporation* is one in which the Secretary of State has accepted the articles and issued a certificate of incorporation, a charter, or a copy of the articles duly certified. Such status is conclusive evidence that the corporation is validly incorporated, even if there are mistakes and omissions, though the state can bring a legal action, called a *quo warranto* (by whose authority) proceeding to compel the corporation to correct any deficiencies or to cancel its charter. A *de facto* corporation is a most interesting concept indeed. In such a case, there is no *de jure* status; yet the corporation nonetheless will be recognized as a valid corporation for all purposes except as against the state. Accordingly, this doctrine can be used to "clothe" the "shareholders" of a defectively formed "corporation" with corporate attributes, in particular limited liability, as opposed to holding the "shareholders" to partner status. Generally speaking, most states would mandate the following three requirements for a *de facto* corporation: 1) a law under which such a corporation might be lawfully organized; 2) a good faith and *bona fide* attempt to organize and incorporate under the law (for example, a director's meeting, shares being issued, bylaws adopted, an attempt at filing of articles); and 3) an actual use and exercise of corporate powers (for example, some business being transacted as a corporation). A *corporation by estoppel* is a legal doctrine which may be used by the "shareholders" even when there is neither *de jure* nor *de facto* status. There is not a real corporation or even a *de facto* one; rather, there is an estoppel (that is, a preclusion) from denying corporate existence. Such an estoppel arises when a third party has dealt with the business as a corporation, for example, by contracting with or extending credit to the "corporation"; and in such a circumstance the third party is estopped (prevented) from even asserting that the corporation does not legally exist.

The limited liability that the corporate form of business organization provides to the investors is naturally a very attractive feature of this way of doing business. However, there is legal doctrine that maintains that even if a corporation has *de jure* status, a court may be able to disregard the corporate entity. This doctrine characteristically is called "*piercing the corporate veil*." Note, however, that the corporate "fiction" is a basic legal assumption, and there usually must be compelling evidence for a court to ignore the separate "corporateness" of the entity. Most often, this "piercing" legal doctrine comes into play when the corporation has sustained some type of liability and the corporation is insolvent; and a third party seeks to recover against the shareholders in their personal capacity. The court may based on this legal doctrine look through the fiction of the corporate entity and hold the persons doing business in the name of the corporation personally liable for corporate debts. However, this "piercing" doctrine can only be applied, if at all, against the shareholders of the corporation. There are two general requirements for a court to disregard the corporate entity. First, there must be demonstrated a unity of interest and ownership to the extent that the separate personalities of the corporation and its individual human components no longer exist. Second, there must be a showing that if the corporate entity is not disregarded, and the acts are treated as those of the corporation alone, the law will be violated or circumvented, or public policy contravened, or an unfair or unjust result will ensue. The "classic" example is when the sole shareholder sets fire to corporate property; and the corporation sues to recover on the fire insurance policy. However, it is important to note that it is not sufficient to "pierce the veil" merely because the primary motive for incorporating was to achieve limited liability. The lack of unity requirement means that the corporation is so organized and controlled to make the corporation merely an instrumentality, conduit, "shell," "dummy," or "alter ego" through which the individual shareholder(s), often a single shareholder, for convenience conduct business activities. There is no precise test to determine whether a corporation is a "dummy"; rather, a variety of factors are used, to wit: 1) the fact that all the shares are owned and controlled by a single shareholder or a small number of shareholders (but note that this fact in and of itself will be inadequate to disregard the corporate entity); 2) the fact that a single person governed or influenced the corporation (but again this factor alone is insufficient); 3) the business commenced without completing the organization of the corporation, for example, no shares were issued, no shareholders meetings were held, no directors were chosen or elected, and no officers were selected; 4) the corporate formalities and "routine" were not adhered to, for example, no dividends were issued, no meetings of shareholders and/or directors were held, no corporate records were kept, and no minute entries were made; 5) corporate property and funds were not kept separate; rather, they were commingled with the shareholders' personal property and funds; 6) corporate affairs are not distinct from the shareholders' personal affairs, for example, the execution of corporate contracts not in the corporate name as well as the use of the same office, attorney, letterhead, mailbox, website; and 7) if the corporate *capitalization* is regarded as "*thin.*" Regarding the final factor, the law expects a corporation to commence and carry on business with adequate capital and assets to meet reasonably foreseeable business needs, obligations, and risks. Unavoidable losses are permissible to suffer; capital is not necessary to cover every conceivable contingency. Yet not having adequate insurance, especially liability insurance to make a tort claimant "whole," as well as siphoning off funds to the shareholders, are consequential "piercing" factors. The rationale of the "unity" requirement is that it is inequitable for the "shareholders" to ignore the forms and rules of corporate organization and behavior, and then to later claim the advantage of the corporate limited liability "shield." The burden of showing that the corporation is a mere "dummy" is on the party alleging the doctrine; and this legal issue is regarded as a question of fact for a jury to decide. Of course, if a third party potential contract or creditor claimant against the corporation is concerned that the corporation may not be able to fulfill its contract or debt obligation, the third party can insist on the personal guarantee of the principal shareholders. Finally, it should be noted that the "piercing the corporate veil" doctrine also may apply in the case of a parent and subsidiary corporation. A subsidiary corporation is a separate and distinct corporation, though its "parent" is usually the sole or majority shareholder. There is nothing inherently wrong with a parent-subsidiary relationship, and the law does permit some commonality in boards, officers, employees, and shareholders, as well as a close functional working relationship; but when the subsidiary is a mere "conduit" for the parent, akin to a department or division, the subsidiary is "thinly" capitalized, the operations and assets too commingled, or the representations or advertising confuses the identities of the two, the corporate entity of the subsidiary can be disregarded. Of course, in such a case, the ultimate defendant is still a corporation, the parent!

Corporation - Director Rights and Responsibilities
The rights and responsibilities of directors and officers as well as shareholders are very important areas of corporate law and practice. The first task is to distinguish between directors and officers and then to describe their role in corporate governance and management. A *director* is a natural person designated in the articles, selected by the incorporators, or elected by the shareholders to act as directors; whereas *an officer* is a person in a position of authority and trust in regular and continuing employment at the corporation. Directors are the governing body of the corporation, while officers are "merely" administrative and executive officials. As such, directors may delegate management of the day-to-day business of the corporation to executive officials, so long as they remain under the ultimate direction and control of the board. Another difference between directors and officers is that individual directors are not regarded as agents of the corporation, while an officer is so regarded. However, as will be seen, when the directors act as a board, the directors collectively are regarded as an agent of the corporation. In most states, a corporation must have the following personnel: 1) a chairperson of the board, 2) a president or chief executive officer who is the general business manager of the corporation subject to the ultimate control by the board, 3) a chief financial officer, and 4) a secretary. These positions are provided for by the articles or bylaws. The same person may hold any number of offices in most states. Agency law principles cover the authority of these corporate officers as well as agents and employees of the corporation. The duty of selecting officers falls on the director(s). Directors are elected annually; whereas officers serve at the "pleasure" of the board; and consequently officers can be removed with or without cause by the board at any time (subject to any binding employment contract, of course). The officer of a corporation or the manager of a limited liability company is not personally responsible for the obligations of the entity so long as the officer or manager clearly indicates that he or she is signing in a representational capacity by naming the entity and indicating one's status as an officer or manager after one's signature.

Although the president of the corporation is the principal executive officer, the general manager, and an agent of the corporation, the president nonetheless "only" has the authority pursuant to agency law principles to make contracts and to do actions appropriate to the ordinary course of business. For example, the president has the authority, even by means of "incidental" agency authority, to make usual and regular hiring and firing decisions and to fix the compensation of employees. However, it is the board of directors that has the authority, the sole authority, to perform extraordinary or unusual transactions, for example, long-term employment contracts, real estate contracts (unless that is the regular business of the corporation), surety and guaranty contracts, employing legal counsel, making litigation decisions, negotiating loans, and incurring debts. The distinction, therefore, between presidential "ordinary" decisions and board "extraordinary" ones emerges as a critical and problematic one in corporate law and practice, as well as a "trap for the unwary." That is, a third party dealing with or contracting with the corporation must ensure that the corporation (the principal) is bound by the contract of the president (the officer-agent) of the corporation. If the president lacks agency authority to bind the corporation because the contract is deemed "extraordinary" for the board, then the corporation is not bound, though the president-officer-agent who exceeded his or her authority is bound. The third party, of course, wants the corporation-principal to be bound. So, what is the solution? If there is any doubt as to the nature of the contract or transaction, the third party must insist on a certified copy of the board resolution that authorized the contract or transaction, thereby empowering the president-officer-agent with actual agency authority.

The election, resignation, and removal of directors are areas that are regulated in detail by state corporate law; but some general observations must be offered. First, as to the qualifications for serving as a director, most states have an age requirement of 18 years of age, and some states require that the director must be a resident of the state and/or a shareholder of the corporation. The standard corporate board consists of 7 to 11 directors. A state corporation statute may specify a certain minimum number of directors; conversely, in some states a corporation may be allowed to have just one director. Directors as a general rule need not be shareholders of the corporation; but the state corporation statute, the articles of incorporation, or bylaws may impose this requirement.

Additional requirements can be specified in the bylaws, including, for example, the posting of a bond. Second, as to the number of directors, most states require that the number be stated in the articles. In some, though, naming the directors in the articles is optional; and if the number is not provided in the articles, it usually must be done in the bylaws. In some states, there is a minimum number of directors – three typically. However, now in most states, a corporation can have only one director. Yet even those states that require three will permit one or two if there are only one or two shareholders to the corporation. Subsequent to the initial board's service, directors are elected to hold office by the shareholders at their annual meeting, and the directors serve until the next annual meeting. Interim vacancies can be filled by either the board or the shareholders, depending on the state statute, and usually by a majority vote. Staggered terms for directors are permissible; and in fact a common practice, designed to ensure management continuity, is to elect one-third of the board each year for a three year period. Directors, any or all, can be removed by the shareholders at any time with or without cause in most states, though some will require a reason to be specified. Director(s) can also be removed by a court pursuant to a shareholder suit. However, a certain percentage of shareholders, usually 10%, will be required to bring the lawsuit; and in addition the shareholders will have to convince a judge that the director(s) engaged in dishonest or fraudulent acts or committed a gross abuse of authority or discretion.

A fundamental principle of corporate law is that for the directors to act and to legally bind the corporation, the directors must act collectively as a board. Most state statutes, however, do not require regular meetings of the board to be held at stated times; rather, the time and place of the meetings are addressed in the articles or bylaws. Regular meetings of the board do not require any notice so long as the time and place are fixed by the articles or bylaws. Special meetings of the board do require notice. Generally, a notice of a special meeting does not have to include its purpose. However, notice can be waived if the directors all meet as a board or a director without notice attends a meeting and does not object to the lack of notice. Moreover, in some states, any board action may be taken without any meeting if all the members of the board consent in writing to the action. Finally, meetings are allowed to be conducted now by conference telephone or other telecommunications equipment. The traditional requirement of the directors' physically meeting has been dispensed with in virtually all states. A quorum for a board meeting is a majority of all directors, that is, a majority of the entire board without vacancies, though the articles or bylaws may provide for a lesser or greater quorum number. When a quorum is present, a majority vote of the board of directors present constitutes a binding act or resolution of the board of directors of the corporation. Again, the articles or bylaws may require a larger voting percentage generally or for certain types of actions by the directors.

The *board of directors* is the governing body of the corporation. Directors collectively have the power to govern, control, and manage the corporation, subject to any restrictions in state statutes, the articles, or bylaws. It is a fundamental principle of corporate law that collective action by the board is required; that is, the powers vested in the directors can be exercised only in a collective capacity. As a result, no act is a valid corporate act unless generally it is done by the directors duly assembled as a board. The realities of everyday business practice, however, especially for a large corporation, mean that the directors' primary role is to formulate major policies, for example, a new product line, and to decide on extraordinary transactions, such as selling or leasing corporate assets out of the ordinary course of business, and very important contracts, such as major labor-management collective bargaining agreements, rather than to be directly involved in the daily management of the corporation. Accordingly, the board of directors can delegate the daily and ordinary management and business affairs to officers, employees, agents, and others, so long as these people are under the ultimate control and direction of the board. However, directors have certain statutory duties, such as declaring dividends and proposing, changing, and adopting bylaws, which cannot be delegated.

A board of directors, furthermore, is allowed to create board committees. That is, a board may appoint specific directors, with two being the standard minimum number, to executive committees to perform certain routine and ordinary board functions, such as the compensation of officers, and such a committee has the full authority of the board. However, the board cannot delegate total control and management to a committee. Again, state statutes will deem certain matters to require full board approval, ordinarily for example, any matter that requires shareholder approval, filling vacancies on the board, fixing the compensation of directors, amending, repealing, or adopting bylaws, or any other extraordinary matter. Because of the many functions of a board of directors as well as the heightened risk of legal liability, the board is allowed to create specialized committees composed of board members. Typical committees would be an executive committee, a compensation committee, an audit committee, a litigation committee, and a nominating committee. The board as a general rule is allowed to delegate to these board committees the power to act on behalf of the entire board. However, the usual state corporation statute would mandate that certain board powers must be exercised by the whole board and thus cannot be delegated to committees, for example, the power to declare dividends and authorize the issuance of stock, approve fundamental corporate change, such as a merger, appointing replacements for board vacancies, and amending the bylaws.

Compensation of directors always seems to emerge as a problematic corporate issue. The first compensation rule is that the articles or bylaws can fix the compensation of directors. The second rule is that absent any internal corporate rule the directors have the power to fix their own compensation unless negated in the articles or bylaws. Regarding the compensation of directors, in the past, directors normally were not compensated for their service to the corporation. However, in modern times, due to the increase in the amount of work and supervision required as a director as well as a marked increase in the legal liability for serving, most corporations in the U.S. today now compensate directors. Directors also may be shareholders of the corporation and thus may have an additional motive to serve, and to serve well, that is, to protect their investment. It is important to note that in many states directors are allowed by the state corporation statute to set their own compensation, but those statutes also allow for the negation of that power if there is a specific contrary provision in the articles of incorporation. In addition to compensation, many companies also pay directors for the expenses of attending meetings.

Directors, however, are regarded as fiduciaries and owe duties of trust and confidence to the corporation (though not directly to the shareholders). In most states, corporations are allowed to indemnify directors for expenses incurred in conducting corporate business, including payments to reimburse the director for legal costs, fees, and judgments sustained as a result of lawsuits against the director for his or her position or actions as a director. Moreover, most states permit the corporation to obtain insurance, called Directors and Officers Insurance (or "D&O Insurance") to protect directors and to cover indemnification. A court in some states may also order that a director be indemnified if the director acted in a fair and reasonable manner and in the best interests of the corporation.

The board of directors of a corporation has the authority and responsibility to oversee the CEO of the company and to make sure that his or her performance is sufficient. Accordingly, it is essential that the board members have point of views that are independent of those of the CEO and that may be at variance with the view of the CEO. That is, boards of directors are not there to merely "rubber-stamp" the CEO's decisions. Important functions of the board of directors regarding the CEO are to review the performance of the CEO each year and to set the CEO's compensation for the next year. Of course, in discharging the latter responsibility, the board can consult with specially formed consultation committees. In addition to overseeing the CEO, the primary functions of the board of directors include: establishing long-term corporate objectives and the policies and strategies to achieve these objectives; hiring and firing a chief executive officer (CEO) as well as other officers to implement policies and to operate the corporation on a daily basis; determining the contract and salaries for the CEO and other officers; declaring dividends and the nature and amount of dividends; deciding and approving fundamental corporate change, such mergers, consolidations, acquisitions, and amending the articles (with shareholder approval also in certain cases); determining new types of business for the corporation as well as exiting certain types of business; deciding whether to borrow money or to extend credit on behalf of the corporation; determining whether to issue new classes of stock or whether to buy back stock; and instituting litigation and hiring attorneys to represent the company. The board of directors of the corporation, as emphasized, does not exist to merely "rubberstamp" decisions of the CEO, but rather must be ready and prepared to have an independent perspective of the firm and to make decisions contrary to that of the CEO. The board thus should review the performance of the CEO each year and set the CEO's compensation for the next year.

The fiduciary status and duties of directors are very important corporate law principles. They are regarded as fiduciaries of the corporation and serve in a relationship of trust, confidence, honesty, and loyalty. Directors, however, at times serve on more than one corporate board. The fact that a director has many business affiliations is not in and of itself a violation of the fiduciary duty. However, a conflict of interest is forbidden, for example, serving on the boards of competing companies. Full disclosure of any potential conflict of interest must of course be made, as well as the disclosure of any transaction or contract in which the director has a material interest. Directors are also under a duty of due care. They are under a legal obligation to use reasonable and prudent business judgment in conducting corporate affairs. They are expected to attend board meetings and presentations, ask questions (and not sit silently as the Enron board did!), be informed, review reports and other materials, seek professional advice from lawyers and accountants and others, study options and alternatives, and make decisions based on information received from officers, professionals, and others. Nevertheless, directors are neither guarantors nor insurers of the corporation's business success. Directors are protected from "bad" decisions by a significant corporate rule, called the *"Business Judgment Rule."* This rule holds that if a director acts in a reasonable, prudent, good faith, and informed manner, but nonetheless makes an honest mistake in judgment or a poor business decision, and the corporation suffers thereby, the director is not liable to the corporation for damages. The "bad" director, of course, may be removed or not re-elected by the shareholders. Furthermore, several states now by statute permit directors to consider the consequences of a particular corporate course of conduct not just on the company and the shareholders, the primary stakeholder group, but also on the company's broader stakeholders, such as the employees, local communities, and society as a whole. If a director or directors breach the duties of trust and due care owed to the corporation, but the corporation (controlled by the directors) does not bring a cause of action for redress, the shareholders may be able to bring a lawsuit on behalf of the corporation by means of a "shareholder derivative suit." The shareholders must first petition the board of directors to bring the lawsuit, the shareholders typically must post a bond, and any recovery belongs to the corporation.

The board of directors of the corporation does not exist to merely "rubberstamp" decisions of the CEO, but rather must be ready and prepared to have a perspective of the firm and to make decisions contrary to that of the CEO. The board thus should review the performance of the CEO each year and set the CEO's compensation for the next year.

Corporate Constituency Statutes and Corporate Governance

Many states today now have statutes called either "constituency" or "stakeholder" statutes which permit the board of directors of the corporation to consider the interests and values of other stakeholders or constituency groups, beyond the shareholders, affected by the corporation's actions, such as the employees, suppliers and distributors, consumers and customers, the local community, and society as a whole. These statutes allow the directors to attempt to balance and align the values and interests of (at times competing) stakeholder groups; and even permit the directors to make decisions that favor one or more stakeholder group over the shareholders, who traditionally have been the sole focal point of corporate decision-making. These state statutes vary in scope and application, so naturally reference should be made to the pertinent state's corporate constituency statute. The vast majority of these statutes are "permissive," that is, the board of directors *may* consider the interests and values of other stakeholder groups beyond the shareholders; but the board is not required to do so. The subject of corporation constituency statutes as well as the new concept of a "social benefit corporation" or "B-corp" is discussed in detail in the *Business Ethics and Corporate Social Responsibility* chapter.

The term *corporate governance* encompasses the laws, rules, and doctrines that govern a corporation and its operations. The basic model of corporate governance entails the shareholders, the owners of the corporation, who elect the board of directors, which sets long-term corporate goals and the policies and strategies to achieve those goals, as well as appoints officers to implement the policies and strategies and run the corporation on a daily basis. Corporate governance in a broader sense includes all the laws and regulations, governmental as well as internal corporate rules, which govern the corporation, as well as ethical and social responsibility doctrines that are used today to evaluate corporate activities. The goal of corporate governance is to have a successful, just, and sustainable corporation. The topic of corporate governance will be further explicated in the *Business Ethics and Corporate Social Responsibility* chapter.

Corporation - Shareholder Rights and Responsibilities

The next important area of corporate law to address is the shareholders, who are in fact the owners of the corporation. What is their status? What are their rights and duties? The technical legal definition of a "*shareholder*" is a "holder of record of shares." Shareholders are the human ownership component of the corporation. Generally, anyone with capacity to contract may be a shareholder; and a corporation can be a shareholder of another corporation. One may become a shareholder by an original purchase of shares or by transfer of another person's shares. The relationship of the shareholders to the corporation is a contractual one, defined principally by state statute, the articles, and the bylaws. Evidence of shareholder status usually is ascertained from the certificate for shares and by the corporate records. Eligibility to vote at corporate elections, it must be emphasized, is determined conclusively in most states by the corporate records, even though a determination as to who possesses title to shares may be later judicially determined. Furthermore, the shareholder retains his or her status and relationship until there is a transfer of shares registered on the corporate books.

Shareholders possess several important rights and interests in the corporation. Generally, a share of stock is regarded as property (of the intangible kind) and gives the shareholder an ownership interest in the corporation. This interest is the right to participate in profits and, upon dissolution and termination, the right to share in any distribution of assets. Shareholders, however, have no right or claim to corporate property in their individual capacities, and as such shareholders cannot dispose of title to corporate property. When dealing with the corporation, the shareholder is regarded as a separate entity separate and distinct from the corporation. As a result, a corporation may enter into a contract with shareholders and may buy and sell property with shareholders. As a general rule, shareholders are not fiduciaries; but a dominant or controlling shareholder may be construed as owing fiduciary duties, and not just to the corporation but also to minority (in number) shareholders. The rule is that such a dominant or controlling shareholder will not be allowed to use his or her power to control the activities of the corporation for only self-benefit and in a manner detrimental to minority shareholders. Shareholders, individually or collectively, are neither regarded as agents or representatives of the corporation, nor are authorized to perform any corporate acts. The shareholder's authority is limited in corporate matters principally to the right to vote for directors. Although shareholders are the ultimate owners of the corporation, they have no power to directly control the corporation as far as the day-to-day management of corporate affairs. Rather, shareholders have several indirect methods of controlling the corporation, such as by electing directors, removing directors, approving amendments to the articles, approving, amending, or repealing bylaws, and approving fundamental change. Shareholders, of course, can always consult with and make recommendations to the board of directors as well as protest to the board. Shareholders also have the right to inspect the corporation's books, records, and properties. Moreover, this right cannot be defeated or unreasonably restricted by the articles or bylaws. However, the purpose of the inspection must be a proper one reasonably related to the shareholder's interest and not for the purposes of harassment or obtaining confidential information. In addition, a written demand is usually necessary; and the inspection must occur at a reasonable time. In some states, a shareholder must hold a minimum number of shares (for example, 5%) for a minimum period of time before the shareholder can exercise the right to inspect. However, a court can order an inspection or appoint an accountant for an audit if any shareholder can demonstrate sufficient grounds, such as fraud or waste being committed.

Shareholders meetings are a very critical component to corporate law and practice. Annual meetings must be held; the place is usually fixed in the bylaws (or the place is deemed to be the principal executive office of the corporation); and the time is also usually fixed in the bylaws. The chief purpose of the *annual meeting* is the election of directors. The power to elect directors is vested in the shareholders at the annual meeting; and the corporation cannot divest shareholders of that vital right and power. However, any other proper business may be conducted (though there may be notice requirements as to the proposed transactions). A *special meeting* is any meeting other than an annual meeting. A special meeting ordinarily is called by the board, its chairperson, the president or CEO, or in most states shareholders holding not less than 10% of the voting shares. The purpose of a special meeting can be for any purpose; but only subjects described in the written notice of the special meeting can be acted upon. As a general rule, when the shareholders are required or permitted to take any action at a meeting, written notice of the meeting must be given to each shareholder entitled to vote. The notice must specify the date, place, and hour of the meeting. If the notice is for a special meeting, the nature of the business to be conducted must be noted. If the purpose of the meeting is to elect directors, the names of the nominees must be stated. In some states, obtaining the written consent of all the shareholders is sufficient to authorize an action, even without a meeting or notice. For a meeting, general or special, a quorum is necessary. *A quorum* is a majority of shares entitled to vote (in person or by proxy); but the articles or bylaws may increase or decrease the quorum requirements, though in the latter case in some states to no less than one third of the shares. Once a quorum is present, a majority of the shares present voted binds the corporation. The articles or bylaws can increase that amount, but not decrease it in most states. A shareholder is entitled to one vote, per share, per subject. A corporation is required to keep a written record, that is, "minutes," of the meeting. Voting at a meeting need not be done by ballot, unless a shareholder demands it before a vote or the bylaws require a ballot. The record date is the day on which eligibility to vote is determined, which date characteristically is set by the directors or bylaws, and which is set usually 10-50 days before each shareholder meeting. "Record holders" are holders of voting shares on the record date and are thus eligible to vote at the meeting. A voting list of shareholders eligible to vote at the meeting must be prepared before each shareholder meeting and must be available for inspection. Shareholders may authorize another person, not necessarily a shareholder, to vote the shareholder's shares as well as to exercise shareholder discretion. Such an arrangement is called a "proxy." The articles cannot deny or unreasonably restrict the proxy rights of shareholders. A proxy must be written but ordinarily there is no required form. Usually, the duration of a proxy is eleven months from its date (and thus a new proxy would be necessary for the next meeting) unless stated otherwise. Proxies are revocable by the shareholder, even if a proxy says it is irrevocable and consideration was present. A proxy can be revoked by a written revocation delivered to the corporation, a subsequent proxy given by the same shareholder, the voting in person by the same shareholder, or by the death of the shareholder once the corporation receives notice thereof. The percentage of shareholder vote required is a majority of voting shares present, presuming a quorum; however, the articles or bylaws usually can increase, but not decrease, the percentage of shares required for the election of directors.

An interesting and important shareholder voting right is called "*cumulative voting.*" Cumulative voting means that a shareholder is entitled to vote one vote for each share in the shareholder's name; and at the election for directors the shareholder may "cumulate" his or her votes. That is, the shareholder's votes equal the number of shares multiplied by the number of directors to be elected; and then the shareholder can vote all these votes for one candidate for director (or the shareholder can distribute the votes as he or she sees fit over one or more candidates). Of course, cumulative voting works only if the there is plurality voting; that is, the directors are running "at large" rather than for specific places; and the candidates receiving the highest number of votes up to the number of directors to be chosen are winners. There are several standard requirements for cumulative voting, to wit: 1) the candidates' names must be placed in nomination prior to voting; 2) at least one shareholder has given advance notice prior to the meeting of his or her intent to vote cumulatively; 3) if one shareholder gives notice of intent, all shareholders may accumulate; 4) all directors to be chosen must be voted for at one time; and 5) in most states, the shareholder's right to cumulative voting must be granted by specific provision in the articles of corporation. The purpose of cumulative voting is not to enable certain shareholders to control the board of directors; rather, the objective is to ensure some minority representation on the board.

Other voting mechanisms for shareholders to exercise (at least indirectly) their authority are the "pooling agreement" and the "voting trust." *A pooling agreement* is an agreement between two or more shareholders who agree that their shares will be voted as specifically provided for in the agreement. The result is that shares are voted in a bloc. The standard requirements for a pooling agreement are that it be written, signed, for a proper purpose, such as to maintain control and to ensure stable management, only to be used for matters within the province of shareholders, and for a limited duration in most states. Pooling agreements can be enforced by a decree of specific performance. *A voting trust* arises when shareholders transfer legal title of shares to a trustee, who becomes the record holder of the shares. The trustee is a fiduciary who in the usual case votes the shares in accordance with the terms in the trust, though the trustee can be accorded discretion in voting. The equitable ownership of the shares, and thus the right to receive dividends, remain with the shareholders who get a voting trust certificate. The standard requirements for a valid voting trust are that it must be written and signed, irrevocable, with a usual statutory maximum period of 10 years, and for a proper purpose, such as maintaining control.

Shareholders also can impose restrictions on the transfer of shares. As a general rule, in the absence of any specific agreement, shares of stock are freely transferable; but restrictions on the transfer of shares may be valid, and may be very important especially in a small or closely-held corporation. The three most common means of restricting the transferability of shares are the option, the buy-sell agreement, and the right-of-first-refusal. An option can be granted to the corporation or to shareholders (usually proportionately) to purchase shares at a designated price. If the corporation or other shareholders refuse to exercise their option, the selling shareholder can offer shares to outsiders. *A buy-sell* agreement makes it contractually mandatory for the corporation or other shareholders to buy shares. The *right-of-first-refusal* gives the corporation or other shareholders the right to meet the best price that the selling shareholder has been able to obtain from outsiders. The reasons for these restrictions on the ordinarily free transfer of shares, which is a traditional positive attribute of a corporation, are to enable the participants in the corporation to decide who will participate, to ensure stable management, to protect against unexpected changes in the corporate ownership interests, and to maintain relative secrecy. The legal validity of such restrictions depends on whether they unreasonably restrain or prohibit the transferability of shares. For example, a total prohibition would usually be struck down, though a long one may be upheld. In most states, the restrictions must appear in the articles or bylaws, or perhaps in an agreement among the shareholders, and must be for a lawful purpose, for example, preventing outsiders or maintaining proportionate shareholder interests. An indispensable requirement is that the restriction must be noted conspicuously on each share subject to the restriction. Without such notice, any restriction is unenforceable against a person without knowledge. One problem with all these transfer restrictions is establishing the price for the stock, especially since in small or closely-held corporations there is generally no established market for the shares. Presumably in all these agreements, there is a stated price; but if not the "book value" of shares or the best offer by an outsider may be used, or failing all those methods, arbitration can be utilized. A stock warrant is a right granted to a person for a given period of time to purchase a stated amount of stock at a stated price. The price is usually equal to the fair market value of the stock when the warrant is issued, thereby allowing the holder of the warrant to benefit from any increase in the value of the stock. The stock warrant is different from the stock option in that the latter is granted only to a company's directors, officers, and employees in connection with their services to the company, whereas the former is sold to investors.

One of the most common forms of share transfer restrictions, typically found in a small, family, or closely-held corporation, is the *right-of-first-refusal*. Pursuant to this legal concept, if a shareholder wants to transfer his or her shares of the company, the company or the shareholders (or who is specifically designated in the agreement) first must be given the opportunity to purchase the stock based on the terms and conditions offered by a third-party purchaser. Usually there is a time period from between 30 to 90 days to purchase the stock which period commences after receiving notice of the proposed sale. Furthermore, if the company or other shareholders are unable or unwilling to purchase the stock the selling shareholder is free to sell to the third-party purchaser.

A *buy-sell agreement* is another legal device used to restrict the transfer of shares of stock and thus to ensure that the ownership of the shares of stock of a company remains with a small group of shareholders. Characteristically, such an agreement allows or even obligates a corporation or other parties named in the agreement to purchase at fair market value another party's stock that a party is obligated to sell when certain events occur, for example, when an employee leaves the corporation.

Dividends are certainly an important part of any corporate legal and practical analysis, obviously for the shareholders. Dividends are the share of corporate profits to be apportioned among the shareholders as a return on their investment. However, until dividends are declared by the corporation, the profits made by the corporation remain with the corporate entity. Once declared, that portion of the profits declared as dividends becomes the property of the shareholders. Moreover, once declared, dividends represent a debt owed by the corporation to the shareholders which can be enforced legally by the shareholders unless funds are not available to pay the dividends. Shareholders who are "shareholders of record," that is, officially on the corporate books as shareholders, on a specific date, the *"record date,"* are entitled to dividends. Dividends can be paid in cash, property, or stock. A stock dividend is the payment of stock to the shareholder from the corporation's own authorized but un-issued. A stock "split" is not a dividend; rather, the value of the share of stock is reduced accordingly. All states have rules as to when dividends can be paid and from what corporate accounts. It is beyond the purposes of this book to examine this complex area of state law. Yet certain important points must be made. First, the states are consistent in holding that if a corporation is insolvent or would likely to be made insolvent, no dividends are permitted. Similarly, if the corporation cannot meet its current obligations, or would be likely as a result of the payment of dividends to be unable to meet its obligations, the payment of dividends is not permissible. Second, in all states, dividends can be paid from retained earnings. Third, in some states, dividends can be paid from current net earnings, that is, yearly net profits; but in most states dividends cannot be paid from current earnings. These prohibited dividends are at times called *"nimble dividends."* If the directors make an improper payment of dividends they may be held personally liable to the corporation and its creditors for the amount. Also, shareholders who receive the dividends, knowing that they are improper, are also personally liable to the corporation and its creditors for the funds. As to the payment, amount, and timing of a dividend declaration, state corporate statutes characteristically repose a great deal of discretion in the board of directors. As a result, the directors' decision as to dividends ordinarily will not be "second-guessed" by the courts, so long as the directors are acting in good faith and with the corporate welfare in mind. Consequently, as a general rule, shareholders cannot compel a corporate board to declare dividends. However, if there is a very large surplus (and not just a "mere" surplus), and the board has no definite plans to use it, the shareholders may be able to convince a court to compel the directors to declare dividends.

The capital structure of the corporation is obviously another central corporate area to examine, though any detailed explanation thereof is beyond the purposes of this book, and is more appropriate for a corporate finance work. However, certain critical definitions and salient points must be made. The corporation's debt securities represent creditor interests that must be ultimately repaid. There are two main types: 1) *a bond* which is a debt obligation secured by a lien or mortgage on corporate property; and 2) *a debenture* which is an unsecured corporate obligation. *Capital stock* consists of 1) authorized capital, 2) common stock, and 3) preferred stock. *Authorized capital* is the total number and kind of shares which the corporation is authorized to issue, and which ordinarily must be stated in the articles. There is no limit on the number of shares that may be authorized; there is no requirement that all or any specific portion of the authorized shares actually be issued; and a corporation may issue fewer shares than authorized, but not more unless the articles are amended. *Common stock* consists of the shares that have no preference over any other class of shares with regard to payment of dividends or distribution of assets upon liquidation. The corporation must have at least one class of common stock because common stock represents the residual ownership of the corporation as well as the ultimate claim to profits and assets. Ordinarily, common stock is voting stock, though it is permissible to have a non-voting class of common stock too. Shares of common stock are also known as equity securities. *Preferred stock* consists of the shares of stock that are not common. Preferred stock can be voting though it usually is non-voting stock. A corporation is allowed to have a variety of preferences or priorities as to dividends and asset distribution; and these preferences must be stated in the articles. Three corporate finance terms are fundamental: 1) par value, 2) stated capital, and 3) capital surplus. The articles generally must state the value of par for each class of shares or state that the shares are without par. Par value refers to the amount designated as such by the incorporators and draftsperson of the articles. Note that usually this amount is a nominal amount and not a true indication of the actual price of the shares. The stated capital is the par value of shares issued with par value and the entire amount of consideration received for no par shares. Stated capital represents the initial investment money placed at risk of the business by the shareholders. Of course, there is no uniform requirement that any specific amount be placed in stated capital. Capital surplus also represents part of the investment capital placed at risk of the business by the shareholders. Capital surplus consists of the consideration paid for par value shares in excess of par as well as that portion of the consideration received for no par shares which is not allocated to stated capital. The distinction between stated capital and capital surplus is very important. Why? In most jurisdictions a corporation has greater legal latitude to issue dividends or make distributions from capital surplus. States also have rules for the quality and amount of consideration to be paid for shares. Generally, shares are issued for consideration as determined by the board of directors. Consideration may consist of money paid, labor done, services rendered, debts or claims cancelled, or tangible or intangible property, such as good will or patent or contract rights. The judgment of directors as to the value of consideration is usually conclusive and binding absent fraud or bad faith, for example, a gross estimation of services performed for the corporation resulting in "watered" stock. Note, however, that in the case of labor or service, consideration is legal payment for shares only if the labor and services are performed; future services and labor do not constitute consideration.

Preemptive rights are an important corporate concept. The purpose of preemptive rights is to protect shareholders' proportionate interests in the event of issue of additional shares. Preemptive rights are defined as the right to preempt, or to purchase before others, a new issue of shares in proportion to the shareholder's present interest in the corporation. There is one significant constraint on preemptive rights; that is, shareholders do not have them in most states unless they are explicitly provided for in the articles of incorporation. Also, preemptive rights only apply to shares previously unauthorized, and not to previously authorized but un-issued shares. In addition, the preemptive right can be exercised only for the same class of stock. The price for a "preemptive" purchase of a share must be a fair one, and thus not more than any subsequent offer to others. If a shareholder does not or cannot exercise his or her preemptive rights, the shareholder ordinarily cannot complain, even if he or she was financially unable to purchase the shares.

Fundamental Corporate Change

The final area of corporate law concerns fundamental corporate change. The major types of change to consider are as follows: 1) amending the articles of incorporation, 2) merging corporations, 3) consolidating corporations, 4) purchasing corporate assets, 5) purchasing controlling shares of stock of a corporation, and 6) dissolving and terminating corporations. First, regarding amending the articles, the rule is that a corporation may amend its articles at any time. The amendment may include any provision which would have been lawful to include in the original articles. The standard amendment procedure is as follows: approval by the board; then approval by the shareholders generally by a majority of shareholders entitled to vote; but if any amendment would affect adversely any class or series of stock, those shareholders are entitled to vote separately, even if their shares are non-voting shares; and finally filing to and approval by the state.

The next type of fundamental change is the *merger*. However, it initially is necessary to distinguish between a merger and a consolidation. A merger is a legal combination of two or more corporations; and after the merger only one corporation continues to exist; and the surviving corporation issues shares or pays consideration to the shareholders of the disappearing corporation. A *consolidation* is the combination of two or more corporations so that each corporation ceases to exist and a new corporate entity emerges. In a merger, the surviving/absorbing corporation is recognized as a single corporation. As such, it possesses all the rights, privileges, and powers of itself as well as the disappearing corporation; it automatically acquires all of the disappearing corporation's property and assets without the necessity of a formal transfer; and it becomes liable for all the disappearing corporation's debts and obligations. The results of a consolidation are essentially the same as a merger; in fact, in some states the concept of corporate consolidation has been abolished; and merger law is used to in essence create a new entity. All states have statutes authorizing mergers under certain conditions; moreover, federal and international antitrust may have to be taken into consideration too. The basic state requirements for a merger are as follows: 1) The board of directors of each corporation must approve the merger plan. 2) The shareholders of each corporation must approve the plan at a shareholder meeting. In most states, merger approval requires a two-third vote. In addition, each class of stock must approve the merger, including the holders of non-voting stock. 3) A merger plan is filed with the state's Secretary of State. 4) When the state merger requirements are deemed to be satisfied, the state issues a certificate of merger to the surviving corporation. There also must be noted a special type of merger, called either a "*short form*" or "*parent-subsidiary*" merger, that some states subscribe to, and which is found in the Revised Model Business Corporation Act. Essentially, this type of merger has a simplified procedure when a parent corporation seeks to merge a substantially owned subsidiary corporation into the parent. This "simple" merger can be accomplished without the approval of the shareholders of either corporation; the only approval that is needed is the approval of the board of directors of the parent. There is one main requirement. The parent must own at least 90% (or 80% in some states) of the outstanding shares of each class of stock of the subsidiary corporation. What if a shareholder objects to the merger? Such a shareholder possesses dissenting rights, usually called "appraisal rights." The rationale behind this legal doctrine is that a shareholder should not be forced to become an unwilling shareholder in a different corporation. The appraisal right is the right to dissent to certain fundamental change, such as the merger, and to be paid a fair value for the number of shares held on the date of the merger. Generally speaking, appraisal rights apply in addition to mergers to consolidations, and the sales of substantially all corporate assets. They do not apply to shareholders in a short-form merger. Once again, the states have detailed statutory procedures that must be followed exactly for a shareholder to take advantage of his or her appraisal. In general, the mandatory steps are as follows: 1) A written notice of dissent must be filed by the shareholder prior to the vote. 2) After the merger or other applicable fundamental change is approved, the shareholder must make a written demand for payment. 3) Then, the shareholder is entitled to "fair value" for his or her shares based on the value on the day of the vote. 4) If the shareholder and the corporation cannot agree, a court will determine the value.

The purchase and sale of assets and the purchase and sale of stock may rise to the level of fundamental corporate change. First, regarding the purchase of assets, when a corporation acquires all or substantially all of the assets of another corporation by direct purchase, the acquiring corporation simply extends ownership control over those physical assets. Shareholder approval of the shareholders of the acquiring corporation generally is not required; however, for the corporation selling its assets, the board of directors must approve the sale and also the shareholders unless the sale is in the ordinary course of business. Dissenting and appraisal rights exist for the shareholders of the selling corporation. As a general rule, the acquiring corporation is not liable for the obligations of the selling corporation unless there is an express or implied assumption of the selling corporation's liabilities, the sale is really a merger (a *de facto* merger), or the acquiring corporation continues the selling corporation's business and retains its same personnel. As an alternative to the purchase of corporate assets, a corporation can purchase a substantial number of voting shares of stock of another corporation. The effect is that the purchasing corporation can control the other corporation. In such a case, the purchasing corporation has to deal directly with the shareholders in an effort to purchase their shares. Such a public offer to purchase is called a "tender offer" and is regulated by state and federal securities laws.

The final fundamental change is the dissolution and termination of the corporation. Dissolution is the cessation of corporate business, except for winding up, which leads to the termination and legal "death" of the artificial corporate person. Liquidation or winding up is the process by which corporate assets are converted to cash and distributed among the creditors and shareholders. Dissolution can occur in a variety of ways, as follows: 1) Dissolution can be voluntary. Usually dissolution must be approved by the board and the shareholders or in some states by the written unanimous consent (or a supra-majority in some states) of the shareholders. 2) Dissolution can occur involuntarily by the state's Secretary of State or other equivalent officer when the corporation fails to comply with the state's administrative requirements, such as the failure to pay its annual taxes, the failure to submit an annual report, or the failure to have a registered office or agent in the state. 3) Finally, dissolution can be effectuated judicially in three main instances: a) The Attorney General of the state or equivalent legal officer can seek a judicial dissolution of the corporation if its articles were procured by fraud, the corporation has exceeded its powers or purposes, or for violating the law. b) The shareholders can seek a judicial dissolution if they have sufficient grounds, for example, when the business has been abandoned for a period of time, usually one year, or the directors are deadlocked and the shareholders cannot break the deadlock and irreparable harm is being suffered by, or is threatened to, the corporation. Other grounds for judicial dissolution by shareholders are when the shareholders themselves cannot elect directors, when corporate assets are being misapplied or wasted, or when there is fraud or abuse of authority. Note in some states the "mere" fact that the business is not profitable and is not likely to be profitable or that the company is being mismanaged is insufficient shareholder grounds for dissolution. Moreover, in most states a designated number of shareholders must join the petition for judicial dissolution, usually one-third of the shareholders, but only one in a small, closely-held corporation. c) A creditor of the corporation can seek judicial dissolution if the creditor possesses an unsatisfied judgment and the corporation is insolvent. The standard dissolution-liquidation-termination procedures in a voluntary action are as follows: 1) The board of directors acts as a trustee for corporate assets. 2) The corporation ceases business except for winding up. 3) No new business is conducted. 4) The corporation must send a notice to each known creditor and claimant. 5) Present rights and claims are not adversely affected by the dissolution; but the board of directors must put a reasonable fund together to satisfy future claimants, who generally have a three year period to present any claims. 6) An "articles of dissolution" is filed with the state, usually after liquidation. 7) The date the articles was received and approved by the state is the official dissolution date and thereby the termination of the corporation. Note that a state will not approve the dissolution if there are any pending claims or lawsuits against the corporation or if there is no provision for future liability. Shareholders are not liable beyond their initial investment in the corporation and for not more than any assets distributed to the shareholder.

How should one compensate employees in a start-up corporation? One effective way is to utilize stock options to attract talented, hard-working, and ambitious employees. Many people may be encouraged to join an entrepreneurial company due to the opportunity to receive equity incentives, in particular, stock options. The smart entrepreneur thus can use stock options as a compensation device. Usually, a start-up company will create a group of shares pursuant to a formal stock option plan that has been approved by the board of directors and the shareholders. Then, options to purchase stock can be made from this group of shares. Typically, an entrepreneurial firm will devote about 20% of its shares for issuance to employees as stock options. The price of such stock is usually the fair market price of the stock at the time the option is granted.

An S Corporation is one that was in essence created by federal tax law in the United States. The Internal Revenue Code allows certain shareholders to have a corporate business while being taxed as individuals. "S" refers to the pertinent section in the tax code. The S corporation entity does not pay income taxes; rather, the profits (or losses) of the entity are "passed through" to the individual shareholders who report them on their individual tax returns. These profits and losses must be allocated based on the share ownership in the corporation. The advantage to the S corporation is thus clear: there is no "double taxation"; profits earned by the S corporation are only taxed once. The S corporation, therefore, would be a very attractive investment vehicle for investors who do not work for the company. However, if the shareholders in the S corporation are also employees who receive salary and bonuses, which are deductible, then the rationale for forming an S corporation is not as strong. There are certain requirements to forming an S corporation. An S corporation can have no more than 100 shareholders; almost all of whom must be individuals; none of whom can be non-resident aliens; and the S corporation can only have one class of stock. These requirements mean that the S corporation will not be able to have access to a wide capital pool due to the shareholder limitations as well as the fact that international and institutional investors, such as other corporations, are prevented from being shareholders. Also, because of the one class of stock requirement, the S corporation cannot issue inexpensively priced stock to promoters and organizers, and must issue stock to employees at the same price paid by investors (assuming during the same time period).

Corporation – Criminal Liability

The corporation as a legal entity can be held criminally liable. The corporation, of course, is an artificial person, so it cannot be imprisoned like a real person, but the corporation can be fined criminally, and it can lose its charter and/or business licenses. For a corporation to be deemed to be criminally liable, the "real" people "behind" the corporation – the directors, officers, employees, and agents – must have acted in the course and scope of their employment on behalf of the corporation. However, to hold the corporation criminally liable there typically must be evidence that the corporation knew of or should have known of the wrongdoing and failed to prevent it or that there was authority for, knowledge of, or consent to the wrongdoing by corporate personnel in executive or managerial positions. Of course, the corporate personnel committing the criminal acts can be held personally criminally responsible too, even if the crimes were committed for the corporation's benefit.

Regarding punishment for corporate wrongdoing, in 2003 the United States Sentencing Commission, which is a federal agency created by Congress to establish fair, consistent, and effective criminal sentences, which a sentencing judge must select within certain guidelines, significantly increased the potential prison time for corporate wrongdoers as well as fines for the corporation. However, there are several mitigating factors, to wit: whether directors, officers, and employees knew of and condoned the criminal conduct or were they purposefully ignorant; whether these personnel cooperated with government investigators and prosecutors in the investigation of the case and the bringing of criminal charges; whether the corporation had an effective compliance program in existence at the time of the wrongdoing; and whether any attempts were made to correct the misconduct and to punish wrongdoing personnel. The government objective is to set severe fines and penalties, but then give companies and their personnel a significant incentive in the form of reduced fines and prison sentences if they have compliance programs, self-report wrongdoing to the government, and cooperate with the government in the investigation and prosecution of wrongdoing.

SEC Corporate CEO Pay Rules

Pursuant to the power granted to it by Congress in the Securities Acts of 1933 and 1934 as well as the Sarbanes-Oxley Act of 2002 and the Dodd-Frank Wall Street Reform and Consumer Protection Act of 2010, the federal Securities and Exchange Commission (SEC) has promulgated rules regarding CEO pay and performance disclosures. The Dodd-Frank Act was an attempt to protect consumers, principally by creating the Consumer Protection Financial Bureau (which takes complaints from consumers about financial companies, publishes the complaints on a website, and attempts to resolve them), as well as to eliminate financial bailouts (particularly created by the pre-recession "too-big-to-fail" mentality for banks and other financial institutions) by restricting banks from investing and trading in hedge funds, establishing new capital and liquidity requirements, and establishing mandatory annual "stress tests" for banks with more than $10 billion in assets (and prohibiting the banks who do poorly on the tests from paying dividends). The SEC has already promulgated shareholder votes to approve or disapprove CEO compensation, called "say-on-pay," but those votes are non-binding; and they only have to occur at least once every three years, though the expectation is that a negative vote will prompt CEOs to respond to shareholder concerns. The vast majority of companies reported shareholder approval of CEO pay. Yet one rare exception occurred in 2018 when shareholders at the Walt Disney Co., in a non-binding vote, by a 52% margin refused to endorse the proposed compensation of Chairman and Chief Executive Robert Iger. Nevertheless, the Disney board of directors, stated that although they would take the shareholder non-binding vote into account for future compensation decisions, the board would go ahead with Iger's compensation plan, which includes the receipt of up to $142 million, a salary of $3 million a possible $500,000 raise, and a possible bonus of up to $20 million, since the compensation, according to the board, was in the best interest of the company and essential to the company's successful purchase of the assets of 21st Century Fox. Also, another major exception occurred too in 2018 when the shareholders of Wynn Resorts, Ltd voted by an 80% margin to register their dissent to the company's executive compensation plan pursuant to the SEC say-on-pay rule, including disapproving former CEO Steve Wynn's compensation package, which included a stock grant of 200,000 shares valued at over $19 million. Wynn resigned in 2017 due to sexual misconduct allegations. Perhaps not coincidentally the company's board of directors' compensation committee will now be composed of three new female directors. Moreover, the SEC also has promulgated rules that would compel companies to disclose the ratio between their chief executives' annual compensation and the median pay of employees. The new disclosure rules, which, as with the previous rules, would only apply to publicly-traded companies regulated by the SEC, would make it easier for shareholders and investors to ascertain whether executive compensation is in conformity with a company's financial performance. The rules would require that companies inform shareholders how well executives' pay followed corporate performance over a several years period. The SEC will require these pay-for-performance disclosures to cover a period of up to five years. Moreover, companies must compare themselves with a corporate "peer group" of their choosing. For the CEO, a company would have to provide his or her actual pay, but only average figures for other top executives. The objective of the rules is to give shareholders and investors greater understanding about the relationship between what corporate executives are paid each year and the total return for shareholders, that is, the annual change in stock price plus reinvested dividends. The expectation is that establishing a consistency between pay and performance would pressure companies to change their compensation practices if there is a big gap between pay and performance or if a company's compensation practices are not in alignment with their peers. Any marked disconnect between pay and performance would certainly be important information for the shareholders, investors, and the public, and likely would cause a loud outcry; consequently, any large gap should emerge as an area of corporate concern and redress. SEC rules, based on the 2010 Dodd-Frank Act, also require that publicly traded companies disclose the ratio between CEOs' total reported pay, including salary, bonuses, and equity rewards as well as any other benefits, and the pay of median workers at their companies. One 2018 study of a group of U.S. top executives, conducted by Equilar, found that the executives earned 140 times more than their workers. Consumer groups argue that publishing such ratios will help to reduce executive pay as well as the ratio between executive and worker pay; yet critics contend that it is difficult to calculate pay as well as pay ratios, especially across different industries and businesses, and that the information produced will have an inflammatory effect and will be used to unfairly condemn executives. Nevertheless, in 2018, 50 major companies reported the ratios. For example, Bank of America reported that its CEO made $23 million in 2017, whereas the median bank employee had total compensation of $87,115, which is about 250 times as much. Whirlpool Corp. reported the median pay of a full-time worker at $19,000 a year compared to the CEO pay of $7.8 million, which was 356 times as much. Heinz Co. reported the median worker's compensation as $46,000 whereas the CEO received $4.2 million, which was 91 times more. To compare, Kellogg Co. paid its CEO $7.3 million and its median employee $40,000, or 183 times more. The biggest disparity reported was at the Marathon Petroleum Corp., where the median worker made just over $24,000 and where the CEO made $19.7 million, which was 935 times more. However, as permitted by the SEC, companies are allowed to provide supplemental explanatory materials along with the ratio disclosures. As such, Marathon explained that many of its employees work at convenience stores and gas stations of its Speedway unit and are part-time employees. If those workers were excluded the median pay would be about $126,000 and thus lower the ratio to 156 to 1.

SEC and Whistleblowers
In order to obtain more evidence securities fraud, the Securities and Exchange Commission pursuant to the power given to it by the Dodd-Frank financial reform act now can pay whistleblowers who disclose information on potential securities law violations. The whistleblowers can receive 10-30% of the sum of penalties collected if the information leads to an SEC enforcement action with sanctions of more than $1 million. This incentive program has been very successful in bringing tipsters and their information to the SEC. However, in order to receive the bounty as well as to be protected from retaliation in employment the whistleblower must report the potential fraud to the SEC. In a 2018 Supreme Court case, *Digital Realty Trust v. Somers*, the

court dismissed a case by the vice-president of a real estate investment trust who was terminated after he filed a complaint with top executives of the company about hidden cost-overruns in an Asian branch office. The Supreme Court ruled that the specific and explicit language in Dodd-Frank required him to first report the potential fraud to the SEC and not just internally to the company. Accordingly, if Congress meant to include a greater scope of protection for whistleblowers the court implied that Congress would have to amend the legislation. The recent Supreme Court decision emphasizes that an employee seeking protection under this statute or for that matter any whistleblower protection statute – federal, state, or local – must strictly adhere to the requirements and conditions of the statute and thus the whistleblowing employee first should seek advice from legal counsel as well as the Whistleblower Protection Organization.

Limited Liability Company

In recent years, a majority of states in the United States have approved a new form of doing business; that is, a new "hybrid" business entity, called *a limited liability company* (LLC). In 1995, in order to promote harmony among the states' LLC laws, a Uniform Limited Liability Company Act was created by the National Conference of Commissioners on Uniform State Laws, but to date not all the states have adopted the Uniform Act. Thus, in order to precisely ascertain one's state LLC law, one must examine the LLC statutes of that particular state. For the purposes of this book chapter, the common elements of the LLC form of doing business will be examined.

The LLC is formed pursuant to an *"articles of organization"*; it is an unincorporated business entity that combines the most favorable attributes of a general partnership, limited partnership, and corporation. The LLC may elect to be taxed as a partnership; the owners can co-manage the business; yet the owners have only limited liability. The foreseeable result is that many entrepreneurs who begin new businesses will choose the LLC as their legal form of conducting business. In some states, the LLC is allowed to have just one member-owner. The LLC is a "creature" of state law, although as noted the states' LLC law predominantly is based on the Uniform Limited Liability Company Act. Note, however, that if the state's LLC statute is silent on a particular matter, the state's partnership law must be consulted. The LLC is a "legal person"; that is, the LLC is a separate legal entity distinct from its members. It is treated as an artificial legal person distinct from its members, which can sue or be sued, enter into and enforce contracts, hold title to and transfer property, and be found civilly and criminally liable for violations of the law. The owners of the LLC are called "members," and, most importantly, these members are not personally liable to third parties for debts, obligations, and liabilities of the LLC, beyond their capital contribution, of course. The members thus have limited liability. Yet, if a member agrees either in the articles of organization or other writing, or if he or she personally guarantees the repayment of LLC obligations, then the member naturally will be personally liable.

Certain formalities are required by statute to form an LLC. Again, make sure to consult the relevant state's LLC statute when contemplating the LLC way of doing business. Generally speaking, an LLC can be organized for any business purpose, lawful of course. However, there are certain regulated industries, such as banking and insurance, which cannot use the LLC form. Moreover, the LLC cannot operate in certain professions, such as accounting, law, and medicine; but these professionals can use the new LLP form. The LLC can be organized in any state, but only in one state, though it can conduct business in all states. Note that the LLC's name must include the phrase "limited liability company" or "LLC." In addition, the LLC name cannot violate any trademarked name or be deceptively similar to other trademarked names. Finally, a name for the LLC can be reserved with the appropriate state official, for example, the Secretary of State of a state (and not the federal government presidential cabinet position).

Why should one operate a business as an LLC? An "S Corporation" has limits on the number of shareholders and classes of stock (only one class). In a general partnership, as we well know, the partners are personally and unlimitedly liable. In a limited partnership, there must be at least one general partner who is personally liable. Limited partners, moreover, are precluded from participating in management. In the LLC, the members can participate in management.

An Articles of *Organization* (and note *not* one of incorporation) must be filed with the appropriate state official. An LLC may be organized by one or more persons; and if only one member, a sole proprietor can obtain the LLC benefit of limited liability. The existence of the LLC begins when the articles of organization are filed. Filing, moreover, is conclusive proof of LLC status. The LLC's articles of organization must set forth the name of the LLC, its address, the name and address of its initial legal agent (for services of legal notices and lawsuits), who is usually its attorney, and the name and address of each organizer. The articles, in addition, must include the following: whether the LLC is a term LLC, and if so, the term; whether the LLC is manager-managed, and if so, the name and address of each manager; and whether any member of the LLC is to be personally liable. The articles also may set forth provisions from the members' operating agreement and any other matters not inconsistent with the law. The articles of organization, finally, can be amended at any time by filing an "articles of amendment." As to the duration of the LLC, it is regarded as at-will unless it is designated as a term LLC and the duration is specified in the articles. An at-will LLC, of course, has no fixed term. A member's capital contribution may be in the form of money, personal property, real property, other tangible and intangible property, services performed, contracts for services to be performed, promissory notes, or other agreements. The LLC's operating agreement may provide that a member's ownership interest may be evidenced by a certificate of interest in, and by, the LLC.

A general partnership, limited partnership, as well as a corporation may be converted to an LLC. A "foreign" limited liability company, note, is a *non-domestic (that is, non-state of organization)* LLC that wants to do business in all other states. Such a foreign LLC needs a certificate of authority from the appropriate state official.

The powers of an LLC are the same powers as an individual. Members of the LLC may enter into an operating agreement, which regulates the affairs of the company and the conduct of its business, and governs relations among members, the LLC's manager, and the company. The LLC is liable for any loss or injury caused to anyone as a result of a wrongful act or omission by a member, manager, agent, or employee of the LLC who commits an act within the ordinary course of business of the LLC or with the authority of the LLC. An LLC, it is important to note, can be either member-managed or manager-managed. An LLC is presumed to be member-managed unless designated as a manager-managed LLC. If the LLC is *member-managed,* all members have agency authority to bind the LLC to contracts. In a *manager-managed LLC,* it is important to note, only the designated managers have authority to bind the LLC to contracts (which, of course, are in the ordinary course of the LLC's business or that the LLC has authorized). In a member-managed LLC, each member has equal rights in the management of the business (regardless of the size of his or her capital contribution). The business of the LLC is decided by majority vote. Note, moreover, that members' and managers' authority to bind the LLC to contracts may be restricted in either the articles of organization or the operating agreement. However, the restrictions do not affect the apparent authority to bind the LLC to third parties who do not have notice of the restrictions. Yet, if the restrictions are in the articles of organization which is filed with the Secretary of State or appropriate state official, then such filing will be deemed to constitute notice to the public. If the restrictions are merely in the operating agreement, then a third party must have actual notice thereof.

As to the sharing of profits and losses, the general rule is that a member has the right to an equal share in the LLC's profits, but the members can change this in the operating agreement, for example, when the members' capital contributions are unequal. As to compensation and reimbursement, a non-manager LLC member is not entitled to remuneration for services performed to the LLC. The exception is remuneration for the winding up of the LLC. The manager of an LLC is paid compensation as specified in the employment contract with the LLC. The LLC, in addition, is obligated to reimburse members and managers for payments made on behalf of the LLC and to be indemnified for liabilities incurred in the ordinary course of business. Regarding information, the LLC must give members access to the records at the LLC's principal office. A member, moreover, has the right on written demand to obtain a copy of the LLC's written operating agreement. Concerning lawsuits by a member, a member of an LLC can bring a direct lawsuit against the LLC to enforce a member's rights under the articles of organization, operating agreement, state LLC law, and other federal, state, and local law. Such a lawsuit, for example, may be used to enforce a member's right to vote, inspect books, and compel dissolution. If the LLC is harmed by a third party, a member/manager has the right to bring a lawsuit on behalf of the LLC against the offending party to recover damages. This type of lawsuit is called a "derivative" suit. Note that it is required that a member must have made an effort to secure initiation of the lawsuit by the LLC. Note also that a member, if successful, can recover reasonable expenses and attorneys' fees. A member's ownership interest in the LLC is called a "distributionist interest." This interest is regarded as personal property and may be transferred. The transfer, however, does not entitle the transferee to be a member of the LLC; the transferee only receives the transferor's distribution rights.

Significantly, note that there is a limited duty of care owed to the LLC. A member/manager owes a duty of care *to the LLC* not to engage in: 1) known violations of the law, 2) intentional wrongful conduct, 3) reckless conduct, and 4) grossly negligent conduct which harms the LLC. It is essential to emphasize that the preceding rules indicate a limited duty of care, *because liability for ordinary negligence is not included.* The LLC, of course, is liable to third parties for injuries caused by a member/manager who is acting on LLC business (including injuries caused by ordinary negligence). A member/manager, of course, is personally liable for injuries caused to third parties by the member/manager's own negligence. As to the duty of good faith and fair dealing, the member/manager owes to the LLC and other members such a duty in discharging responsibilities. Note, however, that there is no fiduciary owed by a non-manager member of the LLC. He or she owes no duty of loyalty and good faith, as well as fair dealing, to the LLC and its other members. Rather, the non-manager member is treated as the ordinary shareholder of a corporation.

To complete the LLC commentary, it is necessary to state a few rules regarding the always perplexing area of dissolution and winding up. LLC laws typically (but not exclusively) use the term "*disassociation*" in place of "dissolution." The first rule is that a member of an LLC always has the *power* to disassociate from the LLC, regardless if the LLC is one at-will or for a fixed term. However, the disassociation from a term LLC before the expiration of the term is deemed to be a wrongful termination; and the member so acting will be liable for any damages caused to the LLC and its members for the wrongful disassociation. If the LLC is one at-will, then the LLC must purchase the disassociating member's distributionist interest. Recall that in the at-will situation, the member has both the *power and the right* to disassociate. As to the amount of the disassociating member's distributionist interest, it is either fixed in the agreement or set by the court (with "fair market value" as the standard). Note that there are some interesting rules regarding notice of disassociation in LLC law. First, for two years after a member disassociates from an LLC, he or she possesses the apparent authority to bind the LLC to contracts in the ordinary course of business. Exceptions arise, however, if the third parties knew of the disassociation or were given notice of the disassociation. Moreover, the LLC can give constructive notice of a member's disassociation with the Secretary of State or appropriate state official. The name of the disassociated member must be included. This notice is effective against any person who deals with the disassociated member, regardless if the third party was actually aware of the notice. The disassociation of an LLC can occur by the happening of several events: 1) an event specified in the agreement; 2) the consent of the % specified in the agreement; 3) its activity becomes illegal; 4) by a court if it becomes impracticable to carry on the business of the LLC or if the economic purpose of the LLC is likely to be unreasonably frustrated; and 5) by the Secretary of State, or appropriate state official, for failure to pay taxes and fees or to file an annual report. At the expiration of the LLC's term, some members may want to continue the LLC. They can do so if: 1) there is a unanimous vote to continue for a specified term, and an amendment to the articles is filed; 2) there is a majority vote to continue the LLC as an at-will LLC. If the LLC is not continued, it is wound up. Winding up, of course, is the process of preserving and selling assets of the LLC and distributing the money to creditors and members. Any member, except a wrongfully disassociating member, can participate in the winding up of the LLC's business. The winding up member can maintain the LLC's business for a reasonable time. The LLC's assets are first applied to pay off creditors; and then to members in equal shares unless the operating agreement provides otherwise. After disassociation and winding up, the LLC can terminate its existence by filing an "articles of termination" with the state Secretary of State official.

When a contract is entered into with a business entity, whether corporation, partnership, or limited liability company (LLC), it is critical to ensure that the person signing the contract on behalf of the entity has the legal authority to do so. Typically, any general partner in a partnership or the managing member of an LLC will have such authority to bind the business. However, for an LLC as well as a partnership situation, it is important to be aware of the fact that state LLC and partnership statutes may require that some major transactions have to be approved by all the LLC members or all the partners in the partnership. Regarding the corporation, the contract with the corporation must be signed by an appropriate corporate officer. The CEO thus generally has the authority to enter into most contracts on behalf of the corporation. However, pursuant to state corporation laws, some types of contracts must be first authorized by the board of directors, such as agreements for the issuance of stock or to sell most of the corporation's assets. Consequently, the prudent person will first seek evidence, characteristically in the form of a board resolution, or perhaps in the corporation's articles of incorporation or bylaws, that specifies that the corporate officer in fact has the appropriate contract authority.

There are two principal documents that pertain to the LLC. The first is its charter document. This document is typically a short document called either the *articles of organization* or a *certificate of formation* which is filed with the Secretary of State. It contains basis information as to the name of the LLC, its address, its agent for service of process, its term (which can be perpetual), and whether the LLC will be a member managed one or a manager managed one (that is, in the latter case the manager is chosen by the members). The other principal LLC document is called its operating agreement, which closely resembles a partnership agreement. This agreement should be detailed, specifying, among other provisions, the LLC's ownership structure, how the LLC will be governed and managed, and how the profits and losses are to be apportioned. As with the partnership, general legal forms should be avoided in creating an operating agreement, and accordingly an attorney should be consulted to draft an agreement tailored to the needs of the LLC members.

Finally, it must be pointed out that certain disadvantages of an LLC are: lack of access to capital markets since there is no stock to be offered and sold to the public; ownership interests are not freely transferable (which could be a major problem if a large number of investors is anticipated); and uncertainty due to the vague definition of an "investment security" as to whether the buying and selling of LLC interests is a securities transaction thus governed by federal and state security laws

Franchise

Franchising is a method of doing business that has existed for many years. However, the growth of the franchising method of doing business in recent years has been dramatic and the use of the franchise format pervasive throughout the United States as well as the global economy. Concomitantly, the franchise way of doing business has become subject to a wide array of laws – international, U.S., federal, state, and local.

This discussion will address some of the major aspects of the franchise way of doing business; but will focus on one important legal aspect to the franchise business relationship – the covenant of good faith and fair dealing pursuant to the law of the United States.

There are many ways for a manufacturer, seller, or supplier to convey its products and services into the marketplace. One principal method of distribution is by means of the legally recognized business relationship of a "franchise." Thus, the first critical term to define and explicate is *franchise*. However, there are various common law and statutory – federal and state – definitions of the term. Generally speaking, a franchise is a method of conducting business that combines the advantages of a recognized, proven, centralized, and unique way of doing business with the capital, initiative, ambition, and "hands-on" management provided by a local and independent business entrepreneur, with the goal of leveraging that business person's success far beyond his or her typically limited resource potential. The franchise owner is a legally independent entity, but is economically dependent on the franchisor and is in fact an integral unit of the franchisor's business system. The benefit to the franchisee is that the franchisor's business system is characteristically a proven way of doing business, encompassing the provision of uniform products and services, advertising, and computer and reservation systems. Moreover, the franchisor is available to provide continuing assistance, guidance, and training to the franchisee. Of course, the franchisor usually obtains an initial fee as well as a percentage of the franchisee's gross profits for sales and a percentage for advertising fees for granting to the franchisee the right to use the franchisor's name in the selling of products and services. The consumer also benefits because the consumer can obtain uniform products and services at numerous distribution points. The franchise, therefore, is a very appealing way of doing business, since a business person with a small amount of capital can become a true entrepreneur; and in addition the pride of owning one's own business surely will motivate the franchisee to make the business successful.

The key issue is to ascertain when a business relationship rises to the level of a franchise, thus triggering special legal rights and responsibilities regarding the covenant of good faith and fair dealing and otherwise. The critical franchise factor is the commonality of the economic situations and legal rights the parties have to contend with in their business. Nonetheless, the immediate, as well as foremost difficulty, confronting and franchise law analysis, regarding the good faith covenant or otherwise, is that the federal and state franchise statutes define the term "franchise" in different ways. The term "franchise" is defined by a variety of state laws, some of which require registration of franchise offerings and/or disclosure to prospective franchises, as well as others which do not require registration or disclosure, but which do regulate the relationship between the franchisor and franchisee. The state statutes thus define "franchise" in an assortment of ways. However, the state definitions do contain common definitional components to the term "franchise," to wit: some type of association by the holder of the franchise, the franchisee, with the franchisor's trademarks and service marks; the payment of a fee or consideration for the right to use the franchisor's trademarks and service marks, that is, the franchise fee; the right to sell goods or services as well as for a system for marketing and doing business; the position of the franchisee as an integral component in the franchisor's distribution system; the providing of material assistance by the franchisor to the franchisee in opening, marketing, and managing the business; and, concomitantly, a significant degree of control exercised by the franchisor over the franchise business; and finally a "community of interest" between the franchisor and franchisee. At times, the requirement of a "community of interest" is used to describe the relationship between the franchisor and franchisee. Of course, differences in the various states' definitions of key terms, such as "franchise," as well as the important terms under examination herein, that is, "good faith" and "fair dealing" and also commercial reasonableness, naturally can be crucial in determining whether legal redress is available in a particular case. The term "franchise" also is defined at the federal level, notably by a Federal Trade Commission Rule, which is similar to the state definitions. The Federal Trade Commission deems a business arrangement a "franchise" if the arrangement, among other factors, is a continuing commercial relationship, for the right to operate a business pursuant to the franchisor's trade name or to sell the seller's branded goods, and the franchisor provides significant assistance to the buyer, or can exercise significant control over the buyer's business operations. A business relationship rises to the level of a "franchise," therefore, if it satisfies one of the many legal definitions of the term.

The essence of a franchise is the *franchise agreement* between the franchisor and franchisee. The franchise relationship is thus a contractual one. Each franchise industry, business, and even relationship has its own distinct contract, of course, but there are certain common and fundamental provisions that must be addressed. There will always be a provision dealing with the franchisee's payment for the franchise. An initial fee is typically required, which is usually a lump sum for the franchise license and for the privilege of being part of the franchisor's business system. Moreover, the franchisee will be obligated to pay a certain percentage of weekly, monthly, or annual gross sales to the franchisor for the continuing right to remain a franchisee, as well as another smaller percentage for advertising costs. Another very important provision in the agreement will be the location of the franchise, which naturally the franchisor must approve, and concomitantly the franchisee's territory, which should be an exclusive area that only the designated franchisee can serve. The agreement will also specify the type of premises for the business, whether the premises are to be constructed, purchased, or leased, the kinds of equipment and furnishings, and who supplies them, and the specific standards for the premises. The agreement will also grant the franchisor the right to inspect the premises in order for the franchisor to maintain quality standards and to protect the franchisor's name and reputation. Furthermore, the agreement will specify the form of the business for the franchise, that is, for example, whether it is owned by a partnership or a Limited Liability Company, as well as the capital structure of the business. There will be provisions in the agreement for standards of operation, for example, sales requirements, quality standards, computer software, record-keeping, as well as standards for the hiring, training, and supervision of personnel. Usually, the franchisor will require the franchisee to purchase certain types of equipment or supplies, but not exclusively from the franchisor as there may be antitrust problems. Typically, the franchisor will give the franchisee a choice of approved suppliers, including perhaps the franchisor. Similarly, due to antitrust concerns, the franchisor cannot contractually set the price by which goods are to be sold or services are to be performed; rather, the franchisor can merely "suggest" the retail prices of goods or services. The duration of the franchise is usually set forth in the franchise agreement. The time period is characteristically a relatively short one (from one to three years) so the parties can ascertain whether they want to continue doing business together. In addition, in the typical franchisee agreement, there will be a "for cause" termination provision which specifies certain circumstances, such as death or disability, insolvency, failure to meet sales quotas or to maintain standards, and breach of the franchise agreement, which will operate to end the franchise, presuming some reasonable notice period is given. One final and important point relating to the agreement must be made; and that is the franchisee agreement is almost always drafted by the franchisor, the party with superior bargaining power, and thus naturally contains provisions that are favorable to the franchisor. Of course, if either party breaches the agreement, the aggrieved party can sue for breach of the franchise contract, receiving contract damages such as the loss of income, profits, and salaries.

One of the main statutory protections afforded to the franchisee stems from a Federal Trade Commission rule that requires the franchisor to provide sufficient accurate information to a prospective franchisee so that one can make an informed business decision. This information includes an *Earnings Claim Document*, which enumerates the requirements for the franchisor's claims about existing profits or projected sales income. Another important document, called a "Basic Disclosure Document," is mandated. That document includes information regarding the business experience, financial picture and history, and backgrounds of the franchisor and its principals. The document also must describe the business of the franchise, the initial funds required to be paid by the franchisee, recurring payments, any personal participation required by the franchisee, site selection, training programs, and a sample franchise agreement. The document also must have information concerning the establishment of the franchise and its renewal, cancellation, or termination. In addition to this federal statute, there also are in some states in the U.S. franchisee protection statutes, which, for example, may prohibit the franchisor from making any misrepresentations in the initial sale of the franchise, and also which may require the franchisor to terminate the franchisee only for certain specified grounds and/or in "good faith." Otherwise, absent any statutory protection, the main source of redress for the franchisee is the old common law implied covenant of good faith and fair dealing.

The common law *covenant of good faith and fair dealing* which is implied in contracts, including franchise agreements, has been defined by the courts in a variety of ways. The covenant means that the parties honestly and reasonably carry out their contractual obligations. The covenant also implies a reasonableness standard to contract obligations. Moreover, the covenant means that neither party to the agreement shall do anything which will have the effect of destroying or injuring the right of the other party to receive the fruits of the contract. The Restatement (Second) of Contracts maintains that every contract imposes on each party a duty of good faith and fair dealing in its performance and its enforcement. The Restatement notes that the phrase "good faith" is used in a variety of contexts, and its meaning varies somewhat with the context. Nonetheless, the Restatement equates "good faith" enforcement or performance of a contract to faithfulness to an agreed common purpose and consistency with the justified expectations of the other party. The Restatement further defines the "good faith" duty by elaborating what is prohibited under a contact, that is, a variety of types of conduct characterized as involving "bad faith," because they violate the community standards of decency, fairness, or reasonableness. The Restatement finally identifies several instances of conduct that generally would constitute a violation of the duty of good faith: evading the spirit of the bargain; lack of diligence and slacking off; willful rendering of imperfect performance; abuse of power to specify terms; and interference with or failure to cooperate in the other party's performance. Finally, the Restatement notes that a party's conduct can contravene the good faith obligation even if the party believes the conduct to be justified; and in addition points out that fair dealing may require more than honesty. The Uniform Commercial Code provides a statutory definition of "good faith" in the case of a merchant, that is, honesty in fact and the observance of reasonable commercial standards of fair dealing. Accordingly, in examining the law, one can discern that the implied covenant of good faith and fair dealing contains both a subjective and objective element – subjective good faith and objective fair dealing and commercial reasonableness. These legal standards are certainly applicable to the franchise relationship, and will provide the parties, especially the franchisee, who is typically the weaker party, a degree of protection, above and beyond statutory law, from abuse and overreaching. For example, even if the franchise agreement does not specify an exclusive territory for the franchisee, the covenant of good faith and fair dealing may preclude the franchisor from granting additional franchises or from operating itself in an area served by the franchisee. Another illustration would occur if the franchisor seeks to terminate a franchise or not renew a franchise when the franchisee has spent a considerable amount of time, effort, and money to open or to develop the business, and the franchisor is aware of that fact. Even if the franchisor has the technical legal right to terminate or to not renew, the covenant of good faith may prevent the franchisor from so acting.

Regardless of the legal nature of the proposed business, certain key questions must be resolved initially, to wit: Who are the key "players" and what percentages of the business will they own? Who will be controlling the business? How, and by whom, will the business be managed? Who is contributing capital, property, and services to the business, and to what extent? How are property and service contributions to be valued? How much time will the participants be required to spend on business matters? What happens if a key "player" dies or become incapacitated or is otherwise unable or willing to stay with the business? How will the participants' tenure with the business be maintained; that is, what protections are there regarding the expulsion of a participant? Answering the ownership issue is, of course, critical, since that arrangement will determine who and to what extent the participants will share in the financial success of the business. The objective is to answer these preceding questions in a clear, precise, and also fair, manner, since the success of the business will depend on everyone knowing their rights and responsibilities as well as knowing that they have a fair share in the "fruits" of the business to be "harvested" by their hard work.

What type of business form should the entrepreneur choose – a corporation, S corporation, partnership, or limited liability company (LLC)? Usually, the entrepreneur will choose the LLC because the LLC provides the limited liability protection of the corporation as well as the favorable tax treatment of the partnership. The S corporation does have the preceding advantages too, but it has other limitations, as pointed out, that the LLC does not have, such as the restriction on the number of shareholders in the LLC and the preclusion of corporations as shareholders. If the entrepreneur expects the business to be a widely and publicly held one, then the traditional corporation is the logical choice. Yet many entrepreneurs are "small" business men and woman who do not anticipate an initial need to sell shares of stock to the public to raise capital, and who thus do not want to undergo the expense and effort of forming and operating a traditional corporation; and thus they logically choose the LLC. If the entrepreneur intends to distribute business earnings presently, then with the LLC the earnings can be distributed without incurring a second level of taxation. Distribution of corporate earnings to the company's employees is a tax deductible expense; but if the distribution of earnings to shareholders is taxed as corporate income first and then taxed again as dividend income to the shareholders. Of course, the gain on the sale of stock held for more than one year is taxed at the more favorable capital gains rate. Since most small businesses distribute earnings on a current basis, the LLC is preferable. Also, if the entrepreneur expects there to be initial business losses, then again the LLC is preferable because the LLC enables its owners to deduct these losses from their personal income.

Summary

As mentioned in the introduction, establishing a business can be complex and cumbersome. Opening a business requires understanding the national and local laws. As discussed in this chapter, entrepreneurs that want to establish a business must become aware of the laws that apply to each type of business prior to deciding whether to have a sole proprietorship, a partnership, a corporation, a limited liability company, a franchise, or a joint venture with another national or international organization. This chapter outlined some of the information that business owners, academic scholars, and entrepreneurs need to know about the various types of business organizations in the United States. The chapter outlined some of the risks and benefits associated with each type of organization so the entrepreneur can decide which format best fits his/her purpose for the business. For example, any person who does business individually without utilizing any of the other forms of business organization is doing business as a sole proprietorship. The sole proprietorship is the most basic form of business organization, as the owner of the business is in essence *the* business. The advantages and disadvantages of this way of doing business as well as the other forms of doing business were examined in this chapter.

Discussion Questions

1. What are the advantages and disadvantages of doing business as a partnership compared to a corporation? Provide examples with brief explanations thereof.

2.   Why is a partnership regarded as a very "fragile" legal form of doing business? Provide an example and a brief explanation thereof.

3.   What is the authority of partners to bind the partnership and other partners contractually? Provide example with brief explanations thereof.

4.   Compare and contrast a partnership to a limited partnership. Provide examples along with brief explanations thereof.

5.   Compare and contrast a partnership to a limited liability partnership. Provide examples along with brief explanations thereof.

6.   Compare and contrast the articles of incorporation with the bylaws of a corporation. Provide examples of provisions that should be in each document together with a brief explanation thereof.

7.   Compare, contrast, and illustrate a *de jure*, *de facto*, and corporation by estoppel.

8.   What is the legal doctrine of "piercing the corporate veil," and why should the owner of a one person or small family corporation be very concerned with this doctrine? Provide examples with brief explanations thereof.

9.   What are some of the shareholders' fundamental rights and obligations? Provide examples with brief explanations thereof.

10. How can shareholders of the corporation seek to control the business of the corporate entity? Provide examples and brief explanations thereof.

11. What are some of the directors' fundamental rights and obligations? Provide examples with brief explanations thereof.

12. Why is the "business judgment" rule the "best friend" of the corporate director? Provide examples with brief explanations thereof.

13. What does the law regard as "fundamental corporate change"? What are some of the legal requirements for effectuating such changes? Provide examples along with brief explanations thereof.

14. What are the advantages and disadvantages of doing business as a corporation compared to a limited liability company? Provide examples with brief explanations thereof.

15. Why is it even more important in an LLC than even a corporation to maintain LLC formalities? Provide examples with brief explanations thereof.

16. What are the advantages and disadvantages of doing business as a sole proprietorship compared to doing business as a franchisee? Provide examples along with brief explanations thereof.

17. Why does the old common law covenant of good faith and fair dealing emerge as a very important legal doctrine for the franchisee? Provide an example with a brief explanation thereof.

8 – COMMERCIAL PAPER AND BANKING TRANSACTIONS

The law of commercial paper, as well as banking transactions, is found predominantly in the Uniform Commercial Code (UCC) specifically in Articles 3 and 4 (as revised in 1990 and 2002). The term "commercial paper" refers to written obligations, promises, and orders to pay sums of money which arise from the use of negotiable instruments, such as promissory notes, drafts, checks, and trade acceptances. There are two basic purposes of commercial paper. The first is the credit function; that is, some forms of commercial paper are used primarily to obtain credit now, to be repaid out of future income. For example, a buyer purchases goods from a seller and pays with a 90 day promissory note. The seller then waits until the maturity date to collect; and thus the seller has extended credit to the buyer. The second purpose is the payment function; that is, some types of commercial paper are used primarily as a paying obligation as a substitute for money. For example, a buyer buys goods from a seller using a check; the check is a substitute for money. This chapter will examine in detail commercial paper law pursuant to the UCC, and then will examine banking transactions laws pursuant to the UCC and certain U.S. Federal statutes.

Part I - Commercial Paper

Types of Commercial Paper
The UCC specifies four types of *commercial paper*: drafts, checks, notes, and certificates of deposit. First, a *draft* (also called a "bill of exchange") is an instrument where the party creating it (called the *drawer*) orders another party (called the *drawee*) to pay money to a third party (called the *payee*). It is very important to observe initially that one of two conditions must exist for a draft arrangement to work. The drawee must owe the drawer a debt or there must be an agreement or a relationship between the parties whereby the drawee consented to the drawing of the draft upon him, her, or it. It also must be emphasized that the mere execution of the

draft by the drawer does not legally obligate the drawee; rather, liability arises when the drawee formally accepts the obligation (typically by signing the instrument). A *trade acceptance* is a type of draft used in the sale of goods. The purchaser of goods agrees to pay the seller of goods at a future time by accepting a time draft drawn on the buyer by the seller; in other words, the instrument is drawn by the seller of goods (the drawer) on the purchaser of those goods (the drawee) and accepted (signed) by the purchaser; the seller of goods is also the payee on the draft. The purpose of the trade acceptance is to enable the seller to raise money on the instrument before the purchaser's obligation matures. The second type of commercial paper is the *check*, which is also a variant of the draft. This variant of the draft must be drawn on a bank and payable on demand. The check is premised on an order by the drawer ordering the drawee-bank to pay a sum of money to the payee of the check. A cashier's check is a check drawn by the bank on itself, payable on demand to the payee. A certified check is a check which has been accepted by the drawee-bank. A traveler's check becomes a "check" once it is completed with the signature (and is negotiable) and the bank is both the drawer and the drawee. The third type of commercial paper is the *promissory note*. The note consists of a promise by one party (the "maker") to pay a sum of money to another party (the "payee"). The "promise" in the note manifests an undertaking to pay, and not the mere acknowledgement of an obligation; and consequently an "IOU" is not a promise and cannot form the basis for a note (though it can form the basis for a contract obligation). A note differs from a draft in two respects: it contains a promise to pay as opposed to an order to pay; and there are only two parties to a note whereas there are three to a draft. Finally, the fourth type of commercial paper is a certificate of deposit (CD), which is a variant of the note. The CD is an instrument whereby a bank (the maker) acknowledges the receipt of money and promises to repay the money at a later date or on demand. CDs may be negotiable or non-negotiable.

Commercial paper can be further divided into demand and time instruments. A *demand instrument* (also called a *sight instrument*) is payable whenever the holder of the instrument chooses to present it to the maker (if a note) or the drawee (if a draft); that is, the holder is entitled to demand payment at any time after the instrument is issued. A *time instrument* is one payable at a specific future date. Notes, drafts, and CDs can be either demand or time instruments; but a check must be a demand instrument. However, a check can be post-dated and can still be negotiated prior to the date shown, but is not payable until the date stated. Thus, if a demand instrument is post-dated, the holder must wait until the date shown on the instrument arrives before demanding payment.

A fundamental differentiation is made in commercial paper law between negotiable and non-negotiable instruments. Generally, all commercial paper is either negotiable or non-negotiable, depending, as will be seen, on the UCC's requirements for negotiability. The distinction is absolutely critical in commercial paper law because the UCC applies only to negotiable instruments; non-negotiable instruments are governed by ordinary contract law. In particular, if an instrument is a negotiable instrument, it is possible for the holder of the instrument to become a "holder in due course" (HDC), which, as will be seen, is a special status for the holder of the instrument that enables the holder to take the instrument free of most defenses of the maker or the drawer of the instrument. Accordingly, the facts that an instrument is a negotiable one and concomitantly that a holder can become an HDC thereon promote the transferability, viability, and value of the instrument, thereby underscoring the paper's role as a substitute for money.

It is also important initially to define the possible parties to commercial paper. As related, a note has two original parties – the maker and the payee; and a draft/check has three parties – the drawer, drawee, and payee. The *acceptor* is a critical party to a draft. After the draft is issued, it characteristically is presented by the payee (or a subsequent holder) to the drawee for the drawee's "acceptance" (which can be mandatory or optional). A drawee who "accepts" the draft is then called an "acceptor." An *acceptance* occurs when the drawee signs his or her name to the face of the instrument. The significant result of an acceptance, as will be seen, is that the acceptor becomes the primary party to the instrument (comparable to the liability of the maker of a note). An *indorser* arises when the payee of a note or draft transfers it to a third party instead of presenting it to the primary party for payment. The payee/transferor almost always "indorses" the instrument by signing his or her name on the back of it; the payee thereby becomes an "indorser." An indorsee is thus a person who receives the indorsed instrument. The *bearer* of an instrument is any person who has physical possession of a bearer instrument (for example, an instrument "payable to bearer" or "payable to cash"). It is also important to note another type of bearer instrument; that is, an instrument originally payable to the order of a named person, which the named person then indorses by signing his or her name on the back, which is called a *blank indorsement*, and which converts the paper into a bearer instrument. The *"holder"* is a person who possesses by means of negotiation a negotiable instrument, that is, a bearer instrument or one payable to the order of a specific person as payee or indorsee. A *holder in due course* (HDC) is a holder who has given value for an instrument and who takes it in good faith and without notice or knowledge of any problems or defenses pertaining to the instrument. An ordinary holder is a person who qualifies as a holder but who does not meet the HDC requirements. Unlike the HDC, the holder cannot enforce the instrument against the primary party if he or she has a personal defense; that is, the ordinary holder is treated as a contract law assignee; however, the holder can enforce the instrument if the primary party does not have any defense. Finally, a "holder through an HDC" arises if a holder fails to qualify as an HDC, but can still enjoy the special status and rights of an HDC by showing that any prior holder qualified as an HDC.

Ambiguities in Instruments

The Uniform Commercial Code provides four general rules to guide parties and courts when an instrument is ambiguous as to terms, parties, and/or legal consequences. The first situation involves language in the instrument which is ambiguous or instruments with omissions. There may be a discrepancy between words and figures in an instrument. The rule of law is that where the sum is expressed in words and also in figures and there is a discrepancy, the sum denoted by words is payable. However, if the words are ambiguous, the figures control. For example an instrument that states "pay five hundred dollars ($5000)" means that the amount payable is $500; and an instrument that states "pay six dollars ($6.00) means that the amount payable is $6.00. If there is a discrepancy among the handwritten, typed, and printed provisions in an instrument, the handwritten provisions prevail, and then the typed over the printed. If there is a clause in an instrument authorizing extension of the maturity date, the clause means according to the UCC a single extension not longer than the original period, though the parties may expressly provide otherwise. The second ambiguity area concerns additional description of the payee, for example, "pay to the order of KA, Vernon Valley, NJ." The rule of law is straightforward, and that is that any additional description of the payee has no legal effect. The third situation deals with the omission of an interest rate in an instrument. The rule of law holds that if a negotiable instrument states that the maker or drawer agrees to pay an amount "with interest," but does not specify the rate, the "judgment rate" is construed as the interest rate. The judgment rate is the interest rate specified by state statutes, typically 12%, for unsatisfied money judgments. The interest accrues from the date of the instrument, or if undated, on the date the instrument was first issued to the payee. Finally, joint signers may sign an instrument; that is, two or more parties may sign an instrument as a maker, drawer, acceptor, or indorser as part of the same transaction; and if so they are "jointly and severally" liable, which means the full amount can be collected from any one of them, even though the instrument may say "I promise to pay" or similar words.

The Negotiability Requirement

The concept of negotiability is a very significant one in UCC commercial paper law. The extensive protection afforded to buyers of commercial paper (for example, attaining HDC status) applies only when an instrument is a "negotiable" one under the UCC. A non-negotiable instrument is "merely" a contract, and thus is only assignable. Recalling contract law, the assignee of a contract merely possesses the contract rights of his or her assignor; that is, the buyer of a non-negotiable instrument takes the paper subject to the claims and defenses of prior parties. There can be no HDC status if the instrument is non-negotiable. A negotiable instrument is more freely transferable, and accordingly serves as a much better substitute of money or an extension of credit, which are two of the fundamental purposes of commercial paper.

There are several requirements for *negotiability*. The term "negotiability" in essence refers to the form of the instrument. "Speaking" generally, in order to be negotiable under the UCC, the instrument must be: 1) in writing; 2) signed by the maker or drawer; 3) contain an unconditional promise or order to pay a sum certain in money, on demand or at a definite time; 4) contain the "words of negotiability"; and 5) be free from other promises as a general rule.

A writing is an indispensable negotiability requirement; the instrument must be written; it cannot be oral. Paper, however, is not essential; the writing can be on other objects; and it is not required that any particular type of writing be used. A signature of the maker or drawer is required. Any mark or symbol placed on the instrument by the maker or drawer with the intent to authenticate the writing is construed as a "signature." A complete formal signature, however, is not required. For example, the use of one's initials is permissible. One's signature, moreover, can be placed on the instrument as the maker or drawer by one's authorized agent.

Furthermore, a trade name is sufficient for a signature. A problem area in commercial paper law concerns unauthorized or forged signatures. An "unauthorized" signature is made without authority, and includes a forgery or a pretense of agency. As to liability on such instruments, the person whose name is signed is not liable, unless there is any ratification or estoppel; but the unauthorized signer is personally liable, just as if he or she had signed his or her own name. Note also that the unauthorized use of an electronic banking card is governed by a federal statute, called the Electronic Funds Transfer Act, which limits liability to the lesser of $50 or the amount obtained before the issuer was properly notified; but if there is no notice by the customer within two business days after knowledge of a theft, the liability amount expands to $500. Finally, as to the location of the signature, it need not be at the bottom of the instrument; and thus may be placed on the letterhead, body, or in any other location.

    A negotiable instrument must contain an unconditional promise or order to pay. The necessity of a promise or order is indispensable. A negotiable note must contain a promise to pay. However, it is not required that the exact word "promise" be used (though it almost always is). Consequently, the mere acknowledgement even in writing of a debt, that is, the "classic" IOU, does not contain the requisite promise. Yet even though non-negotiable, the IOU may be sufficient as a matter of contract law to base a recovery. The draft type of instrument must contain an order to pay. The purpose of such an instrument is for the drawer to order the drawee to pay money to the payee or to his or her order. The language must be an order or a direction to pay, and not merely a hope, expectation, wish, request, or authorization. The promise or order, moreover, must be unconditional. The reason for this requirement is that if the promise or order in an instrument was conditional, the conditions would hinder the transferability of the instrument. That is, it would be necessary for every transferee of an instrument to determine whether the condition was performed prior to taking the instrument. Conditions can be express. The rule of law is that if the instrument is conditioned on some event, it violates the UCC's "unconditional" requirement and is consequently not negotiable. For example, an instrument which states that "I promise to pay if I receive goods from the seller," or "I promise to pay on the marriage of my daughter," is not negotiable. Note, furthermore, that even if the condition or event is very likely to occur, or in fact has occurred, the instrument is still not negotiable. A problem arises when a purported negotiable instrument refers to other agreements. Typically, there can be a separate agreement executed between the immediate parties (that is, the maker or drawer and payee) as part of the same transaction. This separate agreement may in fact be effective in regulating the rights of the parties (though it may not bind later HDCs). However, does this separate agreement destroy negotiability? The first rule is that a mere reference in a negotiable instrument to the other contract or agreement does not impair negotiability. For example, a promissory note can say: "This note arises out of a contract signed by the parties on this date..." Similarly, a mere description of the consideration for which the instrument is given as well as the other transaction connected with the instrument, by itself, is only informative, and thus does not impair negotiability. So, a note can describe in detail the contract which gave rise to the note, including all the contract terms, and the note is negotiable. However, the incorporation of a separate agreement or document into an instrument destroys its negotiability. Why is this so? Because the later purchasers of the instrument cannot determine its applicable terms from the instrument; and consequently must search out the other agreements, which is very impractical. The "bad" incorporation words in an instrument to look for are as follows: "dependent upon," "subject to," and "part hereof." For example, a note that says "it is subject to the terms of a separate contract," or one that says the "terms of the mortgage are made a part hereof," is not negotiable. Yet note that there is some "safe" language, for example, the words "as per" or "in accordance with" which are merely "reference" language, and thus do not impair negotiability. For example, a note that says it is "executed as per another contract" is fine as far as negotiability is concerned. Another "conditional" problem arises with the "particular fund" doctrine. It is a basic tenet of commercial paper law that all the assets of the maker or drawer must be available to pay the instrument. Thus, the rule of law holds that if an instrument says that payment can only be made from some particular source, the instrument is not negotiable because the payment is conditioned upon the continued existence of funds from that source. For example, a note that says it is to be payable "from projects now under construction" is not negotiable; similarly, a promise to pay in a note from the "proceeds of the sale of my Microsoft stock" is not negotiable. However, the mere reference to an expected source of payment is permissible, and does not impair negotiability, so long as payment is not limited to that source. The best example is that checks refer to the number of the account from which the drawee bank is expected to pay the check.

A negotiable instrument must contain an order or a promise to pay a sum certain in money. Money is defined as the medium of exchange of a domestic or foreign government. For example, a promise to pay 1000 Euros is negotiable, even though the instrument is executed in the United States. Such an instrument, even though containing an amount stated in a foreign currency, may be payable in the equivalent U.S. dollars, unless the instrument expressly requires payment in the foreign currency. However, a promise to pay an "ounce of gold" is not negotiable, or to pay bonds, or for that matter to be Shakespearian, "a pound of flesh," is not negotiable because the promise is not one to pay money. The promise or order to pay money must be a "sum certain." It is important to initially point out that absolute certainty as to the sum due at all times is not required; rather, it is sufficient if at any particular time, the amount due on the instrument can be calculated mathematically. So, for example, the sum payable is certain even though it is to be paid: 1) with stated interest or by stated installments; 2) with stated different rates of interest before or after default or a specific date; 3) with stated discount or addition if the instrument is paid before or after a date fixed for payment; or 4) with costs of collection or attorneys' fees upon default. A corollary "sum certain" rule is that the interest rate must be "stated." Generally, interest to be paid at the "prime rate," "bank rate," or at a variable interest rate will render the instrument non-negotiable. The reason is that the rate of interest cannot readily be determined from the face of the instrument, and thus the sum is uncertain. However, interest payable at the "maximum lawful rate" or the "highest lawful rate" probably will not impair negotiability.

The time of payment of the instrument also must be certain. Accordingly, the rule of law holds that unless it can be determined from the face of the instrument when, or upon what events, the obligation will become due, the instrument is not negotiable. The reason is that without certainty as to time, the instrument cannot function as a substitute for money, since the holder will not be able to determine when he or she will be paid. Accordingly, the UCC requires that a negotiable instrument be payable "on demand" or at a definite time. An instrument is a "demand" instrument if it states that it is payable "on demand" (for notes), "at sight" or "upon presentment" (for drafts), or if no time for payment is stated. The key characteristic of demand paper is that the holder can require payment at any time by making a demand for payment to the person obligated on the paper to pay it. If an instrument lacks a maturity date, it is a demand instrument; if an instrument is undated, it is payable on demand. An antedated instrument is payable after the date stated; whereas a postdated instrument is payable on the date stated (though it may be negotiated prior to the date stated). A "time" instrument is one payable at a definite time in the future. Examples of instruments payable at a definite time are ones (dated, for example, January 10) payable as follows: 1) "on February 10, 2010" (or any date in the future); 2) "on or before February 10, 2010" (or any date in the future); 3) "60 days after date" (or any period more or less than 60 days); or 4) "60 days after sight" (or any period more or less than 60 days). However, an instrument payable upon the happening of an event, which is uncertain as to its time of occurrence, is not payable at a definite time, and thus not negotiable, even if the event is very likely to occur or has in fact occurred. Yet the instrument is payable when the event does in fact occur. The reason for this rule is to preclude negotiability for notes payable out of an expected inheritance. Consequently, a note payable "30 days after my uncle's death" is not negotiable, even if the uncle is dead when the note was signed.

Acceleration and extension clauses present challenges to negotiability. An *acceleration clause* is one in an instrument that makes it payable earlier than the stated maturity date. The rule is that an acceleration clause will not impair negotiability. Either the maker or holder may be given an unconditional right to accelerate the maturity date; acceleration may be made automatic upon the happening of the event. Examples of permissible acceleration are as follows: 1) the maker promises to pay to the order of payee "on or before March 15," which means the maker can accelerate; 2) the maker promises to pay to the order of payee "on March 15, or sooner if the holder chooses to accelerate," which means the payee or subsequent holder can accelerate; or 3) a note is payable in monthly installments, but "if any installment is not paid when due, the entire instrument is due and payable." *Extension* clauses are considerably more problematic than acceleration ones. An extension clause makes an instrument payable later than its stated maturity date. However, does such an extension clause violate the definite term requirement for negotiability? There are three important extension rules that answer this question. First, if the extension is at the option of the holder, that is, the current possessor of the instrument with good title thereto, the instrument is deemed to be payable at a definite time and is negotiable. However, unless specified in the instrument, the consent by the holder of an extension authorizes only a single extension for no longer than the original time period. The rationale is that the holder always has the right to delay demand of payment; yet the holder cannot exercise that option if the maker or acceptor tenders full payment when the instrument is due, which means that the holder cannot keep the interest running on the instrument indefinitely. Second, if the extension is at the option of the maker or drawee/acceptor, it is valid only if the new extended maturity date is stated in the instrument; but if the extension is open-ended, the instrument is not negotiable. The rationale is that without a maturity date in the extension clause, a subsequent holder cannot know when the instrument is to be paid. However, if the instrument only states that the maker or drawee/acceptor has the right to extend the time of payment but without stating a time, then the time is definite, because the UCC authorizes only a single extension not longer than the original time period. For example, a note payable at a definite time but extended six months at the maker's option is negotiable; whereas a note payable at a definite time but extended by the maker for "no longer than a reasonable period of time" is not negotiable. Third, if there is an extension automatically upon the happening of an event, the instrument will be negotiable only if a definite time period is stated for the extension.

In order to be negotiable, as a general rule, an instrument must contain the *words of negotiability*. The language clearly must indicate that the maker or drawer intends that the instrument be fully capable of being transferred to person(s) other than to the one the instrument was originally issued. The UCC thus requires that an instrument be payable "to order" or "to bearer"; and if the instrument contains neither order nor bearer language, it is as a general rule not negotiable. The exception to this rule concerns checks which do not require order or bearer language to be negotiable. Order paper is payable to the order of a person specified with reasonable certainty; and requires an indorsement for further negotiation. So, "pay to the order of Stephanie" is negotiable, but "pay to Stephanie" is not. An instrument also may be payable to the order of several payees. If the payees are "joint" (that is, "payable to the order of Stephanie and Silvano") they both must indorse the instrument; but if they are "several" (that is, "payable to the order of Stephanie or Silvano") then either one can indorse. A bearer instrument is one "payable to bearer" or "to cash" or to the "order of bearer" or to the "order of cash." A bearer instrument, it must be emphasized, can be transferred without indorsement, merely by delivery, just like cash; but a transferee will often want an indorsement because an indorser has greater liability on the instrument. The omission of these "magic" words of negotiability renders the instrument, as noted, non-negotiable. However, the rights and liabilities of the parties are still governed by the UCC, but with one very important exception, and that is no one can qualify as an HDC on such an instrument. However, the omission of the consideration for which the instrument is given does not impair negotiability. Similarly, the omission of the place where the instrument is drawn and payable does not impair negotiability; and finally the omission of the date of issue of the instrument does not impair negotiability (unless the date of issue is tied to the date of maturity, for example, an undated instrument "payable 60 days after date").

An instrument in order to be negotiable must also generally be free from other promises. That is, a negotiable instrument cannot generally contain any other promise, order, obligation, or power given by the maker or drawer. For example, a promise to pay "$500 and deliver goods" is not negotiable; similarly, a promise to pay "$500 or deliver goods" is still not negotiable since the holder cannot be given an election of requiring an act instead of the money. However, certain promises are permissible in an instrument, and thus do not impair negotiability. The four main types of permissible promises are: 1) a confession of judgment; that is, a provision authorizing the holder to enter judgment against the maker if the note is not paid when due; but such provisions may be prohibited by state consumer protection statutes as well as Federal Trade Commission rules on consumer sales; 2) a collateral security promise; that is, a statement that collateral is given as security for the obligation and the enumeration of the rights of the payee/holder in the collateral; 3) an additional security promise; that is, a promise by the maker, drawer, or acceptor to maintain, protect, or give additional collateral in specific circumstances; and finally 4) a promise to pay the cost of collection and attorneys' fees upon default of the instrument.

The Negotiation Requirement

The focus of the discussion in this subsection of the chapter is to examine the various ways that negotiable paper can be transferred from one holder to another as well as to address the UCC rules that apply to such transfers. The first area to cover is the difference between an assignment pursuant to contract law and a "negotiation" pursuant to the UCC. A negotiable instrument has no legal significance of and by itself. Its legal "life" does not begin until it is issued by the maker or drawer to the first holder. After issuance to the first holder, it can be transferred further by either negotiation or assignment. Of course, if the instrument is not a negotiable one, it can only be transferred by means of assignment. A "*negotiation*" occurs when the payee or holder of a negotiable instrument transfers it to a third party in the manner required by the UCC; such a transfer is called a "negotiation" and the subsequent transferee is called a "holder." Significantly, it is now possible for a transferee to qualify as a Holder in Due Course (HDC) if he or she meets the other HDC requirements. As will be seen, the HDC can acquire greater rights in the instrument than the transferor. If there is no UCC "negotiation," then a later holder cannot qualify as an HDC. A "mere" assignment is the transfer of an instrument or a right pursuant to contract law and not the UCC; the transferee is merely an assignee, governed by contract law; and the transferee/assignee's rights cannot be greater than the transferor's.

There are several key terms that must be defined so as to clearly explain the negotiation process: 1) *Negotiation* is the process by which a negotiable instrument is issued or transferred to a subsequent party who qualifies as a holder. 2) A *Holder* is a person in possession of an instrument issued or indorsed to him or her, or to his or her order, or to bearer or "in blank." 3) An *Issue* is the first delivery of the negotiable instrument by its maker or drawer to the holder. 4) A *Transfer* is any change in the possession of an instrument other than its "issue" or "presentment." 5) *Good title* means the rightful possession of a negotiable instrument. If the instrument is bearer paper, anyone in rightful possession of it has good title thereto. Note, however, that anyone in possession of bearer paper is a "holder," but the possessor may lack good title unless there was a valid delivery. If the instrument is order paper, the named payee has good title by acquiring possession of the instrument; but before a subsequent transferee can acquire title, the payee must indorse (that is, sign his or her name) and surrender possession of it to the transferee (that is, a "delivery").

The UCC negotiation process is thus different for bearer as opposed to order paper. Bearer paper is negotiated simply by delivery. For example, the drawer writes a check payable "to cash," which means the check is now bearer paper, which means that anyone in possession thereof is a holder. The critical term "delivery," however, means the voluntary delivery by the transferor. Consequently, if a thief steals bearer paper, there is no delivery and no negotiation, but since the thief is technically a "holder," the thief can deliver the paper to a third party, and there is a negotiation. The thief, or finder, does not acquire good title, but can transfer good title to a subsequent transferee. Also, since a thief or finder is a holder, the thief or finder has the power to discharge any person from liability on the instrument, for example, by obtaining payment. An order instrument is negotiated initially by delivery of the instrument to the payee; and then further negotiation requires that the payee indorse the instrument and deliver it to the transferee. It is absolutely essential that the payee's indorsement be valid. The rule of law is that title to an order instrument will not pass unless the payee's indorsement is authorized and valid. Consequently, forging the payee's name breaks the "chain of title," and no subsequent possessors of the instrument can qualify as even a holder, let alone an HDC.

There are many detailed rules governing the negotiation of order paper. Multiple payees in an instrument are permissible; that is, the instrument can be made payable to more than one payee. The payees can be *joint* or *several*. If "joint," the names on the payee line are connected with an "and." The instrument is thus payable to the payees jointly; and any subsequent negotiation is effective only if all indorse. For example, an instrument made payable to "Nancy and Victor" requires both payees to indorse; and if only one signs, then the subsequent transferee is not a holder. If the payees' names are only "several," their names are connected by an "or" or an "and/or," for example, an instrument payable to "Nancy or Victor." The instrument is thus payable severally, which means the valid indorsement of any one payee is sufficient to pass title to a subsequent transferee. As to the location of the indorsement, it must be written on the instrument; it usually is placed on the reverse side, but it also may be placed in front, or in a separate writing, called an "allonge," which must be firmly affixed to the instrument. Note, however, that banks have special rules for the indorsement of checks. What happens when an order instrument is transferred without an indorsement? The legal answer is that the mere delivery of an order instrument without the indorsement is not effective to transfer title to the instrument (merely possession). Accordingly, the transferee is not a holder, and no UCC negotiation has occurred. However, the transferee of the order instrument with the missing indorsement does possess certain rights. The transferee can institute a lawsuit to compel the indorsement, presuming the transferee paid value for the instrument; however, in this suit to enforce the instrument, the transferee must show that the instrument is due, the instrument is valid, and that the transferee is entitled to the missing indorsement. When the transferor's indorsement is later obtained, title is then vested in the transferee, who is now a holder, and who thus can now qualify as an HDC. However, for the purpose of determining whether the transferee had notice or knowledge of a problem with the instrument, which is crucial for ascertaining HDC status, the time period is measured from the date the transferee obtained the missing indorsement, and not from the date the transferee obtained the instrument. As such, any notice or knowledge between the time of possession and the obtaining of the missing indorsement obviates any HDC status. Another important UCC negotiation rule deals with attempted partial indorsements, for example, "pay to Iola one-half of this instrument" or "pay to Iola one-third of this instrument, and pay two-thirds to Melinda." The rule of law holds that an indorsement which purports to convey less than the complete amount of the instrument is not negotiable, and the transferee is thus not a holder. What if the payee's name is misspelled? The UCC allows the payee to negotiate the instrument either by indorsing the name appearing or his or her true name, though banks will usually require both versions.

Indorsements are divided into four kinds: 1) blank, 2) special, 3) qualified, and 4) restrictive. 1) A *blank indorsement* occurs when the payee of an order instrument signs his or her name to the back without naming a new payee. The legal effect is that the instrument is converted into bearer paper (which now can be negotiated without further indorsement). However, the holder of bearer paper can readily convert it into order paper by writing in the name of a new payee above the last indorsement. 2) A *special indorsement* arises when a payee of order paper names a new payee when he or she indorses the instrument. The character of the order paper is maintained and thus any further negotiation of the paper requires an indorsement of the new payee; and only the new payee, called "a special indorser," can now qualify as a holder. An example would be a check payable to the order of Paula, who indorses it: "Pay to the order of Xavier (signed) Paula." It is very important to relate that the words of negotiability are not required in an indorsement. That is, an indorsement "pay to the order of Xavier" is not required; and the indorsement "pay to Xavier" is permissible. 3) In order to explicate a qualified indorsement, it is first necessary to define an unqualified one. An *unqualified indorsement* occurs when an indorser merely indorses an instrument. In such a case, the indorser incurs conditional liability "on" the instrument, which is called "contract liability." The indorser thereby promises to pay the instrument if the holder is unable to obtain payment from the maker or drawee/acceptor. The effect of conditional liability is that the indorser conditionally guarantees payment of the instrument in addition to transferring title to it. A qualified indorsement, however, occurs when the indorser adds the words "without recourse" after his or her indorsement. The effect of a qualified indorsement is that the indorser passes title to the instrument but does not incur any contract liability on the instrument. 4) *Restrictive indorsements* come in four types: a) conditional; b) those that purport to prohibit further transfer of the instrument; c) those that include the words "for collection," "for deposit," or "pay any bank"; and d) those that state that the instrument is for the benefit or use of the indorser or another person. It is very important to point out that a restrictive indorsement does not prevent the further transfer or negotiation of the instrument; and an indorsee or any subsequent transferee may qualify as a holder; but the restrictive indorsement may require the indorsee and subsequent transferees to see to it that funds paid for the instrument are applied in accordance with the indorsement. The first type of restrictive indorsement is the conditional indorsement, which is rare. A conditional indorsement is one in which there is an order to pay an instrument only if a specified event occurs. For example, Julio, the payee of a check, indorses it: "Pay to the order of Yolanda, provided Yolanda finishes painting my portrait by March 15." Such an indorsement does not prohibit further negotiation of the instrument, regardless of whether the condition has occurred; however, until the stated condition has occurred, neither the restrictive indorsee nor a subsequent holder has the right to enforce the instrument. To compare, if the original maker or drawer had used the conditional language in the instrument itself, it would not be negotiable at all due to the fundamental requirement of an unconditional promise or order. There are also special rules for banks. Only the first bank, called the depositary bank, to which an item is transferred for collection is required to comply with the restrictive indorsement; and all other banks, that is, the payor/drawee bank and intermediary banks, may presume compliance with a restrictive indorsement. The rationale for this rule is that due to the immense volume of commercial paper, there is no practical way for banks to consider the effect of restrictive indorsements. The second type of restrictive indorsement is one attempting to prohibit further negotiation of the instrument, for example, "Pay to Masud only, (signed) Bina." The rule of law is that such an indorsement has no effect on negotiation; and further negotiation by the indorsee or any subsequent transferee is permitted. The third type of restrictive indorsement is one for deposit or collection. Such an indorsement does not terminate negotiation; and as a matter of fact, further negotiation is required in the bank collection process. However, this type of restrictive indorsement makes the indorsee the agent of the indorser to collect the funds due on the instrument and to credit the indorser's account. The failure to comply with such an indorsement is construed as a conversion, that is, a civil "theft," of the instrument. The final category of restrictive indorsement is called an indorsement for the benefit of an indorser or another, at times called a "trust indorsement," for example, "Pay to Alan in trust for Bill, (signed) Paul," or "Pay to Susan as agent for Tracie, (signed) Pedro." What is the legal effect? The rule of law is that when the original restrictive indorsee (Alan or Susan) receives payment for the instrument, he or she holds the proceeds in trust for the named beneficiary (Bill or Tracie). That is, the first taker under such a "trust" indorsement must pay or apply value consistently with the indorsement. Moreover, any subsequent purchaser of the instrument takes it free of the restriction, and thus can qualify as an HDC unless he or she had actual knowledge that the restrictive indorsee's negotiation of the instrument is a breach of a fiduciary duty.

The final area of negotiation law deals with *rescission of indorsements*. At times, the indorsement and delivery of the instrument are made under circumstances in which the indorser, based on ordinary contract law, has the right to rescind the indorsement. The most common situations arise when the indorser is a minor, the indorsement and delivery are brought about by fraud or duress by the indorsee, or the negotiation is part of an illegal transaction. The legal effect of such a problematic indorsement is that the negotiation is still effective; that is, the indorser still qualifies as a holder and is capable of indorsing the instrument further; but until the instrument is negotiated to a party who qualifies as an HDC, the indorser can rescind the indorsement.

Holders in Due Course

In order to fully explicate the very important UCC concept of an HDC, it is first necessary to review some contract law, specifically the doctrine of assignment of contract rights. Pursuant to ordinary contract law, an assignment of a non-negotiable right transfers to the assignee the same rights possessed by the assignor. The assignee takes the rights subject to all defenses which might exist between the original parties to the contract, regardless of whether the assignee knows of them. As a result, contract claims are not assigned in large numbers in the business community. Yet there is nothing inherently "wrong" with the assignment of contract rights and the transfer of non-negotiable instruments; and the assignee is entitled to payment unless the party obligated to pay can assert a defense. The policy of Article 3 of the UCC, however, is to insulate remote holders of instruments from disputes between the original parties; and thereby facilitate the negotiation of commercial paper. How is this policy effectuated? The UCC spells out the requirements that must be met by the purchaser of negotiable instruments in order for that person to qualify as a holder in due course (HDC); and then identifies specific kinds of defenses which are cut off when a transferee of an instrument attains the legally elevated status of an HDC. Accordingly, the HDC is free of most defenses which the original obligor on the instrument might be able to assert against the original party, the obligee. The HDC, therefore, acquires greater rights than those possessed by the transferor of the instrument. Yet there are limitations on the HDC doctrine; and thus the HDC does not always prevail over the obligor. First, the obligor may assert certain "real" or "universal" defenses against the obligee, for example, forgery. Second, there are consumer protection statutes that may curtail HDC rights in certain situations, and thus might permit a consumer-obligor to assert personal defenses against the HDC.

Holder in due course standing entails three requirements under the UCC. First, a holder must take a negotiable instrument for "value"; second, the holder must take it in "good faith"; and third, the holder must take it without notice that the instrument is overdue or dishonored or that any defenses exist against it or claims to it on the part of any person. In order to be an HDC, it is imperative to point out that one must first be a "holder"; that is, one must have possession of the instrument (for bearer paper) and have good title to it (for order paper, which requires a valid indorsement and no forgeries of signatures necessary to the "chain of title").

Value is defined in the UCC as the extent to which the agreed upon consideration for the instrument has been performed. Thus, paying for an instrument or delivering goods or performing services for it is "value." One can proportionately possess "value" by partially performing the consideration for the instrument, for example, by making a partial payment or a partial delivery or a partial performance. One can thus be a partial HDC on an instrument. However, an executory, that is, future promise to perform is not "value," since a promise to give value in the future is not "value." Yet there is an exception, which arises when the future promise to give value is embodied in a negotiable instrument, such as a promissory note. The reason for the general rule is that the holder of an instrument can refuse to perform his or her executory promise and thereby avoid harm. It is important to note the distinction between the common law of contracts, where future promises to perform are "consideration," and the UCC, where the future promise to perform, even though consideration, is not "value." Value is also present when the holder takes the instrument either as security for an antecedent debt or as payment for an antecedent debt, regardless of whether the debt is then due. There are also certain special "value" rules for banks. When the holder of a negotiable instrument is a bank which credits its depositor's account, has the bank given "value"? Merely crediting a depositor's account is not "value," since the transaction is only a bookkeeping one, since the bank has the right to set the credit aside if the instrument is returned unpaid. However, when the bank permits withdrawals from the depositor's account, the bank becomes a holder for value to the extent it permits withdrawals of the amount credited to its customer's account.

The *good faith* requirement in the UCC means that the holder must purchase the instrument "honestly" and exhibit honesty in all aspects of the transaction. However, the critical point to good faith is that the test is a subjective one, that is, the only consideration is what is in the holder's mind. The holder is not required to exercise due care, ordinary prudence, reasonable diligence, or even to observe reasonable standards in the business or banking communities. For example, there is no legal duty for the holder to investigate what would appear to the reasonable person to be a suspicious transaction, such as purchasing an instrument from a total stranger for substantially less than its face value. With the "good faith" requirement, one can have an "empty head," and still meet this HDC requirement so long as one has a "pure heart." The test is purely subjective to the holder.

The third requirement to HDC status demands that the holder must purchase the instrument without notice that it is overdue, has been dishonored, or that any defenses to it or claims against it exist. The *notice* test, as opposed to *good faith*, is an objective test. That is, was there actual notice of a problem or was there reason to know of a problem? The test, therefore, is an objective one measured by a "reasonable person" standard. So, if the holder had actual knowledge of a problem or a claim or a defense, the holder could not be an HDC. Similarly, if facts existed from which a reasonable person would infer the existence of a problem or claim or defense, then this "inferable" knowledge is construed against the holder, who consequently cannot be an HDC. As such, if one acquires an instrument knowing or with reason to know that it is already overdue, one cannot qualify as an HDC. The reason is clear, and that is such notice should indicate to the purchaser that there is a defect in the instrument or a defense to it. Facts constituting such notice would include knowledge of the existence of a default, such as when any part of the principal amount is overdue. Furthermore, when the instrument has a fixed maturity date, the purchaser must have acquired it before midnight on the date set for payment, or else it is overdue. Similarly, if the principal is payable in installments, and there is notice that the maker has defaulted on any installments which remain uncured, the purchaser cannot qualify as an HDC. Furthermore, if the purchaser has notice that the instrument has been accelerated due to an event and the instrument is now overdue, the holder cannot be an HDC. However, it is permissible for the purchaser to have knowledge of the obligor's default on interest payments as well as to have knowledge that the obligor has defaulted on other obligations. When the instrument is a demand instrument, the rule of law is that when a purchaser takes a demand instrument with reason to know that a demand for payment has been made or more than a reasonable amount of time after its issue, the purchaser cannot be an HDC. What is a "reasonable time" depends on the nature of the instrument, local business and trade practices, and banking customs. However, when the instrument is a check drawn and payable in the United States, the UCC provides a presumptive time period – 90 days after the issuance of the check. Consequently, although "only" a presumption, anyone acquiring a check 90 days after its issuance date will have serious problems in establishing HDC status.

In order to be an HDC, moreover, the purchaser cannot have actual knowledge, or reason to know, of a defense against or claim to the instrument when the purchaser acquired the instrument. Such knowledge precludes HDC status. Accordingly, knowledge or notice that the obligation of any party is voidable in whole or in part prevents HDC status. For example, knowledge that the obligor has some valid defense to payment, such as breach of contract, failure of consideration, fraud, or mistake, will preclude HDC status. Similarly, knowledge or notice that all parties to the instrument have been discharged prevents HDC status. Yet it is permissible to know that one party has been discharged on the instrument, for example, by the striking out of a party's signature. Knowledge or notice that the instrument has been dishonored will also preclude HDC status. Dishonor occurs when a demand for payment or acceptance has been properly made on a party expected to pay or accept the instrument, and that demand has been refused or cannot be made within the time limits allowed. If an instrument contains the notation "NSF" (insufficient funds) or "payment stopped," the purchaser is charged with knowledge that the instrument has been dishonored.

The time when a purchaser receives notice may affect HDC status. The rule of law is that any notice to the purchaser must have been received in a manner and time to give the purchaser a reasonable opportunity to act. Moreover, notice is determined when the purchaser acquires the instrument as a "holder." As such, if the purchaser of an order instrument fails to obtain the transferor's indorsement at the time of purchase, there is no title passed, and the purchaser is not a "holder." Consequently, if the purchaser is put on notice of a claim or defense prior to obtaining the indorsement, there can be no HDC status for the purchaser since he or she had the notice before he or she became a "holder."

The fact that an instrument is incomplete or irregular may adversely affect one's HDC status. The rule of law is that if an instrument is so irregular or incomplete so as to call into question its validity, the purchaser is placed on notice of a claim or defense and thus cannot attain HDC status. For example, major incompletions or irregularities precluding HDC status would occur in the following circumstances: the holder takes a check from the payee with amount entirely blank; the instrument is payable 20 days after date but the date is blank; or the instrument has visible evidence of forgery or alterations. However, minor irregularities, such as a minor erasure, or minor incompletions, such as the location at where the instrument is to be paid being left blank, or a check without its date of issue, are usually permissible. Moreover, if a holder has knowledge that blanks in the instrument were completed after its issue should not impede HDC status, unless the holder has knowledge that the completion was improper.

Other factors may also have a bearing on HDC status. If the purchaser has knowledge that an instrument was antedated or postdated, generally, that is not construed as notice of a defense or claim, and thus HDC status is permissible. Moreover, notice or knowledge that a party obligated to pay the instrument has defaulted on a payment of interest will not alone preclude HDC status. Problems can occur, however, when an instrument is purchased at a discount. The rule of law is that the existence of a discount does not mean that the holder has not given full value; nor does even a large discount constitute a lack of good faith; yet a very large discount, particularly when coupled with suspicious circumstances, may be grounds for imputing notice of a claim or defense to the instrument.

The final HDC area to examine is called "*successors to HDCs*," which is the area of law that deals with holders who take instruments from HDCs. In certain circumstances, a transferee can acquire the rights of an HDC without actually qualifying as an HDC. An important rule of commercial paper law is *the Shelter Doctrine*, whereby a transferee generally will acquire what rights in the instrument his or her transferor had; that is, the transferee takes "shelter" in the status of the transferor. The legal effect is thus to allow the transferee to "step into the shoes" of the HDC who formerly held the instrument and accordingly to obtain the rights of an HDC, even though the transferee failed to meet HDC requirements, for example, by receiving the instrument as a gift or, significantly, even by possessing knowledge or notice of a defense to the instrument. The purpose of the Shelter Doctrine is to enhance the negotiation of commercial paper by not restricting the HDC's "market" for the instrument. There are, however, exceptions to the Shelter Doctrine. The first exception deals with a prior holder with notice of a problem. The rule of law is that if a person reacquires a negotiable instrument from an HDC, he or she will not receive HDC rights if he or she had notice of a claim or defense to the instrument at the time he or she was formerly a holder. The reason for this rule is that the Shelter Doctrine was designed to protect only those transferees who had no connection to the problems giving rise to the claims and defenses to the instrument. If a transferee was not an HDC on his or her first possession due to knowledge or notice of a problem, he or she will not be allowed to improve his or her status by "washing" the instrument through the hands of a subsequent HDC. To compare, a prior holder without such notice can obtain HDC rights by reacquiring the instrument from an HDC even if the prior holder learned in the interim of a problem with the instrument. Another exception to the Shelter Doctrine involves parties who were part of any fraud or illegality pertaining to the instrument. The Shelter Doctrine never grants HDC rights to persons who were parties to any fraud or illegality affecting the instrument, whether or not such parties are prior holders. A party so implicated cannot sell an instrument through an HDC and re-obtain it in order to free himself or herself from the defense of fraud or illegality. Finally, if the Shelter Doctrine is properly in operation, it is important to note that once a person qualifies as an HDC, all subsequent transferees acquire the same rights of an HDC, no matter how far "down the chain" of transferees they may be.

Claims and Defenses to Negotiable Instruments

There is, as noted, a substantial difference in the legal effects of transferring a negotiable instrument to an HDC as compared to other transferees. The claims and defenses to payment of the instrument may be cut off when an HDC is involved; whereas the non-HDC who "at best" may be forced to litigate the claims and defenses of other parties to the instrument. A "claim" to an instrument is an affirmative cause of action for recovery on the instrument, based on allegedly superior ownership rights. As a general rule, an HDC takes free of all such claims. A "defense" is a reason for refusing to pay all or part of a negotiable instrument. There is a critical distinction the UCC makes in the types of defenses to negotiable instruments. There are "real" defenses and "personal" defenses. A real defense can be asserted against all holders, even HDCs. Accordingly, the maker, drawer, or drawee/acceptor who has available a real defense is under no liability to the plaintiff transferee of the instrument, even if he or she is an HDC. Personal defenses, however, can be asserted only against ordinary holders, but not against HDCs of holders with the rights of an HDC.

There are several real defenses, also at times called *universal defenses*. The first is *infancy or minor status*. The rule of law is that if state law makes the status of being an "infant" (usually under the age of 18) a defense for the minor to a breach of contract cause of action (that is, by rendering the contract void or voidable due to the minor's status as a minor), then the minor has a real defense to payment of negotiable instruments too. The second defense is incapacity to contract, which is a real defense if under state law a contract is deemed void (but not voidable) due to a person's mental incompetence. The third defense is illegality which similarly is a real defense if under state law illegality in the underlying transaction renders the obligation void; but if the obligation is only voidable, the defense of illegality is only a personal one. The fourth defense is duress; and its status as a real defense depends on the type of duress involved. It the duress is extreme, it rises to the level of a real defense. "Extreme" means overwhelming pressure, such as the exertion of force or the threat of force which deprives the victim of his or her free will, for example, a person who is compelled to sign a negotiable instrument at gunpoint. Otherwise, duress is only a personal defense.

The fifth real defense is fraud; yet fraud as a defense is a complicated area of commercial paper law. *Fraud in the factum*, also called fraud in the execution or fraud in the inception, is a real defense. This type of "real" fraud arises when a misrepresentation causes a party to sign an instrument with neither the knowledge of its character as a negotiable instrument nor its essential terms. That is, a person is caused to sign an instrument under circumstances under which he or she honestly and reasonably believes it is something other than a negotiable instrument. This type of fraud perpetuated on the victim rises to the level of a real defense which can be asserted against the HDC. Another type of fraud, fraud in the inducement, where the victim knew what he or she was signing, but was deceptively induced into signing the instrument, is only a personal defense. However, for fraud to be a real defense there is also a requirement that the victim was not negligent in the transaction. That is, even if the victim was unaware that he or she was signing a negotiable instrument, real fraud cannot be asserted as a defense if the victim failed to take reasonable steps to recognize the instrument as a negotiable instrument or to otherwise ascertain the true nature of the transaction.

The sixth real defense is a discharge in bankruptcy or other insolvency proceeding, the latter typically referring to state insolvency, liquidation, or credit rehabilitation proceedings. A discharge in federal bankruptcy proceedings is the most common type of discharge, which excuses the bankrupt from most debts listed in the bankruptcy petition, such as promissory notes. The rule of law is that such discharges are real defenses which can be asserted against an HDC. The seventh real defense involves discharges that are known to the HDC. The basic legal principle is that an HDC takes a negotiable instrument subject to any other discharge which the HDC had notice when he or she took the instrument. "Discharge" refers to events which excuse further liability of a party to an instrument. One example is cancellation of liability. The rule of law is that a holder may cancel liability of a prior party by striking out the signature of that party. The effect is not to give a later purchaser notice of a problem with the instrument (so as to prevent HDC status); but such a striking-out would give an HDC notice that the person whose name is stricken is no longer liable on the instrument. The result, therefore, is that the discharge of a person stricken amounts to a real defense which he or she can interpose against an HDC. Of course, an entire instrument may be cancelled, for example, by marking it "Paid." Otherwise, discharge is usually a personal defense. That is, unless the discharge is apparent from the face of the instrument (for example, a line drawn through an indorsement) or the HDC knows of the discharge, discharge is only a personal defense which cannot be asserted against an HDC. Thus, payment by a party to a holder is a discharge, but unless payment is known or apparent, a later HDC can compel payment again.

The eighth defense is a *material alteration* of an instrument. A material alteration is one that changes the contract of the parties in any respect, for example, by adding a penny to the amount to be paid, or by advancing the payment date by one day. However, correcting the spelling of the payee's name is not considered to be a material alteration. As to material alteration as a defense, the rule of law is that it is a partial real defense. That is, the HDC can enforce the materially altered instrument, but only according to its "original tenor" (as it was originally made or drawn). Consequently, the HDC can only collect the original, non-altered amount. An ordinary holder, of course, usually recovers nothing since a material alteration is typically fraudulent, which fraud serves as a complete defense to a holder. However, there is an exception to the "original tenor" rule, which arises if the material alteration is in the form of a completion of an incomplete instrument in an unauthorized manner. The rule in such a case is that the HDC can enforce the instrument according to its terms as completed. The reason for this exception is due to the risk a person takes by signing an incomplete instrument.

The ninth defense is *forgery*. There is a very basic principle of commercial paper law that a person cannot be held liable on a negotiable instrument unless his or her name appears thereon. In the case of a forgery, a person's name does appear (as a maker or drawer usually), but the signature is made by a person without authority to do so. A forgery can occur to a name necessary to the "chain of title" of an instrument, that is, the payee or any special indorsee. In such a case, the rule of law is that if the name of the payee or any special indorsee is either forged or unauthorized (usually an agent signing without authority), no subsequent taker of the instrument can be an HDC, because no one can obtain good title to the instrument necessary to qualify as a holder. In the case of a forgery of a name not necessary to the chain of title, such as a maker, drawer, acceptor, or an indorser of bearer paper, the forgery does not affect title, and thus a subsequent holder may qualify as an HDC but the forgery or unauthorized signature is a real defense.

Finally, it should be noted that the Federal Trade Commission has enacted rules, which will be covered later in the chapter, which limit the rights of HDCs in certain consumer transactions.

Personal defenses cannot be asserted against an HDC or one with the rights of an HDC. Thus, any transferee of a negotiable instrument without HDC rights takes the instrument subject to all personal defenses. The first personal defense is the lack or failure of consideration. Generally, a negotiable instrument must be supported by consideration; but the existence of consideration is not technically a prerequisite to negotiability. An instrument, for example, can be given as a gift. The rule of law thus holds that the lack or failure of consideration may be asserted by the maker or drawer as a valid defense against an ordinary holder, but not an HDC. The second personal defense is breach of contract, which actually is the most common personal defense. Many instruments are issued to payees in payment for goods and services which the payees are obligated to deliver or perform under contracts with the maker or drawer of instruments. If the contract is breached by the payee, the maker of a note can refuse to pay, and the drawer of a check can stop payment, but if the instrument is negotiated to an HDC, the maker or drawer must pay the HDC and then the maker or drawer can pursue a breach of contract suit against the payees who breached the contract. The third personal defense is breach of warranty. For example, when a merchant sells goods, the UCC implies that a warranty of "merchantability" attaches to the sale, but if the buyer pays for the goods with a negotiable instrument, and the warranty is breached, but the instrument is transferred to an HDC, the breach of warranty as a personal defense will not prevent the HDC from recovering on the instrument from the maker or drawer, who now will be compelled to sue the merchant for breach of warranty. As previously noted, fraud in the inducement, as opposed to fraud in the execution, is only a personal defense. That is, when a person signs a negotiable instrument knowing it to be such, but is induced to sign it by misrepresentation of the other party, such fraud is only a personal defense. Also as noted, the unauthorized completion of an incomplete instrument is only a personal defense, and thus the HDC can enforce the instrument as completed. Finally, also as noted, prior payment of an instrument, which is usually a discharge of a party's liability, is nonetheless only a personal defense unless there is some notation on the instrument that it has been paid in full or in part. Absent that notice, an instrument that has been paid may have to be paid again to the HDC, especially if payment has occurred before the instrument's maturity date. Of course, if an instrument is fully paid, the maker or acceptor has the right to demand the return or surrender of the instrument.

Liability of the Parties

This section will commence the examination of the liability of the various parties to commercial paper transactions. The authors will presume that there are no valid defenses to be asserted. Speaking very generally, persons whose signatures appear on negotiable instruments have different types of liability depending on their status. The UCC authorizes three types of lawsuits on instruments: 1) suits in contract based on signing the instrument; 2) suits based on implied warranties arising from the transfer or presentment of the instrument; and 3) suits in tort for conversion of the instrument.

Before addressing these key liability issues, it is first necessary do examine an ancillary legal area – the liability of an agent on commercial paper. As a basic rule of negotiable paper, called the Signature Rule, no one is liable on an instrument unless his or her signature appears thereon. Usually, the maker, drawer, acceptor, or indorser personally signs the instrument; but the signature of a person may be made by his or her agent (and in the case of an artificial legal person like a corporation must be made by an agent). Two problems arise in such an agency situation: first, the liability of the principal (that is, the person the agent is representing and whose named is signed on the instrument); and second, the personal liability of the agent himself or herself. Regarding the personal liability of the agent, the agent must be very careful to sign the instrument so as to bind the principal but not the agent; otherwise, the agent may be personally liable on the instrument and unable to introduce evidence of forgery. Of course, the authors are presuming the agent has the authority to sign the instrument. If there is an unauthorized signature by the agent, the principal generally is not bound, and the agent is alone liable on the instrument. In order to escape personal liability against all persons, including HDCs, the agent must do two things: first, name his or her principal; and second, indicate that the signature was made in a representative capacity. For example, the name of the agent followed by his or her official title (such as "agent" or "president," or "treasurer") coupled with the principal will be sufficient to relieve the agent of liability. Also, the use of the word "by" in front of the agent's signature coupled with the name of the principal (such as "P, Principal, by A, Agent") will also work to avoid the agent's liability. What is the legal result if both requirements are missing? If the agent signs his or her own name, intending to bind the principal, but the instrument neither names the principal nor shows the agent has signed as an agent, the rule of law is that the agent is alone liable, and evidence to show the agent's agency status is not admissible, even in a lawsuit between the immediate parties to the instrument. What if one of the two requirements is missing? That is, the instrument omits the principal's name, but does indicate that the agent signed in a representative capacity, or the instrument names the principal, but omits any indication of agency status (for example, by failing to use the word "agent" or one's corporate status). In such a case, evidence is admissible between the immediate parties to show the agent did not mean to incur personal liability. However, if the instrument is acquired by a third party transferee from one of the original parties, the agent is personally liable since the lawsuit is no longer between the immediate parties to the instrument.

Another important initial liability area to examine involves lawsuits based on the obligation underlying the instrument. This area of law is at times referred to as the *Merger Doctrine*. Generally, negotiable instruments are issued for some reason, usually to pay an obligation, for example, rent. As a result, when the instrument is issued, the obligation becomes merged into the instrument, and thus is not available as a cause of action (at least temporarily). There are three main Merger Rules: 1) Suspension of the Underlying Obligation – The rule of law holds that where a negotiable instrument is accepted as conditional payment for an underlying obligation, the obligation cannot be the basis for a lawsuit until the instrument is due or if a demand instrument, such as a check, until it is presented and dishonored. On dishonor, the holder of the instrument has the option of suing on the instrument, the underlying obligation, or both (but the holder is only entitled to one recovery). 2) Discharge of the Underlying Obligation – The rule of law holds that if liability on the instrument is discharged in any way (for example, by payment, cancellation, material alteration, or bankruptcy), liability is also discharged on the underlying obligation.

The reason is that since the instrument and obligation have become merged, the discharge of the instrument also discharges the underlying obligation. 3) Cancellation of the Underlying Obligation – The rule of law holds that when the party primarily liable on a negotiable instrument is a bank, such as a cashier's check, the underlying obligation is completely discharged (so long as the person who owed the obligation is not liable on the instrument). The reason is that banks are more solvent and trustworthy than most individuals.

Contract Liability – Suits "on the Instrument"

The general rule of law is that any person who puts his or her name on a negotiable instrument will incur contract liability on the instrument (whether such liability is intended or not). In the following discussion, the authors make two assumptions: first, the party signed the instrument personally; and second, the party does not have a defense against the holder. Contract liability depends on the commercial paper signer's contract status, which for purposes of liability, the UCC divides into two groups – primary parties and secondary parties. First, primary parties are the makers of notes and the acceptors of the drafts and checks. Generally, they are absolutely liable on the instrument, and typically are the parties who will pay the instrument. Second, the secondary parties are drawers of drafts and checks and indorsers of any instrument. They do not expect to pay the instrument, but rather assume that the primary parties will fulfill their obligations. The drawer and indorsers of drafts and checks expect that the acceptor will pay; and the indorsers of notes expect that the maker will pay. As will be discussed in detail, the liability of drawers and indorsers is a conditional or secondary type of liability. That is, they are responsible to pay if the primary parties do not pay, provided that the party entitled to payment has satisfied certain conditions precedent (specifically, presentment of the instrument to the primary party, dishonor by the primary party, and notice of the primary party's dishonor being given to the secondary party).

First, regarding the liability of the *primary parties*, the liability of the maker of a note must be addressed. The rule of law is straightforward regarding the contract liability of the maker of a note – the maker is primarily and absolutely liable on it. The contract the maker has made renders the maker legally obligated to pay the note according to its terms on maturity date (even if the holder does not demand payment at that time). There can be co-makers on the note; and the rule of law is that if two or more people sign as co-makers in the same transaction, they are jointly and severally liable on the note, which means each can be sued for the entire amount (even if the note uses the single pronoun, "I promise to pay"). Of course, if one co-maker is forced to pay the entire amount to the holder, he or she can seek reimbursement from the other, which legal right is called the "right of contribution." If there is late presentment of the note for payment, the general rule is that nonetheless the maker is not discharged (as compared to an indorser who is discharged). Actually, even if the note is presented many months or years after its due date, the maker remains fully liable thereon (at least until the applicable state Statute of Limitations, that is, the time allowed to bring a lawsuit, "runs," that is, expires).

Next, the liability of the acceptor, who is the other primary party under UCC law, must be addressed. It is initially important to emphasize that by merely being named as a drawee does not mean one has incurred any contract liability. An "acceptor" is a drawee who signs the draft or check and thereby agrees to honor the draft or check as presented. "Acceptance" is thus the drawee's signed agreement to honor the draft as presented. Acceptance can occur by the drawee's signature alone written on the draft, or it can occur by stamping "Accepted" with the drawee's name and date on the face of the instrument. If the draft is a check, acceptance is called "certification." It is also important to underscore that the drawee's failure to accept is not a breach of any duty owed to the holder of the draft, who consequently cannot bring a lawsuit against the drawee; but the drawee usually owes a legal duty to the drawer to accept. The purpose of acceptance is to create an acceptor's contract to honor the draft; the draft is then returned to the holder; and the draft, now with the obligation of the acceptor thereon, has greater commercial worth, and thus is easier to sell. The legal effect of the acceptor's contract is to create primary liability identical to the maker of a note. That is, the acceptor promises to pay the instrument according to the terms at the time he or she accepted it (and the acceptor is not entitled to any conditions precedent, that is, the acceptor has no right to presentment, dishonor, or notice of dishonor). If the drawee refuses to accept the draft unless some alteration is made in its terms, the presenter/holder may treat this as a dishonor (and after giving notice of dishonor) may sue the drawer or any prior indorsers. However, if the presenter/holder agrees to the drawee's varied acceptance, the drawer and all prior non-consenting indorsers are discharged. If a draft which is presented for acceptance is dishonored, further presentment for payment is not required. It also must be noted that if a draft is one payable on demand, such as a check, there is no right to acceptance (and the bank has the option to certify the check or refuse to certify it); and thus the failure of a drawee to accept a demand draft is not a dishonor. Once a bank does certify a check, the bank becomes primarily liable thereon, and it is too late for the drawer to stop payment. Bank checks, such as cashier's checks, are deemed to be accepted in advance. If certification is obtained by the holder, the drawer and all prior indorsers are discharged from liability; but if the drawer procures certification, the drawer is still liable on the drawer's contract.

The next major liability area to examine concerns the contract liability of the secondary parties. *Secondary parties* are the drawers of drafts and checks and indorsers of all instruments. They promise to pay the instrument only if certain conditions are met: due presentment, dishonor, notice of dishonor, and perhaps protest. These conditions, unless waived, must be met for the secondary party to be held liable on contract liability. The contract made by the drawer is that he or she promises to pay the amount of the draft to the holder only if the drawer was first accorded the procedural rights of due presentment for payment and/or acceptance, dishonor, notice of dishonor to the drawer, and perhaps protest. However, it is important to relate that a late presentment for acceptance or payment as well as late or no notice of dishonor does not free the drawer of liability on the instrument (unless the drawee goes insolvent during the delay). The other secondary party is the indorser. What is the indorser's contract liability? The indorser promises to pay the instrument to any later holder, but the indorser's promise is conditioned on the indorser first being accorded technical procedural rights of presentment for acceptance and/or payment, dishonor and notice thereof, and protest where relevant.

The conditional liability of the indorser is similar to the drawer except: 1) if either the required presentment for acceptance or presentment for payment is made late, the indorser is entirely freed of contract liability to the holder; and 2) the indorser is also totally freed from liability if the holder gives late notice or no notice of dishonor. It also should be noted that the indorser can indorse "without recourse" after his or her signature, which means that the indorser does not assume contract liability on the instrument, but nevertheless the indorser still can pass title to the instrument. Indorsements are not necessary on bearer instruments to pass title; however, the transferee may insist on the indorser's unqualified indorsement in order to acquire the transferor's contract liability. There also can be multiple indorsers on an instrument. In such a case, each indorser is liable for the full amount to any holder or later indorser. Usually, the holder of a dishonored instrument seeks to hold the last indorser liable, but the holder is not required to do so. That is, an indorser who pays a holder usually proceeds against the immediate prior indorser, but the holder can sue any prior indorser (but not later indorsers since liability under the UCC moves only "up the chain").

The contract liability of the secondary parties, as noted, is conditional. Drawers and indorsers are entitled to certain conditions precedent which must be fulfilled in order to establish their secondary liability. Also as noted, these conditions, or technical procedural rights, are proper presentment, dishonor, notice of dishonor, and protest (where relevant). *Presentment* is a demand for payment or acceptance of the instrument made by the holder of the instrument. In the case of a note, presentment is made to the maker; and in the case of a draft, presentment is made to the drawee. Presentment can be made by personally contacting the primary party, or by mail (effective on receipt), or through bank clearing houses. Presentment usually is made on the location specified on the instrument; otherwise, it occurs at the place of business or residence of the maker or drawee. If presentment is made in an unauthorized manner, the refusal of the maker or drawee or acceptor to accept or pay the instrument is not a dishonor. The "presentee," that is, the maker or drawee, has certain rights on presentment. When presentment is made to the maker or drawer, the presentee may demand: 1) exhibition of the instrument; 2) reasonable identification from the person making the presentment; 3) evidence of the presentee's authority, if the person presenting the instrument is doing so on behalf of another; 4) production of the instrument at a reasonable place and hour; 5) a signed receipt on the instrument for any partial or full payment; and 6) surrender of the instrument if the presentee pays it in full. What is the legal effect of the failure to comply with these demands? The rule of law is that if the presenter cannot or will not comply with the aforementioned demands, "presentment" has not occurred, and thus the presentee's refusal to pay is not "dishonor." When is the proper time for presentment? For presentment for acceptance, if the instrument is payable at a stated date, any presentment for acceptance must be made on or before the date payable. Also, if an instrument is payable "after sight," it must be presented for acceptance within a reasonable time after its date or issue, which is later. For presentment for payment, if the instrument shows the date which it is payable, presentment for payment is due on that date. However, if the presentment is for payment of a demand instrument, the presentment must be made within a reasonable time after the secondary party signed the instrument (and thus is liable thereon). What is a "reasonable time" for presentment? It depends on the nature of the instrument, the local banking and trade practices, and the facts of the case. However, if the demand instrument is an uncertified check drawn and payable in the United States (and not a draft drawn on a bank), a reasonable time for presentment for payment is presumed to be 30 days after date or issue (whichever is later) with respect to the liability of the drawer and indorsers. If presentment is not properly accomplished, the indorser is completely released from liability. With respect to the drawer's liability, the drawer is released from liability only if the drawee becomes insolvent during the delay.

After the secondary condition of presentment comes the requirement of dishonor. The party who presents an instrument wants it accepted or paid. A "*dishonor*" occurs when the presentee refuses to accept or pay or when the maker or drawer returns it after presentment without paying or accepting within the allowed time. What is the time allowed for the decision? If a draft is presented for acceptance, the drawee may delay acceptance until the close of business on the next business day following presentment without triggering a dishonor. The reason is to give the drawee time to ascertain the facts before the drawee assumes the obligations of an acceptor. If a draft or check is presented for payment "across the counter," it must be paid or returned by the close of business on that day. In the context of checks, "across the counter" means that the drawer has an account at the bank to which the holder presents the check for payment. If payment is made through bank collection channels (that is, banks are collecting checks from one another), the operative rule is called the "mid-night deadline" rule, which holds that the drawee (called the "payor" bank) has until mid-night of the banking day following the banking day of receipt to make a decision; and if there is no dishonor by the "mid-night deadline," the bank is accountable for the item. Finally, regarding payment of a promissory note, that is, a note which is presented to the maker for payment, the rule of law is that the maker has until the close of business on the day of presentment within which to pay the instrument or return it; and if the maker fails to do either, his or her inaction is considered to be a conversion of the instrument.

Once an instrument is dishonored, the next secondary condition is notice of dishonor. The rule of law is that once an instrument is dishonored upon proper presentment, the holder must give prompt notice of dishonor in order to have the right of legal recourse against the secondary parties. Failure to give prompt and proper notice of dishonor will discharge all indorsers on the instrument as well as the drawer (but only if the drawee goes insolvent during the interim). Notice of dishonor can be given to any party who may be secondarily liable on the instrument (though the holder typically gives notice to his or her immediate transferor). The notice can be written or oral, given in any reasonable manner, and effective on dispatch, but it must identify the instrument and state that it has been dishonored. As to the time for giving notice, there are two main rules: first, banks must give notice of dishonor before the expiration of their "mid-night deadline"; second, ordinary holders have 30 business days to give notice after a dishonor or their own receipt of a notice of dishonor. However, in the case of a non-certified check which is "stale," that is, one presented more than six months after its date, the bank can dishonor the check and not be sued for wrongful dishonor. Finally, there may be required as a secondary condition a

"*Protest*," which is a certificate stating that a dishonor has occurred and which is signed and sealed by a U.S. Consul or notary at the place where dishonor has occurred. Protests are required when a draft is drawn or payable outside the United States. The failure to make a mandatory protest completely discharges the liability of the indorsers and the drawer.

The failure to perform the secondary conditions may be excused. First, delay in compliance can be excused when the holder acted with reasonable diligence and the delay was not due to any fault of the holder. For example, bank delays due to war, insolvency of another bank, or interruptions in communications would be grounds for excusable delay. Second, compliance can be excused completely. For example, a waiver written into the body of the instrument binds all parties; or a waiver can be written above the signature of an indorser, which binds only that indorser. Also, there may be found in an instrument the term "Protest Waived," which waives all the secondary conditions, even if protest is not technically required. Another example of a complete excuse would be when the primary party is unavailable, for example, he or she is deceased or the subject of insolvency proceedings, or when the primary party has anticipatorily repudiated the instrument, that is, has clearly stated in advance that he or she will not pay the instrument.

Warranty Liability – Suits "off the Instrument"

A note or draft is not only written evidence of contract liability, but also a special kind of property intended for trading, and thus possessing marketability. So, just as there are certain implied warranties that attach to the sale of goods under the UCC, certain warranties attach to the sale and transfer of commercial paper. These warranty suits are regarded as being "*off the instrument*" since the warranties are effective whether or not the transferor or presenter signs the instrument. There are four important, initial, general rules dealing with *implied warranties*: 1) the warranties are created automatically when the instrument is physically shifted from one party to another; 2) the plaintiff in a cause of action for breach of warranty need neither possess the instrument nor comply exactly with the conditions precedent for contract liability; but 3) the notice of a claim for breach of warranty must be given to the warrantor within 30 days after the transferee or holder has reason to know of a breach and the identity of the warrantor (or the warrantor is not liable for any loss caused by the delay); and 4) warranties can be disclaimed (except for checks).

There are three stages in the life of a negotiable instrument: issuance, transfer, and presentment. No warranties are made on issuance; that is, no implied warranties are created by the issuance of a negotiable instrument (that is, the first delivery to the payee). Warranties can be created by the transfer of the instrument and the presentment of the instrument. In the former case, they are called transferor's or transfer warranties; and in the latter case, they are called presenter's or presentment warranties.

The first category of implied warranties is the *warranties on transfer*. A "transfer" is the movement of an instrument other than its issuance or presentment. The rule of law is that any person who transfers an instrument, whether by negotiation or assignment, and who receives consideration, makes certain implied warranties. If the transfer is made by delivery alone, the warranties extend only to the immediate transferee (for example, the transfer of bearer paper without any indorsement); but if the transfer is made by indorsement (whether qualified or unqualified), the warranties extend to any subsequent transferee who takes the instrument in good faith. There are five transfer warranties. First, the transferor warrants that he or she has good title to the instrument and that the transfer is "rightful." "Good title" means that all indorsements necessary to the chain of title (that is, the payee and any special indorsee) are genuine. The "rightful" part of the warranty arises when a thief or finder transfers bearer paper, and thereby breaches the warranty (even though an HDC would have good title to the instrument). The second transfer warranty is that all signatures are genuine and are authorized. For example, a forged signature on bearer paper would breach the warranty, even though there are no title problems. Also, the forged signature of the maker or drawer or drawee or acceptor or an indorser not in the chain of title would be a breach of the warranty, even though there are no title problems. The third transfer warranty is that there is no material alteration of the instrument. Recall that for contract liability, the ordinary holder recovers nothing from an altered instrument, and an HDC only recovers its "original tenor" from the maker or acceptor. However, with warranty liability, any holder or transferee can hold the transferor liable for breach of the warranty, presuming the alteration occurred before the transfer. The fourth transfer warranty is that there is no defense good against the transferor. The rule of law is that the transferor warrants that no party to the instrument has a defense that is good against the transferor. Even if the transferee is an HDC, the warranty is still breached, even though the HDC may be able to enforce the instrument, because the transferee need not undertake to "buy" a lawsuit with the necessity of proving his or her status as an HDC. Note, however, that if there is a qualified indorsement ("without recourse"), then the warranty becomes that the transferor had no knowledge of a defense against the transferor. The fifth and final transfer warranty is no knowledge of insolvency proceedings. The rule of law is that the transferor warrants that he or she has no knowledge of any insolvency proceedings instituted with respect to a party from whom payment is accepted. Note that the warranty is "no knowledge," which is measured by an objective test, and not that no such proceedings exist.

The second category of *implied warranties* consists of those made on *presentment of the instrument*. That is, they are warranties made by the presenter who presents an instrument for payment or acceptance. These warranties are considerably narrower than the transfer warranties. The rationale is that if the presentment warranties are breached, and payment or acceptance has been made, then the transaction will have to be undone and the money paid recovered or the acceptance done nullified. There are three presentment warranties. The first is good title. That is, the presenter warrants that he or she has "holder" status, meaning that no names necessary to the chain of title (the payee and any special indorsee) are forged or not genuine. The second is that the transferor warrants that he or she has no knowledge that the signature of the maker or drawer is forged or unauthorized. However, an HDC even with knowledge avoids the warranty when the HDC is acting in good faith and presents the instrument to the maker or drawer (who presumably knows his or her own signature yet fails to detect the forgery). "Good faith" means that at the time of taking, the HDC had no knowledge of the forgery, but acquired knowledge after taking, but before presentment). The third presentment warranty is that there is no material alteration of the instrument. Note that this is an absolute warranty which does not depend on knowledge. However, once again, the HDC who presents the altered instrument to the maker or drawer can avoid this warranty if the HDC acts in good faith. What are the damages for breach of the implied warranties? The rule of law is that the aggrieved party may recover the difference between the value of the instrument received and its value had it been as warranted.

Conversion of Instruments

The final liability area to briefly examine is the conversion of instruments. Under the common law, unauthorized assumption and exercise of ownership over personal property belonging to another is conversion. Conversion is a tort under the common law. Pursuant to the UCC, conversion is the only tort cause of action recognized. There are several ways that instruments can be subject to conversion under the UCC. The first is the failure to accept or return a draft. When a draft is presented to the drawee for acceptance, he or she must either accept it or return it to the presenter/holder unaccepted. If unaccepted, the holder can proceed against prior parties (the drawer and any indorsers) on their contract liability. If the drawee refuses to return the draft, there has been a conversion. The second similarly is the failure to pay or return the draft, which also is a conversion. The third type of conversion under the UCC is the failure to comply with the terms of a restrictive indorsement. That is, if a party who is required to comply with the terms of a restrictive indorsement fails to do so, he or she is liable for a conversion. Finally, the payment on a forged indorsement is a conversion of the instrument as against the true owner, the party whose indorsement was forged (typically the payee). The true owner can recover from any party who made payment; and the paying party then has recourse against the other parties for breach of the presentment warranty of good title. The measure of damages for conversion is generally the face amount of the instrument.

Statutory Erosion of the Holder in Due Course Doctrine

The original purposes of the HDC doctrine were to enable commercial paper to move more freely through the business community as an equivalent of money and to insulate lenders and sellers from problems between the immediate parties to the instrument. However, dissatisfaction arose with the HDC doctrine in consumer credit transactions. For example, unethical lenders and sellers would victimize consumers by selling defective goods on credit, and then discount the consumer's negotiable instrument payment to a supposedly innocent and ignorant finance company that technically qualified as an HDC. The consumer was unable to obtain repair or replacement of the goods, but had to pay the finance company HDC even though the consumer had valid contract defenses against the seller/lender. Of course, the consumer could sue the seller under products liability law, but that recourse was a problematical one for the consumer. Accordingly, some state governments as well as the federal government began to pass laws that restricted or eliminated the HDC doctrine in consumer financing transactions. For example, some state statutes give the consumer the power to preserve defenses against any assignee/holder by notifying the assignee/holder of claims against the seller (within certain time periods after the instrument is negotiated). Other states simply eliminate the HDC doctrine by providing that any assignee of an installment contract or the holder of any negotiable instrument takes it subject to whatever defenses the retail consumer buyer had against the seller. The federal law in the U.S. is based on a rule of the Federal Trade Commission, called the rule for "Preserving Consumers Claims and Defenses." Pursuant to the federal rule, any consumer sales and credit transaction involving a promissory note must contain a notice that any assignee or holder will be "subject to all claims and defenses which the debtor could assert against the seller of goods and services" covered by the contract. The notice added to the note renders the note not negotiable since the maker of the note has not made an unconditional promise to pay. The holder of such a note, moreover, cannot be an HDC since the holder agrees to be subject to all defenses. It is important to relate that the rule applies to consumer credit contracts, that is, transactions involving either the purchase or lease of consumer goods or services; the rule does not apply to commercial buyers. Also, the rule applies only to consumer purchases on credit, for example by means of a promissory note, and not when a check currently dated is given in full payment, since payment by check is not a credit transaction.

Part II – Banking Transactions
Article 4 of the UCC ("Bank Deposits and Collections) amplifies and alters Article 3 provisions regarding negotiable instruments when the negotiable instrument (particularly a check) becomes part of the bank collection process. If there is any conflict between the two, Article 4 generally prevails. Article 4 has two basic parts: 1) rules for governing the relationship between a bank and its customers; and 2) rules governing the check collection among banks (although the latter has been superseded in part by federal statute).

The Relationship between Banks and Their Customers
The focus of this part of Article 4 is the contractual relationship between the drawee bank (called the "payor" bank) and the drawer (the customer) and the rights and duties that stem from that relationship.

The first area to cover is called *wrongful dishonor*. The bank has a duty to honor checks drawn by its customers when sufficient funds are available in the customers' accounts to cover the checks. A "wrongful dishonor" occurs when a check is properly payable from the drawer's account, but the bank wrongfully refuses to honor it; then the drawer has a cause of action against the bank. Damages for wrongful dishonor are based on two main rules: 1) if the dishonor occurred because of a bank mistake, for example, when the bank accidentally placed its customer's check in a savings account as opposed to a checking account, the drawer must prove that actual damages were suffered, which may include damages for arrest and prosecution; and 2) if the bank's decision to dishonor the check was intentional, some courts will award damages even without direct proof as to the amount of the injury, and even if the bank believed in good faith that it had proper reason to dishonor. However, one must recall the *stale check* rule; that is, the bank is not obligated to pay an uncertified check more than six months after its date of issuance (though the bank has the option to do so). The second area to cover concerns the death or incompetence of the bank's customer. Pursuant to common law agency rules, an agent's authority to act terminates with the death of the principal; thereafter, an agent's act is unauthorized, even if done without knowledge of the principal's death. The problem is that a bank can be both a collecting agent and a paying agent for its customers. There are two important bank agency rules: 1) The first rule concerns pre-knowledge actions. The rule of law is that the bank's collection and payment actions taken prior to knowledge of the death or incompetence of its customer are valid. "Knowledge" means actual knowledge of the bank employee whose job it is to close down accounts. 2) Regarding post-knowledge actions, the rule of law is that even where the bank has knowledge of its customer's death, the bank may elect to pay or certify checks for 10 days following deaths. However, any person who claims an interest in the customer's account, regardless of whether the claim is valid, may order the bank to stop payment on checks or to not certify checks during a 10 day period (and the bank is bound). The third important area to cover examines the requirement that a bank item be *properly payable*. As a general rule, a bank may charge a customer's account for an item (e.g., a check) only if the item is properly payable; and if the item is not properly payable, the bank must replace the money in its customer's account (presuming the customer complains within the relevant time limits). When exactly is an item "properly payable"? This key legal determination depends on the terms of the deposit contract between the customer and his or her bank, who presents the item, the terms of the item, and the possibility of a stop payment order from the customer. There are several important rules: First, regarding overdrafts, if payment of an item would overdraw the customer's account, the bank need not pay, but may do so (even when the bank and its customer have no agreement concerning overdrafts). Second, regarding altered items, if an item is altered, (for example, the item is changed), the bank may charge its customer's account only according to the original terms of the item (unless the customer's negligence led to the alteration). The third rule is called the "proper presenter" rule, which holds that a bank may charge its customer's account with the amount of the item only if the bank pays a person who qualifies as a "holder" (that is, a person in possession of the instrument with good title thereto). The fourth rule deals with a forged drawer's signature. If the drawee bank honors a check bearing a forged drawer's signature, it cannot charge the drawer's account (even if the bank did not know of the forgery) because there was no valid order. The fifth rule deals with completed items. If the customer leaves blanks in an item (that is, signs his or her name to an incomplete check), which are later filled in, the bank may assume that the item as completed is proper, and thus charge the drawer's account (unless the bank knows otherwise). The sixth rule deals with post-dated checks, which a bank cannot pay before the specified date since a customer has the right to stop payment on checks drawn to his or her account because the item is not properly payable; yet a bank may certify the check before the date; however, in some states in the U.S., a customer must give written notice to the bank within certain time periods, as well as bear the expense of a stop payment request, in order to properly stop payment on a check. The seventh rule deals with the bank's right of *set-off*, which is an old common law principle. The bank, regarded as a debtor, as opposed to the customer, regarded as a creditor, can exercise the debtor's traditional right of set-off. That is, the debtor can subtract (set-off) from the amount owed to the creditor any debt the creditor owes to the debtor.

For example if a bank customer misses payment on a school loan borrowed from the bank, the bank is allowed to pay itself out of its customer's checking account, even if the withdrawal causes the customer's checks to "bounce." Notice of set-off is not required by the bank; however, under federal law, banks are prohibited from setting-off unpaid credit card debts of its customers. Finally, it is imperative to relate that a bank customer has a legal obligation to examine his or her bank statements; and the failure of a customer to use reasonable care to examine his or her statement of account, and to report unauthorized signatures and alterations, may validate improper payments, as will be seen later in this chapter.

Bank Collection Procedures

When a bank customer puts cash or a check in his or her account, the bank may or may not permit immediate withdrawal, according to its own rules. However, what is the length of time that a check must be deposited in an account before it must be made available for withdrawals? In the past, the UCC had certain rules, including allowing a bank to wait a "reasonable time" before allowing customers to make withdrawals. However, the U.S. Congress felt that banks were taking advantage of the latitude granted by the UCC and were making their customers wait unreasonably long periods of "reasonable time." The Congress, therefore, promulgated a law in 1987 to deal with this time period, called in banking parlance, the "float." The statute was called the Expedited Funds Availability Act. Pursuant to this statute, which, as federal law, supersedes the UCC, which is state-based law, any "local" check deposited must be available for withdrawal (by check or cash) within one business day from the day of deposit. The Federal Reserve Board has designated check processing regions; and if the depositary and drawee/payor bank are located in the same region, the check is regarded as "local." For "non-local" checks, the funds must be available for withdrawal within not more than five business days. Regarding cash deposits, the funds must be available on the next business day (and also for government checks, cashier's checks, and certified checks). Regarding checks for which the depositary and drawee/payor banks are the same institution, the funds are available on the next business day. There are two exceptions to the preceding rule: first, for "new" accounts (in existence for less the 30 days), the time period is eight days; and second, for deposits over $5000, an extra four days is added to the initial time period.

Electronic and Online Banking

The application of computer technology to banking, especially in the form of electronic fund transfers, certainly has helped to improve the efficiency and accuracy of the banking system, but technology has also raised a whole host of complex legal and practical problems. In the "old days," checks had to be physically transported and transferred in order to be cleared by banks. Now, with the new technology, checks can be processed electronically, which means that presentment can occur on the day of deposit. The UCC had authorized banks to utilize other means of presentment, such as electronic presentment, but such means required agreement among many individual banks, and thus electronic clearing of checks was not used extensively. In 2004, however, Congress enacted an important statute, the Check Clearing in the 21st Century Act, which created a new negotiable instrument called a *"substitute check."*

The statute does not require banks to use substitute checks or to engage in electronic banking, but the act has, and is expected to further, encourage banks to utilize electronic check processing. To facilitate such processing, the statute states that banks now must accept substitute checks as if they were original checks. Another consequence of substitute checks is that now banks can, and most likely do, destroy original checks, which then means that the bank customer can no longer insist on the return of original canceled checks with his or her monthly statement, but rather has to be satisfied with a substitute check for proof of payment.

Another important statute dealing with electronic and online banking is the Electronic Fund Transfer Act of 1978, which was briefly mentioned in the Commercial Paper part of this chapter, and which governs consumer fund transfers. Article 4A of the Uniform Commercial Code, which now has been adopted by most states, governs commercial fund transfers and wire transfers among businesses. An electronic fund transfer is a transfer made by the use of an electronic terminal, a telephone, or a computer. The most common electronic fund transfer systems are automated teller machines, debit cards (also called point-of-sale systems), direct deposits and withdrawals, and Internet pay systems (where bank customers can allow access to their accounts by means of the Internet to transfer funds to pay particular bills). The Electronic Fund Transfer Act requires financial institutions to make certain disclosures to consumers regarding their rights and responsibilities. If a customer's debit card is lost or stolen and used without his or her permission, the customer is only liable for $50; but if the customer does not notify the bank or financial institution which issued it within two days, the customer's liability is increased to $500. Moreover, the customer's liability may be increased to over $500 if the customer does not report the unauthorized use within 60 days after it appears on the customer's statement. The customer has a duty to notify the bank of any error in the monthly statement and to notify the bank within 60 days. The bank then has 10 days to investigate and report its findings to the customer in writing. If the bank takes longer than 10 days, it must return the disputed amount to the customer. A bank must provide receipts for transactions made by means of computer terminals; and a bank must provide a monthly statement for every month in which there is an electronic transfer of funds. Due to the instantaneous nature of an electronic transfer, the statute does not provide for the reversal of an electronic transfer, and thus the old UCC "stop payment" doctrine is not generally applicable to electronic transfers. However, there is one important exception and that is authorized electronic prepayments for utility bills and insurance payments can be stopped three days before the scheduled transfer. Another negative consequence for consumers is that the bank customer can no longer count on the old "float time," that is, the time between the writing and transfer and presentment and clearing of a check and its deduction from the customer's account. It also should be noted that telephone transfers are also governed by the Electronic Fund Transfer Act but only if there is a prearranged plan pursuant to which periodic and regular telephone transfers are contemplated. The Act also makes it a felony, punishable with a prison term of up to 10 years and a fine of up to $10,000 for an unauthorized electronic transfer, defined as one initiated by a person who lacks actual authority to make a transfer, the consumer receives no benefit from the transfer, and the customer did not provide the person with a card, code, or other means of access.

The Act also imposes penalties on banks for failing to comply with the statute, and authorizes consumer lawsuits for damages, including actual damages, attorneys' fees and costs, and punitive damages (though limited at $1000). Moreover, if a bank fails to investigate an error in good faith, it can be liable to the customer for treble damages.

Forgery and Alteration

Pursuant to the UCC, as a general rule, a forged or unauthorized signature is not deemed to be the signature of the person signed unless that person is estopped (that is, prevented) from denying it. There are four circumstances where forgeries, unauthorized signatures, as well as alterations, may be validated. The first is called the "imposter rule." The carelessness of the maker or drawer in issuing an instrument may make it likely that the payee's name will be forged; and if so, the resulting forgery will be effective to pass good title to later transferees. One such example is the issuance of an instrument to an imposter. An *imposter* is one who pretends to be someone else. The rule of law is that if the maker or drawer is duped into issuing an instrument to an imposter, the resulting forgery of the payee's name will be effective to pass good title. The second rule is called the *fictitious payee* rule. A "fictitious payee" is one who was not intended to have any interest in the instrument. The rule of law is that when the maker or drawer issues a negotiable instrument to a payee whom he or she does not actually intend to have any interest in the instrument, the resulting forgery of the payee's name is effective to pass good title to later transferees. The "classic" case is when a company treasurer draws checks on the company payable to phony employees; then the treasurer forges the names of the payees, and cashes the checks at the drawee bank; and pursuant to this rule, the company does not have a cause of action against the bank. The third rule is called the negligence rule. Very simply, the negligence of any person which substantially contributes to an unauthorized signature or alteration of a negotiable instrument will act as an estoppel which prevents the careless person from raising the issues of forgery or alteration against later parties who transfer or pay the instrument in good faith. The final rule, which is a variant of the aforementioned negligence rule, is called the "bank statement" rule. Once a month, a bank will return cancelled checks to its customers with a statement of the customer's account (or the bank can provide the customer with information to reasonably identify checks paid and furnish copies to the customer); and the customer's failure to examine the checks and statement is a form of negligence which can preclude the defenses of forgery and alteration. A bank customer thus has a duty to exercise reasonable care to detect forgeries, unauthorized signatures, and alterations; and the failure to examine and to report such matters to the bank within a reasonable time is a form of negligence which prevents the customer from complaining to the bank that an item is not "properly payable."

Summary

Laws regarding commercial paper and banking transactions are primarily found in the Uniform Commercial Code (UCC); and a foundational knowledge and understanding of this body of law is critical for all managers and entrepreneurs. The chapter defined "commercial paper" as the written obligations, promises, and orders to pay sums of money which arise from the use of negotiable instruments, such as promissory notes, drafts, checks, and trade acceptances. The chapter further mentioned and explored the two basic purposes of commercial paper: the credit function, and the payment function. In the initial section, the chapter explored types of commercial paper, ambiguities in instruments, the negotiability and negotiation requirements, holders in due course, claims and defenses to negotiable instruments, liability of the parties, contract liability, warranty liability, and conversion of instruments, and the statutory erosion of the holder in due course doctrine. In the last section of the chapter, the authors explored the relationship between banks and their customers, bank collection procedures, forgery, and alteration.

Discussion Questions
1. What are the basic types of negotiable instruments and who are the parties to negotiable paper? Provide an example of each with a brief explanation thereof.
2. What are the requirements for a "negotiable" instrument pursuant to the UCC? Why is that initial determination critical in commercial paper law? Provide an example of a negotiable instrument with a brief explanation thereof.
3. How does the UCC treat extension and acceleration clauses regarding negotiability of an instrument? Provide examples of permissible and impermissible extensions clauses along with brief explanations thereof.
4. Compare and contrast "order" paper and "bearer" paper under the UCC. Provide an example of each with a brief illustration thereof.
5. What is a UCC "negotiation" and how does it differ from a common law assignment? Provide examples of the negotiation of order and bearer paper with a brief explanation thereof.
6. What are the fundamental ways of indorsing negotiable instruments? Provide an example of each with a brief explanation thereof.
7. Who is a "holder" of a negotiable instrument? Why is holder status important? Provide an example with a brief explanation thereof.
8. What are the requirements for being a "holder in due course" (HDC) of a negotiable instrument? Provide an example of an HDC with a brief explanation thereof.
9. How does the "good faith" HDC requirement differ from the "without notice" requirement? Provide an example of each with a brief explanation thereof?
10. How does being an HDC under the UCC differ from being an assignee under the common law of contracts? Provide an example of each category with a brief explanation thereof.
11. What are the "real" or "universal" defenses that will be operative against even an HDC? Provide examples with brief explanations thereof.
12. What is the difference between a forgery "inside" as opposed to "outside" of the chain of title on a negotiable instrument? Why is that distinction a critical one under the UCC? Provide an example of each with a brief explanation thereof.

13. What is contract liability on a negotiable instrument? How does it arise? Provide examples with brief explanations thereof.

14. How should an agent sign a negotiable instrument to ensure that the agent is not liable thereon but his or her principal is liable? Provide examples with brief explanations thereof.

15. Who are the parties primarily liable on negotiable instruments and who are the parties who are secondarily liable? Why is that distinction critical pursuant to the UCC? Provide examples along with brief explanations.

16. What are the "conditions precedent" (or secondary conditions) that secondary parties are entitled to? What happens if these conditions are not complied with? Provide examples along with brief explanations thereof.

17. What is the "merger" doctrine and how does it affect liability on negotiable instruments? Provide a merger example with a brief explanation thereof.

18. What is warranty liability on a negotiable instrument and how does it arise? How does it differ from contract liability? Provide examples of warranty liability along with brief explanations thereof.

19. What is presentment warranty liability on negotiable instruments? Why is it narrower than warranty liability? Provide examples with brief explanations thereof.

20. What are some of the special UCC rules that will validate fraud, forgery, or an alteration of a negotiable instrument? Provide examples with brief explanations thereof.

21. What is the special FTC rule that impacts HDC status in consumer goods transactions? What is the rationale for the rule? Provide an example of the FTC rule with a brief explanation thereof.

22. What are some of the fundamental UCC principles that govern the relationship between a bank and its customers? Provide examples along with brief explanations thereof.

23. What is the concept of the "float" when it comes to banks processing checks? How is this concept been drastically reduced by federal statute? Provide examples along with brief explanations thereof.

24. What are some of the benefits of electronic banking, and what are some of the risks? Explain how the latter have been mitigated to a degree by statute? Provide examples along with brief explanations thereof.

9 – CREDITORS AND DEBTORS – RIGHTS AND RESPONSIBILITIES

This chapter will examine creditor and debtor relationships and will analyze the rights and responsibilities of creditors and debtors. The primary creditor rights to be examined will be the legal doctrines of suretyship and secured transactions, and the primary debtor right to be examined will be bankruptcy.

Part I – Creditors

Suretyship
Suretyship is the relationship by which one person becomes responsible for the debts of another person. The relationship arises when one has money to lend or goods to sell, or perhaps services to render, but this person may have doubts about a prospective debtor's ability to pay the obligation, and therefore may want more assurances than the debtor's mere promise to pay, regardless if embodied in a contract or even a negotiable instrument. One legal solution is for the creditor or seller or performing party to reduce his or her risk by requiring some form of security. Suretyship entails a third person joining the debtor's obligation as a "surety." Also, as will be seen in the next subsection to this chapter, the seller of goods is allowed pursuant to Article 9 of the Uniform Commercial Code (UCC) to acquire a legal interest, called a "security interest," in the debtor/buyer's goods. The rationales of these legal doctrines are that the debt or undertaking will be paid or performed.

The problem with suretyship law is that two important legal arrangements are encompassed by the term "suretyship": 1) *suretyship*, in which the person who promises to be liable is called the *surety*; and 2) *guaranty*, in which the person who promises to pay is called the *guarantor*. In both cases, the person who owes the money (or who is under the original obligation to perform) is called the "principal" or debtor; and the person to whom the debt (or obligation) is owed is called the creditor or "obligee." The common feature of both arrangements is that there is a promise to answer for the debt or default of another. There are, however, significant differences between the two relationships. In a suretyship relationship, the surety is generally primarily liable for the debt or obligation of the principal; and thus the moment the debt or obligation is due, the creditor may demand payment or performance from the surety. Yet in the guaranty relationship, the guarantor generally is only secondarily liable; that is, the creditor must first attempt to collect or seek performance from the original debtor; and next if the principal debtor does not pay or perform, then the guarantor must fulfill his or her secondary promise to pay or perform. Both relationships are created by means of a contract, which is usually express and in writing. In a surety situation, the contract is an express one between the surety and creditor, in which the surety assumes primary liability for the principal's debtor's payment and performance. Regarding the Statute of Frauds, for suretyship, no writing is required (because the relationship imposes primary liability). However, for the guaranty arrangement, a writing is required, except for the "benefit to the promisor" exception, one recalls from the contract law chapter. Consideration is generally required for both. However, the usual consideration is the consideration that was given by the creditor in the original transaction, presuming the suretyship or guaranty arrangement also arose as part of that original transaction. Otherwise, if either arrangement is done subsequent to the original transaction, new consideration is required. Also, pursuant to the UCC, it is not required that an "accommodation party" to a negotiable instrument receives consideration in order to be bound in the capacity that he or she signed.

Under the old common law, a "surety" was (and still is) regarded as a "favorite of the law." Accordingly, the surety possesses certain rights under the common law to protect him or her from sustaining a loss. There are four main surety common law rights: 1) exoneration, 2) subrogation, 3) reimbursement, and 4) contribution. *Exoneration* is a right that the surety can exercise against the principal debtor as well as the creditor. Regarding the debtor, at the maturity of the obligation, the surety may bring an equitable action against the debtor to compel the debtor to pay the debt or perform the obligation, and thereby to exonerate the surety. Regarding the creditor, if the surety finds that his or her position may be impaired (for example, the debtor is about to flee the jurisdiction), the surety may call upon the creditor to take action against the debtor; and if the creditor could proceed, but fails to do so, the surety is exonerated from liability to the extent harmed. *Subrogation* arises when the surety is forced to pay the principal debtor's debt; and then the surety is subrogated to (that is, acquires) any rights the creditor had (for example, rights to the collateral or a preferred position in bankruptcy). *Reimbursement* arises when the surety pays the debt of the principal debtor; and then the surety may sue the principal debtor for reimbursement. *Contribution* occurs when two or more sureties are bound on the same obligation. In such a case, each is liable for the full amount. However, between themselves, each is liable for only a proportionate share of the debt; and thus if one surety pays more than his or her fair share, that surety is entitled to demand, and to sue for, contribution from the co-surety. Of course, the sureties can decide expressly as to the proportion of their obligation.

The surety, furthermore, possesses certain defenses. These defenses not only include ordinary contract defenses, but also special surety defenses. As to the ordinary defenses, since the relationship of suretyship is based on contract, the surety may raise any defense that a party to an ordinary contract may raise (such as fraud or Statute of Limitations). There are, in addition, several special suretyship defenses, to wit: 1) the invalidity or lack of the principal obligation; 2) discharge of the principal/debtor, which releases the surety (unless there has been a reservation of rights against the surety); 3) payment of the principal obligation by the debtor (or a tender of payment by either the debtor or the surety which is rejected by the creditor), which releases the debtor; 4) discharge by modification, meaning that if the terms of the original contract backed by the surety are modified in any way (even to the benefit of the surety), any non-consenting surety is discharged; and 5) extending the time of performance by the original debtor and the principal by means of a binding agreement, which the surety does not consent to, releases the surety (but a mere indulgence by the creditor to allow the debtor more time to pay does not release the surety).

Suretyship is also governed by the Uniform Commercial Code (UCC) when commercial paper is involved in the transaction. The UCC calls a surety an *accommodation party*, who pursuant to the Code is a party who signs a negotiable instrument to lend his or her name to some other party to the instrument. The principal debtor is called the "accommodated party." If the surety adds the words of guaranty to his or her signature (e.g. "X, guarantor," or "I, X, guarantee this obligation"), then the surety becomes a guarantor. Note that a guarantor is a special party under the UCC, as will soon be seen, but also that a guarantor as a surety still has the usual common law suretyship rights. Also note that the UCC does not require that an accommodation party receive consideration. There are four basic rules dealing with the contract liability of an accommodation party: 1) a surety who signs in the place where the maker usually signs makes the same contract as the maker; 2) a surety who signs in the place where an indorser usually signs makes the same contract as an indorser; 3) accommodation makers and indorsers have UCC rights of non-surety makers or indorsers as well as the special common law and UCC rights given to sureties; and 4) a surety is not liable to the principal debtor, that is, the person accommodated, regardless of the place where the surety signed the instrument. There are five special rules dealing with the contract liability of a guarantor: 1) if the surety adds words of guarantee which state "payment guaranteed," the surety-guarantor consents to primary liability (that is, agrees to pay the instrument without first requiring that it be presented to the other party for payment); 2) however, if the words of guarantee state "collection guaranteed," before the surety-guarantor can be required to pay the instrument, the holder must first pursue the maker or acceptor to an unsatisfied judgment; 3) guarantors are not entitled to any technical procedural rights merely by being guarantors; 4) all defenses are available to the surety-guarantor (that is, the guarantor's contract liability is not absolute); and 5) if the words of guarantee are ambiguous and do not specify the exact type of guarantee relationship, a guarantee of payment is construed.

Secured Transactions

A large part of business is conducted today "on credit"; and the credit given is typically unsecured credit. For example, the most common types of transactions where unsecured credit is extended by one person or business to another are: 1) sale of goods "on credit," where the buyer promises to pay the purchase in installments; and 2) the loan of money. These examples are regarded as unsecured credit cases because once the seller/creditor delivers goods to the buyer or once the creditor makes a loan to the debtor, the creditor has lost all rights to the goods or money. That is, if the debtor subsequently defaults, the creditor cannot immediately attach any specific goods or money in the debtor's possession. The creditor's remedy is to bring a lawsuit to recover the amount of indebtedness, secure a judgment, and then seek to have any unencumbered property of the debtor sold under court order in order to satisfy the obligation. The problem, of course, is that the debtor may not own any property when and where the judgment is obtained. Moreover, the creditor may have to share limited proceeds with other judgment creditors. The risk, therefore, is evident, and that is the creditor or seller may recover little or nothing from the debtor or buyer.

One solution for the creditor/seller to minimize such risks is found in Article 9 of the Uniform Commercial Code which creates the legal device of a secured transaction. Pursuant to Article 9, the creditor/lender/seller can require the debtor/borrower/buyer to enter into a "security agreement" at the time credit is extended. A *security agreement* is an arrangement whereby the debtor conveys to the creditor a legally recognized interest in specific personal property owned by the debtor. The effect is to give the creditor the right to have specific property sold if the debtor defaults on payments and to receive as much of the proceeds of the sale as necessary to pay off the debt. If the proceeds are not sufficient to pay the total indebtedness, the creditor then has the usual unsecured claim for the balance. Accordingly, there are two main purposes to a secured transaction: 1) to give the creditor a specific interest in the debtor's property; and 2) to grant the creditor a priority claim in that property as against other creditors who may seek to have the property sold in satisfaction of their claims. This critical "priority" may be obtained by the creditor giving notice (usually by means of filing a "financing statement") to all creditors and third parties who may become creditors of the debtor and secure a security interest in the debtor's property. This priority is called "perfection" under the UCC; it is the process whereby the creditor has taken the proper steps in order for the security interest to be valid against other creditors. However, before perfection can be obtained, the security agreement must be effective between the parties; it must "attach" to the collateral, which is the property subject to the security agreement. Article 9 of the UCC applies to any transaction intended to create a security interest in personal property; it does not apply to any security interests in real property, such as mortgages.

How is a *security interest* created? The first step is the presence of a security agreement between the parties. The formal requirements for a security agreement are as follows: 1) A written agreement is required. (However, if the collateral is a good and it is placed in possession of the secured party, which is called a "pledge," no writing is required.) 2) The writing must be signed by the debtor. 3) The writing must contain a description of the collateral sufficient to reasonably identify it. 4) The writing usually contains other provisions, such as a statement of the amount of the obligation, the terms of payment, the debtor's duties with respect to the collateral (e.g., insuring the property), and the rights of the insured party on default. The security agreement, however, is not enforceable unless it "attaches" to the collateral.

Attachment occurs when three conditions are met: 1) There is an agreement that the security interest attaches, that is, the security agreement. 2) The secured party must give value to the debtor. ("Value" can consist of any consideration sufficient to support a simple contract, such as delivering goods or loaning money.) 3) The debtor must have "rights" in the collateral, which means the debtor must have an ownership interest in the collateral or the right to obtain possession. Note that these three events can occur in any order. A security interest may exist in after-acquired property, which is collateral which the debtor does not own now, but which he or she may or will acquire in the future. However, for a security interest to be established for after-acquired property, specificity is required; that is, the security agreement must expressly use that term or clearly refer to collateral to be acquired in the future. Yet if the security interest covers "inventory," the use of that term implies that it covers not only present inventory, but also inventory to be acquired in the future.

Perfection of the security interest is a critical UCC concept. Although the security agreement creates a security interest in the property between the secured party and the debtor, it is not sufficient to give the secured party priority over other persons who may claim an interest in the collateral. In order to have a valid security interest as well as priority over third persons claiming an interest in the property, the secured party must "perfect" the security interest. Perfection is thus the set of actions which when complied with provide the secured party priority over certain other classes of the debtor's creditors. Perfection, in essence, entails giving notice to third persons that the secured party has a security interest in the debtor's collateral. There are three methods to secure perfection of the security interest: 1) possession, 2) attachment, and 3) filing. 1) *Perfection by possession*, called a "pledge," requires the creditor to have possession of the collateral. No written security agreement is required, one recalls; yet this means to perfection has limited practical use because debtors need and want possession of the collateral. 2) *Perfection by attachment* occurs as an automatic means of perfection of the security interest upon its attachment; no further steps are necessary. The classic example is a "purchase money security interest" (PMSI) in consumer goods, which arises from an installment purchase of the goods. Such an interest is perfected automatically and is exempt from any filing requirements. The reason is that it would be too great a burden for retail merchants who typically advance credit by means of retail installment contracts for consumer goods. The essence of a "purchase money" arrangement is that the secured party advances money or credit to enable the debtor/buyer to purchase the consumer goods. Note that for a viable *purchase money security interest* a written agreement is still required; only a filing is not required. However, there is a big problem with the PMSI device. It does protect against claims by other creditors of the debtor; but it does not protect against the rights of another consumer who purchases the goods in good faith from the debtor. Thus, the secured party should file a *financing statement.* 3) *Perfection by filing* is the best way to secure perfection; it is the most common way to perfect too. The financing statement is a document which notes the secured party's interest and generally describes the collateral included under the security agreement. The effect of filing is to put other creditors on notice that the security agreement is in effect. Potential creditors have the duty to investigate and to see if the proposed collateral is already encumbered. The required contents of a financing statement are as follows: 1) the names of both the debtor and the secured party, 2) the address of the secured party (so more information can be obtained), 3) the mailing address of the debtor, and 4) a statement describing the types and items of collateral. Where should the financing statement be filed? The UCC provides different filing systems for the states to choose from, with the majority of the states opting for "local" filing for consumer goods at the county level and filing at the state's Secretary of State's office for most other goods. Of course, it is possible that there may be more than one perfected creditor for a piece of collateral. Who has priority among perfected creditors? Under the UCC, the rule is called the *"first to file or perfect"* rule, which grants priority to whichever secured party is the first to either file or to perfect the security interest. The effect of such a rule is that the party who files first has top priority, even though a later creditor perfected first (for example, by taking possession after the first creditor's filing). Moreover, one creditor's knowledge of the other's unperfected security interest is irrelevant; the time when the competing security first attached is also irrelevant. Regarding priority among perfected creditors, there are special rules for the PMSI if the subject matter of the PMSI is non-inventory consumer goods. The UCC holds that such a PMSI takes priority over conflicting security interests in the same collateral if the interest is perfected when the debtor takes possession of the collateral or within 10 days thereafter. The legal result is to create a "super-priority" that supersedes the "first to file or perfect" rule from the standpoint of time and method of perfection.

When the debtor defaults, what are the rights of the secured party? The basic remedy of the secured party is to repossess the collateral and to dispose of it. The secured party has the right to take possession without any judicial process (presuming no "breach of peace"). Once the secured party obtains possession, the secured party has broad power to sell, lease, or dispose of collateral to obtain satisfaction of obligation. The collateral may be sold at either a public or private sale so long as the sale is effectuated in a commercially reasonable manner. The secured party is required to notify the debtor of the time and place of the sale. Additional notification must be sent to any other secured party from whom the secured party has received a written notice of a claim of an interest in the collateral (but not in the case of consumer goods). A purchaser of the collateral receives all the debtor's rights in the collateral free from the security interest and subordinate security interests and liens. The proceeds from the sale are applied as follows: 1) the expenses of the secured party in retaking, holding, selling, and/or leasing the collateral; 2) satisfaction of the debt to the secured party; 3) satisfaction of the debts of persons who have subordinate security interests in the collateral (if there was a written demand for payment before the proceeds were distributed); 4) any surplus goes to the debtor; and 5) if there is any deficiency, the debtor is liable. Once the debt is paid, the secured party files a termination statement with the office where the filing statement was filed; and when the collateral is a consumer good, the secured party must file the termination statement within one month after the debt paid (but within 10 days if the debtor demands so in writing). In all other cases, the secured party must file or furnish the debtor with the termination statement within 10 days after a written demand.

Other Laws Assisting Creditors

There are several other important laws that protect and assist creditors. The first is called the *artisan's lien* (or *laborer's lien*). A "lien" means there is a legal charge against property. The artisan's lien was originally a common law lien (though in many states it is now in statutory form) given to creditors who perform labor or services on personal property. If the debtor does not pay for the services, the creditor is permitted to obtain a judgment and/or foreclose and sell the property in satisfaction of the debt. However, in most states, the creditor must retain possession of the property in order to exercise the lien. Also, in some states, a "cautionary notice" is required; that is, the creditor must give notice, which must be personal and express, to the debtor and owner of the property so as to enable him or her to reserve a sufficient amount of funds to pay for the labor and material. The failure to give such notice will preclude the lien. A *mechanic's lien* is a lien against real estate for labor, services, and/or material used in improving realty. Originally common law in formulation, the mechanic's lien is now heavily regulated by state statute. To make the real property security for the obligation, the creditor must file a notice of the lien in accordance with state law. If the debt is not paid, the creditor can foreclose and sell the property. However, usually, the lien is paid when the property is sold (since no one will purchase such encumbered property until the lien is paid off). Another creditor protection device is called a *"writ of execution* on a judgment." Once a debt is overdue, the creditor can file suit for payment, and if successful, be awarded a legal "judgment." If the judgment is not satisfied, the creditor can go back to court and obtain a writ of execution. The writ is a court order directing the sheriff to levy (seize) any of the debtor's nonexempt property in the jurisdiction; and the judgment is then paid from the proceeds of the sale, with any balance returned to the debtor.

 Garnishment is an important creditor protection device. It is a court order requiring persons who owe a debtor money or who possess the debtor's personal property to turn over the property or money to the court. The most common types of property garnished are wages and bank accounts. There are federal and state statutory limits as to the types and amounts of property and money that can be garnished, however. Attachment is the seizing of a debtor's property without a court order. This remedy, moreover, is available to the creditor even before a judgment is rendered. The creditor must demonstrate a reasonable belief that the debtor may conceal or remove property from the jurisdiction before the creditor can obtain a judgment. There are, as one would expect, detailed statutory procedures for an attachment to occur. Typically, the creditor files an affidavit with the court attesting to the debtor's default or the creditor's insecurity and the legal reasons why the attachment is sought. The creditor also must post a bond to cover the value of the property, the value of the loss of use of the goods, and the court costs involved (if the creditor later loses). The court then issues a writ of attachment directing the sheriff to seize non-exempt property sufficient to satisfy the creditor's claims. If the creditor's suit is successful, the seized property is sold to satisfy the judgment.

 Receivership is a related remedy which is available to creditors when attachment is inadequate to protect creditors while they pursue their claims because the debtor's property requires care. The grounds are the same as an attachment; but with the main justification being the prevention of the wasting of assets and/or debtor mismanagement of assets. The court upon proper showing will appoint a "receiver" to care for and to preserve the property pending the outcome of the lawsuit. A "composition of creditors" is a remedy that is available to creditors when the debtor and his or her creditors realize that the debtor is in financial difficulty. Instead of bankruptcy, the debtor and creditors make a contractual agreement to resolve the debts. The contract characteristically entails the debtor's immediate payment of a sum less than the original amount owed in consideration for the creditors' immediate discharge of the debt. An "assignment for the benefit of creditors" occurs when a debtor voluntarily transfers title to assets to an assignee for the creditor's benefit. The effect is that the debtor irrevocably gives up any claim or control over the property. The assignee sells the property and makes payment to the creditors (on a *pro rata* basis). The creditors can accept or reject any partial payment but if there is an acceptance, the creditor typically releases the balance of the creditor's claim. A "creditor's committee" arises when the debtor agrees to submit his or her business and financial affairs to the control of a committee appointed by the creditors. The function of the committee is to virtually control the debtor's business operations until the debt is paid.

Part II – Debtors

Bankruptcy
Bankruptcy protection is the most important law protecting debtors. Bankruptcy law, of course, deals with the problems which arise when a person, including a business or corporation, is unable to satisfy his, her, or its obligations due to creditors. Bankruptcy is based on federal law, stemming from Article I of the Constitution, Section 8, which grants Congress the power to establish bankruptcy laws. The most important modern statute is the Bankruptcy Act of 1978, as amended by the Bankruptcy Act of 1984, and the Bankruptcy Reform Act of 2005. The objectives of bankruptcy law are to: 1) provide a method of applying the debtor's assets in an equitable distribution among the debtor's creditors; 2) prevent the debtor from preferring one creditor over another; 3) minimize losses of all the creditors to the extent possible; 4) to relieve "honest" debtors of the weight of oppressive indebtedness; and 5) to allow the debtor a "fresh start" free of his or her former obligations. The Bankruptcy Act of 1978 created a separate system of federal bankruptcy courts to hear and resolve bankruptcy cases. The 1984 statute placed bankruptcy judges under the jurisdiction of the federal courts. Bankruptcy judges serve for 14 year terms. Their function is to administer the estate of the debtor in bankruptcy. Bankruptcy law provides for three different legal proceedings: 1) *liquidation*, which is found in Chapter 7 of the statute; 2) *reorganization* and *continuation* of the business, which is found in Chapter 11 of the statute; and 3) adjustment of the debt's of an individual with regular income. The focus of the discussion herein will be on liquidation, also known as "straight" bankruptcy, and which has been the most common form of bankruptcy; however, as will also be seen, the 2005 Reform Act makes it more difficult for a person to select a "7" as opposed to a "13."

The objective of a Chapter 7 liquidation proceeding is to sell the debtor's assets, pay off his creditors as far as possible, and then have the court legally discharge the debtor from further responsibility to pay. The debtor, of course, has to state his or her debts, and then turn over any asserts to a trustee. Liquidation proceedings can be commenced in a voluntary or an involuntary manner. The former is initiated by the debtor; and the latter by the creditors. In a voluntary case, the debtor files a voluntary petition of bankruptcy, which automatically subjects the debtor and his or her property within the jurisdiction and supervision of the bankruptcy court. The petition consists of several items: 1) a statement that the debtor understands the other bankruptcy proceedings, but is pursuing a Chapter 7 bankruptcy; 2) a list of creditors – secured and unsecured; 3) a list of property and assets; 4) a list of property and assets that the debtor claims to be exempt; 5) a statement of the financial affairs of the bankrupt individual; and 6) a listing of current income and expenses. The purpose of the petition is to provide the bankruptcy court with sufficient information to dismiss the Chapter 7, encourage a Chapter 13, or order a Chapter 13. Any "person" can file a petition, including a husband and wife filing jointly, as well as a partnership and corporation. However, banks, credit unions, insurance companies, and government bodies cannot file. Note that the debtor need not be technically insolvent (that is, debts exceed the fair market value of assets exclusive of exempt property). The petition is signed and sworn to under oath; and concealing assets or providing false information is a federal crime. In an involuntary case, the debtor's creditors force the debtor into bankruptcy. If the debtor has less than 12 creditors, one or more may file; but if there are more than 12, three are required to join in the involuntary petition. Regardless of the number, they must have unsecured claims against the debtor of at least $12,300. If the involuntary petition is not challenged, the debtor and his or her property automatically become subject to the jurisdiction and supervision of the bankruptcy court, which issues an immediate "order for relief," which in effect is an adjudication of bankruptcy. However, if the debtor contests the creditor's petition, the creditors, at a trial in bankruptcy court, must prove either 1) the debtor has not been paying his or her debts as they become due; or 2) the debtor's property has been placed in receivership or an assignment for the benefit of creditors within 120 days before the involuntary petition was filed. If the filing creditors prove either, the debtor and his or her property are under the supervision of the bankruptcy court, which issues the "order for relief"; the debtor must now file information forms with the court. Of course, if the creditors cannot offer sufficient proof, the petition is dismissed. There are, it must be noted, penalties for the frivolous and bad faith filing of petitions by creditors, who cannot use the bankruptcy courts as an "everyday" debt collection instrumentality. The filing of either petition results in an automatic stay, which means that all litigation and actions by the creditors against the debtor and his or her property are suspended (but a secured creditor may petition the bankruptcy court for relief from the stay). There are penalties that can be imposed against creditors who violate the stay.

Once the debtor becomes subject to the bankruptcy court's jurisdiction and supervision, the proceedings, whether voluntary or involuntary, are identical. After the debtor becomes subject to the court's jurisdiction, the court must appoint an *interim trustee*. The trustee's duty is to take over the debtor's property and financial affairs until a *permanent trustee* takes over. A permanent trustee is usually elected by the creditors (by means of a majority in number and amount of claims); but if there is no election, the interim trustee receives permanent status. Generally, the duties of the trustee are to administer the debtor's estate as well as to represent the debtor's estate (under the supervision of the court, of course). The trustee's specific duties include the following: 1) investigate the financial affairs of the debtor; 2) collect the assets and claims owned by the debtor; 3) operate the debtor's business on a temporary basis if necessary; 4) reduce the debtor's assets to cash; 5) receive and examine claims of creditors; 6) challenge in bankruptcy court any claim which the trustee feels is questionable; 7) oppose the debtor's discharge from obligations when the trustee feels there are legal reasons why the debtor should not be discharged; 8) render a detailed accounting to the court of all assets received and the disposition made of them; and 9) make a final report to the court when the administration of the debtor's estate is completed. Creditors' meetings are an important feature of Chapter 7. Within a reasonable time after the commencement of the proceeding, the bankruptcy court must call a meeting of the creditors. The functions of such a meeting are to elect a trustee, examine the debtor (with the trustee) as to the debtor's assets, and, to determine whether the debtor is entitled to a discharge. The debtor in bankruptcy has certain duties. The debtor must file with the court (within a reasonable time after commencement of the proceedings) the following: 1) a list of creditors, 2) a schedule of assets and liabilities, and 3) a statement of financial affairs. The debtor is also obligated to cooperate and to respond truthfully during his or her examination and with all dealings with the trustee. The debtor also must surrender to the trustee all property to be included in the estate, as well as any pertinent documents, books, journals, ledgers, and records. The debtor must appear at the hearing conducted by the court in order to determine if a discharge is warranted. If the debtor fails to fulfill any of these duties, he or she may be denied a discharge from liabilities.

The *debtor's estate* consists of property owned by the debtor which becomes subject to the bankruptcy proceeding, and which is ultimately sold by the trustee. The property included is very broad, including: 1) real and personal property, 2) tangible and intangible property, 3) property in the debtor's possession and property of the debtor possessed by another (and the latter must return such property to the trustee), and 4) the proceeds, income, and production from property (even after the petition is filed, but not after-acquired earnings from the debtor's personal services or labor). Note that after-acquired property does include property in the debtor's estate acquired within 180 of the petition filing date by means of inheritance, being the beneficiary of a life insurance policy, or as a result of a divorce decree or property settlement. A debtor who is an individual, as opposed to a partnership or corporation, may claim certain exemptions. As a result, certain types of property are not included in the debtor's estate. There are federal as well as state exemptions. The effect of the exemptions means that the debtor may keep such property and still receive a discharge from liability. The federal exemptions list includes the following: 1) a homestead residence up to $18,450; 2) a motor vehicle up to $2,950; 3) $475 per item of household furniture/furnishings, appliances, clothes, animals, crops, musical instruments, which are owned primarily for personal and family use (and not business use) with a total amount of such items limited to $9,850; 4) jewelry up to $1,225 (non-business); 5) any property, including any unused portion of the homestead, up to $9,250; 6) implements, tools, and books used in one's trade or profession not to exceed $1,050; 7) any un-matured life insurance policies owned by the debtor with a cash value not to exceed $9,850; 8) health aids which are professionally prescribed; 9) government benefits, such as social security and welfare, and the right to receive such benefits; 10) alimony, child support, certain pensions, and education savings accounts; and 11) the right to receive personal injury awards up to $18,450. Bankruptcy law has allowed a debtor to choose federal or state exemptions of the state where the debtor resides. Usually and historically many states had exemptions that were far more liberal than the federal exemptions, especially states such as Texas and Florida which totally protected one's homestead, regardless of amount. Such liberal state laws created so-called "debtor's havens" for debtors fleeing more conservative jurisdictions with limited homestead protections. However, due to the new federal bankruptcy law, as well as legislative efforts on the state level, the use of states' more liberal exemption laws has been severely curtailed.

Two very important legal doctrines in bankruptcy law which are designed to protect creditors are 1) voidable transfers and 2) voidable preferences. The *voidable transfer doctrine* means that the trustee has the power to sue and to restore to the debtor's estate property and funds which the debtor transferred to a third party. There are three situations where a voidable transfer could occur: 1) The trustee may cancel any transfer of property of the debtor's estate which was made after the debtor became subject to the bankruptcy proceeding. However, the trustee must exercise the power within two years after the transfer was made or before the bankruptcy case was concluded (whichever comes first). 2) The trustee may cancel any fraudulent transfer made by the debtor within one year prior to the filing of the bankruptcy petition. Fraud includes actual fraud against creditors as well as any fraudulent acts that hinder, delay, or impede creditors. Fraud also encompasses a debtor who is insolvent selling assets for less than fair consideration. 3) The trustee has the power to cancel a transfer on any grounds that the debtor could have used, for example, ordinary contract defenses. The voidable preference doctrine is premised on a fundamental rationale of bankruptcy law to ensure equal treatment of most types of unsecured creditors. The reason is that usually the bankrupt debtor's assets are adequate to pay only a fraction of the creditors' total claims. Accordingly, the *voidable preference doctrine* grants the trustee the power to cancel any transfer made by a debtor to a creditor which is deemed to be a "preference." Technically, a "preference" is defined as the transfer of money or property in payment of an existing debt, which causes the creditor to receive more of the debtor's estate than the creditor would ordinarily be entitled to receive in the bankruptcy proceeding. The first rule for voidable preferences is the general rule for canceling preferences. In an ordinary situation, a preferential transfer to a creditor can be cancelled by the trustee and the property and funds returned to the debtor's estate if 1) the transfer occurred within 90 days prior to filing the bankruptcy petition; and 2) the debtor was insolvent at the time of the transfer. Insolvency is presumed, it must be underscored, if there is a transfer within 90 days (and consequently the creditor to whom the "preference" was given must show that the debtor was not insolvent). There are special preference rules for "insiders," who are individuals or businesses which had a close relationship with the debtor at the time of transfer. Examples are a relative or partner of the debtor, a corporation in which the debtor is a director or officer, or the director or officer of a corporate debtor. The special "insider" rule holds that if a creditor receiving a preference was an insider, the trustee's power of cancellation extends to any such transfers made within one year of the bankruptcy petition being filed (if the debtor was insolvent). However, the presumption of insolvency only applies to the 90 day period prior to filing; and if the preference has taken place more than 90 days, the trustee must prove the debtor was insolvent and the recipient knew or had reasonable cause to know of the insolvency. There are exceptions to the voidable preference rules. The payment or transfer to a creditor cannot be cancelled even though it meets the requirements of a voidable preference in three main situations: 1) The transaction involved a "contemporaneous exchange," that is, within a very short period of time, between the debtor and creditor. For example, the debtor buys goods and pays immediately or within a few days (which of course is different from paying off a pre-existing debt). 2) Pursuant to the 1984 and 2005 bankruptcy act amendments a consumer debtor is allowed to transfer any property to a creditor up to $5,000 without triggering an illegal preference. 3) Even though there is no contemporaneous exchange, a payment or transfer to a creditor within a 90 day period cannot be cancelled if the particular debt was incurred by the debtor in the ordinary course of business or personal financial affairs, the payment was made within 45 days after the creation of the debt, the payment was made in the ordinary course of the debtor's business, and the payment was made according to ordinary business terms. An example would be the debtor's payment within the 90 day period of the previous month's utility bill.

Creditors naturally can assert claims against non-exempt property. What are considered to be "claims"? Generally, any legal obligation of the debtor gives rise to a claim against the debtor's estate in bankruptcy proceedings. There are some special situations, however. If a claim is contingent on the happening or non-happening of a future event, or if the amount is in dispute, the bankruptcy court has power to make an estimate of the claim's value. If the claim against the debtor is for breach of contract, the claim includes damages prior to the filing as well as damages from the debtor's failure to perform future obligations, but if the claim arises out of an employment contract or real estate lease, there are limits placed on a claim for damages for future non-performance. For the former, damages are limited to a term of one year from filing date or the date the contract was repudiated (whichever was earlier); and for the latter, damages are limited to one year or 15% of the remaining term of the lease, whichever is greater, up to a maximum of 10 years. If the creditor has received a voidable transfer or preference, the creditor cannot assert a claim of any kind until the wrongfully received property or funds are returned to the debtor's estate. Otherwise, any claim filed with the bankruptcy court is allowed unless it is contested by an interested party (that is, trustee, debtor, or another creditor). If a claim is challenged, the court will rule on the claim's validity after an evidentiary hearing. Claims against the debtor's estate are subject to any defenses that the debtor could have asserted if there was no bankruptcy. The effect of a claim being allowed, of course, does not mean that a particular creditor will be paid in full; rather, it just means that the creditor has a hope of receiving something.

The next area to address is the distribution of the debtor's estate. Secured and secured and perfected creditors can proceed directly against the property for the satisfaction of their claims, even if the debtor presently is or is about to become subject to the bankruptcy. If the secured collateral is insufficient to cover the debt, the secured creditor becomes an unsecured creditor for the difference. When the trustee has collected all the assets of the debtor's estate and reduced them to cash, the trustee commences a distribution to the general creditors. What is the priority of the creditors' claims? First, certain claims are given priority in distribution, and thus must be paid in full in order of priority (assuming sufficient proceeds are available). Each class must be fully paid before the next class is entitled to anything. If the available funds are insufficient to satisfy all creditors within a class, payment to the creditors in that class is made in proportion to the amounts of their claims. There are six classes of debts in order of priority: 1) the costs and expenses involved in the administration of the bankruptcy proceeding (for example, trustee's, accountant's, and attorney's fees); 2) if the proceeding is involuntary, any expenses incurred in the ordinary course of the debtor's business or financial affairs after commencement of the case but before the appointment of the trustee; 3) claims for wages, salaries, and commissions earned by an individual within 99 days before filing of the petition or cessation of the debtor's business (whichever occurs first) but with a limit of $4,925 per individual; 4) claims for contributions to employee benefit plans for services performed within 180 days before filing or cessation, but with a limit of $4,025; 5) claims for individuals for deposits made on consumer goods and services not received but with a limit of $2,225 per person; and 6) claims of government units for taxes (but note that the rules vary depending on the type of taxes owed). If all priority claims are paid, and there are still funds available, the general creditors are paid in proportion to the amounts of their claim on a *pro rata* basis. Any portion of a priority claim beyond the limits of the priority goes to fulfill general claims.

The final event in a Chapter 7 proceeding to review is the discharge. After the debtor's estate is liquidated and distributed to creditors, the bankruptcy court will conduct a hearing to determine whether the debtor should be discharged from liability for his or her remaining obligations. There are certain grounds for refusal of a discharge, which means the court will refuse to grant the debtor a discharge, to wit: 1) only individuals, not corporations and partnerships, can receive discharges; 2) the debtor has previously received a discharge within six years before the present petition was filed; and 3) fraudulent activity by the debtor, such as intentionally concealing or transferring property in order to evade creditors, concealing, falsifying, destroying, or failing to keep business records, failing to adequately explain any loss of assets, refusing to obey a lawful court order or to answer court approved questions, or making any fraudulent statement or claim. If a discharge is granted, the court may revoke it within one year if it is discovered that the debtor has not acted honestly. There are, however, certain non-dischargeable claims. That is, even if the debtor is granted a discharge by the court, there are still some claims that the debtor is liable for. These claims include: 1) claims for back taxes that accrued within two years prior to the bankruptcy; 2) claims arising out of the debtor's fraud, embezzlement, larceny, or breach of fiduciary duty; 3) claims arising out of willful and malicious torts as well as driving under the influence; 4) alimony and child support claims; 5) "unscheduled" claims caused by the debtor's failure to file a complete list of creditors which caused a creditor not to assert a claim; 6) student loans unless there is a showing of undue hardship to the debtor or his or her dependents; 7) consumer debts of more than $500 for luxury goods or services owed to a single creditor and incurred 90 days before the order for relief; 8) cash advances of more than $750 that are extensions of consumer credit that are obtained by the debtor within 70 days before the order of relief; and 9) fees and assessments due to the debtor owning a lot in a homeowners' association.

Chapter 11 of the 1978 Act (as amended in 1984 and 2005) covers business reorganization. The premise is that when reorganization and continuance of a business are feasible, and preferable to liquidation, a petition for reorganization is filed. The reorganization procedure for Chapter 11 is intended for business use; but the owner of a business may be an individual as well as a partnership or corporation. Voluntary and involuntary filings are permissible; the requirements for filing are essentially the same as liquidation. A most important distinguishing aspect of reorganization is that after commencement, the court will appoint a committee of creditors. A trustee may or may not be appointed; and if not, the debtor remains in possession and control of the business. However, the court will appoint a trustee if requested by a creditor or there is a concern that the debtor is mismanaging or wasting assets. The creditors' committee and any trustee investigate the business and financial affairs of the debtor; and then prepare and file a reorganization plan with the bankruptcy court. The plan divides the creditors' (including shareholders) claims into classes, and indicates how claims in each class are to be handled, and to what extent each class will receive less than full payment. The court will approve the reorganization plan if: 1) each class approves the plan; and 2) the plan is fair and equitable to all classes. The required vote is 2/3rds the amount of claims in each class and more than one half of the creditors in each class. If the parties cannot produce an acceptable plan, of if the plan does not work, the court can dismiss the case or dismiss it for other good cause, such as unreasonable delay on the part of the debtor. After a plan is approved, the debtor is discharged from claims not provided for in the plan; but there are claims that are not dischargeable, which are comparable to a liquidation proceeding. It should be mentioned that there are two new provisions for Chapter 11: first, there is a "fast track" procedure for small business debtors whose debts do not exceed $2 million and who also do not own or manage real estate; and second, the 2005 amendments mandate that a debtor's post-petition acquisitions and earnings become the property of the bankruptcy estate.

Chapter 13 covers adjustment of debts. The specific title to Chapter 13 is Adjustment of Debts of an Individual with Regular Income. Chapter 13 provides a method by which an individual can pay off debts from future income over an extended period of time. Its intended use is by an individual whose primary income is from salary, wages, or commissions, that is, an employee. However, there is nothing to prevent a self-employed individual, that is, the owner of a business, from using Chapter 13. The debtor, however, must be an individual. As originally intended by the bankruptcy act, only a voluntary filing by the debtor was contemplated; that is, there was no such doctrine as an involuntary adjustment; but, as will be seen, the 2005 amendments to the bankruptcy act made some important changes to the "voluntary" nature of a 13 proceeding. To be eligible for a Chapter 13 proceeding, the debtor must have regular income and less than $360,475 of unsecured and undisputed debts, and less than $1,081,400 of secured and undisputed debts. In a 13 proceeding, the bankruptcy court will always appoint a trustee, whose main function is to receive and distribute the debtor's income on a periodic basis. The key component to Chapter 13 is the filing of an *adjustment plan* by the debtor with the bankruptcy court. The plan designates a portion of the debtor's future income that will be turned over to the trustee for distribution to the debtor's creditors. The plan must describe how the creditors are to be paid, as well as indicate the period of time during which payment will be accomplished. There is usually a time limit for an adjustment plan – three to five years depending on the debtor's income (but with a five year maximum time period). The plan, significantly, can provide for less than full payment of claims (but must provide for full payment of the types of claims which are given priority in a liquidation case). The court will approve the plan if the debtor prepared it in good faith, and all secured creditors have accepted it; but it is not necessary for unsecured creditors to accept the plan; rather, unsecured creditors are bound by the plan, even if it modifies their claims. The debtor may have the right to convert the plan to a liquidation proceeding; and the court may convert if the debtor fails to perform according to the plan; or if the debtor engaged in substantial abuse of a Chapter 7, the bankruptcy court could convert it to a Chapter 13. If the debtor performs by completing payments provided for in the plan, he or she is granted a discharge; but there is no discharge from claims that cannot be discharged in a liquidation case.

A brief mention should be made of the new Chapter 12 of the Bankruptcy Act which essentially is a Chapter 13 proceeding for "small farmers" and "family fishermen." The procedures and plan and other key aspects are very similar to a Chapter 13.

The U.S. Congress in 2005 passed a bankruptcy law, the *Bankruptcy Reform Act*, which makes some very major changes in bankruptcy law. The law makes it much more difficult for debtors to completely discharge their debts. Many more debtors will now be forced to repay their debts to creditors instead of having those debts completely discharged. The law also will have a significant impact in Florida, which has been known, is a "debtor's haven" due to the state's very generous homestead exemption law which allowed those in bankruptcy to protect the full value of their homes. The bankruptcy bill has been passed by both the House and the Senate; and President Bush signed the bill into law. The law eliminates many of the protections of Chapter 7 of the Bankruptcy Code that allowed consumers and debtors to completely erase their debts. Most significantly, the Bankruptcy Reform Act of 2005 established a new system of "means testing" based on the debtor's income to determine if there is a presumption of substantial abuse of a Chapter 7 proceeding. There now will be standards that will compel debtors who make more than their state's median household income (which of course varies from state to state, but for example, is almost $40,000 in Florida) into Chapter 13 of the Code and into a five year repayment plan. Technically, the debtor's current income is calculated over the last six months' average income, minus certain "allowed expenses" which reflect basic needs of the debtor; next the monthly amount is multiplied by 12; and finally if the resulting income exceeds the state median income by $6000 or more, abuse is presumed. The trustee can then petition the judge to dismiss the 13 proceeding and to convert it to a Chapter 7 proceeding. However, the debtor can rebut the presumption of substantial abuse (for example, by pointing to unanticipated medical expenses not covered by insurance) and thus show there is no reasonable alternative to a Chapter 7 proceeding. That is, the debtor can attempt to demonstrate to the court that he or she will have insufficient disposable income to pay debts under a Chapter 13 repayment plan. Moreover, applying for bankruptcy protection will no longer be a quick legal process, because now pursuant to the new law, debtors will have to go through and pay for credit counseling for six months before any filing can be approved. In the case of Florida, under existing bankruptcy law, the state had opted out of the federal homestead exemption and utilized its own. That state exemption allowed state residents to protect a home of limited value from creditors, so long as the home sits on one half acre or less within an incorporated city, or on a 160 acre lot outside city limits. Iowa, Kansas, South Dakota, and Texas also have unlimited homestead exemptions. The new law will stop anyone from fleeing to a "debtor's haven" just before filing for federal bankruptcy protection from creditors. The law passed by Congress states that anyone who bought a home within the previous 40 months will only be able to protect $125,000 of the home's value. In Florida, for example, for those residents who have owned a home for more than 40 months, Florida's current and unlimited homestead exemption will apply. Florida law and federal law grant retirement savings accounts, pensions, annuities, and insurance policies full protection. Another important change that the new law makes is the means or income test. This test will force people with income above a state's median income, and who can pay at least $100 a month over five years to repay their debts, to do so under Chapter 13 of the Bankruptcy Code. Presently, most consumers utilize the protections of Chapter 7 of the Code, which completely eliminates debts after certain assets are forfeited. People with very low income or very few assets could still qualify for Chapter 7, however, if a bankruptcy judge approves the filing. The new law is making it much more difficult for people to totally erase their debts in a bankruptcy proceeding. Many people will now be shifted into repayment plans.

The automatic stay that occurs when a person goes into bankruptcy has a significant effect on contracts. The legal effect of the stay means that creditors, including contract claimants, are prohibited from instituting any legal action to enforce a contract or to obtain any money owed pursuant to a contract. Moreover, a party that has a contract with the bankrupt party (now called the debtor in bankruptcy) can neither seize, attach, nor foreclose on any collateral or property nor cease performing any promised obligation under a contract without first receiving the permission of the bankruptcy court. Furthermore, a conditional provision in a contract that attempts to give one contract party the right to cancel the contract if the other contract party goes into bankruptcy is not enforceable as it violates public policy as well as the primacy of federal bankruptcy law over state contract law.

Other Laws Assisting Debtors

There are a variety of federal and state laws protecting debtors, particularly by exempting certain property from seizure by creditors. A very important debtor protection law is the *Homestead Exemption*, which is a law found in either state statutes or in state constitutions. Generally, a *"homestead"* is an acreage amount (for example, one half to one and one half acres in most states) of contiguous land within a municipality, including a residence, which is owned by a "natural person" (as opposed to a business entity) or an acreage amount of contiguous land outside a municipality (for example, 100 to 200 acres in most states) including all improvements thereon. Generally, a homestead is exempt from a forced sale and no judgment can be a lien thereon. Moreover, the proceeds from the sale of a homestead are exempt from claims of creditors. There are several exceptions, however, to homestead protection, the standard ones being: 1) mortgage foreclosure, 2) obligations (either from debt or duty) that the buyer contracted for as consideration for purchase of the property, 3) any consideration furnished by a third party, 4) obligations for improvement, repair, and labor on the homestead (e.g., mechanic's liens), and 5) taxes. Note that in some jurisdictions, the sale of the homestead is permitted, but the states exempt a certain amount of the proceeds from the claims of creditors. Statutes in most states, in addition, exempt certain, though limited, amounts of personal property from the claims of creditors. Garnishment is a creditor assistance remedy that is heavily regulated by both the federal and state governments in order to protect debtors. Statutes, both federal and states, accordingly limit the amount of disposable earnings (that is, after taxes) of an employee that may be garnished to pay a creditor. The main federal statute sets a limit to the wages of an employee that can be garnished by using a multiplier of the minimum wage; but in some states the wages for a "head of a family" are totally exempt from garnishment (except for monies due for alimony and child support and money due for personal services or labor performed).

Summary
The intricate and symbiotic relationships between creditors and debtors are often balanced through supply and demand forces. This chapter has thoroughly and comprehensively examined the relationship between creditors and debtors. It further analyzed and discussed many of the rights and responsibilities associated with creditors and debtors in the United States. The primary creditor rights examined were the legal doctrines of suretyship and secured transactions, and the primary debtor right examined was that of bankruptcy in the United States.

Discussion Questions
1. Compare and contrast suretyship and guaranty? Provide an example of each with a brief explanation thereof.
2. What is the concept of a security interest under the UCC and how does it aid creditors? Provide an example with a brief explanation thereof.
3. What is the concept of "perfection" under secured interest law? How is it achieved? Why is it so important? Provide an example of perfection along with a brief explanation thereof.
4. Describe and illustrate some of the other methods that the law provides to protect creditors.
5. Compare and contrast the three main types of bankruptcy proceedings. Provide an example of each with a brief explanation thereof.

6. What are the concepts of a "voidable preference" and a "voidable transfer" under bankruptcy law? What are their rationales? Provide an example of each with a brief explanation thereof.

7. What is considered to be "exempt" property under federal and state bankruptcy law? Provide examples along with brief explanations thereof.

8. How did the Bankruptcy Reform Act of 2005 materially change the rights of debtors to use Chapter 7 proceedings? Provide examples along with brief explanations thereof.

9. Describe and illustrate some of the other methods the law provides to protect debtors.

10 – INTERNET LAW

Internet regulation is an extremely vital topic, as inappropriate use of the Internet can result in criminal and civil liability. This chapter examines the governing bodies that control e-contracts, the extent to which e-contracts are valid and enforceable, as well as the privacy issues that businesses have to bear in mind when conducting business via the Internet. Consequently, businesses have to bear in mind that the Internet is a global and not merely a nationwide system, so managers have to comprehend other nations' Internet policies and rules before they carry out business proposals such as e-contracts. Also, businesses in the United States need to ensure that their Internet practices are in accordance with the respective statutes governing computer transactions.

On-line Contracts
The advent, development, and proliferation of the Internet as a global tool not only of communication but also as a means of doing business presented the legal system itself with a challenge, that is, in a "nutshell," how to keep pace with the rising and spreading technology, as a prime example pertaining to electronic or "e-contracts," particularly since contract law is a field of law where many of the common law rules are literally of ancient heritage. The legal system in the United States, however, has adapted to the new technology of contracting and doing business; and accordingly has promulgated three very important statutes governing e-contracts: the *Uniform Electronic Transactions Act* (UETA), the *Uniform Computer Information Transactions Act* (UCITA), and the federal *Electronic Signature in Global and National Commerce Act*. Each of these important acts will be examined. Yet first it is necessary to point out that UETA and UCITA are "model" acts, prepared by the Conference of Commissioners on Uniform State Laws. These acts provide uniform rules for contracts involving computer transactions and the Internet; but they are not laws until adopted by the various state legislatures in the United States. Initially, it also must be emphasized that an electronic contract or *e-contract* must have all the requirements as a traditional "paper" contract (that is, as discussed in the Contracts

chapter: mutual agreement, consideration, capacity, legality, and a writing if requited by the Statute of Frauds.

Uniform Electronic Transaction Act

The objective of the *Uniform Electronic Transaction Act* (UETA) is to place electronic records and signatures on the same level as paper contracts and written signatures. Thus, electronic contracts should be as enforceable as paper ones. UETA applies only to those transactions between parties or entities which have agreed to conduct their business transactions by electronic means, such as, plainly, from using the Internet. There are two major components of UETA: first, an electronic record will satisfy the writing requirement of the Statute of Frauds; and second, an electronic signature is equal to a written signature on a paper contract. Moreover, UETA maintains that an electronic signature will have the same effect as a notarized signature if the signature includes all the standard information as required in an oath. UETA, it must be underscored, does not displace existing contract law – common law and statutory – but rather "merely" attempts to ensure that electronic contracts and signatures are treated legally as equivalent to paper contracts and written signatures.

Uniform Computer Information Transaction Act

The *Uniform Computer Information Transaction Act* (UCITA) is a model act that establishes a uniform and extensive set of rules that govern computer information transactions. The term computer information transaction is broadly defined as an agreement to create, transfer, or license computer information or information rights. There are several UCITA provisions that have relevance to e-contracts. First, regarding offer and acceptance, if an offer is in an electronic form, and thereby evokes an electronic response accepting the offer, the contract is formed when the electronic acceptance is received. Second, regarding counteroffers, UCITA makes a notable change to the old common law, specifically that counteroffers are not effective against electronic offerors. The rationale is that most electronic entities do not have the ability to evaluate or accept counteroffers or to make counteroffers. Thus, a contract is formed if the electronic offeree takes an action in response to the electronic offer that causes the electronic offeror to perform or to promise to perform the agreement, regardless of any additions, conditions, or qualifications being placed in the acceptance, for example, an acceptance of an offer to purchase software with the proviso stated "but only if I am satisfied with the software." Third, regarding mistakes, the UCITA rule is that a consumer is not bound by a unilateral electronic error if: 1) there is prompt notification of the error; 2) the consumer has not used or benefited from the information; 3) the consumer delivers all copies of information, or destroys the information at the request of the other party; and 4) the consumer pays all costs for shipping, reshipping, and processing. It must be emphasized that this rule only applies to consumers. However, it is equally important to relate that the consumer will not be entitled to any relief if the other party has provided a reasonable method to detect, avoid, and correct errors, for example, an information verification process that must be utilized before an order is processed. It is also important when discussing acceptance to distinguish between a shrink-wrap agreement and a click-on agreement. The former, characteristically used in the sale of computer software, is an agreement in which the provisions are expressed inside a box in which the goods are packaged. When the buyer opens the box, he or she is informed that by retaining the goods in the box, he or she thereby agrees to the terms of the shrink-wrap agreement. As a general rule, the courts will enforce shrink-wrap agreements even if the buyer and user of the goods did not read the terms of the agreement. A click-on agreement is an agreement made by a buyer who, after completing a transaction on a computer, frequently for the purchase of software, is required to specify his or her agreement to the terms of the offer by clicking on an "agree" button. The terms of the agreement usually are found on the seller's Web site. Again, as a general rule, the courts will enforce click-on agreements, maintaining that by clicking on "agree," the buyer-offeree has manifested his or her acceptance. Finally, UCITA has created a novel provision called "authenticating the record." The rule is that if a contract requires a payment of $5000 or more, the contract is enforceable against a party only if that party has authenticated the record. "Authentication" in essence means electronically signing the contract, which signature becomes part of the record, and then verifying the information a second time before an order is placed. Similar to the UCC's merchant's written confirmation doctrine, UCITA holds that if the parties to a contract are merchants, and the contract is for $5000 or more, the contract may be enforced even without authentication, if one party sends a letter or record confirming the contract, and the other party does not reject it within 10 days of receiving it. Of course, since as mentioned UCITA is a model act, one doing business in a particular state in the U.S. must ascertain whether his or her state has adopted the act and in what exact form. The E-Sign Act as well as UETA, in order to protect people who do not want to, or cannot, do business electronically, stipulates that the use or acceptance of electronic signatures be voluntary.

Electronic Signature in Global and National Commerce Act
The United States federal law that made electronic signatures equally as valid as written signatures is called the *Electronic Signature in Global and National Commerce Act*, which also is known as the *"E-Sign" law*, and which was enacted by Congress in 2000. Before this federal law, electronic signatures were already legal in most of the states in the United States; however, there was a problem of lack of uniformity among the states as state statutes differed as to what type of signatures were valid. The E-Sign law, therefore, was not only an effort to legalize electronic signatures but also an attempt to standardize the various state laws. The federal law, however, did not specify what type of technology must be used to create a legally binding signature for an Internet transaction. Another goal of the statute was to place electronic contracts on the same equal footing as paper contracts. Accordingly, the statute deems that electronic contracts in most cases will meet the requirements of the Statute of Frauds. The federal statute, finally, preempts state laws, except if a state has enacted the e-signature provisions of UETA, in which case the state is exempt from the federal statute.

A valid electronic signature can include any mark or process intended to be the signature of an electronic contract, for example, a name typed at the bottom of an email message or a "click-through" process on a computer screen where a person can click on an "I Agree" component of a Web page. However, for an e-signature to be enforceable, the contracting parties must have agreed to use electronic signatures. Consequently, consumers can neither be compelled to accept electronic signature agreements nor be forced to receive records or documents electronically rather than in traditional paper form. Finally, there are certain types of documents that the E-Sign law does not apply to, such as court papers, divorce decrees, evictions, foreclosures, pre-nuptial agreements, and wills.

E-Contracts

As noted, contracts can be formed online; and also, as emphasized, an online contract must contain the same requirements of a traditional contract. The seller of goods and services can make an offer online; but it is advisable to have the entire proposed contract on the seller's website or at least a clearly designated link so the offeree can view the entire contract. As with the old common law, the online seller is still the "master" of its offer; and thus the seller should clearly specify the terms of the offer (and thus the eventual contract), for example, disclaimer clauses, return policy, remedies for a defective product, arbitration clauses, and choice-of-law clauses. It is recommended that the seller include a clause indicating what constitutes the buyer's agreement, for example, clicking in a box that says "I accept." It is also recommended that the seller have a privacy policy statement on its website stating how any information obtained from the buyer will be used and also stating that such information will be kept strictly confidential. The act of the offeree in clicking in the "I accept" or "I agree" box has been construed by the courts as an acceptance of the online offer; and the resulting contract (assuming all the other elements of a contract are present) has been termed a *"click-on agreement"* or at times a *"click-wrap agreement."* And as with traditional requirements the fact that the offeree did not read all the terms of contract is a moot one; the contract is still effective (assuming no fraud).

A click-on agreement must be differentiated from a *"shrink-wrap agreement,"* also called a "click-wrap" agreement, which arises when there are terms expressed in a box in which goods are packaged (and with the shrink-wrap referring to the plastic covering of the box). The party who opens the box is told that by doing so he or she agrees to the included terms. This type of agreement is also used when a buyer purchases a software package, and thus agrees to abide by the manufacturer's terms, including typically a limited license agreement as well as the aforementioned terms concerning disclaimers, remedies, etc. The courts have construed the buyer's acceptance to be the receiving the package, having an opportunity to view all the terms, and then using the product, for example, installing the software, without any objection to the proposed terms.

So, critical to business law, are email contracts, e-contracts, valid and enforceable? The answer is "yes," assuming all the elements to a contract are present. Of course, certain problems inherent in the technology remain. For example, as to securing evidence of the e-contract, one simple and straightforward solution is to print out all pertinent email communications as well as all "electronic" prior negotiations. Regarding the Statute of Frauds and the "writing" requirement to certain contracts, the practical solution is to print a paper version of the electronic contract, which certainly will comply with the Statute of Frauds. Finally, concerning the signature requirement to contracts, an e-contract need not have a personal signature to be valid and enforceable; rather, it is now acceptable for an electronic signature to be legally sufficient. However, there is one caveat; and that is the Acts discussed herein are just U.S. federal and state statutes, and obviously Internet business and contracting are conducted globally, and there is not yet at this writing an international treaty on e-contracts. Thus, one engaging in Internet contracts globally is well advised to be aware of the laws of other countries, or the lack thereof, regarding on-line contracts specifically as well as Internet commerce generally.

Online Jurisdiction

One of the problems of contracting or doing other business online is to determine which jurisdiction's legal system has the power to adjudicate any online dispute that arises since an online agreement can be made by parties from different states or for that matter are from different countries. In the United States, in order for an in-state court to acquire personal jurisdiction over a non-resident party, the putative defendant must have "minimal contacts" with the state. This legal connection (or nexus) is a requirement of the Due Process clause to the Constitution. As such, the more contacts that the non-resident party has with the state, for example, a sales office, distributorship, or sales agents in the state, then the greater the likelihood of a sufficient connection being found. However, if the non-resident defendant is doing business solely by means of the Internet, the critical legal question arises as to whether these "virtual" contacts are sufficient to subject the non-resident to the state's laws and legal system. This area of the law is still developing; but, based on the court decisions to date, it appears that if the non-resident party merely has a passive website, for example, just containing advertising that people voluntarily access, which is accessible from other states, the existence of such a website will not be enough in the way of contacts to satisfy Due Process. However, if in addition to the website there are electronic contacts that are more continuous, systematic, and substantial, for example, entering into contracts, then there would be enough "minimal contacts" to hold the out-of-state website owner or business subject to the state's laws. The problem arises when there is an out-of-state website or business, but no contracting, and information is actively sent to specific people. In the latter case, is the active transmission of information to specific individuals by means of the Internet a sufficient "minimal contact"? The law at present requires further development and clarification. If a single electronic contact is construed by the courts to meet the requirements of Due Process, then the out-of-state defendant website or business owner can be made subject to the state's laws, even if the non-resident defendant has no physical presence in the state whatsoever and even just for perhaps a single electronic contact. However, a major decision was enunciated by the U.S. Supreme Court in 2018, where the court reversed a long-standing precedent ruled that states can now compel online shoppers to pay sales taxes on goods sold by companies even if they do not have a physical presence in the state, such as warehouse, distribution center, or office. The Supreme Court explained that the "physical presence" rule had become removed from economic reality and the rule also resulted in significant revenue losses to the states. The decision was a major victory for the states, of course, but also for large retailers which have an extensive physical presence, such as

Macy's, Wal-Mart, and Target. However, for consumers decision was a loss as now they likely will end up paying sales taxes and thus more money for goods purchased over the Internet.

Internet Privacy – The Electronic Communications Privacy Act

The *Electronic Communications Privacy Act* (ECPA) is a federal statute enacted by the U.S. Congress in 1986 that makes it a crime to intercept an electronic communication at the point of transmission, in transit, when stored by a server, or after receipt by the intended recipient. The statute also makes it illegal to access stored email. In addition to criminal penalties, the statute allows an aggrieved party to sue the interceptor for civil damages. There are, however, two important exceptions whereby stored electronic email communication can be accessed without violating the law. First, access is permitted by a party or entity which in fact provided the electronic communication service. A prime example would be an employer who can access the stored email communications of its employees who used the employer's email system. Second, government and law enforcement entities and personnel can access stored communications when investigating suspected illegal activities, though a valid search warrant may have to be obtained for the ultimate disclosure of the communications.

Internet Domain Names – The Anticybersquatting Consumer Protection Act

The United States Congress in 1999 enacted the *Anticybersquatting Consumer Protection Act* in order to protect Internet domain names. A "domain name" is a distinct designation that identifies a website. In the past, domain names could be registered for a fee with private organizations that maintain databases of domain names; but legal controversies often resulted from the allegedly deceptive use of domain names. "*Cybersquatting*" was the term used to describe such unfair uses of domain names. It results when a person or business registers a domain name that is the same or very similar to another's domain name or trademark or even a "famous" person's name; and then, in the typical case, attempts to sell the domain name back to the original owner. The federal statute now makes this practice illegal if the domain name is identical to or confusingly similar to the name of another and there is evidence of bad faith intent. Examples of bad faith would be the intent to divert the owner's customers, to harm its good will, or "merely" to offer to sell the domain name back to its owner. The act makes cybersquatting illegal, and accordingly provides civil remedies to the victim of cybersquatting who can sue for actual damages, including lost profits, or can sue for statutory damages. Also, the courts have ruled that the registration of a deliberate misspelling of a famous person's name or trademark is a violation of the statute. Finally, it should be mentioned that a private entity, under contract with the U.S. government, called the *Internet Corporation for Assigned Names and Numbers* (ICANN), now is primarily responsible for regulating the issuance of domain names on the Internet. Moreover, ICANN has established an arbitration process, called the Uniform Dispute Resolution Policy, to resolve domain names disputes; and all users of the ICANN registration process are held to agree to use this dispute resolution procedure.

The Computer Fraud and Abuse Act

The most important federal statute in the United States that governs crime on the Internet is the *Computer Fraud and Abuse Act* of 1984 (technically known as the Counterfeit Access Device and Computer Fraud and Abuse Act). This law makes it a crime for a person to access a computer online, without authority, in order to obtain restricted, classified, or protected data or information, financial or credit records, medical records, or military or national security information, as well as any other confidential information stored in government or private sector computers. Note that the crime, commonly called "hacking," entails not "merely" accessing the computer but actually taking the confidential data. Penalties encompass fines and imprisonment (for a felony) as well as a civil lawsuit by the victim against the "hacker" for money damages and to obtain an injunction.

Social Media, Employment, and Lending

The Internet certainly has had momentous effect on employment and business relations. Employers now routinely conduct social media investigations as part of the examination of a job applicant's qualifications for a position. Moreover, employers do the same when conducting investigations concerning wrongdoing by current employees. Employers may even ask applicants and employees for their user names and passwords to check their social media accounts. And refusing to supply this information may be grounds for an applicant to be denied employment or for an at-will employee to be summarily discharged unless there is some statutory protection for the employee or applicant, which protection is very rare.

Presently, however, it is not just employers engaging in this arguably intrusive practice. Banks and lending institutions are now examining social media to determine the creditworthiness or even the identity of a loan applicant. As with its use by employers, the practice of investigating a borrower's social media postings and profile is generating concern and criticism among consumer groups, privacy advocates, and government regulators. Lenders are especially looking for potential problems, such as whether loan applicants put the same employment information on their loan applications as they posted on social media, like Facebook, Twitter, or LinkedIn, or if they posted information that they had been discharged by an employer. Furthermore, an eBay investigation by a lender could uncover, particularly for a small business, poor reviews, which could impede the business' chance of obtaining credit or more credit. Amazon and other e-commerce and accounting sites are being used to assess creditworthiness. For example, PayPal is being accessed by companies to help determine creditworthiness. Social media information is also used for the fundamental reason of verifying the identity of loan applicants. Moreover, a determination can be made as to whether a business wanting a loan gets a lot of "likes" as well as responds well to its customers. Of course, the basic issue is whether information gleaned from social media is predictive of the ability and/or willingness to repay a loan. Regardless, any lending institution which utilizes social media must be careful that they do not violate federal fair credit laws, for example, by discriminating against certain loan applicants based on information derived from social media. Furthermore, "hacking" into a loan applicant's social media accounts without permission would be a federal crime as well as a common law invasion of privacy. Critics of social media investigations in the context of lending are concerned that such examinations will increase the chances that borrowers, including small businesses, will be unfairly denied credit or will have higher interest rates imposed due to information derived from social media. Privacy advocates are concerned that social media investigations will become overbroad and intrusive. Critics are also worried by the fact that there currently are no federal laws governing the use of social media in lending transactions. However, one benefit for borrowers might be that their social media examination might help credit become more available, especially for people who might be denied credit by larger lending institutions. Consequently, borrowers are voluntarily providing social media information so that lending institutions have a more complete, and presumably a better (in a positive sense), picture of a loan applicant. The more information that applicants provide, supporters of the practice say, the better the chances of a loan approval can be. Some lenders make the social media examination voluntary on the part of the borrower; but others require social media access information as part of a credit background check. Some supporters of the practice say that such social media investigations can help certain borrowers get credit when other lenders deny them credit based on traditional credit sources. And other supporters say that people should be used to social media investigations since employers regularly do them now. However, the important point is that people should be keenly aware that anything posted online these days is public information!

Internet Self-Regulation, Disinformation, and Offensive Content
Internet and social media giants, such as Facebook, Google, and Twitter, are increasingly confronting a problem of very harmful content on the Internet, particularly disinformation of a serious political nature, such as terrorist incitement, calls for violence, and hateful speech, including most prominently divisive postings, tweets, and political allegedly by the Russians in the attempt to unduly influence the presidential election of 2016 in the United States of America. Twitter has said that there were over 36,000 Russian-controlled "tweets" during the campaign. Another example was a phony posting spread by Google News that the shooter in the Texas church massacre was a supporter of Hillary Clinton and Senator Bernie Sanders. Accordingly, the legal, ethical, and practical issue has arisen as to how these companies can regulate such disinformation and divisive communications on the Internet. If government takes the lead in regulating speech on the Internet serious constitutional questions would emerge, especially under the First Amendment. Moreover, under the Trump Administration and with a president who likes to Tweet and with a Republican-controlled Congress, at least during this first-two years, and Senate there likely will not be any major attempts to regulate Internet speech. There is one proposal in Congress, however, a bill by the now deceased Senator John McCain that would make online election ads be subject to the same disclosure requirements as conventional broadcast ads; but the bill is opposed by Google and other companies and has little chance of passage. Thus, the responsibility for addressing and rectifying Internet "pollution" lies with the private sector, particularly, the larger Internet content providers, in the form of self-regulation. Some "private" suggestions that companies could do help monitor the Internet and to prevent harmful content would be to have more human oversight of content, especially of automated systems and to

provide better user warnings. Another proposal is for Internet companies to have more transparency in the sense of opening up their data operations to scrutiny by outsiders; yet privacy advocates are worried about the privacy data of consumers. Another proposal is for companies to enhance their data operations and instructions so as to better detect false information. Google has said that it is attempting to detect "clearly misleading" or "offensive" content and return it. The company launched a program called Project Owl to detect disinformation and divisive postings. One example was a posting from a New-Nazi website giving "the top-ten reasons why the Holocaust did not happen," which Google removed. The objective of Project Owl is to make such offensive and false postings "less likely to appear," said Google. Another way to monitor the Internet has been announced by Facebook which is experimenting with a fact-checker program to make sure there is no fake news in its News Feed. The program is based on user reports and other signals as well as sending out stories to third-party fact-checkers. When a posting or story is questioned Facebook notifies users that the story is "disputed," and the company also discourages the sharing of the story. When it comes to postings that are hateful and incite violence Google, Facebook, and YouTube are developing a technique called "hashing" which allows the companies to trace the digital source of videos so that they can be automatically removed if offensive. Recently taken down were sermons of the American-born Muslim cleric, Anwar Al-Awlaki, who was known for recruiting extremists (and who was called in a drone strike in 2011). YouTube, moreover, has said that videos with inflammatory religious or supremacist content would also be taken down. Other videos are branded to be not recommended for "likes" or "comments." They also are made more difficult to search for and they cannot have ads sold and placed next to them. Google, in addition, has developed a search tool called the Redirect Method which can ascertain a user's possible extremist sympathies based on their search words. Once the system has identified such a person the tool redirects them to sites that show terrorist violence in an unflattering way. Companies, therefore, are starting to engage in self-regulation to prevent and to take down offensive and fake postings and other objectionable content on the Internet. This effort will be costly, of course, but it is argued that for many reasons it is the "right" thing to do; and, furthermore, if this self-regulation is not successful there may be more calls for stricter government regulation of Internet content.

Summary
The E-Sign Act and UETA have legalized electronic signatures; yet in order to protect people who do not want to, or cannot, do business electronically, the laws stipulate that the use or acceptance of electronic signatures be voluntary. A valid electronic signature can include any mark or process intended to be the signature of an electronic contract, for example, a name typed at the bottom of an email message or a "click-through" process on a computer screen where a person can click on an "I Agree" component of a Web page.

E-communication has become the order of the day in most organizations; and as a result management has to keep employees informed about the Internet's global and national legislation that they may encounter in their business transactions. E-contracts have become a significant aspect of business partnerships and ventures and they have aided to simplify business processes by saving time and money in addition to decreasing the chances of human error. However, management has to focus on certain strategies when dealing with e-contracts in order to ensure that the contract process is a smooth process and not a very nerve-wracking experience for the parties involved. A very important consideration is that managers should ensure that online contracts are properly formed and enforceable; for example, if this requirement is not imposed, disputes could occur between both parties and that would hinder the business process or result in serious legal risks if there are doubts about effective communication of terms and conditions. Secondly, management should keep abreast of innovative technological systems such as Contracts Online by IBM (which allows clients to review and sign a contract, track its status, and see who made alterations to the document online), as these systems will help to improve their level of business performance. Lastly, management should ensure that they keep employees informed of any current updates with online laws, statutes, or acts, as well as the elements required for a legally enforceable contract; for instance, if people are conducting an online contract in Jamaica, they should be advised that there is no law enforcing e-signatures in that country, so an e-contract which requires an electronic signature would not be recommended in that case. Therefore, management should realize that Internet regulation is a very sensitive issue that needs to be closely monitored.

Internet regulation is a very pertinent issue in today's global marketplace; and therefore this chapter has looked at the essential legal systems that govern computer transactions and the Internet. These statutes include the Uniform Electronic Transaction Act (UETA), Uniform Computer Information Transaction Act (UCITA) and the Electronic Signature in Global and National Commerce Act. Internet privacy and Internet Domain are also discussed with regards to the Acts that they are regulated by, which are the Electronic Communications Privacy Act (ECPA) and the Anticybersquatting Consumer Protection Act. The Computer Fraud and Abuse Act was discussed too. This chapter also examined the validity of e-contracts nationally as well as globally.

Discussion Questions

1. Describe, explain, and provide examples with explanations of the statutes in the U.S. that have allowed the law to "catch up" with technology in the area of contracting.
2. What rights and duties does an employer have regarding the electronic monitoring of its employees in the United States? Provide examples along with brief explanations thereof.
3. What are some best practices for online contracts, online signatures, and online surfing while at work? Provide a list of do's and don'ts.

CHAPTER ELEVEN

11 – INTELLECTUAL PROPERTY LAW

Conceiving, inventing, constructing, and developing useful and creative information and instrumentalities are the hallmarks of the entrepreneur. Such information and devices may have taken considerable effort and expense to create; and may be very valuable to the success of a business and business person. Such information and knowledge can provide a business with a distinct competitive advantage. Problems perforce arise when an employee possessing such vital information and knowledge moves from one firm to another in today's very competitive, knowledge-based, global economy. Therefore, the key legal question emerges as to how one can protect such information or inventions from being misappropriated, and not only in the U.S., but also in the many other legal jurisdictions where the global business person does business. Knowing how to protect such information is not only important to a company, but also important to an individual entrepreneur, who naturally wants to keep such information confidential, yet who may have to share this potentially valuable information with venture capitalists and others. The purpose of this chapter, therefore, is to demonstrate the variety of ways that things and information can be legally protected pursuant to U.S. law.

Intellectual Property Protection in the United States
The term *intellectual property law* has come to designate in the United States a very broad field of law encompassing several forms of law – international treaty, federal and state statutes, criminal and civil, and state common law – as well a variety of legal doctrines from federal patent and copyright law to state trade secret law and contract law. These legal doctrines govern the methods by which a company, inventor, or entrepreneur can safeguard information and inventions and prevent others from wrongfully exploiting such intellectual property. An important rationale animating intellectual property law in the Untied States is the desire to motivate the creation, production, use, and proper disclosure of such creative endeavors by granting to the creators of such information specific legal protection against the infringement and misappropriation of such intellectual property. The law in the U.S.

also attempts to strike a balance by encouraging the disclosure and use of intellectual property as well as seeking to further creative and entrepreneurial activity, and also attempting to protect legitimate competitive advantage and to help instill ethical behavior in the marketplace. Yet, as the line between physical and intellectual property becomes less clear, especially regarding the distinction between computer hardware and software, the challenges in determining the existence and efficacy of legal protection will become more apparent. Moreover, none of the important legal doctrines to be covered in this chapter were originated and developed with computers in mind.

Patent Law

A *patent* is an exclusive legal right granted by the federal government to the inventors of new and useful inventions, processes, improvements. The owner of the patent has the right to exclude others from making, using, or selling the patented invention for up to seventeen years. As such, the patent holder has a legally granted monopoly in that invention by obtaining a patent. A patent is obtained by the filing of an application with the U.S. Patent and Trademark Office and receiving approval. Once accepted, the patent holder must place the words "patent" or "pat" on the product, object, or design, followed by the patent number, which gives notice to all of the existence of the patent. Patents last from twenty years from the date of the application if the subject of the patent is an invention; whereas the time period is 14 years for designs. In addition to be being novel and useful, the invention must be non-obvious. For example, mimicking a mental process, abstract ideas, or premising something on a mathematical formula, destroys "patentability," since the "laws of nature" are not new. This rationale has presented formidable hurdles to the patenting of computer software. However, in 1981, in the case of *Diamond v. Diehr*, the United States Supreme Court ruled that it may be possible to obtain a patent for a process that incorporates a computer program, but only if the process itself is patentable. It is also important to note the "reverse engineering" exception to patent law; that is, a person can take the basic idea and function of an invention, and accomplish the same result through a different series of steps, and then legally resell the "new" device. If a patent is infringed, the aggrieved patent holder can obtain in federal court an injunction as well as damages in the form of lost royalties and profits; and if the infringement was willful the court can award treble damages. Finally, mention must be made of the fact that the U.S. Patent and Trademark Office has a database consisting of patents granted since 1976 which one can search at www.uspto.gov.

Copyright Law

A *copyright* is another exclusive legal right granted by the federal government to the creators of original works of authorship, such as writings, recordings, works of art, and movies. The copyright gives the author the exclusive right to reproduce, distribute, display, and to perform the work and the expressions found in the work as well as to authorize others to do the same. Copyrights can be registered at the United States Copyright Office in Washington, D.C.; and although registration is permissive and voluntary, it is strongly recommended. For authors, the duration of a copyright is the life of the author plus 70 years; for co-authored works, the copyright expires 70 years after the death of the last surviving co-author; and for publishers, the duration is 95 years after the date of publication or 120 years from the date of creation, whichever comes first. It is important to note that copyright law, in essence, "only" protects the expression of an idea; whereas a patent protects the application of an idea, thereby conveying to the patent-holder a greater degree of protection than the copyright-holder. Modern copyright law is based principally on the federal Copyright Act of 1976, as amended, which governs works created after January 1, 1978. Note that it is no longer required that the creator of the work place the copyright symbol © or the word "copyright" on the work in order to have it legally protected.

This statute makes it illegal for a person to duplicate the exact expression, or a substantially similar expression, of a copyrighted work, and then use it or resell it without the permission of the copyright-holder. Copyright infringement does not have to be of the entire work or word-for-word. If a substantial part is reproduced there is a violation. Copyright infringement can also occur if a person or business aids or abets copyright violations by others. Works protected by the Copyright Act must fit into one of the following categories: 1) literary works, broadly defined to encompass not only books but also newspaper and magazine articles, computer and training manuals, catalogues, brochures, and print advertisements; 2) musical works, including accompanying words and also advertising jingles; 3) plays and dramatic works including accompanying music; 4) ballet, dance, pantomime, and choreographic works; 5) pictorial, graphic, and sculptural works, including maps, cartoons, posters, and statues; 6) movies, audiovisual, and multi-media works; 7) sound recordings; and 8) architectural works. However, the ideas, concepts, or principles underlying a work are not subject to copyright; yet the expression of those ideas in a work is copyrightable. Accordingly, it must be emphasized that copyright law does not prevent a person from taking the basic idea of a copyrighted work and then by means of different expressions essentially recreating it as an independent work and reselling it. Moreover, facts widely known to the general public are not copyrightable, though the compilation of facts, if selected, arranged, collated, or coordinated in an original manner, is subject to copyright protection. Remedies for copyright infringement include actual damages (that is, the actual harm caused to the copyright holder by the infringement), statutory damages (not to exceed $150,000), criminal sanctions (including fines and imprisonment), and the issuance of an injunction.

It is very important to note that copyright protection extends automatically to original works of authorship fixed in a tangible medium of expression, that is, the works are expressed, touched, and/or perceived. As such, registration of the copyright with the Copyright Office is not required; registration according to the law is merely permissive. Moreover, using the copyright symbol or word with the work is not required either as the law says it may be placed on publicly distributed copies of the work. However, it is strongly advised that the registration procedure to register a copyright be effectuated and that the copyright symbol or the word be used in order to ensure maximum protection for one's original works of authorship.

A leading copyright infringement case was the 2001 Napster decision, *A&M Records, Inc. v. Napster, Inc.,* where the U.S. Court of Appeals held that Napster was vicariously liable as a contributor to copyright infringement by assisting others to violate copyright law by means of its file-sharing software, which allowed people to obtain copies of copyrighted music without the permission of the copyright holders. Even more important is the 2005 Supreme Court decision in *Metro-Goldwyn-Mayer Studios v. Grokster.* The *Napster* case involved the use of a central server to facilitate copyright infringement. Consequently, after *Napster*, companies began to use peer-to-peer computer programs, which could be installed on users' computers, to facilitate the downloading and sharing, file-to-file, without the use of a central server, of digital music. That is, the computers of the users were communicating directly with one another and not with a central server. Nevertheless, copyright holders, including the recording industry, movie studios, and songwriters, sued two such companies, Grokster and Streamcast Networks, for copyright infringement. The Supreme Court unanimously agreed with the copyright holders, ruling that the companies knowingly and intentionally distributed copyrighted works in violation of the Copyright Act. The Court pointed out that the vast majority of the users' downloads were acts of copyright infringement, as well as the fact that literally billions of files were shared, and thus the probable scope of copyright infringement was "staggering." The court also noted that the companies were not passive recipients, but rather provided the file-sharing software for free, the companies stated that the objective of the software was to download copyrighted works, the companies took active steps to encourage copyright infringement, no filtering tools or other mechanisms were provided to diminish copyright infringement, and the companies made money by selling advertising space. The companies, therefore, had a purpose to commit copyright infringement; and did in fact commit copyright infringement, the Court declared, on a "gigantic scale." After the *Grokster* decision, the recording and movie industries subpoenaed and sued thousands of individual file-sharers, many of them university students, to stop the practice of illegally sharing copyrighted material.

In 1980, Congress passed an important amendment to the copyright statute, called the *Computer Software Copyright Act*, which includes computer programs and software under that legal protection. Specifically, the statute now classifies computer programs and software as creative and literary works. However, another 1980 amendment, as interpreted by the courts, permits people or businesses who buy copyrighted software to make copies and modifications of the software for their own use and under some circumstances to transfer the software. The modification and distribution must be for personal use or for internal business purposes, and not for unauthorized distribution. Nonetheless, to deter such potentially widespread distribution of software, most software manufacturers market their software through licenses rather than sales.

In 1998, the U.S. Congress enacted the *Copyright Term Extension Act* which lengthened the time periods for the protection of copyrighted works. As with patent law, an important exception exists under copyright law, explicitly so in Section 107 of the Copyright Act, called the "fair use" exception, which allows the limited use of copyrighted materials, principally for educational use, without having to pay any royalties for the copyright holder.

Moreover, in 1998, Congress passed the *Digital Millennium Copyright Act*, which extends copyright protection to the creators and owners of digital information, though there are exceptions for libraries and universities as well as "fair use" for educational purposes. There is also a "circumvention" exception which allows the testing of computer security as well as to enable parents to monitor their children's use of the Internet. The Digital Millennium Copyright Act also holds that an Internet service provider (ISP) is not liable for copyright infringement by its customer unless the ISP was aware of its customer's violation.

An example of a copyright legal contest arose when one of the creators of the famous Broadway musical Grease accused several large cruise lines, including Carnival Cruise Lines and Celebrity Cruises, of copyright infringement for staging his play at sea for years without his permission. Under copyright law, any producer of a show that makes use of the story, dialogue, or lyrics of a musical beyond the singing of a few of its songs is required to purchase a license for what the law calls "grand performing rights." There are two very interesting aspects of the case, one practical and the other legal. The practical one is how the purported unlicensed use was discovered; and that was when the wife of one of the co-creators told her husband upon returning from a Hawaiian cruise that she had seen a "full-blown production" of Grease in the ship's theatre. The interesting legal issue is the jurisdictional one. Because many of the cruise line companies are incorporated and registered in foreign locales, principally Liberia and Panama, acquiring jurisdiction in the U.S. represents a major legal challenge. However, the U.S. companies would still be bound by the laws of the nations where their ships are registered, including copyright law, presuming certain countries have copyright law and have signed intellectual property treaties.

Copyright Law – "Fair Use" Exception

Even if material is protected by federal copyright law in the United States, there is an important exception called the "*fair use doctrine*." This exception, found in Section 107 of the Copyright Act, allows people to make limited use of copyrighted materials for "fair use," which includes commenting, criticizing, reporting news, and engaging in scholarship and research. If the "fair use" doctrine applies then a person or organization can use or reproduce the copyrighted material without having to pay fees, that is, "royalties," to the holder of the copyright.

Pursuant to this exception to copyright law, there are four criteria to determine "fair use," to wit: (1) the purpose and character of the use, especially whether the use is commercial or not; (2) the nature of the copyrighted work; (3) the amount and substance of the copyrighted work used; and (4) the effect of the use on the value and potential market of the copyrighted work. As a general rule, if the use amounts to a substantial revision or is transformational, that is, the use adds new information, interpretations, or understanding of the copyrighted work, the use is more likely to be deemed to be a "fair use." However, the more commercial the use is, and the more it diminishes the value of the copyrighted work, the less likely that a use will be construed as a "fair" one. The courts apply these four factors on a case-by-case basis, balancing them all, though it is likely that the final factor is given the greatest weight.

Trademark Law

Trademark law at the federal level in the United States is governed by the Lanham Act of 1946 as amended by the Federal Trademark Dilution Act of 1995. A *trademark* is obtained by registering the mark with the appropriate federal or state government agency. At the federal level, the agency is again the U.S. Patent and Trademark Office. Most states also have comparable trademark statutes and agencies. A trademark is a legal right granted by either the federal or state governments to protect names, logos, marks, mottoes, slogans, images and appearances, and other symbols, as well as combinations thereof, that identify goods and services and that distinguish them from other goods and services. Service marks refer to marks used to distinguish the services of the holder, as opposed to products, from that of its competitors, for example, the logo of an airline, or the NBC television network's peacock symbol. Protection not only is extended to distinctive trademarks but also to famous ones; and a famous mark can be diluted not only by the use of an identical mark, but also by a similar mark that lessens the value of a famous mark. Trademark protection extends to the registering of famous names as domain names on the Internet, that is, cybersquatting. "Trade dress," that is, the design, overall appearance, and image of a product or service is also protected by trademark law.

Trademark law protects the owner of the trademark from others who might use the same trademark or a similar one on their products and services, and thereby mislead and confuse the public. Accordingly, not only is the use of confusingly similar trademarks prohibited, but also the *dilution* of trademarks, that is, an unauthorized use of a trademark even regarding non-competing goods but where confusion is likely to ensure. In the classic "Coke" (no pun intended) case, the U.S. Supreme Court in 1920 gave trademark protection to the Coca-Cola company for its product's "nickname," "Coke," against a company that was attempting to market a rival product called "Koke." Generic terms, however, which refer to a class of products, such as "cell phone" or "laptop computer," cannot be protected by trademark law; nor can the names of products that originally were protected marks but through the years have acquired general and common usage, such as linoleum, corn flakes, nylon, dry ice, and escalator.

Trademark *infringement* occurs when a person uses a protected trademark in such a way as to create a likelihood of confusion about the source or origin of the goods or services. Consequently, when a trademark is copied entirely or copied substantially and used by another whether intentionally or intentionally trademark infringement has occurred. The essence of an infringement lawsuit is confusion in the mind of the consumer. The holder of the mark is entitled to prohibit and to stop any unauthorized use of the mark so that consumers can trust the source of the goods and services they are buying. Trademarks also protect against the loss of reputation and value, for example, when the infringed-on product or service is of poor quality and/or when the supply of the product or service is artificially increased by the unauthorized use. Remedies encompass an injunction, actual damages, including lost profits which the infringer wrongfully obtained from the unauthorized use of the mark, as well as court-ordered destruction of the goods bearing the unauthorized mark.

One major trademark problem created by the "Internet age" is the selling of counterfeit goods, especially with fake "high-end" logos, such as "Coach," online. To address this growing problem, the U.S. Congress in 2006 promulgated the Stop Counterfeiting in Manufactured Goods Act. This statute makes it a crime to intentionally sell counterfeit goods or services or to knowingly use a counterfeit trademark or service mark. Sanctions include fines up to $2 million and imprisonment up to 10 years. Also, the seller of the counterfeit goods must pay restitution to the holder or the mark representing the actual loss to the victim. Moreover, the counterfeit goods will be forfeited and destroyed. As such, online sellers of goods, such as eBay, who are advised by a manufacturer or otherwise become aware that counterfeit goods are being sold on their "virtual" systems, must immediately remove the fake items.

A very interesting as well as controversial trademark case was decided by the U.S. Supreme Court in 2017. The case, *Matal v. Tam*, also colloquially known as the "Slants" case, was an 8-0 decision by the Court holding that a 70-year-old statute that prohibits disparaging and offensive trademarks is unconstitutional because the law violates the First Amendment right to freedom of speech. The ruling was in favor of an Oregon-based, Asian-American rock-n-roll band called the Slants who wanted to obtain that name as a trademark for their band. The founder of the band, Simon Tam, sought to obtain the trademark name for the band in 2001, but Tam was denied the trademark by the U.S. Patent and Trademark Office on grounds that the name was disparaging to Asian-Americans and thus in violation of the law's "disparagement clause." This clause gives the trademark office the power to prohibit trademarks that may disparage persons, living or dead, institutions, beliefs, or national symbols. A trademark is an important grant of authority to its owner because the owner then has the power to sue others, especially competitors, who infringe on the trademark. The term "slant" traditionally has been regarded as a racial slur against Asian-American people. Yet Tam has always insisted that he and the band were not trying to be offensive; rather, Tam contended that he wanted to transform an insulting and derisive term into a statement of pride, like gays have done with the term "queer." Tam stated that he thus wanted to reclaim an ethnic slur and transform it into a term of pride and to use it in a positive light. He also intended to use the name as a rebuke to those people who use the term "slant" in a pejorative and demeaning manner. Tam appealed the trademark office denial of the "Slants" trademark to the federal appeals court in Washington, D.C., which sided with the band and said that the law barring offensive trademarks was unconstitutional. The Supreme Court now has agreed with the lower court. Justice Samuel Alito, writing for the Supreme Court, stated that a "bedrock" principle of the First Amendment is that speech cannot be banned merely because it is offensive or expresses ideas that offend. Speech that offends people based on their race, color, national origin, religion, gender, age, or disability may be hateful, but nevertheless it is protected by the First Amendment. Also, the fact that there was a commercial element to the name did not change the decision. Justice Alito stated that the market for goods includes many goods that disparage prominent people and groups. Moreover, Justice Alito said that the line between commercial and non-commercial speech is not clear. The government does have more power to regulate commercial speech, as opposed to political speech, but the government must have a substantial reason to regulate or prohibit commercial speech and any such regulation or prohibition must be narrowly tailored. Justice Alito also explained that the "disparagement clause" was too broad and sweeping; it is not an anti-discrimination law, he said. However, Justice Alito said that the government still retains an interest in preventing certain types of offensive speech and ideas. Also, important in the decision was the fact that four justices stated that even if the "Slant" speech herein was commercial speech the denial of the trademark was still unconstitutional. One justice, Justice Anthony Kennedy, particularly was concerned that to allow the government ban "offensive" speech could result in government censorship as well as discrimination against unpopular ideas, dissenting views, and minority groups in society.

Trade Secret Law

Because of the difficulties involved with securing federal patent, copyright, and trademark law, the creators of intellectual property can use *trade secret* law, which is based on state statutes or state common law, to protect proprietary information. Trade secret law is considered to be complementary to federal patent, copyright, and trademark law, and thus is not preempted by these federal laws. Trade secret law is predominantly based on state law, with one very important exception – a federal statute which criminalizes the theft of a trade secret. Every state has a body of trade secret law. Generally speaking, trade secret law will protect information that is valuable and is subject to reasonable efforts to maintain its secrecy. The primary state statute on point is the *Uniform Trade Secret Act*, which many states in the United States have adopted. However, the statute follows the old common law definitions and rules for acquiring and protecting trade secrets. There is legal liability – criminal and civil – to the misappropriation of a trade secret. Misappropriation occurs when a person, typically an employee and his or her new employer, acquires another's trade secret, usually the trade secret of the former employer, and the acquiring person knows or should know that the trade secret was secured through improper means. The key "misappropriation" fact is that the trade secret was obtained, conveyed, or used without the consent of the original owner. The remedies for a misappropriation of a trade secret can be both criminal and civil. Civil remedies include an injunction against actual or threatened misappropriation, monetary damages for the actual loss as well as for the unjust enrichment of the misappropriating party, and perhaps punitive damages and attorneys' fees. An injunction can forever prohibit an employee from disclosing a trade secret to a competitor or using it himself or herself. Many state statutes, as well as a federal statute, make the misappropriation of trade secrets a crime; and even if a state does not have a precise criminal statute on point, a state's civil theft statute should be able to encompass the intentional misappropriation of a trade secret. One major advantage to trade secret protection as compared to patent and copyright law is that trade secret protection theoretically can be in perpetuity.

The predicate for any type of legal trade secret protection is *"information,"* which obviously is a broad term, but one that is very liberally construed by the courts. Information can consist of devices, designs, patterns, programs, such as computer software, processes, procedures, techniques, compilations, such as customer and supplier lists, as well as other valuable proprietary information, such as price markups and profit margins and research results. Information can be "hard," in the sense of a scientific formula, such as the formula for Coca-Cola which is the "classic" (no pun intended!) trade secret example, or information can be "soft," in the sense of plans and strategies, such as an entrepreneur's business plan or a company's marketing strategy. To illustrate how "soft" information can be, and how "hard" a jury can be, in one notable Florida case, involving the Walt Disney company, a state appeals court ruled that the idea and detailed business plan for a sports-themed park could be construed as "information" and remanded the case for trial for a jury to determine if this idea was a trade secret that Disney had misappropriated from a development company and its two principals. The jury decided in fact that the idea was a trade secret, and that the Disney company had misappropriated it, and awarded the plaintiff company $240 million in damages. Now Disney is being sued by the family of a now deceased relative who contends that Disney misappropriated the idea for Epcot that their relative had proposed to Disney many years ago, calling his idea for a theme park "Miniature Worlds." Assuming that the major legal impediment of the Statute of Limitations can be overcome, one wonders what a Florida jury will do with such a case, and one can only begin to contemplate the damages that might be awarded for misappropriating the concept of Epcot. Concerning "value," it should be pointed out that even "dead-ends" reached in research and development can be protected, so as to prevent one's competitors from obtaining such knowledge and thereby avoiding similar costly and time-consuming fruitless efforts. The requisite "information" must possess economic value – real or potential; that is, the information gives a business a commercial, economic, or competitive advantage. In order to have value, this information must have some degree of novelty. Consequently, if the information is generally known or readily ascertainable by competent people, it is not trade secret information because it lacks "value."

The final factor in achieving trade secret status to information is the secrecy element. The person or business attempting to convince a court that his or her valuable information is in fact a legal trade secret must demonstrate that reasonable security measures were adopted and continued in order to maintain the secrecy of the information. "Reasonable" means, well, reasonable; and thus depends on the facts and circumstances of the case. Obviously, a high-tech firm with a defense contract will have more elaborate secrecy procedures than a small sales firm or an entrepreneur with a business plan in hand. Designating appropriate information as confidential and proprietary is the first step, and then protecting it by lock-and-key and passwords is a good start on the road to a trade secret destination. Moreover, reasonableness does not mean that the information cannot be disclosed; certain information must be disclosed, for example to key "need to know" employees and outside sales personnel, vendors, subcontractors, and licensees in order for a company to function, and they of course must be clearly, as well as regularly notified only to use the information in the scope of their duties; yet the more people the information is disclosed to, as well as the paucity of precautions with the disclosure, will make it less likely to achieve trade secret status. Having employees and others who need access to the information sign confidentiality and non-disclosure agreements is an extremely important factor in finding "secrecy." When an employee resigns, the employer should discuss the handling of trade secrets as part of the "exit interview"; and also should communicate with the employee's new employer informing it that the employee had access to trade secrets. Plainly, do not put the information out over the Internet and then later expect a court to grant trade secret status to it. Trade secret audits to see what information needs to be protected and how are naturally advisable. To further illustrate "reasonable" measures, the manufacturers of computer software typically use software licensing agreements to preserve secrecy by means of forbidding the licensee to copy the program and also by requiring the licensee to sign a confidentiality agreement. Another more "plebian" example concerns the expiration dates on bottles of beer, which the manufacturers place on the cans by means of unintelligible, cryptic codes that look like hieroglyphics, but which can be deciphered by the manufacturer, of course, as well as its wholesalers and distributors. Using complex codes is certainly an example of a "reasonable" secrecy measure. A new form of security measure for trade secret protection is a new computer technology – fingerprint reading sensors – that requires a computer user to swipe his or her finger on a sensor in order to gain access to a computer or to certain Web sites. Fingerprints are more difficult to mimic or to copy than passwords; and it is more convenient for a user to merely swipe his or her finger than to remember a bunch of passwords, which often are written down in several places as well as used time and time again. Yet trade secret law requires a security measure to be "reasonable" under the circumstances; and it is still not certain if fingerprint sensors for computers are feasible, practical, and cost-effective security devices. Whether the secrecy measures adopted are in fact sufficiently reasonable is regarded as a question of fact for a jury to decide. Once information is established as a trade secret, if it is improperly used by a person individually or in one's capacity as an employee in a new firm, the person and the new employer can be sued for misappropriating a trade secret.

Trade secret protection does not extend to information that is generally known or readily ascertainable. Therefore, any information deemed to be in the public domain cannot be the basis for a legally protected trade secret. Since such information is public it is available to a firm's competitors and customers. For example, the information contained in a company's own product, service, and promotional materials that are distributed to the public will be deemed "pubic," even if they contain technical information. Similarly, information even if confidential, that is mistakenly disclosed by a company's employees is nevertheless "public." Trade secret protection is also not available for information that is "reverse engineered," that is, taking apart a product, examining its components and internal workings, and then reconstructing the product with a different series of steps. Yet, if this process cannot be readily or easily accomplished, then the trade secret protection for the product is not lost.

Trade secret disputes can arise when an employee leaves one firm and brings confidential information with him or her to a new employer who is a competitor of the former employer. What can the new employer do to protect itself? The new employer must first emphasize that no trade secrets from the former employer can be brought to the firm; and then the new employer should try to make sure that the employee has not brought any computer discs or devices, documents or papers, or other material that can be construed as a trade secret. Moreover, the new employer should require the new employee to sign a statement saying that he or she is not bringing any trade secrets or confidential information to the new employer.

On the federal level, misappropriating a trade secret can be a very serious legal wrong because the U.S. Congress has converted the misappropriation of a trade secret into a federal crime by means of the federal *Economic Espionage Act of 1996*. The definition of a trade secret under the federal statute is essentially the same as under the state statutes and the common law. The statute has two separate provisions that criminalize the theft or misappropriation of a trade secret. One is aimed at foreign industrial or economic espionage and requires that the theft of a trade secret be done to benefit a foreign government or an instrumentality or agent of a foreign government. In the latter case, it must be shown that the foreign government substantially owned, controlled, sponsored, dominated, directed, or managed the entity. The second provision in the Act is directed at the more common business and commercial theft or misappropriation of trade secrets. The penalties for violating the Economic Espionage Act are very severe, with substantial monetary fines, forfeiture of any property or proceeds made in violation of the Act, and imprisonment up to twenty-five years. The title to the Act is a bit of a misnomer, since the statute criminalizes any theft of a trade secret, and not just by "foreign agents," though the federal government usually will leave "minor," "domestic" misappropriations to the states to prosecute.

The importance of a firm having a non-disclosure agreement is a critical legal factor. A non-disclosure agreement as part of the employment contract should be seriously considered by the employer. The non-disclosure agreement will require that the party not disclose confidential information to anyone outside the employer's company unless necessary to conduct the employer's business. Such an agreement will protect trade secrets as well as other confidential and proprietary information. Also, recall that one required element of converting information into a legally protected trade secret is a showing that the employer utilized reasonable methods to maintain the secrecy of the information. Accordingly, one "tried and true" way of demonstrating that "secrecy" requirement is for the employer to have a contractually based non-disclosure agreement with its employees and other parties who have access to confidential information. These parties would include, in addition to the employees, independent contractors, suppliers, vendors, distributors, the "outside" sales force, and even actual and potential investors in an entrepreneurial endeavor. Thus, by means of the non-disclosure agreement, the employees and other parties are put on notice that they will have access to confidential information, that they have an obligation to keep this information secret, even after their relationship with the employer ends, and also that the employer can demonstrate to the court that it took a "reasonable" required measure to maintain the secrecy of the information. The importance of a firm having a non-disclosure agreement cannot be over-emphasized. If trade secrets exist, then a reasonable non-disclosure agreement will be upheld by the courts, even in states such as California that will not enforce post-employment covenants not to compete.

In order to fully take advantage of trade secret law, the employer or entrepreneur should first determine if the business in fact has trade secrets, and, if so what exactly are they. Next, a determination must be made as to who in the business must have access to this confidential information; then the business must take steps to ensure that all the people who have access to the trade secrets recognize the information as confidential and promise to treat it as such. Since a non-disclosure agreement is a very efficacious way for the employer or entrepreneur to maintain the secrecy of the information as well as to create the trade secret itself, such an agreement should be required of all employees. Finally, in addition to the non-disclosure agreement, the business must ascertain what other "reasonable" steps it should take to maintain the secrecy of the information.

As the authors have emphasized, non-disclosure and confidentiality agreements are an essential component to protecting intellectual property by means of trade secret law. Employers, however, must be careful about having over-broad non-disclosure agreements as part of their company policies. Initially, employers may think it is advisable to have a policy that prohibits the employees from saying or communicating anything publicly, including on social media that might harm the reputation of the employer and damage its relationship with customers, clients, and the community. Yet, there may be practical as well as legal problems in having a too broad non-disclosure agreement policy. Practically, such a broad policy might have a "chilling effect" in the workplace, thereby inhibiting employees from reporting workplace problems or concerns, which may turn into more serious problems, such as the presence of incompetent employees or employees engaging in wrongful or unprofessional conduct. Legally, too, there may be problems. For example, the National Labor Relations Act (NLRA) protects "concerted activities" by employees (two or more to be "concerted") who are discussing issues at work, that is, the "terms and conditions" of employment, with the aim of improving working conditions. An overbroad non-disclosure policy may thus violate the NLRA. Similarly, the Securities and Exchange Commission may find that an overbroad policy might be illegal for restricting the employee's right under the Sarbanes-Oxley Act to "blow the whistle" on wrongdoing by the employer or co-workers. Finally, some states, for example, New York, New Jersey, California, Vermont, and Pennsylvania, now prohibit non-disclosure agreements in sexual harassment settlements due to a concern that in the past such agreements have kept sexual harassment secret and consequently have allowed sexual harassment in the workplace to continue unabated. However, there is a countervailing argument against these statutes, and that is there may be less incentive for an employer to settle a lawsuit, and thus the victims of sexual harassment might have to go through the effort, expense, and likely embarrassment of a lawsuit, which outcome is always uncertain due to the vagaries of juries. Accordingly, since these statutes are relatively new it is difficult to precisely ascertain what their effect in the workplace will be.

Covenants-Not-To-Compete

Covenants-not-to-compete, also called *non-competition clauses*, were first addressed in the Contract Law chapter. This important legal concept will be more extensively covered in this chapter with particular reference to employment relationships. One recalls that a covenant-not-to-compete can be found in a contract for the sale of a business or in an employment contract. Moreover, the covenant clause must be ancillary to, subordinate of, or part of a larger contract, and also must be supported by the common law contract requirement of "consideration." A covenant not supported by consideration is merely an unenforceable promise. Moreover, a restrictive covenant, standing alone, and not part of a larger contract, usually will be deemed to be an illegal restraint of trade or a violation of public policy. Examples of the "larger" contract would be an employment contract, a sale of business contract, or a partnership agreement, and in most states even an employment at-will employment relationship.

Although covenants-not-to-compete are disfavored in the law, since the law favors economic advancement and competition, and does not want to restrain people from pursuing their careers and entrepreneurial ambitions, the law will restrain competition in a properly drafted covenant situation. Covenants-not-to-compete typically are found in two contract situations, the sale of a business and an employment relationship. In the first case, as noted earlier, a business owner is selling his or her business to a buyer, and the buyer wants assurances that the seller will not resume the same or similar business in the same locale, thereby, in essence, retaking the "good will" that the buyer purchased as part of the purchase of the business. Accordingly, in order to protect himself or herself, the buyer will insist as part of the sales contract a non-competition clause, in which the seller promises not to compete, directly or indirectly, in the same or similar business for a period of time in a designated trade territory. Based on the common law, such a non-competition clause will be upheld if it is reasonable as to time, that is, duration, and also place, that is, trade territory. Both requirements are necessary; and if one or both are not present, the covenant is unreasonable, overbroad, invalid, illegal, and stricken from the contract, though ordinarily the remainder of the contract will not be adversely affected (which means the buyer now has a business but no protection against competition). For example, in the sale of a "high-end" Italian restaurant in Ft. Lauderdale, Florida, a trade territory of a radius of several miles and a time period of two to three years should be deemed reasonable; but certainly not in the state of Florida for a ten year period. The idea is to give the new buyer, who has purchased a going concern with a good reputation, a reasonable opportunity to demonstrate that he or she can continue the business on a prosperous footing. As noted, if the covenant is overbroad, the courts usually will not "reform," that is, rewrite, covenants, and change time periods and territories, to make them reasonable and enforceable.

However, if the covenant-not-to-compete is found in an employment contract, either by statute of by common law interpretation, most courts will impose a third requirement for the validity of the covenant. In this employment situation, the employee is signing a contract, either initially or as a modification of a contract, in which the employee promises when he or she leaves the employer's employ for any reason (that is, fired, quits, "down-sized," "right-sized," laid-off, off-shored, out-sourced, etc.), not to compete against the employer, directly or indirectly, as an employee for another firm or in his or her own business capacity, for a certain period of time and within a designated trade territory. In order to have a legally valid and enforceable non-competition agreement in an employment situation, the first two requirements are the same as in the sale of a business circumstance. However, in most states in the U.S, though not all, either by statute or common law, a third, and very significant requirement is necessary. The party seeking to enforce the covenant, that is, the employer, must show that it is not only reasonable in time and place, but also that it is necessary to support a legitimate business interest of the employer. Before the third requirement is explicated, it is interesting to note how the first two compare in the two restrictive covenant situations. As to the time or duration requirement, the employee is in a more beneficial position compared to the seller of a business, as the courts typically will require much shorter time periods for covenants-not-to-compete in an employment situation. Particularly if the employment is related to the technology field, the courts will insist that a "reasonable" time be a short time indeed. As one court declared, in throwing out a one year covenant-not-to-compete in an Internet publishing company employment case, one year is an "eternity" in such an on-line technical field, due to the very rapid changing and advancing of technology. In Florida, by statute, to illustrate, a time period of six months or less in an employment covenant situation is presumed to be reasonable; but a time period of two years or more is presumed to be unreasonable; and anything in between carries no presumption, and is left to the discretion of the court. Presumptions are merely assumptions, of course, and thus can be rebutted, but one will need evidence to do so. The time period interpretation is the "good news" for the employee; but the trade territory interpretation is the obverse "bad news"; that is, in many companies, which are truly global in nature, the trade territory or geographic area for the restrictive covenant may legitimately be the world. In such a case, presuming the third covenant requirement is present, it may be time for the former employee to rely on family or a spouse or a sympathetic "significant other" and go back to school and wait out the covenant time period.

It is important to note that a court will not enforce a covenant not to compete that is unreasonable in the sense of being overbroad in either duration or territory. Consequently, the employer must avoid a covenant in which the employee promises never to compete or not to compete for an unreasonable amount of time or promises not to compete within an unreasonable trade territory. An employer who is "greedy," and thus who demands too much for an employee, and who gets it, as a consequence may get nothing in the form of legal protection, as the entire covenant may be struck down as overbroad, unreasonable, invalid, and illegal. Accordingly, the employer is well advised to think carefully what legitimate business interests it is seeking to protect by means of the covenant and to what degree (in time and place) the employer reasonably needs protection against competition. Then the employer must consult with an attorney about the creation of the covenant-not-to-compete, since the attorney will be able to advise the employer if its restrictions will likely be upheld by the courts, or conversely whether they may be struck down as overbroad and unreasonable, thereby affording the employer no covenant protection whatsoever.

The third requirement for a valid covenant in an employment situation is that the covenant be necessary to further a *legitimate business interest of the employer*. The burden of proof as well as persuasion is on the employer to demonstrate not only the reasonableness elements but also an adequate interest to support the covenant. Examples of a sufficient employer business interest arise when the employee sought to be constrained from competing has access to confidential, proprietary, or trade secret information of the employer, including business and customer lists and records, has established goodwill with the employer's customers, and when the employer has invested in the employee extraordinary, specialized, unique, or valuable training and/or education in the employee. Regarding the latter, a few seminars on hiring and firing skills, diversity training, and ethics courses most likely would not suffice, but enabling the employee to obtain an MBA degree or a license or certification from a government agency, for example, to repair planes pursuant to an FAA certification, most likely would be an adequate interest to protect. Once these three requirements are present, the covenant is enforceable, and the employee cannot compete in contravention of the covenant. Covenants can be enforced by means of a lawsuit for breach of contract as well an injunction, upheld by a court's traditional "contempt" powers, although for an injunction a showing of "irreparable harm" must be shown. Moreover, it is no defense in most states that the enforcement of the covenant would be harsh or oppressive or unduly burdensome to the employee, perhaps an employee whose job was out-sourced and who cannot take advantage of another opportunity locally due to a covenant. The employee signed the covenant as part of his or her contract, which the employee presumably read (and will be deemed to have read by the law), and the employee will be so bound. In one recent and notable covenant employment case, Microsoft sued a former company vice-president, who had seven years with the company, possesses a doctorate degree, and who is an expert in search technology and was one of the architects of the company's China policy. The former employee was hired by Google and named as the head of that company's China operations and placed in charge of establishing a research and development center in China. Microsoft contended that its former employee had breached his employment contract, specifically the covenant-not-to-compete provision, and requested damages and an injunction to prevent the employee from working for Google. A Washington state court judge, however, ruled that the former Microsoft employee could work for Google and could help that firm establish its operations in China; but the judge restricted the former employee from working on projects, products, and services that were directly competitive with those that he had worked at Microsoft as well as restricted him from making key budgetary and personnel decisions for the China project. Both companies were not pleased with the judge's covenant "reform" decision. One notable exception to the enforceability of covenant-not-to-compete is the state of California where they are completely illegal in employment.

A covenant-not-to-compete in order to be valid must be a part of or ancillary to or subordinate a larger contract. A restrictive covenant, standing alone, usually will be deemed to be an illegal restraint of trade or a violation of public policy. Examples of the "larger" contract would be an employment contract, a sale of business contract, or a partnership agreement, and in most states even an employment at-will employment relationship.

Regarding the time period, as a general rule, courts will find a period of one year or less to be reasonable in an employment contract, and a period of three or more years to be unreasonable. For the sale of a business, time periods of five years have been deemed reasonable. Regarding the geographic area in order for it to be deemed reasonable some courts will require that the geographic area correlate to the employer's actual trade territory. Legitimate employer interests to support a covenant-not-to-compete include the protection of goodwill, long-term customer relationships, trade secrets, confidential information, and business relationship.

Although some states such as California have statutes prohibiting covenants from restraining a person from engaging in any lawful profession, occupation, trade, or business, there are exceptions, for example, when a person sells all of his or her shares in a corporation and the company is sold as an ongoing business, or when a partnership is dissolved but not terminated and continues in an altered form, or when a limited liability company is sold. The prudent approach is naturally to ascertain a state's statutory and common law regarding covenants and their validity, and then to use the aforementioned choice-of-law and forum selection provisions to ensure the desirable legal result.

Anti-Piracy and Non-Solicitation Agreements

Anti-piracy and *non-solicitation agreements* are clauses in contracts which bar a departing employee from soliciting or serving the former employer's customers, clients, and employees. These types of provisions typically are enforceable based on the reasonableness and legitimate business interest standards found in restrictive covenant law. Also related to the aforementioned provisions are clauses in contracts which require the departing employee to repay the company's training and education costs if the employee does not stay with the employer for a reasonable period of time after completion of the training or education. Again, this type of provision will be held legally binding and effective if reasonable.

A *non-solicitation* agreement is typically part of the employer's contract with its employees or independent contractors, for example, an "outside" sales force, which states that when these parties leave the employer's firm or employ they will not solicit the employer's customers, clients, or employees. The non-solicitation agreement also can be used in contracts with the employer's clients and customers by stating that they will not solicit the employer's employees. In the latter case, the employer may be concerned that a client will "hire away" from the employer one of the employer's very good employees who has been serving the client very well, as the client may decide it would be less expensive to have the work done "in-house." It also should be noted that non-solicitation agreements are enforceable in all the states, even ones such as California, which do not enforce covenants-not-to-compete.

Anti-piracy agreements (also called "no-raid" agreements) are similar to non-solicitation agreements. Anti-piracy agreements are typically part of the employee's contract with the employer in which the employee promises when he or she leaves the firm for another firm, or to embark on an entrepreneurial venture, not to solicit other employees to join the departing employee or to hire the employees for a stated period of time. However, even if there is such an agreement, the courts usually maintain that the employee who is leaving is allowed to tell his or her fellow employees of his or her plans. Of course, the employees cannot be solicited; but if they on their own wish to join the departing employee such conduct would generally be permissible. Yet there is, obviously, a "fine-line" between soliciting one's fellow employees and "merely" informing them of one's employment or entrepreneurial plans and aspirations.

Non-solicitation agreements, as well as non-piracy and non-poaching agreements, are prevalent in the franchise industry, for example, at Burger King and H&R Block, as well as in fitness and lodging chains and large retailers. The legal effect of such agreements is to limit the ability of franchise employees to seek employment at another franchise in a designated trade territory. These agreements have been attached as being illegal, anti-competitive restraints of trade under federal and state anti-trust law, but to date they have withstood attack. There is federal legislation sponsored in 2018 in Congress by Senators Cory Booker (D.-NJ) and

Elizabeth Warren (D.-MA) but passage is highly unlikely. There is also state legislation that is being proposed, for example, in Massachusetts, Maine, and Maryland; and one state, Illinois, bans enforcement of such agreements on workers making less than $13.00 an hour. The franchise industry defends these agreements in that a franchise owner typically makes an investment in workers in training, which can be expensive and time-consuming, especially for workers who are new to the franchise industry (or for that matter to employment at all) and consequently these workers need to develop the knowledge and skills necessary to deliver the product or service to the customer. Of course, training and education can be used by an employer to demonstrate a legitimate business reason for a court to uphold a covenant-not-to-compete in an employment contract; and these training and education rationales can be, and have been, asserted legally too with non-solicitation agreements.

Confidentiality and Non-Disclosure Agreements
These types of agreements forbid employees from using confidential, proprietary, and trade secret information that they became cognizant of at their former employer. They can be used to protect a wide variety of trade secret, confidential, and proprietary information. Such agreements can also be drafted to cover meetings, communications, and even conversations. A single employment contract can of course include non-competition, non-solicitation, and non-disclosure provisions. Often, they are used at the hiring stage when an employer requests executives and managers to sign them. The first point is that there is neither a standard type of *confidentiality or non-disclosure agreement* nor a standard set of terms. Generally, the agreement will state that one use the information only for a specific purpose. In addition, usually there will be a provision that the party receiving the information will use a certain level of care, for example, "commercially reasonable efforts," to protect the information. Otherwise, there may be provisions to the effect that the party receiving the information will not disclose it except to people with a "need to know" or perhaps only to certain named individuals. Yet it is possible for the non-disclosure agreement to state that one party is prohibited from even revealing that he or she has any information. One should also be as specific as possible in the agreement as to exactly what the confidential information is that is protected by the agreement. Moreover, one typically finds in such agreements a clause dealing with the length of the agreement, which usually limits the time the agreement is in effect. Frequently one will find in such agreements a clause that confidentiality is waived in certain circumstances, such as when a court or government agency requires disclosure. When the agreement ends there should be some type of provision as to what happens to the information, for example, its return or its destruction. As with any contract agreement, one can and should attempt to negotiate the best agreement as possible, and naturally with the advice of legal counsel.

Employee Inventions
Another perplexing intellectual property problem arises when an employee creates certain knowledge or invents some device which is potentially valuable to the employer as well as naturally the employee. Who possesses the property rights to such employee creations? This field of law has always been a problem area. The rules

governing this area are predominantly common law formulations and they are not precise by any means. The problem – legally, ethically, and practically – is exacerbated when the employee does his or her creating on his or her own time and with no or minimal use of employer resources, but the creation does relate to the employee's job and the employer's business. The best way to describe the law governing employee inventions is to categorize employee inventions into three main groups: 1) "service" inventions, 2) "shop right" inventions, and 3) "free" inventions. First, a *"service" invention* occurs as a product of one's employment. The employer and employee usually have a contractual agreement that states that the employee is hired to make inventions or to create intellectual property. In such a case, the common law holds that the employee is legally obligated to turn over the invention to his or her employer. Here, the invention or creation characteristically entails a considerable utilization of the employer's resources. The employee in this first situation is ordinarily given a fixed amount of money, as per the contract, with characteristically a bonus amount for a valuable invention. Second, a *"shop right" invention* materializes when the employee is neither obligated by contract to invent or create nor is there any understanding, explicit or implicit, that the employee is hired in whole or in part to invent or create; yet nonetheless the employee invents. However, the employee so inventing or creating does use the employer's resources extensively and substantially, for example, by using equipment, supplies, facilities, materials, other employees, and confidential and trade secret information. In such a case, absent a contract provision to the contrary, the employee must give his or her employer the "right of first refusal" to the invention; and if the employer decides to use the invention, the employee must share in the royalties and profits therefrom; but if the employer decides after a reasonable period of time not to use the invention, the employee-inventor can use it or take the device and knowledge to a new employer. The third type of invention, the *"free" invention*, arises when there is no contract or understanding of any type between the employer and employee, and the employee does not use or materially use the employer's resources. The invention or creation is made on the employee's own time, using wholly or principally his or her own resources and thoughts, the invention or creation may result to the employee's job or the employer's business. In the "free" case, absent any contractual agreement to the contrary, the employee is legally entitled to the profits and royalties of his or her invention.

If an employee is expressly hired to invent, then clearly as a matter of contract law, any inventions belong to the employer. Also, the employer can have an employee sign an *invention assignment agreement* whereby the employee agrees to transfer to the employer the rights to any inventions created or developed by the employee during the course of his or her employment and also for a certain time thereafter, usually a one-year period. Furthermore, it should be noted that federal copyright law in the U.S. holds that the copyright to any work created by an employee during the scope of his or her employment belongs to the employer, even if the employee has not signed any assignment agreement. In order to avoid patent and copyright problems, the employer and entrepreneur should specify in the employment contract that any work created by the employee during the course of his or her employment, such as an invention subject to patent or a computer program or software subject to copyright, belongs to the employer. The language of such an agreement can extend beyond works that are subject to patent and copyright, of course. Yet, in order to motivate the employer's more creative employees, the language in the agreement can specify that the employer and the inventing employee jointly share the ownership rights in the invention or work, or at least that the inventing or creating employee will receive type of recognition and bonus for the idea or invention.

In today's highly competitive, and perhaps morally relativistic, global economy, applicants for employment must be very careful during the application and interview process not to disclose too much, and to protect the rest, of their inventions and other intellectual property. Submitting a business plan or even a more limited version of a work sample or invention typically is considered to be part of the investment process for the former and the hiring process for the latter. However, the applicant and interviewee must be aware of unscrupulous employers or for that matter fake employers who may reject the applicant but use his or her work for their own benefit. Naturally, an applicant wants to secure a position and thus is prepared to demonstrate in a tangible way his or her competence; yet one does not want to be taken advantage of by some "Machiavellian" schemer. When submitting a business plan, as previously recommended by the employer, it is best to convert the business plan or strategy document into a legally protected trade secret using the principles explicated therein, most importantly letting the recipient of the plan know that he or she is dealing with a confidential work and securing a non-disclosure agreement (NDA). However, for more modest work samples using trade secret law or for that matter even an NDA might not be practical, and actually might be off-putting to the prospective employer. Another more practical suggestion would be the applicant or interviewee to ask if his or her work will be used in any way, outside of the employment process, and if so, in what manner. Moreover, if there is any doubt as to the extent of use "get it in writing," as the old maxim says; and if a written acknowledgement is refused the refusal certainly can be viewed as a warning of potential problem. Another warning sign arises when the applicant or interviewee is asked to provide information beyond the scope of the duties of the position applied for at the firm. Moreover, an applicant can informally ask other applicants about the hiring process and what is entailed therein; and one can do some research to make sure the company and/or position being advertised is a legitimate one and not a device to defraud one of his or her intellectual property. Obviously, one wants and needs to be employed, entrepreneurs need investors, and similarly prospective employers and investors want to see some substance of one's work; so one must be cautious and heedful and do some research, and most importantly, when it comes to providing one's intellectual property, it is best to be cognizant of another old maxim, that is, "to be forewarned is to be forearmed."

Summary

The practically-minded manager, inventor, and entrepreneur must first be keenly aware that obtaining patent protection is not easy, not fast, and definitely not cheap. Moreover, it is still an ongoing legal debate as to whether certain creations, such as computer software, are even patentable. Regardless, the eminently practical constraint is that by the time one secures, if one can, a patent for one's product, especially if it is computer hardware, or perhaps even software, or technologically-related, the "march" of technology moves so rapidly and is so ever-changing, that one may find oneself the owner of a very expensive, and quite useless, patent.

Trade secret protection, in comparison to patent and copyright protection, is very broad and relatively easy to attain. The "information" component to a trade secret can encompass not only the expression of an idea, as in copyright law, not only the application of the idea, as in patent law, but the very idea itself. Trade secret law requires no registration, no filing fees, no notice, no disclosure (as opposed to patents and copyrights), and no lengthy, expensive, and time-consuming procedures. Moreover, a covenant-not-to-compete and a confidentiality agreement are not required for trade secret protection, though both are certainly advisable. All one needs is "information," which conceivably can be any concept or notion, some potential value to the information, and the adoption and maintenance of reasonable measures to safeguard the information. For example, an entrepreneur, before showing his or her business plan to potential investors in the business, can prominently indicate on his or her business plan the words "confidential" and "secret" and further indicate that the plan is being disclosed for limited business review purposes and is not to be disclosed to or shared with others. Customer or client lists, as compilations, as noted, may be protected under trade secret law. However, even if an employee has personally compiled a customer or client list, but no considerable effort or expense was involved and the names are readily obtainable from public sources, the employee may be able to take the list with him or her to a new employer or use it entrepreneurially, absent other restrictive contractual provisions.

All these intellectual property legal protections must be of heightened concern to the global business person and entrepreneur. Creating and developing intellectual property is characteristically an expensive and time-consuming process. Moreover, the advent of the Internet and the relative ease of transmission and duplication of information on a truly global basis means that the gain the creator expects to accrue from his or her creative efforts may be imperiled unless actions are taken to legally safeguard the intellectual property.

Discussion Questions

1. What are the major ways that the federal government in the U.S. can provide protection to intellectual property? Provide examples with brief explanations thereof.

2. How can intellectual property be protected pursuant to state trade secret law? Provide an example of a legally protected trade secret along with a brief explanation thereof.

3. How can trade secret law protect both "hard" and "soft" information? Provide examples along with brief explanations thereof.

4. What steps would you consider to be "reasonable" on the part of an employer to maintain the secrecy of its purported trade secret? Provide examples with brief explanations thereof.

5. Why should an entrepreneur developing a business plan find trade secret law a very valuable legal doctrine? Explain, providing an example.

6. What are the key legal differences between a covenant-not-to-compete in the sale of a business and in an employment contract? Provide an example of each together with a brief explanation thereof.
7. What would you consider to be a legitimate business interest of the employer that is a perquisite to a valid covenant not to compete in an employment contract in some jurisdictions? Provide an example and a brief explanation thereof.
8. What would you consider to be "specialized" or "extraordinary" training or learning to support the validity of a covenant-not-to-compete in an employment contract? Provide an example and a brief explanation thereof.
9. How can the employer use confidentiality and non-disclosure agreements to protect information? How can they be used in conjunction with trade secret law? Provide examples along with brief explanations thereof.

12 – REAL PROPERTY LAW

This chapter on real property law is divided into two parts. Part I covers real estate law and Part II covers real estate leases. Ownership of property and the rights to property are very important and strongly held beliefs in Western civilization law, history, and society, and especially in the Anglo-American tradition. Property can be defined generally as anything that can be owned, possessed, used, or disposed of. Property law in the U.S. is based on the old English common law; and property law today in the U.S. is still predominantly common law, though now there are many statutes that regulate the ownership, transfer, and use of property. The two basic types of property are real property, or real estate, which is not moveable, and personal property, which is moveable. There is also the concept of a "fixture," which is a piece of personal property that has become so firmly attached to real property that it is considered part of the real property. This chapter examines the nature of property, paying particular attention to real property, and also discusses how ownership rights to property are transferred. The approach to real estate law taken in this chapter is transactional in nature. It begins in Part I with a discussion of the sources of real estate law. Next, it moves progressively through the stages that are typical of real estate transactions: acquisition, ownership, financing, permitting, and entitlements. Personal property is comprehensively covered in a separate chapter. Part II covers real estate leases and landlord tenant law. The types of tenancies are described, the rights and obligations of the landlord and tenant are explained, and commercial leases are compared and contrasted to residential leases.

Part I – Real Estate Law[2]

The Sources of Real Estate Law
The real estate law in the United States springs from several different sources. Initially, the states constituting the original thirteen colonies and several other states

---

[2] Part I to this chapter is co-authored with John Wayne Falbey, Attorney at Law.

in the eastern portions of the country adopted the laws of England, generally referred to as the common law. It consisted of case law (i.e., judge-made law) that developed from centuries of court rulings in England, as well as various statutes enacted by the British Parliament. Examples include the rule in Shelley's Case from a case decided in Elizabethan England and now largely abolished in several states in the U.S., as well as the Statute of Frauds enacted by Parliament in 1677. English jurisprudence recognizes two major branches or systems. Actions at law are based upon a body of principles and rules, written or unwritten, determined by judges and legislative bodies as well as custom, which are of fixed authority, and which must be applied to controversies with the same or similar facts. An example of an action at law is a lawsuit seeking monetary damages for breach of a contract. Proceedings in equity, on the other hand, are intended to achieve justice to parties by affording redress where the courts of law were not capable of adequately dispensing justice by means of traditional legal remedies. In other words, there are situations the remedy for which is unattainable in an action at law. Equity is designed to fill this void. An example of a proceeding in equity is a suit for specific performance of a real estate contract. Originally, separate judicial bodies heard actions at law and proceedings in equity. That is still the case in Great Britain, but many states in the United States have combined these jurisdictions into a single judicial body. Many of the states in the western and southwestern portions of the country were settled originally under the flag of Spain. Louisiana's laws derived initially from French law. French and Spanish laws differ from the common law of Great Britain in that they were based on the Roman civil law system. Under these systems, laws were developed in the form of codes enacted by legislatures, then interpreted and applied by the respective court systems. Over time, the federal law, which is paramount to state and local laws in certain areas, and the laws of several states and their respective agencies and divisions have been modified, reinterpreted, and expanded by appellate court cases, statutes, laws, and regulations.

Acquiring Real Estate

It is important at the outset to differentiate between real property, personal property, and fixtures. *Real property* generally is considered to be land and the improvements constructed upon it. *Personal property* generally is property which is moveable and not affixed to the land. It can be tangible, meaning generally that it can be seen and touched, such as furniture, or intangible, meaning generally that it exists as a right or idea, such as a patent. *Fixtures* are items that originated as personal property but became permanently affixed to the real property, and consequently cannot be removed without damage to the real property. An example would be tile flooring in a residence or place of business. The individual tiles would be considered personal property, but, when affixed to the floor, the tile becomes part of the real property. Initially, acquiring an interest in real estate can be facilitated in various ways, such as by use of contracts or options. Pursuant to the previously mentioned Statute of Frauds, which still exists in some form in most jurisdictions, an agreement to acquire an interest in real estate must be in writing and signed by all of the parties to the transaction. There are narrow exceptions to this standard, such as the doctrine of part performance. This exception generally requires that the purchaser has relied on representations made by the seller to sell the property, has taken possession of the property, and has made improvements to the property and/or paid the purchase price.

Contracts and contract law emerge as indispensable components of real estate law and practice. Contracts can be bilateral or unilateral in nature. A contract is considered to be bilateral if all parties to it have to take some sort of action. For example, a contract for the sale and purchase of real estate requires the seller to sell and convey the title to the property to the buyer as of a certain date. The real estate contract also requires the buyer to take action in the form of paying the agreed consideration for the property to the seller as of a certain date. Typically, there are many other actions that also are required of each party along the road to the "closing" of the transaction. The *closing* is the legal term to indicate the transaction where the real estate contract is effectuated and the deed to the property is transferred from the seller to the buyer. A contract is considered to be unilateral in nature if it obligates one of the parties to perform, but not the other. An option to purchase real estate is a classic example of a unilateral contract. The seller has agreed to sell the property for a certain price and under certain conditions. The buyer, however, is not obligated to go through with the transaction unless he or she affirmatively notifies the seller that they have decided to do so. This is called "exercising the option." Options must be exercised within a determinable period of time and supported by a consideration, or they may be deemed to be illusory, and thus unenforceable. Options often are used in situations where a buyer wants to "tie up" the property, that is, take it off the market for a period of time so that it won't be sold to another party. This can occur where the buyer needs to achieve or attain certain things in order to be in a position to move forward with the purchase. It may be that the buyer needs to line up the acquisition capital with certainty, or enhance the entitlements for the property, such as by rezoning. Another common scenario involving the use of options is the situation where the buyer is assembling two or more separately owned properties and needs to be sure that all parcels are tied up before closing on any of them. An acquisition technique known as "rolling options" often is used where the buyer wants ultimately to acquire a large property, but does not need all of the land at once or does not have all of the capital necessary to do so. The buyer and seller agree to divide the land into several parcels each of which is under option to the buyer. The options are to be exercised sequentially within certain time constraints, such as every two years. Generally, there is an escalator clause that effectively increases the price over time on the parcels for which the options have not yet been exercised. The buyer acquires the parcels one at time, develops them, and then exercises the next option.

There are certain key elements of contracts in general, which were covered in the Contracts chapter in this book, and certain specific elements for contracts involving the sale and purchase of real estate. In addition to the requirements for the validity of contracts in general, there are a number of key specific elements for real estate contracts:

- The parties must be identified clearly and distinctly;
- The property must be identified by a description that is such that a survey, following the description, could locate the actual boundaries of the property;
- The purchase price must be clearly determinable within the express language of the contract;

- The timing of payment of the purchase price and manner in which it is to be paid is critical;
- When and where closing of the transaction will occur must be specified. Other matters generally covered in the real estate contract include:
- Limiting conditions;
- Conditions precedent, or things which must occur in order for the transaction to move forward;
- The quality of the title to be conveyed by the seller;
- How title discrepancies are to be managed;
- Who pays which closing costs and how probations are to be adjusted;
- Remedies in the event a party defaults;
- Whether various warranties and representations of the parties are to survive the closing of the transaction;
- Whether the contract is assignable to another party.

There are occasions where a party defaults or breaches the terms of the contract by failing to perform some action or obligation required. In these situations, there may be a number of remedies available to the aggrieved party. One of these is to bring an action at law for money damages. This requires that the monetary damages can be determined. For example, if the seller took the property off the market pending closing with the buyer and property values declined in the interim, then the buyer defaulted, the seller might be able to prove a specific sum as the difference between the contract price and the current fair market value. Another remedy is the right of rescission. This allows the aggrieved party to rescind, or terminate, the agreement and to receive reimbursement for expenses incurred in the effort to perform the contractual obligations. A third remedy is that of specific performance. This is an action that arose originally in equity rather than at law. It is based on the idea that each parcel of real property is so unique that money damages cannot be determined and would be inadequate as a form of compensation. In this instance for example, the court orders the defaulting seller to convey the title of the property to the buyer and perform according to the terms of the contract. Fourth, there is a remedy referred to as liquidated damages. This remedy is available when the parties to the contract have agreed in the contract that, in the event of a default or breach of contract, damages will be limited to a specific sum or amount of money as stated in the contract.

Finally, mention must be made of another potential remedy for the buyer of real estate – the *implied warranty of habitability*. Implied warranties were discussed in the *Sales Law and Uniform Commercial Code* chapter; implied warranties by virtue of the UCC attach to the sale of goods and not real estate. Moreover, under the common law, a seller of real estate was not held to have made any warranties regarding the soundness, fitness, or habitability of real estate (unless those warranties were expressly made in the real estate contract and/or deed). However, based on certain state statutes, the seller of a new home is deemed to make a warranty (typically only to the first buyer) that the house is fit for human habitation (and typically using the "reasonable person" standard to measure fitness). Moreover, in many states, based on court decisions, the implied warranty of habitability has been applied to the sellers of any homes. The warranty usually states that the seller has a duty to disclose material defects to the home or land which the seller knew of and the buyer could not have discovered by means of a reasonable inspection. Failure to disclose the defect will cause a breach of the warranty, thus affording the aggrieved buyer the right to rescind the contract or sue for damages for the breach. However, there typically is a time limit, usually one year from the date that the buyer knew of the defect, for the buyer to sue for breach. Again, it must be underscored that these warranties are imposed on sellers by operation of the law.

Ownership of Real Estate

The ownership or title to real estate may be acquired in a number of ways. For instance, and as will be explained further, real estate can be purchased, inherited, received by gift, or acquired simply by occupying it adversely to the interests of the true owner for a certain period of time. Most often, however, title to real estate is acquired by purchasing it from the legal owner. The most common form of title obtained is known as fee simple absolute, meaning that it is the most complete bundle of ownership rights extant. Title generally is acquired pursuant to a contract between the buyer and the seller. In the period between the signing of the contract by all parties concerned and the closing, which is where the title to the property passes from the seller to the buyer, there generally is a period known as due diligence. The length of this period is determined by the parties and agreed to in the contract. During this time, the buyer attempts to learn everything about the property that might have an adverse effect upon his or her ownership and planned use of the property. This could include title, roof, and termite inspections for a residence, or geotechnical, ecological, hydrological, and environmental studies for a larger-scale development. The purpose of the due diligence period is to avoid post-closing surprises. If the buyer discovers matters that are adverse to the planned use of the property, he or she generally has a right to rescind the agreement of purchase and receive a return of all deposit monies.

At the closing, the seller provides the purchaser with a *deed* to the property. This is a written instrument that evidences the conveyance of title to the property and establishes the buyer's legal right of ownership. The deed generally contains warranties of title. These are guarantees by the seller that the title being conveyed is free and clear of defects except as specifically mentioned in the deed, such as a mortgage being assumed by the buyer. The deed then is recorded in the public records of the county in which the land is located. This provides constructive notice to the world that the buyer is the legal owner of the property. Laws require that all persons are charged with knowledge of whatever is recorded in the public records, which generally are maintained at the county courthouse and available for all to inspect. There also is the concept of actual notice of ownership. This can be provided by the buyer taking possession of, and occupying, the land. There are two main types of deeds: 1) quitclaim deeds, and 2) warranty deeds. In a *quitclaim deed*, the grantor gives up any claim which he or she may have to the real property; the grantor neither makes any warranties that the title is good nor even that the grantor has a title claim; the grantor conveys only the interest that the grantor has, and no more. Note that in the typical real estate transaction in the United States, a quitclaim deed is not used because the contract specifies a warranty deed. A warranty deed not only conveys the grantor's interest in the real property, but also makes certain warranties or guarantees.

There are two types of warranty deeds. The first is a *general warranty deed* wherein the grantor warrants the following: 1) the grantor has good title to the property; 2) the grantee will have quiet and peaceful possession free from all claims; 3) the grantor will defend the grantee against all claims against the property; 4) all prior grantors had good title; and 5) there are no defects in any prior grantor's title. The second type of warranty deed is the *special warranty deed* wherein the grantor warrants that the grantor has the right to sell the property. The grantor does not warrant the genuineness of any prior grantor's title. In the United States, this type of deed ordinarily is used by executors and personal administrators of estates, trustees, and sheriffs at foreclosure sales; and as such they only warrant that they have the legal right to sell whatever interest the owner of the property has.

A deed possesses certain fundamental characteristics. The parties to the deed are the grantor and the grantee; and they both must be named in the deed. If the grantor is married, the grantor's name and his or her spouse should be named in the deed. If the grantor is unmarried, the deed should indicate such status by using the words "single" or "single person." Consideration is the amount paid by the grantee to the grantor for the real property. A statement of consideration must be made in the deed, although the amount specified need not be the actual price paid for the property. The *covenants* in a deed usually refer to promises made by the grantee. Covenants can be affirmative, whereby the grantee promises to do something, such as maintaining a driveway used in common with an adjoining property; and covenants can be negative, whereby the grantee promises not to do something, for example, not using the property for business purposes, or not constructing a certain type or size of dwelling. The *description* in a deed refers of course to the description of the property to be conveyed. The property must be correctly described; and any description that identifies the property is sufficient. Typically, the description in a deed is the description by which the present owner acquired title to the property. The deed requires a signature, specifically the signature of the grantor; and if the grantor is married, the spouse also should sign. Finally, a deed contains an acknowledgement; that is, the deed must be formally acknowledged before a notary public, whereby the grantor acknowledges the instrument as a deed. Typically, states in the U.S. also require that there be two witnesses to the signing of a deed. *Delivery* of the deed is an essential requirement to the transfer of title to real property. The rule of law in the U.S. is that a deed is not effective until delivered. Delivery from a technical legal standpoint means the grantor giving up possession and control of the deed. Consequently, if the grantor maintains control of the deed, or reserves the right to demand its return before the deed is delivered to the grantee, there is no legal delivery. For example, the grantor leaving the deed with his or her own attorney is not a delivery, since the attorney is the agent for the grantor, until the grantor's attorney delivers the deed to the grantee.

Title to the property is complete and vested in the grantee upon delivery of the deed. The deed need not be recorded in order to effectuate a title transfer. However, most certainly a deed should be recorded. All states in the U.S. have *recording statutes*, the purposes of which are to establish clarity and certainty to property ownership and to prevent fraud. Copies of deeds as well as other instruments pertaining to real property can be recorded in government offices where they become part of the public record. Fees are required, of course; but the fees are well worth it since recording gives notice "to the world" that a particular person owns a particular piece of property. Furthermore, recording allows the deed to be used as evidence in court without further proof of its authenticity; and recording also protects the grantee against a second sale of the property by the grantor. As noted, the grantor in a warranty deed has an obligation to transfer good title.

Yet one way for the grantee to ensure that he or she has obtained good title is to purchase *title insurance* from an insurance company. Then if there is any loss to the insured grantee caused by undiscovered defects in the title, the grantee will be reimbursed by the insurance company. An *abstract of title* is usually a component of the title insurance process; the abstract shows the complete history of the real estate, encompassing prior deeds, mortgages, taxes, judgments, liens – paid and unpaid.

Real property is divided into two major classifications: 1) the fee simple, and 2) the life estate. The *fee simple* or fee simple estate is the largest and most complete ownership right which an individual can possess in real estate under U.S. law. Fee simple status gives the owner the right to the surface of the land, the subsoil beneath, and air space above, subject, of course, to certain government regulations. The *life estate* is an estate in land in which the owner owns the land (and structures and attachments thereto) only for the owner's lifetime, and at the death of the present owner, the title to the land passes as directed by the original owner. A life estate with a "reversion" means the title to the property passes back to the original owner; whereas a life estate with a "remainder" means the title does not pass back to the original owner; rather, it "remains" away and passes to some third party. Reversions and remainders are called future interests.

As initially noted, there are several ways of acquiring ownership to property. Property, of course, can be purchased; that is, the buyer pays the seller and the seller conveys title to the property to the buyer. In addition, *accession* is a means of acquiring property by an addition or increase in property already owned, for example, the product of land or the young of animals. *Accretion* occurs when the boundary to property is a river, stream, lake, or ocean, and the land is increased by the shifting flow of the water or the depositing of silt or sand on the bank. "*Confusion*" is the mixing of goods by different owners so that the parts belonging to each owner cannot be identified and separated. If such a case, if the confusion is willful, title to the entire mass passes to the innocent party, unless the person causing the confusion can clearly prove who exactly owns what. Property ownership can be based on creation, for example, inventing or authoring, and then title to such creations can be made secure through patent and copyright law. *Adverse possession* is a method of acquiring title to real property by occupying for a period of time fixed by statute in the particular jurisdiction, usually 21 years. The occupancy, however, must be continuous, open, visible, exclusive, uninterrupted, and "hostile" (that is, asserting ownership of the property against the legal interests of the title holder). Sometimes this specified time period is shorter if the adverse possessor also has paid the taxes on the property for a specified length of time.

Ownership of property can be held jointly by two or more persons or entities. There is *joint tenancy* with right of survivorship where each of the joint tenants has an undivided interest in the property and the title to the property automatically passes to the last surviving joint tenant. A joint tenancy requires the "four unities": time, title, interest, and possession. In a *tenancy in common*, each of the co-owners has an equal right to the entire property, but there is no right of survivorship. As is true in the case of joint tenancies with survivorship, a tenancy in common may be terminated by an action to partition the ownership. This generally is accomplished by a court ordering the property to be sold and the proceeds divided among the co-tenants. In the case of a husband and wife, title may be held as *tenants by the entirety* in the states that recognize this form of ownership. The spouses are considered to be a single titleholder, and, upon the death of one, the survivor automatically becomes the sole owner. Conveyance or encumbrance of title requires both spouses to join in conveying the property. In the event of divorce, the former spouses become tenants in common. Some states recognize the concept of community property between spouses. This provides that each spouse has a one-half interest in all property acquired during the marriage.

Ownership of property in a condominium or cooperative provides a few different aspects from what has been discussed above. Typically, a *condominium* property is a multistory residential property, but can be single story and can involve commercial properties, as well. In a typical condominium, a unit owner has fee simple title to the space enclosed by the interior surfaces of all exterior walls of the unit as well as its floor and ceiling. All other parts of the structure and the land on which it is located are known as common elements and are owned in common with the other unit owners. Those areas that are shared by more than one unit owner, but not by all of the condominium's unit owners, are known as limited common elements. A *cooperative* often has the appearance of a condominium, but offers at least one significant difference. Whereas each of the condominium unit owners holds fee simple title to their respective units, a corporation generally owns the land and improvements of a cooperative. The individual unit occupants own stock in the corporation which permits them to enter into long-term leases for their respective units.

While they do not provide ownership of property per se, *leases* do provide the right of possession and use. In this situation, the owner of the property, known as the lessor or landlord, enters into an agreement with the occupier of the land, known as the lessee or tenant. Pursuant to this agreement, the lessor agrees that the lessee can occupy the land for a specific period of time in exchange for rent payments or other consideration. Generally, in the case of a valid lease, the right of the lessee to continue to occupy the property under the terms of the lease survives the sale of the property by the lessor. There are a number of types of leasehold estates. A *tenancy for years* means that the lease agreement sets out a specifically determinable period of time and automatically terminates at the end thereof. A *periodic tenancy* is one that continues automatically from rent period to rent period until one of the parties provides proper notice of termination. A *tenancy at will* continues until either party elects to terminate it. In the situation where a lease has expired or been terminated and the tenant continues to retain possession of the property, a tenancy at sufferance exists. It is also important to note that once a tenant so securely attaches a piece of personal property to the leasehold building or land that it becomes a fixture, the fixture absent any agreement to the contrary passes at the end of the lease to the landlord with the leasehold.

Non-possessory Interests in Real Estate

The rights involved in real estate described thus far have been possessory, whether by virtue of holding fee title or by way of lease agreement. In addition, there are certain non-possessory rights in real estate. These are rights to use all or a portion of another person's property for some limited purpose. One of these rights is the concept of the *easement*. For example, utility companies often have easement rights to a portion of a homesite for the purposes of installing and maintaining sewer, water, gas, electric, and cable facilities. The owner of the homesite has legal title to and possession of, the land, not the utility companies, but they have a legal right to use a specific portion of the homesite for the purposes specified. Easements can be created in a number of ways. The most common method is by grant, meaning that an instrument such as a deed specifically describes the location of the easement and who is to be benefited by it. Similarly, the instrument may reserve an easement in lands being conveyed to another. This is known as an easement by reservation. There also are *easements by implication* and *easements by prescription*. *Easements by implication* generally arise out of a legal action in which the court determines that the parties to a conveyance intended to create an easement, but for some reason failed to do so, such as where property sold would require access across the property still owned by the seller. The court therefore creates the easement. An easement by prescription is similar in concept to adverse possession. It can arise in situations where the owner of real property allows another to make some use of a portion of the owner's land for a specified period of time without interruption. This could occur, for example, where the owner of waterfront property allows others to cross the property from a road to access the water body. While easements are considered to be interests in land, although non-possessory, *licenses* are not. They simply permit someone to enter on property owned by another for some specific purpose, such as to attend a concert. *Profits à prendre* are a type of easement that generally allows someone to enter upon the land of another and remove some part of it such as timber.

Financing Real Estate

The capital that a buyer invests from his or her own pocket or from other investors is called equity. Capital borrowed, for example, in the form of a loan, and which must be repaid, is termed debt. The *Truth-in-Lending Act* of 1968, which applies to residential loans, requires lenders to disclose the terms of a loan in clear and understandable language so that a borrower can make an informed decision. In particular, the amount of the loan principal, the interest rate at which the loan is made, the annual percentage rate, called "APR," which is the actual cost of the loan on a yearly basis, as well as any and all costs and fees pertinent to the loan, must be disclosed. The statute also gives the borrower the right to cancel the residential real estate loan within three business days.

In real estate transactions, the most common form of debt is the *mortgage*. The mortgage does not actually evidence the debt; rather, it merely secures it, which means it provides a source from which funds can be realized by the lender through the foreclosure of the mortgage and sale of the property encumbered by the mortgage. The mortgage transfers equitable title to the mortgagee but the legal title remains with the mortgagor. The instrument that actually evidences the debt – the "IOU" – is the note or promissory note, literally a promise to repay the debt. Technically, any mortgage used to secure the purchase price of the property is called a purchase money mortgage. The classic example of a *purchase money mortgage* is when the seller agrees to take back a mortgage from the buyer for some portion of the purchase price. A purchase money mortgage enjoys certain priorities over other debts of the purchaser. When the buyer, also known as the mortgagor, defaults on the terms of the mortgage, such as by failing to make payments, the lender, also known as the mortgagee, can institute a foreclosure action in the court having proper jurisdiction. Typically, the court orders the property sold and proceeds distributed in payment of the outstanding principal and interest due. Some jurisdictions recognize deeds of trust. These are instruments wherein the mortgagor transfers the legal title to the property to a trustee who holds it for the benefit of the mortgagee. Upon repayment of the debt, the trustee must re-convey the legal title to the mortgagor.

A mortgage, therefore, is a lien given on real property to secure a debt. The mortgage is not the debt itself, but only the security for the debt. The land, as well as any interest in the land, or improvements thereon, may be mortgaged. The mortgagor is the person who gives the mortgage as security for the loan of money. The mortgagee is the person or business that holds the mortgage as security for the debt. The mortgagor has possession of the property. If the debt is defaulted, the mortgagee takes possession of the property or sells the property at a foreclosure sale. The mortgage contract is a written instrument, generally in the same form as a deed. It usually is given to raise money for the purchase price of real estate; but one can borrow money for any reason and secure the loan by means of a mortgage. The mortgage is a lien that attaches to the real property described in the mortgage. A mortgage should not be confused with a "security interest," which is a creditor's or seller's lien on personal property, and is governed extensively by the Uniform Commercial Code. Security interests as well as other liens on personal property, such as artisan's liens, were covered in the Creditors and Debtors chapter of this book.

The mortgagor has certain obligations and duties by virtue of granting a mortgage. The mortgagor's first duty is to make all payments of interest and principal when due. The failure to pay either is a default, which gives the mortgagee the right to foreclose on the property. Typically in a mortgage there will be an acceleration clause which states that if any payment of interest or principal is not made when due, the entire principal automatically becomes due immediately. Conversely, if the mortgagor wishes to pay off the mortgage debt before it is due, and thereby to save interest, he or she must have expressly reserved that right at the time the mortgage was given; otherwise, the mortgagor can still pay off the debt, but must also pay the full interest amount. A second fundamental obligation of the mortgagor is to pay all taxes, assessments, and insurance premiums on the property. If the mortgagor does not pay them, the mortgagee can pay them, and then seek reimbursement from the mortgagor. Moreover, if the mortgage contract requires the mortgagor to pay, the failure to pay is regarded as a default. As a general rule, the mortgagor does not have to keep the property insured for the benefit of the mortgagee, but the mortgage contract can impose a duty to insure on the part of the mortgagor. The mortgagee can also insure the property. The third duty of the mortgagor is not to do any act that materially impairs the security of the mortgage, such as tearing down a structure. Any acts that are deemed to be a "waste" of assets give the mortgagee the right to foreclose. The mortgagor has certain rights, however. The first and foremost is possession of the property. Of course, upon default, the mortgagee takes possession. Second, if there are any rents or profits that accrue from the property, they belong to the mortgagor. Next, when the mortgagor has made final payment, he or she has the right to have the mortgage lien cancelled. The final right is the mortgagor's right to redemption. After default and foreclosure, the mortgagor has the right to redeem the property by paying the amount of the mortgage plus all costs. As noted, if the mortgagor fails to pay the mortgage debt when due, there is a default and foreclosure, and consequently the mortgagee can force a sale of the mortgaged property. The proceeds from such a sale go first to pay any taxes, then the costs of the foreclosure, next to pay off any mechanic's liens (that is, claims by workers who have performed work on a home or building or who have furnished materials for construction or renovation), and finally the mortgagee is paid. If the proceeds from the sale are greater than the aforementioned debts, the surplus belongs to the mortgagor. Yet if the proceeds are insufficient, the mortgagee can obtain a judgment against the mortgagor for the remaining balance due. Furthermore, if one is contemplating buying mortgaged property one must know the very important distinction between "*assuming a mortgage*" and buying property "*subject to a mortgage.*" In the former case, the buyer becomes primarily liable for the payment; that is, the buyer is liable on the mortgage as fully as the original mortgagor. However, if a buyer takes property "subject to a mortgage," the buyer is not personally liable for the mortgage debt, which still exists on the property, of course. In either case, the original mortgagor is still liable.

There are occasions when there is more than one mortgage encumbering a property. In this case, depending on when each mortgage was recorded in the appropriate public records, there will be an order of priorities – first mortgage, second mortgage, etc. In most cases, when the buyer signs the note and mortgage, he or she has personal liability on the debt, meaning that the mortgagee, in satisfaction of the debt, can come after their personal assets in addition to the encumbered land. Loans for which the debtor does not have personal liability are said to be nonrecourse. In situations involving larger parcels of property, such as development parcels, the buyer may want to have portions of the land released from the mortgage as it is paid down. It is important to have the release provisions clearly spelled out in the contract and incorporated into the mortgage, as there is no automatic right to releases. Some jurisdictions recognize installment sales contracts for the purchase of real estate. Pursuant to these instruments a buyer makes payments to a seller over time, much like a purchase money mortgage situation. In this instance, however, the seller retains title to the property until the buyer has paid the purchase price in full. After receipt of the final payment, the seller conveys the title to the buyer. The original attractiveness of these instruments was the ability of the seller to avoid having to foreclose a mortgage against the buyer in the event of default, as the title had not been conveyed prior to the final payment. Many jurisdictions today, however, require foreclosure of the buyer's equitable title to the property; thus, these instruments are no longer found with any frequency. Mortgages are not the only liens that can encumber the title to real property. Mortgages are voluntary liens, meaning that the owner has agreed to place a lien against the title to the property. There also are involuntary liens created by law to safeguard the interests of others in their dealings with the owner of the property. Construction or mechanic's liens are designed to secure payment for services rendered or materials supplied in the improvement of the real property in the event the owner fails to pay. Judgment liens are created when a party to a lawsuit wins a judgment for monetary damages in the jurisdiction in which the property is located. Tax liens can be imposed at local, state, and federal levels to secure payment of taxes owed by the property owner. Laws generally afford tax liens priority over other liens, even preexisting ones.

Regulation of Use of Real Estate

The key to successful investment in and development of real property is the ability to obtain the requisite permits for development as well as the optimization of the entitlements for the property. There are two key legal concepts involved in this process: permitting and entitlements. *Permitting* is the official government sanction to perform a regulated activity. *Entitlements* mean the right to benefits specified by law, or as some developers view them, the limitations on the use of the land or its improvement. Permits and entitlements typically must be obtained at a number of different levels of government. For example, there are federal permitting requirements, state permitting and growth management regulations, and local and regional authorities to deal with. Each level can prevent a project from going forward. In addition, not all reviewing agencies share the same perspective on approval criteria – resulting in a disjointed and non-linear process. There are multi-jurisdictional levels to the real estate regulatory process.

Local Government Process

Today, in many jurisdictions where there is any market activity occurring, the result is the creation of negative impacts on the area, such as transportation, emergency services, and school issues. In response to these negative impacts, state and local authorities often create comprehensive growth management plans. These are intended to be primary long-range growth management tools to plan for future development in an orderly fashion and respond to anticipated changing conditions, and usually include both map and text. Key elements of the plan include general land use categories, as well as goals and objectives. Land development codes and regulations, which are detailed regulations implementing the Comprehensive Plan, typically establish zoning, setbacks, and buffers, among other things. They also typically define approval and administrative processes. Among these are:

- Zoning (Right-to-Use) which specify use, density, intensity, height, setbacks, and mid-range issues consistent with the Comprehensive Plan.
- Planned Development Approvals which initially offer a more flexible zoning technique, but usually require another post-approval process to tie down details. Typical elements include an approved master concept plan and approved resolution by the governing authority.
- Subdivision/Plat Approvals set out the requirements of dividing land, as well as impact fees, exactions, and other government requirements.

- Development Orders & Engineering Approvals are the final plans which detail civil engineering or related requirements. These are necessary in order to construct horizontal improvements on the property.
- Temporary Use Permits govern uses on the property such as sales or event tents or trailers. One must plan ahead and consider these for major events on the property.
- Special Exceptions are intended to govern situations excluded from a zoning code or regulation.
- Zoning Variances, on the other hand, govern items covered by a regulation, but are allowed to vary from the code if a certain approval process is followed.
- Administrative Variances differ from special exceptions and variances because they are approved by administrative staff without public hearing or legislative body approval.
- Building Permits constitute the official documents or certification that authorizes construction, alteration, enlargement, or the like, of a building or structure on the property.
- Dock and Shoreline Permits often must be obtained in order to construct structures in or adjacent to water bodies or along shorelines.
- Vegetation Removal Permits are required prior to any cutting, trimming, removal, or other impact on vegetation.
- Consumption on Premises is governmental permission to consume alcohol on certain premises, such as clubhouses, restaurants, and others uses of the property where alcoholic beverages are to be served.

State Environmental Resource Permit Process

Moving up a notch from the local governmental level, the property owner encounters the land use regulations promulgated by the state. These may include:

- State Wetland Resource Permit Process which sets up areas designated as wetlands.
- Environmental Resource Permit (ERP) which regulates both environmental and surface water management. These may exist in two or more varieties, including: 1) Standard General ERPs, which are designed for predetermined impact and are usually easier to obtain due to their standardized nature; and 2) Individual ERPs, which are unique and require specialized evaluation.
- Consumptive Water Use Permit (CUP) provides official allowance for consumption of water from the aquifers beneath the property's surface.
- Individual De-Watering Permits are required in order to remove surface or ground water prior to construction in certain areas.
- Works of the District are permits that apply to government construction.
- Sovereign Submerged Lands Authorizations set out requirements prior to building upon government owned submerged lands.
- Coastal Construction Control Line Permits (CCCL) usually are required to perform construction along coastlines.
- Endangered Species Take Permits apply to habitats of species determined to be endangered by federal law.

State Development of Regional Impact Process

States that have been experiencing rapid growth that previously outstripped the government's ability to control impacts of development on the lands within its jurisdiction have developed special bodies of regulations to deal with large-scale developments. In Florida, for example, these are known as DRIs, or Developments of Regional Impact, while in California they are referred to as CEQA, or California Environmental Quality Act rules. Their purpose is to establish thresholds for larger projects in order to review in advance of development what the impacts of these projects will be on the environment and quality of life in the area that will be impacted. Generally, they relate project scale to population levels of the jurisdiction. These governmental reviews identify regional issues that impact more than one jurisdiction, such as two or more counties. These issues usually relate to transportation, environment, and affordable housing.

Community Development Districts

These are the creations of state statute and may not exist in every state. Their purpose is to enable the creation of a special governmental geographic district to finance infrastructure and similar improvements. Generally, the process works as follows:

- Petition to Create District – including identification of geographic boundaries.
- Assessment Methodology – to determine how funds raised for development will be repaid, by whom, and in what amounts.
- Engineer's Report – this is an independent engineer's finding that improvements are justified, necessary, and benefit the land.
- Preliminary Offering Statement is prepared and approved.
- Adoption of Final Assessment that is to be placed on the land to be improved. This may allow the owner-developer to pass on costs to end-users (i.e., home buyers). This often is critical to the viability of many master-planned communities.
- Bonds are validated.
- Issuance of Bonds is authorized.
- Construction Management Agreement is entered into between the governing authority of the district and the Developer.

Federal Permitting

The third major level of land use permitting involves the federal government. These regulations apply uniformly in every state. Often the role of a number of federal agencies is that of commenting agency, rather than permitting agency. Their requirements frequently are more onerous than those of the primary agency. Among the principal regulations are the following:

- Federal Wetland Jurisdictional Determination which involves a complex review of wetlands areas on the property. Upland areas also are included in the review, although the review is not as complex.
- Dredge and Fill Permits are required for excavation activities on the property.

Post-Permit Compliance
The owner's or developer's efforts are completed with the issuance of the requisite permits. Steps must be taken to ensure permit conditions are continuing to be met. This is an often overlooked step. Plans must be made to assign permit conditions to another entity or developer maintains significant liability. A commonly accepted way of doing this is to assign permit conditions to continuing entity, such as a homeowners' association or the community development district.

Construction, Mitigation, and Monitoring
The permitting process typically consists of additional steps beyond the planning and preconstruction stages. For example, the following activities often are required:
- Invasive / Exotic Plant Removal is a frequent and often expensive step.
- Environmental Monitoring Guidelines require careful adherence. Documentation is required at turnover of the project.
- Tree Protection regulations require clear direction be given to the land clearing crew. Otherwise the developer or property owner may face consequences such as fines and/or loss of permits.
- Surface Water Management System regulations require that both functionality and aesthetics must be considered.
- Conservation Easements are often required or offered by the developer or owner as a bargaining chip in the permitting process. Typically, the developer maintains ownership of the land, but meets environmental regulations. The remaining rights may be used to provide amenities to end users.
- Mitigation Banks enable the developer to restore off-site areas in exchange for clearing and filling onsite environmental areas impacted by the development activities.

Tactical and Strategic Entitlement Considerations
The owner or developer of real property is not totally adrift in this seeming miasma of onerous, confusing, and often conflicting regulatory schemes. Certain tactical and strategic moves should be considered, depending on the nature of the development situation. For example, tactical ploys might include any or all of the following:
- Good design components may convince local governments to allow higher density or intensity of use. However, basic changes to allowances for density (number of dwelling units on the site) and intensity (degree of commercial usage on the site) need to be carefully evaluated to determine the overall effects. For example, increased density may trigger impacts or exactions because of increased road or school usage.
- On the other hand, careful integration of uses, such as incorporating a public access park in the development often reduces impact of exactions.
- Development agreements allow complex terms to maximize benefits to a development.

Strategic entitlement considerations might include:

- Planning for large areas, known generally as sector planning, may be required to make changes for small areas. This occurs when several large property owners band together to do long-range, overall planning for their combined properties.
- Specific Plans are local government plans which might eliminate problems and open up long range opportunities.
- TDR or transfer of development rights from one area (sending area) to another (receiving area) can increase the density allowances on the receiving area, thus increasing its value and lowering per unit acquisition and development costs.
- Smart Growth Initiatives often are regional in nature and address complex issues such as integrating land uses, transportation systems, and environmental systems into a single comprehensive plan. The objective is to solve regional problems and improve quality of life.
- Safe Harbor Agreements are long-range environmental permitting strategies and are critical for long-range projects with issues such as endangered species that are expected to move around on large properties.
- Habitat Conservation Plans usually plan for survival of endangered species and protect property owners from incremental problems. Examples in the United States include the Fringe-toed lizard (Desert Southwest), the Red-cockaded woodpecker (East), and the Gnatcatcher (West)

Land use permitting and entitlements, therefore, emerge as absolutely critical components to the successful investment in, and development of, real property.

Zoning and Eminent Domain
In the United States, even though the ownership of property is a very important, indeed sacred right, government can control the use of property. As noted in the constitutional law discussion, state and local governments pursuant to their sovereign "police power," that is the power to make laws to benefit the health, welfare, and safety of their citizens, enact zoning regulations. *Zoning* laws, as noted, are one of the main types of land use regulation in the United States. The major purpose of zoning law is to designate certain types of permissible uses for property within a county or municipality or zoning district. The objective of the local zoning authority is to formulate a comprehensive zoning plan that promotes growth and development but in an organized and sustainable way. The usual "uses" are for residential (perhaps divided into low-density single family homes and high density multiple family homes, apartments and condominiums), commercial or business use, such as retail businesses, offices, supermarkets, hotels and motels, and movie theatres, light industrial, heavy industrial, or mixed use. If an owner of property seeks to use property for a use that is not allowed, he or she must seek a "variance," that is, an exemption, from a government authority, usually a local zoning commission, at a public hearing. The owner ordinarily has to demonstrate undue hardship if the variance is not granted. In addition, the owner typically will have to show that the variance will not materially change the essential character of the neighborhood.

Moreover, similar to the old common law doctrine that one "cannot move to a nuisance," a person cannot create his or her own hardship by buying property in a zoned area and then seeking to obtain a variance for an intended use not permissible under the zoning laws. Even more significant than regulation, and as pointed out in the constitutional law discussion, government at all levels – federal, state, and local – in the U.S. possesses the power to seize and to take private property for "public" use or purpose; but the Constitution also requires that government pay the owner of the property "just" compensation for the property. Also, as underscored in that chapter, what is a truly a "public" purpose, as well as what is really "just" compensation, are ongoing and very controversial and contentious issues – legally, morally, and practically.

Part II - Real Property Leases[3]
If one does not own the real property but rather occupies it, then most likely one has a tenancy, which thereby has created a leasehold interest. Tenancies come in various forms and often are represented by a written contract known as a lease. This part of the chapter thus will address the following subject matters: types of tenancies; the obligations and covenants between the tenant, also known as the lessee, as well as the landlord, also known as lessor; and the remedies if there is a breach of the lease agreement. Keep in mind that, like all other contracts, the necessary elements identified in the Contracts chapter must exist for a promise to become a lease. If the term of the contract is to be a year or longer, then the Statute of Frauds will require the lease to be in writing.

Types of Tenancies
A *term tenancy*, also referred to as a tenancy-for-years, is an interest in land which a tenant has exclusive rights to the land for a certain time period, which is often for a year or more. These are fixed duration leases; and once they have expired, by operation of law, they become periodic tenancies unless the parties expressly renew them for another defined term. While most residential term leases are for one year, commercial leases can vary in length from a few months to ninety-nine year leases. Most commercial leases range from two to five years, with options to renew and extend the lease for a longer term should the tenant desire to continue a successful business at that particular location. The longer the term of the lease, the more likely that it will contain rental escalation clauses, which provide for a formula to raise the rental so that the lease payments keep pace with inflation, and over-and-above any rental increases the parties contemplate over the term of the lease. Term leases can expire naturally upon completion of the term; and also may terminate early by agreement of the parties; or terminate through a court action. Leases, moreover, can be terminated due to the destruction of the real property or by merger into the freehold estate if the tenant ultimately becomes the owner of the real property, either through a written option to purchase provision within the lease, or if the tenant exercises a written right of first refusal found within the written lease to match a third party's offer to buy the real property.

---

[3] Part II of this chapter was contributed by Stephen C. Muffler, Attorney at Law, Adjunct Professor, Nova Southeastern University.

A *periodic tenancy* is one that continues from a period-to-period. Often this time frame is one month; and unless one of the parties gives proper notice, the period resets after its expiration and continues automatically for another like period of time. This situation could last for many years if the parties continue their landlord/tenant relationship and both voluntarily allow the periodic term to continue. Most state laws require prior notice to the other party should one of the parties to a periodic tenancy wish to end the relationship and tenancy. Depending on the state, the required minimum time period to deliver the termination notice to the other party may be equal to one full term or half of the lease term. It is not unusual for these periodic tenancies to not have a written lease since they are, by their very terms, less than one year in length. However, it is recommended that all periodic tenancies be represented by a written lease so that all parties clearly understand their rights and obligations in regard to the leasehold interest. Periodic tenancies allow the flexibility to both parties to end their contractual relationship at the end of each term, but they do not guarantee any long term tenancy between the parties, for better or worse. Commercial leases tend not to be periodic tenancies since businesses must have stable, predictable, leasehold "duration terms" to build-up and continue a successful commercial venture at the site.

If a lease interest is not a term or periodic tenancy, then it most likely will be considered a *tenancy-at-will*. Tenancy-at-will is a leasehold interest that is terminable at the option of either party for any reason whatsoever. A common state legislative effort to clarify this area of law and distinguish among the types of tenancies is represented by Florida Statute Section 83.01 which provides:

> *Any lease of lands and tenements, or either, made shall be deemed and held to be a tenancy at will unless it shall be in writing signed by the lessor. Such tenancy shall be from year to year, or quarter to quarter, or month to month, or week to week, to be determined by the periods at which the rent is payable. If the rent is payable weekly, then the tenancy shall be from week to week; if payable monthly, then from month to month; if payable quarterly, then from quarter to quarter; if payable yearly, then from year to year.*

A tenancy-at-will is, by its very nature, at the whim of the parties who can cancel the tenancy at any time for, for any reason, or no reason.

Finally, the last type of tenancy is called *tenancy-at-sufferance*. Technically, it is more of a "hold over" of an occupant of property under a lease that has expired without the permission of the landlord. At common law, this type of tenancy was created by operation of law by the continued holding over of a tenant, whose initial possession was lawful but has since expired. A tenancy-at-sufferance, unlike the other aforementioned tenancies, provides no rights to the occupier as a tenant and no estate interest in the land. Consequently, there is a "thin-line" between a trespasser and a tenant-at-sufferance. The former is unlawfully on the property without the permission or consent of the owner, while the latter is a hold-over tenant who once had rights under a valid tenancy, but those rights have now expired and lapsed, leaving the occupier susceptible to immediate removal through proper court process.

Obligations and Covenants between the Parties

Regardless of the type of tenancy, there are some common rights and responsibilities by and between the parties. If there is a written lease, then the terms and conditions of that written agreement will dictate the parties' relationship. Common covenants that are found in all leasehold interests can be classified as landlord duties and tenant duties.

Landlords have duties to deliver the leasehold premises to the tenant, free from other occupants. A landlord also has the obligation to make sure that the premises has no code violations and the walls, roof and concrete slab are in good repair. Further, the landlord in a residential lease warrants that the premises is "habitable," even if the lease does not specifically require the landlord to make repairs. *"Habitability"* is an implied warranty that arises by operation of law in residential leases and generally cannot be waived by the tenant; and accordingly any provision within a residential lease that attempts to do so is often held void or unenforceable as a violation of public policy. Another closely aligned warranty that landlords must provide to tenants is called the *covenant of quiet enjoyment.* Quiet enjoyment is a tenant's right to the undisturbed use and enjoyment of real property without unreasonable disturbance by hostile claimants or neighboring tenants. Finally, landlords are held responsible for unreasonably dangerous conditions, physical or otherwise, on the property or in the common areas of the premises pursuant to a specific negligence theory called "premises liability." What constitutes a breach of habitability, quiet enjoyment, and/or premises liability is often a factual matter, decided on a case-by-case basis by a jury. Generally, many state statutes allow for the landlord to shift the responsibility of some landlord duties upon a commercial tenant, so long as such a shifting of duties will not be a violation of public policy. Conversely, courts often void the shifting of these landlord duties upon a residential tenant's shoulders as such a burden shifting is *per se* (that is, automatically) a violation of public policy. Should the property be sold, then the new owner often "stands-in-the-shoes" of the prior landlord, and as such is under the duty to perform under the lease's terms and the aforementioned obligations.

Tenants likewise owe duties to landlords under a leasehold relationship. The most obvious is to pay the rental. In a residential lease, often this payment is structured on a month-to-month basis due at the beginning of each month. In a commercial lease, this payment may be classified as a "triple net lease," which means the tenant will pay, in addition to rent, some or all of the real property expenses, which can include its pro-rata share of real estate taxes, insurance on the real property, special assessments, and common area expenses shared by other tenants in a multi-use commercial center, and insurance on the real property. A "gross lease" rental rate arises when a commercial tenant is charged on lump-sum per square foot of the premises, which includes all the aforementioned related expenses. Sometimes, commercial leases define the rental on a percentage of profits earned by the tenant over a period of time, such as a month or year, and such leases also allow the landlord to audit the tenant's business records to accurately determine the rental payments due under such lease payment provisions. In both commercial and residential leases, often landlords require prepayment of last month's rental and also a security deposit. It is not unusual for commercial leases to require the principal owners and/or officers of the tenant's business entity to personally guarantee the performance under the lease. That is to say, if the tenant's business entity fails to pay rental, or otherwise fails to perform under the lease, the landlord has the ability to sue the personal guarantors for damages which are caused by the tenant's breach of the lease. Tenants also are under a duty not to commit "waste" to the premises, which means they will not physically damage the real property, normal wear-and-tear excepted. Tenants may assign or sublease the premises or property, unless the written lease prevents such actions.

Remedies for Breach of Lease
If one of the parties fails to perform the duties and/or obligations under a lease, then a breach has occurred; and that breach generally relieves the other party from performing under the agreement. Landlord and tenant law is very state-specific, which means each state has a set of statutes that control and govern the parties' relationships and provides for remedies in case of a breach. Often these state statutes require notice of a breach be provided to a party as well as an opportunity to cure said breach prior to the lease being terminated or vesting a party with a legal cause of action. Similarly, it is typical that written leases have detailed notice provisions which require the non-breaching party to notice the breaching party of the breach, prior to exercising a right to terminate and/or seek other remedies.

If a tenant breaches the lease, these statutes or contractual provisions often allow the landlord to seize security deposits, accelerate and recover the remaining rental due under the lease for the remaining balance of the term, terminate the leasehold, evict the tenant from the premises, and also seek re-letting costs and expenses, including real estate commissions incurred in securing a replacement tenant for the premises. One principle common in almost all states is the landlord's inability to use "self-help" evictions, which is a term that describes a landlord taking matters into "their own hands" and physically changing the locks or preventing the tenant from access to the premises or physically removing the tenant from the premises, extra-judicially. Failure of a landlord to seek remedies via the court system and to abstain from using "self-help" can result in a costly separate tort action by the tenant against the landlord, even if the tenant breached the lease first and should have and could have been dispossessed from the premises. Finally, often written leases have indemnification provisions, which require the tenant to reimburse the landlord for any losses suffered by the landlord due directly to the tenant's actions or inactions at the premises.

Tenants are also afforded a number of remedies should the landlord breach the lease. These include withholding of rental, directing rental to pay for expenses to cure a physical defect in the premises, interpleading the rental into the court registry for the judge to decide the proper ownership of the funds in light of a landlord's breach, lease termination, and/or seeking consequential damages. Consequential damages are money damages which flow naturally from the landlord's breach of lease and can include costs of moving the business to a suitable replacement location or loss of business due to the landlord's breach. If a landlord wrongfully evicts a tenant through "self-help," many courts will issue an injunction against the landlord from interfering with the tenant's continued business at the premises, or a court could grant punitive damages payable to the tenant by the landlord to punish the landlord's improper and unacceptable anti-social behavior. In commercial tenancies, sometimes a tenant specifically negotiates a provision within a retail center that exclusively allows that tenant the ability to furnish services or goods to the public from the premises, precluding any other competing tenants in the common shopping center or commercial complex. If such a provision exists, and a landlord breaches this provision by allowing a competing tenant to commence business transactions at the common shopping center or commercial complex, then the tenant may sue the landlord for monetary damages and loss of business. These "use exclusivity" provisions in commercial leases awarded to tenants do not violate anti-trust laws since they cover only the specific shopping center or commercial complex owned by the landlord, so competing businesses can still rent locations outside the property lines on a contiguous parcel of land.

Summary

After reading Part I to this chapter, one should be able to understand the definition and nature of real property law, to distinguish between real and personal property, owning versus leasing real property, and the real estate contract and the deed. One as well should be able to understand the types of ownership interests in property, the legal complexities of transferring and financing real property, particularly real estate mortgages, and the regulation of the use of real property, especially land use permitting and entitlements in the United States. Part II to this chapter examined various types of leasehold interests in real estate and also discussed the legal rights and responsibilities of the landlord and the tenant in a leasehold relationship. The covenants between the parties that can arise in the leasing of property were also discussed. Residential leases were compared and contrasted to commercial leases.

Discussion Questions

1.   What are the definitions and distinctions among real property, personal property, and fixtures? Why are the differences important, especially under contract law? Provide examples with brief explanations.
2.   What are the definitions and distinctions between the real estate contract, the closing, and the deed in a real estate transaction? Provide examples with brief explanations.
3.   What are the definitions and distinctions between a warranty deed and a quitclaim deed? Why are the differences important? Provide examples along with brief explanations.
4.   What are the two major classifications of warranty deeds and why are the differences between the two important? Provide examples with brief explanations.
5.   What are the definitions of and distinctions between the covenants and the description in a deed? Why are the distinctions important? Provide examples with brief explanations.
6.   What are the definitions and distinctions between a fee simple and a life estate? Why are the differences important? Provide examples along with a brief explanation.

7. What are the definitions of and distinctions among a joint tenancy, tenancy in common, and a tenancy in the entirety? Why are the distinctions important? Provide examples along with brief explanations.

8. What are the definitions and distinctions between acquiring property by accession and accretion? Why are the distinctions important? Provide examples with brief explanations.

9. What is the concept of adverse possession? Provide an example with a brief discussion. Is this legal concept a realistic one today? Why or why not?

10. What are the definitions and distinctions between a condominium and a cooperative? Why are the differences important? Provide examples along with a brief explanation.

11. What is a mortgage and why is it such a critical part to real estate financing?

12. What is the difference between buying real property subject to a mortgage as opposed to assuming a mortgage? Why is the distinction between the two critical? Provide examples with brief explanations.

13. What are the definitions and distinctions between an easement and a license? Why are the differences important? Provide examples along with brief explanations.

14. What are the definitions and distinctions between an easement by prescription and an easement by implication? Why are the differences important? Provide examples along with brief explanations.

15. What are some of the major components of state and local land use regulation? Provide examples along with brief explanations.

16. Discuss and provide examples of the different types of leasehold interests.

17. Discuss and provide examples of the rights and responsibilities of the landlord and the tenant in a lease situation.

18. Compare, contrast, and provide examples of the warranty of habitability and the covenant of quiet enjoyment in a leasehold situation.

19. Compare and contrast the rights and responsibilities of the parties in a residential lease and a commercial lease.

13 – INTERNATIONAL BUSINESS LAW

With the evolving and expansive economic growth around the world, many entrepreneurs seek to expand their operations into new and exciting territories. Today, even a small or medium sized company may do business in numerous countries. Understanding and obeying domestic laws are a critical component of each manager's and entrepreneur's job doing business in these different countries. Since today's managers and entrepreneurs often deal with customers, suppliers, and employees in different parts of the world, understanding international business laws in regards to each specific country becomes very important for success. This chapter briefly discusses international business law as it applies to domestic and global firms. It further provides recommendations and sources where managers and entrepreneurs can gain relevant insights as they work on successfully expanding their dealings across diverse countries, cultures, and borders.

Sources of International Law[4]
While starting or developing a business overseas can prove to be a profitable endeavor, every company is charged with the task of compliance with the local law of each jurisdiction. An important factor that the entrepreneur or manager considers when making his or her decision to enter a new foreign market is the country's legal scheme, particularly if the industry is a heavily regulated one. Although it is impossible for managers and entrepreneurs to keep up with all the laws and regulations of the different sovereignties without the assistance of legal counsel, they should familiarize themselves with the basic legal principles and different legal systems. Although there is no single international legal system, various legal systems around the world exhibit patterns and parallels. Each national legal system varies in philosophy and practice, and each maintains a court system that is independent of those legal systems in each and every nation. However, most nations in the world use only a few legal systems as the foundation of their laws. Countries that were colonies

---

[4] This chapter is co-authored with Miguel Orta, Attorney At Law, Adjunct Professor, Nova Southeastern University.

of more than one power may use a mixture of legal systems. A manager or entrepreneur will be able to understand the basics of the legal system of any given country if he or she understands the foundation of the legal system upon which the laws of that country are based. Most countries derive their legal system from the common law, the civil law, or Islamic law.

Common Law

Common law is a tradition oriented legal system, the body of law that has grown out of legal customs and practices that developed in England. Common law prevails unless superseded by other law. It serves as precedent or is applied to situations not covered by statute. Under the common law system, when a court decides and reports its decision concerning a particular case, the case becomes part of the body of law and can be used in later cases involving similar matters. If there is no specific precedent or statute controlling, common law requires a court to make a decision that will create new law. This use of precedents is known as *stare decisis*. Common law has been administered in the courts of England since the Middle Ages in a pure form; it is also found in the United States, (except Louisiana state courts), Canada, Australia, Nigeria, and in most of the British Commonwealth. The influence of common law is also found in the laws of India and Pakistan.

Civil Law

Civil law is based on a set of laws that is well-organized and detailed and written into comprehensive codes. It is a body of law developed from Roman Law and German Law, and used in continental Europe and most former colonies of European nations, including the province of Quebec and the U.S. state of Louisiana. The basis of law in civil-law jurisdictions is a code or statute that is intended to spell out the law in all possible situations. Thus, the law is all inclusive leading to general principles, but also supple enough to allow application to many different facts and circumstances. In civil law, judges apply principles embodied in statutes, rather than turning to case precedent. They do not give any consideration to prior court decisions. There are about 70 civil law countries. French civil law forms the basis of the legal systems of the Netherlands, Belgium, Luxembourg, Italy, Spain, most of France's former possessions overseas, and many Latin American countries. German civil law prevails in Austria, Switzerland, the Scandinavian countries, and certain countries outside Europe, such as Japan, that have "westernized" their legal systems. Both Japan and the former Soviet Republics that make up the new Commonwealth of Independent States also use codes or statutes as their main source of law.

Islamic Law

More than 30 of the world's nations that stretch from the Atlantic coast of Northern Africa across the center of Asia and the Indian subcontinent, and continue all the way to Indonesia in the Pacific as well as the Arabian Peninsula, are part of the Muslim legal system. Islam's greatest difference with other legal systems is that the source of its law is considered to come directly from God. All laws in the Islamic system are to be interpreted in harmony with Sharia's or God's rules and the Koran. The Koran is not a code of laws, but the expression of Islamic ethic. It contains about 80 firm rules in its more than 6,000 verses. Moral conduct is the preeminent concern. Muslim law governs all aspects of life. Most countries follow Islamic law to varying degrees. The system is usually mixed with common, civil, or indigenous law, depending on colonial ties. The Muslim law holds that the prophet Muhammad had interpreted the divine law sufficiently, and thus there was no need for further independent reasoning. Under the Sharia, which prohibits unearned or unjustified profits, the modern use of interest on loans can be problematic. In modern Islamic countries, the prohibition is circumvented by having banks finance businesses by buying shares in the enterprise borrowing the funds and receiving a share of the profits. A bank may also loan money to purchase assets, and then could be paid over a period of time, but without interest. However, an additional payment is mandated from the borrower to show appreciation. Many countries are now adopting new commercial codes to facilitate business transactions. When engaging in business in countries following the Islamic legal system, one must be sensitive to these beliefs, and also must use ingenuity in dealing with these laws.

International Law
International law consists of rules and principles which govern the relations and dealings of nations with each other. International Law, which is in most other countries referred to as Public International Law, concerns itself only with questions of rights between several nations or nations and the citizens or subjects of other nations. In contrast, Private International Law deals with controversies between private persons, natural or juridical, arising out of situations having significant relationship to more than one nation. In recent years, the line between public and private international law has become increasingly uncertain. Issues of private international law may also implicate issues of public international law; and many matters of private international law have substantial significance for the international community of nations. International Law includes the basic, classic concepts of law in national legal systems -- status, property, obligation, and torts. It also includes substantive law, procedure, process, and remedies. International Law is rooted in acceptance by the nation states which constitute the system. Customary law and conventional law are primary sources of international law. Customary international law results when states follow certain practices generally and consistently out of a sense of legal obligation. That is, the practice, action, or decision is followed in a regular manner and a country recognizes this practice as binding. Recently the customary law was codified in "conventional" international law, which is law derived from international treaties, agreements, or conventions, and which may take any form that the contracting parties agree upon. A *treaty*, also called a "convention," is an agreement or contract between two or more countries that must be legally authorized and ratified by the legal system in each country. For example, in the U.S., Article II of the Constitution empowers the President to enter into treaties on behalf of the United States, but with the "advice and consent" of the Senate (manifested by a $2/3^{rd}$'s vote concurring vote of the Senators present). An example of a treaty is the Organization of Economic Cooperation and Development Anti-Bribery Convention (which treaty is patterned after the Foreign Corrupt Practices Act outlined in this chapter). Another example would be NAFTA – the North American Free Trade Agreement – between

the U.S., Mexico, and Canada which regulates trade among those countries. Treaties and agreements may be made in respect to any matter except to the extent that the agreement conflicts with the rules of international law incorporating basic standards of international conduct or the obligations of a member state. International agreements create law for the parties of the agreement. They may also lead to the creation of customary international law when they are intended for adherence generally and are in fact widely accepted. Customary law and law made by international agreement have equal authority as international law. Parties may assign higher priority to one of the sources by agreement. However, some rules of international law are recognized by international community as peremptory, permitting no derogation. Such rules can be changed or modified only by a subsequent peremptory norm of international law.

Comity, Act of State, and Sovereign Immunity

The doctrines of comity, Act of State, and sovereign immunity are also very important international law principles. *Comity* means that countries *should* comply with international treaties, conventions, customary law, and other sources of international law due to the mutual respect that countries should have for one another as well as the need for effective and harmonious relationships. Of course, comity assumes that a particular country has signed a treaty or convention or has participated in international customs. Comity also entails one country deferring and giving effect to the laws and judicial decisions of another country (assuming they are consistent with the laws and public policy of the country asked to defer). Accordingly, U.S. courts ordinarily will not review laws, acts, or judicial decisions of foreign countries or interfere with foreign government legal and judicial proceedings which are taking place in foreign countries. However, it is important to note that comity is not law *per se*; that is, countries should abide by international agreements and they should honor foreign legal determinations, but they are not legally required to do so. Related to comity is the *Act of State* doctrine. This doctrine holds that the judicial system in one country does not have the power or authority to challenge and overrule the acts of another country within that country. To illustrate, if a U.S. citizen has property in a foreign country and that property is seized and expropriated by the foreign government (presumably pursuant to proper legal procedure, for a legitimate public purpose, and with payment of just compensation), nevertheless, based on the Act of State doctrine, that expropriation cannot be challenged in a U.S. court, for example on grounds that the compensation was not sufficient and that the property was really confiscated by the foreign government.

The doctrine of *sovereign immunity* is another fundamental principle of international law, which is based on the premise that the jurisdiction of a country within its own territory is exclusive and absolute. Consequently, as a general rule, sovereign immunity exempts foreign countries from the jurisdiction of U.S. courts. However, there is a statute in the United States, called the Foreign Sovereign Immunities Act (FSIA), which provides the exceptional circumstances when a foreign country can be sued in a U.S. court, to wit: 1) the foreign country has waived its immunity and has consented to be sued; 2) the lawsuit is based on commercial activity by the foreign country in the U.S. or commercial activity outside the U.S.

which has a direct effect in the U.S.; 3) the lawsuit is based on personal injuries caused by the commission of a tort in the U.S. or any torture, extrajudicial killings, aircraft sabotage, hostage-taking, or providing material support and resources for the aforementioned acts. Furthermore, based on U.S. judicial interpretation, the FSIA only provides immunity to foreign governments and not to foreign officials even if they are acting in an official capacity.

International Jurisdiction

As with residents of different states in a federal system, such as the United States, jurisdictional issues also arise with citizens of foreign countries in the international arena, especially regarding the adjudication of disputes and the enforcement of judicial decisions against foreigners. Generally, a country can exercise its jurisdiction to adjudicate and enforce against foreigners when: 1) a person is physically present in a country's territory, except if he or she is merely in transit; 2) a person is domiciled in or a resident of that country; 3) a person regularly carries on business in that country; 4) a person has carried on an activity in the country and that activity is the subject matter of the dispute; or 5) a person has done something outside of a country but that action has a direct and substantial effect within another country. The international jurisdiction issue becomes even more problematical when the Internet is involved (as was discussed in the U.S. national context in the Internet Law chapter). As difficult as it is to determine the jurisdictional issue involving an out-of-state website owner and business in the U.S., resolving the jurisdiction question will be even more daunting when the website or business owner is located in a foreign country. What is considered a "direct and substantial effect" in the "virtual" world of cyberspace? For example, if a foreign business uses the Internet to target consumers in the U.S., is that action sufficient for the U.S. courts to exercise jurisdiction? Will the courts and legislative bodies in other countries move to the U.S. "minimal contacts" Due Process standard? These difficult global jurisdictional issues will eventually have to be dealt with by the courts.

Another significant jurisdictional legal issue, as well as an ethical one, concerns human right abuses overseas and the use of the courts in the U.S. to seek redress therefor. In 2013, in an important international jurisdiction case involving the Shell oil company, *Kiobel v. Royal Dutch Petroleum Co.*, the Supreme Court ruled that U.S. courts do not have jurisdiction to hear cases of victims of human rights violations and other international law violations that occur in foreign countries and not in the United States. The lawsuit was premised on an 18th century law – the Alien Tort Statute, a very old and vague statute that grants the federal courts the power to resolve claims arising under the "law of nations." The lawsuit was brought by Nigerian refugees who contended that Shell had aided and abetted the Nigerian government in inflicting human rights abuses while suppressing protests against Shell's operations in Nigeria. Shell had denied the allegations; regardless, the Court ruled that the U.S. courts even lacked jurisdiction to decide the case because the allegations were too remote from the United States. The only U.S. connections were that the Nigerians bringing the suit had received political asylum in the U.S. and that Shell, an Anglo-Dutch company, does business in the United States. As construed by the Court, the statute provides redress against violations of international law that occur only within the United States. To hold otherwise, explained Chief Justice John Roberts, would make the courts in the U.S. the forum for deciding disputes from around the world and the U.S. the enforcer of international norms.

International Intellectual Property Agreements

Globally, there are several international agreements in place which protect intellectual property. The main agreements are: the Paris Convention of 1883; the Berne Convention of 1886; the TRIPS Agreement of 1994; the GATT Agreement of 1994; the WIPO Treaty of 1996; and the Madrid Protocol of 2003. The *Paris Convention*, known fully as the Convention of the Union of Paris, which approximately 175 countries adhere to, allows a party in one signatory country to sue for patent and trademark protection in the other member countries. The *Berne Convention* is the international copyright treaty, which affords legal protection to copyrighted works in all the member countries. Copyright notice on the work itself is not required for works produced after March 1, 1989 (though such notice is strongly recommended as it will rebut an assertion of "innocent" infringement). *TRIPS* stand for Trade-Related Intellectual Property Rights. It is an agreement that over 100 countries have signed, which grants legal protection to patents, copyrights, and trademarks. The most important part to TRIPS is the provision that each signatory nation provide in its own domestic laws legal protections for intellectual property rights as well as legal mechanisms and sanctions to enforce these rights. In essence, TRIPS forbids a signatory nation from discriminating in legal processes against foreign owners of intellectual property in favor of their own national citizens. The TRIPS treaty also extends legal protection to computer programs. *GATT* is the General Agreement on Tariffs and Trade, which established the World Trade Organization (WTO), which is an international trade organization of which the U.S. is a member. GATT's intellectual property provisions, which were ratified by the U.S. Congress, changed U.S. patent law to make patents valid for 20 years, and also changed U.S. law to make the time period run from the date the patent application was filed. *WIPO* stands for the World Intellectual Property Organization Treaty. The WIPO Treaty upgraded intellectual property protection, particularly on the Internet. It also should be noted that the U.S Digital Millennium Copyright Act (discussed in the Intellectual Property chapter) implemented the provisions of the WIPO Treaty and established civil and criminal penalties for those violators who circumvent encryption software and anti-piracy protections for protected digital works. Finally, the *Madrid Protocol* is an international treaty dealing with trademark protection, which has been signed by approximately 80 countries, that seeks to facilitate international trademark protection, in particular by having a simplified and less costly process for multi-country trademark registration.

International Organizations

International organizations play an increasingly important role in the relationships between nations. An international organization is one that is created by international agreement or which has membership consisting primary of nations. There are many international organizations that will be of importance to the entrepreneur seeking to reach global markets, among them the United Nations (UN), the World Bank, and the

International Monetary Fund (IMF). However, the organization that has the most impact on business is the World Trade Organization (WTO). The World Trade Organization (WTO) is the only global international organization dealing with the rules of trade between nations. At its heart are the WTO agreements, negotiated and signed by the bulk of the world's trading nations and ratified in their parliaments. The goal is to help producers of goods and services, exporters, and importers conduct their business. The organization has been the major driver behind trade liberalization, which has led to increased trade in goods and services, and has improved quality of life around the world, reducing barriers for entrepreneurs to trade and invest worldwide. The past 50 years have seen an exceptional growth in world trade. Merchandise exports grew on average by 6% annually. Total trade in 2006 was 25 times the level of 1950. The WTO has helped to create a strong and prosperous trading system contributing to unprecedented growth. The system was developed through a series of trade negotiations, or "rounds." The first rounds dealt mainly with tariff reductions, but later negotiations included other areas such as anti-dumping and non-tariff measures. Through the WTO, member nations have promoted international business through agreements on telecommunications services, tariff-free trade in information technology products, and financial services deals covering more than 95% of trade in banking, insurance, securities, and financial information. Today, negotiations continue among countries on issues related to agriculture and services.

Through the efforts of the United Nations, 72 countries have adopted The United Nations Convention on Contracts for the International Sale of Goods (CISG). The CISG creates a uniform, international, commercial law, which unless excluded by the express terms of a contract, is deemed to be incorporated into and supplant any otherwise applicable domestic laws with respect to a transaction in goods between parties from different contracting nations. As of 2006 it had been adopted by countries that account for three-quarters of all world trade. The CISG establishes uniform legal rules to govern the formation of international sales contracts and the rights and obligations of the buyer and seller. The CISG is given automatic application to all contracts for the sale of goods between traders from all countries that have adopted the CISG. The CISG only applies to international commercial sales of goods. The following elements constitute important limitations on the scope of the CISG applicability. First, the sale must be international in character. A sale is considered international if it involves parties whose places of business are in different nations. Second, the CISG covers the sale of goods, and may not apply to contracts that include services. Where a contract includes both goods and services elements, the CISG will apply unless the preponderant part of the obligations of the party who furnishes the goods consists in the supply of labor or other services. Finally, the CISG only applies to commercial transactions, and does not apply to sales of goods that are bought for personal, family, or household use, unless the seller, at any time before or at the conclusion of the contract, neither knew nor ought to have known that the goods involved were bought for such use. Additionally, the CISG does not apply to the following types of sales: by auction; on execution or otherwise by authority of law; of stocks, shares, investment securities, negotiable instruments or money; of ships, vessels, hovercraft, or aircraft; or of electricity.

The CISG's rules closely follow Article 2 of the Uniform Commercial Code (UCC), which is in force in 49 of the 50 United States. Under the CISG, a proposal to create a contract is not sufficiently definite as an offer unless it indicates the goods and expressly or implicitly fixes or makes provision for determining the quantity and the price. By contrast, the UCC is more flexible in contract formation, and accordingly will find an agreement valid, despite missing terms including performance and price, if the parties intended to be bound by the agreement, and a reasonably certain basis exists for granting a remedy.

Under the CISG, an offer becomes irrevocable if it indicates through a fixed time for acceptance or otherwise that it is irrevocable, or if the offeree reasonably relies on the offer as being irrevocable, and acts in reliance on it. Under the UCC, an irrevocable offer must be in a signed writing that by its terms assures that the offer will be held open. Contract acceptance occurs upon receipt thereof by the offeror under the CISG. Many UCC jurisdictions hold that acceptance occurs when it is mailed or transmitted by the offeree to the offeror. The CISG does not require that a sales contract be reduced to a writing. Under the UCC's Statute of Frauds, oral contracts for the sale of goods for a price of $500.00 or more are generally not enforceable, unless, for example, the existence of a contract is conceded to, or payment or delivery and acceptance have occurred. The CISG generally leaves questions relating to the validity of a contract and the effect that the contract may have on the goods sold to be determined by applicable domestic law.

International Business Operations

There are more than 200 nation-states in the world. Entrepreneurs must strive for profits and growth in the global marketplace that is characterized by enormous movements of products, technology, capital, and enterprise across international borders. In today's economy, no business is free from foreign competition. Whether or not a firm goes global, it should plan for growth and even survival in a global marketplace. Firms are confronted with several closely related challenges: the decision of which foreign market to enter, when to enter the market, to what scale, and ascertaining the choice of entry mode. There are six market entry strategies that a firm may chose: exporting, "turnkey" projects, licensing, franchising, establishing joint ventures in a host company, or setting up a new wholly-owned subsidiary in the host company. Firms may decide to enter a foreign market by exporting and later switch to another mode for serving a foreign market. An export is any good or service transported from one country to another country, typically for use in trade. An *import* is any good or commodity brought into one country from another country. Import goods or foreign producers provide services to domestic consumers. Import of commercial quantities of goods normally requires involvement of the customs authorities in both the country of import and the country of export.

Prior to discussing the market entry modes in detail, it should be pointed out that a number of U.S. laws apply to U.S. companies which conduct international business transactions. The following laws are applicable when a U.S. company establishes a business operation in a foreign country:

1. Export controls under the Export Administration Regulations (U.S. Department of Commerce):

- Prohibit export transactions regarding certain products and/or certain country destinations; requires export licenses for certain transactions
- Export controls apply to (i) exports by a U.S. company to its foreign affiliates; (ii) sales by the foreign affiliate within the foreign country; and (iii) sales by the foreign affiliate to third countries
- Export controls apply to the export of both goods and "technical data" including software, technology, trade secrets, and other information
- Under the "deemed export rule" technical data can be "exported" by disclosing it to foreign persons in the U.S. and to foreign nationals who are employees of U.S. companies both in the U.S. and abroad; posting information on the Internet and similar computer networks can be deemed an "export" since such information is accessible in foreign countries
- Export controls apply to "re-exports" to third countries of U.S. products, U.S. technical data and foreign products based on U.S.-origin technical data
- Civil and criminal sanctions; up to ten years imprisonment; Justice Department may attempt to hold officers and directors of U.S. company liable for acts of its overseas affiliates.

2. Commercial Embargoes Under the Trading With the Enemy Act and the International Emergency Economic Powers Act (Treasury Department):
   - Prohibit commercial transactions with specified countries including Libya, North Korea, Cuba, Yugoslavia, Iraq, Iran (certain restrictions); this list is subject to change
   - Prohibit U.S. companies from setting up business operations in certain designated foreign countries
   - Civil and criminal sanctions.

3. Export Controls Under the Arms Export Control Act (State Department):
   - Prohibit export of products on the U.S. Munitions List
   - Note that encryption software is on the U.S. Munitions List, and consequently export is strictly prohibited without a license
   - Civil and criminal sanctions

4. Anti-boycott laws include:
   - Requirements to report and not cooperate with foreign boycotts
   - Separate anti-boycott laws under Export Administration Act and Internal Revenue Code.

5. Foreign Corrupt Practices Act (FCPA):
   - The FCPA is a U.S. statute that makes bribery in international business illegal.
   - The law applies to U.S. nationals and businesses that do business anywhere in the world; and this law also applies to foreign nationals and

companies doing business in U.S. territory as well as foreign companies listed on a U.S. stock exchange; that is, the U.S. law has "extra-territorial" effect.

- The FCPA is enforced in the U.S. by the Securities and Exchange Commission for civil sanctions and the Justice Department for criminal sanctions.

- The FCPA prohibits payments of things of value, typically money, to foreign government officials in order to wrongfully obtain business.

- Bribes can be "purchase bribes" (that is, to wrongfully obtain a contract or business from the government) or "variance bribes" (that is, to get one's firm or company wrongfully exempted from some aspect of the host country's law).

- Paying a "*bribe*" is a civil and criminal wrong, including a felony sanction of up to ten years imprisonment and fines of up to $2 million for a company and $250,000 for a person (and the latter fine cannot be paid by the company).

- Bribery can be "direct," such as a cash payment to the foreign official, or "indirect," such as renting an office space from a relative of the foreign official but not using the office or contributing to a purported charity run by the spouse of the foreign official.

- A U.S. company can be liable for payments made by its employees as well as payments made by its foreign distributors, sales representatives, and agents.

- The FCPA applies to company directors, officers, employees, shareholders, and agents.

- The FCPA provides special accounting controls and reporting rules for public companies; accurate and detailed financial records must be maintained (so as to prevent "slush funds" for bribes)

- However, the government needs evidence of a "corrupt" motive; that is, the bribe-payer knowingly and wrongfully was attempting to direct business to his or her firm; this requirement of having "bad intent" or an "evil motive" is called "scienter."

- Evidence of "corrupt" intent can be direct or circumstantial, such as use of aliases and "shell" companies and offices, which give rise to an inference of bad intent; and for criminal conviction proof of wrongdoing must be "beyond a reasonable doubt" as well as a unanimous jury verdict by 12 federal jurors, who are, it must be emphasized, allowed to make inferences of bad intent.

- An exception to the FCPA (that is, a legal payment) exists if the payment to foreign government official is authorized by express written law of host country.

- Another exception also exists for "*facilitating and expediting payments*," that is, relatively small payments to lower level foreign government officials with merely ministerial and clerk-like authority to induce them to perform routine government services that a firm is entitled to, such as issuing visas, customs declarations, licenses, and processing other documents or turning on utilities, which one is legally entitled to, more smoothly and more quickly (at times called "petty bribery")

- Note, however, that the larger the sum of money or transfer of something of value to the foreign official as well as the higher level of the official and the more discretionary power the official has, the less likely that the government will construe the payment as a "facilitating and expediting" payment and the more likely the government will deem it an illegal bribe.

- A final exception for reasonable and legitimate payments, for example, reimbursement for travel, meals, and lodging, as well as "good will" gifts, directly related to the demonstration and/or explanation of a company's products or services; note that gifts should be modest, given at culturally appropriate times, and not be lavish; note too that any trips should have a predominate business and educational purpose and not be merely "junkets" for fun and entertainment, which latter case could be construed as an illegal bribe.

- Warning: FCPA is a very vague statute, thereby giving some latitude to business people in their dealings with foreign government officials, but also giving a great deal of discretion to government regulators.

- Bribery criminal convictions: Although many companies have been fined for violating the FCPA, criminal convictions against individual corporate executives are difficult to obtain due to the burden of proof on the government that an executive knew or should have known of the bribe and had the requisite corrupt intent to wrongfully direct business to his or her firm. However, there have been two notable successes for the government. First, former Halliburton Co. chief executive, Albert Stanley, pleaded guilty to violating the law and sentenced to two years in prison. Specifically, he pleaded guilty to orchestrating the payment of $180 million in bribes to Nigerian government officials over a nine-year period in order to secure very large construction contracts for his firm. His major role was to determine exactly which Nigerian government officials to bribe since, apparently, so many had "their hands out." Stanley could have received 10 years imprisonment pursuant to the FCPA, and the government requested a seven-year sentence; but perhaps the judge was a bit lenient when Stanley blamed his transgression on alcohol abuse as well as ego and ambition. Halliburton and a subsidiary paid almost $600 million in fines. In the second case the founder of the high-end, women's accessories company Dooney & Bourke, Frederic Bourke, was sentenced to a prison term of one year for violating the FCPA. He also was ordered to pay a $1 million fine. A jury convicted Bourke of paying bribes in the form of cash and jewelry by means of a middle-man to secure oil deals in post-Soviet Republics. The middle-man was a Czech citizen known as the "Pirate of Prague," which nick-name just might possibly be some evidence of bad intent.

- J.P. Morgan Chase & Company and Bribery: A recent allegation of a U.S. company violating the Foreign Corrupt Practices Act involved the giant bank, J.P. Morgan, which was accused by the U.S. government of bribing high-level Communist party officials, who are responsible for running large state-owned, -dominated, or -controlled companies, such as the China Railway Group. The method of bribery was to hire the sons and daughters of these officials allegedly for the *quid pro quo* of the bank being granted very lucrative consulting contracts. Bribery under the FCPA can be effectuated as the transfer of "anything of value" to a foreign government official with a "corrupt" or bad intent, that is, to wrongfully direct business to one's firm. Now the hiring of one's relatives is certainly a way to transfer value; but the issue of corrupt intent is very difficult to establish particularly when evidence of motivation must be obtained in foreign jurisdictions. In the J.P. Morgan case, the government was investigating as to whether jobs even existed for the sons and daughters of the officials, whether their children were qualified for the jobs, and for that matter whether the children even showed up for the jobs and did any work. The bank claimed that it did nothing wrong, that the practice of all big companies doing business in China is to curry favor and produce good will by hiring the relatives of high-placed government officials. Moreover, the bank even had a program to that effect called, appropriately, the Sons and Daughters program. Of course, complying with ethical norms is being culturally competent, and the fact that "everyone is doing it" means that one is simply complying with societal mores and practices; yet neither is a defense to the FCPA. However, due most likely to the government's inability to get sufficient evidence on the "corrupt" intent requirement of the FCPA the government settled the case civilly with the bank with no admission of liability, no criminal liability, and the payment of a "mere" fine of $226 million (and the authors use the word "mere" because in that year JP Morgan bank was number one in bank profits to the tune of over $1 billion dollars.

- The United Kingdom Bribery Act: The United Kingdom in 2010 passed a new anti-bribery act that parallels in many respects the U.S. Foreign Corrupt Practices Act (FCPA). One significant difference is that the British law also makes illegal bribes between private business people. The law also increases the maximum penalty for bribery from seven to ten years in prison, and, unlike the U.S. FCPA, there are no limits on fines. Another major difference in the United Kingdom law is that the act criminalizes the payment of "grease money, that is, small payments to lower level foreign government officials for routine government actions, such as establishing mail, phone, or utility services. These "tips" are very common practices in many countries and are legal pursuant to the FCPA. One problem area in the British law, like the U.S. law, is the issue of permissible "good will" gifts or "corporate hospitality." Gifts to government officials could be construed as illegal bribery in both countries. In resolving this issue for British companies the British government provided some guidance, to wit: the norms of a particular industry would be taken into account assuming the hospitality was "reasonable," for example, tickets to the Wimbledon tennis tournament, but if the gifts were more "lavish," such as travel and accommodations, the gifts could be construed as illegal bribes if they were viewed as attempts to improperly influence government officials. The British government also counseled that gifts must be "sensible" and "proportionate" to be proper hospitality expenditures. The British business community has been concerned about the criminalization of "grease payments" as well as by the lack of clarity as to the level of permissible "hospitality."

- Note that there is now an international treaty against bribery – the Organization of Economic Cooperation and Development Convention Against Bribery – which has been adopted by many nations and which is patterned after the FCPA; yet the question emerges as to whether the signatories to the treaty, especially the U.S.' main trading partners and competitors for international business are as aggressively attempting to enforce their government treaty obligations as the U.S. government seeks to do against U.S. business people.

- Note too that there is also an international private organization, called Transparency International, which has as its goal to create a world where government business and civil society, especially the daily lives of people, are free from bribery and corruption. Corruption and bribery engender dishonest officials and broken institutions which cause inequality, exploitation, and poverty. The organization is based in Berlin and has more than 100 chapters. Among its many anti-corruption educational and lobbying activities Transparency International puts forth each year a Corruption Perceptions Index based on expert opinions around the world of perceived corruption in 176 countries. Consistently, Denmark has been number one, that is, the least corrupt country, followed by mainly the Scandinavian countries and Singapore, with the U.S. usually in the high "teens" or low "twenties," and with Somalia, Sudan, and Yemen usually at the bottom spot as the most corrupt countries in the world (which in the authors' humble opinion may not be fair due to the extreme poverty and war-torn nature of these distressed countries). The Index also explains based on geographic sectors of countries some of the "good" and "bad" illustrations of anti-corruption efforts and corrupt activities, respectively, and briefly states what needs to be done to eliminate corruption. The organization is a valuable resource for the international business person, academic, and government leader.

Host Country Laws

A U.S. company operating in a foreign country will be subject to the laws of that country; and as a starting point, the company's operations in the country (e.g., subsidiary, branch office, etc.) will be subject to such laws; in certain instances the foreign country may also claim that the parent would be subject to its jurisdiction or be legally responsible in the event the local operation violates local law. Any U.S. company that is operating through a subsidiary means that the subsidiary will be subject to a host of local corporate laws, such as provisions for permitted activities of the subsidiary, requirements regarding officers, directors, control, minimal capital, and protection of minority shareholders. Many countries also have laws regarding currency and finance, such as restrictions on currency conversion and foreign exchange, restrictions on repatriation of dividends, etc.; these could place significant obstacles on the parent company withdrawing its profits to its home country. A major area of concern for many U.S. companies is local employment and termination laws; many countries impose severe restrictions on termination of employees, such as requiring substantial severance payments, requirements for obtaining government approval for layoffs, etc. Similar restrictions often apply to termination of distributors. Other areas of local laws which may be applicable include: 1) local labeling, advertising, and marketing laws; 2) local tax laws; 3) local environmental laws; 4) local product, liability, and consumer liability laws; 5) local health, safety, and inspection laws; and 6) local antitrust and competition laws. U.S. firms doing business abroad will also have to be concerned with the extraterritoriality of U.S. regulatory law, especially Civil Rights and antitrust law. Extraterritoriality means that the U.S. law will reach out and apply to the activities of U.S. companies doing business in foreign countries.

Export Regulations and Licenses

In the United States, most export transactions do not require specific approval in the form of licenses from the U.S. However, there are several areas that are highly regulated, and all regulations must be strictly followed. Specifically, these areas are: the exportation of sophisticated and high-technology products; short supply items; technical information and products that have defense, strategic, weapons development, proliferation, or law enforcement applications can be subject to export licenses. Major factors in determining whether an export license is required include the destination and end-use of the product. To determine whether a license is needed to export a particular commercial product or service, an exporter must first classify the item by identifying what is called an Export Control Classification Number (ECCN) for the item, according to the Export Administration Regulations (EAR); and then the exporter must reference the Commerce Control List (CCL).

There are several federal agencies that have export licensing responsibilities. The following is a list of the agencies and their area of jurisdiction:

- Department of State, Directorate of Defense Trade Controls (DTC): Licenses defense services and defense (munitions) articles.
- Department of the Treasury, Office of Foreign Assets Control (OFAC): OFAC administers and enforces economic and trade sanctions against

targeted foreign countries, terrorism sponsoring organizations, and international narcotics traffickers.

- Nuclear Regulatory Commission, Office of International Programs: Licenses nuclear material and equipment.
- Department of Energy, Office of Arms Controls and Nonproliferation, Export Control Division: Licenses nuclear technology and technical data for nuclear power and special nuclear materials.
- Defense Technology Security Administration: The Defense Technology Security Administration (DTSA) administers the development and implementation of Department of Defense technology security policies on international transfers of defense-related goods, services, and technologies.
- Drug Enforcement Administration, Office of Diversion Control, Import-Export Unit: Oversees the export of controlled substances and the import and export of listed chemicals used in the production of controlled substances under the Controlled Substances Act.
- Food and Drug Administration, Office of Compliance: Licenses medical devices.
- Food and Drug Administration, Import/Export: Licenses drugs.
- Patent and Trademark Office, Licensing and Review: Oversees patent filing data sent abroad.

Harmonized Commodity Description and Coding System

In order to facilitate the importation of goods worldwide, an intergovernmental organization, the World Custom Organization (WCO), consisting of 170 members, has established an international standard classification of commodities called the Harmonized Description and Coding System (HS). The Harmonized Tariff Schedule consists of a list of numbers recognized throughout the world to classify commodities for importing and exporting. The harmonized code number is also used to assist customs with duty assessments.

The Harmonized Tariff Schedule of the United States (HTUS) is the primary resource for determining tariff classifications for goods imported into the United States; and it is also used for classifying goods exported from the United States. This two volume U.S. government publication is updated periodically by the United States International Trade Commission and is available in various electronic formats. The HTUS, like Harmonized System tariff schedules generally, classifies a good (assigns it a ten-digit tariff classification number) based on such things as its name, use, and/or the material used in its construction. The tariff schedule is divided into Chapters 1 through 99 plus numerous additional sections, such as various appendices and indices. Chapters are divided into a varying number of headings, and headings are divided into a varying number of subheadings. Raw materials or basic substances often appear in the early chapters and in earlier headings within a chapter, where highly processed goods and manufactured articles often appear in later chapters and headings.

Payments in Export Transactions

Naturally, all entrepreneurs and managers view being paid for the export transactions a major concern. There are several methods of payment when selling to overseas buyers. The most commonly used methods of payment for an export transaction are the following: 1) cash in advance; 2) documentary letter of credit; 3) documentary collection or draft; 4) open account; and 5) other payment mechanisms, such as consignment. Now listed in order from most secure for the exporter to the least secure, the basic methods of payment are: cash in advance; documentary letter of credit; documentary collection or draft; open account; and other payment mechanisms, such as consignment sales. Receiving payment by cash in advance of the shipment might seem ideal. In this situation, the exporter is relieved of collection problems and has immediate use of the money. A wire transfer is commonly used and has the advantage of being almost immediate. Payment by check may result in a collection delay of up to six weeks. Therefore, this method may defeat the original intention of receiving payment before shipment.

Many exporters accept credit cards in payment for exports of consumer and other products, generally of a low dollar value, sold directly to the end user. Domestic and international rules governing credit card transactions sometimes differ, so U.S. merchants should contact their credit card processor for more specific information. International credit card transactions are typically done by telephone or fax. Due to the nature of these methods, exporters should be aware of fraud. Merchants should determine the validity of transactions and obtain the proper authorizations. For the buyer, however, advance payment tends to create cash flow problems, as well as increase risks. Furthermore, cash in advance is not as common in most of the world as it is in the United States. Buyers are often concerned that the goods may not be sent if payment is made in advance. Exporters that insist on this method of payment as their sole method of doing business may find themselves losing out to competitors who offer more flexible payment terms. Documentary letters of credit or documentary drafts are often used to protect the interests of both buyer and seller. These two methods require that payment be made based on the presentation of documents conveying the title and that describe the specific steps that have been taken. Letters of credit and drafts can be paid immediately or at a later date. Drafts that are paid upon presentation are called sight drafts. Drafts that are to be paid at a later date, often after the buyer receives the goods, are called time drafts or date drafts.

Since payment by these two methods is made on the basis of documents, all terms of payment should be clearly specified in order to avoid confusion and delay. Banks charge fees - based mainly on a percentage of the amount of payment - for handling letters of credit, and smaller amounts for handling drafts. If fees charged by both the foreign and U.S. banks are to be applied to the buyer's account, this should be explicitly stated in all quotations and in the letter of credit. The exporter usually expects the buyer to pay the charges for the letter of credit, but some buyers may not agree to this added cost. In such cases, the exporter must either absorb the costs of the letter of credit or risk losing that potential sale. Letters of credit for smaller amounts can be somewhat expensive since fees can be high relative to the sale.

The following are the typical steps of an irrevocable letter of credit that has been confirmed by a U.S. bank:

1. After the exporter and buyer agree on the terms of a sale, the buyer arranges for its bank to open a letter of credit that specifies the documents needed for payment. The buyer determines which documents will be required.

2. The buyer's bank issues, or opens, its irrevocable letter of credit and includes all instructions to the seller relating to the shipment.
3. The buyer's bank sends its irrevocable letter of credit to a U.S. bank and requests confirmation. The exporter may request that a particular U.S. bank be the confirming bank, or the foreign bank may select a U.S. correspondent bank.
4. The U.S. bank prepares a letter of confirmation to forward to the exporter along with the irrevocable letter of credit.
5. The exporter reviews carefully all conditions in the letter of credit. The exporter's freight forwarder is contacted to make sure that the shipping date can be met. If the exporter cannot comply with one or more of the conditions, the customer is alerted at once.
6. The exporter arranges with the freight forwarder to deliver the goods to the appropriate port or airport.
7. When the goods are loaded, the freight forwarder completes the necessary documentation.
8. The exporter (or the freight forwarder) presents the documents, evidencing full compliance with the letter of credit terms, to the U.S. bank.
9. The bank reviews the documents. If they are in order, the documents are sent to the buyer's bank for review, and then transmitted to the buyer.
10. The buyer (or the buyer's agent) uses the documents to claim the goods.
11. A draft, which accompanies the letter of credit, is paid by the buyer's bank at the time specified or, if a time draft, may be discounted to the exporter's bank at an earlier date.

A draft, sometimes also called a bill of exchange, is analogous to a foreign buyer's check. Like checks used in domestic commerce, drafts carry the risk that they will be dishonored. However, in international commerce, title does not transfer to the buyer until he or she pays the draft, or at least engages a legal undertaking that the draft will be paid when due. A sight draft is used when the exporter wishes to retain title to the shipment until it reaches its destination and payment is made. Before the shipment can be released to the buyer, the original ocean bill of lading (the document that evidences title) must be properly endorsed by the buyer and surrendered to the carrier. It is important to note that airway bills of lading, on the other hand, do not need to be presented in order for the buyer to claim the goods. Hence, risk increases when a sight draft is being used with an air shipment.

In actual practice, the ocean bill of lading is endorsed by the exporter and sent via the exporter's bank to the buyer's bank. It is accompanied by the sight draft, invoices, and other supporting documents that are specified by either the buyer or the buyer's country (e.g., packing lists, consular invoices, insurance certificates). The foreign bank notifies the buyer when it has received these documents. As soon as the draft is paid, the foreign bank turns over the bill of lading, thereby enabling the buyer to obtain the shipment. There is still some risk when a sight draft is used to control transferring the title of a shipment. The buyer's ability or willingness to pay might change from the time the goods are shipped until the time the drafts are presented for payment; there is no bank promise to pay standing behind the buyer's obligation.

Additionally, the policies of the importing country could also change. If the buyer cannot or will not pay for and claim the goods, returning or disposing of the products becomes the problem of the exporter.

A time draft is used when the exporter extends credit to the buyer. The draft states that payment is due by a specific time after the buyer accepts the time draft and receives the goods (e.g., 30 days after acceptance). By signing and writing "accepted" on the draft, the buyer is formally obligated to pay within the stated time. When this is done the time draft is then called a trade acceptance. It can be kept by the exporter until maturity or sold to a bank at a discount for immediate payment. A date draft differs slightly from a time draft in that it specifies a date on which payment is due, rather than a time period after the draft is accepted. When either a sight draft or time draft is used, a buyer can delay payment by delaying acceptance of the draft. A date draft can prevent this delay in payment though it still must be accepted. When a bank accepts a draft, it becomes an obligation of the bank and, thus, a negotiable investment known as a banker's acceptance. A banker's acceptance can also be sold to a bank at a discount for immediate payment. International consignment sales follow the same basic procedures as in the United States. The goods are shipped to a foreign distributor who sells them on behalf of the exporter. The exporter retains title to the goods until they are sold, at which point payment is sent to the exporter. The exporter has the greatest risk and least control over the goods with this method. Additionally, receiving payment may take quite a while. It is wise to consider risk insurance with international consignment sales. The contract should clarify who is responsible for property risk insurance that will cover the merchandise until it is sold and payment is received. In addition, it may be necessary to conduct a credit check on the foreign distributor.

International countertrade is a trade practice whereby one party accepts goods, services, or other instruments of trade in partial or whole payment for its products. This type of trade fulfills financial, marketing, or public policy objectives of the trading parties. For example, a firm might trade by bartering because it or its trading partner lacks foreign exchange. Many U.S. exporters consider countertrade a necessary cost of doing business in markets where U.S. exports would otherwise not be sold. One consideration for smaller firms is that this type of trade may cause cash flow problems. Therefore, many smaller exporters do not consider this an option as they wish to do business in U.S. dollars. There are several types of countertrade, including counterpurchase and barter. Counterpurchase is quite common. In this situation, exporters agree to purchase a quantity of goods from a country in exchange for that country's purchase of the exporter's product. These goods are typically unrelated but have an equivalent value. Another form of this practice is contractually linked, that is, parallel trade transactions that involve a separate financial settlement. For example, a countertrade contract may provide that the U.S. exporter will be paid in a convertible currency as long as the U.S. exporter (or another entity designated by the exporter) agrees to purchase a related quantity of goods from the importing country. Barter arrangements in international commerce are not as common, because the parties' needs for the goods of the other seldom coincide and because valuation of the goods may be problematic. This type of countertrade occurs without money exchanging hands as merchandise is traded directly for other merchandise or services.

Barter might occur by swapping (one good for another) or by switching (using a chain of buyers and sellers in different markets to barter). U.S. exporters can take advantage of countertrade opportunities by trading through an intermediary with countertrade expertise, such as an international broker, an international bank, or an export management company. One drawback to this type of exporting is that there are often higher transaction costs and greater risks than with other kinds of export transactions.

Summary

This chapter has attempted to shed some light on understanding and obeying domestic and international laws as they are a critical component of each manager's and entrepreneur's success in today's global workplace. Since today's managers and entrepreneurs often deal with customers, suppliers, and employees in different parts of the world, having a functional understanding of international business laws in regards to the specific country becomes very important to success of the organization. This chapter discussed international business law as it applies to domestic and global firms, and provided sources where managers and entrepreneurs can gain relevant insights as they work on successfully expanding their dealings across diverse countries, cultures, and borders.

Discussion Questions

1. What is international business law and how does it apply to foreign firms?
2. How are local and international laws different?
3. Should a firm obey the headquarters' laws or the local country's laws, if they differ? Why or why not? Provide examples.
4. What are some laws and regulations that you became familiar with when you traveled to a different country? How would the awareness (or lack thereof) of these laws impact a person's success?
5. How do Islamic laws impact managers and entrepreneurs who are coming from non-Islamic countries?

14 – LIABILITY OF ACCOUNTANTS AND OTHER PROFESSIONALS

Accountants are members of a profession who provide a variety of professional services: for example, tax, consulting, bookkeeping (compilations), and various assurance services. Assurance services provide information enhancement and include audits and reviews of financial statements. An audit is the examination of financial statements performed by a certified public accountant in accordance with specific professional standards. The product of this work is the auditor's opinion which, according to the Public Company Accounting Oversight Board's (PCAOB) standard auditor's report, gives the users of financial statements reasonable assurance that the entity's statements are free from material misstatement and "...present fairly, in all material respects, the financial position,...results of...operations, and...cash flows...in conformity with accounting principles accepted in the United States of America." A certified public accountant, known as a CPA, is an accountant who has attained certain educational requirements, typically five years of college study, and who has passed the rigorous Uniform CPA Exam administered in 55 U.S. jurisdictions.

In the performance of their professional services, accountants, like members of the legal and medical profession, are exposed to legal liability. Legal liability against accountants is based on both the common law and statutory law. In the former category, the accountant can be sued for breach of contract, negligence, and fraud. In the statutory category, the accountant faces legal liability based on a variety of federal and state statutes, especially federal securities laws. Moreover, accountants may confront legal liability not only from their clients but also third parties. This chapter[5] will examine the legal liability of accountants under the common law and selected statutory law, particularly federal securities laws, as well as briefly address the

---

[5] This chapter is co-authored with Donald L. Ariail, Texas A&M University-Kingsville. Accounting case studies and discussion questions contributed by Donald L. Ariail can be accessed at the following link: http://www.huizenga.nova.edu/course-materials/business-law/

accountant-client legal privilege and some practical steps an accountant can take to minimize his or her legal liability. Mention will also be made of the liability of other professionals, especially lawyers.

Common Law Liability

As previously discussed in the first chapter of this book, common law is derived from case law. That is, it is based on prior adjudicated precedent (which is the legal opinion of judges). Pursuant to the common law, accountants are exposed to legal liability from their clients and potentially third parties based on three doctrines: 1) breach of contract, 2) negligence, and 3) fraud.

Breach of Contract

Accountants are retained by their clients to perform a variety of professional accounting services; as such, accountants regularly enter into contracts with their clients; these contracts are at times called "engagements" or *engagement letters*. The standards of the accounting profession require an engagement letter for each audit and review. The failure of the accountant to perform or to substantially perform his or her contract duties subjects the accountant to a lawsuit for breach of contract premised on common law contract principles. Money damages would be the primary redress the aggrieved client could obtain; and these damages would encompass compensatory damages for the expense the client incurred to obtain another accountant to perform the services or to perform them correctly as well as consequential damages for any fines, penalties, legal expenses, and perhaps lost business opportunities and loss of goodwill the client suffered due to the accountant's non-performance or inadequate performance. The client, though aggrieved, must be aware of the common law Mitigation Rule, covered in the Contracts chapter, which would require the client to make a good faith and reasonable effort to secure other accounting assistance and to otherwise lessen the client's own losses.

Negligence

Accountants, as members of a profession, like lawyers, are under a legal duty to perform their professional accounting and auditing services in a careful, reasonable, and prudent manner. They must exercise the degree of care and skill and possess the requisite knowledge of the ordinary, reasonable, and prudent member of their profession. Accountants are thus held to the old common law negligence standard of the "reasonably prudent person," but in the specific, reasonably prudent, accountant professional context. The failure to adhere to this legal duty, referred to as *due care*, subjects the accountant to legal liability for negligence, which on the professional level is deemed "malpractice," and thereby accounting malpractice. The two most important sources for the legal standards that certified public accountants must adhere to are: 1) the generally accepted accounting principles (*GAAP*), promulgated by the Financial Accounting Standards Board and other authoritative bodies, which govern the proper reporting of financial information; and 2) the generally accepted auditing standards (GAAS), promulgated by the Auditing Standard Committee of the American Institute of Certified Public Accountants, which govern the procedures and methods that must be used to conduct audits of nonpublic companies, and by the

Public Company Accounting Oversight Board which governs procedures and methods that must be used to conduct audits of public companies. The accountant's failure to adhere to these standards of the profession is evidence of professional malpractice, that is, negligence as applied to the profession. These accounting standards are uniform national ones, which means that an aggrieved party as a plaintiff will have a much easier time finding an expert witness to testify in a professional malpractice case as to the requisite standard of care and the breach thereof. Note, however, that accountants are not insurers or guarantors that every decision they make will be the correct one for the client and benefit the client. Moreover, an accountant is not required to discover every impropriety, fraud, or embezzlement in the client's books or records. Rather, the accountant is liable if his or her negligence or failure to perform a legal duty caused the fraud to go undetected and the client to thereby incur a loss. Of course, if the reasonably prudent accountant would have investigated a suspicious matter further, and the accountant does not, or does not even inform the client, then the accountant could very well be liable for any resulting loss to the client. Accountants, therefore, based on the common law, are "merely" liable for their negligent actions that cause harm. They are liable for not performing their professional duties with due care.

Fraud
An accountant may be liable for fraud, which (as explained in the Contracts and Tort chapters), is a very broad term encompassing liability for intentional misrepresentation, called deceit in the old common law, and negligent misrepresentation. In the former more serious formulation of fraud, the accountant could be subject to punitive damage liability. Also, accountants are regarded as fiduciaries; and thus are in a relationship of trust and confidence with their clients; consequently, the breach of this fiduciary relationship, for example, by purposefully omitting a material fact which is relied on by the client, is regarded in the law as the equivalent of fraud, thereby subjecting the accountant to punitive damage liability. Thus, under the common law, accountants are liable for actual fraud and constructive fraud. Constructive fraud is committed by an accountant when professional standards are recklessly or carelessly disregarded.

Liability to Third Parties
Most negligence lawsuits instituted against accountants are brought by their clients who contend that the accountants' carelessness has caused them some harm. However, it is possible that another party also suffered harm and thus seeks to sue the accountant. This party is characteristically a third party, such as a corporate shareholder or financial institution, who relied on the information supplied (or not supplied) by the accountant. This area of the accountant's negligence liability to third parties is a very difficult one in the law because there are three competing legal principles: 1) the *Ultramares* rule, 2) the *Restatement (Second) of Torts rule*, and 3) the negligence "foreseeability" rule.

The Ultramares Rule

The *Ultramares* rule is based on a seminal 1931 state case, called *Ultramares* v. *Touche*, by the Court of Appeals of New York (which is the highest court in the state). The court ruled that an action for ordinary negligence could only be brought against an accountant by a party in *privity*. Thus, a party not in privity was barred from bringing an action against an accountant for ordinary negligence. Subsequently, this doctrine was extended to parties in "privity-like" contracts by the 1968 federal district court decision in *Rusch Factors v. Levin*. Accordingly, the accountant would be liable to the third party for negligence if the client contractually retained the accountant to prepare financial statements or to perform an audit to be used by a third party for a specific purpose, for example, to secure a bank loan for the client, *and* the accountant was made aware of the special purpose for the work. In such a case, the third party, for example the bank, would be able to sue the accountant for the damages it sustained for the accountant's negligent performance of the engagement. The *Ultramares* rule, though an old one, still remains as the majority rule for the accountant's negligence liability to third parties; however, this rule has been substantially eroded in recent years by the next rule, the *Restatement (Second) of Torts* rule.

Section 552(2) of the Restatement (Second) of Torts Rule

The *Restatement (Second) of Torts* in Section 552(2) provides a second and broader standard for holding accountants liable to third parties who have been harmed by the accountant's negligence. Pursuant to the *Restatement* standard, an accountant is liable for his or her negligent actions to any members of a limited class of users for whose benefit the accountant has been employed by the client to prepare financial statements or to whom the accountant knows the client will supply the financial statements. Under this more expansive standard, the accountant does not have to be in a contractual relationship with the third party, and does not even have to know the specific name of the third party. Therefore, this standard makes the accountant liable to foreseen third parties. Several states have now adopted this legal standard.

The Foreseeability Rule

The final rule impacting the accountant's negligence liability to third parties is based on the *H. Rosenblum v. Adler* case, decided in 1983 by the New Jersey Supreme Court. The ruling followed the traditional "foreseeability" standard to the causation element in negligence law. Pursuant to this "foreseeability" rule, an accountant would be liable to any foreseeable user of the client's financial statements prepared by the accountant who is harmed thereby. The accountant, of course, would not be liable to indirect, remote, and unforeseeable users of the negligently prepared statements. The accountant's liability under the "foreseeability" rule would not be contingent on either the accountant's knowledge of the identity of the third party who used the information or even the intended class of users. Therefore, under this rule, the accountant is liable to third parties who could reasonably have been foreseeable users of the financial statements. This very broad rule of legal liability has only been adopted by a few states.

Statutory Liability
There are several statutes, both federal and state, that impact the liability of the accountant. First, the civil liability of the accountant under major statutes will be addressed; and then in the next statutory section, the criminal liability of the accountant will be examined.

Sarbanes-Oxley Act and the Public Company Accounting Oversight Board
The *Sarbanes-Oxley Act (SOX)* of 2002 was a Congressional response to the spate of corporate scandals as exemplified by the famous (infamous) Enron collapse. SOX emerged as one of the most important modifications of federal securities laws since the enactment of the 1933 and 1934 acts. The main purposes of SOX are to protect investors by improving the accuracy and reliability of corporate disclosure and to increase and improve corporate accountability and governance. The Act also imposes very harsh, some would say draconian, penalties for violations of the securities laws and SOX provisions. One of the principal provisions of SOX is to require corporate chief executives to take legal responsibility for the accuracy and completeness of financial statements and reports that are filed with the SEC. Chief Executive Officers (CEO) and Chief Financial Officers (CFO) now must personally certify that the statements and reports are accurate and complete. The days of Enron CEO Ken Lay claiming "ignorance and innocence" as to the "financials" are long gone! The Act also created a new federal agency, the *Public Company Accounting Oversight Board (PCAOB)*, which reports to the SEC, to oversee and regulate public accounting firms. The Board consists of a chair and four other members. In the "pre-Enron days," the accounting profession was regarded as an independent, autonomous, and self-regulating profession, governed by a code of ethics, like law and medicine; but the failure of the accounting profession to regulate itself, let alone others, brought down on itself a new federal regulatory agency to "police" the now delimited profession.

The certification requirements of SOX are a very important and consequential feature of the statute. Section 906 mandates that CEOs and CFOs of most major companies whose stock is traded on public stock exchanges now must certify the financial statements and reports that are required to be filed with the SEC. These corporate executives have to certify that the statements and reports fully comply with SEC requirements, and, in addition, that the information therein fairly represents in all material respects the financial conditions and operations of the company. Specifically, Section 302 requires the CEO and CFO of reporting companies to sign the reports and to certify that they reviewed the report, and that to the best of their knowledge, the report neither contains any untrue statements nor omits any material facts. Furthermore, the signing officers must certify that their firms have established internal control systems to make certain that any relevant material information is ascertained and is placed in the report. Finally, the signing officers must certify that they disclosed to the auditors any significant deficiencies in the internal control systems of the firm. Certain reports are required to be filed quarterly as well as annually with the SEC.

In addition to the certification requirements, there are other important corporate governance provisions in SOX. Section 402 prohibits any reporting company as well as a company which is filing an initial public stock offering from arranging, extending, renewing, or maintaining a personal loan for a director or executive officer, though there are some exceptions in the Act for consumer and housing loans. The objective of this provision is to prevent companies from making personal loans to corporate directors and officers and then forgiving the loans to the detriment of shareholders.

Section 806 of SOX provides protections for *"whistleblowers."* This provision prohibits publicly traded companies from discharging, demoting, suspending, threatening, harassing, or otherwise discriminating against an employee who provides to the government or assists in any government investigation regarding activities that the employee reasonably believes constitute a violation of securities fraud laws. The whistleblowing employee is protected if he or she discloses information internally or to federal regulatory and law enforcement agencies or to a member of Congress or a Congressional committee. The employee is not protected if he or she makes a report to the media. It is important to emphasize that the SOX whistleblower protection provisions will protect an employee who has a reasonable belief of wrongdoing, even if that belief later is determined to be unfounded. To compare, some state whistleblower protection statutes, such as the one in Florida, although allowing the employee to report the violation of any law, rule, or regulation, also will require that the employee report actual violations of law. A belief even if reasonable as to a violation will be insufficient for whistleblowing legal protection if the employee is erroneous as to his or her "illegal" conclusion. SOX also requires that regulated companies set up confidential whistleblowing reporting systems so that employees can express their concerns about illegal accounting and auditing practices and securities fraud. Employees should be able to anonymously contact, electronically or otherwise, an independent ethics center, which will then alert the company directors, officers, executives, and managers as to a possible problem.

Section 406 of the statute deals with codes of ethics for senior financial officers. Initially, it must be underscored that the Act neither mandates that SOX regulated companies adopt codes of ethics, nor if such codes are in existence does the Act make them legally binding. Rather, the Act does require that publicly traded firms report to the SEC whether or not the firm has a code of ethics for senior financial officers, and if not, the reasons for the lack thereof. The objective of this provision is to let the potential investor know that he or she may be making an investment in a firm that does not have a code of ethics. Moreover, SOX also requires that if a regulated company changes its codes of ethics, or makes any exceptions or waivers thereto, the company must make an immediate disclosure to the SEC as well as disseminate the information publicly by means of the Internet or other comparable electronic means. Again, the objective is to warn current shareholders and potential investors of possible problems at the firm. This ethics "exception" disclosure provision directly resulted from the Enron disaster, where the company did have a fine-sounding code of ethics, but many exceptions were made thereto by and for company executives.

Securities Act of 1933

The *Securities Act of 1933* is a disclosure type of statute. It is designed to promote fairness and stability in the securities markets by requiring that certain essential information concerning the issuance of stocks and the principals behind the issuance are made available to the investing public. There are two major sections of the Act: Section 5, which details the requirements for a registration statement as well as a prospectus; and Section 11, which sets forth the penalties for non-compliance with Section 5 requirements. The basic principle of Section 5 of the Act is that, unless a security qualifies for an exemption, a security must be registered before it is offered to the public through either interstate commerce or through a securities exchange. The issuing corporation must file a registration statement with the Securities and Exchange Commission. Moreover, investors must be provided with a prospectus, which is a document that describes the securities to be sold, the issuing corporation and principals behind the sale, material facts concerning the financial operations of the corporation, the nature of the investment, and, most importantly, the risk of the investment. The objective of the prospectus, as well as the registration statement, is to provide adequate information to the investing public to enable the unsophisticated investor to evaluate the financial risk involved, and thereby to make an informed investment decision.

Accountants are retained to certify the financial statements that are included in the registration statements filed with the SEC as well as the prospectuses that are given to potential investors. Again, as underscored, the SEC does not formally approve or disapprove the issuance of securities or certify the risk or the degree thereof of a security. It is beyond the purpose of this book to cover in detail the registration process, or for that matter all the contents of the registration; yet, regarding the latter, the registration statement must contain certain key information, such as a description of the security offered for sale, the issuing corporation, the principals and management of the business, any current or potential litigation, as well as how the corporation intends to use the proceeds of the sale of the securities. Most importantly, a detailed financial statement certified by an independent Certified Public Accountant (CPA) is required.

As noted, however, there are certain exemptions to the 1933 Act by which a company will not have to comply, either totally or partially, with all the registration requirements of the Act. Again, it is beyond the purpose of this book to cover in detail all the exemptions and the precise nature thereof. Yet a brief and very general mention should be made of three important exemptions: 1) the "small offering" exemption, which eliminates the complicated and costly registration requirements for offers to sell securities below a specified dollar amount and/or to a specified number of investors; 2) the "sophisticated investor" exemption, which pertains to offerings made to investors with sufficient knowledge and experience in business and financial matters that the investor is capable of evaluating the merits and risks of the prospective investment; and 3) the "private offering" exemption, which pertains to non-public offerings to a limited number of people who would have the necessary knowledge to make an informed investment decision, for example, management personnel who are offered stock by their corporation.

Section 11 of the Act imposes legal liability on accountants and others when either the registration statement or prospectus contains material false statements and, most notably, material omissions. Evidently, pursuant to securities law, as opposed to the common law, "silence" very well can be fraud. The key qualifier "*material*" means that the information, if stated accurately or disclosed, would have deterred or tended to deter an average ordinary and prudent investor from purchasing the securities at issue. Minor errors, minor omissions, and irrelevant information are not grounds for liability. Rather, the thrust of Section 11 is to ensure the disclosure of those facts which would be an important indication of the nature of the investment, its risk, and the condition of the issuing corporation and its business affairs; examples include an overstatement of revenues, an understatement of liabilities, and the criminal records of corporate executives.

There are criminal and civil penalties for violating the provisions of the 1933 Act. The SEC can impose civil fines and is also authorized to bring an injunction to stop an improper offering. Finally, investors are permitted to bring a private cause of action for damages in federal court for monetary losses caused by the violation of the Act. It is important to note that a private plaintiff bringing a lawsuit within one year of the offering does not have to show that he or she relied on the false or misleading statements, as the reliance element to the lawsuit is presumed. An accountant, however, may have the legal defense of *due diligence*, which means that when the accountant audited the financial statements, the accountant made a reasonable investigation and had reasonable grounds to believe that there were no inaccuracies or material omissions therein and that the statements were true and not misleading. The test of due diligence is that of the prudent CPA. That is, would a prudent CPA make the same decision in the same or similar circumstances?

When should a company "go public"? That is, when should a company contemplate selling shares of stock to the public? Offering shares of stock to the public will surely result in access to broader financial markets from which to obtain capital. Moreover, once the company goes public, it can use shares of stock as opposed to cash to acquire employees, technology, products and services, as well as other businesses. "Going public" will certainly enhance the visibility of the company, and assuming the company does well, it can return to the public market for additional capital. "Going public" also will typically result in the shares of the company's stock being valued at a much higher price than that originally set by the promoters and organizers of the company (which will afford these original participants as well as early investors) a ready market for the sale of their stock. Yet there are many critical questions to answer in making this determination. First, does the company need significant new amounts of capital that only can be obtained by a public offering of stock? Are the initial investors "tapped out"? That is, are they now unwilling or unable to provide additional capital? Second, can the company make a public offering viable – financially and practically? That is, is the company at the stage where it is ready to expand into new markets, to introduce new products and services, and to engage in sufficient research and development? Does the company have or can it obtain the working capital to sustain the expansion created from initially "going public"? Third, is the company and its principals (directors, officers, major shareholders) prepared – legally, financially, and practically – to assume the extensive legal obligations, particularly in the area of disclosure to government regulators and shareholders, that will now be necessary? Are these principals prepared to reveal substantial information about their experiences, background, financial transactions, business dealings, and legal proceedings? Is the company prepared to provide detailed audited financial statements to government regulators? Is the company prepared to spend the time, effort, and money to comply with federal and state security laws? Can the company afford the attorneys' and accountants' fees, which easily could cost several hundreds of thousands of dollars, for the initial offering and to maintain compliance with the laws, particularly the Sarbanes-Oxley Act which mandates much more strict controls and procedure for corporate governance, disclosure, verification, and internal accounting processes?

Securities Act of 1934

The *Securities and Exchange Act of 1934* has several purposes. It provides for the registration and regulation of security exchanges, securities brokers and dealers, and national security associations. It also provides for the regulation of proxy solicitations for voting. Most importantly, the 1934 Act is a very broad anti-fraud statute, which applies to all purchases and sales of securities, and which seeks to police, punish, and deter fraudulent, deceptive, and manipulative practices in the securities marketplace. It is very important to observe that the Act prohibits affirmative false, deceptive, and misleading statements and conduct, but also the omission of material information in the purchase and sale of securities. The Act also seeks to prevent and punish insider trading, that is, the use of material, "inside" (non-public) information in the purchase and sale of any security.

There are very serious penalties, civil and criminal, for violating the 1934 Act, including individual fines up to $5 million and corporate fines up to $25 million, and imprisonment for up to 20 years. Private actions for damages are also allowed. However, only purchasers and sellers of securities can sue; but privity of contract is irrelevant. Yet violations of the Act are specific intent wrongs; that is, evidence of purposeful wrongful conduct is required (called the *scienter* requirement, meaning the presence of the requisite "evil mind"). The 1934 Act's anti-fraud and insider trading provisions cover all cases of securities trading, whether on organized exchanges, over-the-counter markets, or in private transactions. The Act covers any form of security, and regardless of whether a company's securities are registered under the 1933 or 1934 Act. Of course, federal jurisdiction must be present, which is readily accomplished in any case since virtually no commercial transaction can be effectuated in the U.S. today without some connection to, or use of some instrumentality of, interstate commerce. However, if a particular case is deemed too small for the SEC or the Justice Department to get involved, there are, as will be seen later in this chapter, state security laws and agencies which parallel the federal laws and the SEC.

Section 14(a) of the 1934 Act regulates the solicitation of proxies from shareholders of Section 12 corporations. A Section 12 company is one that has assets of more than $10 million and 500 or more shareholders. Such a company among other requirements must file a registration statement with the SEC for its securities. Section 14(a) authorizes the SEC to regulate the content of proxy statements sent by a corporation to shareholders who are seeking the power to vote on behalf of the shareholders in a particular corporate election. This law requires that the proxy solicitation materials must fully and accurately disclose all the facts that are relevant to the matter to be voted on. The law also prohibits false and misleading statements in proxy materials sent to shareholders. Section 14(a) also regulates *tender offers*, that is, the public invitation to shareholders of a public corporation to sell their shares. If an offeror is seeking 5% or more control of a company, the offeror must disclose sufficient facts about his or her background and intentions; and there is liability for false or misleading statements or omissions in the "tender offer."

Section 18(a) of the 1934 Act is particularly applicable to accountants. This section makes it a civil wrong for any person to make false or misleading statements in any application, report, or document filed with the SEC. Since accountants are frequently engaged to assist their clients in the filing of this type of material with the SEC, the accountant is exposed to legal liability. However, a violation requires a showing of intentional fraudulent conduct; mere negligence or carelessness is insufficient. Potential defenses available to the accountant or other defendant include demonstrating that the misleading statement was made in good faith and that the plaintiff had knowledge of the false and misleading statement when the securities were bought or sold; such knowledge rises to the level of a defense to liability.

One major problem that the 1934 Act seeks to remedy is the wrong of insider trading. That is, corporate insiders, such as directors, executives, officers, and managers, due to their position, often have access to non-public, confidential, "inside" information, that can materially affect the price of their company's stock; and the possession of such information very well could provide them with a distinct, and unfair, advantage over the general public and average shareholder. Pursuant to the common law, as noted in the Torts and Business chapter of this book, liability for fraud is attached only to intentional, affirmative misrepresentations. Silence as a general rule was not deemed to be fraud. However, there was an exception in the case of silence by a fiduciary which would be construed as fraud. Yet the problem for insider trading wrongs was that even though corporate directors, executives, and officers were deemed to be fiduciaries, their fiduciary duty was owed only to the corporation and not to the purchasers or sellers of their company's stock.

The 1934 Act attempts to redress this potential fragrant insider trading inequity in two ways. One is in Section 16(b) that regulates "short swing" profits by insiders. The other, which will be covered in the next section to this chapter, is the very significant Section 10(b), as elaborated and implemented by SEC Rule 10b-5. Section 16(b) makes such corporate directors and officers, as well as large shareholders (that is, those holding 10% or more of a company's stock), turn over to the corporation all short-term (or "*short-swing*") profits, that is, within a six month period, made from the purchase and sale or sale and repurchase of the company's stock. It must be emphasized that it is irrelevant as to whether the corporate insider actually used inside information; regardless, all "short-swing" profits must be returned to the corporation. This section of the Act in essence presumes, irrebuttably, that such an insider possesses inside information and is taking advantage of such information. Section 16(b) applies not just to the purchase and sale of stock, but also to stock warrants and options. Section 16(b), finally, requires directors, officers, and large shareholders to report their ownership interests and stock trading activities to the SEC.

Section 10(b) of the 1934 Act is one of the most important anti-fraud provisions in federal securities law as well as the section of the Act under which the liability of the auditor often arises. Pursuant to this very broad law and its related SEC

Rule 10b-5, it is illegal to make any false, deceptive, or misleading statements regarding the purchase or sale of securities, as well as to fail to state material facts regarding the purchase and sale of securities. It is also illegal to employ any fraudulent, deceptive, or manipulative device or scheme that harms another person who participates in the securities market. The Act and SEC Rule also prohibit insider trading; and it is very important to emphasize that the coverage of these laws is not restricted "merely" to insiders as is Section 16(b); rather, potentially, any person having access to or receiving material information of a non-public nature and who trades thereon is subject to Section 10(b) and Rule 10b-5.

Securities fraud crimes are specific intent crimes. That is, the government must demonstrate that the alleged wrongdoer acted purposefully, intentionally, and knowingly to misrepresent facts, to deceive or mislead, or to omit facts. This intent requirement is called "scienter," which is an old common law requirement for fraud, though the term is Latin in origin. Basically, it means the presence of an "evil mind"; that one committed a wrongful act knowingly and purposefully. It also must be underscored that if the U.S. government is prosecuting a person for criminal violations of federal securities laws, the government must convince a jury, "beyond a reasonable doubt," that the defendant possessed scienter, as well as the other elements of the crime. "Materiality" is another requirement to liability – civil and criminal – under the securities laws. That is, liability attaches only to misrepresentations and omissions of "material" facts in connection with the purchase or sale of a security. A fact will be regarded as a material one if it likely would have affected the price of a company's stock. Another definition of materiality is that a reasonably prudent investor would have attached importance to the fact in making his or her investment or sale decision. For example, changes in a firm's financial position, dividend payments or adjustments, sales and profit information, new discoveries (of products, processes, minerals, or oil), the sale or purchase of substantial assets, illegal activity by corporate directors, executives, and officers, as well as an impending merger or take-over, all very probably would be deemed "material" facts, and thus legally must be stated accurately and disclosed fully. Furthermore, in a private cause of action for violation of the securities laws, a plaintiff in addition to scienter and materiality must prove reliance, that is, he or she reasonably relied on the false or misleading statement or omission to his or her detriment (that is, suffered damages).

Section 10(b) and SEC Rule 10b-5 prohibit and punish insider trading. Moreover, as will be seen, the term "insider" is broadly construed by both the SEC and the courts. However, securities law in the U.S. does make a critical distinction between *insider trading*, which is illegal, and trading on *inside information*, which generally is illegal, but there are two important exceptions. In order to fully explicate this very complex and consequential area of the law, it is first necessary to point out that in the U.S. there historically have been two competing legal theories regarding the use of inside information in the purchase or sale of securities. One is called the narrow, or insider, or misappropriation theory; and the other is called the broad, outsider, or level-laying-field theory. Under the first theory, only certain people are liable for trading on inside information; and under the second theory, potentially anyone is liable for trading on inside information. The prevailing legal view in the U.S. is the first theory. However, even before this legal liability theory can be discussed, it is first necessary to establish certain prerequisites. For legal liability to attach to insider trading, one needs first, "information," second, "material" information, and third, "inside" material information. Since "materiality" has been briefly discussed, the crucial terms "information" and "inside" will be examined. The problem with these terms, as well as "materiality" for that matter, is that there are no precise definitions of them, perhaps by design as the SEC and the Justice Department very well may want people, particularly insiders, to think very carefully when they start trading and especially in their own company's stock. Information ordinarily means factual information, that is, concrete, actual, historical, or scientific information; whereas predictions and opinions are ordinarily not regarded as sufficiently factual to be "information"; and rumors and speculation similarly are not regarded as information. Furthermore, statements in the form of questions are not regarded as sufficiently factual for liability. Of course, it can be a "fine-line" between a mere opinion or rumor and a fact, especially if either is based on some underlying actual facts. For example, if the staff research assistant to a company's high-level executive reports to a friend that his/her "boss" has been asking for a lot of information about a potential merger partner, is that sufficiently factual to be "information"? It is certainly not public, which brings one to the next foundational requirement. Even if "information," it must be "inside," that is, non-public, confidential, and proprietary. How is the information characterized? Who knows of the information? How many people? How did they come to know of it? Did the recipients of the information know, or should they have known, that the information was private? Did they know that someone breached a fiduciary relationship or duty of loyalty in obtaining or passing on the information? These are key questions that must be answered, ultimately perhaps by a jury; and they indicate what the wise reader has already discerned – that the law is not physics!

Nevertheless, presuming that information is factual, material, and inside, exactly who is liable under the "narrow" theory? There are three categories of people who can be liable for insider trading under the narrow theory: 1) misappropriators, 2) insiders, and 3) "tippees" of insiders. The first classification, misappropriators, is a rather simple and straight forward one. These are people who steal inside information, spy it out, or bribe for it, and then trade on it. In addition to their initial crimes, they are subject to securities law liability. The second category is the one the government is most concerned with, since that is the situation where there exists the greatest chance for abuse. As a result, if an *insider* knowingly and purposefully trades in his or her own company's stock based on the possession of material, inside information, the insider commits a very serious legal wrong. The term "insider," it must be emphasized, is broadly construed. It covers not only traditional insiders, such as directors, executives, officers, managers, employees, and agents of the company, but also people known as "temporary insiders," such as the firm's attorneys, accountants, auditors, stockbrokers, investment bankers, and financial printers. Of course, what if the insider – permanent or temporary – does not trade directly, but rather tips off someone to trade. That circumstance brings the reader to the third classification of liable people – *tippees*. A "tippee" is a person to whom material inside information is transmitted to from an insider. The "usual suspects" when it comes to "tippees" are the relatives, friends, and business associates of the insider. The leading tippee case is the famous Supreme Court *U.S. v. Chestman* decision, in which the Court upheld the conviction of a former stockbroker who was deemed to be a tippee and conspirator with a family insider in the trading of company stock before the sale of the company to a large competitor. What makes the case unique is that the stockbroker was a "remote tippee" in the sense that the information was passed on to him from the insider by means a very attenuated chain of family personal and business conversations. However, regardless of how remote, tippees are liable only if they were in conspiracy with an insider; that is, that they knew they were acting improperly in concert with the insider to commit a legal wrong. There is, of course, a big difference between being a co-conspirator and acting to trade, and merely hearing a comment from an insider and trading thereon. Yet, there is an exceptional form of liability for a special type of tippee, called an inadvertent tippee, who is under some type of recognized fiduciary duty. So, for example, if an ordinary person not connected to an insider hears at a public place a comment by an insider regarding the company, and trades thereon, there is no liability, since there is no conspiracy and no legal tippee status. However, if the member of a profession, such as a doctor, lawyer, or CPA (for example in tax practice), hears even inadvertently from an insider some private fact pertaining to the company, the professional cannot trade on it due to the obligations of their profession and especially their fiduciary duty to their clients and patients. The leading inadvertent tippee case was a Supreme Court case in which the court upheld the insider trading conviction of a psychiatrist who traded on private information obtained from a patient-insider during treatment. The psychiatrist, although not in conspiracy with his patient, was legally liable due to the breach of the fiduciary relationship and the confidential nature of the professional relationship.

Insider Trading, Rule 10b-5, and the Benefit to the Tipper Saga

As emphasized throughout this book, there are many lines the law in the U.S. draws between legal and illegal conduct, and oftentimes not too precisely. One critical distinction the law makes occurs in securities law and this line is the differentiation between insider trading, which is illegal, and trading on inside information, which *may* be legal. A difficult problem confronting the courts has been when insider trading occurs and subsequently the issue arises as to the type of benefit the tipper of the information must receive in order to be held liable criminally. However, before attempting to explain this vexing area of the law it is first necessary to state some core principles of securities law in the United States. First, in order for any liability to arise there first must be trading on material inside information. "Information" means information of a factual, objective, scientific, and historical nature, and not mere rumors, speculation, opinions, or predictions. "Material" means the information will be likely to affect the price of the stock up-or-down. And "inside" means the information is confidential, secret, and, obviously, not public. Assuming the predicate of material inside information there have been in the history of U.S. jurisprudence two competing legal theories dealing with the liability of trading on inside information. One is called the narrow or insider theory; and the other is called the broad or level-playing-field theory. Under the broad theory there would be culpability for trading on inside information no matter how the information was acquired. However, the current and prevailing legal theory is the narrow one. Pursuant to the narrow theory there are three types of people who can be liable for trading on inside information: 1) misappropriators, that is, people who steal, hack, eavesdrop, or bribe to obtain the information; 2) insiders, that is, company directors, officers, employees as well as "outsiders" who have a professional relationship with the company, such as its lawyers, accountants, stock brokers, and financial printers; and 3) tippees of insiders, that is, people in conspiracy with insiders who have communicated the information by the company insiders. As noted, a problem in the field of securities law has been to determine what exactly the insider has to receive or how the insider must benefit from the trading by the tippee for there to be liability.

There are four important cases to examine; two are Supreme Court cases and two are from the U.S. Courts of Appeal. The first is the Supreme Court case of *Dirks v. the United States* where the court first dealt with the issue of what type of benefit must accrue to the insider tippee for there to be criminal liability. The court in *Dirks* emphasized that a violation of the law could arise when an insider makes a gift of confidential information to a relative, friend, or someone the insider has a personal relationship with, even a casual friendship.

However, in the Second Circuit Court of Appeals case of *Newman v. the United States* the court narrowed the *Dirks* ruling by holding that the benefit to the insider tipper had to be objective, consequential, and represent a pecuniary gain, real or potential, or something of a similarly valuable nature. Without money going back to the tipper there would be no liability. Thus, according to the court, being a friend of the tipper or even a relative would be insufficient if the insider tipper did not receive something of value. The court in *Newman* was concerned that an overly broad interpretation of insider trading law would give the federal government prosecutors too much power to charge people with questionable, perhaps unethical conduct, which was not technically illegal.

Next, in the 2016 case of *Salman v. the United States*, the Supreme Court, in upholding an insider trading conviction of a California man, unanimously ruled that an insider tipper can be held liable for insider trading even when the tipper who provided the tip did not receive any money or even did not try to make any money. The court thus rejected the appeals court decision in *Newman* saying that their narrow interpretation of the law was a mistake. The *Salman* case dealt with a tip originally provided by Maher Kara, at the time a Citigroup Investment banker, who gave the information to his brother, who passed it on to his brother-in-law, Bassam Salman, who made over $1.5 million in trades. The court stated that it is enough for criminal liability if the insider provided the information as a gift to a tippee who is likely to trade on it. The court thus rejected a ruling from the court of appeals in the *Newman* case that held that the insider tipper must receive something of pecuniary or similarly valuable nature. The personal relationship of being a friend or relative with the tipper would be sufficient for a "benefit" for the tipper. Justice Samuel Alito, who wrote the opinion for the court, focused on the conduct of the tipper and the fact that he violated a duty of trust and confidence to his employer, Citigroup, as opposed to the tipper receiving a financial benefit. Accordingly, the decision will prevent insiders from giving an advantage to their friends and relatives at the expense of the trading public who would not have access to the tipper's information.

Moreover, in 2017, in the case of *Martona v. the United States*, the Second Circuit Court of Appeals considerably broadened insider trading liability by holding that the government no longer needed to show a meaningful and close personal relationship between the provider of the inside information, the tipper, and the recipient of the information, the tippee. The court further provided an example, to wit: a situation where a business person gives an inside to his doorman as an end-of-year gift which would be construed as illegal insider trading even if the insider and the doorman were not friends. The ruling materially expands the liability of a person who passes on inside information to another person. However, it is still the law that if one happens on inside information accidentally or by luck or happenstance there is no insider trading liability and one can legally trade on the information that one fortuitously and propitiously came upon. Accordingly, the critical distinction in the law holds, that is, that insider trading is illegal, but trading on inside information *may* be legal.

Securities and Exchange Act of 1994

The Securities and Exchange Act of 1994, as amended by the U.S. Congress in 1995, in Section 10A imposed significant new duties on auditors to investigate, detect, and report illegal acts committed by their clients. Specifically, unless the illegality is clearly inconsequential, the auditor is required to disclose to the client's management and audit committee the illegal act. Moreover, if the management of the firm fails to take timely and proper remedial action to correct the illegal activity, the auditor must report the illegal act to the firm's board of directors; but only if the illegal conduct would have a material effect on the client's financial statements and the auditor intends to issue a non-standard audit report or intends to resign for the audit engagement. Finally, once the auditor reports the matter to the firm's board of directors, if the board does not notify the Securities and Exchange Commission of the auditor's conclusion within one business day, then the auditor must notify the Securities and Exchange Commission on the next business day.

Private Securities Litigation Reform Act of 1995

Mention must be made of the Private Securities Litigation Reform Act of 1995. As noted, there is liability under federal securities laws for misrepresenting as well as omitting material facts, but generally there is no liability for "mere" opinions or predictions since they are not "facts." Nonetheless, companies were reticent to make future projections of financial results, due to the fear of being sued if the projections were not accurately forecast. There is, plainly, a "fine-line" between an opinion/prediction and a fact, especially when the former are based in part on the latter. Therefore, the U.S. Congress passed the 1995 Act to in essence give companies a "safe harbor" to make such forecasts. Specifically, the Act legally protects "forward-looking" statements if they contain "meaningful cautionary statements" which explain why the projections may not be achieved or that the statements were made without the knowledge that they were misleading. Significantly, the 1995 statute also changed the liability rules to benefit accountants and other professionals. The Act made it more difficult for plaintiffs to bring class action lawsuits. Furthermore, the act replaced the traditional legal principle of "joint and several" liability (where any one of culpable defendants could be made to pay the plaintiff's entire judgment regardless of degree of fault) with a rule of proportionate liability where a defendant need only pay that part of the plaintiff's judgment equivalent to the defendant's degree of fault. However, there is an exception whereby the traditional "joint and several" rule is imposed when the defendant acted in a knowingly wrongful manner.

Criminal Liability

Accountants as well as other professionals and members of the public can be held criminally liable under federal and state laws, especially securities laws. Section 24 of the 1933 Act makes it a crime for any person to make an intentional false statement of material fact in a registration statement filed with the SEC. It is also a crime for any person to purposefully omit any material fact that would be necessary to ensure that the registration statement is not misleading. Since accountants typically certify the financial statements included with registration statements, accountants are exposed to criminal liability pursuant to this section of the 1933 Act. The 1933 Act contains criminal penalties of fines up to $10,000 and imprisonment for up to five years, or both. Pursuant to the 1934 Act, in addition to the criminal penalties mentioned in the preceding discussion, Section 32(a) of the 1934 Act makes it a crime for any person intentionally and knowingly to make or cause to be made any false or misleading statement in any application, document, or report given to the SEC. Again, like the 1933 Act, accountants are exposed to criminal liability due to the types of material (audited annual financial statements and reviewed quarterly financial statements) provided to the SEC. Under Section 32(a), criminal penalties include fines of up to $1 million and imprisonment of up to 10 years, or both.

The Sarbanes-Oxley Act substantially increases the penalties for securities fraud and related crimes. Specifically, Section 906 holds that a CEO or CFO who certifies a financial report or statement filed with the SEC and who knows that the report or statement does not fulfill SOX reporting requirements can be subject to up to $1 million in fines and up to 10 years in prison, or both. In addition, if the CEO of CFO willfully certifies a report knowing that it is does not fulfill SOX requirements, the CEO or CFO is subject to a penalty of up to $5 million in fines and 20 years in prison, or both. Section 801, which was a major result of the shredding activities of the Enron era accounting firm, Arthur Andersen, imposes criminal penalties, including fines and/or imprisonment for not more than 20 years, on anyone, including auditors, "…who knowingly alters, destroys, or makes a false entry in any record or document with the intent to impede, obstruct, or influence…" any government investigation. Furthermore, this section requires auditors to retain their working papers for at least five years from the date of the financial statements being audited or reviewed. Section 1106 of the Act increases the penalties for willful securities law violations of the 1934 Act, in particular by increasing the fines up to $5 million and an individual's imprisonment up to 20 years. Section 1107 deals with retaliation against whistleblowing employees, although in the statute Congress used, to the dismay of the authors of this book, the pejorative term "informants" is used instead of the neutral term "whistleblowers." Regardless, the penalties are very severe for an employer of a publicly traded firm who retaliates against a whistleblower. The Act decrees a punishment of a fine as well as up to 10 years in prison, or both, for knowingly and purposefully taking any adverse action against a person, including interfering with a person's lawful employment or livelihood, for making whistleblowing disclosures or assisting with a government investigation. Of particular importance to accountants is the SOX provision that holds that if there is a securities filing accompanied by a false or misleading certified audit statement, the accountant can be fined up to $5 million and imprisoned up to 20 years, or both.

Criminal liability can also be imposed against accountants, other professionals, and members of the public pursuant to the Racketeer Influenced and Corrupt Practices Act (RICO) and the Internal Revenue Code. Pursuant to RICO, securities fraud can be construed as a "racketeering" activity; and thus the government can institute a RICO prosecution in addition to the securities fraud criminal case. RICO also authorizes private civil lawsuits for damages (as well as permitting triple damages) for RICO violations (but only if a defendant has been criminally convicted). However, for a third party independent contractor, such as an accountant (or lawyer or other professional), to be liable civilly under RICO, he or she must have participated in the management or operation of the business or enterprise. The Internal Revenue Code imposes criminal liability on accountants and other professionals who prepare federal tax returns. Aiding and assisting in the preparation of a false tax return is a felony punishable by a fine of up to $100,000 (and up to $500,000 in the case of a corporation), and imprisonment up to three years, or both. Criminal fines also range from $250 for the negligent understatement to $1,000 for the willful understatement of a client's tax liability. The Code also imposes a fine up to $1,000 per document for an accountant's aiding and abetting a person's understatement of tax liability (and for corporations, the penalty is increased up to $10,000). Furthermore, accountants who violate the Act can be prevented by means of an injunction from further federal income tax practice.

State Laws
In the United States today, not only the federal government, but all the states have their own bodies of securities laws, which usually parallel the federal laws. These laws regulate the theoretically purely intrastate purchase or sale of securities, but characteristically are employed in securities cases in which the federal government has declined jurisdiction. Thus, it is quite conceivable for both the federal government and a state government to have concurrent jurisdiction of a securities case; and as a matter of fact, the federal securities laws specifically preserve state remedies. The purposes of the state laws are to prevent the issuance and sale of worthless securities and to protect the investing public from fraudulent and deceptive practices. State securities laws colloquially are referred to as "blue sky" laws, which title plainly indicates their main objective of preventing the sale of securities as worthless as the blue sky! Although it is beyond the purposes of this book to examine all the states' securities laws, a few common features should be pointed out. First, as noted, the state statutes are usually patterned after the federal statutes, especially as to the anti-fraud and insider trading prohibitions. Second, most states regulate securities brokers and dealers. Third, most states provide for the registration of securities offered or issued within the state with an appropriate state agency or official, together with the filing of

detailed background and financial information, unless there is a state exemption. Finally, most states take the approach of the federal government and "merely" mandate that certain disclosures be made before stock is offered for sale. Most states thus will not pass judgment as to the wisdom of a particular stock investment. However, there are a few states that have fairness standards that a company must meet in order to sell its stock in the state; and if these standards are not complied with, the state can forbid by virtue of its "police power" the issuance of the securities. Similarly, it is possible for a state to provide more securities law protection than the federal government. Finally, many states have now adopted the Uniform Securities Act, which makes it a criminal offense for accountants and others to intentionally file fraudulent financial statements and other reports.

Confidentiality and Privilege

Accountants and attorneys are regarded as members of a profession in a fiduciary relationship with their clients. One of the characteristics of this professional relationship is a duty of confidentiality. The legal system also recognizes this duty of confidentiality as a legal privilege, but to a much greater degree for lawyers than accountants.

Attorney-Client Relationship

The *attorney-client privilege* is the privilege a client has to reveal information given to his or her attorney in confidence without fear of disclosure. The common law has long recognized such a privilege. The privilege is also constitutionally protected on the federal and state levels by the right against self-incrimination and the right to legal counsel. In order for a person to secure effective legal representation, and particularly to obtain a viable defense to criminal prosecution, the client must feel confident that he or she can fully tell the attorney the facts of the case without any apprehension that the attorney will be called as a witness against the client. If such a privilege was not recognized by the law, then the attorney could be called to testify against his or her client, and consequently the client might decide to withhold critical information from their attorney. Not only the client but also the attorney can raise this privilege. The privilege will then protect the confidentiality of communications between the client and his or her lawyer from being used in a lawsuit or prosecution. However, for the privilege to work, the communication must be made to the attorney in his or her capacity as an attorney, and not as a family member, friend, or informal advisor.

Accountant-Client Relationship

Although the rationales for the legal privilege arguably are just as compelling for the accountant and his or her client, the legal status of the *accountant-client privilege* is definitely more problematic. The reason is a significant Supreme Court case in 1973, called *Couch v. United States*, where the court refused to find a corresponding privilege under federal law for accountants and their clients. Accordingly, an accountant could be compelled to be a witness against his or her client pursuant to federal law, for example, tax and securities law, including criminal prosecutions. However, several states in the United States now have enacted statutes to create the accountant-client privilege. For example, some states have work product immunity statutes for accountants, which would prohibit the discovery of the accountant's working papers prepared for the client in lawsuit against the client. Of course, those privilege and immunity statutes would apply just to state legal proceedings and only in those states that have recognized the privilege. Finally, it must be mentioned that the accountant's work papers prepared in the course of the CPA's engagement are the property of the auditor and not the client. However, the books and records of the client, which may include certain working papers of the CPA that are deemed to constitute books and records of the client, are in fact the property of the client.

Practical Recommendations for Avoiding Legal Liability

As one can clearly discern from the preceding legal explication of the potential liability of an accountant, the prudent professional must know the law and the standards of the accounting profession; and he or she would also be very well advised to take heed of the following very practical suggestions on how to avoid legal problems and thus legal liability.

1. An accountant should never promise more than he or she can deliver. Accountants often fall into the habit of trying to please their clients by telling them, usually untruthfully, that their work will be prioritized. Thus, when their work is completed later than was promised or anticipated, the result is an unhappy client; and unhappy clients are more apt to sue.
2. Do not take on work that you cannot competently complete. That is, know your limitations.
3. Screen your new clients; and do not accept ones that appear to be unethical. More practically, if a current client exhibits unethical behavior, cease your engagement with that client.
4. Make notes for the client's file of all telephone conversations. This procedure is particularly important when the client verbally communicates tax or accounting information. You need to be able to show the source of all information you used in performing the agreed upon services. As a senior partner told the co-author of this chapter during his first months in the CPA profession, "A short note is better than the longest memory." Remember, if you are sued, the client's file and working papers need to "stand alone" as proof of your "due care."
5. While written engagement letters are required for audits and reviews, they also are recommended for other types of engagements. There should be a clear understanding between you and the client regarding the service you are performing. Thus, for example, it should be clear that you are performing a compilation engagement, instead of a review or audit, and that the financial statements are based entirely on the information provided by the client. In the same regard, it is advisable to have taxpayers "sign off" that they have provided you with the complete and accurate information needed to prepare their tax return in order that they understand that they are solely responsible for the accuracy of the return, and that they reviewed the tax return before it was signed or electronically transmitted to the IRS.
6. You should make it a practice to promptly return telephone calls and e-mails. In addition to this practice being just "good business" (in that it tells the

client that his work is important, no matter how small the job), it may also help you avoid missing deadlines or failing to give the client time sensitive advise.

7. Do not joke around about tax evasion. You need to make it clear to the client from the very first day of an engagement that you are not going to be a party to doing anything that does not abide by the rule and spirit of the law.

8. Use a "tickler" system (manual or computerized) to avoid missing critical due dates. The missing of IRS deadlines for filing and paying the IRS is a major area of litigation for CPAs.

9. Do not start down the "slippery slope" of unethical conduct. If the client knows that you will overlook small errors/discrepancies, the amounts of the errors and the frequency of their occurrence are bound to grow. Do not even start down this path. Let the client know from the very first day of an engagement that you are meticulous, and thus will not overlook even the slightest unethical or illegal act. Honest and ethical behavior is definitely the best long term policy, and the policy that will minimize your exposure to legal problems.

10. You should be very careful with clients that are potentially insolvent. Once they go bankrupt, the creditors and other stakeholders will be looking to recover from anyone with "deep pockets." That includes you as the accountant as well as your malpractice insurance carrier.

11. When working on a tax or accounting engagement that may involve the client having committed an illegal act, be sure to work through an attorney. You should sign a "three cornered" agreement with an attorney so that you have privileged communication with the client. With such an agreement, the accountant becomes a subcontractor (agent) of the attorney and thus shares his or her privilege. Without such an agreement, you may be called on in a criminal proceeding to testify against your client. Recall that the accountant-client privilege is definitely not as extensive and protective as the attorney-client one.

12. You must maintain your professional competence. While this standard is a general requirement of being a professional accountant, it is particularly important if the practitioner is specializing in a particular niche. For example, if you are specializing in working with real estate agents, you need to not only keep current on the tax laws that affect such agents' returns, but also keep up to date on what is happening in the real estate business. That is, you not only need to know the tax and accounting laws and standards that apply to your niche, you also need to know your clients and their industry.

13. All tax and accounting work must be adequately supervised. This requirement includes the checking of work completed by everyone in the firm. Thus, all work that includes compilations, reviews, audits, and tax work needs to be checked by a person other than the one that completed it. A second "set of eyes" looking at work can avoid costly mistakes. The correcting of mistakes before the work "gets out the door" will raise the quality standards of the firm and show due diligence in the performance of engagements. Nothing should leave the firm without it having been

competently checked. The accountant's mantras should be supervise, supervise, supervise, and check, check, check.

14. When performing any engagement, follow up on "red flags" (clues of a problem). While this procedure is particularly important in an audit, it is also important when performing any accounting or tax service. Ignoring clues of a problem may result in accusations that your engagement lacked the due care that would have been used by other reasonably prudent accountants.

15. When doing accounting or tax work, if the client fails to provide you with all of the information needed to complete the engagement, make a list of the missing documents or data. Then, as subsequent information is provided, note where the information came from, the date it was received, and the method of delivery. This process is especially important when dealing with verbally communicated information.

16. While communicating with the predecessor auditor is required by Generally Accepted Auditing Standards, it is also important that the accountant communicate with prior accountants when performing accounting engagements. As part of the start-up procedures for a new client, have them sign a release form that allows the predecessor accountant to not only provide you with various documents or copies of working papers, but also to verbally communicate with you. In addition to providing a "clean" transition, this procedure may help the CPA firm avoid association with an unethical client.

17. Treat your clients as you would want to be treated. For example, when billing for your services, ask yourself, if you were the client getting the bill, how would you react? Would you think that the bill was fair? If not, either revise the bill or try to answer any potential objections up front. Clients that know you are a fair person are apt to talk to you about a problem they have with you, instead of first seeking legal advice. Maintaining good communication with a client is imperative to avoiding legal problems.

18. No matter how careful you are, you may still be confronted with legal liability. Thus, it is imperative that you maintain adequate insurance coverage. It is "best" to assume that you will be sued on each and every engagement. With this attitude, you will take the defensive actions necessary to avoid getting into legal difficulties.

19. Retain client-prepared tax organizers and copies of source documents used in preparing tax returns. It is suggested that any interview notes made by the accountant be clearly indicated (possibly in a color different from the client's writing), thereby specifying answers given by the client to verbal inquiries.

20. Do not help the tax client estimate (without a reasonable basis) critical tax return or accounting numbers! For example, if a self-employed taxpayer, who uses his or her car extensively in his or her business fails to provide a realistic number for the business miles traveled, do not accept a verbally provided estimate, such as about 70% or about the same as last year. You, as the professional, know that the taxpayer is required to keep a contemporaneous written record of his or her business travel mileage. By accepting a verbal estimate that is used in preparing the tax return and by

checking "yes" to the questions about whether the taxpayer has the required documentation, the accountant is potentially aiding the taxpayer in filing a false tax return. Moreover, by accepting "rough" numbers instead of demanding accurate numbers, you are communicating to the client that the accuracy of accounting and tax numbers is not that important. If or when the client subsequently gets into trouble with the IRS or some other regulatory agency, the client's defense is apt to be that you are the one, not the client, that falsified the numbers.

21. It is imperative that an accountant at all times follows the applicable professional standards: for example, Generally Accepted Accounting Principles (GAAP), Generally Accepted Auditing Standards (GAAS), Statements of Standards for Accounting and Review Engagements, Statements of Standards for Tax Services, and Public Company Accounting Oversight Board (PCAOB) Standards and Related Rules.

22. Ethical behavior is not an option, it is a necessity. An unethical accountant will not long avoid legal problems. Accordingly, it is imperative that accountants abide by applicable codes of professional conduct: for example, the American Institute of Certified Public Accountants (AICPA) Code of Professional Conduct for CPAs, the International Federation of Accountants (IFAC) Code of Ethics for Professional Accountants, the Institute of Management Accountants (IMA) Code of Ethics for management accountants, etc.

By adhering to these legal and ethical norms, following these practical suggestions, as well as by using his or her common sense, the prudent accountant will be able to professionally serve his or her clients in an efficient and effective manner as well as uphold the legal and ethical standards of the accounting profession.

Summary

This chapter has examined the legal liability of the accountant as well as other professionals under a variety of laws – federal and state, statutory and common law, civil and criminal. Regarding the liability of the accountant for negligence to third parties, this chapter underscored that there are three competing legal theories, and thus the prudent reader is well advised to check his or her state's law to determine which legal approach applies. This chapter also underscored the very important Sarbanes-Oxley Act of 2002, and discussed how it impacted corporate governance, the securities laws, and the accounting profession. This chapter compared and contrasted the privilege of confidentiality and non-disclosure between lawyers and their clients and accountants and their clients. Finally, this chapter provided certain practical recommendations for the accountant to avoid legal liability.

Discussion Questions

1. What are the three major common law legal theories that would impact the liability of the accountant? How could they be applied to accountants?

2. What are the three competing legal theories dealing with the liability of a negligent accountant to third parties? Which one is preferable? Why?

3. Why is the Securities Act of 1933 known as a disclosure type of law? Provide examples of stock offerings subject to the 1934 Act and the types of disclosure required.
4. How can the accountant be civilly and criminally liable under the 1933 Act? Provide examples along with a brief discussion thereof.
5. How can the accountant be civilly and criminally liable under the 1934 Act? Provide examples along with a brief discussion thereof.
6. What is the difference between insider trading and trading on inside information? Why is that distinction critical pursuant to U.S. securities laws? Provide an example of each along with a brief explanation thereof.
7. Who is an "insider" pursuant to U.S. securities law? Why is that definition critical when it comes to liability under the securities laws? Provide an example of an accountant as an insider along with a brief discussion thereof.
8. What is the difference between an "inadvertent tippee" and an "inadvertent tippee" under a fiduciary duty? Why is that distinction a critical one in U.S. securities laws? Provide an accounting example of both types along with a brief explanation thereof.
9. How can the "lucky" and the "smart" legally trade on inside information? Provide examples with a brief discussion thereof. Is it morally fair to legally allow ANY trading on inside information? Why or why not?
10. Discuss some of the ways that the Sarbanes-Oxley Act (SOX) has impacted the accounting profession. Provide examples along with brief explanations thereof.
11. Discuss some of the ways that the Sarbanes-Oxley Act (SOX) has impacted corporate governance. Provide examples along with brief explanations thereof.
12. How does SOX treat the issues of corporate whistleblowing and codes of ethics? How would the accountant be affected by this aspect of SOX? Provide examples with brief explanations thereof.
13. Compare and contrast the attorney-client privilege with the accountant-client privilege. Provide examples. Why is the distinction important?
14. What are some of the ways that accountants can avoid legal liability? Provide examples with brief explanations thereof.

15 – Wills and Trusts

This chapter reviews two important areas of the law, wills and trusts, which are important subject matters not only for their business, estate planning, and tax and accounting applications, but also for their personal family ramifications. The two legal areas, wills and trusts, are treated separately for academic purposes in two distinct sections to the chapter, but in the "real-world" they are often interrelated, especially because, as will be seen, one very common way of creating a trust is by means of a will. It is also very important to point out that these two important areas of the law are governed in detail by state laws, which may differ. Thus, this chapter will provide certain fundamental concepts and general rules applicable to these legal areas. Naturally, one must consult his or her own state's law to determine the exact legal rules that apply to a will or trust situation.

Part I – Wills

Intestate Descent and Distribution
Before one can examine the legal concept of a will, traditionally called a Will and Testament, one must be cognizant of the laws of *intestate descent and distribution*, that is, the rules governing the disposition of property upon one's death when one dies without having a will. Initially, it should be noted that most states make no distinction between real and personal property in descent and distribution; moreover, the terms "heirs" and "next of kin" are treated synonymously. Other important terms to be aware of are: lineal v. collateral heirs, and *per capita* v. *per stirpes* distribution. *Lineal heirs* are people who stem from one another in a line which includes the intestate decedent, for example, one's mother and father, and grandmother and grandfather. *Collateral heirs* stem not from each other, but from a common ancestor, for example, one's brother and sister or one's cousins. *Per capita* distribution means that if the relationship among all members in a class of "takers" is the same, for example, all are children of the decedent, then they all take the same equal share. *Per stirpes* means that when a relationship between "takers" is unequal, then each person takes by

representation, that is, a person takes his or her ancestor's share. For example, a decedent leaves one son and two grandchildren by a previously deceased daughter; the son takes one half of the estate, and the grandchildren take one quarter each, that is, they split their deceased mother's share.

All states have a statutory pattern for the intestate distribution of the property of an intestate decedent (and also for the undisposed property of a testate decedent). If there is a surviving spouse, and no lineal descendants, all of the estate goes to the surviving spouse. If there are lineal descendants, and all of them are also lineal descendants of the spouse, then typically the surviving spouse gets one half of the estate. The remaining one half of the estate (or the entire estate if there is no surviving spouse) goes to the lineal descendants *per stirpes*; if there are no lineal descendants, the estate goes to the decedent's mother and father equally; and if neither to the decedent's brothers and sisters and their descendants. However, if there are none of the foregoing situations, the estate usually is divided into two shares, with one share going to the decedent's maternal kindred or her survivors and the other going to the paternal kindred or his survivors. If there is no one to inherit the estate, the estate goes to the kindred of the last deceased spouse of the decedent. Three special intestate cases are "half-bloods," adopted children, and illegitimate children. A half-blood is a child having one, but not both parents in common. Usually, a half-blood inherits only one half as a whole blood. An adopted child, however, is treated as a natural child of the adopted parents for intestate descent and distribution. An illegitimate child is considered a lineal descendant of his or her mother; but only a lineal descendant of the father if the natural parents participated in a marriage ceremony before or after the child's birth, or paternity has been established by legal adjudication. Finally, it should be noted that simultaneous death, for example, of a husband and wife in a plane crash, means that the property of each person is disposed of as if he or she had survived.

Execution of Wills

A *will* or *will and testament* is a legal instrument disposing the property of one's estate that only takes effect on the death of its maker; it "speaks at the time of death." A *testator* is the person who executes a will. In order to be admitted to probate, a will must either dispose of property, appoint an executor (or in some states a personal representative), or revoke another instrument. *Testamentary intent* is a requirement for a valid will. Testamentary intent means that that the testator must have had the intention to make a particular instrument his or her will. Moreover, present intent is required; that is, the testator must have the present testamentary intent to make a will now. Consequently, there is no such thing as a future will; that is, a written statement of one's intention to make a will in the future is not legally sufficient. There are several formalities for a will. These requirements are set forth in state statutory law. Generally speaking, however, a valid will requires the following formalities: First, a writing is required; and any type of writing material is usually permissible. Second, the signature of the testator is required. Any mark affixed by the testator, or by another in the testator's presence and at the testator's request and direction, will suffice so long as the testator possesses the intent that the mark operate as the signature of the testator. Where should the testator sign? Typically, state laws require that a will be *subscribed*, which means signed at the end. Consequently, if there are provisions after the signature of the testator, the general rule is that the will is invalid since it was not subscribed. However, there is an exception if the provisions after the testator's signature are merely "formal" and not substantive or dispositive, for example, the date of the will, maps, a statement that the executor serve without bond (but not the appointment of an executor as most states would construe such a provision to be substantive). Third, *publication* is required. Publication occurs when the testator declares to witnesses that the instrument is his or her will. Fourth, *attestation* by competent witnesses is required. The rule of law is that the witnesses must attest that the testator signed the will in the presence of the witnesses, all of whom were present at the same time. Therefore, typically the law will require: 1) a signing by the testator in the joint presence of witnesses; and 2) the witnesses signing in the presence of each other and in the presence of the testator. However, it is important to note that the "single continuous transaction" rule, which holds that if the witnesses signed before the testator signed, the will is still valid if the signings occurred as part of a single continuous transaction. Characteristically, witnesses must sign at the end of the will after all the provisions of the will as well as the testator's signature. Most states will require at least two witnesses for a valid will. The witnesses must be physically and legally competent; that is, they must be able to observe the testator signing and comprehend the nature of the testator's act. In some states, a witness is allowed to be a beneficiary of the will, and thus the will is valid and the witness' provisions thereunder valid too. Finally, mention should be made of a *holographic will*, which is an unattested will completely in the testator's handwriting and signed, and a *noncupative will*, which is an oral will. In most states, these types of wills are not recognized.

Revocation of Wills
As a general rule, a testator is entitled to revoke his or her will at any time prior to death. There are three principal revocation areas to examine: 1) revocation by written instrument, 2) revocation by physical act performed on the will, and 3) revocation by operation of the law. The first category is revocation by written instrument. An express revocation by a subsequent instrument is recognized by the law. The rule of law is that a will may be revoked in whole or in part by the express terms of a later written instrument. The instrument can be a will or an amendment to a will, called a codicil (which will be covered shortly). Even partial revocation by the express terms of a subsequent instrument is permissible. Moreover, an implied revocation by subsequent instrument also is permissible. The rule is that a will may be revoked in whole or in part by implication from the terms of a subsequent inconsistent instrument. For example, A in her first will gives all her property to B; but in A's second will gives all her property to C; thus, even without any express revocation clause, C gets all the property. Note, also, that any non-inconsistent provisions will remain in force and will not be revoked. For example, in her first will A gives all her property to B; in her second will, A gives her house to C, her classic auto to D, and her diamond ring to E; thus, with no express revoking clause in the second will, both wills are read together, meaning the specific devises are valid, and B obtains the residue of the estate. The second area to examine, which is a major problem area under revocation of wills, is the revocation of a will by a physical act performed on

the will. There are two requirements to have a valid physical revocation: 1) the will must be burnt, torn, cancelled, defaced, obliterated, or destroyed; and 2) the testator must possess the simultaneous intent to presently revoke the instrument. It is important to relate that the majority rule in the United States forbids a partial revocation by physical act. That is, crossing out or interlining a portion of the will is legally ineffective; and accordingly the part attempted to be revoked may be admitted into probate, if it can be recreated, of course. Furthermore, it must be noted that the revocation of a will revokes all amendments/codicils to the will, but the act of revocation of an amendment/codicil to a will does not revoke the will, even if the testator so intended. The third category to examine is revocation by operation of the law. In such a case, the law deems that the testator would not want his or her will to stand. Marriage is the first situation. The testator makes a will and then gets married. In such a case, the law holds that the will is not revoked, but the surviving spouse gets his or her intestate share. Birth of children is another circumstance. The testator makes a will, and then a child is born or adopted after the execution of the will. The law holds that the will is not revoked, but the child gets his or her intestate share. Divorce is a major problem area. The general rule is that a divorce revokes a provision in a will in favor of the divorced spouse when the will was executed prior to the divorce.

Components of a Will – Codicils and other Instruments and Documents
The most important legal concept to examine in this section is the *codicil* to a will. A codicil is a testamentary instrument executed with the same formalities as a will, executed subsequent to the will, which typically modifies, alters, or expands the will. Initially, it must be noted that a codicil can "save" a will; that is, if the original will was not legally sufficient, but then the testator subsequently executes a codicil, the will and the codicil are read together and treated as a single testamentary instrument executed on the date of the codicil. The original will is thus made to "speak" on the date of the codicil. It is also permissible for a document, for example, a separate list disposing of the testator's personal property, to be incorporated into a will by reference, and thus be considered part of the will, but only if it is in existence at the time the will was executed and the document is sufficiently described in the will. Oral instructions by the testator, however, cannot be incorporated into a will since a writing is required. Finally, it is permissible in a will for the testator to devise property to a trust so long as the trust was created before or concurrently with the will, existed at the time of the testator's death, the trust was clearly identified in the testator's will, and in some states that some trust property was transferred to the trust during the life of the testator.

Will Substitutes
The three main substitutes to a will are the joint ownership of property, both real and personal, the use of deeds to transfer real property, and the device of a trust. The first two will substitutes were covered in the Real Property chapter to this book, and the important legal concept of a trust will be covered shortly in the next major part to this chapter.

Restrictions on Testation – Family Protection

The most important restriction on testation is a statutory one, found in most states, usually called the *elective share*. The elective share rule maintains that if a surviving spouse is dissatisfied with not only his or her provisions in a will but also if no will the intestate share of the estate, the surviving spouse may elect to take an elective share of the estate, typically 30%. This share is in lieu of any interest under the will or by means of intestacy; and the share only applies to property owned by the decedent at his or her death. Moreover, in many states, either by statute or constitutional provision, real property deemed to be a "homestead" cannot be subject to a devise by a testator/owner if the testator is survived by a spouse or a minor child or children (except if there is no minor child/children, the testator may devise the homestead to his or her surviving spouse). Finally, in many states, charitable devises in a will executed six months prior to the testator's death may be voidable by the testator's surviving spouse or his or her lineal descendants. There is one exception, though, and that is when the testator in a prior will had a similar charitable devise.

Restrictions on the Power of Testation

There are five principal legal doctrines to consider when discussing restrictions on the power of testation: 1) testamentary capacity, 2) undue influence, 3) fraud, 4) mistake, and 5) ambiguities in wills. First, *testamentary capacity* means the requisite legal degree of mental capacity to make a will. The rule of law is that in order to have the mental capacity to make a will, the testator must know and understand the following: a) the nature and extent of his or her property, b) the natural objects of his or her bounty, c) the disposition he or she is making, d) and how to interrelate the above factors and form an orderly scheme of disposition. A person, it must be emphasized, must have this mental capacity at the making of his or her will, and not at the time of death. A person, however, can have testamentary capacity, but nonetheless suffer from an insane delusion. That is, a person may have the sufficient mental capacity to make a will, but may be suffering from an insane delusion so as to invalidate the will or a portion of the will, for example, a particular gift. The rule is that the will or provision would be set aside to the extent the delusion caused the testamentary disposition. An insane delusion is a conception of reality which has no foundation in reality and is not supported by any evidence. Note, finally, that the burden of proof as to mental capacity is on the person contesting the will; that is, the testator is presumed to be sane. Second, *undue influence* will render a will or a provision in a will invalid. Undue influence means that the will or the provision was obtained through force, duress, menace, or a degree of persuasion exerted on another which is sufficient to destroy the testator's free will and true intentions. Again, the burden is on the person contesting the will. However, a presumption of undue influence arises when: a) there is a confidential relationship, for example, attorney and client, or a close personal relationship, caretaker and ward, between the testator and the beneficiary; b) the beneficiary participated in the procuring or drafting of the will; c) the will was retained by the principal beneficiary after its execution; and/or d) the provisions in the will are "unnatural," for example, the testator disinherits his children in favor of a "stranger." Finally, it should be noted that a will can fail partially or entirely due to the presence of undue influence. Third, fraud can cause a will or a particular gift in a will to be invalid. Fraud, generally, was covered in the Contracts and Torts chapters, and the distinction, applicable here, between fraud in the *factum* and fraud in the inducement was covered in the Commercial Paper chapter. Fourth, mistake, also applicable in the will context, was covered in the Contracts chapter too; yet it is important to note in the context herein that the majority of states will not provide relief if the testator makes a mistake as to the contents of a will. All, including the mistaken part, will be probated. Fifth and finally, if there is an ambiguity in a will, for example, two gifts to two nephews with only their same first name mentioned, or a gift to my granddaughter when the testator has two granddaughters, most states will allow extrinsic evidence to explain the ambiguity and construe the testator's intent. However, the old contact "plain meaning" rule is applicable to wills too. Accordingly, when the testator accurately and clearly describes a person or thing, no extrinsic evidence will be allowed to show that the testator meant a different meaning or thing. For example, if the testator makes a gift "to my cousin A," and the testator has a cousin A and a cousin B, the law will not permit B to introduce evidence to show that the testator really intended cousin B to take the gift.

Estate Administration and Probate

Estate administration and probate are very complex procedural and substantive areas of the law, as well as ones that are set forth specifically and in detail by the various states' laws; and as such any precise explication of these areas is beyond the scope of this book. Nevertheless, certain basic definitions, concepts, and principles must be pointed out. First is to define the *probate process*, which is the process where a will is legally proved. In most states, the Circuit Courts of the state have exclusive original jurisdiction; and the venue for probate is the county of the decedent's residence. Probate proceedings are commenced by the filing of a petition for administration. Any "interested person," that is, a person who may be reasonably affected by the probate proceedings, can file such a petition. To secure "proof of will," the petition must contain the oath of the witnesses, or if they are dead or unavailable, the oath of the personal representative or executor or any disinterested person that the writing offered for probate is in fact the will of the testator. A will, however, may be a *self-proving will*, which is one signed by the testator and the witnesses before a notary in accordance with state statutory requirements. Such a will can be admitted to probate without further proof. A personal representative must be appointed by the Probate Court. The *personal representative*, also called, depending on the state, the executor or administrator, must be appointed by the Probate Court. The petition for the administration of the estate will state the person whose appointment is sought. In a testate case, the person usually is named in the will; and in an intestate case, the person usually is the surviving spouse or a person selected by a majority of the heirs closest in degree to the decedent. The next major step is the publication, usually by the personal representative or executor, in a paper of local circulation of the *Notice of Administration*, also called the Letters of Administration. The type of paper for the notice and the time periods for the publication are set forth by state statute. The purpose is to give notice to all persons who may have claims or demands against the estate of the decedent so these people can file claims. There will also be a time limit to submit claims, which again is set by state law, and usually three months from the date the statutory notice was published, for people to file claims against the estate or objections to the will with the Probate Court. The duty of the personal representative is to secure the assets of the decedent and to preserve the estate. The personal representative, therefore, can take possession and control of the decedent's property; however, property can be surrendered to or left with the person entitled to it pursuant to the will or the laws of intestacy. The personal representative must take all steps necessary for the management, protection, and preservation of the estate. The personal representative is under an obligation not to commingle assets; that is, he or she must keep the decedent's estate separate from his or her own. There is also a duty to keep records, to file an inventory, and to hire attorneys, accountants, and appraisers if necessary. The personal representative must also pay the decedent's debts; and then as his or her main duty must distribute the decedent's estate. The personal representative is regarded as a fiduciary, and thus must exhibit good faith and fairness and avoid any conflicts of interest; and the personal representative is also held to a standard of reasonable care in the management of the estate. It should be noted that in most states a court order is needed for the personal representative to sell the decedent's real property. In most states, when the personal representative completes the administration, except for the distribution, he or she files a formal accounting and a petition for discharge with the Probate Court. If no objections are filed, the personal representative can distribute the estate without any court order. Finally, it should be noted that most states have special forms of administration, called *Summary* or *Family Administration*, for small estates, as defined by state statute, and not including any real property, when the beneficiaries of the decedent are the spouse and/or lineal descendants.

Distribution of the Decedent's Estate
The first area to deal with is the order of the payment of claims against the estate. State statutes will prescribe the order of payment of claims; and all claims must be provided for before the estate can be distributed. The order is as follows: 1) expenses of administration, 2) funeral expenses (usually with a maximum amount), 3) taxes and debts, 4) medical and hospital bills (usually from a prescribed time period before the decedent's death), 5) family allowances as determined by statute, 6) debts from a business continued after death, and 7) all other claims (for example, legal judgments against the decedent).

The second area to deal with is the classification of *devises* (or *bequeaths*) which is the name the law gives to the gifts a testator makes in his or her will. A *specific devise* is a gift of a particular object distinct from all other objects, for example, of a piece of described land or a diamond ring. Whereas, a *general devise* is a gift of general economic benefit payable out of the general assets of the estate, for example, a gift of "$10,000 to A." An important rule of law holds that if the testator does not have the cash at the time of his or her death, items in the estate must be sold by the personal representative to raise the cash. A *residuary devise* is a devise of what remains of the testator's estate. An important rule impacting only specific devises is the *ademption* rule, which maintains that a specific devise will be adeemed (that is, revoked) if it is not in the testator's estate at the time of his or her death, regardless of the testator's intent. Another important legal doctrine, which applies to all gifts, is called *abatement*. Abatement is the process of reducing gifts to beneficiaries because the testator's estate is not sufficient to pay all the estate obligations and gifts under the will. Any property not disposed of by the will is used first, then residuary gifts, next general gifts, and finally specific gifts. Finally, many states have *anti-lapse statutes*, which generally hold that if the recipient of a gift is a lineal descendant of the testator, and that person is dead at the execution of the will or fails to survive the testator, the gift to the descendant does not lapse (that is, fail), but rather the descendants of the deceased beneficiary of the testator take the gift *per stirpes* (that is, they take their deceased ancestor's share). The anti-lapse statute also usually applies when the testator makes a devise to a class of descendants and one of the class of beneficiaries has died. So, for example, the testator leaves $15,000 to his three children, A, B, and C; but B dies, leaving two children, D and E. Thus, A and C get $5000 each and D and E get their deceased parent's share, $2,500 each.

Part II – Trusts

Express Private Trusts

A *trust* is the transfer of legal title to property to another person, called the *trustee*, who is to manage the property for the benefit of the beneficiaries of trust. There are a variety of trusts that the law recognizes. The first to be examined, and the most common one, is the *express private trust*. An express private trust is a fiduciary relationship regarding property, real or personal, wherein the trustee holds legal title to the trust property (called at times the trust principal or *res*), subject to enforceable equitable rights in the beneficiary or beneficiaries of the trust. The trustee possesses legal title; the beneficiary or beneficiaries hold equitable title. The person who creates the trust is called the *settlor* (or at times the grantor, but *not* "settler").

An express private trust must have five elements: 1) an intention on the part of the settlor to create the trust; 2) a trustee; 3) trust property or *res*; 4) a beneficiary or beneficiaries; and 5) a valid trust purpose. It is important initially to underscore that no consideration is required to create a trust; it can be created gratuitously. Note also that the temporary absence of one element does not necessarily destroy the trust or prevent the creation of the trust.

First, for a valid trust, the intention on the part of the settlor to create a trust must be present. The manifestation of this intent is indispensable to the legal existence of the trust. When the trust *res* is real property, the intent must be evidenced by words; yet if personal property is the subject matter of the trust the words evidencing intent can be oral. For either, no particular form of language is necessary, so long as the intent is indicated. An important intent trust rule holds that the intention to create a trust must have been manifested by the settlor at the time the settlor owned the property. That is, one cannot convey property outright and then later execute a trust instrument declaring it a trust. Thus, there is no such thing as a future trust. The settlor must have intended for the trust to take effect immediately and not at such future time. However, the settlor does not have to communicate this future intent to the beneficiary; rather, delivery of the trust instrument and the manifestation of intent to the trustee are sufficient. Yet if the settlor is also the trustee, and no one is notified, the trust may fail for lack of intent unless the settlor has somehow segregated and identified the property as trust property. Another problem area regarding intent involves *precatory language* in the purported trust. Precatory language means that the transferor has merely expressed his or her hope, wish, or suggestion that the property be used for certain purposes, but with no requirement that the transferee actually do it. The rule of law is that precatory language does not create a trust since the intent by the settlor to clearly direct the trustee to carry out the terms of the trust is lacking.

The second requirement for a valid trust is a trustee. However, though a trustee is essential to a trust, a trust will not necessarily fail for the lack of a trustee. If a trustee dies, becomes incapacitated, resigns, or is removed, the rule of law is that a successor trustee will be appointed by the court. Yet there is an exception to the foregoing rule which can occur if there is an absence of a trustee in a trust of real property by deed because the trust may fail due to lack delivery of the deed, which requires a present and effective transfer. Another important rule of law regarding trusts is that the trustee must have some duties for a valid trust. That is, the trust must be an *active trust*, meaning that the trustee has duties, even if the trustee's only duties are to convey title to the beneficiaries. A *passive trust* is one in which the trustee has no duties; such a trust fails. Another important area of trust law concerns the court's power to remove a trustee. A court always has the power to remove the trustee; and the beneficiaries can compel removal but only on certain grounds, for example, conflict of interest, unfitness for position, crimes of dishonesty, insolvency of the trustee, and extreme friction and hostility between the trustee and beneficiaries. Finally, a trustee can refuse to accept a trust appointment, and for any reason too; however, once the trustee accepts the assignment, he or she cannot resign unless the trustee has the permission of the court, the resignation is authorized by the trust, or all the beneficiaries consent.

The third requirement of the trust is the presence of a trust *res* or *corpus* or principal. Because a trust involves the duties to manage specific property, there must be specific assets for the trust duties to relate to. Furthermore, the trust principal must be of existing property which the settlor has the power and right to convey. The property need not be tangible property, but the settlor must have an assignable interest. Consequently, property which the settlor expects to own in the future cannot be the subject of a present trust. Finally, the property must be adequately and specifically described in the trust. The fourth requirement for a valid trust is the presence of beneficiaries. The general rule is that a beneficiary or beneficiaries are necessary to the validity of every trust. The exception, as will be seen, deals with charitable and honorary trusts. There generally can be no valid trust without the beneficiaries who have the right to enforce the trust. A private express trust requires, therefore, definite beneficiaries or beneficiaries who will be definitely ascertainable. If a trust fails for the lack of beneficiaries, a resulting trust in favor of the settlor is created. The unascertained beneficiary precept means that the beneficiaries need not be identified at the time the trust was created; rather, they must be definitely ascertainable when their interests come into fruition. The classic example would be "unborn children" as beneficiaries; such a trust would be valid. The fifth and final requirement for a trust is trust purposes. The rule of law is that a trust can be created for any purpose not deemed contrary to the public policy of the state. For example, a trust that is illegal in subject matter or purpose, or calls for the commission of a tort, or engenders immorality or the neglect of parental, family, or civic duties, would be an invalid trust.

The Creation of Private Express Trusts

The first category of trusts to examine is the *inter vivos* trust, which is a trust created by a settlor when he or she is alive. An *inter vivos* trust can be created in two ways: 1) An *inter vivos* trust can be created by a present *declaration of trust*. A declaration of trust is a statement by the owner of the property that he or she holds the property as trustee in trust. This act creates an *inter vivos* trust with the settlor as trustee. 2) An *inter vivos* trust can be created by transfer of property by the settlor in his or her lifetime. A present transfer to the trustee is required; the trustee takes legal title upon the delivery of the deed to the trust property, document of title, or physical delivery of the property. Are there any formal requirements for a trust? If the subject matter of the trust is personal property, the Statute of Frauds will not require a written trust instrument. However, if the principal of the trust is real property, such as land, a written trust instrument will be required by the Statute of Frauds to make the trust effective. The second category of trusts to examine is testamentary trusts. A *testamentary trust* is one created by a person's will. In order to create a trust by will, the essentials of the trust must be ascertainable in ways permissible by a state's will statutes. If a will reveals the existence of a trust, but not its terms, the usual remedy is for a court to impose a constructive trust for the benefit of the beneficiaries of the trust, and if they cannot be determined a constructive trust is imposed for the benefit of the testator's estate.

Charitable and Honorary Trusts

A *charitable trust* is a trust for the benefit of society, the public, the community, or for some indefinite portion thereof. Such a trust must have a charitable purpose. It is critical to note that for such a trust the beneficiary or beneficiaries must be indefinite. The permissible recipients must be unnamed and a changing class, for example, the "needy," and not particular individuals, even if very poor. The charitable purpose, moreover, can be expressed in very general terms, for example, a trust for "charitable" or "humanitarian" purposes. The law will imply a charitable trust when a charitable purpose is clear. As such, if a person makes a gift to the needy, a court will appoint a trustee and name a beneficiary. The trustee, of course, need not be a charity. An important legal doctrine governing charitable trusts is the *cy pres* doctrine. This legal principle maintains that a court can name a charitable beneficiary or substitute one charitable organization or group for prior beneficiaries if the prior beneficiaries cease to exist or cease to be charitable. However, a court can only alter the charitable purpose if it appears that the settlor had the general intent to aid charity or some particular type of charity; otherwise, the court will impose a resulting trust for the settlor or his or her estate. An *honorary trust* is a trust, recognized in some states, for the care of graves or animals. This type of trust is not a true trust since there is no beneficiary to enforce the direction to the trustee (though the attorney general of the state may enforce the trust). The trust is "honorary" because the trustee is on his or her honor to carry out the settlor's wishes.

Trust Administration

The initial important point to make regarding trust administration is to define the trustee. The *trustee* is the person named in the trust, who has legal title to trust assets, and is charged with the duty of effectively managing and administering the trust. The trustee has certain powers as well as duties in handling trust affairs. Most states have statutes that set forth the powers of the trustee; and these statutes typically hold that the trustee has virtually all powers regarding the trust property as a fee simple owner would have with respect to the property. Of course, the trust instrument may set forth the exact powers of the trustee, which may be narrower than the state law provisions; and in such a case the explicit trust language would prevail. Nonetheless, state laws prohibit the trustee to engage in any "self-dealing" with the trust, regardless if the settlor permits such conduct, unless there is court approval. The trustee has a duty to segregate trust property; and accordingly the trustee cannot commingle trust property with his or her own property. There is no duty, however, for the trustee to perform his or her trust duties personally; rather, the trustee can employ lawyers, accountants, and financial advisors, and other agents. A trustee has a duty to account, that is, to keep the beneficiaries reasonably informed. A bond is usually not required for the trustee. The trustee also has a duty to make the trust principal productive, which means the trustee has the power to make investments of trust property. In so doing, the law holds the trustee to the "prudent investor" rule, which means that the trustee must exhibit good faith, reasonable prudence and care, and sound judgment in making investments. To fulfill this "prudent" requirement, the law will require a reasonable diversification of investments; and consequently even if a particular investment is proper, it may become improper if too great a portion of the trust principal is invested in it. However, if the assets received by the trustee are all in one investment at the creation of the trust, then the trustee does not have to diversify unless the investment is not a good one. Regardless, it must be emphasized that the trustee is not a guarantor of the financial success of his or her investments; rather, the investment must have been a prudent one at the time the investment was made. The trustee is also under a duty of fairness to both the income beneficiaries of the trust and the remainder beneficiaries when it comes to investment decisions. The income beneficiaries naturally want investments that yield the greater income, but the remainder beneficiaries who receive the trust *res* would prefer to see more growth investments. As a result, the trustee as a prudent trustee must strike a fair balance between the two categories of beneficiaries. If the trustee breaches his or her duties, the beneficiaries can force the trustee to pay damages or be removed from office. A trustee, however, is not generally liable for the acts of third party agents the trustee retained to help manage the trust, unless the trustee was negligent in selecting or supervising the agents.

Beneficiaries' Interests: Transfer, Modification, and Termination

Generally, beneficiaries can freely transfer their equitable interest in the trust. In addition, the law can involuntarily reach the beneficiaries' interest in the trust to satisfy creditors; but the creditor can only obtain the beneficiaries' income interest and not the principal of the trust. In essence, pursuant to a court order, a judge will order the trustee to pay the creditors of the beneficiary the income from the trust the debtor beneficiary is entitled to. However, there are three types of trusts that impose certain restraints on alienation: 1) the spendthrift trust, 2) the discretionary trust, and 3) the support trust. 1) A *spendthrift trust* is one with a restraint on alienation (transfer) imposed expressly or impliedly by the terms of the trust. The reason is that the settlor deems the beneficiaries incapable of managing their own affairs. No particular language is required to impose the restraint, so long as the settlor's intention is clear. The significant legal consequences of the spendthrift trust are that the beneficiaries cannot transfer their interests voluntarily, and creditors cannot reach the beneficiaries' interests to sell them; creditors cannot compel the trustee to directly pay them the beneficiaries' income; but creditors can reach the beneficiaries' income after it is distributed to the beneficiaries (since it is no longer protected by the spendthrift provision of the trust). 2) A *discretionary trust* is a trust that gives the trustee the discretion to apply or withhold payments of income and/or principal to beneficiaries. Before the trustee exercises his or her discretion to make payments to the beneficiaries, the creditors have no right to reach the beneficiaries' interests. However, after the creditor makes payments to beneficiaries, the creditors can reach them (unless of course the beneficiaries' interests are also protected by spendthrift provisions). Similarly, before the trustee exercises his or her discretionary power to make payments to the beneficiaries, the beneficiaries can neither transfer their interests nor interfere with the trustee's exercise of discretion (unless there is abuse, bad faith, or dishonesty present). 3) A *support trust* is a trust that allows the trustee to pay the beneficiaries only so much income and principal as necessary for the beneficiaries' support. Even without any spendthrift provisions, the beneficiaries' interests in a support trust are neither assignable by the beneficiaries nor reachable by their creditors.

A final area to cover is the modification and termination of trusts. In most states, the settlor of a trust can only revoke or modify it if the settlor expressly reserved those rights in the trust instrument. The settlor's creditors, moreover, have no power to terminate the trust (unless there was some type of fraudulent conveyance). When the term of the trust expires or the trust purposes are accomplished, the trustee is then obligated to wind up the affairs of the trust and to distribute the remaining trust principal to the beneficiaries. The beneficiaries, however, only have very limited rights to terminate or modify a trust. In most states, the beneficiaries can modify or terminate the trust only if they all consent and the termination or modification will not interfere with the material purposes of the trust. Thus, the possibility of unborn children as beneficiaries will preclude modification or termination. In addition, the presence of a spendthrift provision in a trust will preclude termination or modification. There also exists judicial power to modify trusts. Pursuant to the doctrine of "changed circumstances," a court may direct the trustee to deviate from the terms of the trust, including permitting unauthorized or forbidden acts if: 1) compliance with the terms of the trust would impair or defeat trust purposes; and 2) the settlor did not know and did not anticipate the changed circumstances. However, there is an important limitation to the "changed circumstances" doctrine. That is, the doctrine cannot be used to change the beneficial rights of the beneficiaries. To illustrate, a court cannot permit an invasion of the principal of the trust for the benefit of the income beneficiaries (unless the settlor has expressly or impliedly reserved this power in the trust instrument).

Trusts Arising As a Matter of Law: Resulting and Constructive Trusts

Certain trusts arise not by express declaration of trust by a settlor, but they are implied by a court when one person obtains legal title to property which the court feels equitably belongs to another. A *resulting trust* arises when one person buys property, real or personal, and obtains legal title from the seller, but the consideration for the property is supplied by another person. In such a case, a court will deem that the person with title to property becomes a trustee, who must convey title to the person who supplied the consideration, who now is construed as a beneficiary. The amount or form of consideration is immaterial; but it must be it must be given before or at the time that title passes. Moreover, a presumption of a resulting trust arises when one person proves that another has supplied consideration for property. However, this presumption can be rebutted when the title holder to the property show that the money used for consideration for the purchase was a gift, loan, or the payment of a debt. A resulting trust can also arise from the failure of an express trust, for example, if the trust becomes unenforceable or void for any reason. The trustee's basic duty in a resulting trust is to convey title back to the settlor. A *constructive trust* is one imposed by a court in favor of the settlor or the beneficiaries when the trust was procured by fraud, duress, undue influence, or mistake, or when the trustee has abused his or her fiduciary relationship or contravened his or her duties of care. A constructive trust over property will also be imposed when a person has fraudulently or by theft or embezzlement or otherwise wrongfully obtained title to property. The sole legal obligation of the trustee of a constructive trust, as with a resulting trust, is to convey legal title to the property to the proper beneficiaries or recipients thereof.

Summary

This chapter has examined two very important areas of the law, not only for business but also for the family and estate planning reasons. The wills part to the chapter discussed what a will is, how wills are created, and how they can be revoked and amended. The wills part also examined briefly the legal doctrines that impact a person's ability to draft a will and for the will to transfer property. The administration, or probate, of wills was also briefly mentioned. The trusts part to this chapter examined the concept of a trust, discussed how trusts can be created, and defined and differentiated the variety of trusts the law recognizes.

Discussion Questions

1. List and briefly explain the requirements for a valid will. Provide an example of a valid will with a brief discussion thereof.
2. What are the differences between revoking a will by means of a subsequent instrument and revoking a will by means of performing a physical act on the will? Why are the differences very significant? Provide an example of each with a brief discussion thereof.
3. What is a codicil and how can it operate to modify a will? Provide an example and a brief explanation thereof.
4. What is an elective share? Why is it very significant when it comes to inheritance? Provide an example along with a brief explanation thereof.

5. What is testamentary capacity? Why is it so critical to the validity of a will? Provide an example along with a brief explanation thereof.

6. What is the concept of undue influence? How can it invalidate a will? Provide an example along with a brief explanation thereof.

7. What is the difference between specific and general devises? Why is the difference important when it comes to the doctrines of ademption and abatement? Provide examples along with brief explanations thereof.

8. What are anti-lapse statutes and how do they operate when it comes to devises in a will? Provide an example along with a brief explanation thereof.

9. What are the requirements of a valid private express trust? Provide an example of such a trust with a brief explanation thereof.

10. What are the differences between an *inter vivos* trust and a testamentary trust? Why are the differences significant? Provide an example of each along with a brief discussion thereof.

11. What are the legal powers and duties of a trustee? Provide examples of each with brief explanations thereof.

12. What is a charitable trust and why is the *cy pres* doctrine such an important feature of charitable trust law? Provide an example of a charitable trust as well as the application of the aforementioned doctrine together with brief explanations thereof.

13. Compare and contrast the spendthrift, discretionary, and support trusts. Provide an example of each along with a brief explanation thereof.

14. Compare and contrast the resulting and constructive trusts. Provide an example of each with a brief explanation thereof.

15. How can will and trust law be integrated as a family estate planning tool? Provide examples with brief explanations thereof.

16 – PERSONAL PROPERTY, GIFTS, AND BAILMENT

Ownership of property is the highest status recognized by the law with respect to a particular piece of property. The distinction between real and personal property as well as the types of ownership of real property were discussed in the Real Estate chapter. This chapter focuses on the ownership of personal property. In particular, the chapter examines the acquisition of ownership of personal property through possession and by means of gifts. The chapter also discusses the important and interrelated personal property legal concept of a bailment.

Part I – Personal Property
Ownership rights to personal property can be obtained by a variety of methods. One can acquire ownership of personal property, that is, things or (to use the old English term) chattels, simply by finding them, which of course is rare in the "real-world." That is, the ownership of certain types of chattels can be acquired merely by taking them into possession. Two examples would be abandoned goods and wild animals. Also, as will be seen, the finder may acquire ownership of lost property through possession as well as certain procedures for publication. Yet most acquisitions of ownership involve some type of conveyance or by dealings with the former owner. The obvious illustration is a purchase and sale of goods, which subject was covered extensively in the Sales chapter; yet there are many non-sale methods, both voluntarily and non-voluntarily, of securing ownership over personal property.

Ownership of personal property, moreover, can be acquired through *accession* and *confusion* (or commingling). *Accession* is improvement of personal property by artificial means. The legal problem arises as to ownership of such property as well as damages when the personal property of one person has been improved or increased in value through the labor and materials of another person, but without the owner's consent. The first issue to resolve is the title, if any, the "trespasser by accession" acquires to the property. There are two principal rules: 1) one deals with an accession that is a willful taking; and 2) the other deals with an accession that is an innocent taking. First, if the taking by accession is willful or fraudulent, the "trespasser by accession" generally does not obtain any legal title to the property. Accordingly, the owner of the property is entitled to all increment and augmentation even the there is a change to the form or identity of the property. For example, the owner of sugar is entitled to the rum into which the sugar was converted. The rationale for this rule is that to allow the "trespasser by accession" to gain title would permit him or her to benefit from wrongdoing and encourage the theft of property. However, there is an exception. When the value of the original property is negligible, and the identity of the property is so changed that it acquires great value, then the "trespasser by accession" can claim value. For example, if one steals a junk car, and turns it into a "classic car," the exception would apply, though damages would still have to be paid for the wrongful initial taking (presuming the property was not abandoned). Note that if the taking is willful, the owner of the property can elect to sue the "trespasser by accession" for conversion, which was covered in the Torts chapter, and get the full present value of the property in its enhanced state as damages in lieu of recovery of the property. Second, if the taking by accession is innocent, a different rule applies. The rule of law holds that if an innocent taker, though a wrongdoer, has nonetheless made a substantial expenditure of labor and materials on the property, and thereby has greatly increased its value, the "trespasser by accession" can acquire title to the property. The key fact is the relative value of the property before and after the taking. Title will pass to the innocent taker only when there is great disparity in value between the original article and the new product. The owner, of course, is still able to obtain money damages for the loss of property. The standard of damages would be the value of the property before its enhancement. To illustrate, if grapes are innocently taken and converted to wine, or clay to bricks, there is a great change, and the "trespasser by accession" acquires title (and pays damages to the original owner). Another way to acquire ownership of property is by *confusion*, which also is known as commingling. Confusion is the intermixture of different owners' goods in such a way that the property of each cannot be distinguished. Legal as well as practical problems perforce arise when fungible goods, such as wheat, cattle, or oil, are accidentally or intentionally intermingled so that the separate interests can no longer be identified. Confusion, literally as well as legally, also occurs when property is affixed to other property and cannot be removed, for example, paint sprayed on a car. Again, there are two principal rules: 1) one deals with willful intermixture and 2) the other with innocent intermixture. The first rule holds that generally when one person willfully, fraudulently, or wrongfully intermixes goods with those of another, the commingling party forfeits ownership to the goods entirely to the innocent party. The innocent party thereby acquires ownership and title of all the goods and concomitantly is under no obligation to compensate the wrongful party. However, there is an exception to this general rule, which maintains that if the goods, though intentionally commingled, can be readily identified, and the commingling party can prove which specific items are his or hers, or if the goods are exactly the same and the commingling party can prove exactly what portion is his or hers, then the commingling party can keep his or her goods, minus any damages to the aggrieved party. The second rule deals with innocent intermixtures. Where the commingling is innocent or inadvertent, the aforementioned forfeiture rule does not apply, and the parties become tenants in common in proportion to their interests in the commingled mass of goods. However, the exception maintains that if it is impossible to tell the quantities intermingled and to apportion their values, the loss is placed on the party who caused the intermixture, even though innocent.

Ownership rights to personal property also can be obtained by finding property that the owner has somehow relinquished possession thereof. The most common ways involve *abandoned*, *lost*, or *mislaid* property. If property is *abandoned*, the person who discovers and takes possession of it acquires title thereto. Property is considered abandoned when the owner has actually discarded the property and without any intention of reclaiming it. If property is *lost*, the finder thereof has the right to possession against everyone but the true owner. Property is lost when the owner through carelessness, neglect, or accident unintentionally and involuntarily leaves the property somewhere; but there is no intention of the owner to part with the title to the property; yet the owner has no knowledge of the location of the property. Typically, there are statutes regarding the finding of lost property with statutory notice and posting procedures, which if followed, will enable the finder to obtain title to the property. Usually, if the property is found on public premises, the finder of the property, after a statutory notice period, will become the owner; but if the lost property is found on private premises, most states would hold that the owner of the private property will become the owner. Usually the notice period is for a six month period. Property is designated as *mislaid* if it is intentionally and voluntarily left in someplace by the owner and then forgot by the owner; but the owner could recollect the location and thus have resort to the property. Again, there are state statutory procedures that deal with converting the possession of mislaid property to title ownership thereof, but most states, if the original owner cannot be found, will grant title to the owner of the "locus in quo," that is, the owner of the place where the property was first mislaid. The rationale is that since the property is merely mislaid, the true owner of the property will return to the place where the property was mislaid, and then be able to recover the property from the owner of this *"locus in quo."*

Part II – Gifts
One can acquire ownership of personal property by means of a gift. Of course, real property can also be the subject matter of a gift; but this chapter for practical reasons will concentrate on the gift of personal property. A *gift* occurs when the owner of property, called herein the *donor*, voluntarily transfers ownership of the property to another, called the *donee*, without any consideration being paid by the recipient. There are two main types of gifts: *inter vivos gifts* and *gifts causa mortis*.

An *inter vivos* gift is a gift between two living persons. There are three requirements for an effective present transfer of property; and all three must be present; they are: 1) donative intent, 2) delivery, and 3) acceptance of the gift. Note again that the common law contract requirement of consideration is not necessary. *Donative intent* means that the donor of the gift must intend to make an effective present gift of the property. That is, the donor is transferring ownership, and not merely possession or the right to use the property, which latter situations are typically bailment scenarios, as will be seen. The requisite intent is determined from the language and conduct of the donor. The intent must be a present intent, and not the intent to make a future gift. Consequently, the expression of the intent to transfer property in the future is not a gift because the intent to make a present gift is lacking. So, if a father tells his son that the son will have the father's yacht when the father dies, there is no gift since there is no present intent to invest any rights in the boat in the son. The second requirement is the *delivery* one. To be legally effective, an *inter vivos* gift requires some act by the donor giving up dominion over the property and passing control to the donee. As such, the retention of a degree of control by the donor over the property is not a gift. For example, if one person indicates to another the desire to make a gift of a rare coin to another; and the coin is placed in a safe deposit box which both have access to, there is no gift since there is insufficient delivery. The type of delivery act, however, depends on whether the personal property is tangible or intangible. Intangible delivery methods will be discussed shortly. The rationale for this rule is to have evidence to prove the existence of donative intent as well as to prevent fraudulent claims of gifts. There are, however, four exceptions to the delivery rule: First, if the property is already in the possession of the donee when the donor indicates his or her present intent to make a gift, the law dispenses with the formal delivery requirement. Second, according to the majority view, a written document in lieu of physical delivery conveying the gift will be sufficient evidence of donative intent. However, the minority view would insist that if the gift is at hand at the time of gifting, and it is capable of being physically delivered, then a written conveyance is not acceptable. Third, delivery to a third person or agent may be permissible. That is, the donor need not personally make delivery to the donee, but rather the delivery can be made by the donor's own agent with instructions to delivery the gift to the donee. However, there is no gift until the donee actually receives the item (because the donor can revoke instructions and avoid the gift). Finally, constructive delivery is another delivery option. The rule of law is that when physical delivery of a tangible chattel is too inconvenient or impossible, for example, the item is too large or located too far away, delivery of something that gives the donee control of the item will be sufficient, for example, the keys to a car or building. Regarding intangible property, there are special gift delivery rules when the donor is contemplating the gift of stock, bank accounts, bonds, insurance polices, promissory notes, or other commercial paper. Obviously, the physical delivery of the intangible property is impossible; yet some act is required; oral words are insufficient. The doctrine that applies to such an intangible delivery situation is called the *constructive delivery* principle. This legal precept holds that when a token or symbol of an intangible piece or property exists, the delivery of the token or symbol is construed as delivery of the intangible property. To illustrate, the delivery of a stock certificate, a bank account passbook, or even the delivery of a safe deposit box key for the gifting of the contents of the box, may be sufficient delivery methods. The third requirement for a valid gift is the acceptance. The rule of law is that the donee must accept the gift; the donor cannot force the gift on the donee. There usually is a presumption of ownership when the gift is beneficial to the donee; but not when the gift has burdens of ownership with it such as taxes or liability. Finally, there is no right of revocation of a gift as a general rule. The rule of law is that when there is a valid *inter vivos* gift complete ownership vests in the donee, and as a result the donor has no power to revoke. The exceptions would be cases of fraud or mistake. Also, under the common law, if there is a gift in contemplation of marriage, the rejected suitor and his or her family are allowed to recover gifts made in contemplation of the marriage, such as an engagement ring.

The final type of gift to examine is the *gift causa mortis*, which is a gift motivated by the prospect of imminent death. These types of gifts are not favored in the law because they may contravene state statutes regulating wills. One thus will need in most states "clear and convincing" evidence to make such a gift. They are, moreover, limited only to personal property. The same donative intent is required as for an *inter vivos* gift, but also a required frame of mind, that is, the fear of an imminent death. Note that if a person makes a gift intending it to be effective on his or her death, there usually is no legal gift because neither the present intent to make a gift exists nor is there compliance with the state's statutes for wills. Furthermore, for there to be a valid gift *causa mortis,* actual physical delivery of the item or a written conveyance is necessary; allowing the donee to be in constructive delivery is insufficient. Finally, this type of gift is always revocable by the donor; and automatic revocation can occur if the donor recovers from the illness or escapes the peril which motivated the gift, and also if the donee dies before the donor.

Part III – Bailment

A *bailment* is the delivery of the possession of personal property from one person, called the *bailor*, to another, called the *bailee*, pursuant to an agreement by which the bailee is obligated to return the identical property to the bailor or deliver it to a third party. The agreement can be written or oral; it can be gratuitous or for consideration. The most important points are that in a bailment the title to the property remains with the bailor; the bailee is entitled only to possession. Bailment situations arise only regarding personal property and not land, though it is possible to have a bailment of intangible personal property, such as by means of the delivery of a stock certificate.

The first requirement of a valid bailment to examine is delivery of possession. The general rule of law is that delivery of possession requires: 1) physical delivery and transfer of possession, 2) the recipient being given a substantial measure of control over the property, and 3) the delivery was knowingly accepted by the recipient. Here are some illustrations of the preceding rules: If a customer hangs his or her coat in a restaurant coat rack, the restaurant owner is not a bailee because the owner is not in possession; whereas if the patron checked his or her coat with an attendant in a coat room, then there would be a bailment. Similarly, if a car owner parks a car at a car lot and keeps his or her keys, the owner of the car lot is not a bailee because the owner of the lot has insufficient control over the car (and is really only a lessor of space); whereas if the car owner is required to leave his or her keys with the car lot attendant, then there is a bailment. There is also a legal concept of constructive delivery. That is, the law will imply a delivery, for example, when the owner of a car gives the bailee keys as well as well as the title to secure the car from a third party. Note that it is not necessary for the bailor to be the owner of property; rather, the bailor just must have a superior interest over the bailee. For example, if an owner loans his boat to a neighbor for the summer, and the neighbor takes the boat to a marine mechanic before returning it to the owner, a bailment has occurred. It is required, however, that the prospective bailee realizes that he or she has possession of the property belonging to another. Knowledge of possession is an indispensable requirement for a valid bailment. To illustrate, one checks a coat into a restaurant coat room with an attendant. The owner of the restaurant is the bailee of the coat, but not the valuable jewelry left inside unless there was knowledge of the jewelry. Bailment agreements can be express (though there is no requirement of a writing), implied (for example, when one takes his or her clothes to the dry cleaners), or constructive. In the latter case, the law will create a bailment, even though there is no express or implied bailment, when the law deems it necessary to impose the duties of a bailee on a person. For example, if a person finds property, he or she is deemed to be a constructive bailee of the property. As a requirement of bailment, the general rule holds that the identical property must be obtained. There are two exceptions. One arises when the subject matter of the bailment is fungible goods, and in such a case the same quantity and description of goods can be returned, for example, grain in a grain elevator. The second exception arises when the bailment is with an option to purchase, which is still regarded as a bailment even though the bailee has the option to give the bailor money instead of the property.

There are different types of bailments; and there are different types of rights and obligations depending on the type of bailment. The first is a bailment for the sole benefit of the bailee, for example, the loan of one's car or tool to a friend. The second is a bailment for the sole benefit of the bailor, for example, when the owner of a car leaves the car in a neighbor's garage while on vacation. The third type of bailment is one for the mutual benefit of the bailor and bailee, where the bailor and/or the bailee are compensated, and/or the bailee has the right to use the property. For example, a bailor tool rental business that receives a fee for leasing the tools and the bailee uses the property. The bailee has certain rights to the property. First is the right of possession. Once the property is delivered to the bailee, the bailee has the right to exclusive use and control of the property during the course of the bailment (naturally so long as that use is consistent with the terms and conditions of the bailment). This right empowers the bailee to sue any third party who destroys or damages the property. In addition, the bailee can even sue the bailor if the bailor wrongfully interferes with the bailee's use of the property. Second, the bailiee also may have the right to use the property; but the extent and type of use must be determined from the bailment agreement. Such use must be within the scope of the bailment agreement as well as reasonable. If there is substantial abuse or misuse of the property, then there is a breach of the bailment agreement, and the bailee is liable for damages. Note that in most cases, the bailee allowing a third party to use the bailor's property is considered abuse of the property. As to any right of compensation, the general rule is that in the absence of any agreement, the bailee is not entitled to compensation for his or her own services, for the expenses in keeping the goods or using the goods, or for minor repairs or incidental expenses incurred. However, the bailee is entitled to compensation for the actual expenses which were reasonably necessary to protect and to preserve the goods. To illustrate, if the bailed property is a horse, the costs of feeding, stabling, and shoeing the horse would not ordinarily be compensable expenses for the bailee renter of the horse; but the veterinarian's expenses for caring for the horse due to a serious illness would be recoverable.

The duties of the bailee are mainly twofold: 1) to exercise care and 2) to return the property to the bailor. First, the bailee is under a duty to exercise reasonable care under the circumstances to protect and to preserve the bailed property. If the bailee fails to exercise such care, the bailee may be liable for the tort of negligence. However, it is important to note that the law does not regard the bailee as an insurer or guarantor of the property; and thus the bailee is not liable absent some fault. Also, significantly, there is a presumption of negligence when the bailed goods are destroyed or damaged while in the bailee's possession. That is, the bailee under such circumstances is presumed to be negligent; yet such a presumption can be rebutted, but then the bailee must affirmatively show that he or she was without fault. How much care need be exercised by the bailee? There are three "care" rules: 1) if the bailment is a mutual benefit one, the bailee must exercise reasonable and ordinary care; 2) if the bailment is for the sole benefit of the bailor, the bailee need only exercise slight care; and 3) if the bailment is for the sole benefit of the bailee, the bailee must exercise great care. However, if the bailee substantially deviates from the terms of the bailment agreement, and a loss results while the bailee is using the property in an unauthorized manner, then the bailee is liable even without negligence. The second major duty of the bailee is to return the property to the bailor. If there is a misdelivery of the property, the bailee is absolutely liable for such a misdelivery, that is, when the bailee mistakenly delivers the property to someone other than the bailor. This liability is premised on the breach of the bailment agreement.

The bailor also has certain rights and duties. The rights of the bailor are: 1) the return of the property at the end of the bailment period; 2) the exercise of reasonable care by the bailee; and 3) the use of the property in conformity with the terms of the bailment agreement. The bailment agreement may also give the bailor the right to compensation and the right that the bailee performs any work on the property in a non-defective manner. The duties of the bailor are: 1) to disclose any defects in the property (including in a mutual benefit bailment defects which the bailor knows or should know; but in a sole benefit for the bailee bailment, only defects which the bailor actually knew); and 2) if the bailor is a commercial bailor, or as usually called a commercial lessor, the Uniform Commercial Code will impose warranty liability on such commercial lessors.

A bailment is terminated under the following circumstances: 1) If a bailment is for a specified period, when the period elapses, so does the bailment. 2) If the bailment is one at will, that is, not for a definite time period, the bailee may terminate at any time. 3) If the bailment has an express purpose, when the purpose is accomplished, the bailment ends. 4) A bailment may automatically end by operation of the law if the bailee acts improperly, for example, violates the terms of the bailment agreement or substantially misuses or abuses the property.

Finally, it should be noted that most states have special bailment rules dealing with common carries and innkeepers. A "common carrier" is a person or company willing to furnish transportation services to the general public. A common carrier is regarded as a bailee when goods are delivered to it. Under the common law, common carriers are absolutely liable for all loss or damage to the goods, unless the carrier can prove that the loss or damage was caused by an Act of God, a criminal act, an act by public authorities, an act by a shipper, or due to the inherent nature of the goods. Most states, however, have by statute allowed common carriers to contractually curtail their common law bailment liability, and also have imposed on the bailor the obligation of proving that the carrier was negligent. Similarly, under the common law innkeepers were required to be bailees of their guests' goods, and were strictly liable for any loss or damage to the goods. However, most states now by statute have rules that innkeepers are not under any obligation to accept the goods of their guests; and that if goods are accepted, the innkeeper is only liable to a certain monetary extent unless the guest can prove that the innkeeper was negligent.

Summary

This chapter reviewed three important areas of the law which are important subject matters not only for their business applications, but also for their individual and family financial ramifications. The three legal areas were personal property, gifts, and bailment, which were treated separately for academic purposes in three distinct sections to the chapter, but which in the "real-world" are often interrelated, especially because, as was seen, one very common subject matter of a gift is personal property.

Discussion Questions

1. Compare and contrast gifts *inter vivos* and gifts *causa mortis*. Why are the differences significant? Provide an example of each along with a brief explanation thereof.
2. What are the requirements for a valid bailment? Provide an example of a valid bailment along with a brief explanation thereof.
3. What are the duties of the bailee and how do these duties differ depending on the type of bailment involved? Provide examples together with brief explanations thereof.
4. Compare and contrast securing ownership to abandoned, lost, and mislaid property. Provide an example of each along with a brief explanation thereof.
5. Compare and contrast acquiring property by means of accession and confusion. Provide an example of each along with a brief explanation thereof.

17 – BUSINESS ETHICS AND CORPORATE SOCIAL RESPONSIBILITY

In addition to the legal ramifications of business decision-making, business today is being called upon to act not "merely" legally, but also in a moral, ethical, and socially responsible manner. Accordingly, this chapter has two components. Part I will examine ethics, which is a branch of philosophy; and the authors will demonstrate how ethics can be applied to business decision-making to determine if business is acting in a moral manner. Moreover, Part II of this chapter will examine the related, but distinct, concept of corporate social responsibility; and accordingly the authors will discuss what it means in a modern-day business context for a business, particularly a corporation, to be a "socially responsible" one.

Part I – Business Ethics

Determining whether an action, rule, or law is moral or immoral, right or wrong, or just or unjust perforce brings one into the realm of *ethics*, which is a branch of *philosophy*, and then logically one proceeds to ethical theories, ethical principles, applied ethics, and ethical reasoning to moral conclusions. In the ethics part to this chapter, the authors will explain and then apply four major ethical theories – Ethical Egoism, Ethical Relativism, Utilitarianism, and Kantian ethics – to the subject of bribery to determine if paying a bribe to a foreign government official is moral. These ethical theories were chosen because they represent the essence of ethics as a branch of philosophy in Western Civilization, which obviously is not the only civilization, but it is one that the authors are the most familiar with, including, of course, the ethics component to Western knowledge and thought, as opposed to, for example, Confucian ethical principles and the application thereof, which, although most interesting and intriguing to learn and to apply, practically would be beyond the scope of the authors' objectives for this chapter. These four Western theories also were selected because they are reason-based ethical theories; as such, the authors assume that the readers of this book possess intellect, reason, and logic, and thus will be quite "comfortable" in following the authors' ethical "train of thought," though, of course, perhaps not agreeing with their ultimate moral conclusions. Furthermore, religion-based ethical theories were not chosen because not all the readers of this book will be of the same religion and, for that matter, some may have no religion at all; and, moreover, bringing in a religious-based ethical component to this chapter would be to expand the book beyond the authors' aims. The focus is on Western ethics; and the ethical theory to be examined will be Ethical Egoism. However, it is first necessary for the authors to explain some key ethical terms and concepts.

Values

The authors believe it is very harmful for people to use continually a wide variety of very general terms without clear meanings. The lack of any fixed meaning, the inability of people to provide proper explanations, the individualistic, expedient decision-making, as well as an emphasis on rhetoric and persuasion, engenders relativism, skepticism, and a great deal of confusion, People then will be talking at cross purposes and their discussions will make no progress. Only confusion, skepticism, chaos, and perhaps even conflict, will ensue. Therefore, it is very important for a business leader, academic, and manager to look for, ascertain, and pay special attention to definitions and terms. When one initially encounters the fields of ethics, corporate governance, social responsibility, and stakeholder analysis in a business context, one is confronted with some confusion due to a lack of an agreed-upon terminology and set of definitions. What is social responsibility? How does it differ from the law, ethics, and morality? What exactly do the terms "corporate social responsibility," "stakeholder values," "sustainability," "people, planet, and profits," "going green," and "socially responsible investing" mean? What is a corporate "constituency" statute and how does it compare and contrast to a "social benefit" corporation? So, as will be seen in Part II of this chapter, if one is going to understand what social responsibility is and how it works in a modern global business environment, there must be some agreement on, and some insight into, the meaning and nature of the value of social responsibility especially when juxtaposed with the values of legality, based on the law, and the value of morality, based on ethics. There is, therefore, a need for words, terms, and definitions with precise meaning.

In order to arrive at a precise as possible meaning of the terms ethics and "social responsibility," it is first necessary to define some fundamental terms and concepts. A value is something that possesses worth. *Values* can be *intrinsic* (also called terminal), meaning that they possess value and worth in and of themselves, for example, happiness and aesthetics. Whereas values that are "merely" *extrinsic* (also called instrumental) possess worth and are valuable because they are the means to produce something else of value, for example, money (which can buy happiness!). The value of legality is, of course, based on the law. The value of morality stems from ethics; yet the terms ethics and morals or morality are not synonymous. *Morality* is the conclusion of what is right or wrong or good or bad; whereas ethics is the philosophical framework, consisting of ethical theories and principles that one uses to reason to moral conclusions. Whether morality is an intrinsic value or merely and instrumental one is an issue which the authors will leave to the philosophers. Social responsibility too is a value, related to, but distinct from law and ethics. Social responsibility, particularly in a business sense, as will be addressed in Part II to this chapter, is concerned with a business going "above and beyond" the law as well as acting beyond morality by taking an active part in community and civic affairs and charitable endeavors.

Ethical Egoism

The ethical theory of *Ethical Egoism* harkens back to ancient Greece and the philosophical school of the Sophists and their teachings of relativism and promotion of self-interest. This ethical theory maintains that a person ought to promote his or her self-interest and the greatest balance of good for himself or herself. Since this theory is an ethical theory, one thus has a moral obligation to promote one's self-interest; and so "selfishly" acting is also morally acting; and concomitantly an action against one's self-interest is an immoral action; and an action that advances one's self-interest is a moral action. An ethically egoistic person, therefore, will shrewdly discern the "pros" and "cons" of an action, and then perform the action that performs the most personal good, which also is the moral course of action. However, the Ethical Egoists counsel that one should be an "enlightened" ethical egoist; that is, one should think of what will inure to one's benefit in the long-run, and accordingly be ready to sacrifice some short-term pain or expense to attain a greater long-term good – for oneself, of course. Also, the prudent ethical egoist would say that as a general rule it is better, even if one has a lot of power as well as a big ego, to treat people well, to make them part of "your team," and to "co-op" them. Why should one treat people well? One reason is certainly not because one is beneficent, but rather because one is "selfish." That is, one is treating people well because typically it will advance one's own self-interest in the long-term to do so. One problem with ethical egoism is that one's own "good" must be defined. What exactly is one maximizing? Is it one's knowledge, power, money, pleasure, comfort, prestige, success, or happiness? Ethical egoists agree that people ought to pursue and advance their own good; but they disagree as to the type of good people should be seeking. Yet in business the "good" typically means making money! Another problem with Ethical Egoism is that the doctrine counsels that everyone should pursue his or her own self-interest. Yet what if there is just one job position or one promotion opportunity and two people want to advance themselves by attaining the job or promotion? Now, one would hope that as rational egoists there would be clearly defined, legitimate, job-related criteria for the job or promotion. Yet that is no always the case. Consequently, there is the distinct possibility that the two egos seeking self-advancement will clash; and conflict may result; but there is no mechanism in Ethical Egoism that acts as an arbitrating principle to decide whose ego gets advance. So, who will "win" the job or the promotion? "Might makes right," the Sophists long ago said!

Ethical Relativism

Ethical Relativism as an ethical theory also harkens back to ancient Greece and the philosophical school of the Sophists as well as the philosophical school of the Skeptics. Ethical relativists deny that there are any objective, universal moral rules which one can construct an absolute moral system. Ethical relativists deny that there are moral rules applicable to all peoples, in all societies, and at all times. There thus are no universal moral standards by which to judge an action's morality; rather, morality is merely relative to, and holds for, only a particular society at a particular time. "When in Rome, do as the Romans," said the Ethical Relativists. Morality, therefore, is a societal-based notion; it is nothing more than the morality of a certain group, people, or society at a certain time. What a society believes is right is in fact right for that society; the moral beliefs of a society determine what is "right" or "wrong" in that society. However, different societies may have different conceptions of what is right or wrong. What one believes is right, the other may believe as wrong. Consequently, the same act can be morally right for one society but morally wrong for another. So, one society can believe that the use of partial nudity in advertising is moral; whereas another society may condemn such a practice as immoral. Since pursuant to Ethical Relativism there are no moral standards which are universally true for all peoples, in all societies, and at all times, and since there is no way to demonstrate that one set of beliefs is true and the other false, the only way to determine an action's morality is to determine what the people in a particular society believe is right or wrong at a given time. So, "simply" discern the societal moral precepts, and then conform and adapt; and one will be acting morally, at least pursuant to this ethical theory.

Of course, ascertaining exactly what a society is a daunting challenge. Even within a homogeneous society, there are diverse cultures, subcultures, social classes, kinship, and work groups; and in a heterogeneous society there will be many smaller sub-societies that co-exist. All these components of society may reflect different standards, mores, customs, and beliefs, including moral standards and beliefs. Yet pursuant to the doctrine of Ethical Relativism, one must attempt to find the pertinent "society" and then try to ascertain that society's moral beliefs; but when one does ascertain the societal beliefs, standards, and practices regarding morality, one simply has to conform and adopt, and one will be acting morally, at least according to the ethical theory of Ethical Relativism.

Utilitarianism

Utilitarianism is a major ethical theory in Western civilization; it was created principally by the English philosophers and social reformers Jeremy Bentham and John Stewart Mill. Their goal was to develop an ethical theory that not only was "scientific" but also would maximize human happiness and pleasure (in the sense of satisfaction). Utilitarianism is regarded as a consequentialist ethical theory, also called a teleological ethical theory; that is, one determines morality by examining the consequences of an action; the form of the action is irrelevant; rather, the consequences produced by the action are paramount in determining its morality. If an action produces more good than bad consequences, it is a moral action; and if an action produces more bad than good consequences it is an immoral action. Of course, ethical egoism is also a consequentialist ethical theory. The critical difference is that the Utilitarians demand that one consider the consequences of an action not just on oneself, but also on other people and groups who are affected directly and indirectly by the action. The scope of analysis, plainly, is much broader, and less "selfish," pursuant to a Utilitarian ethical analysis. In business ethics texts and classes, the term "stakeholders" is frequently used to indicate the various groups that would be affected by a business decision. Furthermore, the Utilitarians specifically and explicitly stated that society as a whole must be considered in this evaluation of the good and/or bad consequences produced by an action. The idea is to get away from a "me, me, me" mind-set and consider other people and groups affected by an action.

Utilitarianism is a very egalitarian ethical theory since everyone's pleasure and/or pain gets registered and counted in this "scientific" effort to determine morality. Yet, there are several problems with the doctrine. First, one has to try to predict the consequences of putting an action into effect, which can be very difficult if one is looking for longer-term effects. However, the Utilitarians would say to use one's "common storehouse of knowledge," one's intelligence, and "let history be your guide" in making these predictions. Do not guess or speculate, but go with the probable or reasonably foreseeable consequences of an action. Also, if one is affected by an action, one naturally gets counted too, but if that same one person is doing the Utilitarian analysis, there is always the all-too-human tendency to "cook the books" to benefit oneself. The Utilitarians would say that one should try to be impartial and objective in any analysis. Next, one now has to measure and weigh the good versus the bad consequences to ascertain what prevails and thus what the ultimate moral conclusion will be. The Utilitarians said that not only was this ethical theory "scientific," but it was also mathematical ("good old-fashioned English bookkeeping," they called it). But how does one do the math? How does one measure and weigh the good and the bad consequences? And for that matter how does one measure different types of goods? The Utilitarians, alas, provided very little guidance. Finally, a major criticism of the Utilitarian ethical theory is that it may lead to an unjust result. That is, the "means may justify the ends." Since the form of the action is irrelevant in this type of ethical analysis, if the action produces a greater overall good, then the action is moral, regardless of the fact that some bad may be produced in this effort to achieve the overall good. The good, though, outweighs the bad; accordingly, the action is moral; and the sufferers of the bad, who perhaps were exploited or whose rights were trampled, got counted at least. Such is the nature of Utilitarianism.

After determining the action to be evaluated, the next step in the Utilitarian analysis is to determine the people and groups, that is, the stakeholders, affected by the action, then make a determination as to how they are affected (that is, are the reasonably foreseeable consequences good or bad ones), and next make an overall determination if putting the action into effect results in more good or bad. If the former, the action is moral; if the latter, the action is immoral pursuant to Utilitarianism. Although the Utilitarians claim that their ethical theory is objective and scientific, it is difficult to predict, measure, and weigh consequences. Nonetheless, in the next section the authors present a Utilitarian model, specifically a stakeholder, pleasure v. pain, consequentialist version of the Utilitarian ethical theory, originally developed by Professor Richard T. DeGeorge in his book, *Business Ethics* (2006).

In order to determine the morality of an action, practice, rule, or law pursuant to the stakeholder, pleasure v. pain, consequentialist model of the ethical theory of Utilitarianism:

1. Accurately and narrowly state the action to be evaluated (e.g., Is it moral for a particular company or organization to...?);

2. Identify all people and groups who are directly and indirectly affected by the action (including the company's or organization's constituent groups or "stakeholders" as well as society as a whole);

3. Specify for each stakeholder group directly and indirectly affected all the reasonably foreseeable good - pleasurable and bad - painful consequences of the action, as far as into the future as appears appropriate, and consider the various predictable outcomes, good and bad, and the likelihood of their occurring;

4. For each stakeholder group, including society as a whole, measure and weigh the total good consequences against the bad consequences, and determine which predominates for each stakeholder group;

5. Overall, measure and weigh all the good and bad consequences assigned to the stakeholder groups;

6. If the action overall produces more good than bad it is a morally right action; and if the action overall produces more bad than good it is morally wrong based on this model of the Utilitarian ethical theory.

By following the aforementioned Utilitarian, and being as objective and precise as possible, one can make a determination of what it means to be moral pursuant to the Utilitarian ethical theory. However, as noted, the lynchpin to the Utilitarianism is the focus on consequences. Yet some moral philosophers believe that focusing on consequences is the wrong approach to take in determining the morality of an action.

Kant's Categorical Imperative
The German professor and philosopher, Immanuel Kant, condemned Utilitarianism as an immoral ethical theory. How is it logically possible, said Kant, to have an ethical theory that can morally legitimize pain, suffering, exploitation, and injustice? Disregard consequences, declared Kant, and instead focus on the form of an action in determining its morality. Now, of course, since Kantian ethics is also one of the major ethical theories in Western civilization, a huge problem arises since these two major ethical theories are diametrically opposed. Is one a Kantian or is one a Utilitarian? (Or is it all relative as the Sophists and Machiavelli stated?) For Kant, the key to morality is applying a formal test to the action itself. This formal test he called the *Categorical Imperative*. "Categorical" meaning that this ethical principle is the supreme and absolute and true test to morality; and "imperative" meaning that at times one must command oneself to be moral and do the right thing, even and especially when one's self-interest may be contravened by acting "rightly." The Categorical Imperative has three ways to determine morality. One method is called the *Universal Law* test. Kant is not referring to legal law here; rather, Kant asks one to imagine what would happen if a practice theoretically could be made into a universal law. Would one want to live in such a society where the universal moral norm is that it is permissible to steal, to lie, and to cheat? Of course, one would not want to live in such a society; but then one can logically conclude pursuant to the Universal Law test that stealing, lying, and cheating are immoral actions. Now, Kant does admit that people do steal, lie, and cheat, but he calls these people immoral "parasites" for living off an otherwise moral system where the vast majority of people do not steal, lie, or cheat.

Another method of determining morality is called the *Kingdom of Ends* test. Pursuant to this Kantian precept, if an action, even if it produces a greater good, such as an exploitive but profitable overseas "sweatshop," is nonetheless disrespectful and demeaning and treats people as mere means, things, or as instruments, perhaps as badly as broken pieces of office furniture, then the action is not moral. The goal, said Kant, is for everyone to live in this "Kingdom of the Ends" where everyone is treated as a worthwhile human being with dignity and respect. Related to the Kingdom of Ends precept and also part of the Categorical Imperative is the *Agent-Receiver* test, which asks a person to consider the rightfulness of an action by considering whether the action would be acceptable to the person if he or she did not know whether the person would be the agent, that is, the giver, of the action, or the receiver. If one did not know one's role, and one would not be willing to have the action done to him or her, then the action is immoral. Do your duty, be ethically strong, have a good moral character, declared Kant, and obey the moral "law," based on his Categorical Imperative, and thus do the "right" thing regardless of consequences.

The authors have attempted to explain and illustrate the field of ethics as a branch of philosophy by discussing four major ethical theories. Yet, as the discerning reader can see, these ethical theories can conflict; and there is no "Supreme Court of Ethics" to tell one which ethical theory is the correct, true, and right one! The ethical situation gets even more complicated when these ethical theories are applied to factual situations to determine whether a person or a business is acting morally. In the next section to Part I of this chapter, the authors will show how "applied ethics" works, that is, how these ethical theories can be applied to practices to make moral determinations. The authors will use as their factual situation the paying of a bribe by a U.S. business person to a foreign government official in order to secure a government contract with the business person's corporation.

Applied Ethics - Payments to Foreign Government Officials

Doing business globally raises the difficult issue of payments to foreign officials. A multinational company or international business person may feel pressured into paying money or transferring something of value to a foreign official in order to protect a business investment, secure a business opportunity, to facilitate the performance of some service in the host country. The *Foreign Corrupt Practices Act*, as will be seen in the International Business Law chapter, makes *bribery* a civil and criminal wrong; yet the statute has exceptions which have the potential to legalize "bribery." Yet, assuming a U.S. multinational's or business person's ethical analysis extends, as it should, beyond the law, the issue emerges as to whether it is moral to bribe legally (or for that matter illegally!).

In order to explicate the ethical aspects of bribery in an international setting, assume a situation, as originally proposed by Professor Richard T. DeGeorge in his book, *Business Ethics* (2006), where a sales and marketing representative of a U.S. multinational in precarious financial condition is in the final stages of negotiating a contract for the sale of a substantial quantity of goods to the government of a rapidly developing foreign country. The contract is very important to the company because it provides a significant infusion of money as well as an entry to a foreign market. The contract, moreover, personally is very important to the company's marketing/sales representative and would secure the representative a promotion and substantial raise. All appears to be proceeding very well; and actually the company's offer is viewed very favorably by the foreign government, and the foreign country would in fact secure a very good deal by accepting the U.S. multinational's offer to contract. The U.S. multinational's representative seems assured of success until the representative is confronted by a key foreign government official, who also looks upon the company's offer favorably but demands a large "consulting fee" to process properly the paperwork and thus secure the contract. If the fee is not paid, the official will reopen the bidding and the contract may go to a competitor. The representative is acutely aware of the critical nature of the deal, knows that the sum is immaterial when compared to the contract price and the profits to be realized, and has heard that such payments are a common and lawful practice in the foreign country, but feels that making such payments are not quite right and may be illegal under U.S. law. What is the right and moral decision for the representative to make? Such an inquiry leads one directly into the field of applied ethics.

If one is a Legal Positivist, that is, a person who equates acting legally with acting morally too, one simply would advise the representative to determine the legality of the payment. If it is legal under the foreign country's law, and it is legal under the Foreign Corrupt Practices Act exception for expediting and facilitating payments for ministerial actions (such as, perhaps, the mere processing of the lowest bid), then this legal action is also a moral action pursuant to legal positivism.

If one is an Ethical Emotist, that is, a person who makes moral decisions based on conscience, one would advise the representative to get in "touch" with his or her feelings. If he or she feels "bad" about the payment, then it's immoral; if "good," then it is moral. Of course, he or she can always have a change of heart by merely having a different emotion about the payment at a later, perhaps more critical, date.

If one adheres to the doctrine of Ethical Egoism, the analysis is twofold: is it in the representative's best long-term interest, as agent of the multinational, to pay the bribe; and is it in the interest of the multinational, as the corporate entity, for its representative to pay the bribe? The representative must calculate whether the risks to his or her career, reputation, conscience, and even freedom will supersede the potential personal benefits from paying the bribe, securing the contract, and thus the promotion and raise. The multinational must determine whether the assertion and defense of its legitimate and critical business interests in the foreign country are worth the legal risks as well as risks to the company's reputation. An intelligent ethical egoist also could argue that even if the "bribe" is deemed immoral, the fact that its nonpayment is such a dangerous threat to the company's very existence, the issue of duress as a moral defense arises to counter any charge of immorality.

An Ethical Relativist simply would tell the company and its representative to ascertain whether such payments are an accepted standard and locally unobjectionable practice in the foreign country; if so, paying the "bribe" may be quite moral.

A Utilitarian, of course, would be concerned with the consequences of paying or not paying the bribe. If the bribe is not paid, the company, its shareholders, employees, and suppliers all will suffer a severe financial loss. If, however, the bribe is paid, all these preceding groups benefit, as well as the sales representative, who gets a promotion and raise; the foreign official, who gets the money; the foreign government, which gets a "good" price for a "good" product; and the foreign consumers, who get a quality product. If the bribe is paid, the competition does not get the contract; yet none of the company's competitors had the low bid anyway, so what is the real harm? Paying a bribe, however, usually is construed as adversely affecting the society of the "host" country. Bribery's net effect is to reduce market competition by engendering unequal competition and by erecting additional barriers to market entry. The "best" bribers thus begin to achieve monopoly status, with the distinct possibility of exhibiting the inefficiencies characteristic of monopolies, such as higher prices and lower quality. However, if this instance of bribery under consideration is viewed as an exception, and if one is an Act utilitarian, the harm to society is reduced accordingly and this "pain" is subject to being outweighed by the greater good produced for all the other affected groups and people.

Disregard these consequences, good ones or otherwise, of paying the bribe, a Kantian would argue. Rather, apply the Categorical Imperative to determine if bribery is moral. Applying the first test, a Kantian would argue that bribery cannot be realized as a consistently universal practice. Assuming everyone bribed in a similar fashion, the action "bribe" would no longer be able to sustain itself. Since everyone is bribing, "bribing" loses its efficacy; it contradicts itself, becomes nonsensical, and self-destructs. Bribery, therefore, is immoral. Bribery with qualification, however, is a different matter. Bribery, in the case herein, saves one's company from financial ruin, secures a contract that is a "good deal" for the host government and country when the bribing company is in fact the lowest bidder, and induces the foreign government official to perform his or her public duty of merely awarding the contract. With such qualifications, "bribery" can be made consistently universal. Not everyone is bribing, and the bribe, because it is qualified, will secure results in the limited circumstances presented.

Although bribery qualified arguably can pass Kant's first test, the issue arises as to whether a qualified bribery action will pass the second and third parts of the Categorical Imperative. Does bribery treat all the parties involved with dignity and respect, particularly the official and the company's representative "pressured" to pay the bribe? Would paying the bribe be acceptable to a rational person one did not know one's status as the "giver" (or agent) of the action or the receiver? Would a rational person want to be placed in the role of the competition in a bribery scenario? Such questions clearly illustrate the strictness of Kantian ethics and the difficulty of even a qualified "wrongful" action passing the Categorical Imperative.

So, is bribery in the preceding context moral or immoral? Well, the answer is it depends! That is, determining whether a bribe or for that matter any action is moral or immoral often depends on the ethical theory that one is using to make the determination. Differing ethical theories can lead, even logically so, to differing moral conclusions. Yet, the truly egoistic goal of the ambitious yet moral person would be to take a long-term approach and naturally seek to benefit oneself and one's company or organization, but to do so without offending the moral norms of a society where one does business (that is, be "culturally competent"), always seeking to achieve the greater good for all the stakeholders, including society as a whole, but also always mindful not to demean or disrespect anyone in an effort to attain this personal and societal good. The idea is to do well, but also to do good – and "good" meaning in the full ethical sense. In order to keep a company or organization and its employees and associates on this "good" ethical path many companies today have adopted Codes of Ethics.

Corporate Codes of Ethics

Ethics codes have always been adopted by the profession, such as law and medicine. In recent years, however, they also have been adopted by many corporations and businesses. A strong legal impetus for codes of ethics emerged from the Sarbanes-Oxley Act of 2002 (SOX) (discussed in the Liability of Accountants chapter in this book), which was promulgated as a result of the Enron and other corporate accounting and financial scandals, and which was intended to help restore confidence in the corporate financial system. SOX has many provisions; and regarding ethics codes the statute states that companies must have such a code for senior financial executives and officers or to state (to the Securities and Exchange Commission and to the public) why they have not done so. SOX defines an ethics code as one having written standards that are reasonably designed to deter wrongdoing and promote honest and ethical conduct, as well as full disclosure, compliance with the law, prompt reporting of violations, and methods to conform to the standards of the code.

Codes of ethics usually are developed for a company as a whole and form the foundation of the company's ethics program. Codes of ethics serve as the major vehicle for stating the ethical principles, core values, and moral rules the company believes in and follows. A code of ethics helps to make managers and employees aware that moral considerations, as well as economic and legal factors, must be considered when business decisions are made. The code also demonstrates to other stakeholders that the corporation is aware of, and fully committed to, acting morally as well as in a socially responsible manner.

If the corporate code of ethics is to serve as a means by which business managers legitimately can begin to claim "profession" status, like the doctors and lawyers have, the code ideally should contain: a statement of adherence, that is, a statement that the corporation, as well as its employees, will be bound by the principles of the code; an ethical preamble, stating the fundamental ethical principles and core values motivating the code; a statement and description of the corporation's basic mission and purpose, how this mission coheres with the ethical preamble, thus demonstrating that the corporation serves an inherently moral purpose; a statement and description of the main stakeholders or constituencies to whom the corporation believes it is obligated in the pursuit of its mission; an enumeration of the specific obligations the corporation believes it owes to these groups; a listing of precise standards of conduct required, permitted, or forbidden by the code; and a statement of the types and severity of sanctions the corporation will impose upon violators of these principles, obligations, and standards.

The process by which the code of ethics is put together is very important. The initial, and ultimate, responsibility, of course, lies with the company's board of directors. However, it is critical that employees and departments at all levels and sectors of the corporation take part in drawing up the code. The legal department, human resources, public and community relations, and ad hoc committees of employees from different departments, for example, must be drawn into the process.

If a wide variety of employees are not drawn into the process, the company risks the perils of a code that does not address real concerns and that engenders a feeling by the employees that the code is not "owned" by them, but rather is merely another set of rules and regulations imposed on them.

A company should be prepared to expect certain objections to be raised to the creation of a code of ethics. A code might invite increased scrutiny of the corporation by members of the public, the press, and consumer and environmental groups. These "outsiders" now will be able to ask if the company is complying with its code of ethics and, if there have been any violations, what is being done to rectify them. An open examination of the company, however, should be encouraged, not feared. Such an examination affords the company an opportunity to explain its positions and demonstrate its commitment to morality. If a corporation desires to maintain or regain the confidence of the public, it must demonstrate that it is taking the interests of its stakeholders into account.

A code also may appear to be an act of self-condemnation on the part of the company. Of course, if the company has been acting morally, the code can be phrased as a formal embodiment of long-standing moral policies and practices. However, if the company has engaged in immoral past conduct, the promulgation of a code may appear in some sense to be an admission of responsibility. Yet, the very creation of the code clearly demonstrates that the company's problems have been confronted, that the company does not now tolerate such misconduct and intends to redress it in a formal manner, and that the company wants to signal this new attitude to managers, employees, and other stakeholders.

Whistleblowing

"*Whistleblowing*" may be defined as an attempt by a member of an organization to disclose what he or she believes to be wrongdoing in or by the organization. This section focuses on whistleblowing by employees of a corporation. "Wrongdoing" entails not only conduct or conditions that the employee believes are illegal, but also behavior that the employee considers to be immoral. Whistleblowing can be internal, that is, to those higher up in the corporate hierarchy; or it can be external, that is, to the government, such as a regulatory agency, to a public interest group, or to the media. A "*whistleblower*," of course, is the person, the employee, who attempts to make known the wrongdoing. He or she usually "blows the whistle" for right, as well as rightful, reasons; yet one should not always assume that the whistleblowing employee's motives are meritorious or that he or she is even correct as to the underlying premise of wrongdoing.

Whistleblowing and the Law

While there may exist federal and state statutes that protect public sector employees who blow the whistle from retaliation by their government employers, as well as statutes in the areas of civil rights, labor law, and health and safety law, that prohibit employers from taking retaliatory actions against employees who report statutory violations, there is no general federal statute, and little state law, extending similar protection to private sector employees, the vast majority of whom are employees and "at will." The state *Whistleblower Protection Acts* that do exist usually only protect disclosures of actual legal violations by a company and by its employees. Therefore, reports of suspicious unfounded illegality are usually not protected, nor are disclosures of immoral and unethical conduct which are also not illegal. Thus the whistleblower must be certain of the legal wrongdoing, as in most states erroneous but good faith whistleblowing is not protected. Moreover, the state statutes are uniform in that to be protected the whistleblowing must be made to a government agency or public official and not to the media or a public interest organization. Some, such as Florida's, even require that the whistleblowing employee report the legal wrongdoing to his or her supervisor, then up the corporate "chain-of-command," and also give the employer a reasonable opportunity to correct the problem. Furthermore, in most states, the successful and legally protected whistleblower "only" gets his or her job back (with lost wages, benefits, seniority, etc. but no money damages (though in New Jersey the wrongfully discharges whistleblower can also sue for emotional distress damages. Even if a state does not have a whistleblower protection statute, the wrongfully discharged employee can attempt to bring a suit under the *Public Policy doctrine* (covered in the Agency and Employment Law chapter) if the employee can convince a court that his or her discharge was in violation of the "fundamental public policy" of the state, for example, when the employee disclosed pollution or workplace hazards on the part of the employer. There is also a federal whistleblowing statute in the Sarbanes-Oxley Act (SOX) of 2002 (discussed in the Liability of Accountants chapter), but that law only protects whistleblowing employees of public companies regulated by the Securities and Exchange Commission. Moreover, SOX only protects employees who disclose information pertaining to securities fraud or some other type of fraud or embezzlement against the shareholders. Thus, SOX provides only some protection to whistleblowers. Whistleblowing, finally, should not be confused with disclosing wrongdoing pursuant to *False Claims Acts*, which are federal and state statutes that provide that a whistleblowing employee who discloses wrongdoing by his or her employer in the form of embezzlement or fraud against the government, such as Medicare or Medicaid fraud, is entitled to a percentage (ranging from 10-30%) of the award or settlement against the employer that the government receives. It also should be noted that the 2010 Dodd-Frank Wall Street Reform and Consumer Protection Act has a provision that extends whistleblower protection and rewards to those employees, as well as any others, disclosing financial fraud in private sector contracting and bribery in overseas contracting with foreign governments. Thus, whistleblowing may, or may not be, legally protected, let alone rewarded; and consequently the issue arises, therefore, as to whether ethics extends any moral protection to private sector whistleblowing employees, especially in the corporate context and particularly regarding at-will employees.

Morally Justifying Whistleblowing
A problem inherent in Kantian ethics is the possibility that two secondary moral rules, both of which "pass" the Categorical Imperative, conflict! This problem is particularly apparent in a corporate whistleblowing context. It can be argued that employees have an ethically "certified" moral obligation of loyalty and confidentiality. Yet it also can be argued persuasively that employees have a moral right to free speech, which at a minimum should include a right to "blow the whistle"

on wrongful corporate activities. All these secondary moral rules theoretically pass the Categorical Imperative, yet they clash in practice. What is the ethical solution to this problem? Perhaps the solution is to qualify the general duties of loyalty and confidentiality. That is, to maintain generally that employees do owe a moral duty of loyalty and confidentiality to their employers, but also to maintain that this duty is not unlimited. The general duty can be superseded by special circumstances, such as when the employee not only has a moral free speech right, but also an obligation to blow the whistle in order to stop or prevent harm.

Ethical Examination of Whistleblowing
As has been pointed out, there does not yet exist a uniform corpus of whistleblower law to protect private sector, at-will employees. There is yet no general federal law, though the new federal, securities fraud, whistleblower provision in the Sarbanes-Oxley Act is a start. There are some state statutes, but only a relatively small number of truly comprehensive state statutes. Most of these contain strict reporting requirements, and, moreover, are strictly construed by the courts. Finally, as will be seen in the chapter on employment relationships, there is a rather large, but loose, state-by-state collection of at times widely divergent, common law, "public policy" formulations that may encompass whistleblowing protections. The statutory and case law, of course, eventually will determine the legalities of a whistleblowing situation. Ethics, as a branch of philosophy, will be used to determine what is morally required in a whistleblowing situation. Ascertaining whether whistleblowing is morally permissible, or in particular, whether it is morally required, or concomitantly whether it is morally justified, is a very difficult task. Such a moral whistleblowing inquiry first necessitates an examination of the field of ethics as a branch of philosophy. Accordingly, one important moral philosophical issue that emerges is whether ethics, as a branch of philosophy, grants, or should confer, any moral protection to private sector employees, especially at-will employees in a corporate context. Do employees have the moral right, and perhaps the moral responsibility, to "blow the whistle"? Those are the seminal moral questions for ethical analysis. Employers, therefore, must look to both the law and the philosophy of ethics when deciding issues relating to whistleblowing my employee.

The Ethical Principle of Last Resort
One recalls from the Torts and Business chapter that as a general rule (though with exceptions, as noted) based on the common law doctrine of nonfeasance one does not have a *legal* duty to help, aid, or rescue anyone. Consequently, one, again as a general rule, cannot be held legally liable for negligence for not rescuing someone even if one is able or for not warning someone of a peril. That is the law – nonfeasance, not acting, is not actionable legally. Yet when does one have a positive moral obligation to act? Acting morally may involve more than merely avoiding negative harm; acting morally also may require one to perform an affirmative positive action, even though legally one may not be required to take the action. The ethical principle of "*last resort*" indicates when one has a moral duty to act, to aid another, or to rescue. One morally must act when there is a need, proximity, capability, one is the last resort or chance to avoid the peril, and when acting would not cause harm, or threaten to cause

harm, equal to or greater than the original peril. The principle is based partially on Kant's admonition that "ought implies can," that is, that one is obligated to do only what one can do. Thus, if one is unable to act and help, due to lack of opportunity, means, or resources, one is not obligated morally to act.

The "last resort" principle usually involves an obligation of immediacy and high priority posed by an emergency; it thus generates a moral obligation to act that one cannot ignore without moral condemnation. The classic example is a drowning case when the five "last resort" factors are present. The problem in successfully applying the "last resort" principle to business, however, emerges the fourth and fifth factors. Who is the last resort for people unemployed and in need, business or government? Would business "rescuing" in fact harm the corporation, or its shareholders, or other stakeholders? A "friendly takeover," a corporation helping an employee pay his or her children's college tuition, may be praiseworthy actions, but are they morally required under the "last resort" principle? Is a corporation immoral for choosing not to act in the preceding circumstances? One example is the case of the Malden Mills Company, whose very compassionate owner rebuilt the facility after a fire without terminating any employees; but due in part to the added financial strain of keeping those employees, he forced his company to file for Chapter 11 bankruptcy protection in order to reorganize its finances, thereby resulting in a considerably, and permanently, diminished workforce. Another example concerns the large, multinational pharmaceutical companies who are providing for free or at greatly reduced cost their patented anti-AIDS drugs to African nations. Yet are they so doing because it is their moral responsibility as the "rescuer" of "last resort" or due to other social pressures? Similarly, corporations may not be the "last resort" to take care of their employees' disabled children, yet companies such as Toyota and Raytheon do provide assistance, for example, by hosting dinners with speakers and holding "networking" events, as well as expanding insurance coverage for "special needs" children. If not moral duty, what motivates these meritorious actions? A most interesting and thought-provoking example concerns Wal-Mart's very meritorious response to the Hurricane Katrina disaster in New Orleans and the Gulf Coast. Was Wal-Mart's "trucking in" tons of relief supplies (literally!) "merely" a socially responsible action, or was Wal-Mart the "last resort" to bring rapid relief to this devastated region of the country; and if the latter, what does that say about the government—all levels of government—federal, state, and local?

A critical point is that even though a company or person may not have a legal obligation to help, aid, or rescue, and, moreover, even if a company or person does not have any moral obligation to act based on the "last resort" principle, nonetheless many people and businesses do "help out" in the community by taking part in charitable and civic affairs. These philanthropic and civic-minded individuals and business today are deemed to "socially responsible" ones. The value of social responsibility will be covered in Part II of this chapter.

In summary, what does it mean to be moral? Being moral means being ethical, that is, reasoning from ethical theories and principles to moral conclusions as to right and wrong. This chapter has introduced the reader to the field of ethics, which is a branch of philosophy, and has sought to demonstrate how ethical theories can be applied to modern day business problems to reason to moral conclusions. The four ethical theories examined in this chapter – Ethical Egoism, Ethical Relativism, Utilitarianism, and Kant's Categorical Imperative – are major ethical theories in Western Civilization intellectual thought and tradition. These theories are not, of course, the only ethical theories in Western Civilization; and obviously there are many other ethical theories stemming from other civilizations as well as religions. As noted, the authors selected these four since they are very important ones as well as the fact that the basic tenets of each should be familiar to the reader. Ethics is thus a very large intellectual endeavor. And, as emphasized, to really complicate matters, there is no "Supreme Court of Ethics" to tell the readers, and for that matter the authors, which ethical theory is the "true" and "right" one. There is, however, an element of truth and rightfulness in all four theories. Accordingly, the authors would advise the reader to do the following: first, pursuant to Ethical Egoism improve oneself, empower oneself, and achieve success for oneself and one's company or organization; second, pursuant to Ethical Relativism, when achieving this success be "culturally competent" and thus strive not to contravene a society's moral norms; third, pursuant to Utilitarianism, in addition to achieving one's own and one's company's success similarly strive to find "win-win" scenarios where the good of all the stakeholders including society as a whole is maximized too; and finally, pursuant to Kantian ethics, in attaining this individual and societal good make sure that no person or stakeholder group is disrespected or demeaned. These principles should be manifested in any true Code of Ethics. Then, one will be successful, and rightfully so, in the sense that individual and organizational success will be secured in a truly moral manner. Of course, now that one and one's company has achieved so much success, stature, and money, there very likely will emerge an expectation from the community and society that the company and organization will be not "just" a legal and moral one, but also a "socially responsible" entity. The next part to this chapter, therefore, deals with the very current and relevant topic of social responsibility, or when the term is applied to business – "corporate social responsibility."

Part II – Corporate Social Responsibility
Stakeholder analysis has emerged as a critical concern for the modern business leader. Typically, *stakeholder* considerations, above and beyond the interests of the shareholders of the corporation, have been interpreted and examined under the concept of "*corporate social responsibility*." Corporate social responsibility (CSR) now also has become a central issue for business leaders. Moreover, today stakeholder analysis as well as CSR is converging with the notion of "corporate governance," which traditionally has had mainly legal connotations. In this Part II to the chapter, the authors examine stakeholders and CSR in the context of corporate governance. The authors take a broad approach to corporate governance and stakeholders, encompassing legal, moral, social responsibility, and economic values. Stakeholder analysis and CSR are addressed in a global context. The authors discuss the traditional nature of the corporation, with its emphasis on maximizing shareholder value; and then examine corporate constituency statutes which allow corporate boards to consider the values of other stakeholders. Next, the authors examine new socially responsible ways of doing business, social benefit corporations, or B-Corps, and low-profit limited liability companies, which give primacy to stakeholder values beyond

the interests of the shareholders in corporate decision-making. The authors principally analyze U.S. law but global legal perspectives are presented too. The critical relationship of corporate social responsibility and stakeholders to corporate governance is emphasized and explicated; and finally implications and recommendations for business leaders are provided to incorporate not only legal and ethical values but also corporate social responsibility and stakeholder values into corporate governance. The imperative of governing the corporation in a profitable, legal, moral, and socially responsible manner is underscored; so that the corporation achieves sustainable economic growth and development and also produces positive value for all the stakeholders of the corporation and betterment for society as a whole.

Corporate Social Responsibility

What exactly is a corporation's "social responsibility"? Does a corporation have a social obligation to take care of the poor, educate the public, give to charity, and fund cultural programs? Social projects and social welfare in the United States traditionally have been viewed as the appropriate domain of government, not of business. Business, of course, is taxed and such taxes may be used for social purposes. The traditional purpose of business as viewed in the U.S., moreover, is the profitable production and distribution of goods and services, not social welfare. Yet by raising the issue of social responsibility, business is forced to concern itself with the "social" dimension of its activities. This issue is now a critical one for business today.

Accordingly, what is the "social responsibility" of business today? The term at a basic philanthropic level may be defined as a business taking an active part in the social causes, charities, and civic life of one's community and society. Newman's Own is a private sector company praised for its philanthropic mission since it donates all of its profits and royalties after taxes for charitable and educational purposes. However, corporate social responsibility (CSR) certainly can be more than "mere" philanthropy. The social responsibility of business can also be thought of in a broader constituency or stakeholder sense, that is, by the corporation considering the values and needs of employees, suppliers, consumers, local communities, and society as a whole. One can also take a "strategic" as well as stakeholder approach to corporate social responsibility by integrating stakeholder, social, environmental, as well as economic concerns into the organization's values, culture, governance, strategy, and decision-making.

The World Business Council for Sustainable Development views social responsibility in a corporate context as a company's continuing commitment to act legally and morally and also to contribute to the economic development of society while improving the quality of life of their employees and their families as well as the local community and society as a whole. This definition evokes another, and even more expansive, concept of the "social responsibility" of business – "sustainability." The sustainability approach to corporate social responsibility is premised on the idea that a company must remain economically viable in the long-term, and that in order to be viable the company must take into consideration other stakeholders beyond the shareholders. The objective is to simultaneously produce economic value for the company, but also value for society as a whole by helping to solve societal needs, particularly by improving the lives of the people (and potential consumers) who live in the communities where the company does business. "Sustainability" is often used when discussing such concepts as corporate citizenship, social responsibility, stakeholder analysis, and social enterprise. Sustainability is at times discussed as part of a broader conception of social responsibility; but it also is discussed in a narrower discrete sense of a company being environmentally responsible, that is, not "merely" obeying all environmental laws and regulations, but also seeking to reduce waste and energy and water consumption, to conserve energy and water by means of "green buildings" and "offices," and even to produce energy by wind or solar means.

Some recent examples of socially responsible and sustainable actions by companies and organizations are as follows:

- Starbucks has embarked on a program to provide free job-skills training classes to people in certain local communities. The National Urban League as well as other community organizations are partnering with Starbucks to bring in the jobless for training, especially young people, veterans, and the homeless. Starbucks views this laudable effort as not "merely" an exercise in social responsibility designed to have a beneficial social impact in the communities it serves but also a strategic opportunity to hire people, to help achieve a more diversified workforce, and to motivate employees, all of which should help to produce eventual financial value to the shareholders.

- The Carnival Corporation cruise company has embarked on a social impact "volun-tourism" program in the Dominican Republic, where travelers can choose from socially responsible shore excursions in addition to the usual "sand-and-surf" ones. Examples of the former are working on the production-line in a locally-run chocolate factory, visiting an artisan's center and working with local people to recycle products, pouring concrete in local homes, and teaching English. The company expects that the program will be fulfilling and an inspiration for the cruise passengers, will provide a new perspective on life for them, will help the local communities and people in the Dominican Republic, as well as achieve for Carnival some very positive and appropriate publicity for being a socially responsible cruise company.

- The city of Rome, Italy, has commenced a program whereby companies can sponsor a ruin by paying into a fund to restore the hundreds of ruins, statutes, fountains, as well as other artwork and historic sites. The luxury good companies, Fendi and Bulgari, are sponsoring the Trevi fountain and Spanish steps, respectively. However, there is a concern that the big and "big-name" monuments will readily find sponsors and those smaller and less well-known ones will lack patrons.

- Disney and Royal Caribbean are no longer using plastic straws, replacing them with paper ones, because as per Disney a "commitment to environmental stewardship".

- Kroger Supermarkets is discontinuing the use of plastic bags in its stores but will provide brown paper bags for free as well as sell customers reusable bags for $1 to $2 a piece.

- Kraft Heinz is now planning on using eggs only from cage-free hens in its global operations as well as only sustainably sourced palm oil. The company intends to spend $200 million on the project.
- Mondelez, the global snack food company, has as part of its broader social responsibility plan the Cocoa Life program wherein the company works with more than 90,000 coca farmers in Ghana, the Ivory Coast, and other countries to develop a sustainable network of cocoa farms for the future. As part of the program the company sends 15 employees, called "joy ambassadors" to help the local farmers and to work on local projects to improve the quality of life in their villages. Mondelez is investing $400 million over 10 years in the Cocoa Life program. To oversee the successful implementation of all those social responsibility and sustainability activities and budgetary outlays the company has a vice-president of global sustainability. What the company gets in return is a stronger and more reliable supply chain as well as employees who are excited and motivated and a reputation for "doing good" that can be marketed to consumers.
- The Hilton Hotel in Ft. Lauderdale, Florida has a very artistic-looking wind turbine system on its roof that produces renewable, "clean" energy, will pay for itself after several years, is collapsible during hurricanes, and impresses customers, tourists, and community, not only due to the turbines unique design but also because of the company's commitment to environmental protection, conservation, and production.
- An example of sustainability as well as an illustration of social entrepreneurship is a bank in Makassar, Indonesia, called the Mutiara Trash Bank, which will take the "deposits" of recyclable trash, such as plastic bottles and paper, from poor people in the community, at designated collection points, weight it, give it a monetary value, transfer it to the government, and then make a monetary deposit in the account of the "depositor." The objectives are to help reduce pressure on the ever-growing landfills, help clean up the environment, convert the trash to energy and other products, and to introduce poor people into the country's financial and banking system.
- Another example of sustainability and social entrepreneurship is a Kenyan company called M-Kopa Solar (note that kopa means "to borrow" in Swahili) that lends money to poor people on very favorable credit terms to enable them to buy expensive solar-power systems from the company. The objectives are to improve the lives of the people and for the company to do well too.

A corporation, of course, is a profit-making entity that exists in a competitive environment, and thus may be limited in its ability to solve a multitude of social problems particularly at the expense of the owners of the corporation – the shareholders. Where are the philanthropic guidelines for corporate contributions and improvements? How should a corporation's resources be allocated, and exactly to whom, to what extent, and in what priorities? What is the proper balance between shareholder and stakeholder interests? The corporate governance policies of the organization must seek to answer these important, yet, difficult questions. If a corporation unilaterally or too generously engages in social betterment, it may place itself at a disadvantage compared to other less socially responsible business entities. Being socially responsible costs money, and such efforts cut into profits. In a highly competitive market system, corporations that are too socially responsible may lessen their attractiveness to investors or simply may price themselves out of the market. One example is the clearly socially responsible firm – Ben & Jerry's, which has long been known and lauded for its civic, community, and environmental efforts. Yet the company may have been too socially responsible and consequently neglectful of basic business concerns. Ultimately, the original former "hippies" Ben Cohen and Jerry Greenfield of Ben & Jerry's sold their interests in their company in 2000 to global consumer products giant, Unilever, which carried on the social responsibility activities of the brand to a degree, but in a more prudent and strategic manner. Nevertheless, despite the saga of Ben & Jerry's, social responsibility, at least to some reasonable degree, may be in the long-term self-interest of business, so long as these activities align with the corporation's long-term objectives. Furthermore, there is some evidence that these socially responsible strategies have been successful.

A corporation cannot long remain a viable economic entity in a society that is uneven, unstable, and deteriorating. It makes good business sense for a corporation to devote some of its resources to social betterment projects. To operate efficiently, for example, business needs educated and skilled employees. Education and training, therefore, should be of paramount interest to business leaders. A corporation, for example, can act socially responsible by providing computers to community schools and by releasing employees on company time to furnish the training. Business also gains an improved public image by being socially responsible. An enhanced social image should attract more customers and investors and thus provide positive benefit for the firm.

Other examples of companies engaging in socially responsible marketing as one way to persuade consumers to spend in a difficult economy, to wit: Sketchers USA launched a brand called BOBS, meaning Benefiting Others By Shoes, which results in the company donating two pairs of shoes for every one sold; Urban Outfitters features clothes by Threads for Thought, which gives part of its sales proceeds to humanitarian groups; Nordstrom sells hats made by Krochet Kids International, which enlists impoverished people in Uganda and Peru, for example, to make hats which are sold in the U.S. for $24; and Feed Projects, which makes T-shirts, handbags, and accessories, donates a percentage of its profits to United Nations anti-hunger programs. When implemented correctly, these socially responsible retailing efforts are "good works" and also good strategies, which may be young consumers who may not have the means to make large charitable contributions but who admire brands that are "trendy" but which also reflect a save-the-planet theme. To further illustrate, the Walt Disney Company, in an effort to portray a socially responsible message, as well as to attract customers to its theme parks, commenced a program, called "Give a Day, Get a Disney Day," whereby the company will give away a million one-day, one-park tickets to people who volunteer at select charities. A corporation that acts more socially responsible not only secures public favor, but also avoids public disfavor. To illustrate, for many years the large multi-national pharmaceutical companies were criticized for not providing AIDS drugs for free or at greatly reduced prices to African governments. In response to public criticism, the pharmaceutical responded in a socially responsible (and also egoistic manner) by giving the drugs away or selling them at cost. Moreover, certain pharmaceutical companies, such as Roche and GlaxoSmithKline, on their social responsibility and sustainability websites, have statements indicating preferential pricing and accessibility as well as limited patent policies for AIDs drugs going to African and other less developed countries. Accordingly, social responsibility and also good public relations are achieved. Wal-Mart, the giant retailer, in response to criticisms from environmentalists and labor activists, now has a director of global ethics, who will be responsible for developing and enforcing company standards of conduct, as well as a "senior director for stakeholder engagement," whose role will be to develop a new model of business engagement that produces value for society. Similarly, clothing and apparel manufacturers, such as Nike and the Gap, in response to criticism by labor and consumer groups about exploitive working conditions in overseas "sweatshops," have ended poor working conditions, and now also report on their social responsibility efforts and achievements overseas. Business is part of society and subject to society's mandates; and if society wants more "responsibility" from business, business cannot ignore this "request" without the risk of incurring society's anger, perhaps in the form of higher taxes or more onerous government regulation. Socially responsible activities may also improve a company's reputation when viewed by external stakeholders, such as bankers, creditors, investors, and government regulators, which not only may avoid economic harm, but also may bring about economic benefits. As such an egoist and rational actor will surely see the instrumental value of a prudent degree of social responsibility and sustainability in today's global business marketplace. Hannah Jones, head of social responsibility and sustainability for Amazon, states: "Sustainability was always framed as something that was counter to business success, that if you made a product that was sustainable, somehow it would be less good or more expensive.....The reframe that happened is that we stopped seeing sustainability and labor rights as a risk and burden, and instead as a source of innovation....If you flip it to be about innovation opportunity, people step into that space with less fear. And that creates possibility" (Bernstein, 2018, p. 1).

The topics of social responsibility and stakeholder analysis emerged as a critical one for global business leaders too. A global example would be the Coca-Cola's company's efforts to provide clean water to parts of the developing world, which Coke also hopes to promote goodwill, boost local economies, and broaden its customer base. Royal Caribbean Cruise Company is teaming up with a Haitian non-profit organization to build a primary school, which is located on land the company leases from the government as a stop for its ships in the port town of Labadee. Wal-Mart is now selling online handicrafts made by women artisans in developing countries, such as dresses made in Kenya and jewelry from Guatemala and Thailand. Over 500 items from 20,000 female artisans will be offered for sale, which certainly will help the female artisans but also improve the company's global image. "Sustainability" is also used to support corporate social responsibility efforts globally: "For transnational corporations doing business in developed countries, sustainability may require investment in community-level infrastructure development projects, technological innovation, education, and health care. Two excellent examples of global "sustainable" CSR are the Norwegian company, Yara International, the world's largest chemical fertilizer company, has sponsored public/private partnerships to develop storage, transportation, and port facilities in parts of Africa with significant untapped agricultural potential, thereby developing local agriculture, providing jobs and improved incomes for farmers, and at the same time benefiting the company through an increased demand for its fertilizer products. Second, the Nestle Company is working to improve milk production in certain regions of India, by investing in well drilling, refrigeration, veterinary medicine, and training, thereby significantly increasing output and enhancing product quality, certainly beneficial to the company, and at the same time allowing the company to pay higher prices for farmers and their employees, resulting in a higher standard of living for the local community.

The United Nations now has a business initiative on corporate social responsibility, called the United Nations Global Compact, whereby companies can join and thus voluntarily agree to make improvements in human rights, labor, the environment, and combating corruption. The World Bank, moreover, now has an Internet course on social responsibility, called "CSR and Sustainable Competitiveness," offered by its educational and training division. The corporate social responsibility course is designed for "high-level" private sector managers, government officials and regulators, practitioners, academics, and journalists. One major purpose to the course is to provide a conceptual framework for improving the business environment to support corporate governance policies and social responsibility efforts by corporations and business. The course is also designed to assist companies to formulate a social responsibility strategy based on moral and economic values as well as one with a long-term perspective.

Stakeholder Values

Stakeholder theory...considers the enterprise as a community with a number of stakeholders – in other words, social groups that are directly and indirectly connected to the enterprise and that are dependent on its success and prosperity. These groups include employees, customers, suppliers, distributors, local communities, and especially the society or societies in which the business has operations.

The stakeholder groups typically are the following: shareholders and owners, employees, customers and consumers, suppliers and distributors, creditors, community, government, competition, and society. Shareholders as the owners are always listed first. Obviously, a corporation cannot survive unless it serves and benefits its shareholders in a financial sense. However, today, shareholders may view their investment as one that benefits society too and perhaps in a direct manner by means of the social benefit corporation. Regardless, all shareholders are entitled to the honest and efficient management of their investment as well as a fair return on their investment. Employees are of course interested in obtaining and maintaining employment. They value a just wage, fair employment practices and working conditions, and job security. They also may value working for a company that is regarded as a "socially responsible" one. Customers and consumers want access to good and services that are of good quality, at a fair price, and that come with good customer service. Suppliers and distributors want financially rewarding, long-term contractual relationships with the company. Local communities want to see the corporation located in their cities and towns so as to provide employment for the citizens and residents and to support the local tax-base. The local community also values, and very well may expect, that the corporations in its presence participate in civic, charitable, philanthropic, and socially responsible activities. Creditors naturally value being repaid and also expect a fair rate of return as well as adequate assurances of security for the obligation. Government values legal compliance with business laws and business regulations. Government also values business as an important component of its tax-base. Government also values and thus desires to promote entrepreneurship and competition. As to the competition, the competition values its own market share, yet expects in a capitalistic model "tough" and "hard-hitting" competition, but the competition also values completion that is legal and ethical. Society values its survival, of course, and also growth, prosperity for its members, and the sustainability of business and society. Members of society also value today, and thus expect, that the corporation will be a socially responsible one, particularly regarding its stewardship of the environment and efforts to improve the environment.

The goal of the business leader today is to balance and harmonize these values and thus attempt to devise corporate governance policies that maximize these values in a legal, moral, socially responsible, and practically efficacious manner, thereby resulting in "win-win" scenarios for the business and all its stakeholders and attaining a level of continual sustainable business success.

Corporate Constituency Statutes

Socially responsible entrepreneurs and corporate directors and officers who wanted to engage in activities to benefit corporate stakeholders other than shareholders have in the past confronted a serious legal problem. Traditionally, pursuant to state corporation law the directors and officers of a corporation owed legal and fiduciary duties solely to the corporate entity. This overarching duty of the traditional *corpus* of corporate law is to maximize shareholder wealth. In fulfilling this duty, the directors and officers, based on the conventional Business Judgment Rule of corporate law, were required to act based on informed consent, with reasonable care, and in good faith. These legal duties were owed strictly and exclusively to the corporation and to the shareholders and not to any other people or groups, though the shareholders might have to enforce these duties on behalf of the corporation, if a breach of these duties by the directors and officers occurred, by means of a shareholder derivative lawsuit.

Today, however, many states have enacted statutes, called "*constituency statutes*," or have amended their corporation statutes, to allow the directors and officers to consider other constituent groups, often called "stakeholders," who are directly or indirectly affected by the corporation's activities. To illustrate express constituency statutes in the United States, the Minnesota corporation statute states that "in discharging the duties of the position of director, a director may, in considering the best interests of the corporation, consider the interests of the corporation's employees, customers, suppliers, and creditors, the economy of the state and nations, community and societal considerations, and the long-term as well as short-term interests of the corporation and its shareholders" (*Minnesota Statutes* Section

302A.251(5)). Similarly, in Florida, directors are now permitted to consider in making decisions a variety of factors not directly related to maximizing value for the shareholders. These broader stakeholder factors encompass the long-term interests and prospects of the corporation and its shareholders, as well as the social, economic, legal, or other effects of any corporate action on the employees, suppliers, customers, the communities where the corporation and its subsidiaries operate, and the economy of the state or nation (*Florida Statutes* Section 607.0830(3)). There is some variety among the provisions in the state statutes in the United States; but most statutes limit the consideration of stakeholder interests to those of customers, employees, creditors and the local communities. These permissible constituency groups typically include employees, creditors, suppliers, consumers, and the community at-large. Consequently, constituency statutes typically are limited, since the definition of "constituents" is a "narrow" one which, although including customers, employees, suppliers, and the local communities where the company does business, does not encompass the international community, environmental concerns, or broader human rights issues. Nevertheless, these statutes, whether separate enactments or amendments to state corporation statutes, usually are called "constituency" statutes.

It is critical to note, however, that constituency statutes generally are permissive, and not mandatory; that is, the directors and officers may take into consideration the interests of non-shareholder stakeholders, but the directors and officers are not required to do so. Significantly, however, these statutes only permit a balancing of interests rather than requiring a balance. Corporate boards of directors would thus be free to pursue socially responsible policies, but cannot be sanctioned for choosing not to do so. That is, directors can weigh competing interests at their discretion, and they also can freely disregard particular interests without fear of legal consequences at the hands of shareholders or any other group. These constituency statutes, therefore, do not impose any legal duty on the directors to any stakeholders or constituencies; and also these statutes do not furnish a corporate constituency or stakeholder group with a legal cause of action against the corporation's directors. Rather, these statutes allow boards of directors to consider stakeholder interests in the decision-making process, thereby enabling corporations to justify and to possibly defend a decision that they believe to be in the best interest of the corporation without contravening the duties owed to shareholders. Therefore, regarding non-shareholder interests, these constituency statutes are not mandatory but rather merely "permissive."

Social Benefit Corporations
In marked contrast to the corporate constituency statutes, as well as the traditional corporation itself, is a new legal business concept – the *"social benefit corporation."* These new entities also are called "benefit corporations," or simply "B-corporations" (as opposed to the traditional business or "C-corporation" of state corporate law). At times, the general term "social enterprise" is used to describe a social benefit corporation. Very recently in the United States, this new form of business enterprise has been created to provide a corporate legal structure for "social entrepreneurs," that is, those business people who aim to deliver not only financial benefits to the shareholders but also social benefits for other stakeholders, including local

communities and society at large by means of a "double bottom-line" of profits and social benefits or a "triple bottom-line" of social, environmental, and economic concerns. Social entrepreneurs firmly believe that social good can be produced along with profits, and thus they desire hybrid forms of business organizations to effectuate the achievement of both goals.

The critical difference between a social benefit corporation and a constituency statute in the U.S. is that in a corporation constituency statute the directors of a corporation *may* consider other stakeholder groups than the shareholders, but with a social benefit corporation, the directors *must* consider other stakeholders. In a social benefit corporation, typically in the company's articles of incorporation (which becomes its charter when approved by the state), the corporation will specify its intended social purposes or benefits as well as the stakeholders or constituent groups that it is legally obligated to consider in achieving these objectives. That is, it is pursuant to this new form of doing business the legal duty of corporate directors to consider the consequences of corporate actions, such as moving facilities from one state to another or overseas, lay-offs and downsizing, and takeovers and mergers, on groups other than the shareholders. Moreover, the directors are allowed to consider social responsibility and environmental objectives equal to or even greater than achieving profits. Traditionally, pursuant to state corporation laws, directors were held to a legal duty – a fiduciary duty – to act in the best interests of the corporation and its owners – the shareholders; and consequently directors could not consider stakeholders other than the shareholders. Furthermore, even under constituency states, where directors could consider other non-shareholder stakeholders, the directors had to do so with the aim of maximizing the long-term good, not of the public, but ultimately of the shareholders. For the law in the form of a social benefit corporation to now say that directors have a legal duty, that is, *must*, as opposed to *may*, consider the interests of other stakeholders affected by corporate activities is a very momentous change in the law indeed. It must be emphasized that consideration of the other constituencies beyond the shareholders is mandatory.

Several states in the United States, including Vermont, Hawaii, California, New York, New Jersey, Virginia, North Carolina, Pennsylvania, and Maryland, which in 2010 was the first state, have now promulgated legislation to allow "social benefit" corporations. As of the writing of this book, legislation has been introduced in Colorado, Michigan, Pennsylvania, North Carolina, and Oregon. The states generally have based their social benefit corporation statutes on a "model" act, called the "Model B-Corp Act." Pursuant to the Model Act as well as the state corporation benefit statutes, typically, the social benefit corporation must be cleared designated as a benefit corporation, and must specify in its social responsibility and environmental objectives in its charter and articles of incorporation, and also in some cases in its bylaws. In Maryland and other states the stock certificates also must be labeled to include the term "benefit corporation." The benefit corporation can pursue a "general public benefit" and/or "specific public benefits," such as providing low income or underserved people or communities with beneficial products or services, promoting economic opportunity for people and communities, preserving, protecting, and improving the environment, improving human health, promoting the arts and sciences, advancing knowledge, and increasing the flow of capital to entities with a public benefit purpose. The Maryland law allows businesses to commit to a specific public good; and that the specific public benefits in Maryland can encompass the following: 1) providing individuals and communities with beneficial products and services; 2) providing economic opportunity for individuals or communities beyond the creation of jobs; 3) preserving the environment; 4) improving human health; 5) promoting the arts, sciences, or the advancement of knowledge; 6) increasing the flow of capital to entities with a public benefit purpose; and 7) accomplishing any other particular benefit for society or the environment. However, there are concerns as to the lack of clarity in not only the definition of benefits but also the ranking of benefits, perhaps engendering intra-corporate disagreements or conflict between the B-corporation and its stakeholders. The social benefit corporation statutes require the directors of the corporation to consider the impact of their decision-making not "merely" on the shareholders, but also other corporate stakeholders, such as the employees of the corporation, subsidiaries, suppliers, distributors, customers, the local community, society, and the environment, whether local or global. The social benefit report corporation also must publish an annual "benefit report" to disclose the level of performance in attaining those goals as well as any circumstances the corporation's ability to achieve its beneficial purposes. The report must be delivered to shareholders, posted on the company's website, and, in some case, delivered to the state's Secretary of State (who is typically the state cabinet level official who typically is in charge of corporate affairs).

One very serious concern with the creation of a social benefit corporation is that the law is still developing for this new form of doing business; and consequently the major risk of this new corporate entity is the still un-chartered legal liability of the directors, who not only may be sued by shareholders for not achieving social responsibility goals, but who also may be sued by other stakeholders who are adversely affected by a corporation action which they contend is socially irresponsible to a discrete stakeholder group or injurious to the societal good. This new legal cause of action against directors in the U.S. typically is called a "benefit enforcement proceeding." It is quite possible that in the U.S., shareholders, directors, employees, and any other persons or groups that may be specified in the articles of incorporation of the benefit corporation to bring an action against the corporation. The causes of action available to these parties in the benefit enforcement proceedings may include a failure to pursue the general public benefit or any specific public benefit set forth in its articles of incorporation. Consequently, serious question exist about the full legal implications of the B-corporation form. The main legal concern is that unlike other types of corporations or business associations, where executives and managers are merely permitted to consider stakeholder interests, in the benefit corporation there is a clear affirmative legal duty to do so. Furthermore, as emphasized, the state social benefit statutes in the U.S. provide scant guidance as to the scope of the expanded legal duties of the directors, particularly whether the social benefit duties are separate and distinct from traditional corporate duties, as well as to what the relationship is between the two sets of duties. One point is evident, though, and that is shareholder primacy among stakeholders cannot be the motivation behind corporate decision-making. Consequently, a paradoxical situation well could arise because the directors of B-corporations would be legally required to disregard the traditional notion of shareholder primacy and thus take other stakeholder values and interests into account, but they would not be legally entitled to completely ignore shareholder interests. Moreover, to further complicate matters, some of the state statutes also decline to address the key issue as to what non-shareholder stakeholder groups have legal standing to sue to enforce the expanded legal duties of the directors. Now the shareholders of a social benefit corporation may have expanded rights to bring derivative lawsuits (that is, suits pursuant to traditional corporate law against the directors on behalf of the corporation when the directors fail to act) on behalf of other stakeholders. Accordingly, shareholders now may be able to bring a lawsuit against the corporation because its directors failed to consider or adequately consider the values and interests of other non-shareholder stakeholder groups. The social benefit corporate way of doing business in the United States is thus today a vague one, and also one that engenders conflict between pursuing desirable social objectives and striving to maximum profits. As such, there will be inescapable legal conflicts as the courts attempt to define and to reconcile the principles of the legal and fiduciary duty in the context of corporate directors seeking to achieve business objectives and also to fulfill social obligations. So, based on the current state of the law and the legal commentary examined for this chapter, the logical conclusion from the authors' perspective is that the new way of doing business in the U.S. as a social benefit corporation, though well-intended, should be abjured, at least for the present, until the attendant legal rights and responsibilities can be explicated by the courts. Yet social responsibility pursuant to corporate constituency statutes can be a viable legal activity for a company as well as a smart, sustainable, and socially beneficial one, of course.

Social Responsibility, Stakeholders, and Corporate Governance
Corporate governance today has emerged as significant subject for business; and the topic of social responsibility also arises in the context of corporate governance. Initially, one may think of "corporate governance" as having strictly legal components, especially business law and regulatory law. In the traditional governance models, the corporation's primary focus is on shareholder rights, and the primary governance rule is based on maximizing shareholder value. Directors, therefore, have a duty to ensure that companies fulfill their legal obligations, protect shareholder interests, and provide accurate and timely information to investors, markets, and government regulators. Yet corporate governance also has social responsibility as well as ethical ramifications. That is, corporate governance, in the expansive meaning that the authors wish to give to this concept, means the legal, ethical/moral, and social responsibility considerations for regulating business today. Business decision-making cannot be decoupled from the responsibility – legal, ethical, and social - of business leaders for their own risk-taking; otherwise, the whole business and entrepreneurial system will be undermined.

The idea is not "just" to maximize profits by "merely" obeying the law, for example, SEC regulations, but rather to also include ethical, moral, and social responsibility concerns into corporate decision-making. Making profits in a legal manner is obviously an essential component to corporate governance; but the focus on "just" the law is too narrow, the authors contend. To illustrate a more expansive meaning of corporate governance, the American Law Institute in its Principles of

Corporate Governance sets forth fundamental principles of corporate governance. The primary principle is for the corporation to conduct the business with an objective of enhancing corporate profit and shareholder gain. However, the corporation may take into account ethical considerations that are reasonably regarded as appropriate to the responsible conduct of business; and also the corporation may devote a reasonable amount of resources to charitable, philanthropic, humanitarian, and educational purposes; and the corporation may do so in both situations even if shareholder profit and shareholder gain are not thereby enhanced. So, although the primary focus is on the monetary value, this objective is moderated by ethical and social responsibility values. The idea is that the corporation will engage in self-governance; and thus regulate, not only by the strictures of the law, but also by morality and ethics, as well as stakeholder and societal concerns, the manner by which it generates profits. In essence, corporations will act legally, morally, and in a socially responsible manner only if those people who exercise control over the corporation, whether directly or indirectly; that is, the directors, officers, and shareholders together, have the vision to see that the collective future of the business, its stakeholders, and society as a whole is inextricably tied to the sustainability of the entity and the society in which it operates and flourishes, as well as the strength of character and leadership ability to implement and act on that vision.

For the traditional corporation some suggestions on how to structure corporate governance to maximize long-term shareholder, stakeholder, and societal value creation are as follows: empower and motivate business leaders to manage for the long-term by using incentive and compensation systems. That is, compensation should be aligned with long-term objectives, and financial rewards should be linked to the period over which results are realized. Incentive structures should also reflect a more full measure of socially responsible performance, for example, by including environmental sustainability, in these incentive programs. The companies it to make these social responsibility considerations contribute to long-term, successful, financial performance. Business leaders, therefore, must exert – leadership – to improve incentive and compensation systems as well as other aspects of corporate governance to enhance sustainability.

Corporate governance guidelines for social responsibility should be premised on fundamental principles. First the company should formulate a corporate social responsibility policy to guide its strategic planning and provide a roadmap for its CSR initiatives. Second, that policy should be an integral part of the organization's overall business policy and aligned with the company's business goals. Third, the policy should be created and framed with the participation of various level executives as well as representatives of other stakeholder groups, and the policy must be approved and overseen by the board and implemented by top management. The corporate social responsibility policy should cover the following core elements: (1) adherence to the law; (2) acting in an ethical, honest, and transparent; (3) consideration of the values and interests of all stakeholders, including shareholders, employees, customers, suppliers, local communities, society at large, and the environment; (4) treating all stakeholders with dignity and respect and as worthwhile means and not as mere means; (5) charitable and philanthropic activities; and (6) activities that promote social and economic development.

A socially responsible firm, however, must also be a realistic one; that is, socially responsible, stakeholder considerations, and environmental efforts must be sustainable economically and should have some relationship to the firm's business. These prudential considerations should be reflected in the company's corporate governance polices. Employees, for example, should also be engaged directly in the company's social responsibility activities so as to engage them, inspire them, motivate them, and thereby enhance morale and productivity. Moreover, a firm's social responsibility program does not have to be a multi-million dollar effort; rather, something as simple as an employee social responsibility "suggestion box," or as straightforward as a recycling or energy saving program, will do to promote employee involvement as well as to promote and give credence to employee social values. Nonetheless, despite the size, a firm's social responsibility efforts should be publicized widely within the company, for example, in company newsletters, as well as externally, for example in company annual "social responsibility" reports and on its website. Being socially responsible, therefore, is a smart and sustainable business strategy the company's corporate governance policies must be tailored to promote this type of social responsibility.

Corporate governance emerges as a particularly challenging endeavor in the social benefit corporation considering its dual mission of profit-making and societal betterment, the concomitant trade-offs among competing stakeholders, including shareholders, of course, the ensuing competition for corporate resources, the lack of a specific B-Corp government regulator, and the absence in the state legislation as to how the conflicting stakeholder demands should be balanced. To solve this corporate governance dilemma, the management of the social benefit company can refer to the standards set forth by the third party evaluator to whom the B-Corp must report. Yet since the social benefit corporation legislation provides no concrete guidance, the legislation envisions that the top management team will weigh the company's social responsibility goals in light of their business objectives, and then arrive some reasonable determination that advances profit and all stakeholder values. Moreover, to advance social responsibility accountability, it will be important that the views of top management team should be balanced within the company by using participatory mechanisms that allow for stakeholder representation, invite stakeholder participation, and keep internal channels of communication open and flowing. At the very least, due to the mixed mission, vague corporate socially responsible standards, conflicting stakeholder demands, as well as citizen and interest group pressure, the activities of the corporation will be, and should be, carefully monitored – principally by its management as part of their governance function, but also by company stakeholders, government legislators and regulators, and citizens.

Implications and Recommendations for Business Leaders
The new corporation structure of the social benefit corporation is a clearly meritorious way of doing business, indeed. Yet the authors believe that at this time it also is plainly a problematic one for business people, directors, and entrepreneurs, even very socially responsible ones. The law is just too new and unsettled as to nature of the public benefit and especially as to the legal risks of being a director of a "B-corp." As such, no corporate board of directors wants to be the "test case" in determining the

parameters of legal liability under a social benefit corporation model. Similarly, with the very new L3C way of doing business socially until the IRS promulgates some precise rules, this entity, again, though similarly laudatory, is to be avoided. Nonetheless, socially responsible people who plan to incorporate can always include social responsibility goals in the articles and bylaws and corporate governance policies of a traditional corporation; and the typical state's constituency statute expressly allows the consideration of other stakeholder groups. So, the legal latitude exists to be socially responsible, yet without mandating a legal duty on the board to be socially responsible. Moreover, the authors assert that it is in the long-term, egoistic, self-interest of the corporation to be a socially responsible one and thus to be active and engaged in community, civic, and charitable activities.

Accordingly, it is the job of the business leader to educate the shareholders, and perhaps corporate management as well, of the benefits that will accrue to the company and the shareholders by the company acting in a smart, shrewd, and strategic socially responsible manner. Corporate social responsibility, as such, should be treated as an investment, not a cost, comparable to quality improvement and employee training. Business leaders, executives, and managers, therefore, must be cognizant of and appreciate the instrumental strategic value of social responsibility in its constituency and sustainability formulations. Business leaders, executives, and managers today surely are well aware of societal expectations regarding the social responsibility of their companies. Business leaders want their businesses to be successful and to sustain that success on a long-term basis.

The term "*sustainability*" also has emerged, along with social responsibility and corporate governance, as important subject matters for business today. A sustainable business is one that is governs itself in a long-term, stakeholder centered, and environmentally conscious manner. To be a sustainable one, the business must be concerned not "merely" with profits, but also must pay attention to, and seek to balance, stakeholder interests and environmental concerns. Sustainability has legal and ethical predicates too; and as such will result in legal and moral decision-making by companies. In order to better illustrate as well as explicate the values of practicality, legality, morality, social responsibility, and stakeholder interests, and their relationship to sustainability, the authors have developed the model presented in Figure 17.1 (Mujtaba and Cavico, 2013; Mujtaba, 2014), called the Business Sustainability Continuum (BSC).

The BSC illustrates that the continual success and "sustainability" of the business can only be achieved by an adherence to four core values (Mujtaba, Cavico and Plangmarn, 2012): *Economic*, indicating that a business obviously must have a viable business model which fulfills a need and enables the business to make a profit; *Legal*, indicating that this profit must be achieved in legal manner by aligning the conduct of the business with all applicable local, national, and international law; *Ethical*, indicating that since there may be no law or "gaps" in the law nonetheless the business must act in a moral manner and also must act in conformity with its values, promises, and obligations; and *Social Responsibility*, indicating that the business must focus on the community and engage in civic, philanthropic, and charitable endeavors as part of the business' overall strategic plan. Sustainability will help the business; but also help the business help governments solve pressing social problems; and, as such, sustainability provides a means to rebuild trust in the economic and political systems, which naturally is good for business and good for society. Accordingly, corporate governance policies must be devised to give credence and implementation to these "sustainable" values; and thereby will enable the business to achieve success and to sustain that success in a continual manner, thus benefiting the business, its shareholders, communities where it does business, and all the stakeholders affected by the business, including society as a whole. To do so is to act in a truly socially responsible and sustainable manner.

Figure 17.1 – The Business Sustainability Continuum

Economic	Legal	Ethical	Social Responsibility
Have a viable business model to fill a need while earning a profit. Filling an existing need is the goal and profit is the consequence of doing it well.	Align behavior with applicable local, national and international laws that apply to your business employees, associates, partners, clients, and customers.	Act morally and according to your universal values, promises, and obligations. The business must do what it says it will do.	Focus on community, philanthropy, and charity as a strategic part of the business. Successful firms operate on this ultimate end of the continuum.
New Businesses		*Leading and Established Businesses*	

Business Sustainability Continuum

Summary
This chapter has sought to build on the previous chapters' legal materials by introducing the readers to and examining the fields of ethics and social responsibility and showing how, and why, ethics and social responsibility can, and should, be applied to business today. Legality, ethics, and morality are very important values; and today social responsibility is such a value too. Business leaders must be cognizant of these values. Furthermore, the emphasis on stakeholders or constituency groups is an essential component of business leadership and corporate governance today too. The business leader must take an enlightened approach to satisfying the values of stakeholders in order to achieve long-term sustainable success. As emphasized, the ultimate goal is to attain "win-win" resolutions where all the company's stakeholders receive value. Social responsibility emerges as a key element in achieving stakeholder symmetry and success and business sustainability. Furthermore, given the apparent positive relationship between successful financial performance and social

responsibility, and the critical need of both these values for society and the economic system, corporate social responsibility, stakeholder analysis, and corporate governance have emerged as most relevant and profound topics for business today.

Discussion Questions –Business Ethics

1. What is the philosophic distinction between ethics and morality? Why is the difference important? Provide an example.
2. What is the doctrine of Ethical Egoism? What are some of the constraints on the doctrine? Provide an example of an ethically egoistic action with a brief explanation.
3. What is the "conflict" problem in Ethical Egoism? How is it often resolved? How should it be resolved? Provide examples in business with brief explanations thereof.
4. What is the doctrine of Ethical Relativism? What are some of the advantages as well as disadvantages of using this ethical theory to make moral determinations in business? Why is this ethical theory called the international business person's ethics "best friend"? Provide an example of the doctrine in operation along with a brief explanation.
5. How does on go about defining the pertinent "society" for the purposes of Ethical Relativism? Why is that determination critical? What does one do in a society that is very heterogeneous culturally? Provide an example of a "society" as well as a moral precept in that society that would impact business along with a brief explanation of the example.
6. What is the doctrine of Utilitarianism? What are some of the advantages as well as disadvantages of using this ethical theory to make moral determinations? Provide an example of a moral action in business pursuant to this ethical theory with a brief explanation.
7. Why did Kant condemn Utilitarianism as an immoral ethical theory? Provide a business example illustrating Kant's criticism of Utilitarianism.
8. What is Kant's Categorical Imperative? How is it used to make moral determinations in business? Why did Kant call his ethical principle "categorical" and "imperative"? Provide an example of a moral as well as an immoral action in business pursuant to Kantian ethics together with a brief explanation.

Discussion Questions –Social Responsibility

1. One cannot be sued for acting in a socially irresponsible manner (unless some other law is contravened). So, why should one, or one's business, be socially responsible?
2. The conservative economist and Nobel Prize winner, Milton Friedman, said in a famous essay that the "social responsibility of business is to make money," legally, of course, and pay taxes, and not be concerned with charitable or philanthropic endeavors. Do you agree with Friedman? Why or why not?

3. What do the terms "social responsibility," stakeholder analysis, "sustainability" and "people, planet, profits" mean to you in a modern global business environment? Provide examples.

4. Corporate social responsibility (CSR) is viewed by some as a positive phenomenon since CSR helps to "bridge the gap" of social inequality in the world and thus helps to contribute to sustainable development. What organization or company exemplifies this level of CSR in the modern era? Why?

5. Why would anyone invest in a company, such as a social benefit corporation, when the economic returns are very likely to be diminished by the benefit objectives when certainly other investment opportunities exist offering the likelihood of greater returns?

6. Should socially responsible behavior by business be mandated by government or will the self-interest of business promote socially responsible conduct?

7. What does "sustainability" mean to you in the context of business? What actions should a business take to be a "sustainable" one?

8. What is an example of a national or international company or organization that is considered to be "sustainable" because their leaders adhere to economic, legal, ethical, and social responsibility values in the modern workplace? Explain how these leaders govern the company or organization to implement these values.

Case Studies[6] on Law, Business Ethics, and CSR

Case 1- Supreme Court Sports Betting Decision 2018

Betting on sports games has been illegal in the U.S., except for Las Vegas, Nevada, until recently. However, in 2018 the U.S. Supreme Court in the case of *Murphy v. National Collegiate Athletic Association*, ruled, in a 6-3 decision, that the federal law that prohibited the states from legalizing sports betting, called the Professional and Amateur Sports Protection Act, which was passed to protect the integrity of sports, was unconstitutional pursuant to a Constitutional rule, called the anti-commandeering doctrine, which, as interpreted by the Supreme Court, does not allow the federal government to prevent the states from legislating to regulate activities in their states. It is important to note that the federal government can still directly regulate sports betting, based on the power granted to Congress in the Interstate Commerce clause to regulate foreign and domestic commerce; but the federal government cannot indirectly regulate state government regulation by simply not acting on the federal level and enacting a blanket prohibition on state regulation. The Supreme Court interpreted the 10th Amendment to the Constitution, which reserves to the states those powers not expressly granted to the federal government, as prohibiting Congress from directly ordering state legislatures not to pass laws regulating a specific subject matter or activity. Accordingly, now, the states are free to legislate or to pass by a ballot

---

[6] Additional case studies on law, ethics, corporate social responsibility, and sustainability, as well as subject matter videos and other supplemental material, can be accessed at the following link: http://www.business.nova.edu/course-materials/business-law/

referendum laws authorizing, licensing, and taxing sports gambling in their states. The states that do legalize sports betting should see a substantial increase in tax revenues.

The federal law was challenged by the state of New Jersey when Chris Christie (R) was governor; and that state is expected to pass legislation in 2018 to authorize and regulate sports betting at casinos in Atlantic City as well as online for residents. Moreover, at least three other states - Mississippi, West Virginia, and Pennsylvania - are also expected to join New Jersey. As such, in the aforementioned states the crime of sports betting will be essentially nullified. Consequently, the former illegal "underground" and "bookie" activity of sports betting, valued at about $150 billion in annual revenues, will become legal and taxable at least in some jurisdictions. Of course, it remains to be seen what the state regulations will look like as well as the fact that Congress may decide to act and regulate the field, superseding any conflicting state laws, and if the federal regulation is extensive and pervasive perhaps the federal law may preempt state regulation. The dissenting judges in the Supreme Court's opinion stated that the majority should not have entirely struck down the federal law but should have tried to salvage it by eliminating any unconstitutional parts but keeping the rest of the law. Yet the majority said that it was not the job of the Supreme Court to basically write federal legislation especially since the Court does not know exactly what the intent of Congress is regarding a regulatory scheme on the federal level for sports betting.

In addition to Congress and opponents of gambling, the ruling was also a defeat for the NCAA, NBA, NHL, and NFL, which urged the Supreme Court to uphold the federal law due to concerns for the integrity and reputation of college and professional sports. Now, with the federal law struck down the leagues are arguing for one uniform law at the federal level to regulate sports betting and not a patch-work of federal laws. The leagues also want a "cut-of-the-action," perhaps in the form of integrity fees as well as some type of monitoring; and the players' unions want a "piece-of-the-action" too. There are also proposals to pay college athletes, but with the bulk of the money coming when they graduate as an inducement to graduate as well as to provide the money when it is most necessary to the college athletes, most of whom will not be going to the "pro's."

Once legal, sports betting will allow people to bet on which team will win a game, but theoretically on every aspect of the game, for example, each quarter of a football game or each inning of a baseball game or for that matter every play of a game. Sports betting, though profitable, of course, "only" has a profit ratio of 4-5% of a total wager, compared to 20% for horse betting. However, sports betting, as has been the case in Las Vegas, draws people to casinos and hotels for sporting events where large profits are made by the hotel and hospitality industry. Sports betting should also draw more people to sporting events (as well as increase their enthusiasm and rooting interests) as well as increase viewership on media outlets, especially ESPN. Caesar's Entertainment Corp. immediately said that it would expand into sports betting wherever and whenever it is legalized. Moreover, fantasy sports companies FanDuel and DraftKings said that they are planning to enter the sports betting market. With sports betting now to be legal in some states, illegal sports betting, often controlled by "organized crime," should be significantly reduced.

There are concerns now that many states seeking additional revenues will legalize sports betting which would create more gambling, thereby getting more people, especially young people, involved with gambling, and perhaps causing more problems for people with gambling problems and addictions, especially poor people and people of modest incomes who may squander their incomes and savings on sports wagering. There is also concern that the reputation and integrity of sports would become tarnished by allowing the betting not only on the winners and losers of games but theoretically on all aspects of a game (maybe every and any pitch, pass, serve, kick, toss, shot, or swing!). "Match-fixing" is a concern, but it has not been a problem in Great Britain where sports gambling is legal and very popular. Furthermore, placing bets maybe now will be able readily and easily made on computers and mobile devices if states allow online gambling. A trip to a casino may not even be necessary, let along going "off-shore" to bet or going "underground" to see the local "bookie." And informal "office pools" for betting may become moot too. Consequently, sports betting is expected to expand greatly. Nevertheless, the majority of the Supreme Court said that the sovereignty of the states and the supremacy of the Constitution superseded any problems or concerns. Accordingly, until the federal government acts to directly regulate sports betting each state now is free to act on its own.

Bibliography:

Kendall, Brent, Kirkham, Chris, and Beaton, Andrew (May 15, 2018). *Wall Street Journal*, pp. A1, A2.

Klas, Mary Ellen (May 15, 2018). Ruling opens door to sports betting in Florida. *Miami Herald*, pp. 1A, 4A.

Liptak, Adam (May 15, 2018). Justices Nullify Law That Bans Sports Betting. *New York Times*, pp. A1, A15.

Questions for Discussion:

1. Do you agree with the Supreme Court's decision on legal grounds? Or do you agree with the dissenting judges? Why or why not?
2. Why do you think the major sports leagues wanted the Supreme Court to uphold the federal law?
3. Assuming federal regulation of sports betting what should some of the major provisions of the federal law be? Why? Should federal regulations take over the whole field of sports betting, precluding any state regulation? Why or why not?
4. Assuming no or minimal federal regulation and that the states will be allowed to regulate sports betting what should some of the major provisions of a state law be? Why?
5. Is the Supreme Court's decision pursuant to Ethical Egoism, Utilitarianism, and Kantian ethics? Why or why not?
6. What should a "socially responsible" and "sustainable" (that is, environmentally responsible) casino industry, for example, in Atlantic City, NJ or Biloxi, Mississippi, be doing for the local communities and for society as a whole? Provide examples and rationales for so acting.

Case 2 - Electric Motorized Scooters: Legal and Ethical Issues

A controversial new product (as well as service) is now appearing in local communities - electric motorized scooters; and this product is creating legal, ethical, and practical issues. Electric scooters are now available in more than 100 cities worldwide. They are left on the city streets during the day, where they can be accessed by an app on a Smart phone. They can weight up to 200 pounds and can go up to 15 mph. However, because they are dock-less they can be left almost anywhere once a rider has finished riding, including being left on a crowded and busy sidewalk. However, generally, scooters cannot be left in loading zones, handicapped parking areas, bicycle lanes, residential driveways and within 15 feet of a fire hydrant. Two of the biggest companies that make and provide scooters are Lime and Bird. Two other companies are Bolt and Gotcha. They all require a driver to upload a driver's license to confirm that the rider is at least 18 years of age. However, a major problem is that the scooters can cause injuries to riders who do not drive carefully regardless of age. Another major problem confronting cities that allow scooters is that they can be left on the sidewalks, thereby causing injuries to pedestrians. Hospitals and doctors are now reporting an influx of injuries caused by scooters with some injuries being very severe, especially to elder pedestrians who are hit by the scooters or who trip over them. Obviously, there is a real risk to pedestrians who are visually impaired and who physically impaired. Moreover, disabled people using wheelchairs may find their route blocked if a scooter is left in the middle of a sidewalk. Furthermore, accidents can occur more readily and seriously when minors ride the scooters or people double-up on them.

Some cities completely ban scooters, for example, Lauderdale by the Sea, Florida. Other cities permit them but ban driving on sidewalks. Other cities, like Denver permit them on sidewalks. And in some cities, like Washington, DC and Austin, Texas, riding on some sidewalks is permitted but not others. San Diego and Cincinnati permit scooters on the streets, but not on sidewalks. Some cities allow scooters in bike lanes; others do not, like Ft. Lauderdale. San Diego also restricts their speed to eight miles an hour. Most ordinances say that the scooters cannot impede pedestrian traffic on sidewalks. Ft. Lauderdale is considering permitting scooters but not during Spring Break as well as other very congested times. Consequently, there is a hodge-podge of conflicting laws throughout the country. Moreover, Cincinnati requires scooter companies to create a $1 million fund to cover injuries, including medical costs and lost wages, to pedestrians injured by scooters. In some cities, scooters are allowed in the streets. Certain cities like scooters as they help deal with traffic as well as a lack of public transportation. Many people enjoy riding them too. They are an easy and fun way to get around, and some say they are not more dangerous than riding a bike.

Yet there are emerging legal issues pertaining to scooter use. One area of the law that may be triggered by the use of electric scooters is the common law tort of negligence, whereby scooter manufacturers, riders, pedestrians, as well as cities, must act in a reasonably prudent manner, A failure to act in such a carful manner, perhaps by leaving a scooter in the middle of a sidewalk where someone can trip on it, may render the rider liable for negligence, and perhaps a city too if they knew or should have known that scooter riders were improperly leaving their scooters. Presently, the liability of the parties is undefined, but one surely can expect some precedential cases in the near future, which will be highly dependent on where the accidents take place, the circumstances, and the local laws. One point is clear, though, and that is the scooter's owner as well as rider will be able to be identified. Furthermore, the insurance aspects of scooter accidents will have to be ascertained, for example, if local governments are forced to compensate injured pedestrians. Another area of law that could be triggered is nuisance law, specifically public nuisance law, if the scooter riders'€™ actions or inactions, particularly leaving scooters around in an irresponsible manner, prevent other people from using and enjoying public roads and sidewalks.

Lime and Bird stress that safety is a top priority and that they encourage riders to obey all local rules and regulations. Moreover, Lime says it is investing more than $3 million to promote safe driving behavior and proper conduct. Bird says that it provides safety information in an app which is tailored to local regulations. Also, Bird says it encourages riders as well as others to report irresponsible behavior to local authorities. Moreover, in some cities, the company employs "Bird Watchers" whose function is to ensure that the company's scooters are parked and picked up correctly.

Bibliography:
Holley, Peter, "Scooters Upend Sidewalks," *Sun-Sentinel*, January 22, 2019, p. 5b.
Sweeeny, Dan, "Rolling Debate," *Sun-Sentinel*, January 23, 2019, p. 17A.
Wallman, Brittany, "Officials: Spring Break, scooters bad combination," *Sun-Sentinel*, January 23, 2019, pp. 1A, 17A.

Questions for Discussion:
1. Discuss the laws of nuisance and negligence and how they might be applied to electric motorized scooters as well as provide examples of wrongful behavior on the part of the scooter companies, the riders, and the municipalities that allow scooters. Provide examples. Can you envision a situation where the defenses to negligence and comparative negligence and assumption of the risk would be applicable to pedestrians? Provide an example.
2. How should a municipality treat electronic motorized scooters - ban them completely or allow them with restrictions, and if the latter, what type of restrictions should be imposed on the companies and riders? Provide examples.
3. Pursuant to Utilitarian ethics do electric motorized scooters produce more good consequences for the stakeholders involved, including the local communities and society as a whole, or do they produce more bad consequences? That is, pursuant to the Utilitarian ethics are they a moral product and service? Explain your reasoning.
4. Are scooters moral pursuant to Kantian ethics? Why or why not?
5. Pursuant to the doctrine of Ethical Egoism what should the scooter companies be doing to ward off local legislative bans? Explain your rationale and provide examples.

6. What should a "socially responsible" scooter company be doing for its riders, pedestrians, the local community, and society as a whole? Explain your rationale and provide examples.

Case 3 - Royal Caribbean, a Cruise Tragedy, and Tort Liability

In 2016, a tragedy occurred during a Royal Caribbean Christmas cruise out of Port Everglades, Ft. Lauderdale, Florida, when a passenger, Nathan Skokan, a 22-year-old man, fell overboard, was lost at sea, and presumably drowned and died. His parents, Todd and Lisa Skokan, as plaintiffs, brought a lawsuit against the Royal Caribbean cruise line, contending that the company was legally responsible for the death of their son, and specifically alleging that the company committed the common law tort of negligence and also committed the common law intentional torts of infliction of emotional distress and false imprisonment. In October of 2018, a federal judge ruled that there was sufficient evidence to have a jury trial on all tort counts.

The evidence indicated that Nathan went overboard from the 12th level deck of the Independence of the Seas shortly before 2 in the morning on the last night of a five-night cruise with his family. He disappeared on December 22, 2016, when the ship was about 33 miles from Key Largo, Florida. The parents claim that Royal Caribbean was negligent in two aspects: first, because the cruise line served their son too much alcohol; and second, because they failed to institute immediate search-and-rescue efforts after Nathan was reported as falling overboard. Regarding the alcohol consumption, several witnesses testified that they observed that Nathan was intoxicated before his death and that they saw him lose his balance and accidentally go overboard. Apparently, while intoxicated, Nathan went with several other passengers he met on the cruise to the exterior part of the 12th floor deck. Then, one of the passengers suggested as a joke that they should pretend to jump overboard, pointing to a hand-railing. As a result of the suggestion, Nathan threw himself up on the handrail, but when he went to sit on the handrail, he lost his balance, slipped, flipped over the railing and fell over the side of the ship to the water. The evidence indicated that in the 12 hours before his death Nathan was served at least 30 ounces of alcohol, including six full-sized martinis at the martini-making class earlier in the day and at least seven vodka drinks, two vodkas mixed with Red Bull, and a cognac. Nathan's blood alcohol was at least .256%, which an expert witness testified presented an extreme risk of harm to him.

Regarding the search-and-rescue efforts, the evidence indicated that eyewitnesses to the falling overboard immediately told the cruise ship personnel that Nathan had fallen overboard from the 12th floor deck. However, the cruise ship did not begin search-and-rescue efforts by lowering the rescue boats for Rescue Team 1 until two hours after being notified. In addition, the second rescue team, Rescue Team 2, did not get underway until one-hour-and-a-half after Rescue 1 was ready. Moreover, the Skokans alleged that Royal Caribbean committed two intentional torts: first, that the cruise line intentionally caused the family emotional distress by informing them, the ship, and the media that Nathan intentionally went overboard, causing the family to believe that their son had committed suicide, although multiple witnesses told the ship's officials that Nathan had slipped from a handrail while pretending to go overboard in response to a joking suggestion by another passenger.

Furthermore, the Skokans alleged that Royal Caribbean committed the intentional tort of false imprisonment. The parents contend that the cruise line ordered them back to their stateroom during the search-and-rescue efforts and posted a large guard to prevent them from leaving until the ship had returned to port. The Skokans testified that the cruise line's head-of-security directed a security guard to escort the family to their cabin and told them to stay there. Then, the parents related that a big, tall, and "intimidating" security guard was immediately posted outside the cabin door. Also, the parents and one of the brothers of Nathan testified that the guard did not allow them to leave the cabin. Royal Caribbean countered by saying that the Skokans were not told they could not leave, they never asked to leave, and that the crew member posted by their door was for their assistance. The cruise line said that the family had misconstrued the company's offer of hospitality for confinement.

Bibliography:
Hurtibise, Ron, "Judge Oks jury in Royal Caribbean cruise case," *Sun-Sentinel*, October 19, 2018, pp. 6-7B.

Questions for Discussion:
1. Negligence - Count I - Alcohol Serving - The essence of negligence is the failure to act in a reasonable and prudent manner under the circumstances, when one has a duty to act, and which failure to act causes injury or harm to a party. Do you think that the defendant, Royal Caribbean, was negligent by providing Nathan with the amount of alcohol he consumed prior to his death? Why or why not?
2. Negligence - Count II - Rescue Efforts - Do you think that Royal Caribbean was negligent in its search-and-rescue efforts for Nathan? Why or why not?
3. Negligence - Damages - Assuming liability for negligence, what monetary amount of damages would you grant to the plaintiffs, Nathan's parents, to compensate for the loss of their son? Explain your determination. What additional damages, again assuming negligence, would you grant to the Skokans for their emotional distress and pain-and-suffering for the loss of their son? Explain your determination.
4. Negligence - Punitive Damages - If negligence is committed in a gross and/or reckless manner, a jury is allowed to grant additional damages - punitive damages - at the jury's discretion in order to punish the wrongdoer and to act as a deterrent to future wrongdoers. Do you think there should be an award of punitive damages in this case, and if so, how much? Explain your reasoning.
5. Comparative Negligence - Alcohol Consumption - Assuming a defendant is negligent, a jury pursuant to the doctrine of Comparative Negligence is allowed to apportion fault if the plaintiff was also negligent. Do you think that any recovery by Nathan's parents should be reduced by a percentage attributed to the negligence of their son in causing in part his own death? If so, how much should Nathan be responsible for his own death? Explain your determinations.

6.   Intentional Infliction of Emotional Distress - The essence of this tort is the purposeful and intentional performance of conduct, actions, or words, which a civilized society would regard as atrocious or outrageous and which would cause severe emotional distress to a reasonable person. Do you think that Royal Caribbean intentional severe emotional distress on Nathan's parents? Why or why not?

7.   False Imprisonment - The essence of this tort is the intentional confinement of a person to a bounded area by means of force or threats of force that would cause a reasonable person to remain in the bounded or confined area. Do you think that Royal Caribbean committed the intentional tort of false imprisonment? Why or why not?

8.   Intentional Tort - Damages - If you think that Royal Caribbean committed either or both intentional torts, what monetary damages would you grant them, knowing that punitive damages are an appropriate remedy for the commission of an intentional tort? Explain your determinations and rationales.

9.   Moral Responsibility of Royal Caribbean - Ethical Principle of Last Resort - Pursuant to the afore mentioned ethical principle, one is morally obligated to rescue another if there is: 1) need, 2) proximity, 3) capability, 4) the would-be rescuer is the "last resort," that is, the last realistic opportunity to avoid the peril, and 5) the rescuing would not cause harm equal to or greater than the original peril. As such, and regardless, of legal liability is Royal Caribbean morally responsible for the death of Nathan pursuant to the Last Resort principle? Why or why not?

10. Moral Responsibility of Nathan's fellow passengers - Is the passenger who Nathan met on the cruise who jokingly suggested to him that they all pretend to throw themselves overboard morally responsible for Nathan's death? Why or why not? Are the other passengers who were with Nathan morally responsible for his death? Why or why not?

Case 4 - Board of Directors Quotas for Women

Legally imposed quotas to ensure that women are represented on corporate boards of directors has been an issue in Europe and now the topic is emerging as an issue in the U.S. too. The issue first came to the fore in Italy a few years ago. In Italy, compared to other industrialized countries, fewer women work, especially in high level corporate positions. Italy has the second lowest level of women in the workforce in Europe, next to Malta. In Italy, 46.5% of the women between the ages of 15 and 64 work, compared to a European average of 58.5%. The low Italian average was partly for "cultural reasons" as well as for the fact that Italian law makes it difficult for women to work part-time, and thus many women leave the job market after having children. The Italian government, however, is trying to reverse that situation by a new law that requires Italian listed and state-owned companies to ensure that one-third of their board members are women by 2015. Presently, only about 6% of corporate board members in Italy are women, and this low rate of participation is one of the lowest in Europe. Also, at the end of 2011, 48% of Italian companies at all male boards. A female member of the Italian parliament, who co-authored the law, said that the country thus needed a "shock to the system," and she also stated her hope that the law would produce a "cultural change." The law is part of a European effort to get more women into corporate boardrooms and executive positions. In the Northern European countries, such as Finland, Sweden, and Norway, women to play a large role in corporate life; but the rest of Europe falls behind the United States regarding women's participation. In the U.S., 16% of board members are women, compared to an average of 13.7% in the European community. The EU figures are higher, however, due to the Scandinavian countries. Currently, the European Commission is deciding whether to make female board quotas mandatory for the entire European community. The Italian legislation is starting to encourage change. For example, Fiat, Italy's largest car manufacturer by sales, appointed in 2012 two women as members of its board of directors, and this appointment was for the first time in the company's 100-plus year-old history. A principal goal of the law is for it to serve as a stimulus for working women as well as a means to force companies to think about women for high-level positions. Pursuant to the new law, companies that do not comply will face progressive sanctions, including fines of up to 1 million euros (about $1.25 million). However, there are critics of the new law. They assert that the law is an affirmative action policy aimed at gender equality, but one will harm business by further curtailing the traditional business prerogative of hiring people solely on merit. Moreover, critics assail the law by declaring that it interferes disproportionately with the freedom that businesses and shareholders traditionally have had to organize and run their affairs. Yet, in Italy, supporters of the law counter, the law was the only way to prevail over cultural barriers and to bring about needed change.

Recently, in the United States the issue of legally mandated representation of women on corporate boards of directors is emerging as a contentious legal, ethical, and practical issue, specifically in the state of California. In October of 2018 California became the first state to required companies that have headquarters in the state to have at least one female member to the company's board of directors by the end of 2019. Moreover, the law requires in 2012 that companies with at least five directors would need to have two or three female members on the board, depending on the size of the board of directors. The goal of the law is to promote the inclusion of women into high-level corporate policy-making positions. Other states have passed legislative resolutions encouraging companies to improve the diversity of the boards of directors of companies in those states, including Illinois, Pennsylvania, and Colorado. Yet these are non-binding resolutions and do not have the effect of law like the California statute. However, the California law does present some legal issues. For instance, if the mandatory female representation is deemed to be a fixed quota it could face challenges pursuant to Title VII of the Civil Rights Act which prohibits discrimination based on gender as well as the Equal Protection Clause of the 14th Amendment which prohibits government classification based on gender unless the classification is substantially related to an important government interest. Another legal and practical problem deals with the jurisdictional reach of the statute. Assuming it is otherwise legal it would apply to companies that are incorporated in California. Yet the attempted reach of the statute goes further to extend to companies that are headquartered and based in California even though they are incorporated in another state. Many companies, however, are incorporated in Delaware since that state has very favorable corporate laws, but they may be based in California as well as in many other states. The Due Process Clause of the 14th Amendment requires that for a state to regulate a company the state must have a sufficient "nexus" or connection to the company. If the California law is interpreted to just apply to companies that are incorporated in California, the law would have a diminished practical effect since it would apply just to those companies that are incorporated in the state. Moreover, under traditional corporate law principles the internal governance of a corporation is determined by the law of the state where the company is incorporated. Consequently, while the goal of promoting gender diversity on corporate boards may be a very laudable one that objective may encounter serious legal pitfalls.

Bibliography:

Fuhrmans, Vanessa, "State Sets Board Quota for Women," *The Wall Street Journal*, October 1, 2018, pp. B1, B5.
Zampano, Giada, "Italy to Push 'Pink Quotas,'" *The Wall Street Journal*, June 6, 2012, pp. B1, B7.

Questions for Discussion:
1. Would the California law be legal in the U.S. pursuant to constitutional principles of Equal Protection and/or Title VII of the Civil Rights Act? Or would the women's mandatory placement be an illegal female "quota" or illegal "reverse discrimination" against men who want to be on corporate boards? Why or why not?
2. Do you think it is legal under the Due Process clause for the California law to apply to companies that are not incorporated in California but are headquartered in the state and/or are mainly based in the state? Why or why not?
3. What would some of the cultural factors be that might inhibit the participation of women in business in California as well as in Italy? How does one go about changing cultural norms?
4. Is the California law moral pursuant to Utilitarian ethics? Why or why not?
5. Is the California law moral pursuant to Kantian ethics? Why or why not?
6. How should an Ethically Egoistic company treat the participation of women in the workplace, particularly at a high-level in business? Explain your rationales.

Case 5 - Legal Marijuana and Employer Drug Testing Policies
The *Sun-Sentinel* (Ft. Lauderdale, Florida) newspaper in 2018 had a front-page story about the developing conflict between traditional employer drug-testing policies and the relaxation of marijuana laws in those states where medical marijuana is legal as well as those states where recreational marijuana is legal. As of the writing of this case study 29 states and Washington, D.C. have passed laws making medical marijuana legal. Moreover, recreational marijuana is now legal in nine stated as well as Washington, D.C. with California legalizing marijuana in 2017. However, to complicate matters legally and practically marijuana is still classified as an illegal

drug under federal law, and, as a matter of fact, it is included in the same classification as heroin. During the past Obama Administration there was essentially a "hands-off" "pot" policy by the federal government regarding marijuana unless there was evidence that the drug was being sold to minors or "gangs" were involved. However, in the current Trump Administration that prior policy was abrogated; and Attorney General Jeff Sessions has stated that the administration will leave it up to federal prosecutors in the several states to decide whether to enforce federal drug laws. The prosecutor for the Denver region in Colorado, where marijuana is legal in both categories, has stated that he will not enforce federal drug laws unless there is evidence of minors and gang involvement.

Accordingly, a dilemma arises not just for the sellers of the drug, but, as per the discussion herein, employers who have drug testing policies, especially in those states where marijuana is legal medicinally or recreationally. The *Sun-Sentinel* (Pounds, February 4, 2018) reported that some employers are now not testing for marijuana at all or are ignoring positive results on tests. For example, the large national auto retailer, Auto Nation, based in Ft. Lauderdale, and which employs about 26,000 people nationwide no longer eliminates candidates who test positive for marijuana. Of course, the company as well as others are still "drug-free" workplaces; and consequently drug use on the job-site is prohibited, as well as an employee showing up for work impaired; and if there is an accident at work or when the employee is performing work duties off-site, such as delivering goods, then the employee will be tested and appropriate sanctions imposed if the drug test results in a positive finding. Another example is the technology company, Citrix, which has major operations in Florida and California, and which does not require mandatory drug testing. Moreover, a report from the Society of Human Resource Professionals indicated that employers in states that have legalized marijuana are gradually removing the drug from pre-employment drug-testing programs.

The rationales given for the change in employer policies are the competitive nature of the job market, especially for technological, creative, and/or innovative personnel. The CEO of Auto Nation, Mike Jackson, was quoted in the Sun-Sentinel (Pounds, February 4, 2018) stated that traditional drug policies prohibiting marijuana are a "barrier" to attracting talent at the company, and "that's not where society is today." The company has 300 dealerships in the states that have legalized marijuana medicinally and/or recreationally, including Florida where medical marijuana is now legal. The Sun-Sentinel (Pounds, February 4, 2018) quoted a recruiter who stated that drug use is common in the tech industry and specifically that regarding software developers, marijuana is part of their "cerebral culture" which needs constant creativity which apparently the drug is said to provide. Another vexing legal issue emerges when employees who have a disability use marijuana off-the-job for medicinal purposes. Are they protected by the Americans with Disabilities Act? Is an employer required to make a "reasonable accommodation" to its employees who are legally using medical marijuana in their state? So far, there is not much case law on point, but a Massachusetts court did rule in 2017 that under state law an employer had to make the reasonable accommodation to permit off-site use of marijuana by an employee who was taking medical marijuana to ease her digestive issues as she was suffering from Crohn's Disease. One point is clear, though, and that is as more and more people use marijuana - legally and otherwise - employers will have to consider changing and updating their hiring and employment policies regarding marijuana use.

Bibliography: P
ounds, Marcia Heroux (February 4, 2018). Smoke pot? You might be hired anyhow. *Sun-Sentinel*, pp. 1A, 20A.

Questions for Discussion:
1. Discuss the legal issues involved in the clash between employer drug-testing policies and the relaxation of marijuana laws for medicinal and recreational. How should these issues be resolved?
2. 2. Pursuant to the doctrine of Ethical Relativism are societal norms now so changed that using marijuana recreationally is no longer a "big deal" for employers and otherwise in society? Why or why not? Are software developers a separate society with their own norms regarding marijuana use? Why or why not?
3. Is it moral pursuant to Utilitarian ethics for an employer to ignore a positive drug test for marijuana by an employee? Why or why not?
4. Is it moral pursuant to Kantian ethics for an employer not to accommodate a medical marijuana user? Why or why not?
5. What type of drug policy should an Ethically Egoistic employer have in states where medical marijuana is legal as well as in states where recreational marijuana is legal? Explain the rationales for the policy.
6. How should a socially responsible employer be a "good corporate citizen" when it comes to drug use - legal as well as illegal - in the communities where it does business and society as a whole? Provide examples.

Case 6 - Self-Driving Cars and Strict Liability
Google as well as other companies are now testing self-driving, completely autonomous, cars. The company has developed a completely autonomous prototype which it wants to test on public roads. However, in California state law by the Department of Motor vehicles requires that a physical driver must be able to take immediate control of the vehicle if necessary. As such, the car must have a steering wheel, accelerator, and brake. Of course, Google could still test its self-driving vehicle on private roads or outside the state of California. Florida is another state that allows some testing of experimental self-driving vehicles; and there actually have been controlled tests with Google engineers in the state at speeds of 70 mph. Michigan is another state that has a pilot program to test autonomous cars. Google's ultimate goal is to develop a completely autonomous self-driving car without a wheel and pedals that can be operated without any human intervention. A key technological component to a self-driving car developed by the company is called "lidar," which is a laser-radar technology, which helps a driverless car to navigate obstacles and other cars. Google started its self-driving project in 2015. Now the major car companies as well as Uber are beginning to develop the technology; and some of the major car companies have said that they will have a self-driving vehicle on the market in a few years. Google has said its product will be available in 2018. Today, in fact, many car

companies have taken the more limited steps of introducing and integrating such autonomous features as collision-avoidance systems, emergency braking systems, lane-straightening, and self-parking into their existing vehicles. However, Google also wants to experiment with self-driving trucks and motorcycles. Presently, Google is making about 100 prototype autonomous cars; and the company is capping their top speed at 25 mph in order to make the vehicles easier to handle and to limit harm if there is an accident. Google now is asking the state of California to allow tests of autonomous cars without wheels or pedals on public roads. Google is planning to offer the autonomous cars first to taxi and courier service companies. A company spokesperson said that the public will be able to drive in an autonomous vehicle in a few years, though not necessarily be able to buy one.

Two major problems are emerging in the effort to develop self-driving cars; first, public acceptance of this new product; and second legal liability under traditional products liability principles, especially strict liability for "defective" products. One legal as well as practical problem that can arise when there is no driver is the issue of who is to blame - legally as well as morally - if there is an accident. The possible "guilty," that is, liable, parties could include the manufacturer, the company that designed the technology, the owner of the vehicle, and the passengers who were riding in the car at the time of the accident. How should liability be apportioned? That vexing issue will have to be ascertained too. The concern about accidents and liability has led California to require $5 million in insurance or self-insurance or an equivalent bond for the makers of self-driving vehicles. The additional insurance costs could be too much of a burden for smaller companies and would also most certainly increase the cost of a self-driving car. Accidents could come from defects in the driverless car technology as well as from a mix of driverless technology and human drivers. Accidents are thus expected, and consequently so are lawsuits. For example, a tire blowout or a crippling power surge could occur while the human is asleep or otherwise engaged in non-driving activities. And what if a driverless and non-driverless car collide? Who will be at fault and how is that issue determined? There also could be a loss in privacy as the driverless car will record where and when everyone has been. Another worry is that a terrorist or mentally imbalanced person will use the autonomous car as a weapon to deliver a bomb or to cause harm in a crash.

Yet one societal benefit for self-driving cars would be the reduction in land, especially in urban areas, that is used for parking cars. That is, why would you own a car that you would have to park (and pay a lot for in a big city) when a self-driving car would pick you up to take you to work and back home as well as to do your other chores. The unused parking lots could be converted into parks, playgrounds, and bike-paths which would be very nice "green" (literally) additions to life, especially in the big cities. People could even join clubs or fleets of autonomous cars. Traffic jams could be reduced too as the technology will direct driverless cars into convoys of vehicles going smoothly at uniform speeds. Travelling by car should be more enjoyable too as one could now take a nap or read a book in one's self-driving car. And who knows what would happen to the concept of private car ownership, which has been a solid staple to social, commercial, and business life in the U.S. since the days of Henry Ford and the Model-T. Currently, the U.S. Department of

Transportation is trying to promulgate rules to regulate autonomous self-driving cars, including testing with sensors and wireless communication technology in order to determine if driverless vehicles can pass on warnings to other vehicles so as to avoid collisions.

Bibliography:
Barr, Alistair, "Google's Bumpy Road Trip," *Wall Street Journal*, August 25, 2014, p. B4.
Garvin, Glenn, "Driverless cars will be here sooner than you think, and Florida is getting ready for them. *Miami Herald*, March 17, 2014, p. 1A.
Rosenblatt, Joel and Bergen, Mark, "A Slow-Motion Self-Driving Car Crash," *Businessweek*, September 11, 2017, pp. 22-23.

Questions for Discussion:
1. Discuss the legal issues involved with self-driving cars and how these issues should be resolved, particularly pursuant to the laws of negligence and strict liability for products.
2. Are self-driving cars moral pursuant to Utilitarian and Kantian ethics? Why or why not?
3. How should an Ethically Egoistic manufacturer of self-driving cars approach the issue of legal liability for the product?
4. What should a socially responsible and sustainable manufacturer of self-driving cars be doing for society and the environment? Provide rationales and examples.

Case 7 - Johnson & Johnson Baby Powder Cancer Lawsuit
In 2017, a civil jury in Los Angeles, California issued a verdict ordering Johnson & Johnson (J&J) to pay $417 million in damages to woman, Eva Echeverria, 63, years old, and now hospitalized, who contended in a products liability lawsuit that the talcum powder in the company's baby powder caused her ovarian cancer when she applied the powder regularly to her genital area for feminine hygiene and to prevent chafing. She started using the product when she was 11 years old. The verdict represents the largest one in a series of talcum powder lawsuits against J&J as well as one of the largest jury verdicts ever. Echeverria argued that J&J was negligent in failing to warn of the risks caused by its product and also that the talcum powder was a defective product pursuant to strict liability law due to the lack of a warning. Specifically, she contended that the company's product was the factual and actual as well proximate (that is, reasonably foreseeable) cause of her harm. The evidence indicated that Echeverria used the product on daily basis beginning in the 1950's until 2016, when she was diagnosed with ovarian cancer. She was too sick to testify in court but rather submitted a video deposition; and she is currently undergoing cancer treatment.

The jury awarded $68 million in compensatory damages and $340 million in punitive damages. Punitive damages are awarded at the discretion of the jury when there is evidence of malice, spite, ill will, as well as bad faith or reckless behavior and gross negligence. The evidence in the case included internal J&J documents going back several decades that demonstrated to the jury that the company knew about the ovarian cancer risks of talcum powder. A key study linking talcum powder to ovarian cancer, according to the *New York Times*, came out in 1971 when scientists in Wales discovered particles of talc embedded in ovarian and cervical tumors. Other studies have linked talcum powder use to ovarian cancer, but the *New York Times* reported that the research findings have not been consistent. Moreover, there is not yet a definitive study of a cause-and-effect between talcum powder use and ovarian cancer, the *New York Times* reported. Moreover, the National Cancer Institute reported in April of 2017, according to the *New York Times*, that "the weight of evidence does not support an association between talc exposure and an increased risk of ovarian cancer." However, the International Agency for Research on Cancer, also as reported in the *New York Times*, in 2006, classified talcum powder as a possible human carcinogen if used in the female genital area. Yet no federal agencies in the United States have acted so far to remove talcum powder from the market place or to compel warnings on the product. Yet talc is a mineral that is mined near asbestos, which is a known carcinogen, and as such the U.S. Food and Drug Administration has asked talc manufacturers to avoid contaminating the powder with asbestos.

Echeverria argued that the scientific evidence was sufficient to support the causation element to the lawsuits; and that the company thus had a legal duty to warn of the risk but failed to do so. There have been several other similar successful lawsuits against J&J but the Echeverria verdict is the largest ever against the company. Nevertheless, J&J still contends that the scientific evidence supports its long-held assertion that its product is safe and does not cause cancer. Two similar cases against the company in New Jersey were dismissed by a judge who stated the plaintiff's lawyers failed to present reliable evidence linking the talcum powder to ovarian cancer. A company spokesperson stated that the company sympathizes with the women who have been stricken with ovarian cancer; but the company will appeal the jury's decision. Currently, there are, according to the *New York Times*, thousands of women who are suing the company on the same grounds but only a few cases have gone to trial yet. J&J said it will fight these cases since its product is safe. Talc, moreover, is also used in many cosmetics.

Bibliography:

Bellon, Tina, "Massive California verdict expands J&J's talc battlefield," *Reuters*, August 22, 2017. Retrieved August 23, 2017 from https://www.reuters.com/article/us-johnson-johnson-cancer-lawsuit

CBS/AP, "Johnson & Johnson ordered to pay $417M in baby powder lawsuit," CBS News, August 21, 2017. Retrieved August 23, 2017 from: https://www.cbsnews.com/news/john-johnson-baby-powder-lawsuit

Rabin, Roni Caryn, "Jury Awards $417 Million in Woman's Suit Tying Baby Powder to Ovarian Cancer," *New York Times*, August 22, 2017, p. B6.

Questions for Discussion:

1. Should the jury's verdict be overturned on appeal or upheld? Why? Specifically, are elements of a lawsuit for negligence and for strict liability

for failure to warn sufficiently present? Do the facts support these legal theories? Why or why not?

2. Do you agree with the jury's award of compensatory damages, and if so, do you feel the amount is proper? Why?

3. Do you agree with the jury's award of punitive damages, and if so, do you feel the amount is proper? Why?

4. Is the decision a moral one pursuant to ethics? Specifically, is the award of punitive damages moral in this case? Why or why not?

5. How should an Ethically Egoistic and Socially Responsible J&J now proceed in the fact of this jury verdict as well as the other lawsuits and potential lawsuits? Explain your reasoning.

Case 8 – Pro-Golfer Phil Mickelson and Allegations of Insider Trading

In 2016, several media outlets, including the *Wall Street Journal and* the *New York Times*, reported that the U.S. Department of Justice and the Securities and Exchange Commission (SEC) announced the commencement of legal proceedings against a corporate executive, a sports gambler, and the famous professional golfer, Phil Mickelson. The corporative executive is Thomas C. Davis, the former chairman of Dean Foods Co., as well as a retired investment banker from Credit Suisse, who was very heavily in gambling debt to legendary sports gambler, William "Billy" Walters, who is considered one of the most successful sports bettors in the country. Phil Mickelson, who has a reputation for betting on sports, was also in debt to the gambler.

The government alleges that Mr. Davis passed on inside information to Williams, who then passed the info on to Mickelson. The government has been conducting an investigation for over two years. As a result of the charges, Davis has pled guilty to criminal charges and is cooperating in the case against Billy Walters. Davis has also pled guilty to perjury for initially lying to government investigators when he said that he had never given information to Billy Walters. Walters has been arrested and has been charged with 10 counts of securities fraud, insider trading, and wire fraud. His attorney said that any trading was based on mere speculation and not based on trading on sufficiently objective and factual information.

The government, however, is just proceeding civilly against Mickelson, who was not charged with any criminal wrongdoing. Mickelson has agreed to pay to the SEC more than $1 million, including interest, based on the trading he did based on a tip from Billy Waters, who is a long-time friend, a member of the same country club, and a golfing buddy of Mickelson. Actually, Billy Walters is an accomplished amateur golfer as well as a developer of golf courses. He also knows Davis well as he Davis on a golf course when they both lived in Southern California. They have known each other for more than 20 years. Apparently, Mickelson owed a gambling debt to Billy Walters, which was to be repaid in part from the profits Mickelson was to make from trading in Dean Foods' stock based on the tip from Davis given to Mickelson by Billy Walters. The government also said that Mr. Davis was "desperate for money" and thus sought financial help from Billy Walters. For example, Davis owed a casino debt of $100,000, which he paid by taking money from a Dallas charity for battered women and homeless children. So, in one instance, Billy Walters gave Davis $1 million to repay this amount and other obligations. In exchange for this help Davis regularly provided Walters with a large number of tips regarding Dean Foods' earnings and other market-moving information. Another alleged tip dealt with a plan by certain investors to take a stake in the restaurant conglomerate, Darden Restaurants, the parent company of Olive Garden restaurants, and then break it up and spin-off certain divisions. Mr. Davis was under a confidentiality and non-disclosure agreement with the investment group at the time. The SEC says that as a result of this tip and others from Davis, Billy Walters made illegal profits and avoided losses totaling more than $6 million over a six-year period. Moreover, the government alleges that Billy Walters instructed Davis to use the secret code term, "Dallas Cowboys," when referring to Dean Foods, and he also gave Davis a pre-paid cell-phone. As a result of the tips by phone or after personal meetings Billy Walters repeatedly called his Las Vegas broker to buy tens of millions of dollars in Dean Foods' shares. After Billy Walters learned of the planned Darden breakup and "spinoff" from Davis, Billy Walters then allegedly told Mickelson, who then purchased 240,000 shares of Dean Foods' stock in three separate brokerage accounts; and Mickelson then sold his shares, making a $931,000 profit when the stock rose 40% when news of the "spinoff" became public. Mr. Mickelson then paid his gambling debt to Billy Walters in part with those trading profits. Mickelson was then sued by the SEC to recover those profits, but he was not charged with insider trading. Technically, Mickelson was named as a "relief defendant" in a civil case, wherein the government argued that Mickelson was "unjustly enriched" from the trades, and thus he must return is "ill-gotten" gains. Attorneys for Mr. Mickelson said that the golfer did not engage in any wrongdoing. And when the SEC's Enforcement Director was asked why Mickelson was not charged, he said that charges have to be justified "based upon the evidence and the law."

Bibliography:
Viswanatha, Aruna, Hong, Nicole, and Rothfeld, Michael, "The Golfer, the Gambler and the Needy Executive," May 20, 2016, pp. A1, A5.
Goldstein, Matthew, Protess, Ben, and Stevenson, Alexandra, "Insider Trading Case Links Golfer, Banker, and Gambler," May 20, 2016, pp. A1, B4.

Questions for Discussion:
1. Did Mickelson receive material, non-public information in the form of stock tips? Why or why not? Was the planned breakup and "spinoff" of Darden sufficiently factual and objective information or was it mere speculation? Why?
2. Do you believe Mickelson was a tippee in conspiracy with the insider, Davis, by means of the sports gambler? Why or why not?
3. Criminal convictions require evidence of an "evil mind" or bad intent, that is, the wrongdoers knew what they were doing, knew it was wrong, and intentionally did the wrongful acts anyway. Was the fact that a secret code and pre-paid phone were used for Dean Foods' trading sufficient evidence of bad intent? Why or why not?
4. And assuming that the answers to the preceding questions are "yes," then why did the government proceed only civilly against Mickelson and not

criminally? Do you agree with the determination of the SEC's Enforcement Director that charges were not warranted in Mickelson's case? Why or why not?

5. Did Mickelson act morally? Why or why not?

6. What should a "socially responsible" professional athlete such as Mickelson, who is very famous and very wealthy, be doing for society? Provide examples.

7. Phil Mickelson recently said that he was considering changing his residence from the high-tax state of California to Florida, a low-tax state without a state personal income tax. As a result, Mickelson was criticized by California community groups and others for being socially irresponsible for planning to leave the state? Do you agree with his critics? Why or why not?

8. Should professional athletes like Mickelson place bets with "professional" sports gamblers? Why or why not? Should they even associate with them? Why or why not? Actually, should they bet on sports at all? Why or why not?

18 – THE INTERNAL REVENUE SERVICE (IRS)

The Internal Revenue Service[7] (IRS), which is a part of the treasury department, is the official agency for the collection of and enforcement of taxation and tax law. The Internal Revenue Code (IRC) is the official general and permanent law of the United States for taxation purposes and is enacted by Congress (CCH Tax Law Editors, 2018). The IRS is organized around a service delivery model with 4 operating divisions:
1. Wage & Investment
2. Small Business/Self Employment
3. Tax Exempt & Government Entities
4. Large Business & International

The IRS
The Wage & Investment Division is responsible for individual taxpayers who receive wage and/or investment income. Most of these taxpayers receive refunds mainly due to over withholding. Most of the compliance matters focus on dependency exemptions, credits, filing status, and deductions.

The Small Business/Self Employment Division is responsible for all self-employed individuals or small business owners. This division includes corporations or partnerships with assets less than or equal to $10 million dollars. It also has the responsibility of estate and gift returns, fiduciary returns, and all individuals who file international returns. Tax obligations include personal and corporate income taxes, employment taxes, excise taxes, and tax withheld from employees.

The Tax Exempt & Government Entities Division is responsible for employee plans, exempt organizations, and governmental entities. Employee plans cover retirement plans, employee sponsors, and beneficiaries. Exempt organizations include

---

[7] This chapter is prepared by Nicolas-Michel Polito.

section 501 organizations and other not for profit entities. Governmental entities include federal, state, and local governments, as well as tax exempt bonds.

The Large Business & International Division is responsible for businesses with assets over $10 million. Collection issues are rare, but many complex issues such as law interpretation, accounting, and regulation issues are common (Watson, 2016).

The IRS Structure

The Commissioner of the IRS serves under the Secretary of the Treasury and is appointed by the President of the United States with the advice and consent from the Senate. The commissioner has a term of five years. The Commissioner has principal offices, and two deputy commissioners, who directly report to the commissioner. Under the national officer structure, there are two deputy commissioners, one for operations support and the other for services and enforcement (Watson, 2016).

The Deputy Commissioner for Operations Support oversees the integrated internal IRS support functions, facilities economies of scale, and instills better business practices. Their responsibilities include information technology, agency wide shared services, human capital, financial privacy, government liaison and disclosure.

The Deputy Commissioner for Services and Enforcement oversees the four primary operation divisions, the Return Prepare Office, Office of Online Services, Criminal Investigation Division, Office of Professional Responsibility, and the Whistleblower Office (Watson, 2016).

The IRS has many oversights to help administer the laws of the land. The Governmental Accountability Office (GAO) periodically studies how well the IRS is performing and administers the internal revenue laws. There is also the IRS oversight board and the Treasury Inspector General for Tax Administration. Both oversee the function and efficiency of the IRS.

The IRS Oversight Board is a 9-member independent body who are appointed by the President of the United States with the advice and consent of the Senate, Secretary of Treasury, and Commissioner of the IRS. The board is in charge of overseeing the IRS and the administration of the Internal Revenue Laws.

The Treasury Inspector General for Tax Administration (TIGTA) was established by the IRS Restructuring Act of 1988 (RRA). Its purpose is to provide independent oversight of internal IRS activities. TIGTA promotes efficiency and effectiveness of tax administration by its internal inspections and reports on administration programs. TIGTA also prevents and detects fraud, waste, and abuse within the IRS (Watson, 2016).

The Office of Chief Counsel

The Office of Chief Counsel of the IRS is appointed by the President of the United States to provide legal services. There are 4 major areas in which the office is responsible for:

1. Technical Counsel
2. Operating Counsel
3. Field Counsel

4. National Taxpayer Advocate Counsel

The Technical Counsel, located in the National Office, provides authoritative legal interpretations of the tax law. This includes issuing regulations, revenue rulings, private letter rulings, technical advice, and advance pricing agreements.

The Operating Counsel provides legal advice and representation and participates in the plans and activities of operating division management. The operating counsel is responsible for the operating divisions of the IRS, except tax exempt and governmental entities, which are covered by the Technical Counsel.

The Field Counsel is organized using a matrix management structure, is comprised of 49 managing counsels, 6 area teams and 1 national field leadership.

The National Taxpayer Advocate Counsel provides advice to national taxpayer advocates with respect to its authority and legislative recommendations (Misey, Goller, & Meldman, 2016).

Offices of the IRS

The Office of Appeals, located Washington, DC, is primary responsible to resolve tax controversies without litigation. The field operations of Appeals are divided into 9 areas under which there are Area Directors. Each area director reports either to the West or East director of field operations.

The Taxpayer Advocate Service is designed to help taxpayers who have problems with the IRS that could not be resolved under normal administrative processes. It is organized around 2 main functions:

1. The Casework Function - in order to resolve all individual taxpayer problems
2. Systemic Analysis Function - works with the operating division to identify systemic problems, analyze roots causes, implement solutions, and proactively identify new potential problems (Watson, 2016).

The Communication & Liaison Division's primary responsibility is to communicate to those affected by the mission of the IRS. There are 3 primary offices:

1. The Equity, Diversity, and Inclusion Office-oversees the IRS's compliance with federal legislation, statutory requirements, and executive order to uphold taxpayer civil rights.
2. The Research, Analysis, and Statistics office- helps develops data, supports tax research, statistical analysis, and business solutions to improve tax administration processes.
3. The Office of Compliance Analytics- seeks to improve compliance with tax laws and to make data analytics a key part of the IRS's strategy.

The other offices include:

1. The Criminal Investigation Division Office-reports directly to the IRS Commissioner and Deputy Commissioners and operates a nationwide unit with 2500 special agents. It closely coordinates with the operating divisions and is supported by specific attorneys within the Chief Counsel Office

whose mission is to investigate potential criminal violations of the IRS code and related financial crimes.

2. The Whistleblower Office - processes tips received of reported tax issues and problems. There are monetary awards paid to whistleblowers between 15%-30% of the total proceeds that the IRS receives. However, the IRS must act on the information, and the amount identified by the whistleblower must meet certain criteria.

3. The Return Prepare Office –seeks to improve taxpayer compliance by providing comprehensive oversight and support of tax professionals.

4. The Office of Online Service - is responsible for online experience and operations management.

5. The Office of Professional Responsibility - enforces consistent professional standards for tax professional and other individuals and groups subject to IRS circular 230 entitled "Rules of Practice Before the IRS".

Circular 230

Treasury Department Circular 230 is the official IRS publication for regulations governing to practice before the IRS. The publication is divided into subparts addressing different practices:

1. Subpart A - rules governing the authority to practice before the IRS
2. Subpart B - the duties and restrictions relating to practice before the IRS
3. Subpart C - the sanctions for violating the regulations
4. Subpart D - the rules applicable to disciplinary proceedings
5. Subpart E - the general provisions.

In order to have the authority to practice before the IRS, the individual must have a "license". The rules governing practice before the IRS apply to attorneys, certified public accountants, enrolled agents, enrolled actuaries, enrolled retirement plan agents, and certain individuals providing appraisals used in connection with tax matters (J. K. Lasser Institute, 2019).

If the IRS requested any information or records, the practitioner must provide them with no unreasonably delay to the IRS. However, the practitioner may withhold information or records believed to be "in good faith" and on "reasonable grounds" to be privileged. Also, if the practitioner does not possess the IRS-requested information or records, but knows who does, they must inform the IRS on that person (J.K Lasser Institute, 2019).

Former IRS/Government Employees

There are many former government employees who practice taxation and represents clients before the IRS, which might cause a conflict of interest. For instance:

1. If a former government employee, "personally and substantially participates" in a particular matter involving specific parties, that individual can never represent or assist those parties with that matter later
2. If he/she only had an "official reasonability" he/she must wait two years after leaving the government before he/she can represent those parties

3. Former government employees must wait one year after leaving the government before he/she can represent clients before the IRS to influence any U.S. Treasury Department rules if he/she participated in the development of the rule or had "official responsibility" to that rule (Misey, Goller, & Meldman, 2016).

Fees, Conflicts and Advertising

A practitioner can never charge an unconscionable fee. Generally contingency fees are not allowed unless they are for an IRS examination or audit, a claim solely for a refund of interest and/or penalties, or a judicial proceeding arising under the IRC. Conflicts of interests do happen, but the practitioner may represent a clients if the practitioner reasonably believes that he or she can competently represent the client, there is no state or federal law that prohibits, and the affected client waives the conflict of interest in writing within 30 days (Misey, Goller, & Meldman, 2016).

A practitioner may not have any false or misleading advertising with respect to any IRS matter. A practitioner that publishes a written fee must honor them for a 30-day period following the last date that the fees were published. If additional fees may be charged for certain matters, the statement must indicate if clients could be responsible for those costs. All practitioners must retain records for fees that are charged for a client. A practitioner cannot endorse or otherwise negotiate any check including directing or accepting payment by any means, into an account owned or controlled by the practitioner (Misey, Goller, & Meldman, 2016).

Documents and Information

A practitioner may not willfully or recklessly sign a tax return or advise a client to take a tax position that the practitioner knows or should know lacks a reasonable basis. The IRS and the courts consider this fraud. A practitioner cannot advise a client to take a tax return position on a document that will be submitted to the IRS, unless the position is not "frivolous", meaning that it must have a "reasonable basis". The practitioner must inform the client of any penalties that are reasonably likely to apply to a position taken on a tax return (J. K. Lasser Institute, 2019).

A practitioner can rely on client-furnished information only if it appears reasonable. Generally, a practitioner who signs the tax return may rely in good faith without verification upon client-furnished information as long if it appears reasonable. However, the practitioner cannot ignore contradictory information and must make reasonable inquiries if the client-furnished information appears to be questionable or incomplete. If the practitioner knows of any noncompliance, errors, or omissions by a client, he/she must advise the client of the consequences under the law. A practitioner cannot notify the IRS, but might consider withdrawing if the client will not rectify the matter (Misey, Goller & Meldman, 2016).

The practitioner must exercise due diligence regarding preparing returns and other documents and determining the correctness of her/his representations to the IRS. If the practitioner relies on the work of another, there is a presumption that the practitioner exercised due diligence if the practitioner took reasonable care. Generally, at the request of the client, the practitioner must return all original client records. The practitioner, however, may retain copies of the records returned to a client. In the case of a fee dispute and if the state law allows it, the practitioner can retain the original records until the dispute is rectified (Watson, 2016). A practitioner:

1. May give written advice if the advice is based upon reasonable factual and legal assumptions
2. Must reasonably consider all relevant facts and circumstances and use reasonable efforts to relate applicable law and authorities to the facts
3. Cannot rely upon representations, statements, findings, or agreements
4. Cannot consider the possibility that a tax return will not be audited or that a matter will not be raised during an audit
5. May only rely on the advice of another person if the advice was reasonable, the person is competent, has no conflicts, and the reliance is in good faith
6. Must possess the necessary competence to engage in practice before the IRS. A practitioner may become competent through various methods, such as consulting with experts in the relevant area, or studying the relevant law

Compliance

A practitioner's potential failures to comply with circular 230 include if the individual:

1. Fails to have adequate procedures to comply with Circular 230
2. Fails to ensure the procedures for compliance are followed
3. Is grossly incompetent
4. Knows or should know of a pattern of noncompliance and fails to act in a reasonable time to correct the noncompliance.

There are many sanctions by the Secretary of the Treasury for violations of the regulations. These violations are considered as "not acting in good faith". These violations include if a practitioner:

1. Is convicted of any criminal offense involving dishonesty, breach of conduct, or giving false or misleading information
2. Solicits any business prohibited by Circular 230
3. Willfully fails, evades, attempts to evade, counsels, or assist any assessment or payment of federal tax for themselves or another individual
4. Fails to timely remit to the IRS any funds received from a client for the purpose of paying any tax or other obligation owed to the U.S. government
5. Threatens, false accuses, or offers gifts as bribes
6. Is disbarred or suspended from practicing as an attorney, CPA, or actuary
7. Knowingly helps another person to practice before the IRS while that person is suspended, disbarred, or otherwise ineligible to practice before the IRS
8. Knowingly, recklessly, or through gross incompetence gives false opinions on questions arising under the tax laws
9. Willfully fails to sign a tax return
10. Willfully discloses a tax return or tax return information without the owner's permission. This does not apply if it is authorized by the IRC, contrary to the order of any court, or contrary to the order of an administrative law judge in connection with a disciplinary proceeding.

Some possible sanctions include censure and suspension or disbarment from practice before the IRS. The IRS may also impose monetary penalties, not exceeding the gross income derived (or to be derived) from the conduct-giving rise to the penalty (CCH Tax Law Editors, 2018).

Tax Return Preparer

A tax return preparer is any person who prepares for compensation, or employs individuals to prepare for compensation, any tax return required, any claim for refund, or of tax imposed by the IRC. However, a tax return preparer does not include a person who merely furnishes typing, reproducing, or provides other mechanical assistance. Any tax professional with an IRS preparer tax identification number (PTIN) is authorized to prepare federal tax returns. However, if a tax preparer holds a PTIN and does not hold a professional credential, he/she has no authority to represent clients before the IRS (CCH Tax Law Editors, 2018).

There are two types of tax return preparers - ones who sign and ones who do not sign a tax return. A signing tax return preparer has the primary responsibility for the overall substantive accuracy of the preparation of the return or claim for a refund. A non-signing tax return preparer is any tax return preparer who does not sign the tax return, but who prepares all, or a substantial portion of a return or claim for a refund or offers advice to a taxpayer when that advice leads to a position or entry that constitutes a substantial portion of the return (J. K. Lasser Institute, 2019).

Claims

An overpayment of tax is simply an amount paid that exceeds the amount owed. Claims for refund of income taxes overpaid are filed on Form 1040 and for previous years on Form 1040X. All claims other than income taxes are made on Form 843. To get a back any overpayment of taxes either the IRS will automatically refund the amount, or the taxpayer will file a claim for a refund. All claims furnished by the taxpayer need to be carefully prepared to comply with all the requirements on the specific amount to be refunded (Misey, Goller, & Meldman, 2016).

Refund claims are filed with the IRS services center/campus in the region in which the tax was paid. A separate claim must be filed for each taxable year and for each type of tax. The taxpayer bears the burden of responsibility for establishing that the claim was filed timely. IRC §6402 (a) states that the IRS will refund or credit the amount of an overpayment to the person who made the overpayment. A claim for a refund of overpayment taxes must filed on or before 3 years from the date the return was filed or 2 years from the date of the tax was actually paid. However, the statutes of limitations can be extended. §6511 (a) states that if the statute of limitations has been extended by an agreement between the taxpayer and the service under §6501 (c)4, a refund clam may be filed any time within 6 months after the expiration of the extended period. §6511 (c)1 further states the amount of the refund or credit cannot exceed the portion of the tax paid (Watson, 2016).

The IRS services center/campus will process any refund claimed for overpayment for the current year. If the claim for a refund is for a previous year, the claim will be examined by the Compliance Team of the Operating Division. If the government denies the claim under §6325 (a)1 or 6 months passes and the refund claim is not granted, the taxpayer may then file a refund suit in court. If the taxpayer does not want an administrative appeal, he/she must request so in writing.

Overpayments

An overpayment of taxes can occur because of many different reasons. The most common reason is an over withholding of taxes on wages or compensation. This is common for many taxpayers who received a W-2 each year because most of the time the amount paid is more than what is required by the government for the year. A less common overpayment is an error in calculating a tax liability. IRC §6511 (b)1 and §6514 state that unless there is a math error on the return, the IRS has no authority to refund the credit unless the tax payer files a claim with the IRS.

Another example of an overpayment that may occur is if the taxpayer has a carryback from another taxable year in which he/she will be entitled for a refund. However, claims from other pervious years must set forth in detail each ground on which a credit or refund is claimed. Another less frequent way an overpayment may occur is if a tax payment is made after the close of the statute of limitations. §6401 states that if the taxpayer makes any payments made after the close of the statute of limitations, he/ she is entitled to a refund. However, once the statute of limitations has expired the taxpayer may not amend a claim to fix a defect in a return or bring up new grounds. This is known as the "Substantial Variance Doctrine", which state that issues raised before the court for a refund, cannot vary substantially from the refund claim. (Watson, 2016)

Deposit Overpayments

If the taxpayer is suing the IRS not in Tax Court, the amount owed to the government must be paid before entering the court. In some cases, this can cause an overpayment of taxes. The taxpayer may make a deposit against the tax owed in order to stop the running of interest. IRC §6603 states that the taxpayer is entitled to recover a deposit at any time without a specific procedure for a refund. However, he/she is not entitled to interest on a deposit. The date of remittance that constitutes a payment or a deposit is important because there is a 2-year statute of limitations. The statue runs from the date the tax is paid. A deposit will have no effect on the statute of limitations for the taxes owed.

An informal claim is one that is timely filed but inadequately specific. A taxpayer can use a Form 870 as an informal refund claim. The taxpayer can file a formal claim later if it is filed before the expiration of the statute of limitations and before the IRS rejects the informal claim. If a refund claim fails to fully state the facts, but the claim otherwise satisfies the requirement imposed by the statue, the claim may be valid. However, the taxpayer must prove in court that the IRS is aware or had reason to be aware of the underlying basis of the claim. (Watson, 2016)

Audits

The federal income tax system is referred to as "enforced voluntary compliance" which is based on the self-assessment of taxes. The audit process helps ensure that this voluntary assessment and payment is occurring. The IRS describes an audit as "a review/examination of an organization's or individual's accounts and financial information to ensure information is reported correctly according to the tax laws and to verify the reported amount of tax is correct" (Misey, Goller, & Meldman, 2016).

Only a tiny minority of returns are audited which equates to about 2% of all returns. A return may be audited for a variety of reasons, and the examination may take place in many ways. It is important that the IRS acts before the statutes of limitations runs out because they cannot challenge a tax liability once it does. After the audit, if there are any changes to the return, the taxpayer either can agree with the changes and pay the additional tax on which interest may also be due, or can disagree with the changes and appeal the decision.

Audit Methods
The IRS has a variety of ways for the selection of returns that they will audit. The IRS selects most of their returns using "Statistical Models" through a computer. This analysis is called the Discriminant Function or "DIF" system, which is designed to identify returns with a high probability of error and resulting in a significant tax change. A higher "DIF score" would increase the changes of the return to be selected for an audit. Examples that could increase the "DIF score" would be high-income individuals, large amounts of itemized deductions, and self-employment. Just because a return has a high "DIF score" does not mean the return will be audited. Each return that is selected by the computer will be examined manually and the IRS will eliminate returns that do not need further examination. This method yields a significant amount of additional tax revenue each year for the government (Watson, 2016).

Another method the IRS uses for selecting returns for an audit is through the Information Reporting Program (IRP). This is where the IRS manually exams a return. The return is verified by the matching of information the IRS has received with the taxpayer reports on their return. Examples of items that the IRS matches are W-2s and 1099s. If these items do not match the amounts reported on a return, the return will normally be selected for an audit.

A small number of additional returns are manually selected each year. If a prior year's return was audited there is a high chance that a subsequent year may be audited. Some audits are just handled through the mail. However, ones that are more complex will normally involve a meeting between the taxpayer and an IRS employee. Most individual returns are audited within 2 years from the date of filing of the return. However, returns may be audited at any time before the expiration of the statute of limitations (Misey, Goller, & Meldman, 2016).

Types of Audits
The lowest level of audits performed by the IRS are ones that are normally conducted through the mail. These are referred to as a "correspondence examinations". The most common issues are information errors (incorrect Social Security numbers or missing signatures), matching issues (income reported on tax return does not match their W-2 or Form 1099) and mathematical errors. A correspondence examination involves a written request from the IRS campus to the taxpayer to substantiate items.

The IRS will either mail a Letter 55 (CG) "Initial Contact Letter" which advises the taxpayer that their return has been selected and includes a listing of items needed to be verified. Examples of these are charitable contributions, medical expenses, or business deductions. Or the IRS could mail a CP 2000 notice, which will contain proposed adjustments to the return, which are based on documents that are issued by third parties. Examples are Forms W-2, 1099-MISCs, and 1098, Mortgage Interest Statements. If the taxpayer requests an interview or is unable to substantiate their claims, the case will become dealt with an office audit or field audit (CCH Tax Law Editors, 2018).

An "Office Audit" occurs at the IRS office and is conducted by tax auditors. These are restricted to specific items identified during the screening process. If the tax auditors uncover significant items that were not detected before, the audit can be expanded. However, more complex cases are usually handled by revenue agents who are not as restricted. Revenue agents are normally more educated and experienced than tax auditors and usually will expand the scope of the audit (Watson, 2016).

A "Field Audit" might be requested either by the taxpayer or the IRS. This audit is conducted at the taxpayer's home or business. The field agent will examine issues by:

1. First: Identifying the items that may need adjustment
2. Second: Verifying the accuracy of amounts reported by the taxpayer's book and records
3. Third: Analyzing the transactions and determine if the taxpayer has compiled with the law.

A field audit examination must be accordance with the Internal Revenue Manual (IRM) with the standard of "to provide top quality services and apply the law with integrity and fairness to all" IRM 4.10.1.4 (1999). The IRM list examination techniques which are applicable to all field audits, as well as specialized guidelines for specialized industries or circumstances (Misey, Goller & Meldman, 2016).

Safeguards to Audits

The Omnibus Technical and Miscellaneous Revenue Act of 1988 (TBRA 1) have safeguards for taxpayers under §7521. It requires:

1. The IRS deliver a comprehensive notice of taxpayer rights covering the collection of tax. This must explain the taxpayers' rights, appeal, and how the IRS can collect the tax
2. The IRS must act in a reasonable time and place
3. The taxpayer has the right to representation and consultation. If a taxpayer wants representation in an interview, that interview must be stopped immediately
4. The taxpayer or the IRS (with the taxpayer's permission), may request an audio recording (not video).
5. The Taxpayer must be given a "Notice of Right" during an audit and collection. However, in the case of criminal investigations these safeguards do not apply
6. The taxpayer must be notified that their case is being transferred to Criminal Investigation Division (CI)

The IRS Resurrecting Act of 1998 (also known as TBRA 3) was passed in response to complaints that the legislation prohibits financial status or economic reality audit unless there is a reasonable indication that unreported income exists (RRA section 312; IRC §7602). This act and code section prohibit any audit on a taxpayer who lives a lavish lifestyle (Watson, 2016).

Findings of the Audit

Following an audit, the revenue agent may either accept the return or recommend certain changes. If the audit finds that no changes are to be made, the taxpayer will sign Form 870 and nothing will proceed further with the IRS. When an examiner has completed the examination and he/she recommend certain changes, the/she must explain any proposed adjustments to the taxpayer. If the taxpayer agrees to the adjustments, they will sign a document preventing any challenging of deficiency in Tax Court. The examiner could give either the Form 4159 Income Tax Examination Changes or Form 870 Waiver of Restrictions on Assessment and Collection of Deficiency in Tax and Acceptance of Over Assessment (Misey, Goller, & Meldman, 2016).

Form 870 is used to reflect the agreement between the taxpayer and the government prior to an appeals conference (Form 890 for estates and gifts). Form 870's effect is to waive the Notice of Deficiency "90-day letter" and consent to an immediate assessment and collection of tax. A taxpayer who signs, may not litigated in Tax Court, nor prevent the IRS from assessing additional deficiencies. However, the taxpayer may sue the IRS after paying the fine, filing a refund, and the IRS denying that refund.

If agreement cannot be reached at the revenue agent level, the taxpayer receives a copy of the report and a preliminary notice, "The 30-Day Letter", notifying the taxpayer of the right to appeal. The taxpayer has 30 days to submit a request for an administrative appeal with an appeals officer (appeals conference). If the taxpayer takes no action after receiving the preliminary notice, the IRS will issue a Notice of Deficiency, which is commonly referred to as "the 90-Day letter". This means the taxpayer has 90 days to pay the tax or file a petition in tax court. (CCH Tax Law Editors, 2018)

Administrative Appeals:

Failure to reach an agreement with the IRS and an examining agent does not mean Tax Court is then necessary. Factually, a majority all disagreements are settled out of court. The taxpayer could request and Appeal Office Conferences. An appeal will save expense and a delay of litigation and is desirable to the IRS (IRM 8.1.1.1, 2012).

The Appeals Office of the IRS has exclusive and final authority to settle tax cases 26 CFR §601.106 (a) (1). Appeals decisions are not reviewable by any member of the IRS. The taxpayer in deciding to go through the appeals process, can open himself or herself to raise new issues with their return. However, IRM section 8.6.1.6 (2013) makes raising new issues from the IRS infrequent, but it is still a possibility. Also, the tax court can impose a §6673 penalty for frivolous cases or cases maintained for delay. Another reason for an appeals conference is that the taxpayer will not qualify for an award of attorney fees against the government if they bypass the conference or other administrate remedies. If the tax court petition is docketed, the appeals office will become involved whether a conference request happens or not. It is advised to seek an appeals conference to avoid penalties and a possible settlement (Watson, 2016).

If the taxpayer can settle the dispute, he/she is typically asked to sign a Form 870-AD (Form 890-AD for estates and gifts). These are a "Waiver of Restrictions on Assessment and Collection of Deficiency in Tax and Acceptance of Over Assessment". Form 870-AD is binding on the taxpayer and the government. Interest stops accruing when the form is received and accepted by the IRS. If some issues remain unresolved, the form can and must be modified. Unlike Form 870, which does not prevent the Government from assessing additional deficiencies, Form 870-AD does. Form 870-AD is final and binding on both parties. The taxpayer cannot claim a refund or credit, and the government cannot reopen the case unless there is evidence of fraud, misrepresentation, concealment of material facts, or gross mathematical errors (Watson, 2016).

Protest and Closing Agreements:

There is no specified form to file a protest, but it is advisable for the taxpayer to influence their cases thorough explaining and documenting their position.

IRS publication #5 recommends the taxpayer's content of protest to have the taxpayer's:

1. Name, address, and identification number
2. The taxpayer representative's name and a Power of Attorney on signed on Form 2848
3. A copy of or reference to, the preliminary notice "30-day letter" and the audit report identifying the tax years involved and the proposed adjustments
4. A statement that the protest filed is timely
5. A description of the issues and a statement of the taxpayer's position on each issue they are disputing
6. The taxpayer's request for an appeals conference
7. The taxpayer's signature, under penalties of perjury, that the facts alleged are true or the representative's statement that they prepared the protest and know the facts alleged to be true and correct.   The exhibits supporting or amplifying the taxpayer's position may be attached to provide additional evidence.

Forms 866 and 906 are used for closing agreements and collateral agreements with the taxpayer and the IRS and are based upon the IRC §7121 and 7122. §7121 prescribes the rules governing closing agreements while §7122 contains rules for compromises that are final and binding. Form 866 is used to settle conclusively the taxpayer's total and tax liability for the years in question. Form 906 is used to settle one or more issues that will affect a future tax liability. It is up to the taxpayer to convince the IRS and Government that entering into a closing agreement will not disadvantage them. This may be filed at any time before the case involving that period is docketed in Tax Court (Watson, 2016).

Court

If the taxpayer has an issue with the IRS based on a deficiency of tax, it is up to the taxpayer to decide whether to pay the disputed tax or to litigate the controversy. If the taxpayer decides to pay the tax, he/she might abandon the possibility of recovery for a claim for a refund. If the Taxpayer decides to litigate disputed tax the in civil controversy, he/she can select among 3 different forums "courts". They are: The United States Tax Court, The Unite States District Courts, and The United States Court of Federal Claims. Each court has different procedures, precedents, and levels of expertise. The U.S. Court of Appeals, the Federal Court of Appeals, and the U.S. Supreme Court are considered appellate courts (Misey, Goller, & Meldman, 2016).

In most litigation, the party bringing the case has the burden of proof. In most civil tax cases, the taxpayer has the burden of proof. In criminal taxes cases and fraud cases, the burden of proof shifts to the IRS. The doctrine of "Stare Decisis" states that judges are required to respect the precedents established by prior judicial decisions on the same set of facts. Any forum the taxpayer wishes to litigate in must also follow the stare decisis of precedents found in prior tax cases of the same facts and circumstances (Watson, 2016).

The taxpayer and their legal counsel must decide on what forum would most likely to rule in their favor, this is known as "forum shopping". Other factors that may determine the appropriate selection include:

1. Whether a jury trial is available
2. Whether the taxpayer must first pay the disputed tax in order to litigate
3. The apparent expertise of the judges
4. The precedents governing decisions in the tribunal

This is unique as in other judicial systems there in no way to select among multiple different courts and to select one that is likely to rule in their favor.

Tax Court

The United States Tax Court is a specialized trial court that hears only federal tax cases (income tax, estate tax, gift tax, or certain excise taxes). Tax Court judges are experts in tax matters and of the more complicated and technical issues litigated in Tax Court. Tax Court is the only forum that has the deficiency jurisdiction where the tax payer is not required to pay the disputed tax first in order to file suit. Tax Court is the most chosen forum for taxpayers. It also statistically has mostly ruled in favor of the IRS over the taxpayer. The cases are normally "pro s", meaning to be represented by oneself (Tax Court Rule 24(b)). Because the taxpayer doesn't pay the tax before the trail can begin, more frivolous cases are docketed in the Tax Court than in other forums (Watson, 2016).

Trial by jury is not available in the Tax Court. As a result, the Federal Rules of Evidence, which apply in Tax Court proceedings, are enforced much less stringently than in the U.S. District Court or the U.S. Court of Claims. Tax Court has their own rules of practice and procedure, which is differ from the Federal Rules of Civil Procedure (FRCP) (CCH Tax Law Editors, 2018).

Tax Court requires parties to generally resolve factual disputes which FRCP has parties first engage in informal communication for propose of discovery. Tax

Court unlike the other available courts, the Tax Court permits non-lawyers such as accountants and enrolled agents to represent taxpayers in cases. However, they first must pass an examination to do. The exam is given every other year and has a passing rate of less than 15% (Watson, 2016).

Tax Court is an Article I "legislative court", which means that it was established pursuant to Article I of the U. S. Constitution, rather than Article III which established many other federal courts. The Supreme Court has ruled that the Tax Court is a Court of law that is different from other legislatively created tribunals because it exercises judicial power (Misey, Goller, & Meldman, 2016).

Tax Court judges serve for terms of 15 years not a lifetime as in other courts and must retire at age 70 (IRC §7443). Tax Court consists of 19 judges appointed by the President with the advice and consent of the U.S. Senate. The court is based in Washington, D.C., but judges travel through the country to hear cases (Misey, Goller, & Meldman, 2016).

A Notice of Deficiency

Tax Court jurisdiction is dependent on exact compliance with statutory prerequisites.
1. The commissioner must determine that a tax deficiency exists,
2. The IRS must mail a Notice of Deficiency "90-Day Letter"
3. The taxpayer must file a petition.

Once a taxpayer has invoked the Tax Court's jurisdiction election, it is irrevocable, and the taxpayer may not dismiss the petition and seek a refund trial. The taxpayer initiates a suit in Tax Court by filing a petition seeking a redetermination of the tax deficiency computed by the IRS. The commissioner is named the respondent and is represented by the attorneys from the office of chief counsel. In the other forums, the government is represented by trial lawyers from the Tax Division of the Justice department (Watson, 2016).

IRC §7521 requires a Notice of Deficiency to describe the basis for and identify the amounts sought as tax due, interest, penalties, and additions to tax. Failure by the IRS will not automatically invalidate the notice. Tax Court may also consider facts from other taxable years that may have an effect on the determination of the deficiency for the taxable year before the court §6214(b).

A deficiency is defined in IRC §6211 as "the amount which tax imposed over amount tax shown". Meaning that a deficiency is the correct amount of tax liability over the tax liability reported by the taxpayer. The correct amount is not absolute as each department of the IRS might have a different deficiency amount. If the IRS determines that there is a general determination of deficiency, the IRS must send a Notice of Deficiency by certified mail to the taxpayer's last known address (§6212).

The last known address is considered sufficient for all tax purposes. This notice also known as a "90-Day Letter" because it gives the taxpayer 90 days to file a petition in Tax Court. Tax Court will not allow a case without a notice of deficiency (Watson, 2016).

When the IRS sends the Notice of Deficiency, it must disclose the nearest taxpayer advocate location and phone number §6212(b). Additional notices can come if there is fraud, concealment, misrepresentation, mathematical error, or jeopardy assessments §6212(c). The taxpayer has the right, even of a Notice of Deficiency has been issued or not, to their wave rights and pay the deficiency whole or in part §6212(d).

If Notice of Deficiency is sent to an address outside United States, the taxpayer has 150-Days to file in Tax Court. If the taxpayer does not file in time, the deficiency must be assessed and shall be paid upon notice and demand from IRS.

The Statue of limitation for the IRS to collect is 10 years from the start date of assessment, except in the case of jeopardy. When a Tax Court decision is rendered, the taxpayer has 90-days to the appeal the decision. If the taxpayer does not appeal, the Tax Court decision it becomes final after the 90 days (CCH Tax Law Editors, 2018).

After receiving a Notice of Deficiency the taxpayer has 90 days to respond to the notice IRC §6213 (a). The 90-day time frame starts on the date in which the post office stamps the envelope IRC §6501. The IRS cannot assess or collect the deficiency until the 90-day period has expired except in the case of jeopardy. Once a petition is filed with Tax Court, the IRS cannot assess or collect until the Tax Court decision becomes final.

After the Tax Court decision is rendered, the taxpayer has the right to appeal the decision within 90 days, if not, the decision becomes final. The IRS has the statute of limitation of 3 years after the taxpayer files a return to assess or make assessment of any deficiency §6503 (a). The actual mailing of the Notice of Deficiency suspends the statute of limitations on the assessment of deficiency. IRC §6503 (a)1 states that the statute of limitation shall be suspended for assessment and will be picked up at a later date.

If the taxpayer never receives a Notice of Deficiency, one course of action is to seek an injunction barring collection of the deficiency, as it was "never" mailed by the IRS. This is very difficult to prove, as there are many procedures outlined in the Internal Revenue manual for keeping records of mailing Notices of Deficiencies and compliance with these procedures for proof of mailing.

If the last known address is wrong, the deficiency of assessment is wrong, and the statute of limitation might run out for the IRS. If the statute of limitation has not expired, the IRS can send a new Notice of Deficiency to the correct address, and the notice will be valid. If the statute of limitation has expired and if the court finds that it was mailed to the last known address, the taxpayer is deemed to have received the notice (even if the taxpayer never received it). If the notice was not mailed to the last known address and the taxpayer receives it, then the court deems they have received it in due course. If a representative (such as a lawyer or attorney) of the taxpayer has received the notice, it also is deemed that the taxpayer has received it (Watson, 2016).

Small Tax Court
A taxpayer with a deficiency of $50,000 or less has the option to elect a more informal procedure known as a "Small Tax Case" or an "S-case" §7463. Special trial judges, appointed by the Chief Judge of the Tax Court, conducts these cases. Decisions by the trial judge in Small Tax Cases are final and non-appealable and are

not treated as precedent for any other case §7463(b). Tax Court Rule 177(b) requires that trial of Small Tax Cases be conducted as informally as possible, consistent with orderly procedure, and any evidence deemed by the court to have probative value, shall be admissible. Tax Court Rule 177(c) states that neither briefs nor oral arguments are required in Small Tax Cases. Small Tax Case decisions are called "Summary Opinions" and do not set any precedents for other cases. (Watson, 2016)

Decisions in Tax Court:

Tax Court issues 3 types of decisions: reviewed, regular and memorandum.

1. "Reviewed Decisions" have the greatest precedential value in Tax Court. A reviewed decision depends on if the Chief Judge decides an issue will be reviewed by all 19 judges and if their decision will be published.
2. "Regular Decision" normally involves a new or unusual point of law. A ruling of a regular decision will be published and set a precedential value with only one judge ruling on this decision.
3. Memorandum Decision" concerns only the application of existing law or an interpretation of facts and will set no additional precedential value.

Governing precedent in Tax Court is "The Golsen Rule". It was developed after the case of Golsen v. Commissioner, 54 T.C. 742 (1970) which states that the Tax Court will follow the governing precedent in the Court of Appeals. Before this change Tax Court did not follow the appellate court. This created many frivolous cases after a decision would be rendered. The U.S. Court of Appeals will review appeals that are set from Tax Court with the venue generally determined by the taxpayers' residence (Watson, 2016).

U.S. District Courts:

The U.S. District Courts are the general trial courts of the U.S. Federal Court system. Both civil and criminal cases (not just tax cases) are filed in district courts. There is at least one district court for each state and other district courts for territories.

If the taxpayer files a tax case in the United States District Court, the IRS has refund jurisdiction, in which the taxpayer must pay the disputed tax in full including interest first and then file a claim for a refund of the tax paid §7422(a). The suit is filed before the government and not an officer or agent. These suits can be for any amount large or small (Misey, Goller, & Meldman, 2016).

There are two types of taxes in United States District Court: non- divisible and divisible taxes.

1. A Non-Divisible tax is one that includes income, estate, and gift taxes.
2. Divisible "Transactional" Tax permit refund-suit jurisdiction without full payment of the entire amount assessed. These included some excise taxes and penalties imposed. Unlike Tax Court, there is the option of a jury trial at the request of the taxpayer.

U.S. Court of Federal Claims is a nationwide court that has jurisdiction over most claims for monetary damages against the United States, one type of which is a tax refund. The court hears mainly docketed cases because the judges of the court are viewed to have a higher tax expertise. It is an Article III court, and the president appoints 16 judges. Judges have 15-year terms and can be appointed for second term. Like Tax Court, it is based in Washington, D.C., but hold sessions throughout the country. The court has concurrent jurisdiction with U.S. District Courts when the claim is for less than $10,000, and there is a statute of limitations of 6 years. The taxpayer must pay the disputed tax and sue the IRS for a refund. The Court of Federal Claims does not allow jury trials on any matter (CCH Tax Law Editors, 2018).

Courts of Appeals
Court of Appeals and the U.S. Court of Appeals for the Federal Circuit, is the first level of federal appellate courts. A Court of Appeals hears appeals from the U.S. District Courts and the U.S. Tax Court. The U.S. Circuit Court of Appeals hears appeals from the U.S. Court of Federal Claims. Decisions of the court are reviewable by the U.S. Supreme Court on a petition for "writ of certiorari". There are nine justices, who hear all cases that the Supreme Court agrees to consider. However, tax cases are very rare (CCH Tax Law Editors, 2018).

What Forum to Choose
There are many strategic considerations in choosing a forum.
1. First: Attention should focus on cases involving the same or closely related issues under the same or similar factual circumstances.
2. Second: Consider the statistics of the total winning of past taxpayers.
3. Third: The taxpayer should have precedential questions such as if a higher court has previously ruled on the subject).
4. Fourth: The willingness or financial ability to pay the disputed tax before litigating the controversy.

Tax Court gives the taxpayer the option as to whether to pay the tax before or after litigation. If the taxpayer wins, the government must pay the interest in the amounts overpaid.

Tax Court may assert additional taxes due. The taxpayer can make a full payment of the tax, interest, and penalties in a deposit against any potential underpayments of tax IRC §6603. Making a deposit will stop the running of interest. The filing of the tax court petition suspends the statute of limitation on assessment of tax until the court decision becomes final. However, this opens the door for the IRS to determine additional tax as the IRS can raise new issues. The new issues cannot result in a net amount due to the government; they can only reduce the amount the government must pay the taxpayer. Expenses involved is generally cheaper for the taxpayer to file in Tax Court, as there are many "pro se" cases and a more informal setting. District Court or Court of Claims is much more formal and will be more costly. (Watson, 2016)

The Burden of Proof
It is up to the taxpayer to support a finding contrary to the Commissioner's determination. This means that the taxpayer has the burden of proof and is known as "Prima Facie Evidence". Tax Court Rule 142(a) also provides that the burden of proof

shall be upon the petitioner (taxpayer), except as otherwise provided by the statute or determined by the Court.

When the IRS uses statistical information to reconstruct a taxpayer's income, the IRS has the burden of proving the reconstructed income in any court proceeding (§7491). IRC §7491 states that in any litigation, (except criminal cases), the Commissioner bears the burden of proof on any factual issue, if the taxpayer introduces credible evidence relating to the issue and meets 4 conditions.

1. First: The taxpayer must comply with the substantiation requirements of the Code and Regulations.
2. Second: The taxpayer must maintain records required by the Code and Regulations.
3. Third: The taxpayer must cooperate with reasonable requests by the IRS for meetings, interviews, witnesses, information, and documents. Cooperation also includes providing reasonable assistance to the IRS in obtaining access to and inspection of witnesses, information, or documents not within the control of the taxpayer. Also, the taxpayer must exhaust all administrative remedies (all appeals).
4. Forth: The taxpayers must meet the net worth limitations that apply for awarding attorney fess under §7430.

In a refund suit the taxpayer bears a double burden of proof. The taxpayer must establish that the commissioner's assessment is wrong, and they must prove the exact amount of tax due. The government may offset the taxpayer's alleged overpayment of taxes with alleged underpayments not raised in the refund compliant. If the refund complaint is filed, the government will look for previous years returns to reduce the taxpayer's recovery. The Service may issue a deficiency notice for the year(s) in question after the taxpayer has filed a refund suit. If the commissioner's determination of a tax deficiency has developed in a line of cases involving illegal activity, the commissioner will determine a deficiency without a foundation. This is known as a "naked assessment" (Watson, 2016).

Relitigation

Issues of preclusion bars relitigation of a claim after a final judgment on the merits have been issued in a suit involving the same parties or their privies. This is based on the law principal "Res Judicata" - "Let it Rest", found both in civil and criminal law (CCH Tax Law Editors, 2018).

"Collateral Estoppel "also bars relitigation of an issue, even if the parties in the subsequent suit are not identical to those in the first suit. The test for collateral estoppel are:

1. First: Whether the issues presented in the latter case are substantially the same as those involved in the first case.
2. Second: Whether controlling facts or legal principles have changed significantly since the first judgment. Third,
3. Third: Whether other special circumstances warrant an exception to the application of the doctrine of collateral estoppel.

IRS Monitoring of Cases
The IRS monitors dockets of federal and state courts to identify defendants who have been found liable for misappropriation of funds or other illegal income-producing activities. Conviction of a willful attempt to defeat or evade a tax under IRC §7201, will collaterally stop denial of the fraud in a civil fraud case because the elements of civil fraud, as denied in IRC §6663, are identical to the necessary element of criminal fraud as contained in IRC §7201. Just because in a criminal case the taxpayer was exonerated, issues can still be borough up in a civil case (Watson, 2016).

The Statutes of Limitation
Taxpayers generally pay any tax due at the time of filing the return. However, if a taxpayer has either not reported all their income on the return or taken an improper deduction, the IRS can examine the return and seek additional tax in the form of a deficiency.

Tax policy suggests that at some point, a taxpayer should no longer have the responsibility to pay additional tax and the IRS should no longer expend its resources in rising additional amounts of tax for a given year. The Statutes of Limitations are laws that specify the amount of time to perform an act to be legally binding. The IRC contains a number of Statutes of Limitations contained in Subtitle F (Misey, Goller, & Meldman, 2016).

3-Year Statutes of Limitation
The IRS must make an assessment of additional tax within three years of the date a taxpayer files a return. Determining the date, the return is filed is a key issue. A general rule is that a tax return is considered filed on the date of receipt by the IRS. A condition to the general rule provides that a return received by the IRS prior to the original due date is treated as received and therefore filed on the original due date. If the taxpayer mails their return before the original due date, but the IRS receives the return after the original due date, the return is deemed filed on the original due date (Watson, 2016).

The 3-years statute of limitations also applies to the filing date of an extended tax return. An extended return is when a taxpayer mails their return before the extended due date. There are two different rules to determine the date of the filing and when the IRS "receives" the return.
1. First: If the IRS receives the return on or before the extended due date, the return is treated as received and, filed on the extended due date.
2. Second: If the IRS receives the return after the extended due date, the filing date is the date of receipt by the IRS.

Electronically filed returns are deemed filed on the date of the electronic postmark. The general 3-year statutes of limitations for assessment applies to all income tax returns, as wells as estate and gift tax returns. However, the IRS may assess a deficiency attributable to the carryback for a net operating loss, capital loss, or unused tax credit, within 3 years of the date of filing the return for the year of the loss or credit.

6-Year Statutes of Limitation for a Substantial Omission of Income

If the taxpayer omits income exceeding 25% of the gross income reported on their return, the IRS has a 6-year statutes of limitations period to assess any additional tax. A similar rule applies to estate tax or gift tax returns where there is an amount omitted that exceed 25% of the amount of the gross estate or total gifts reported.

On an income tax return reflecting a trade or business, the term "gross income" refers to gross receipts (total of the amounts received or accrued from the sale of good or services without the reduction for the cost of such sales or services). Therefore, in determining whether there has been an omission in excess of 25%, the IRS will calculate the gross receipts figure, not the gross profit figure (Misey, Goller, & Meldman, 2016).

Gross income from the sale of stocks or other capital assets is not treated the same way regarding the 6-year statutes of limitations. Regarding this purpose only the gain is reported, not the gross proceeds of the sale. Even if the deductions are overstated so that they would produce a tax deficiency equivalent to a failure to report gross income, the 6-year statutes of limitations will not apply. This is because an overstated deduction is not an omission from income. The IRS rationale for this ruling is that claiming the deductions fully apprises the IRS of the nature of the items and their amounts (Watson, 2016).

The rule that overstated deductions are not gross income does not apply to an overstatement of cost or other basis. Where a taxpayer overstates the cost basis of property sold, reducing the profit on sale, the 6-year statutes of limitations will apply. The IRS rationale is that overstating the cost basis will have the same effect as not reporting the gross sale proceeds. If there is a substantial omission of gross income from the taxpayer, the 6-year statutes of limitations apply to the entire deficiency. This will include some items comprising the deficiency that were not included in calculating the omission (Watson, 2016).

An item is not considered omitted if the taxpayer discloses its existence in the return or in a statement attached to the return in a manner that informs the IRS of the nature and amount of the item. For either partnerships with ten or fewer partners (before 2018), or for partnerships with 100 or fewer partners that have elected the new unified partnership procedure in 2018, discloser of an item in the partnership return constitutes sufficient discloser on the individual return of the partner. This will avoid the 6-year statutes of limitations to assess additional taxes (Watson, 2016).

Statutes of Limitation for a Filed Return

If a taxpayer never filed a return or if a taxpayer files an incomplete return, the IRS may assess the tax at any time, without any statute of limitations. A return to sufficiently start the running of the period of limitations generally must be properly signed and contain "substantial information" necessary to compute tax (CCH Tax Law Editors, 2018).

A document described as a "tentative" return that fails to include items of substantial information is not a proper return and would not be considered filed. The Tax Court has held that a return which has declared the taxable income, but the taxpayer omitted their social security number, occupation, and any personal exemptions while the return was marked "tentative", was insufficient to start the running of the statute of limitation. Even if a taxpayer files a document titled "return", it may not constitute a return that is sufficient to trigger the statute of limitations.

Any alternation of the jurat (the attestation statement) will not constitute a return as filed. The IRS has determined that a form that lists zeroes on each line and that the taxpayer signs without modification to the jurat, should be treated as a return of Statute of Limitations purposes. Any form filed without a signature is not a completed return. If a taxpayer fails to file a return, the IRS can prepare a return for that taxpayer. However, if the return that the IRS prepares on behalf of a non-filing taxpayer is not treated as a return filed, this will not start the running if the statute of limitations (Watson, 2016).

False or Fraudulent Returns Statutes of Limitation
When a taxpayer files a false or fraudulent return with the intent to evade tax, the IRS may assess a deficiency at any time, as the statute of limitations will remain open forever. However, the IRS has the burden of proving by clear and convincing evidence that the taxpayer intended to evade tax. The conviction of the taxpayer in a tax evasion prosecution sufficiently meets the IRS's burden of proof and will stop the taxpayer from contending that they did not intend to evade tax (Misey, Goller, & Meldman, 2016).

Amending a false return does not have any impact on the statute of limitations. In Badaracco v. Commissioner, the Supreme Court held that the IRC does not explicitly provide for either the filing or acceptance of an amended return. The Court ruled that an amended return is "merely a creature of administrative origin and grace". The Supreme Court further stated in the case that only the original return, not an amended return, determines on which the statute of limitations on assessment applies. An amended return, therefore, will not trigger the 3-year statute of limitations. The time to assess a deficiency remains open forever on the basis of the fraudulent original return (Watson, 2016).

Tax Shelters – Listed Transactions
A listed transaction is a transaction that the IRS specifically identifies as a tax avoidance transaction. Treasury Department has determined that even having a potential for either tax avoidance or tax evasion, it can be declared a listed transaction. If a taxpayer fails to include any information that is required to be disclosed for a listed transaction, the statute of limitations will not expire. If the IRS receives information, the statute of limitations will close 1 year after the earlier of the date of when the IRS receives the required information or the date that a material advisor provides the IRS with a list identifying each person to whom the advisor had acted as a material advisor (CCH Tax Law Editors, 2018).

Gift Omission of Gift Tax Return
If a donor erroneously omits a gift from a gift tax return, the IRS, at any time, may either assess the tax on such gift or proceed in court to collect such tax without assessment. The statute of limitations does not run on omitted gifts regardless if the fact that a donor filed a gift tax return for other transfers in the same period. Assessment at any time for tax on an omitted gift does not apply if the gift tax return

discloses the transfer in a manner that adequately apprises the IRS of the nature of the omitted item (CCH Tax Law Editors, 2018).

Statutes of Limitation for a Partnership
The pass-through adjustments to an individual's reported income resulting from the IRS examination of partnerships raises questions regarding the period of limitations for an assessment. For taxable years prior to 2018, The Tax Equity and Fiscal Responsibility Act (TEFRA) had placed forth partnership procedures that would bind the individual partners to the partnership (Watson, 2016).

Pursuant to the Tax Court, these rules effectively create a two-part analysis.
First: If the partnership is open, the IRS can assess all the partners
Second: If the partnership's statute is closed, the IRS can only assess the partners whose individual statute of limitations remain open.

For taxable years beginning in 2018 and going forward, the new unified audit procedures state that the IRS can assess the tax 3-years after the date the partnership files the Form 1065, the due date for the Form 1065, or the date the partnership files an administrative adjustment request (an overpayment) (CCH Tax Law Editors, 2018).

There are three special operating rules that impact the new unified audit procedures, which assess taxation at the highest rate in effect for the partners.

1. First: The IRS has another 270 days to assess tax after receiving documentation from the partnership that a lower tax rate should apply.
2. Second: If the IRS issues a Proposed Partnership Adjustment to a partnership, the IRS has an additional 330 days to assess a tax.
3. Third: A small partnership (100 or few partners) can annually elect out of the new unified audit procedures, which would result in the filing of each partner's return (and not the partnership return) triggering the statute of limitations.

Statutes of Limitation for a S-Corporation
The statute of limitations begins to run on items that flow through from S-corporation returns (Form 1120S) on the date that individual owner files their return. Neither The Tax Equity and Fiscal Responsibility Act (TEFRA, nor the new unified partnership procedures apply to S-corporations or their shareholders. However, a shareholder of an S-corporation must notify the IRS if they are filing a return that is inconsistent with the S-Corporation's Form 1120S (Watson, 2016).

Computation of Time from the Date of Filing
A return is deemed timely filed for purposes of determining the commencement of the limitation period when it is postmarked. Even if a return is received after the last date prescribed for filing, the return is timely filed if postmarked on or before the due date. This rule in the IRC and regulations applies only to returns timely filed where the envelope containing the return has the proper address and bears the proper postage (CCH Tax Law Editors, 2018).

The timely mailing filing rule applies to the United States Post Office, as well as to returns sent by other private delivery services. In addition to the transmittal of returns by conventional means, a special provision deems electronically transmitted documents as filed on the date of the electronic postmark.

The timely mailing filing rule also applies to foreign postmarks. A return baring an official foreign postmark dated on or before midnight of the last date prescribed for filing, including any extension of time, is timely filed. The IRS bases this position on the general authority granted in Code §6081(a) for the IRS to "grant a reasonable extension of time for filing any return". The decision to accept return as timely when mailed and officially postmarked in a foreign country, is a reasonable and proper exercise of the IRS Commissioner's administrative authority (Watson, 2016).

Despite the timely mailing filing rule described in the IRC and the Regulations, the Supreme Court has extended the law so that the date of the postmark does not control or superseded so long as the taxpayer timely placed the document in the mailbox. However, the taxpayer will have to prove that they timely mailed the document.

For purposes of computing the 3-year statute of limitations period, the return's due date (the date filed) is excluded. When the due date falls on a Saturday, Sunday, or a legal holiday, the return will be considered timely filed if it is filed on the next business day. This weekend and holiday rule similarly applies to the date the statute expires. A claim for refund must be filed within either 3 years of filing the original return or 2 years of the time the tax was paid, whichever is later. If the taxpayer did not file a return, the 2-year statute of limitations rule applies (Misey, Goller, & Meldman, 2016).

Consent to Extend the Statutes of Limitation

The taxpayer can voluntary agree with the IRS to extend the statute of limitations to assess tax. However, this extension by consent is not available for estate tax assessment. Form 872, "Consent to Extend the Time to Assess Tax", is the form the IRS uses when a taxpayer voluntarily agrees to extend to a specified date the period the IRS can assess tax. However, neither the IRS nor the taxpayer can unilaterally terminate the extended statute of limitations once elected (Watson, 2016).

A Form 872-A is a special consent form to extend the statute of limitations to assess tax. The extension will not terminate until 90-days after either the IRS receives a notice of termination on Form 872-T, Notice of Termination of Special Consent to Extend the Time to Assess Tax executed by the taxpayer, or the IRS mails the taxpayer a Statutory Notice of Deficiency.

An extension on Form 872-A can terminate only pursuant to these provisions and will not expire by operation of law simply as a result of the passage of a reasonable period of time. Neither the execution of a closing agreement nor a letter sent by the taxpayer (or even the IRS) terminates the statute of limitations. It may not be sufficient to start the running of the 90-day period following the notice of termination if the taxpayer just sends the Form 872-T to the IRS office considering the case and that office delivers the form to another IRS office (Watson, 2016).

Extended Statutes of Limitation for a Partnership

The IRS uses special consent forms to extend the limitations period for partnerships subject to the unified Tax Equity and Fiscal Responsibility Act (TEFRA) audit procedures. These forms are similar to Form 872 and 872-A, but are given special letter designations. These forms extend the statute of limitations to assess the individual partners or shareholder for any tax resulting from an audit adjustment to partnership items. Other special consent forms are available for extending the time to assess excise taxes on investment income earned by private foundations or to assess the tax return prepared penalty (Watson, 2016).

Rules on the Forms to Extended Statutes of Limitation

The forms for the extension of the limitations period require execution both by the taxpayer or the taxpayer's representative and by an authorized representative of the IRS. Both parties must execute the extension prior to expiration of the statute of limitations within which the assessment can be made. If the taxpayer executes the consent prior to the expiration of the Statute of Limitations, but the IRS does not execute it until after the expiration, the extension will not be valid. Before the expiration of the previously extended statute of limitations to assess the tax, the IRS and the taxpayer may further extend by an additional properly executed consent (Misey, Goller, & Meldman, 2016).

The taxpayer and the IRS must have a meeting of the minds to ensure a valid consent. An extension of the statute of limitations is invalid and void if the IRS obtains the consent of the taxpayer by coercion or under duress. Similarly, where the IRS threatened to impose the fraud penalty in order to secure an extension, the court rejected the extension of the statute of limitations as void.

Issues that Cannot be Resolved

If, in the course of an examination, there is one issue that cannot be resolved prior to the expiration of the statute of limitations, even though all other issues have been resolved, the IRS will generally request that the taxpayer extend the statute of limitations. The taxpayer normally will be reluctant to subject the entire return to the possibility of additional assessment when only one issue remains in controversy. In such a situation, a procedure exists for the IRS to secure a restricted consent. Under such consent, the IRS and the taxpayer extend the statute of limitations only with regard to the remaining unagreed issue. The parties execute restricted consent on both Forms 872 and Form 872-A (Watson, 2016).

Fraud

If any portion of any return is fraudulent, both the deficiency and the fraud penalty maybe assessed at any time. Fraudulent returns have no statute of limitations even if the taxpayer later repents and files a non-fraudulent return §6501(c)1. If the commissioner assets the fraud penalty after the 3-year statute of limitations has expired and the court refuse to uphold the fraud penalty, then the asserted tax deficiency and penalty will be barred due to time (CCH Tax Law Editors, 2018).

A deceased taxpayer who filed a fraudulent return during their lifetime will not be relived of the civil fraud penalty by their death. The penalty may be asserted against their estate, since it is considered an addition to the tax, and is remedial rather than penal in nature.

Fraud in the Regards to Relationships

Common relationships that could give rise to liability for a fraud penalty can be cause by someone other than the taxpayer. This includes spouses, shareholders and corporations, partners and partnerships, executors and estates, trusses, and trust. In a joint return the fraud of a taxpayer may not be imputed to their spouse unless some part of the underpayment is attributed to the fraud of that spouse. The unlimited statute of limitations still applies. But only the spouse who is convicted of criminal fraud is subject to collateral estoppel (CCH Tax Law Editors, 2018).

Acts of the corporate officer can be imputed to the officer's principal, the corporation. There is not a defense for the corporation against which a civil fraud penalty has been asserted, to claim that is not responsible for the officer's actions, particularly when the officer is a controlling shareholder and the corporation received a benefit as a result of those actions. If it can be shown that the officer was acting principally in benefit to himself or herself and corporation did not benefit from it, then the courts have held that the corporations should not impute the fraud.

For partners in a general partnership who participate in fraudulent reporting, the fraud penalty can be upheld against the partners. The partnership would not be liable for the fraud penalty, as a partnership returns are informational only. Each partner can be held liable individually for the civil fraud penalty (Watson, 2016).

Frivolous Position, Delay or Impeded Assessment of Taxation

Under IRC §6702 authorizes the IRS to impose a $5000 penalty on anyone who files a return that does not contain sufficient information from which the correctness of the tax liability can be judged or that contains information that on its face indicates that the tax liability shown on the return is incorrect (J. K. Lasser Institute, 2019).

The actual penalty imposed is based on the taxpayer's frivolous position or a desire to delay or impeded the administration of the tax laws. Once it has been determined that an adjustment is warned, the method of making the adjustment depends on whether the adjustments results in a deficiency or an overpayment. In either case, the adjustment will bear interest and be subject to additional tax, under the laws governing deficiency and overpayments for the year in which the adjustments relate (J. K. Lasser Institute, 2019).

Regarding any determination of a deficiency in the government's favor, the commissioner has 1-year from the date of the agreement to mail a Notice of Deficiency and collect under the deficiency procedures §1313(a)4. With an overpayment in the taxpayer's favor, the taxpayer has 1-year from the date of the agreement in which to file a claim for a refund unless the government refunds the amount without a formal claim being filed §1313(a)4. If the claim is denied or is not acted on by the IRS within 6-months, the tax taxpayer may sue for a refund. The statute of limitations on any assessment or a claim for a refund resulting from an adjustment, begins on the date the "determination" is made. This often is on the date the court decision becomes final and expires 1 year afterwards (Watson, 2016).

Equitable Recoupment

Equitable Recoupment is a judicially created doctrine that permits the bar of statute of limitations to be avoided in certain circumstances in which equity demands relief. It is permitted when the same transaction or taxable event has been subjected to two taxes bases in inconsistent legal theories.

The Statue of Limitations does not bar equitable recoupment so long as the main action itself is timely. The doctrine permits the court to examine the transaction or event as a whole to reach a fair result. The government can invoke it to prevent unfair tax avoidance and the taxpayer can invoke it for double taxation. IRC §6214(b) provides that the Tax Court may apply equitable recoupment to the same extent that it may be applied in the Federal District Court or Court of Claims. IRC §6511 states that the Doctrine of Equitable Tolling of the Statue of Limitations will not apply for filling a refund suit (Misey, Goller, & Meldman, 2016).

Attorney-Client Privilege

Although the IRS has broad investigatory powers, the IRS may not obtain information or documents that are subject to evidentiary privileges. The primary evidentiary privileges are the attorney-client privileges, which the Code extends on a limited basis to cover other tax practitioners and the work-product doctrine.

The attorney-client privilege protects confidential communication between an attorney and client for the purpose of obtaining or providing legal advice. This extends to communications with non-layers provided the purpose of the communication is to assist the attorney on rendering legal advice to the taxpayer. When an attorney retains an agent to assist them in a tax controversy, any work produced by the accountant subsequent to such engagement will be protected in the same manner as if the attorney prepared it. This doesn't extend to an accountant that communications made before the attorney seek them (Misey, Goller, & Meldman, 2016).

A letter that an attorney is retaining the accountant is called a "Kovel Letter". The engaged letter to the accountant should include a recital that the attorney is hiring the accountant to assist them in rending legal advice. The attorney should outline the nature and scope of the accountant's engagement. There should be an acknowledgement that payment will come from the law firm and the client is not to be billed. There should be an explicated acknowledgement that all records, schedules, documents, or anything of that matter of the accountant-agent will be the sole property of the attorney. There also must be a recital that on competition of the assignment, the accountant will deliver their files to the attorney and not retain any copies. To ensure the communications between the client and the accountant will continue to be privileged under Kovel, the attorney, as opposed to the accountant, must act as the taxpayer's primary representative and play a visible role.

Penalties

The IRS imposes a penalty for not filing a return on time, which can be 25% of the amount owed to the IRS. IRC §6651(a) states that the IRS can impose a penalty of up to 25% of the net tax due for delinquency in filing a return. The penalty is imposed at the rate of 5% per month to the 25% ceiling (5 months). The IRS also imposes a complete separate penalty for not paying the tax owed; this also can be up to 25% of the amount owed to the IRS. IRC §6651(a)2 states that the IRS can impose a separate penalty of up to 25% of the net tax due for delinquency in paying the tax. The failure to pay penalty is imposed at the lesser rate of 0.5% per month (50 months) (CCH Tax Law Editors, 2018).

Penalties for Understating Tax
The penalty for an individual taxpayer for the understatement of tax is 20% of the correct tax due. An understatement is considered substantial if it exceeds the greater of 10% of the correct tax or $5,000. For C-corporations other than personal holding companies, an understatement is substantial if the amount of the understatement exceeds the lesser of $ 10,000,000, or the greater of $10,000 or 10% of the correct tax (J.K Lasser Institute, 2019).

Penalties for Fraud
Filing a fraudulent return with the IRS can impose both civil and criminal penalties to the taxpayer. However, the IRS must prove beyond a reasonable doubt that the taxpayer criminally, willfully, and deliberately attempted to evade tax. The civil penalties can be as high as 75% of the understatement of tax due to fraud the criminal penalties can be as high as $100,000 for an individual or $500,000 in the case of a corporation and in both cases there can be potential imprisonment (J.K Lasser Institute, 2019).

Tax Court Penalties
The Tax Court has reasonable basis standards. This means that a taxpayer or tax preparer cannot file a frivolous position with the court. Frivolous positions have no basis in law or other authority which is defined as a less than a 20% chance of succeeding. The penalty for frivolous positions is equal to the greater of $1,000 or 50% of the income the preparer received for tax return preparation services IRC §6694(a).

In addition to the various defenses that are available, a taxpayer generally can avoid a penalty for frivolous positions by showing that the taxpayer had reasonable cause to support the tax return position, acted in good faith, and did not have willful neglect (Watson, 2016).

Penalties for Failing to File
If the taxpayer files a fraudulent return, the return is subject to additional penalties. IRC §6651(f) state that fraudulent failure to file a return is subject to a penalty of 15% per month to a maximum of 75% of the net tax due. A taxpayer who nonfraudulently fails to file a return and pay the tax due in a timely fashion, is subject to a maximum penalty under §6651 of 47.5%. A taxpayer who fraudulently fails to file a return and pay the tax due in a timely fashion, is subject to a maximum penalty under §6651 of 75%. Protesters who file incomplete returns are subject to the failure to file and failure to pay penalties of §6651. These documents are not considered returns and are not filed.

The burden of proving fraud is on the IRS because it is considered criminal in nature §7454(a). If the IRS does not sustain its burden, its ability to impose any penalty for failure to timely file depends on the contents of the notice of deficiency. If in the notice of deficiency, the IRS determines the basic §6651 penalty in the alternative to fraud penalty, then the court may consider the §6651 penalty, and the taxpayer will bear the burden of proof. If the Notice of Deficiency does not contain an assertion of the §6651 penalty, but the IRS asserts the penalty in its answer, then the court may consider the §6651 penalty, but the burden of proof will be on the IRS. If the IRS fails to asset the §6651 penalty, either in the notice of deficiency or in its answer, and fails to sustain its burden of proving fraud, then the court may not consider the §6651 penalty and the taxpayer will not be held liable for it (Misey, Goller, & Meldman, 2016).

Reason that Could Release a Taxpayer from Penalties
Both the §6651(a)1 and the §6651(a)2 penalties apply to the net tax due. This is the amount of tax owing, less any amounts paid or withheld before the due date, and less any credits allowable. Both the §6651(a)1 and the §6651(a)2 penalties are subject to the statutory defense of reasonable cause and absence of willful neglect.

The Supreme Court has held that the duty to file a return and pay the tax is personal and reliance on an attorney to file an estate tax return does not constitute reasonable cause. IRM §20.1.1.3.2 list other defense the services will recognize as satisfying the reasonable cause standard, including death or serious illness of the taxpayer or a member of their immediate family, destruction by fire or other casualty of the taxpayer's residence, business premises, or businesses records, and through no fault of the taxpayer, they are unable to obtain records necessary to complete the return (Watson, 2016).

There are other circumstances and situations that are not covered in the IRM that could release a taxpayer from a penalty. If the taxpayer believes the penalty is not properly imposed, they should summit a request for abatement of the delinquency penalty with the delinquent return or in response to the deficiency notice stating the reasons why it would be unfair to impose the penalty. If the person lacks the funds to pay the tax, regulations state that a failure to pay will be due to reasonable cause if the taxpayer shows that they exercised ordinary business care and prudence in providing for payment of the taxes, but was unable to pay the tax or would suffer undue hardship if forced to pay. Living beyond your means does not constitute reasonable cause (Watson, 2016).

Penalties for Failure to Pay Estimated Taxes
The IRS imposes a separate penalty for failure to pay, or for underpayment of, estimated taxes IRC §6654. The penalty also applies to under withholding of federal income tax from wages. Unless the taxpayer falls within one of the exceptions to liability, the imposition of the penalty is mandatory, and reasonable cause and lack of willful neglect, are irrelevant.

If the balance of tax owed at filing is under $1,000 then there is no penalty. The IRS may waive the penalty if it was the result of casualty, disaster, illness, or death of the taxpayer.

For estimated tax purposes, a year has four payment periods. Taxpayers must make a payment each quarter. For most people, the due date for the first quarterly payment is April 15. The next payments are due June 15 and Sept. 15, with the last quarter's payment due on Jan. 15 of the following year. If a taxpayer receives wages in the form of a W-2 these are taking out of your taxes by your employer.

When filing a return at the end of the year, the taxpayer must pay either 90% of the current year's tax shown or 100% of last year's tax shown on the individual return. If a taxpayer had an adjusted gross income in excess of $150,000 ($75,000 married filing separately) in the prior year, then 110% of the prior year's tax liability is owed instead of the 100%. This applies even if the taxpayer files a tax return with a zero-tax liability in the prior year (J. K. Lasser Institute, 2019).

Overpayment Interest
The government must pay interest to taxpayers who have overpaid on their taxes. Interest on overpaid taxes begins to accrue on the date of overpayment §6611(b). The date of the overpayment for taxes withheld from wages or for estimate taxes is the date the return is due §6611(d).

Taxpayers must pay interest to the government for underpayment of taxes. IRC §6621(a)1 and §6621(a)2 state that overpayments and underpayments applies the interest rate of the short-term federal rate plus 3%. For corporate overpayments taxpayers will receive 1.5% plus the short-term federal interest rate for any amount that exceeds $10,000, and 5% plus the short-term federal interest rate for any amount that exceeds $100,000 IRC §6621(c). IRC §6621(b) state that the short-term federal rates are determined in the first month of each calendar quarter to become effective on the first day of the next calendar quarter §6621(b) (CCH Tax Law Editors, 2018).

Interest from an Underpayment of Tax
Interest in a tax deficiency begins to accrue on the due date of the tax return. If civil penalties are assessed, the taxpayer also must pay interest on the penalties. Valuation penalties and the delinquent filing penalty begin to accrue on the date of the return and runs until the is tax paid in full, plus interest and penalties accrued IRC §6601(e)2B. There is no interest owed (net rate will be zero) on equal amounts of overpayment and underpayment that run simultaneously, provided none of the years in question is barred by the statute of limitations §6621(d). This also applies in the same taxable year or different taxable years (CCH Tax Law Editors, 2018).

Deposits to Stop Interest
A taxpayer who disputes a proposed tax liability and losses, might face a significant amount of interest accrued from the original due date of the return, the actual tax liability, plus interest and penalties. To avoid this, the taxpayer can pay, file for a return, and then sue in District Court or the Court of Claims. However, by using this method the taxpayer will lose access to filing their claim in Tax Court.

The taxpayer can make a deposit to suspend the running of interest. IRC §6603 (a) states that the taxpayer may make a deposit to hold onto tax assessed at time of deposit. If the deposit is used to pay the tax liability the tax should be treated as paid with some payback interest, normally in a very small amount §6603 (b). By making a deposit the taxpayer can still file their suit in Tax Court and if the taxpayer should lose, he/she will not be face with accruing any interest. A deposit will be given back unless the service decided that assessment or collection of tax was in jeopardy or that there was another outstanding tax liability against which the deposit could be credited. A deposit has no Statute of Limitation, but a payment has a 2-year Statute of Limitation to be paid (Watson, 2016).

When the tax is assessed, the amount of the deposit will be applied as a payment against the tax liability, but interest on the underpayment equal to amount of deposit will cease as of the date of the deposit. Prior to assessment of tax, the deposit is not considered a payment. The taxpayer is entitled to interest at the applicable Federal rate on any amount of deposit that is returned, provided the deposit is attributable to a disputable tax.

A disputable tax is any tax attributable to a disputable item. A disputable item has a reasonable basis for the treatment on the return and has a reasonable basis for disallowing their treatment of such item §6603(d)3A. All items that are mention in a 30-day letter are deemed disputable for this purpose (Misey, Goller, & Meldman, 2016).

Tax Preparer Penalties

A tax practitioner has a legal liability for anyone he/she prepares returns for and can be subject to a suit base on a breach of contract, tort, or violating statutes. Civil actions for tax malpractice are usually based on either traditional contract or traditional tort principles.

The contract principles impose the obligation to prepare the tax return diligently and competently. The tort principles provide that a professional has a duty to exercise the level of skill, care, and diligence commonly exercised by other members of the profession under similar circumstances.

To prove malpractice against a tax preparer, the plaintiff must demonstrate that the tax preparer owed a duty to the taxpayer, there was a breach of that duty, the plaintiff suffered injuries, and there was a determinable cause between injury suffered and the duty of the tax preparer (Watson, 2016).

If a tax practitioner does not fulfill the terms of engagement in a contract, the client can hold the practitioner liable for breach. Contract liability generally requires privacy, so only a party to the contract can sue. For a tax practitioner the beset defense for a breach of contract is the taxpayer's failure to cooperate with the practitioner. A tax practitioner liability can also arise from commission of a tort, which include negligence, gross negligence and fraud (CCH Tax Law Editors, 2018).

"Ordinary" Negligence requires a breach of the duty to exercise due care. The standard of care owed by a tax practitioner is to perform with the same skill and care expected of a prudent tax practitioner. To make out a case for negligence, the plaintiff must show the defendant owed a duty of care to the plaintiff, the defendant breached that duty by failing to act with due care, the breach caused plaintiff's injury and damages were suffered by the breach. In the case of negligence, there is a limit to a person's privacy and third-party beneficiaries, or a limited class of persons who foreseeably cannot sue (CCH Tax Law Editors, 2018). Gross Negligence has five elements:

1. A misrepresentation of material fact,
2. There is an intent to deceive,
3. There is actual and justifiable reliance by plaintiff on the misrepresentation,
4. The defendant acts recklessly, and
5. When damages were suffered.

In the case of fraud, the 5 elements are present with the addition that there was an intent to induce the plaintiff's reliance on misrepresentation the tax practitioner can be held liable to anyone who proves these elements.

Privacy is not a defense to gross negligence or fraud. Liability is not limited to persons in privacy, third-party beneficiaries or a limited class of persons who foreseeably can sue (CCH Tax Law Editors, 2018).

Tax Preparer Overpayment Penalties

In some situations, the tax practitioner can be held liable for the amount by which taxes were overpaid, if the overpayment cannot be reclaimed through the filing of an amended return. This is based on the reason that mistakes were reported on the tax return and there was a lost investment or income opportunity. A taxpayer may be awarded by the court's costs incurred to correct the tax return. This includes fees that will be incurred to file amended returns and/or challenge penalties that have been assessed and the extent that the taxpayer has suffered actual damages related to the interest charged (Misey, Goller, & Meldman, 2016).

Failures of Tax Practitioner

Under §6695 a tax practitioner has a $50 penalty for each time they fail to provide a copy of the return to taxpayer, sign the return or furnish their identification number. There is a maximum penalty of $25,500 per calendar year for each one of these issues. The penalty does not apply to the extent the failure is due to reasonable cause and not due to willful neglect. The tax return preparer is required to keep, for 3 years following the last day of the return period, either: a copy of the return or claim or a listing of the name and identification of each taxpayer for whom the preparer prepared a return or claim. The penalty is $50 for each such failure with a maximum penalty of $25,500 per return period. A tax practitioner who endorses or otherwise negotiates an IRS refund check issued to a taxpayer, shall pay a penalty of $510 for each check (J. K. Lasser Institute, 2019).

Due Diligence of Tax Practitioner

A tax practitioner has due diligence requirements that must be met at all times. Some items that the due diligence requirements addresses are eligibility checklists, computation worksheets, reasonable inquires to the taxpayer, and proper record retention. An example of improper due diligence requirements in respect to determining eligibility for, or the amount of, the earned income credit. A penalty of $510 for each failure will be accessed for each incident.

The penalty for aiding and abetting understatement of tax liability applies to any person, not just to tax return preparer, who is found aiding and abetting an understatement of tax liability. The IRS has the burden of proof to establish that any person is liable for this civil penalty of $1,000 for all taxpayers and corporations $10,000 (§6703(a) (J. K. Lasser Institute, 2019).

Duty of Confidentiality for a Tax Practitioner

A tax practitioner has duty of confidentiality. This includes the tax refund and any work papers that were used to develop the return. A tax return preparer who discloses or uses information for any purpose other than to prepare a tax return, shall pay a civil penalty of $250 for each such disclosure or use (maximum annual penalty shall not exceed $10,000), and be guilty of a misdemeanor and fined not more than $1,000 and/or be imprisoned for not more than 1 year (IRC §6713, §7216). Exceptions to the penalty and/or fine for wrongful disclosure and/or use of tax return information are disclosures allowed by any provision of the IRC and disclosures pursuant to a court order, allowable uses and consent by the client, and disclosures and uses permitted by U.S. Treasury regulations for quality and peer reviews (IRC §6713, §7216) (Misey, Goller, & Meldman, 2016).

Summary: IRS Disciplinary Actions

The IRS can impose penalties on any tax practitioner who counsels or prepares a tax return in a fraudulent or false manner. The IRS must prove beyond reasonable doubt in a criminal trial, that the tax practitioner was fraudulent in preparing the return.

A tax practitioner found guilty of making a false or fraudulent statement in connection with a return, is guilty of a felony and may be imprisoned for not more than 3 years and/or fined for $100,000.The IRS may also impose civil penalties, which has a much lower standard of only a "preponderance of evidence". The IRS may prohibit a tax practitioner from practicing before the IRS and may impose fines for various infractions (Misey, Goller, & Meldman, 2016).

19 – CONCLUSION

This chapter first provides a brief summary of what was covered in this book and the objectives of the authors. The chapter then provides a brief conclusion – one which harkens back to the "theme" of Venice.

Book Conclusion
Today's entrepreneurs, managers, and their employees are impacted by law each day; and almost all human activity is affected by the law. In the business world, when contemplating a business transaction or decision, an entrepreneur or manager not only must consider the physical, financial, personnel, and managerial aspects, but also the legal ramifications. Moreover, as the business and entrepreneurial "world" is now a truly diverse workplace, an entrepreneur or manager must be cognizant of laws impacting his/her employees, suppliers, and customers. The main purpose of this book, therefore, has been to introduce the reader to fundamental principles of the laws regulating business as well as their practical application in the United States. The first chapter began by discussing law and the basic legal principles impacting entrepreneurs and managers; the last chapter concluded with some basic business principles that current and aspiring entrepreneurs and managers in the United States must become aware of and understand. The other chapters in-between expanded on other important legal concepts and precepts that will be beneficial to entrepreneurs and managers. The authors wanted the discerning reader to be conscious of the scope and complexity of laws affecting business. The authors accordingly intended to help the reader recognize legal situations in business as well as everyday life; and the authors especially wanted to impart an awareness of potential legal problems, and how to avoid them.

This book is designed to help readers become familiar with important legal issues and concepts so they can make appropriate decisions about their company's status. Entrepreneurs and managers deal with "laws of the land" every day, and consequently must be aware of its nuances and complexities in order to successfully and interdependently work with others in the community, industry, and country. Thus, entrepreneurs and managers should become aware of the fundamental aspects of the legal system so they can avoid legal problems and can seek the help of experts when dealing with complex issues. *Business Law for the Entrepreneur and Manager* has been designed to provide the foundational aspects of the "American" legal system, as practiced in the United States, for current and aspiring entrepreneurs and managers. By reading and becoming familiar with the various topics presented, it is hoped that the readers will be better prepared to more effectively deal with legal challenges.

Business Law for the Entrepreneur and Manager introduced the reader to fundamental principles of the laws regulating business as well as their practical application in the United States. The various chapters covered such topics as the law and the basic legal principles impacting entrepreneurs and managers; the foundational business laws that entrepreneurs and managers in the United States must become aware of and understand, as well as other important legal topics such as constitutional law, torts, products liability, contract law, sales and agency laws, commercial paper, various forms of business organizations, and debtors and creditors laws. The study of this legal material will be very beneficial to all current and prospective entrepreneurs and managers.

Business Law for the Entrepreneur and Manager has been designed to be used academically for foundational business law courses, as well as practically, as a guide and an enlightening learning tool that the hard-working and on-the-go manager or entrepreneur can find useful. Overall, the authors hoped that all the stated and aforementioned objectives were attained in a stimulating, thought-provoking, perhaps at times provocative, and enjoyable manner; and as a result the knowledge of the reader is increased, the mental acuity of the reader is enhanced, and the mental discipline of the reader is strengthened.

The authors of this book selected a picture of Venice for the cover of this book – a picture showing the "hustle and bustle" of this beautiful and unique city, a World Heritage site – as well as the initial quotes from William Shakespeare's Merchant of Venice, for a decided reason, and not "merely" because the city is a major world attraction and tourist destination. Yes, today, the city's activity is predominantly tourist-oriented; but for many years through the Middle Ages and the Renaissance, Venice was known as the premier international business, banking, shipping, and trade center in the world – the trans-shipment point for the "spices" and other valuable items from the Middle East, Turkey, and India to Europe. The art and architecture the tourists flock to the city to enjoy and in fact the physical city itself, all were products of the wealth the city generated from this international business finance and trade. International business was the key to Venice's greatness. That is why this book, in addition to the explication of U.S. business law, included a chapter on international and comparative law. The cover of this book and the aforementioned quotes, therefore, underscore the primacy and indispensable nature of the law in the conducting of business, then as well as now, and on a global basis. Venice could not have survived, let alone prospered, and achieved fame and glory, as The Venice now known famously as the World Heritage site, if the city's international business foundation was not built solidly on the "rock" of the law. International trade, finance, and business could not, and cannot, be beneficially engaged in unless there are rules of law – rules which are clearly stated, communicated effectively, consistently implemented, and fairly enforced. As a matter of fact, the commercial paper and negotiable instrument law that the reader has learned from this book was brought to the Western nations by the Venetians, who learned this very useful body of business law from the Arabs with whom the Venetians traded extensively. All people from all places did business in Venice; and all under the protection of Venetian law. Regardless of their city, nation, race, and religion, the laws of Venice were impartially applied to all people. Venice grew and prospered, as did its people, and so too the city's global business, trading, and investment partners. All prospered under a system of "communally controlled capitalism"; and all was for the "Honor and Profit of Venice."

Chapter TWENTY

20 – Case Problems

This chapter provides many real world cases, problems, and dilemmas that business entrepreneurs and managers are likely to face in their day-to-day operations in the "American" workplace. The cases and dilemmas can serve as a laboratory for students, managers, and entrepreneurs as they prepare to effectively deal with such legal challenges in their workplaces.

Case Problems and Dilemmas[8]
This chapter has various case problems and dilemmas which you can individually or as a group read and "brainstorm" upon and seek to resolve. Try to follow the suggested standardized format of Decision, Rule(s) of Law, and Application. First, you are offered some suggestions for answering the cases and dilemmas. Then, you are given a sample case with the answers in regard to Decision, Rules of Law, and Application. Finally, there are many case problems and dilemmas that you can reflect upon, analyze, and answer.

The following are some suggestions for answering the upcoming case problems and dilemmas:

1. Notice that the decision is usually one word.
2. The Rule of Law is always expressed in a complete sentence, which means a predicate must be used. Consequently, "Minor's Contracts" or "Offers to Contract" are not rules of law.
3. The Rule of Law is a principle of law, which is found herein in the chapters of the book. It need not be stated word-for-word; the writer may phrase it differently; but it must "speak" about the law. For example, the sentence "Susan was a minor and therefore can disaffirm the contract" is not a Rule of Law, but rather a conclusion which properly belongs in the Application

---

[8] Additional case problems can be accessed at the following link: http://www.huizenga.nova.edu/course-materials/business-law/

section. Another example, the sentence, "As there was not a valid offer, no contract was formed," also belongs in the Application.

4. The Application is where you "tie" the matter together. Sometimes, when your Rule of Law is not too specific for the case, you will find it necessary to bring legal rules into the Application section. This is what the writer did in the following *Manser v. Susan* case, suggested answer No. 2b.

5. Be precise. For example, the Rule of Law stated in *Junior v. Sam* is a precise formulation. The Rule of Law, "A valid contract requires an offer and an acceptance," although correct, is too general to fully resolve the problem.

6. Multiple Issues – Case problems may contain more than one issue or legal question to resolve. For example, the *Susan v. Manser* case requires a discussion of general rules of law and exceptions to rules.

Sample Dilemmas and Answers

1. Junior v. Sam
Junior had heard from a friend that Sam might be willing to sell his classic 1973 Capri automobile. Junior therefore wrote to Sam: "I have learned that your car is for sale. How much do you want for it"? Sam replied: "When I get ready to sell, I will want at least $50,000." Junior then responded: "I accept your offer. My check for $50,000 is enclosed herewith." Sam, however, returned Junior's check, stating that he was not ready to sell. Junior sues Sam for breach of contract. Sam defends on the grounds that no contract was ever formed.

Decision:
Junior v. Sam

Rule(s) of Law:
The terms in an offer to contract must be reasonably definite and certain.

Application:
Here, Sam's reply was too indefinite, both as to his decision to sell ("When I get ready...") and as to price ("...at least..."). Therefore, there was not a valid offer for Junior to accept; and without a valid offer, there was no contract.

2. Manser v. Susan
Susan was 17 years only but looked 20. She was interested in purchasing a "sound system" from Manser, a retail dealer. She negotiated well, offering him $1700 for the particular system. Manser, before accepting her offer, asked Susan about her age. She was insulted, until Manser explained that he had lost money last month selling a system to a minor. Susan assured Manser, however, that she was of legal age, saying "just put me down...over 19." Manser was satisfied, and thus accepted the contract, which called for delivery and payment in two weeks. Susan was fickle, however. The next day she purchased a compatible system from Manser's competitor. When Manser called Susan to tell her that he was ready to make delivery, Susan declared, "Push off, I am only 17 years old." Manser then sued Susan for breach of contract. Susan defends on the grounds that she is a minor.

Decision a:
Manser v. Susan

Rules of Law:

When the minor repudiates the contract while it is entirely executory, most courts will permit the disaffirmance just as if there had been no misrepresentation.

Application:
Susan lied to Manser. This lie is called a misrepresentation of fact; and sometimes it has a bearing on the voidability of a contract. Yet it appears to have no effect in the majority of jurisdictions where neither contract party has yet performed the contract, that is, the contract is still executory. It then follows that Susan can indeed disaffirm the contract, which means Manser loses.

Decision b:
Manser v. **Susan**

Rules of Law:
All minor's contracts are voidable at the minor's option.

Application:
This was a contract with a minor, Susan. Generally, such contracts can be disaffirmed, but there is some question as to this right when the minor misrepresents his or her age. The majority rule in the United States allows such disaffirmance; however, only when the contract is still in the executory stage. This contract is in such a stage because neither party has performed. Therefore, Susan will win.

Part I - Contract and Agency Law

1.1- Samir v. Bernstein

Bernstein owns a lot and wants to build a house according to a specific set of plans and specifications. She solicits bids from building contractors and receives the following three bids: one from Chavez for $60,000, one from Freda for $58,000, and one from Samir for $53,000. She accepts Samir's bid. One month after construction of the house has begun, Samir contacts Bernstein and informs her that because of inflation and a recent price hike in materials, he will not finish the house unless Bernstein agrees to pay an extra $3,000. Bernstein reluctantly agrees to pay the additional sum. After the house is finished, however, Bernstein refuses to pay the additional $3000. Whereupon Samir brings a lawsuit in order to require Bernstein to pay the additional amount.

Decision: *Samir v. Bernstein*

Rules of Law: _____
Application: _____

1.2- McKenna v. Big Insurance Company

Elio sues McKenna due to an auto collision. McKenna then asserted a claim against Big Insurance Company, and its agent, Stephanie. McKenna demonstrated that Stephanie was known as an agent for Big Insurance Company, and that there was an official Big Insurance Company sign in Stephanie's office, which was placed by a representative of Big Insurance Company, and which contained their motto. However, nothing indicated that Stephanie was only a soliciting agent for Big Insurance Company. McKenna also demonstrated that he had paid the first premium to Stephanie, and that she had told him that he was then covered by insurance. Nonetheless, Big Insurance Company claimed that it was not liable since it had never issued a policy of insurance to McKenna and it never received the premium which he had paid. Moreover, Big Insurance Company contended that Stephanie had no authority to make contracts of insurance, but was only authorized to receive applications and forward them to the home office for its ultimate action. Is Big Insurance Company liable?

Decision: *McKenna v. Big Insurance Company*

Rules of Law: _____

Application: _____

Part II - Sales Law and Products Liability

II.1- Seller v. Buyer
Seller and buyer orally agree that Seller will manufacture and sell to Buyer 1000 "Success" model calendars at a price to be determined in a mutually consistent manner. The calendars are to have Buyer's name and advertising slogan permanently imprinted thereon. After the Seller had completed production but before shipment was made, the Buyer canceled his order. Seller then sues Buyer for breach of contract.

Decision: *Seller v. Buyer*

Rules of Law: _____

Application: _____

II.2 - Kilgore v. Big Electric Company
Kilgore, an electrician, was testing various fuses with a standard tester. Kilgore had not purchased any of these fuses but had been supplied them by a friend, a fellow electrician. While Kilgore was testing a Royal Crystal fuse manufactured by Big Electric Company, the fuse explodes, injuring Kilgore's eye. Upon later examination, it was discovered that this fuse had been incorrectly wired during manufacture, despite the fact that Big Electric Company had exercised the highest degree of care and maintained the highest standards of product quality control, testing, and inspection. Kilgore sues Big Electric Company for negligence, breach of warranty, and strict liability for her injuries.

Decision: *Kilgore v. Big Electric Company*

Rules of Law: _____

Application: _____

Part III - Business Organizations

III.1- Thelma v. Able, Baker, and Calleti
Able, Baker, and Calleti form a corporation. The state laws governing the incorporation require that the articles of incorporation be signed by three incorporators. A corporate charter is issued, and the corporation begins to do business. Thelma extends credit to the corporation. Because of a national recession, the corporation becomes insolvent. At this time, Thelma learns that Able failed to sign the articles of incorporation. Thelma claims that the corporation's formation was improper, and that Able, Baker, and Calleti are personally liable.

Decision: *Thelma v. Able, Baker, and Calleti*

Rules of Law: _____

Application: _____

III.2- Helena v. Partnership

Helena brought a legal action against a partnership that owned a movie theatre for specific performance of a contract for the sale of land. Vicky, the managing partner of the partnership, had signed a contract for the sale to Helena of real estate adjacent to the theatre and belonging to the partnership. The agreement reserved an easement for use as a driveway into the premises. The partners are claiming that Vicky did not have the authority to sell the property.

Decision: *Helena v. Partnership*

Rules of Law: _____

Application: _____

Part IV - Commercial Paper and Banking Transactions

IV.1- Ike v. Tina

Sal Sharpe steals Danny's checkbook, expertly forges Danny's signature as drawer, and names himself as payee. Sal then indorses the instrument and sells it to Ida, who indorses it, and sells it to Tina. On October 1, Tina indorses and transfers it for consideration to Ike. On October 10, Ike presents the check to Danny's bank for payment, which is refused, as the bank teller spots the forgery. On October 16, Ike gives notice of the bank's dishonor to Tina, who totally ignores Ike's demand for payment. Sal has fled and Ida cannot be found. So Ike sues Tina on her contract *and* warranty liability.

Decision: *Ike v. Tina*

Rules of Law: _____

Application: _____

IV.2- Last National Bank v. Crunch Credit

Rex drafted a check payable to the order of Freda. Ted stole the check from Freda, expertly forged her name, and cashed it at Crunch Credit. Crunch Credit, which was ignorant of the forgery and acted in good faith, indorsed the check, presented it to the Last National Bank, which paid Crunch cash for the check. Freda told Rex about the stolen check. When Rex received his bank statement from Last National, he told it to re-credit his account, which the bank did. Since Ted is nowhere to be found, Last National sues Crunch to get its money back.

Decision: *Last National Bank v. Crunch Credit*

Rules of Law: _____

Application: _____

Part V – Wills and Trusts

V.1- Educational Trust and Common Stock

Williams wants to create an additional educational trust to pay for her children's college expenses. She executes a trust document naming herself the sole trustee. She establishes as the *corpus* of the trust 10,000 shares of Exxon-Mobil common stock, and names as beneficiaries her two children, Alexandra and Melissa. Has she created a valid express trust?

Decision: Yes or No

Rules of Law: _____

Application: _____

V.2- Leprosy Research Fund

In 1958, Juana established a trust at the University of the Pacific for the purpose of "providing funds for leprosy research and the elimination of this disease." Today, leprosy is believed to be non-existent in the world. Juana's heirs contend the trust has failed for want of a beneficiary, and the heirs want the *corpus* of the trust returned to them. The University wants to keep the trust and use the funds for malaria research.

Decision: *Juana's Heirs v. University of the Pacific*

Rules of Law: _____

Application: _____

Part VI – Personal Property, Gifts, Bailment, and Real Property

VI.1-Melissa v. Frankie's Pizza

Frankie's Pizza consisted of one small rectangular room. Along one of the walls, near the cash register, was a series of coat hooks and a sign, "Patrons must place their coats and hats here." Melissa, without saying anything to Frankie, hung her English wool sweater on one of these hooks. After finishing her whole wheat "veggie" pizza, she went to get her sweater, but it was missing. Eventually, Melissa sued Frankie's for the value of her sweater and for her gold sorority pin which was in the sweater's side pocket. Frankie denied any responsibility, contending that the public had access to the coat hooks.

Decision: *Melissa v. Frankie's Pizza*

Rules of Law: _____

Application: _____

VI.2-Joe Martino v. Mr. Blanco

Joe Martino loaned his expensive digital camera to Mr. Blanco to be redelivered to Joe by Friday. On Friday, Mercy, representing herself as Mrs. Martino and Joe's wife, produced a letter purportedly signed by Joe, instructing Blanco to deliver the camera to Mercy. Blanco requested further identification and Mercy provided Blanco with numerous cards indicating that she was Joe's wife. Satisfied, Blanco delivered the camera to Mercy. Later in the day, Joe approached Blanco and requested the camera. Blanco explained what happened; and Joe informed Blanco that Mercy was his ex-wife and the letter was a forgery. Blanco asserts that he was a victim too and denies any responsibility. Whereupon Joe sues Blanco.

Decision: *Joe Martino v. Mr. Blanco*

Rules of Law: _____

Application: _____

Part VII – Accounting Liability Challenges

VII.1 – City v. Tire Company[9]

This case involves a municipality (plaintiff) and a tire company (defendant), and the case centers on allegations of over-billing. The plaintiff solicited sealed bids on a one year contract to supply the city with tires for its fleet of vehicles. The defendant was awarded the contract based on having the lowest price per tire bid. The contract required the tire company to maintain an inventory of the different tire sizes used on the city's vehicles. The bid accepted by the city was for a price per tire that was about 60% of the retail price. About three months into the contract, the finance department discovered that the defendant had repeatedly (about 100 invoices) charged the city the retail price instead of the lower bid price. The plaintiff city inadvertently paid these over-billed invoices. The amount of the overcharge was approximately $35,000. The plaintiff filed an action for breach of contract, fraud, civil theft by deception, and negligence seeking recovery of the overcharge. To support the case for fraud, the plaintiff city emphasized that numerous incorrect invoices were issued by the defendant which indicated that the overcharging was purposeful. The defendant denies all allegations and also contends that the plaintiff city was culpable of contributory and comparative negligence for paying the defendant tire company's invoices for three months before discovering the overcharges.

Decision: *City v. Tire Company* (circle winner)

Rules of Law: _____

Application: _____

VII.2 – PAC v. Carlos Alonso[10]

Upon completion of his military obligation, Carlos Alonso was eager to put his newly-minted finance degree to use. Fortunately for Carlos, John Best & Company, P.C., a large local CPA firm, was experimenting with hiring non-accounting majors and teaching them the "BEST way" of doing accounting. Consequently, Best hired him as a junior accountant. After about a year in that position, he moved on to another CPA firm that offered him greater career opportunities. In the meantime, he had been working on a Master of Professional Accounting (MPA) degree, which he completed while he was employed at a third CPA firm. Carlos had about seven years of accounting experience when he was offered a partnership in the firm of Paulding, Anderson & Clark, CPAs (PAC); unfortunately, he lacked the requisite CPA designation. With almost four years having elapsed since the completion of his MPA degree, and a total of 7 years' experience as an accountant, Carlos decided to quit work for about five months in order to prepare for the rigorous exam. As it turned out, because of this break in his work experience, he had to restart the State of Georgia's two-year experience requirement. In the meantime, he worked for PAC with the understanding that he would become a partner as soon as he received the CPA designation. He signed an employment agreement that barred him from taking any of PAC's clients with him should he leave the firm. Unfortunately, Wesley Winston, PAC's senior partner, had become romantically interested in Carlos' fiancée, Laura,

---

[9] Contributed by Joe Durden, Nova Southeastern Univeristy, Donald L. Ariail and Josephine Sosa-Fey, Texas A&M University-Kingsville.

[10] Contributed by Donald L. Ariail and Josephine Sosa-Fey, Texas A&M University-Kingsville.

who was the firm's executive assistant. Relationships became frayed, and Carlos and Laura both quit their jobs. Carlos had some clients who had been doing business with him since he first started his career at Best. These clients had, over the years, followed him from firm to firm. When he left PAC's employment, these (and only these) clients left with him. PAC (plaintiff) sued Carlos (defendant) for breach of contract. Subsequently, Carlos heard from several of his loyal clients that Winston was "badmouthing" him, claiming that Carlos had been fired for incompetence. Interestingly, one of Carlos' clients taped Winston making derogatory comments about Carlos on the telephone. Carlos (plaintiff) countersued PAC (defendant) for defamation of character. Did these clients become clients of PAC? Is Carlos correct in asserting that these clients were exempt from the employment contract since they already were his clients prior to signing the contract?

Decision: *PAC v. Carlos Alonso* (circle winner); *Carlos Alonso v. PAC* (circle winner)

Rules of Law: _____

Application: _____

Part VIII – Constitutional Law[11]

VIII.1 – Geier v. American Honda Motor Company
The United States Department of Transportation is the federal government agency which is responsible for administering and enforcing federal traffic safety laws, including the National Traffic and Motor Vehicle Safety Act. Pursuant to this statute, the Department of Transportation adopted a federal motor vehicle safety standard which required that in 1997 vehicles be equipped with passive restraints, including air bags or seat belts. In 1992, Alexis Geier was driving a 1987 Honda Accord vehicle which crashed into a tree, consequently seriously injuring her. The car was equipped with manual seat and shoulder belts, which she had used at the time of the accident; but it was not equipped with air bags. Whereupon, Geier sued American Honda Motor Company in tort, based on District of Columbia law, contending that the company had negligently designed the car and also that the car was a defectively designed product because the vehicle lacked a driver's side air bag. Honda defended by arguing that the federal safety standard preempted the District's common law tort law.

Decision: *Geier v. American Honda Motor Company*

Rules of Law: _____

Application: _____

VIII.2 – Janet Reno, Attorney General of the United States v. Condon
State motor vehicle agencies typically register automobile and issue drivers licenses. Many state motor vehicle departments also sell personal information, such as names, addresses, telephone numbers, and social security numbers. However, many people objected and complained that their personal information had been sold. As a result, Congress enacted the Driver's Privacy Protection Act of 1994. This law prohibits a state from selling the personal information of a person unless one gives affirmative consent. Whereupon, South Carolina sued the United States, contending that the

---

[11] All Constitutional Law case problems herein and on the supplemental website are based on actual court cases.

federal government exceeded its authority under the Commerce Clause of the Constitution in enacting the law.

Decision: *Janet Reno, Attorney General of the United States v. Condon*

Rules of Law: _____

Application: _____

DEFINITIONS

- **abandoned property** - when the owner of property has actually discarded the property and without any intention of reclaiming it.
- **abatement** - the process of reducing gifts to beneficiaries because the testator's estate is not sufficient to pay all the estate obligations and gifts under the will.
- **abstract of title** - usually a component of the title insurance process; the abstract shows the complete history of the real estate, encompassing prior deeds, mortgages, taxes, judgments, liens – paid and unpaid.
- **accession** - a means of acquiring property by an addition or increase in property already owned, for example, the produce of land or the young of animals or by substantially improving personal property.
- **accretion** - occurs when the boundary to property is a river, stream, lake, or ocean, and the land is increased by the shifting flow of the water or the depositing of silt or sand on the bank.
- **acceleration clause** – a clause in a negotiable instrument that makes it payable earlier than its stated maturity date.
- **acceptance** – in contract law, the expression of assent by the offeree to the terms of the contract; in commercial paper law, when a drawee signs the face of a draft, thereby becoming an acceptor.
- **acceptor** – a drawee who accepts a draft by signing on the face thereof and thereby consents to primary liability on the instrument.
- **accommodation** – pursuant to the Uniform Commercial Code, when a seller notifies and then ships nonconforming goods to a buyer as a courtesy; construed as a counteroffer.
- **accommodation party** – in commercial paper law, when a third party lends his or her name to an instrument as a surety or a guarantor.
- **accord and satisfaction** – an agreement whereby the contract parties agree that one will render and the other will accept a performance different from the original contract.
- **accountant-client privilege** – legal privilege of confidentiality that to a degree protects a client's disclosures to the client's accountant.
- **action *in personam*** – a legal action in which the plaintiff is seeking to hold the defendant liable on a personal obligation.
- **action *in rem*** – a legal action in which the plaintiff is seeking to enforce a right against certain property owned by the defendant.
- **active trust** – a trust in which the trustee has duties, even if the trustee's only duties are to convey title to the beneficiaries.
- **Act of State Doctrine** – the international law principle that holds that the legal system of one country will not examine and challenge laws, acts, and judicial decisions of a foreign country made within its own territory.
- **actual authority** – the power that the principal has expressly or impliedly granted to the agent to accomplish the purposes of the agency.

- **ademption** – when a specific devise in a will is adeemed (that is, revoked) because it is not in the testator's estate at the time of his or her death, regardless of the testator's intent.
- **adjustment plan** – pursuant to bankruptcy law, the plan that a debtor files with the bankruptcy court in a Chapter 13 bankruptcy proceeding.
- **adverse possession** - a method of acquiring title to real property by occupying for a period of time fixed by statute, usually 21 years; the occupancy must be continuous, open, visible, exclusive, uninterrupted, and "hostile" (that is, asserting ownership of the property against the legal interests of the title holder).
- **agency by estoppel** – when a person either intentionally or carelessly creates the appearance of an agency relationship.
- **agency coupled with an interest** – when an agency relationship is created primarily for the benefit of the agent who has been given some type of legal interest in the subject matter of the agency.
- **agent** – a person who works for another, called a principal, but who also acts for and represents the principal in order to effectuate legal relations with third parties.
- **aggregate view of partnership** – the view that partners are merely an association of individuals.
- **annual meeting** – pursuant to corporate law, the yearly meeting fixed in the bylaws, the chief purpose of which is to elect the board of directors.
- **answer** – the defendant's response to a lawsuit, filed with the clerk of the court, in which the defendant either admits or denies the plaintiff's allegations.
- **anti-lapse statutes** – laws that generally hold that if the recipient of a gift is a lineal descendant of the testator, and that person is dead at the execution of the will or fails to survive the testator, the gift to the descendant does not lapse (that is, fail), but rather the descendants of the deceased beneficiary of the testator take the gift *per stirpes.*
- **Anticybersquatting Consumer Protection Act** – the federal statute that protects Internet domain names.
- **anti-piracy agreements** – also called non-solicitation agreements; agreements in contracts that prevent departing employees from soliciting or serving the former employees' customers.
- **apparent authority** – pursuant to agency law, authority created in the agent when the principal by his or her own words or conduct manifested to third parties has misled third parties to believe that the agent is authorized to act on the principal's behalf; pursuant to the Uniform Partnership Act, the rule that an act by a partner for apparently carrying on the business of the partnership in the usual way binds the partnership.
- **articles of incorporation** – also called in some states a certificate of incorporation or corporate charter; the document required to be filed with the appropriate state authority in order to form a corporation.
- **articles of organization** (also called a **certificate of formation**) - the principal limited liability company charter document, which is filed with the secretary of state, and contains basis information as to the name of the LLC, its address, its agent for service of process, its term, and whether the LLC will be a member managed one or one managed by a manager selected by the members of the LLC.
- **artisan's lien** – also known as a laborer's lien; the common law lien, or charge against property, given to people who worked on or who performed services on personal property.
- **assault** – an act by a defendant which causes a reasonable apprehension of fear in the victim of an immediate harmful or offensive contact to the person of the victim.
- **assignee** – the third party to whom contract rights are transferred by the original contract party.
- **assignment** – the transfer of contract rights to a third party.
- **assignor** – the original contract party who transfers his or her contract rights.
- **assumption of the risk** – a defense to negligence which arises when the defendant knowingly and voluntarily encounters a known risk.
- **assuming a mortgage** – when the buyer buying property becomes primarily liable for the payment; that is, the buyer is liable on the mortgage as fully as the original mortgagor.
- **attestation** – when the witnesses attest that the testator signed the will in the presence of the witnesses, all of whom were present at the same time.
- **attorney-client privilege** – legal privilege of confidentiality that protects a client's disclosures to the client's attorney.
- **bailment** - the delivery of the possession of personal property from one person, called the bailor, to another, called the bailee, pursuant to an agreement by which the bailee is obligated to return the identical property to the bailor or deliver it to a third party.

- **basis of the bargain** – pursuant to Uniform Commercial Code warranty law, when the buyer has relied on the warranty of the seller in making his or her decision to buy the goods.
- **battery** – an intentional act by a defendant that causes a harmful or offensive contact to the person of the plaintiff.
- **battle of the forms** – pursuant to the Uniform Commercial Code, the situation that arises when an acceptance of the offer contains additional and/or contradictory terms.
- **bearer instrument** – a negotiable instrument made payable to bearer or to cash.
- **bilateral contract** – a contract based on mutual return promises.
- **Bill of Rights** – the first 10 amendments to the U.S. Constitution which guarantee certain individual rights from government infringement.
- **blanket warrant** – the name given to an administrative agency search warrant that allows government regulators to inspect certain types of businesses or neighborhoods for health and safety violations without any showing of probable cause or reasonable suspicion.
- **blank indorsement** – when a person indorses a negotiable instrument but does not name a new payee, thereby converting the instrument to bearer paper.
- **board of directors** – the governing body of the corporation, which collectively has the power to control, manage, and to bind the corporation
- **breach of duty** – occurs when a defendant's conduct fails to conform to the required standard of care.
- **bribe or bribery** – the payment of anything of value to a foreign government official to wrongfully direct business to oneself or one's company or organization; a civil and criminal wrong in the United States.
- **business judgment rule** – the rule absolving a director from liability for actions that do not benefit the corporation so long as the director has acted in a good faith, reasonable, prudent, and informed manner.
- **business sustainability continuum** – a model for a business to achieve continual success by adhering to the values of legality, morality, and social responsibility.
- **buy-sell agreement** - another legal device used to restrict the transfer of shares of stock and thus to ensure that the ownership of the shares of stock of a company remains with a small group of shareholders; it allows or even obligates a corporation or other parties named in the agreement to purchase at fair market value another party's stock that a party is obligated to sell when certain events occur; an agreement that makes it contractually required for the corporation or shareholders to buy shares of stock; also known as a right-of-first-refusal.
- **bylaws** – the private rules and regulations governing the internal affairs of the corporation.
- **CAN-SPAM Act** – fully known as the Controlling the Assault of the Non-Solicited Pornography and Marketing Act; the federal statute which prohibits certain types of spamming activities.
- **capital stock** – stock consisting of authorized capital, common stock, and preferred stock.
- **case law** – also called the common law; law expressed by judges in court decisions.
- **Categorical Imperative** – the key ethical principle whereby morality is based not on the consequences of an action but rather on the application of a formal ethical test to the action to ascertain its morality; a three part principle to determine morality consisting of the universal law test, the Kingdom of Ends test, and the Agent Receiver test.
- **causation** – the presence of a causal connection between the defendant's careless conduct and the resulting harm to the plaintiff.
- **Chapter 7 bankruptcy** – the liquidation of a debtor's debts pursuant to federal bankruptcy law; also called straight bankruptcy.
- **Chapter 11 bankruptcy** – reorganization and continuation of a bankrupt business pursuant to federal bankruptcy law.
- **Chapter 13 bankruptcy** – the adjustment of the debts of an individual with regular income pursuant to federal bankruptcy law.
- **charge to the jury** – when the judge instructs the jury as to the relevant rules of law governing the particular case.
- **charitable trust** - a trust for the benefit of society, the public, the community, or for some indefinite portion thereof; such a trust must have a charitable purpose.
- **check** – a variant of a draft; a negotiable instrument drawn on a bank and payable on demand.
- **checks and balances doctrine** – the fact that the Constitution gives each branch of the federal-national government powers to limit the actions of the other branches.

- **choice-of-law provision** – part of a contract that states which country's or state's law will govern any disputes arising from the creation of performance of the contract.
- **circuit courts** – "inferior" or lower courts in the state court system, possessing original jurisdiction.
- **civil law** – in the U.S. legal system, law dealing with legal wrongs committed by one private party against another private party.
- **civil lawsuit** – a lawsuit involving disputes between individuals.
- **clerk of the court** – the court officer whose function is to keep accurate records of cases and to enter cases on the court calendar.
- **click-on agreement** – also called a "click-wrap" agreement; a contractual agreement that arises when a buyer indicates on a computer a willingness to accept a seller's offer by clicking in a box that says "I agree" or "I accept."
- **closely held corporation** – a corporation with relatively few shareholders where all or most of them participate in management.
- **closing** - the legal term to indicate the transaction where the real estate contract is effectuated and the deed to the property is transferred from the seller to the buyer.
- **codes of ethics (or conduct)** – internal rules, certain ones of which go beyond the law, which govern the professions, such as law and medicine; and now which are typically part of the corporate organization and thus an aspect of corporate governance.
- **codicil** - a testamentary instrument executed with the same formalities as a will, executed subsequent to the will, which typically modifies, alters, or expands the will.
- **collateral heirs** – people who stem not from each other, but from a common ancestor, for example, one's brother and sister or one's cousins.
- **collateral promise** – the secondary promise to pay or perform made by the guarantor of a contract.
- **comity** – the international law doctrine that holds that a country must respect and thus defer to the laws and judicial determinations of another country.
- **commercial paper** – negotiable instruments consisting of promissory notes, drafts, checks, and certificates of deposit.
- **commercial speech** – speech which is intended to further economic and monetary interests, such as advertising, but which is still constitutionally protected to a degree.
- **common stock** – corporate shares that have no preference over any other shares of corporate stock with regard to payment of dividends or distribution of assets upon liquidation.
- **comparative negligence** – not a complete defense to negligence, but the reduction of a party's liability based on his or her contributing fault.
- **compensatory damages** – damages awarded when there is a breach of contract and an actual loss, the purpose of which is to make the aggrieved party whole.
- **Computer Software Copyright Act** – federal statute that extends copyright protection to computer programs.
- **Copyright Term Extension Act** – federal statute that extended the time periods for protecting copyrighted works.
- **complaint** – also called a petition; the document filed with the clerk of the court which sets forth the nature of the claim and the remedy sought.
- **Computer Fraud in Abuse Act** – federal statute that makes accessing a computer without authority and taking confidential information a crime and civil wrong.
- **concurrent powers** – powers that can be exercised by both the federal government and the states in the United States.
- **condition precedent** – a clause in a contract stating that a party's duty to perform does not become operative until a stated condition occurs.
- **condition subsequent** – a clause in a contract stating that a party's duty of continual performance comes to an end when a stated condition occurs.
- **condominium** – property which is a multistory residential property, but can be single story and can involve commercial properties as well; a unit owner has fee simple title to the space enclosed by the interior surfaces of all exterior walls of the unit as well as its floor and ceiling; all other parts of the structure and the land on which it is located are known as common elements and are owned in common with the other unit owners.
- **conflict of laws rules** – body of laws which indicate what state's laws apply to a multi-state case.

- **confidentiality agreements** – also known as non-disclosure agreements; provisions in employment contracts in which the employee promises not to disclose confidential information.
- **confusion** - the mixing of goods by different owners so that the parts belonging to each owner cannot be identified and separated.
- **consent defense** – the defense that holds that a defendant is not liable for a wrongful act if the plaintiff has consented to that act.
- **consequential damages** – damages above and beyond compensatory damages which resulted from the breach of contract and which were foreseeable at the time of the contract.
- **consideration** – a requirement of a legally binding contract.
- **consolidation** – the combination of two or more corporations, with both ceasing to exist and a new corporate entity emerging.
- **constructive delivery** - when a token or symbol of an intangible piece or property exists, the delivery of the token or symbol is construed as delivery of the intangible property.
- **constructive trust** - one imposed by a court in favor of the settlor or the beneficiaries when the trust was procured by fraud, duress, undue influence, or mistake, or when the trustee has abused his or her fiduciary relationship or contravened his or her duties of care.
- **contempt power** – the inherent power of a judge to fine or imprison a party for failing to carry out the judge's order.
- **contract** – an agreement between two or more parties that is enforceable at law.
- **contribution** – when there are two or more sureties, and one pays the entire amount, the paying surety can seek proportionate contribution from his or her co-surety.
- **conversion** – in commercial paper law, the unauthorized assumption and exercise of ownership of a negotiable instrument; an intentional tort civil wrong.
- **cooperative** – property which often has the appearance of a condominium, but whereas each of the condominium unit owners holds fee simple title to their respective units, a corporation generally owns the land and improvements of a cooperative; the individual unit occupants own stock in the corporation which permits them to enter into long-term leases for their respective units.
- **copyright** – an exclusive legal right granted by the federal government to the creators of original works of authorship.
- **counteroffer** – a purported acceptance by the offeree which varies, qualifies, conditions, or adds to or subtracts from the offer, and which is treated as a rejection of the offer.
- **court** – a tribunal established by government to hear and decide cases and controversies.
- **court of equity** – a court empowered to issue equitable remedies.
- **corporate constituency statutes** – state statutes in the United States where the board of directors of a corporation may consider the interests of other stakeholders other than the shareholders.
- **corporate governance** – a term encompassing the mechanisms that can regulate the corporation, encompassing statutory and case law, government regulation, internal company rules, such as embodied in Codes of Ethics and Codes of Conduct, and social responsibility policies.
- **corporate social responsibility** – a concept encompassing a company acting legally and morally and also taking an active part in civic and community activities and charitable actions.
- **corporation** – a form of business organization; an artificial legal entity created pursuant to state law upon the filing of an articles of incorporation.
- **corporation by estoppel** – when a third party has dealt with a business as a corporation, and thus is prevented from denying the existence of the corporation.
- **covenants not to compete** – also called non-competition agreements; promises in contracts for the sale of a business or employment contracts in which one party promises not to compete with the other.
- **covenant of good faith and fair dealing** - the common law covenant implied in all contracts, including franchise agreements, which means that the parties must reasonably and honestly carry out their contract obligations; the explicit Uniform Commercial Code covenant requirement for all contracts for the sale of goods for the parties to act in an honest and commercially reasonable manner.
- **covenant of quiet enjoyment** – a warranty that landlords must provide to tenants; the tenant's right to the undisturbed use and enjoyment of real property without unreasonable disturbance by hostile claimants or neighboring tenants.
- **covenants** in a deed - usually refer to promises made by the grantee; covenants can be affirmative, whereby the grantee promises to do something regarding the property; and covenants can be negative, whereby the grantee promises not to do something.

- **cover** – the Uniform Commercial Code rule that allows an aggrieved buyer to purchase comparable goods elsewhere in a commercially reasonable manner and receive damages.
- **criminal law** – law dealing with legal wrongs committed against society and punished by society.
- **cross-examination** – the stage in a trial where the attorneys ask the opposing witnesses questions in an effort to disprove their prior answers.
- **cumulative voting** – a voting device created under corporate law designed to ensure some minority shareholder representation on the board of directors.
- **cure doctrine** – Uniform Commercial Code rule that allows the seller who shipped non-conforming goods to correct the shipment.
- *cy pres* **doctrine** - the legal principle that maintains that a court can name a charitable beneficiary or substitute one charitable organization or group for prior beneficiaries if the prior beneficiaries cease to exist or cease to be charitable.
- **debtor's estate** – in bankruptcy law, all property owned by the debtor which becomes part of the debtor's estate and subject to the bankruptcy proceeding.
- **declaration of trust** - a statement by the owner of the property that he or she holds the property as trustee in trust, which creates an *inter vivos* trust with the settlor as trustee.
- *de facto* **corporation** – a corporation not technically a legal one but recognized as legal except as against the state.
- **deed** - the written instrument that evidences the conveyance of title to the real property and establishes the buyer's legal right of ownership.
- **defamation** – the intentional tort of falsely impugning the character or reputation of another.
- **defect** – in products liability law, pursuant to the strict liability doctrine, when a product is flawed, contains an inadequate warning, or is defectively designed.
- **defective design** – pursuant to strict liability law, when a product could have been made safer with modifications that were economically and practically feasible based on the state-of-the-art when the product was made.
- **defense to commercial paper** – is a reason for refusing to pay all or part of a negotiable instrument; a real defense can be asserted against all holders of commercial paper.
- *de jure* **corporation** – a corporation whose existence is evidenced by an accepted articles of incorporation and a corporate charter from the state.
- **delegatee** – the new third party to whom contract duties are transferred by one of the original contract parties.
- **delegation** – transfer of contract duties by one of the original contract parties.
- **delegated powers** – pursuant to the United States Constitution, the powers delegated by the states to the federal-national government.
- **delegator** – the original contract party who transfers his or her duties to a third party.
- **delivery** of the deed - an essential requirement to the transfer of title to real property; a deed is not effective until delivered; delivery from a technical legal standpoint means the grantor giving up possession and control of the deed.
- **demand instrument** – also called a sight instrument; a negotiable instrument payable whenever the holder of the instrument chooses to present it for payment.
- **description** in a deed - refers to the description of the property to be conveyed; the property must be correctly described; and any description that identifies the property is sufficient.
- **detour and frolic** – when an employee, while performing duties for the employer, goes out of his or her normal scope of duties to do some personal business.
- **devise** – also known as a bequeath; the name the law gives to the gifts a testator makes in his or her will.
- **Digital Millennium Copyright Act** – the federal statute that extends copyright protection to the creators and owners of digital information.
- **director** – a person designated in the articles of incorporation or chosen by the shareholders to be part of the governing body of the corporation.
- **disaffirmance** – the right that a minor has to cancel a contract.
- **disassociation** – the power, though not necessarily the right, that a member of a limited liability company has to disassociate himself or herself from the firm.
- **disclaimer** – pursuant to Uniform Commercial Code law, when a seller of goods can exclude a warranty from the sales transaction.

- **discovery** – the process in a lawsuit where the parties ask for and receive pertinent factual information regarding the case.
- **discharge** – when contract obligations come to an end; when the contract duties of the parties are terminated.
- **discretionary trust** - a trust that gives the trustee the discretion to apply or withhold payments of income and/or principal to beneficiaries.
- **dishonor** – in commercial paper law, when the presentee of a negotiable instrument refuses to accept or to pay it.
- **district courts of appeal** – intermediate courts in the state court system, possessing appellate jurisdiction.
- **dissolution** – pursuant to the Uniform Partnership Act, the change in the relation of the partners caused by any partner ceasing to be associated with the carrying on of the business of the firm.
- **diversity of citizenship** – where the parties to a lawsuit, that is, the plaintiff and defendant in the lawsuit, are citizens of different states.
- **dividends** – the share of corporate profits to be apportioned to the shareholders as a return on their investment.
- **Do-Not-Call Implementation Act** – law passed by Congress in 2003 enabling the Federal Trade Commission to create a Do-Not-Call List, which is a registry of names of persons not wanting to receive telemarketing calls.
- **draft** – also called a bill of exchange; a three party negotiable instrument in which the party creating it, called the drawer, orders another party, called the drawee, to pay money to a third party, called the payee.
- **due diligence** – a legal defense that an accountant possesses that he or she made a reasonable investigation, acted in a reasonable manner, and had reasonable grounds to believe in the truthfulness and accuracy of financial statements and reports.
- **due process of law** – the notice and fair hearing that are constitutionally required before government deprives a person of "life, liberty, or property."
- **duty of care** – the existence of a legal duty to act according to a legally established standard of care.
- **duress** – forcing a person to enter into a contract by means of threats of force.
- **earnings claim document** – document that the Federal Trade Commission requires the franchisor to provide to a prospective franchisee with sufficient accurate information so that the franchisee can make an informed business decision.
- **easement** – a non-possessory interest in land which gives the possessor of the easement the right to use a specific portion of another's land for the purposes designated in the easement; the most common method is by grant, meaning that an instrument, such as a deed, specifically describes the location of the easement and who is to be benefited by it.
- **easement by reservation** – when an instrument reserves an easement in lands being conveyed to another.
- **easement by prescription** - similar in concept to adverse possession; it can arise in situations where the owner of real property allows another to make some use of a portion of the owner's lands for a specified period of time without interruption.
- **easement by implication** - generally arises out of a legal action in which the court determines that the parties to a conveyance intended to create an easement, but for some reason failed to do so, such as where property sold would require access across the property still owned by the seller; the court therefore creates the easement.
- **E-contract** – a contract containing all the required elements of a traditional contract that was entered into "virtually" or in "cyberspace" utilizing computer transactions.
- **economic duress** – also known as business compulsion; wrongful threats of economic harm or financial ruin which force a party to enter into a contract.
- **Economic Espionage Act** – federal statute that makes the theft of a trade secret a federal criminal wrong.
- **elective share** - when a surviving spouse is dissatisfied with his or her provisions in a will or also, if no will, his or her intestate share of the estate, the surviving spouse may elect to take an elective share of the estate, typically 30%.
- **Electronic Communication Privacy Act** – a federal statute that makes it a crime to intercept certain electronic communications.
- **Electronic Fund Transfer Act** – federal statute that governs consumer funds transfers.

- **Electronic Signature in Global and National Commerce Act** – also know as the E-Sign law; federal law that made legal electronic signatures.
- **employee** – a person who is employed to render services and who remains under the control of another in performing those services.
- **employer** – one who hires another to render services and who controls the manner in which those services are performed.
- **employment at-will** - where an employee is hired for an indefinite period and there is no contract or no contract provision limiting the circumstances by which the employment relationship can be terminated, then the employee can be discharged at any time, with no warning, notice, or explanation, for no reason or cause, for no good reason or cause.
- **engagement letter** – the agreement between an accountant and his or her client; professional standards require an engagement letter for each audit and review.
- **entitlements** - the rights to benefits specified by law, or as some property developers view them, the limitations on the use of the land or its improvement.
- **Ethical Egoism** – the ethical theory that maintains that morality consists of advancing one's own long-term self-interest but in a rational, prudent, and self-enlightened manner.
- **Ethical Relativism** – the ethical theory that maintains that what a society believes is right for that society is the moral standard for that society.
- **ethics** – the branch of philosophy, consisting of ethical theories and principles, that one uses to reason to moral conclusions.
- **equal dignity rule** – agency rule requiring an agent's authority to enter into a contract to be in writing if the contract the agent enters into is governed by the Statute of Frauds.
- **equal protection of the law** – the Constitutional guarantee that the government must have legitimate legal reasons to classify people.
- **exclusionary rule** – a criminal law rule that holds that any evidence obtained in violation of the 4th amendment's protection against unreasonable search and seizure is inadmissible against a defendant in a criminal trial.
- **exculpatory clause** – a clause in a contract where one party attempts to free himself or herself from liability for negligent harms.
- **executed contract** – a contract whose terms have been fully performed by all contract parties.
- **executory contract** - one in which the terms of the contract have not yet been fully performed by all the contract parties.
- **executive power** – the power conferred in the U.S. Constitution to the President to take care that the laws be faithfully executed and to serve as Commander-in-Chief.
- **exoneration** – a legal action that the surety can bring against the original debtor to compel the debtor to pay the debt to the creditor.
- **expectation damages** - damages which compensate the aggrieved contract party for the amount lost as a result of the other contract party's breach of contract; that is, the damages are the amount required to place the aggrieved party in the position he or she would have been in if the contract had been performed. This form of compensatory damages is also called the "benefit of the bargain" standard for damages.
- **express contract** – an agreement based on words – oral or written.
- **express private trust** - a fiduciary relationship regarding property, real or personal, wherein the trustee holds legal title to the trust property (called at times the trust principal or *res*), subject to enforceable equitable rights in the beneficiary or beneficiaries of the trust.
- **express warranty by affirmation of fact or promise** – pursuant to the Uniform Commercial Code, the warranty that arises when the seller makes a statement of fact or promise regarding the goods.
- **extension clause** – a clause in an instrument that makes it payable later than its stated maturity date, and which may have an adverse effect on the negotiability of the instrument.
- **facilitating and expediting payments** – a legal "bribe"; a relatively small payment to a lower level foreign official with merely ministerial authority in order to induce the official to do more smoothly and quickly routine government actions that one is entitled to.
- **fair use doctrine** – exception to copyright law that allows fair use of copyrighted works in limited circumstances.
- **False Claims Acts** – federal and state statutes that give a whistleblowing employee who discloses wrongdoing in the form of embezzlement or fraud against the government a percentage of the award against or settlement with the employer.

- **federalism** – a system of government composed of a national government and constituent government entities, for example, states.
- **federal question case** – when the person bringing a law suit is basing the case on the federal constitution, federal statute or administrative regulation, or a U.S. treaty.
- **fee simple** or fee simple estate - the largest and most complete ownership right which an individual can possess in real estate under U.S. law; gives the owner the right to the surface of the land, the subsoil beneath, and air space above, subject to certain government regulations.
- **fictitious payee** – in commercial paper law, a person who was not intended to have any interest in a negotiable instrument.
- **fiduciary** - a legally recognized relationship of trust and confidence, for example in the principal-agency relationship, the breach of which is treated as fraud.
- **financing statement** – pursuant to secured transactions law, the document required to be filed to perfect a security interest.
- **firm offer** – an offer that includes a statement that it will be held open for a certain period of time.
- **first to file or perfect** – rule of law in secured transaction law that gives priority to the creditor possessing a security interest who is the first to file or perfect.
- **fitness for a particular purpose** - the Uniform Commercial Code's implied warranty that arises when a buyer relies on a seller's judgment to select suitable goods.
- **fixtures** - items that originated as personal property but became permanently affixed to the real property, and consequently cannot be removed without damage to the real property.
- **Foreign Corrupt Practices Act** – a federal statute in the United States that makes the payment of a bribe by a business person or business to a foreign government official in order to wrongfully secure a contract or business a criminal and civil wrong; but with exceptions for "facilitating and expediting payments" and legitimate and reasonable expenses related to the demonstration and/or explanation of a firm's products or services.
- **forgery** – in commercial paper law, when a person's name is signed on a negotiable instrument by another person without authority to do so; a real defense.
- **forum selection provision** - a provision in a contract stating that any disputes arising from the contract will be decided by the courts and law in a specifically designated jurisdiction.
- **franchise** – a method of conducting business in which one party, the franchisor, grants to another party, the franchisee, the right to do business under a certain name, in a certain territory, and pursuant to the terms of a franchise agreement.
- **franchise agreement** – the contract between the franchisor and franchisee which sets forth the parties' rights and duties in the franchise business relationship.
- **fraud** – the civil wrong encompassing intentional misrepresentation, also known as deceit, negligent misrepresentation, and innocent misrepresentation; in commercial paper law, called fraud in the inducement.
- **fraud in the** *factum* – also called real fraud; a real defense in commercial paper law; when a misrepresentation causes a person to sign a negotiable instrument with neither the knowledge of its character as a negotiable instrument nor its essential terms.
- **free invention** – when an employee makes an invention related to his or her employment and the employee is not contractually obligated to invent and the employee does not extensively or substantially use the employer's resources.
- **frustration of purpose** – legal doctrine which holds that a party's duty to perform a contract comes to an end when the purpose or value of the contract has been destroyed, although performance is still technically possible.
- **GAAP**– the generally accepted accounting principles, promulgated by the Financial Accounting Standards Board.
- **GAAS**– the generally accepted auditing standards, promulgated by the Auditing Standards Committee of the American Institute of Certified Public Accountants.
- **garnishment** - a court order requiring persons who owe a debtor money or who possess the debtor's personal property to turn the property over to the court for eventual payment to the debtor's creditors.
- **general devise** - the gift of general economic benefit by the testator payable out of the general assets of the estate.
- **general warranty deed** – a deed in which the grantor warrants the following: 1) the grantor has good title to the property; 2) the grantee will have quiet and peaceful possession free from all claims; 3) the

grantor will defend the grantee against all claims against the property; 4) all prior grantors had good title; and 5) there are no defects in any prior grantor's title.

- **gift *causa mortis*** - a gift motivated by the prospect of imminent death.
- ***inter vivos* gift** - a gift between two living persons.
- **good faith** – honesty in fact; a Uniform Commercial Code requirement for being a holder in due course of commercial paper.
- **goods** – moveable, tangible, personal property; the sale of which is governed by the Uniform Commercial Code.
- **good title** – in commercial paper law, the rightful possession of a negotiable instrument.
- **guaranty contract** – a contract where a third party, called a guarantor, makes a secondary promise to perform the agreement.
- **habitability warranty** - an implied warranty that arises by operation of law in residential sales of home and leases and generally cannot be waived by the buyer or tenant; seller or landlord warrants that the leased premises are fit for human habitation.
- **holder** – a person in possession of a bearer instrument or one in possession of an order instrument properly negotiated to him or her or one in possession of an instrument issued to him or her in blank.
- **holder in due course** – a holder of an instrument who pays value for it and who takes it in good faith and without any knowledge or notice of problems with and defenses to the instrument.
- **holographic will** - an unattested will completely in the testator's handwriting and signed by the testator.
- **homestead** – a certain amount of real property protected from seizure by a debtor's creditors pursuant to a state's homestead exemption.
- **honorary trust** - a trust, recognized in some states, for the care of graves or animals.
- **implied contract** - an agreement that is implied from the acts and conduct of the parties.
- **implied transfer warranties** – in commercial paper law, the warranties that are deemed to be made by a person transferring a negotiable instrument; also called liability off the instrument.
- **implied presentment warranties** – in commercial paper law, the warranties that are deemed to be made by a person who presents a negotiable instrument for payment or acceptance.
- **implied warranty of good title** – Uniform Commercial Code warranty that the seller of goods is deemed to guarantee good title thereto.
- **implied warranty of habitability** – pursuant to certain state statutes and court decisions, a warranty that is implied in real estate transactions that a home sold or residential property leased is free of defects.
- **impossibility of performance** – legal doctrine which holds that a party's duty to perform a contract comes to an end when that performance is impossible to perform.
- **imposter** – one who pretends to be someone else; in commercial paper law, one who dupes a maker or a drawer into issuing a negotiable instrument to the imposter.
- **imputed knowledge and notice** – one consequence of the agency relationship whereby the principal is charged with knowledge of facts that have been disclosed to the principal's agent.
- **incidental beneficiary** - a third party beneficiary who is only incidentally benefited by a contract, and who cannot sue to enforce the contract.
- **incorporators** – the persons who sign and execute the articles of incorporation.
- **independent contractor** – a person who renders services in the course of an independent occupation.
- **indorser** – the person, typically the payee or transferor, who signs on the back of a negotiable instrument, thereby becoming secondarily liable thereon.
- **information** – the very broadly construed predicate for a legally protected trade secret.
- **injunction** – an order from a judge commanding a defendant to stop doing a wrongful act.
- **intestate descent and distribution** – the state laws covering the disposition of the property of one's estate when one dies without a will.
- ***inter vivos* trust** - a trust created by a settlor when he or she is alive.
- **IOU** – literally, "I owe you"; a mere acknowledgement of a debt, but not a negotiable instrument due to the lack of a promise to pay.
- **inside information** – the confidential, secret, proprietary, private, and non-public information of a business.
- **insiders** - a broad term under securities law referring to corporate employees, officers, directors, and shareholders, as well as certain "outsiders" who deal with the corporation.

- **insider trading** – illegal stock trading on inside information by a corporate insider.
- **integration or merger clause** a clause in a contract which states that the contractual agreement embodies the entire agreement of the parties and prevails over all prior as well as contemporaneous agreements, promises, and/or representations of the parties.
- **intellectual property law** – a very broad legal term indicating the variety of methods that will legally protect intellectual property.
- **intentional infliction of emotional distress** – the intentional tort which arises when a defendant purposefully acts in an extreme, outrageous, and atrocious manner and thereby causes the plaintiff to suffer severe emotional distress.
- **intentional interference with contractual or business relations** – the intentional tort which arises when a defendant intentionally, knowingly, and improperly interferes with the contract, business relationship, or business expectancy of another.
- **intentional tort** – a legal wrong committed when a person or his or her property is purposefully invaded or harmed by another.
- **interim trustee** - a temporary trustee appointed by the bankruptcy judge to manage the bankrupt debtor's estate until a permanent trustee is elected by the creditors.
- **Internet Corporation for Assigned Names and Numbers** – the entity primarily responsible for regulating the issuance of domain names on the Internet.
- **invasion of privacy** – the intentional tort of purposefully intruding on or unduly publicizing the private life of a person.
- **invention assignment agreement** – an agreement in an employment contract whereby the employee agrees to transfer to the employer the rights to any inventions created or developed by the employee during the course of his or her employment.
- **invitations to make offers** – not real offers, but rather invitations to the public to make offers.
- **issue** – in commercial paper law, the first delivery of a negotiable instrument by the maker or drawer to the holder.
- **joint and several liability** – the legal doctrine that holds that when there are more than one defendant who have caused the plaintiff's damages, they are equally responsible for paying the judgment, regardless of their percentage of fault.
- **joint payees** – in commercial paper law, names on the payee line of a negotiable instrument connected with the word "and."
- **joint tenancy** – joint ownership of real property with right of survivorship; each of the joint tenants has an undivided interest in the property; the title to the property automatically passes to the last surviving joint tenant; a joint tenancy requires the "four unities": time, title, interest, and possession.
- **joint venture** – a business arrangement very similar to a partnership but more narrowly focused to a single transaction or undertaking.
- **judge** – the primary court officer, whose function is to preside over and manage trials.
- **judicial power** - a court's power of adjudication, judicial review, and statutory interpretation; in the U.S. Constitution, the power vested in the U.S. Supreme Court and other such "inferior" courts as Congress deems to establish.
- **jurisdiction** – the original authority of a court to hear a case.
- **jurisdiction over the subject matter** – when a case falls within a court's general, special, limited, or monetary jurisdiction.
- **jury** – the body of citizens sworn by the court to decide questions of fact and to render a verdict in a trial.
- **"last resort"** – an ethical principle which sets forth the conditions under which one has a moral duty to act even though there is no legal duty to do so.
- **law** – the entire body of principles that govern conduct and which can be enforced by the courts or other government tribunals.
- **lease** – property interests which do not provide ownership of property per se, but which do provide the right of possession and use; the owner of the property, known as the lessor or landlord, enters into an agreement with the occupier of the land, known as the lessee or tenant, under which the lessor agrees that the lessee can occupy the land for a specific period of time in exchange for rent payments or other consideration.
- **legal detriment** – the key test under contract law for consideration; whether the promisee has made a return promise or performed an act in return for the promisor's promise.
- **legal reasoning** – process of critical legal thinking that judges use to analyze and resolve a case.

- **legislative power** – the power of the U.S. Congress and the state legislatures to promulgate statutory laws.
- **legitimate business interest** – in some states, a requirement that an employer must demonstrate in order to have a binding covenant not to compete with an employee.
- **libel** – written defamation.
- **license** - legal right that permits someone to enter on property owned by another for some specific purpose.
- **life estate** - an estate in land in which the owner owns the land (and structures and attachments thereto) only for the owner's lifetime, and at the death of the present owner, the title to the land passes as directed by the original owner.
- **limited liability company** – a new hybrid form of business entity combining aspects of a corporation and a partnership.
- **limited partnership** – a special variant of a partnership created by the Uniform Limited Partnership Act.
- **limited liability partnership** – a special variant of a partnership created by state statute and designed for professionals, such as lawyers and accountants.
- **lineal heirs** - people who stem from one another in a line which includes the intestate decedent, for example, one's mother and father, and grandmother and grandfather.
- **liquidated damages** – an explicit provision in a contract which fixes the amount of damages to be recovered if one party breaches the contract.
- **liquidation** – in partnership law, also known as winding up, when all partnership affairs are settled, and which ultimately leads to the partnership's termination.
- **Long Arm Statute** – a state statute that permits a lawsuit to be instituted against an out-of-state defendant in the plaintiff's home state.
- **lost property** - when the owner through carelessness or accident unintentionally and involuntarily leaves the property somewhere; there is no intention of the owner to part with the title to the property.
- **manager-managed limited liability company** – a limited liability company where only the designated manager has the actual authority to bind the company contractually.
- **market share liability** – legal doctrine that holds that damages to an injured person caused by a defective product must be apportioned based on the market share of the manufacturers who made the product when the victim cannot ascertain the exact source of the product.
- **material** – in securities law, if information, if stated accurately or disclosed, would have deterred or tended to deter an average ordinary and prudent investor from purchasing the securities at issue.
- **material alteration** – in commercial paper law, an alteration of a negotiable instrument that changes the contract of the parties in any respect; a partial real defense.
- **mechanic's lien** – a lien against real estate for labor, services, and/or material used in improving realty.
- **member-managed limited liability company** – a limited liability company where all members have the power and right to manage the entity as well as to bind the company contractually.
- **merchant** – a person or business that regularly deals with goods of a particular kind.
- **merchantable quality** – the standard of quality for goods pursuant to the Uniform Code's implied warranty of merchantability.
- **merger** – in corporate law, the legal combination of two or more corporations, with only one corporation continuing to exist after the merger.
- **merger doctrine** – in commercial paper law, when a negotiable instrument becomes merged with an underlying obligation, and thus the latter is not available as a legal cause of action.
- **mirror image rule** – contract law rule that holds that the acceptance must be identical to the offer.
- **mislaid property** – property which is intentionally and voluntarily left in some place by the owner and then forgot by the owner.
- **mitigation rule** – a rule which requires the aggrieved party in a breach of contract situation to make a good faith and reasonable effort to mitigate his or her own damages.
- **morals or morality** – the ethically derived conclusion as to what is good or bad or right or wrong.
- **mortgage** – a legal instrument used to finance the purchase of real property; the mortgage does not actually evidence the debt; rather, it merely secures it, which means it provides a source from which funds can be realized by the lender through the foreclosure of the mortgage and sale of the property encumbered by the mortgage.

- **Motorist Implied Consent Statute** – a state statute that maintains that when a non-resident operates a motor vehicle within the borders of the state, he or she impliedly consents to appoint the state's Secretary of State as an agent for accepting service if the non-resident is involved in a motor vehicle accident in the state.
- **mutual agreement** – the first requirement to a valid contract, consisting of an offer and an acceptance.
- **mutual mistake** – a mistake made by both parties to the contract, and which makes the contract voidable by the party adversely affected.
- **mutuality of obligation** – contract law rule which holds that for a promise to be legal detriment it must impose a real obligation on a party and not a fake or illusory one.
- **necessary and proper clause** – found in Article I of the Constitution; the power that the federal-national government has to enact laws that are necessary and proper to the carrying out of its enumerated powers in the Constitution.
- **negligence** – the name given to a civil unintentional tort lawsuit against a person for acting in unreasonable manner; also conduct which falls below the standard of care of the reasonable prudent person.
- **negligence *per se*** – the breach of a legal duty of due care which is established by a statute.
- **negligent infliction of emotional distress** – the legal wrong of carelessly causing mental anguish, usually requiring some impact on the person of the plaintiff.
- **negotiability** – the Uniform Commercial Code's requirement that converts an instrument into a negotiable one.
- **negotiation** – the Uniform Commercial Code method of transferring a negotiable instrument to a third party who qualifies as a holder.
- **nimble dividends** – corporate dividends which are paid from current corporate earnings, and which are prohibited in most states.
- **nominal damages** – token damages awarded when there is a breach of contract but no real loss.
- **noncupative will** - an oral will; in most states, these types of wills are not recognized.
- **non-existent principal** – the situation that arises when an agent acts for a non-existent principal, for example, a promoter who acts for a corporation that is not yet formed.
- **non-reliance clause** – a contract clause which states that the parties attest that they have not relied on any representations or promises that may have been made during the course of contract negotiations and drafting that are not explicitly set forth in the written contract.
- **nonfeasance** – not acting; and the general rule that holds that there is no legal liability for not acting.
- **Notice of Administration** - legal notice required to be published in a newspaper of the probate of a decedent's estate.
- **novation** – an agreement by which one of the original contract parties agrees to accept performance by a new party and also agrees to release the other original contract party.
- **obligor** – the original contract party who must perform contract duties for the assignee.
- **offer** – the legally recognized beginning to a contract; a proposal to enter into a contract.
- **officer** – a person in a position of authority and trust in regular and continuing employment in the corporation.
- **option** – a firm offer in which the offeror has received something of value from the offeree to keep the offer open.
- **parol evidence rule** – contract law and evidence law rule that holds that generally a contract which is the final agreement between the parties cannot be modified or contradicted by parol evidence.
- **partially disclosed principal** – when an agent acts for a principal in a transaction with a third party, and the third party knows the agent is an agent but does not know the identity of the principal.
- **partnership** – an association of two or more persons to do business as co-owners for a profit.
- **partnership by estoppel** – pursuant to the Uniform Partnership Act, a partnership based on the words or conduct of a person who represents himself or herself as a partner.
- **passive trust** – a trust in which the trustee has no duties.
- **patent** – an exclusive legal right given by the federal government to the inventors of new and useful inventions, processes, and improvements.
- ***per capita*** distribution - when the relationship between all members in a class of "takers" is the same then they all take the same equal share.

- *per stirpes* - when a relationship between "takers" is unequal, then each person takes by representation, that is, a person takes his or her ancestor's share.
- **perfection** – in secured transaction law, the means by which the secured party acquires priority in the collateral over other secured parties; perfection can be by possession, called a pledge, attachment, or the filing of a finance statement.
- **perfect tender rule** – Uniform Commercial Code rule that goods must conform in every detail to the terms of the contract.
- **periodic tenancy** – a tenancy that continues from a period-to-period; often this time frame is one month; and the tenancy continues unless one of the parties gives proper notice.
- **permitting** - the official government sanction to perform a regulated activity typically pertaining to property development and use.
- **personal property** - generally is property which is moveable and not affixed to the land; can be tangible, meaning generally that it can be seen and touched, such as a furniture, or intangible, meaning generally that it exists as a right or idea, such as a patent.
- **personal representative** - also called, depending on the state, the executor or administrator; the person, usually named in a will, appointed by the Probate Court to administer the estate of the decedent
- **periodic tenancy** - one that continues automatically from rent period to rent period until one of the parties provides proper notice of termination.
- **personal defenses** – in commercial paper law, those defenses to the payment of a negotiable instrument that cannot be asserted against a holder in due course.
- **philosophy** – the study of thought and conduct, including the fields of ethics, logic, and metaphysics (the ultimate reality).
- **piercing the corporate veil** – when the "corporateness" of the corporation is disregarded, and the corporation is treated as an association of individuals.
- **police power** – the sovereign authority that a state legislative body has to promulgate laws to promote and protect the health, safety, and welfare of the citizens and residents of a state.
- **pooling agreement** – in corporate law, an agreement between two or more shareholders who agree that their shares will be voted in a certain way.
- **power of attorney** – an express written instrument that confers authority to an agent.
- **predominant feature test** – the major aspect of a mixed contract with sale of goods and performance of service elements.
- **precatory language** – when the transferor has merely expressed his or her hope, wish, or suggestion that the property be used for certain purposes, but with no requirement that the transferee actually do it.
- **preemption** – in constitutional law, the presence of detailed and pervasive regulation in a field to the extent that no state legislation will be allowed.
- **preemptive rights** – in corporate law, the rights of shareholders to preempt, or to purchase before others, a new issue of shares in proportion to their present interests.
- **preferred stock** – shares of stock that are not common and that have a variety of preferences regarding payment of dividends and distribution of assets.
- **primary parties** – in commercial paper law, the parties to a negotiable instrument, who are primarily liable to pay it; the maker of a promissory note and the acceptor of a draft.
- **principal** – in agency law, a person who retains another, called an agent, to represent the principal, to stand in the principal's place, in order to bring about contractual relations.
- **privity**– the existence of a contractual relationship between parties.
- **probate process** - the legal process where a will is legally proved.
- **profits à prendre** - a type of easement that generally allows someone to enter upon the land of another and remove some part of it such as timber.
- **promisee** – the contract party to whom a promise is made.
- **promisor** - the contract party who makes a promise.
- **promissory estoppel** – a substitute for consideration; the reasonable reliance by a party on a promise to his or her great inconvenience or substantial change of position.
- **promissory note** – a two party negotiable instrument where one party, called the maker, promises to pay a sum of money to another, called the payee.

- **protest** – in commercial paper law, a certificate used in international business stating that a dishonor of a negotiable instrument has occurred; must be signed and sealed by a U.S. Consul or notary at the place where dishonor has occurred.
- **pre-incorporation transaction** – a transaction done on behalf of the corporation or in the corporation's name which occurs before the articles of incorporation are filed.
- **premises liability** – the area of negligence law dealing with the liability of landowners to people who come upon their property.
- **preponderance of the evidence** – the standard burden of proof in a civil case.
- **presentment** – in commercial paper law, a demand for payment or acceptance of a negotiable instrument made by the holder of the instrument.
- **private law** – law dealing with the legal problems, relations, and interests of private individuals.
- **privileges and immunities** – the rights of national and state citizenship provided by the Constitution.
- **promoter** – a person who develops and organizes a corporation.
- **properly payable rule** – a bank can charge its customer's account for a check only if the item is properly payable.
- **proximate cause** – the legal doctrine that holds that even a carelessly acting defendant is not liable for the remote, unusual, and unforeseeable consequences of his or her wrongful act.
- **Public Company Accounting Oversight Board** – new federal agency, created by the Sarbanes-Oxley Act of 2002, which reports to the Securities and Exchange Commission, and which oversees and regulates public accounting firms.
- **public law** – law affecting the people as a whole; law intended to serve the societal interest as well as to achieve justice.
- **public policy** – actions as determined by the high court of a state that promote and protect the health, safety, and welfare of the people of that state.
- **public policy doctrine** - when an employee, even an at-will employee, cannot be discharged for engaging in an activity that public policy encourages, or conversely for not engaging in an activity that public policy discourages.
- **publication** - when the testator declares to witnesses that the instrument is his or her will.
- **purchase money security interest** - a special type of security interest recognized pursuant to the Uniform Commercial Code arising when the creditor advances the debtor money to acquire consumer goods.
- **purchase money mortgage** - when the seller agrees to take back a mortgage from the buyer for some portion of the purchase price; the purchase money mortgage enjoys certain priorities over other debts of the purchaser.
- **qualified indorsement** – pursuant to commercial paper law, when an indorser indorses a negotiable instrument, but adds the words "without recourse," thereby eliminating the indorser's contract liability on the instrument.
- *Quantum Meruit* (also called **Quasi-Contract**) – a common law legal device used to recover the value of products or services that were provided in good faith in the absence of any contract in circumstances where the products and services were plainly necessary, but the party receiving them could not contractually agree to purchase them.
- **quasi-contract** – not a real contract; a legal fiction created by the law to prevent unjust enrichment.
- **quitclaim deed** – a deed in which the grantor gives up any claim which he or she may have to the real property; the grantor neither makes any warranties that the title is good nor even that the grantor has a title claim; the grantor conveys only the interest that the grantor has, and no more.
- **quorum** – for shareholders' meetings, the majority of shares entitled to vote in a meeting.
- *quo warranto* – by whose authority; a legal proceeding brought by the state to compel a corporation to correct any deficiencies or to cancel its charter.
- **ratification** – in contract law, when a minor upon reaching the age of majority approves a contract made while a minor; in agency law, when a principal accepts the benefits of an unauthorized contract made by his or her purported authorized agent, thereby authorizing the contract.
- **real property** - generally is considered to be land and the improvements constructed upon it.
- **record date** – the date that ownership of stock is determined for voting and dividend purposes.
- **recording statutes** – state statutes the purposes of which are to establish clarity and certainty to property ownership and to prevent fraud; copies of deeds as well as other instruments pertaining to real property can be recorded in government offices where they become part of the public record.

- **reformation** – an order from a court rewriting the terms of a contract.
- **regulatory taking** – when government so extensively regulates private property that no viable economic use can be made of the property; considered to be an eminent domain "taking" for the purposes of the 5th amendment.
- **rejection** – a statement by the offeree to the offeror that the offeree does not accept the offer.
- **reimbursement** – when a surety pays the debt of the principal debtor, the surety can then sue the debtor for reimbursement.
- **reliance damages** – damages which compensate the aggrieved party for any expenditure made in reliance on a contract that was subsequently breached; he purpose is to return the aggrieved party to the position he or she was in before the contract was formed.
- **renunciation** – the power, though not necessarily the right, the agent has to terminate the agency relationship.
- **rescission** – an order from a judge canceling a contract.
- **rescission of indorsements** – when an indorser, based on ordinary contract law, has the right to cancel his or her indorsement on a negotiable instrument.
- *res* – the *corpus* or principal of a trust.
- *res ipsa loquitur* – "the thing speaks for itself"; the legal doctrine that holds that the fact that a particular injury has occurred may in and of itself establish the breach of duty element to negligence.
- *respondeat superior* – "let the master answer for the wrongs of the servant"; the legal principle that holds that the employer is responsible for the torts committed by the employer's employees acting within the course and scope of their employment.
- **restrictive indorsement** – when a person indorses a negotiable instrument but adds a condition to his or her indorsement.
- **resulting trust** – a trust that arises when one person buys property, real or personal, and obtains legal title from the seller, but the consideration for the property is supplied by another person; it also can arise from the failure of an express trust.
- **revocation** – in contract law, the retraction or withdrawal of the offer by the offeror; in agency law, the power, though not necessarily the right, the principal has to terminate the agency relationship.
- **right of first refusal** – a legal agreement stating that if a shareholder wants to transfer his or her shares of the company, the company or the shareholders (or whomever is specifically is designated in the agreement) first must be given the opportunity to purchase the stock based on the terms and conditions offered by a third-party purchaser.
- **risk of loss rules** – pursuant to the Uniform Commercial Code, the rules which determine which party, the buyer or the seller, bears the loss when the goods, without the fault of either party, are lost or harmed during shipment.
- **Sarbanes Oxley Act of 2002** – a major federal statute impacting corporate governance and securities laws as well as creating the Public Company Accounting Oversight Board.
- **satisfactory performance** – a clause in a contract which states that the performance must be satisfactory to a party.
- **scienter** – the requisite "evil mind" or wrongful intent needed for certain civil and criminal wrongs, such as common law fraud and securities fraud.
- **scope of employment** - when an employee acts within the normal course of his or her duties.
- **secondary parties** – in commercial paper law, the parties to negotiable instruments who are secondarily liable thereon; the drawer of a draft and the indorser of any instrument.
- **security interest** – a security arrangement whereby a debtor conveys to a creditor a legally recognized interest in specific personal property; created by the existence of a security agreement between the debtor and the creditor.
- **Securities Act of 1933** – a major federal securities law which is primarily a disclosure type statute.
- **Securities and Exchange Act of 1934** – a major federal securities law which is primarily an anti-fraud statute.
- **self-defense** – the use of force reasonably necessary to protect oneself from attack.
- **self-proving will** - one signed by the testator and the witnesses before a notary in accordance with state statutory requirements; a will which can be admitted to probate without further proof.
- **separation of powers doctrine** – the fact that the Constitution divides the powers of the federal government into three separate and equal branches – legislative, executive, and judicial – with distinct powers.

- **service invention** – an invention that occurs as an express contractual part of the employee's employment.
- **set-off** – the common law right that a bank, regarded as the debtor, possesses to pay itself from its customer's, regarded as the creditor, account any obligation that the customer owes to the bank.
- **settlor** – the person who creates a trust.
- **several payees** – in commercial paper law, the names on the payee line who are connected with the word "or."
- **shareholder** – a holder of record of shares in a corporation, representing an ownership interest in the corporation.
- **share subscription** – an offer to pay for and to purchase a specified number of the un-issued shares of stock of a corporation.
- **shelter doctrine** – the commercial paper doctrine that holds that ordinarily the transferee of a negotiable instrument acquires whatever rights his or her transferor possessed.
- **slander** – spoken defamation.
- **shop right invention** – when an employee makes an invention related to his or her employment and the employee is not contractually obligated to invent, but the employee does extensively and substantially use the employer's resources.
- **short form merger** - also known as a parent-subsidiary merger; a simplified merger procedure when a parent company wants to merge a wholly or substantially owned subsidiary into itself.
- **shrink-wrap agreement** – an agreement, typically containing a licensing agreement, contained in a document in a box in which goods, for example, software, are packaged; by opening the package and using the good, the buyer is construed to have accepted the agreement.
- **social benefit corporation** – a special type of corporation with a public benefit, which is for-profit and has shareholders, but where the board of directors *must* when making business decisions consider the interest of stakeholders and not just the shareholders and also must fulfill the public benefit.
- **social responsibility** – the doctrine that holds that a person or business should contribute to charities and take an active part in community and civic affairs; in business, typically called "corporate social responsibility."
- **sole proprietorship** – the most basic form of business organization where the owner is in essence the business.
- **sovereign immunity** – an international law doctrine that holds that as a general rule a country is exempt from the legal jurisdiction of another country's legal system.
- **special indorsement** – when the payee of order paper names a new payee when he or she indorses an instrument.
- **specialized federal courts** – specialized courts created by the U.S. Congress to decide specialized matters, such as the Patent Court and Tax Court.
- **special meeting** – in corporate law, any other meeting than an annual meeting.
- **special warranty deed** – a deed in which the grantor warrants that the grantor has the right to sell the property; the grantor does not warrant the genuineness of any prior grantor's title.
- **specific performance** – an order by a judge commanding the defendant to live up to the terms of a contract made with the plaintiff.
- **specific devise** - a gift by the testator of a particular object distinct from all other objects.
- **speculative damage rule** – contract law rule which requires that damages be reasonably certain of computation.
- **spendthrift trust** – a trust with a restraint on alienation (transfer) imposed expressly or impliedly by the terms of the trust.
- **stakeholders** – also at times called constituent groups; those groups, such as shareholders, employees, consumers, suppliers and distributors, local communities, and society as a whole, that have a stake in the decision-making of a business, typically a corporation.
- **stale check rule** – when the bank does not have to pay an uncertified check more than six months after its date of issuance, though the bank has the option to do so.
- **state action** – government action, and not the actions of private parties and business.
- **state supreme court** – the high court in the state court system.
- **Statute of Frauds** – state statute which requires that certain types of contracts be evidenced by a writing.

- **Statutes of Limitations** – state statutes which set forth the period of time in which a law suit must be instituted.
- **Statutes of Repose** – state statutes which set forth the time period in which a products liability lawsuit must be instituted against a manufacturer or seller.
- **statutory interpretation** – the power and role of a court to interpret the meaning of a statute.
- **statutory law** – law enacted by legislative bodies, for example, the United States Congress and state legislatures, as well as county and municipal ordinances and codes.
- **stock option** – the right granted to a person for a given period of time to purchase a stated amount of stock at a stated price; the price is usually equal to the fair market value of the stock when the option is issued, thereby allowing the holder of the warrant to benefit from any increase in the value of the stock; the option is granted only to a company's directors, officers, and employees in connection with their services to the company.
- **statutory process** – the power that legislative bodies have as well as the processes they use to enact law.
- **stock warrant** - a right granted to a person for a given period of time to purchase a stated amount of stock at a stated price; the stock warrant is different from the stock option in that the latter is granted only to a company's directors, officers, and employees in connection with their services to the company, whereas the former is sold to investors.
- **strict liability in tort** – modern common law doctrine holding manufacturers and sellers of defective products liable without fault for harms caused.
- **subject to a mortgage** – when the buyer buying property is not personally liable for the mortgage debt, which still exists on the property; the original mortgagor is still liable.
- **subrogation** – when a surety pays the principal debtor's debt, and then is subrogated, that is, acquires any rights the debtor's creditor had.
- **subscribed** – the requirement that a will be signed at the end.
- **substantial performance** – common law contract doctrine holding that a contract need only be substantially performed.
- **substitute check** – a new variant of a check, and regarded as a negotiable instrument, created by the Check Clearing in the 21st Century Act.
- **successors to holders in due course** – holders who take a negotiable instrument from holders in due course and who thereby may acquire the rights of a holder in due course.
- **summary judgment motion** – a request by a litigant to the judge for the judge to decide the case as a matter of law since there are no genuine issues of fact for a jury to resolve.
- **Summary or Family Administration** – probate administration for small estates, as defined by state statute, but usually not including any real property, when the beneficiaries of the decedent are the spouse and/or lineal descendants.
- **support trust** - a trust that allows the trustee to pay the beneficiaries only so much income and principal as necessary for the beneficiaries' support.
- **supremacy clause** – the clause in Article IV of the Constitution that the Constitution and the laws made pursuant thereto are the "supreme law of the land."
- **suretyship contract** – a primary promise made by a third party, called a surety, to perform a contract.
- **sustainability** – the objective of a business to achieve long-term financial success; attained by the business acting in a legal, moral, and socially responsible manner.
- **tenancy-at-sufferance** – a tenancy arising by a "hold over" of an occupant of property under a lease that has expired without the permission of the landlord; created by operation of law by the continued holding over of a tenant, whose initial possession was lawful but has since expired.
- **tenancy-at-will** - a leasehold interest that is terminable at the option of either party for any reason whatsoever; a lease which continues until either party elects to terminate it; where a lease has expired or has been terminated and the tenant continues to retain possession of the property, a tenancy at will or at sufferance exists..
- **tenancy by the entirety** – joint ownership of real property by husband and wife.
- **tenancy for years** – when the lease agreement sets out a specifically determinable period of time and automatically terminates at the end thereof.
- **tenancy in common** – joint ownership of real property in which each of the co-owners has an equal right to the entire property, but there is no right of survivorship.
- **tender of delivery** – pursuant to the Uniform Commercial Code, when a seller places and holds conforming goods at the buyer's disposition and gives the buyer notice to take delivery.

- **tender offer** – a public invitation to shareholders of a public corporation to sell their shares.
- **term tenancy** - also referred to as a tenancy-for-years; an interest in land where the tenant has exclusive rights to the land for a certain time period, which is often for a year or more.
- **testamentary capacity** - the requisite legal degree of mental capacity to make a will.
- **testamentary intent** – the requirement that the testator must have had the intention to make a particular instrument his or her will.
- **testamentary trust** – a trust created by a person's will.
- **thin capitalization** – when a corporation is inadequately capitalized and does not possess sufficient assets to carry on business.
- **third party beneficiary** – when the parties to a contract agree to have the performance or benefit rendered to a third party.
- **time instrument** – a negotiable instrument payable at a specific future date.
- **time is of the essence** – a clause in a contract requiring performance on a set date.
- **time of performance** – when a contract must be performed; a "reasonable time" when no specific time is stated.
- **tippees** – people in conspiracy with insiders who illegally trade stocks based on inside information.
- **title insurance** – insurance purchased from an insurance company; if there is any loss to the insured grantee caused by undiscovered defects in the title to real property, the grantee will be reimbursed by the insurance company.
- **tort** – a civil wrong; a wrongful act against a person or his or her property for which a legal cause of action may be brought.
- **trade acceptance** – a special type of draft used in the sale of goods.
- **trademark** – a legally recognized mark that identifies goods or services granted by the federal or state governments.
- **trademark dilution** – unauthorized use of a distinctive or famous trademark regardless of a showing of competition between the holder and unauthorized user, or the creation of confusion on the part of the consumer.
- **trademark infringement** – a violation of a person's legally protected right to goods or services protected by trademark law by unauthorized use of the mark.
- **trade secret** – information that is legally protected by federal or state trade secret law, particularly the Uniform Trade Secret Act on the state level.
- **transfer** – any change in the possession of a negotiable instrument other than its issue or presentment.
- **trespass to chattels** – trespass to personal property as opposed to real property.
- **trespass to land** – the intentional tort which arises when a person purposefully and physically invades another's land or real property.
- **trustee** - the person named in the trust, who has legal title to trust assets, and who is a fiduciary and is charged with the duty of effectively managing and administering the trust.
- **Truth-in-Lending Act** – federal statute that requires that the terms of a residential real estate loan be set forth in a clear and understandable manner.
- **undisclosed principal** – when an agent representing a principal deals with a third party but makes no disclosure that the agent is in fact an agent for a principal.
- *Ultramares* **rule** – the majority state legal view in the U.S. dealing with the accountant's liability for negligence to third parties.
- **undue influence** – when a will or a provision in the will was obtained through force, duress, menace, or a degree of persuasion exerted on another which is sufficient to destroy the testator's free will and true intentions.
- **Uniform Commercial Code** – state statutory law governing contracts for the sale of goods as well as regulating commercial paper and other commercial transactions.
- **Uniform Computer Information Transaction Act** – the major statute governing computer information transactions
- **Uniform Electronic Transaction Act** – statute that holds that an electronic signature is equal to a written signature.
- **unilateral contract** – a contract in which an act is done in consideration of a promise.
- **unilateral mistake** – a mistake made by one party to the contract, and which generally has no affect on the validity of the contract.

- **United States Constitution** – the "supreme law of the land"; the document that creates the government and provides individual rights in the Bill of Rights.
- **United States Courts of Appeals** – intermediate federal courts in the United States, possessing appellate jurisdiction only.
- **United States District Courts** – federal courts of original jurisdiction in the United States
- **United States Supreme Court** – the highest court in the United States, possessing both original and appellate jurisdiction.
- **unenforceable contact** – a valid contract, but not enforceable by the courts because a party has an affirmative defense.
- **usury** – illegal interest charged beyond the maximum allowable legal rate.
- **Utilitarianism** – the ethical theory that maintains that morality is based on consequences and that holds that an action is moral if it produces the greatest amount of good for the greatest number of people.
- **value** – pursuant to commercial paper law, when the consideration that has been agreed upon for the payment of an instrument has been performed.
- **values** – things that possess worth either intrinsically (in and of themselves, such as happiness) or instrumentally (because they are the means to obtain something else of value, such as money).
- **venue** – where geographically a lawsuit will be heard by a court.
- **vicarious liability** – the legal principle which holds that an employer is indirectly liable for the wrongs committed by the employer's employees acting within the course and scope of their employment, regardless of the employer's fault.
- **voidable contract** – an enforceable contract, but one or both parties to the contract has the choice to withdraw from the contract with no legal liability.
- **void contract** – a legal nullity; an agreement that has no legal effect and thus is not enforceable by the courts.
- **voidable preference** – in bankruptcy law, the power that the trustee has to cancel any transfer made by the debtor to a creditor that is deemed to give the creditor a preference over other creditors.
- **voidable transfer** – in bankruptcy law, the power that the trustee has to set aside certain transfers the debtor makes to third parties and to restore the property to the debtor's estate.
- *voir dire* – the process of selecting a jury to hear a case wherein the judge and the attorneys ask the prospective jurors questions to ascertain their qualifications, abilities, and biases.
- **voting trust** – a legal relationship that arises when shareholders transfer legal title to their shares to a trustee, who becomes the record holder of the shares.
- **whistleblowers** – people, usually employees, who disclose wrongdoing by their companies or organizations, usually to government regulators, but also to the media.
- **Whistleblower Protection Acts** – federal and state statutes that provide protection to employees wrongfully discharged for disclosing to government agencies legal wrongdoing on the part of their employers but in conformity with the requirements of the various statutes.
- **wholesomeness** – the Uniform Commercial Code's implied warranty that food and beverages sold must be fit for human consumption.
- **words of negotiability** – words to the effect that an instrument be payable to bearer or to the order of a named payee; one of the requirements for negotiability under commercial paper law.
- **writ of execution** – when a legal judgment is not satisfied, the creditor can obtain a court order from judge directing the sheriff to seize the debtor's non-exempt property and sell it.
- **wrongful dishonor** – when a check is properly payable from the drawer's account, but the drawee bank refuses to honor it.
- **zoning** – typically local government laws that designate certain types of permissible uses for property within a county or municipality or zoning district.

SOURCES

44 Liquormart, Inc. v. Rhode Island, 517 U.S. 484, 116 S.Ct. 1495 (1996).

Abdalati, Hammudah (1993). Islam in Focus. LCCN: 75-4382. The Islamic Propagation and Guidance Center.

Abelson, Reed, "Surge in Bias Cases Punishes Insurers, and Premiums Rise," The New York Times, January 9, 2002, Business Day, pp. 1, 5.

Ackerman, Andrew and Lublin, Joann S., (April 29, 2015). SEC Set to Propose New Rules on CEO Pay. *Wall Street Journal*, p. B2.

Ackerman, Andrew and Lublin, Joann S., (April 30, 2015). SEC Votes on Rules for Pay and Performance Disclosures, *Wall Street Journal*, p. B2.

Adarand Construction, Inc. v. Pena, 515 U.S. 200, 115 S.Ct. 2097 (1995).

Adler, I. (2006). Comparing Management Differences: Mexico with Canada & the United States. Retrieved July 20, 2006, from http://www.mexconnect.com/mex_/culmngt.html

Adler, I. (2006). Racism and Business in Mexico. Retrieved July 20, 2006, from http://www.mexconnect.com/mex_/travel/bzm/bzmadler0705.html

Adler, N.J. (1984). "Women in international management: Where are they?" *California Management Review*, 26 (4): 78-89.

Adler, N.J., (1984a). "Women do not want international careers: And other myths about international management." *Organizational Dynamics*, 13 (2, Autumn): 66-79.

Adler, Nancy J. & Bartholomew, Susan 1992. Academic and professional communities of discourse: Generating knowledge on transnational human resource management. *Journal of International Business Studies*, 23(3), 551-569.

Administrative Procedure Act, 5 United States Code Annotated, Sections 551-706 (Thomson/West 2006).

Advertising, "Complaints bring down Spanish ads in Miami," The Miami Herald, March 18, 2006, p. C1.

Aero Kool Corp. v. Oosthuizen, 736 So.2d 25 (Florida Appeals 1999).

Age Discrimination Act of 1967, 29 United States Code Annotated, Sections 621-634 (Thomson/West 2006).

Alfonso, M.E. (2005). Deloitte Mexico Named Socially Responsible Enterprise for the Fifth Consecutive Year. Retrieved July 20, 2006, from http://www.deloitte.com/dtt/press_release/0,1014,cid%253D77003%2526pv%253DY,00.html

Allen, Michael, "U.S. Retirees Fuel Yucatan Land Grab," The Wall Street Journal, April 18, 2006, pp. D1, D2.

Allen, Moira, "Here Comes the Bribe," Entrepreneur, October 2000, p. 48.

All Pro Sports Camp, Inc. v. Walt Disney Co., 727 So.2d 363 (Florida Appeals 1999).

American Civil Liberties Union v. Michael B. Mukasey, 534 F.3d 181 (3rd Circuit 2008), *cert. denied Mukasey v. ACLU*, 2009 U.S. LEXIS 598 (2009).

Americans with Disabilities Act of 1990, 42 United States Code Sections 12102-12118).

A&M Records, Inc. v. Napster, Inc., 239 F.3d 1004 (9th Circuit 2001).

Amdur, Eli (August 6, 2017). Excellence is not an act, but a habit. *Bergen Record*, Section J, p. 8.

Armour, Stephanie (January 9, 2014). Borrowers Hit Social Hurdles. *Wall Street Journal*, pp. C1, C2.

Armour, Stephanie and Feintzeig, Rachel, "Ruling Raises Question: What Does 'Closely Held' Mean," *Wall Street Journal*, July 1, 2014, p. A6.

Anticybersquatting Consumer Protection Act of 1999, 15 United States Code Section 1125-1129.

Appleby, Julie, "Judge overturns Wal-Mart law," USA TODAY, July 30, 2006, p. 3B.

Article 35 in the Official Gazette (*Resmi Gazete*) dated July 19, 2003 and numbered 25173, and dated January 7, 2005 and numbered 26046.

Jones, Ashby, "Court Might Consider Concealed Weapons," The Wall Street Journal, April 12, 2013, p. A5.

Associated Press (October 31, 2018). Google spinoff to test truly driverless cars in California. *Miami Herald*, p. 5A.

Associated Press (November 17, 2006). Spain Chews Out Burger King. *Miami Herald*, p. 3C.

Associated Press (August 24, 2018). Kroger chain looks to ban plastic bags at stores by '25. *Sun-Sentinel*, p. 7B.

Associated Press (May 4, 2018). U.S. indictment alleges top VW exec knew of emissions cheating. *Miami Herald*, p. 6A.

Associated Press (May 5, 2018). Wells Fargo agrees to pay $480 million to settle shareholder suits. *Miami Herald*, p.6AAdams, S. M. (1999). Settling cross-cultural disagreements begins with "where" not "how". *Academy of management executive, vol. 13* retrieved September 9, 2004 from EBSCO database.

Associated Press, "Judge OKs $143 million in CD antitrust lawsuit," Sun-Sentinel, December 5, 2003, p. 9A.

Associated Press, "Martha Stewart to Fight Civil Case," The Wall Street Journal, May 27-28. 2006, p. B3.

Ayman, Roya & Chemers, Martin M. 1983. Relationship of supervisory behavior ratings to work group effectiveness and subordinate satisfactions among Iranian managers. *Journal of Applied Psychology*, 68(2): 338-341.

Bagley, Constance E., Managers and the Legal Environment (4th edition), West-Thomson Learning (2002).

Bagley, Constance E., and Dauchy, Craig E. (2008). The Entrepreneur's Guide to Business Law (3rd Edition). United States: Thomson/West Publishers.

Baier, Elizabeth, "Court's gay marriage ruling has impact on South Florida," Sun-Sentinel, March 31, 2006, p. 1B.

Bakhtari, Hassan 1995. Cultural effects on management style: A comparative study of American and Middle Eastern management styles. *International Studies of Management and Organization*, 25(3): 97-118.

Ball, Jeffrey, "Chrysler-Case Jury Orders Big Payment, The Wall Street Journal, February 19, 1999, p. B1.

Bankruptcy Abuse Prevention and Consumer Protection Act of 2005, Public Law No. 109-8m 119 Statutes 23 (2005).

Barber, Tom, "Beyond Noncompete Agreements: Using Florida's Trade Secrets Act to Prevent Former Employees from Disclosing Sensitive Information to Competitors," The Florida Bar Journal, March 1998, pp. 10-19.

Baris, Tan, Overview of the Turkish Textile and Apparel Industry, Harvard Center for Textile and Apparel Industry, 8-9, 2001. This is a report providing an overview of the Turkish textile sector.

Baro-Diaz, Madeline, "Terror arrests prompt outcry," Sun-Sentinel, June 30, 2006, pp. 1B, 2B.

Barr, Alistair (August 25, 2014). Google's Bumpy Road Trip. *Wall Street Journal*, p. B4.

Barrett, Paul A. (November 27, 2017). Facebook, Google, and Twitter have to be more transparent about the way they work with data. *Bloomberg Businessweek*, pp. 11-12.

Batson, Andrew, "Antitrust Measure Wins Backing Of China's Cabinet," The Wall Street Journal, June 8, 2006, p. A7.

Batson, Andrew, "China Antitrust Law May Alter Global Acquisitions Landscape," The Wall Street Journal, November 3, 2005, p. A11.

BBC News. Mexico Fines US Hotel in Cuba Row. Retrieved July 20, 2006, from http://news.bbc.co.uk/2/hi/americas/4778268.stm

Beatty, Sally, and Simons, John, "FTC Eyes Liquor ads' Kid-Appeal," The Wall Street Journal, August 7, 1998, pp. B1, B6.

Belasco v. Gulf Auto Holding, Inc., 707 So.2d 858 (Florida Appeals 1998).

Bensinger, Greg (February 10-11, 2018. Uber Settles Trade Secret Case. *Wall Street Journal*, pp. B1, B4.

Bernstein, Jill (February 4, 2018). You just can't rail – you have to have solutions. *Sun Sentinel*, Jobs, p. 1.

Berzon, Alexandar (August 24, 2012). U.S. Judge Gives Poker a Break. *Wall Street Journal*, p. B1, B2.

Bennett-Alexander, Dawn D., and Harrison, Linda F. (2012). *The Legal, Ethical, and Regulatory Environment of Business in a Diverse Society.* New York: McGraw-Hill Irvin.

Ben-Zion, Yael, T., "The Political Dynamics of Corporate Legislation: Lessons from Israel," 11 Fordham Journal of Corporate and Financial Law, pp. 185-339 (2006).

Bergen, Kathy, and Kleiman, Carol, "$34 Million Mitsubishi Settlement A Wake-Up Call To Employers," Chicago Tribune, June 11, 1998, Business News, pp. 1, 5.

Bianco, Anthony, "Ken Lay's Audacious Ignorance," Business Week, February 6, 2006, pp. 58-59.

Bierman, Noah, "Verdict against gun firm in teacher's death is rejected," The Miami Herald. January 28, 2003, 1A, 2A.

Bhargava, V. (2005). *The Cancer of Corruption.* Retrieved April 2, 2006, from http://web.worldbank.org/WBSITE/EXTERNAL/EXTABOUTUS/0,

Black's Law Dictionary (5th edition), West Publishing Company, St. Paul, MN (1979).

Black, J. Stewart & Mendenhall, Mark 1990. Cross-cultural training effectiveness: A review and a theoretical framework for future research. *Academy of Management Review*, 15(1): 113-136.

Black, J. Stewart & Porter, Lyman W. 1991. Managerial behavior and job performance: A successful manager in Los Angeles may not succeed in Hong Kong. *Journal of International Business Studies*, 22(1): 99-113.

BMW of North America, Inc. v. Gore, 517 U.S. 559, 116 S.Ct. 1589 (1996).

Boreale, Michael, "Beachfront Property in Arizona? Loosening Restrictions on Foreign Acquisition of Mexican Real Estate and the Implications for Arizona Investors," 22 Arizona Journal of International and Comparative Law, pp. 389-412 (Summer 2005).

Boslet, Mark, "U.S. Court Likely Will Force Google To Turn Over Data," The Wall Street Journal, March 15, 2006, p. B2.

Boudreaux, Karol C., "The Human Face of Resource Conflict: Property and Power in Nigeria," 7 San Diego International Law Journal, pp. 61-102 (2005).

Bowen, Brian D., "Drafting and Negotiating Effective Confidentiality Agreements," Texas Bar Journal, June 1996, pp. 524-532.

Branch, Karen, "Suit against gun industry takes broad aim," The Miami Herald, January 23, 1999, p. 11B.

Branch, Shelly, "Is Food the Next Tobacco"? The Wall Street Journal, June 13, 2002, pp. B1, B9.

Branom, Mike, "Family files suit over Epcot," Sun-Sentinel, November 20, 2002, p. 3D.

Branon, Mike, "Disney: Epcot ideas not stolen," The Miami Herald, November 14, 2000, p. A22.

Bravin, Jess, "Court Hears School Diversity Cases," The Wall Street Journal, December 5, 2006, p. A2.

Bravin, Jess, "Court: Police Can't Force Blood Tests," The Wall Street Journal, April 18, 2013, p. A5.

Bravin, Jess, "Justices Limit Law's Reach for Acts Overseas," The Wall Street Journal, April 18, 2013, p. A5.

Bravin, Jess, "Court Upholds Eminent Domain," Wall Street Journal, June 24, 2005, pp. A3, A10.

Bravin, Jess, and O'Connell, Vanessa, "High Court Rejects Limits on Out-of-State Wineries," Wall Street Journal, May 17, 2005, pp. A1, A6.

Bray, Ilan, "A Company's Threat: Quit Smoking or Leave," The Wall Street Journal, December 20, 2005, pp. D1, D6.

Breed, Allen G., "Company wants to recruit Hispanics," The Miami Herald, February 18, 2006, p. 3C.

Briefs, "Europe: MasterCard Faces Price-Fixing Charge," The Miami Herald, July 1, 2006, p. 2C.

Browning, Michael, "Jury: RJR tobacco not liable," The Miami Herald, May 6, 1997, pp. 1A, 12A.

Brown v. Entertainment Merchants Association, 2011 U.S. LEXIS 4802 (2011).

Bryant, Howard, "Yankees tell El Duque to speak English," Sun-Sentinel, July 2, 2001, pp. 1C, 5C.

Buchan, David, "French put new take on bribes," The Financial Times, February 8, 1997, p. 9.

Buckley, Cara, Consumers stake claim for CD settlement," The Miami Herald, January 23, 2003, p. C1.

Buckman, Rebecca, "China Hurries Antitrust Law," The Wall Street Journal, June 11, 2004, p. A7.

Burkins, Glen, "Grower Tanimura & Antle Agrees to Pay Nearly $1.9 Million in Harassment Case," The Wall Street Journal, February 24, 1999, p. B2.

Burlington Industries v. Ellerth, 524 U.S. 742, 118 S.Ct. 2257 (1998).

Burstein, John, "Gym found liable in man's death," Sun-Sentinel, March 30, 2006, p. 6B.

Business Briefs, "Cruise Lines: Regulators Approve Roman Terminal," The Miami Herald, May 6, 2006, p. 3C.

Business Briefing, "Alamo loses bias lawsuit," Sun-Sentinel, May 31, 2006, p. D1.

Butler, John K. Jr. & Cantrell, R. Stephen 1997. Effects of perceived leadership behaviors on job satisfaction and productivity. Psychological Reports, 80: 976-977.

Boitnott, John (September 17, 2017). 7 beliefs that hamper success – and how to change them. Sun Sentinel, Jobs, p. 1.

Bravin, Jess (July 1, 2014). Court Grants Health Law Exception. Wall Street Journal, pp. A1, A6.

Brummitt, Chris (May 30-June 6, 2016). This is a Bank. Bloomberg Businessweek, pp. 38-39.

Bryan-Low, Cassell (March 31, 2011). U.K. Sets Bribery Law Guidance. Wall Street Journal, p. B2.

Bunge, Jacob (February 3, 2018). Chicken Price Rigging Alleged. Wall Street Journal, pp. B1, B2.

Calamari, John D., and Perillo, Joseph M., Contracts (3rd edition), West Publishing Company Hornbook Series, St Paul, MN (1987).

Carney, Dan, "Predatory Pricing: Cleared For Takeoff," Business Week, May 14, 2001, p. 50.

Calder, Rich and Jaeger, Max (July 27, 2018). It's the last straw for Disney, Barclays. New York Post, p. 4.

Cavico, F.J. (2014). Corporate Social Responsibility and Leadership. Davie, Florida: ILEAD Academy.

Cavico, F. J. (2015). J.P. Morgan Recruitment Practices in China and the Foreign Corrupt Practices Act: Legal Networking or Illegal Bribery. Open Ethics and Law Journal, Vol. 1, pp. 30-37.

Cavico, Frank J. and Mujtaba, Bahaudin G. (2014). Business Law for the Manager and Entrepreneur. Davie, Florida: ILEAD Academy, LLC.

Cavico, Frank J. and Mujtaba, Bahaudin G. (2018). Defamation by Libel and Slander in the Workplace and Recommendations to Avoid Legal Liability. Public Organization Review, available online at: https://doi.org/10.1007/s1115-018-0424-8.

Cavico, Frank J. and Mujtaba, Bahaudin G. (2016). Developing a Legal, Ethical, and Socially Responsible Mindset for Sustainable Leadership. Davie, Florida: ILEAD Academy.

Cavico, F. J. and Mujtaba, B. G. (September 2016). The Intentional Tort of Invasion of Privacy in the Private Employment Sector: Legal Analysis and Recommendations for Managers. International Journal of Business and Law Research, 4(3): 37-57.

Cavico, F. J. and Mujtaba, B. G. (August 2016). Insider Trading and the Case of Pro Golfer Phil Mickelson: Understanding the Legal, Ethical, and Social Responsibility Consequences. Global Journal of Social Sciences Studies, 2(3): 112-130. DOI: 10.20448/807.2.3.112.130.

Cavico, F.J. and Mujtaba, B.G (2016). Insider Trading v. Trading on Inside Information: A Primer for Management. European Journal of Business and Management, Vol. 8, No. 17, pp. 72-85.

Cavico, Frank J. and Mujtaba, Bahaudin G. (2018). Teaching Law, Ethics, and Social Responsibility in a School of Business: A Value-Driven Approach to Leadership and Sustainability. Marketing and Management of Innovations Journal. Issue 4, pp. 263-281.

Cavico, F. J. and Mujtaba, B. G. (April 2016). Volkswagen Emissions Scandal: A Global Case Study of Legal, Ethical, and Practical Consequences and Recommendations for Sustainable Management. Global Journal of Research in Business & Management, 4(2), 433-411.

Cavico, F. J. and Mujtaba, B.G. (2017). Wells Fargo Fake Accounts Scandal and Its Legal and Ethical Implications for Management. SAM: Advanced Practice Journal, Vol. 82, No. 2, pp. 4-19.

Cavico, F.J., Mujtaba, B.G., and Muffler, S.C. (2016). Covenants Not To Compete in Employment: The Education and Training Criteria to Enforceability. SAM Advanced Management Journal, Vol. 81, No. 2, pp. 45-59.

Cavico, F. J. Mujtaba, B.G., and Muffler, S.C. (2018). The Duty of Loyalty in the Employment Relationship: Legal Analysis and Recommendations for Employers and Workers. Journal of Legal, Ethical, and Regulatory Issues, Vol. 21, No. 3, pp. 1-27,

Cavico, F. J., Mujtaba, B.G., and Muffler S.C. (2018). Examining the Efficacy of the Common Law Tort of Intentional Infliction of Emotional Distress and Bullying. *Business Ethics and Leadership Journal*, Vol. 2, No. 2, pp. 14-31.

Cavico, F.J., Mujtaba, B.G., Muffler, S.C., and Samuel, M. (2018). Manufacturer, Supermarket, and Grocer Liability for Contaminated Food and Beverages due to Negligence, Warranty, and Liability Laws. *Economy*, Vol. 5, No. 1, pp. 17-39.

Cavico, F.J., Mujtaba, B.G., Muffler, S.C., and Samuel, M. (2017). Restaurant Liability for Contaminated Food and Beverages Pursuant to Negligence, Warranty, and Strict Liability Law. *Global Journal of Social Science Studies*, Vol. 3, No. 2, pp. 63-100.

Cavico, F., Mujtaba, B., Nonet, G., Rimanoczy, I, and Samuel, M. (2015). Developing a Legal, Ethical, and Socially Responsible Mindset for Business Leadership. *Advances in Social Sciences Research*, Vol. 2, Number 6, pp. 9-26.

Cavico, F.J, Mujtaba, B.G., and Rosenberg, R. (2015). Unionization and College Athletics: An Emerging Legal, Ethical, and Practical Quandary. *Management and Administrative Sciences Review*, Vol. 4, No. 1, pp. 1-22.

Cavico, F. J., Mujtaba, B. G., and Samuel, M. (June 2014). E- Cigarettes: An Unfolding Legal, Ethical, and Practical Quandary. *Journal of Psychology and Behavioral Science*, 2(2), 01-44. Website: http://aripd.org/journal/index/jpbs/vol-2-no-2-june-2014-current-issue-jpbs.

Cavico, F.J., Mujtaba, B.G., Samuel, M., and Muffler, S. (2016). The Tort of Negligence in Employment Hiring, Supervision and Retention. *American Journal of Business and Society*, 1(4): 205-222. Website: http://www.aiscience.org/journal/paperInfo/ajbs?paperId=3190

Cavico, F.J., Orta, M., Muffler, S.C., and Mujtaba, B.G. (December 2014). Business Plans as Legally Protected Trade Secrets under the Uniform Trade Secrets Act. *Journal of Business Studies Quarterly*, Vol. 6, No. 2, pp. 42-66.

Cavico, F.J., (2003). The Tort of Intentional Infliction of Emotional Distress in the Private Employment Sector. *Hofstra Labor and Employment Law Journal*, Vol. 21, No. 1, pp. 109-182.

Cavico, F. J., (2002). Tortious Interference with Contract in the At-Will Employment Context. *University of Detroit Mercy Law Review*, Vol. 79, No. 4, pp. 503-569.

Cavico, Frank, "Business Plans and Strategies as Legally Protected Trade Secrets: Florida and National Perspectives," Vol. 9, Numbers 1 & 2, *University of Miami Business Law Review* 1-66 (Winter 2001).

Cavico, Frank, "Extraordinary or Specialized Training as a Legitimate Business Interest in Restrictive Covenant Employment Law: Florida and National Perspectives," Volume 14, No. 1 *St. Thomas Law Review*, 53-107 (Fall 2001).

Cavico, F.J. (1999). Defamation in the Private Sector: The Libelous and Slanderous Employer. *Dayton Law Review*, Vol. 24, No. 3, pp. 405-489.

Cavico, Frank J., "Fraudulent, Negligent, and Innocent Misrepresentation in the Employment Context: The Deceitful, Negligent, and Thoughtless Employer," Vol. 20 *Campbell Law Review*, 1-90 (Winter 1997).

Cavico, Frank J., "Private Sector Whistleblowing and the Employment At-Will Doctrine: A Comparative Legal, Ethical, and Pragmatic Analysis," Vol. 45 *South Texas Law Review*, 543-645 (Summer 2004).

Cavico, F. J. (2006). The covenant of good faith and fair dealing in the franchise business relationship. *Barry Law Review*, Vol. 6, pp. 61-104.

Cavico, F. & Mujtaba, B. G., (2008). *Legal Challenges for the Global Manager and Entrepreneur*. Kendal Hunt Publishing Company. United States.

Cavico, Frank J. and Mujtaba, Bahaudin G. (2011). *Baksheesh or Bribe: Cultural Conventions and Legal Pitfalls*. Davie, Florida: ILEAD Academy, LLC.

Cavico, Frank J. and Mujtaba, Bahaudin G. (2010). Baksheesh or Bribe: Payments to Government Officials and the Foreign Corrupt Practices Act. *Journal of Business Studies Quarterly*, Vol. 2, No. 1, pp. 83-105.

Cavico, Frank J. and Mujtaba, B.G. (2010). *Business Ethics: The Moral Foundation of Effective Leadership, Management, and Entrepreneurship (Second Edition)*. Boston, Massachusetts: Pearson Custom Publishing.

CCH Tax Law Editors. (2018). *2019 U.S. master tax guide*. Riverwoods, IL: Commerce Clearing House.

Chamber of Commerce of the United States v. Whiting, 2011 U.S. LEXIS 4018 (2011).

Chazan, Guy, "Russia to Tighten Access to Oil and Gas Reserves," The Wall Street Journal, June 14, 2006, p. A7.

Check Clearing in the 21st Century Act of 2004, 12 United States Code Section 5001-5018.

Cheeseman, Henry R., Business Law (5th edition), Pearson/Prentice Hall, 2004.

Cheeseman, Henry R., The Legal Environment of Business and Online Commerce (5th edition), Pearson/Prentice Hall (2007).

Chemers, Martin M. 1969. Cross-cultural training as a means of improving situational favorableness. *Human Relations*, 22(6): 531-546.

Chemers, Martin M. & Ayman, Roya 1985. Leadership orientation as a moderator of the relationship between job performance and job satisfaction of Mexican managers. *Personality and Social Psychology Bulletin*, 11(4): 359-367.

Christopher Deliso, *Investing in Turkey: Incentives, Conditions, Getting Started*, from http://www.escapeartist.com/efam/38/CD_Turkey.html.

Christensen, Jon (July 13, 2018). Talcum powder case: Johnson & Johnson to pay $4.69 billion. *CNN.com*. Retrieved July 13, 2018 from: https://www.cnn.com/2018/07/13/health.

Cihan New Agency: Economy News, *Turkey Attracts Record Foreign Investment of $8.1 Billion in January – May 2006*, July 13, 2006, from http://www.cia.gov/cia/publications/factbook/geos/tu.html#Econ.

CIA Government, (2006), Retrieved on July 30, 2006 From www.cia.gov.

Circuit City Store, Inc. v. Adams, 532 U.S. 105, 121 S.Ct 1302 (2001).

Citizens United v. Federal Election Commission, 130 S.Ct. 876 (2010).

Civil Rights Act of 1964, Title VII, 42 United States Code Annotated, Sections 2000e-2000e-17 (Thomson/West 2006).

Clark, Kim, "Noncompete contracts: Be loyal or see you in court, employers warn workers," U.S. News & World Report, December 18, 2006, pp. 63-64.

Clarkson, Kenneth W., Miller, Roger LeRoy, Jentz, Gaylord A., and Cross, Frank B., Business Law (9th edition), Thomson-West, 2004.

Clarkson, Kenneth W., Miller, Roger LeRoy, and Cross, Frank B. (2012). *Business Law Text and Cases: Legal, Ethical, Global, and Corporate Environment* (12th edition).

Clayton Act of 1914, 15 United States Code Annotated, Section 14, as amended by the Celler-Kefauver Act of 1950, 15 United States Code Annotated, Section18 (Thomson/West 2006).

Clean Air Act, 42 United States Code Annotated Sections 7401 et seq. (Thomson/West 2006).

Clean Water Act, 33 United States Code Annotated Sections 1251-1387, as amended by the Water Quality Act of 1987 (Thomson/West 2006).

Coca-Cola Company v. Koke Company of America, 254 U.S. 143, 41 S.Ct. 113 (1920).

Coffee, John C., Jr., "Outsider Trading, That New Crime," The Wall Street Journal, November 14, 1990, p. A16.

Cohen, Adam, "China's Draft Antitrust Law Sows Worries in West," The Wall Street Journal, January 30, 2004, p. A12.

Cohen, Adam, and Jacoby, Mary, "EU's Kroes Puts Consumers First in Merger Cases," The Wall Street Journal, September 26, 2005, p. A17.

Cohen, Laurie P., "Court Says Prosecutors Pressure White-Collar Defendants Unfairly," The Wall Street Journal, June 28, 2006, pp. A1, A12.

Collins, Erika C., "International Employment Law," 39 International Lawyer, pp. 449-481 (Summer 2005).

Coltri, Laurie S. (2010). Alternative Dispute Resolution: A Conflict Diagnosis Approach (Second Edition). Boston: Prentice Hall.

Commission for Environmental Cooperation (CEC). Retrieved July 20, 2006, from http://www.cec.org/home/index.cfm?varlan=english.

Communications Decency Act of 1996, 47 United States Code Section 230.

Comprehensive Environmental Response, Compensation, and Liability Act, 42 United States Code Annotated Sections 9601-9675 (Thomson/West 2006).

Computer Fraud and Abuse Act of 1984, 18 United States Code Section 1030.

Computer Software Copyright Act of 1980, Public Law No. 96-517, 17 United States Code Section 101..

Consolidated Omnibus Budget Reconciliation Act of 1985, 29 United States Code Annotated, Sections 1161-1169 (Thomson/West 2006).

Continental T.V., Inc. v. GTE Sylvania, Inc., 433 U.S. 36, 97 S.Ct. 2549 (1977).

Copyright Law of the United States, Title VII of the *U.S. Code*. Retrieved November 27, 2017 from: www.copyright.gov./title17.

Copyright Act of 1976, 17 United States Code Sections 101 et. seq.

Copyright Term Extension Act of 1998, 17 United States Code Section 302.

Consumer Credit Protection Act, 15 United States Code Annotated, Sections 1601-1693 (Thomson/West 2006).

Consumer Product Safety Act, 15 United States Code Annotated Sections 2051-2083 (Thomson/West 2006).

Controlling the Assault of Non-Solicited Pornography and Marketing Act of 2003, United States Code Annotated Sections 7701-7713, (Thomson West 2006).

Cooper, Phillip J., Public Law and Public Administration (3rd edition), F.E. Peacock Publishers, Inc., Itasca, Ill., 2000.

Copeland, Libby, "The fat suit," Sun-Sentinel, November 17, 2002, pp. 1E, 8E.

Corkery, Michael, "New Twist in Vacation Homes," The Wall Street Journal, February 25-26, 2006, pp. B1, B4.

Couch v. United States, 409 U.S. 322, 93 S.Ct. 611 (1973).

Crock, Stan, and Moore Jonathan, "Corporate Spies Feel a Sting," Business Week, July 14, 1997, pp. 76-77.

Cross, Frank B., and Miller, Roger LeRoy, Legal Environment of Business (6th edition), Thomson/West, 2007.

Crutsinger, Martin and Sell, Sarah Skidmore (February 3, 2018). *Miami Herald*, p. 12A.

Curtis, Henry Pearson, "Ex-Disney employee sues over dress code," The Orlando Sentinel, May 23, 2004, p. A7.

Dash, Eric, "Pay Rules Adopted by S.E.C.," The New York Times, July 27, 2006, pp. C1, C10.

Davidson, Daniel V. and Forsythe, Lynn M. (2011). *The Entrepreneur's Legal Companion*. Boston, MA: Prentice Hall.

Davies, Frank, "Senate Ok's Homeland Security Bill, "The Miami Herald," November 20, 2002, pp. 1A, 20A.

Davis, Ann, "English-Only Rules Spur Workers to Speak Legalese," The Wall Street Journal, January 23, 1997, pp. B1, B6.

Davis-Bacon Act of 1931, 40 United States Code Annotated, Sections 276a-276a-5 (Thomson/West 2006).

DeCarlo, Thomas E. & Leigh, Thomas W. (1996). Impact of salesperson attraction on sales managers' attributions and feedback. *Journal of Marketing, 60*, 47-66.

DeGeorge, Richard T., Business Ethics (6th edition), Pearson/Prentice Hall, 2006.

DeGeorge, Richard, Business Ethics (5th edition), Prentice Hall, 1999.

Dehart, Philip, "The NAALC and Mexico's Ley Federal Para Prevenir Y Eliminar La Discriminacion," 34 Georgia Journal of International and Comparative Law, pp. 657-688 (2006).

Delaney, Kevin, "Ruling Lets Lee Go to Work at Google," The Wall Street Journal, September 14, 2005, p. B2.

Diamond v. Diehr, 450 U.S. 175, 101 S.Ct. 1048 (1981).

Diamond, Randy, "McGreevey signs law requiring 'smart' guns," Bergen Record, December 24, 2002, pp. A1, A7.

Diamond v. Diehr, 450 U.S. 175 (1981).
Digital Millennium Copyright Act of 1998, 17 United States Code Sections 1201-1205.
District of Columbia v. Heller, 208 U.S. LEXIS 5628 (2008).
Dobbs, Dan B., The Law of Torts, West Group, 2001 (and Supplement 2006).
Dobbs, Dan B., Keeton, Robert E., and Owen, David G., Prosser and Keeton on the Law of Torts (5th edition), West Publishing Company, 1984.
Domrin, Alexander N., "From Fragmentation To Balance: The Shifting Model of Federalism in Post-Soviet Russia," 15 Transnational Law and Contemporary Problems, pp. 515- 549 (2006).
Do-Not-Call Implementation Act (2003). Public Law No. 108-10. 15 United States Code Section 6101
Dorsey, Patrick, "Woman files suit against Marlins," Sun-Sentinel, May 6, 2006, p. 6B.
Dowling, Donald C., and Rose, Proskauer, "The Practice of International Labor and Employment Law for Multinational Employer Clients," 730 Practicing Law Institute Litigation and Practice Course Handbook Series, pp. 773-815 (2005).
Dunham, Kemba J., "Banking on Boomers in Baja," The Wall Street Journal, reprinted in The Miami Herald, February 15, 2006, Business Monday, pp. 6-7.
D'Emilio. Frances (May 29, 2016). Friends, countrymen: Sponsor a Roman ruin. *Sun-Sentinel*, p. 13.
Desmarais Chrustina (September 3, 2017). Executives tell how they make it work. *Sun Sentinel*, Jobs, p. 1.
Ensign, Rachel Louise (March 13, 2018). BofA CEO Receives 250 Times Staff Pay. *Wall Street Journal*, p. B10.
Ensign, Rachel Louise (February 26, 2015). Treatment of Tipsters Is Focus of SEC. *Wall Street Journal*, pp. C1, C2.
Flitter, Emily and Thrush, Glen (April 20, 2018). Wells Fargo will be fine $1 billion. *Miami Herald*, p. 6A.
Fort, Timothy L. and Presser, Stephen B. (2017). *The Legal and Ethical Environment of Business*. West Academic Publishers.
Francis, Theo and Fuhrman, Vanessa (March 12, 2018). In a First, U.S. Firms Reveal Workers' Pay Gap With CEO. *Wall Street Journal*, pp. A1, A2.
Fritz, Ben and Lublin, Joann S. (March 9, 2018). Disney Rebuffed Over Pay for CEO. *Wall Street Journal*, pp. B1, B2.
Earley, P. Christopher 1987. Intercultural training for managers: A comparison of documentary and interpersonal methods. *Academy of Management Journal*, 30(4): 685-698.
Economic Espionage Act, 18 United States Code Annotated Sections 1831-1839 (Thomson/West 2006).
EEOC v. Waffle House, Inc., 534 U.S. 279, 122 S.Ct. 754 (2002).
Ehrenreich, Barbara, "Zipped Lips," Time, February 5, 1996, p. 80.
EIU Business: Industry Overview, *Turkey: Manufacturing*, June 30, 2006; From http://www.toyotatr.com/tr/company.asp; Business Digest, Turkish News in Brief, Toyota Turkey, July 13, 2006.
Electronic Communications Privacy Act of 1986, 18 United States Code Annotated, Sections 2510-2521 (Thomson/West 2006).
Electronic Communication, "Employer's e-mail policy is unfair to union organizing effort, judge rules," Florida Employment Law Letter, Vol. 15, No. 2, April 2003, p. 5.
Electronic Communications Privacy Act, 18 United States Code Annotated Sections 2510-21 (Thomson/West 2006).
Electronic Communications Privacy Act of 1986, 18 United States Code Annotated 2510-2521 (Thomson/West 2006).
Electronic Fund Transfer Act of 1978, 15 United States Code Sections 1693-1693r.
Electronic Signature in Global and National Commerce Act, 15 United States Code Annotated, Section 7002 (Thomson/West 2006).
Emerick v. Kuhn, 737 A.2d 456 (Connecticut Appeals 1999).
Employee Polygraph Protection Act of 1988, 29 United States Code Annotated, Sections 2001 et seq. (Thomson/West 2006).
Employee Retirement Income Security Act of 1974, 29 United States Code Annotated, Sections 1001 et seq. (Thomson/West 2006).
Emshriller, John R, Smith, Rebecca, and Murray, Alan, "Lay's Legacy: Corporate Change – But Not the Kind He Expected," The Wall Street Journal, July 6, 2006, pp. A1, A10.
Ergun Özbudun, *Constitutional Law*, in 19-22 INTRODUCTION TO TURKISH LAW, (Tugrul Ansay et al. eds.., 2005). Kluwer Law International.
Ervin, C. (n.d.). *OECD Actions to Fight Bribery in International Business Transactions*. Retrieved April 2, 2006, from http://magnet.undp.org/Docs/efa/corruption/Chapter10.pdf
Executive Agencies in Jamaica: The Story Thus Far and the Central Management Mechanism. (2001). Retrieved July 19, 2006 from http://www.cabinet.gov.jm/docs/pdf/ExecAgenciesThusFar.pdf.
Expedited Funds Availability Act of 1987, 12 United States Code Sections 229.1-229.42.
Fair Labor Standards Act of 1938, 29 United States Code Annotated, Sections 201-260 (Thomson/West 2006).
False Claims Act of 1863, as amended by the False Claims Reform Act of 1986, 31 United States Code Annotated, Sections 3729-3733 (Thomson/West 2006).
Family Medical Leave Act of 1993, 29 United States Code Annotated, Sections 2601 et seq. (Thomson/West 2006).
Farah, C. E. (1994). *Islam*. ISBN: 0-8120-1853-2. Barron's Educational Series, Inc.
Faragher v. City of Boca Raton, 534 U.S. 775, 118, S.Ct. 2275 (1998).
Federal Arbitration Act, United States Code Annotated, Sections 1-16 (Thomson/West 2006).
Federal Courts Improvement Act of 1982, 28 United States Code Annotated, Sections 1292-95 (Thomson/West 2006).
Federal Trade Commission Franchise Rule, 16 Code of Federal Regulations Section 436.1.
Federal Trademark Dilution Act of 1995, 15 United States Code Annotated Sections 1114-25.

Federal Patent Act of 1952, 15 United States Code Annotated Section 1125(a) (Thomson/West 2006).

Federal Trade Commission Act, 15 United States Code Annotated Sections 41-58 (Thomson/West 2006).

Federal Unemployment Tax Act of 1935, 26 United States Code Annotated, Sections 3301-3310 (Thomson/West 2006).

Feeley, Jeff, "Shoe-seller Nine West to pay $34 million to settle antitrust suit, The Miami Herald, March 7, 2000, p. 10C.

Feld, Louise, "Along the Spectrum of Women's Rights Advocacy: A Cross-Cultural Comparison of Sexual Harassment Law in the United States and India," 25 Fordham International Law Journal, pp. 1205-1281 (2002).

Felsenthal, Edward, "Big Weapon Against Insider Trading is Upheld," The Wall Street Journal, June 26, 1997, p. C1.

Fiedler, Fred E. 1967. *A theory of leadership effectiveness.* New York: McGraw-Hill.

First National Bank of Boston v. Bellotti, 435 U.S. 765, 98 S.Ct. 1407 (1978).

Flint, Joe, "Breaking Longtime Taboo, NBC Network Plans to Accept Liquor Ads," The Wall Street Journal, December 14, 2001, pp. B1, B6.

Fong, Mei, "China May Force Foreign Firms to Allow Unions," The Wall Street Journal, July 7-8, 2006, p. A2.

Fong, Mei, and Zimmerman, Ann, "China's Union Push Leaves Wal-Mart With a Hard Choice," The Wall Street Journal, May 13-14, 2006, pp. A1, A6.

Foreign Corrupt Practices Act of 1977, 15 United States Code Annotated Section 78m , as amended by the Omnibus Trade and Competitiveness Act of 1988, 19 United States Code Annotated Section 2903.

Foreign Sovereign Immunities Act of 1976, 28 United States Code, Sections 1602-1611.

Forster, Julie, "Gotta Get That Gator," Business Week, November 27, 2000, pp. 91, 94.

Fowler, Geoffrey A., and Qin, Juying, "China Threatens Rolling Stone's Ability to Publish Local Edition," The Wall Street Journal, March 31, 2006, p. A13.

Fowler-Hermes, J., "Appearance-based Discrimination Claims Under EEO Laws," The Florida Bar Journal, April 2001, pp. 32f.

Foy, Paul, "Olympic defendants off the hook," The Miami Herald, December 6, 2003, p. 7A.

France, Mike, "Europe: A Different Take On Antitrust," Business Week, June 25, 2001, p. 40.

Fracchia, Fabrizio, "Administrative Procedures and Democracy: The Italian Experience," 12 Indiana Journal of Global Legal Studies, pp. 589-598 (2005).

Frick, Helen L. 1995. The relationship of national culture, gender, and occupation to the work values of the employees of an international organization. Unpublished D.E. Dissertation, School of Education and Human Development, The George Washington University, Washington D.C.

Furchgott, Roy, "Workers Sign Away a Day in Court," The New York Times, July 28, 1996, p. 9.

Gardner v. Loomis Armored, Inc., 913 P.2d 377 (Washington 1996).

Gebert, Diether & Steinkamp, Thomas (1991). Leadership style and economic success in Nigeria and Taiwan. *Management International Review,* 31(2): 161-171.

Gerlin, Andrea, "Seminars Teach Managers Finer Points of Firing," The Wall Street Journal, April 26, 1195, pp. B1, B8.

Gender Watch, "Now No Means No in China," Business Week, March 28, 2005, p. 12.

Gelles, David (October 24, 2016). Megadeal Sends Signal of Assurance. *New York Times,* p. B4.

Gellman, Lindsay (February 3, 2016). Deepak Chopra Offers Guidance to M.B.A.s. *Wall Street Journal,* p. B5.

Gilbert Daniel (February 24, 2012). Ego, Alcohol To, Says KBR's Ex-Chief. *Wall Street Journal,* pp. B1, B2.

Goldstein, Matthew, Protess, Ben, and Stevenson, Alexandra (May 20, 2016). Insider Trading Case Links Golfer, Banker, and Gambler. *Wall Street Journal,* pp. A1, B4.

Greenfield, Rebecca (May 25-31, 2015) Software: Testing Workers' Digital Privacy Protections. *Bloomberg Businessweek,* pp. 33-34.

Gibson, Richard, and Brat, Ilan, "Whirlpool-Maytag Deal Gets Antitrust Approval," The Wall Street Journal, March 30, 2006, p. A2.

Gierczyk, Yvonne, "The Evolution of the European Legal System: The European Court of Justice's Role in the Harmonization of Laws," 12 International Law Students Association Journal of International and Comparative Law, pp. 153-180 (2005).

Gilmer v. Interstate Johnson Lane Corporation, 500 U.S. 20, 111 S.Ct 1647 (1991).

Gingrich, Newt, and Kies, Ken, "Our Taxed Expats," The Wall Street Journal, June 28, 2006, p. A14.

Glick, Norman D. 2001. Situational Leadership in cross-cultural environments: The relationship between cross-cultural experience, culture training, leadership style, and leader effectiveness in the U.S. Foreign Service. Doctoral Dissertation, School of Business and Entrepreneurship, Nova Southeastern University; Ft. Lauderdale, Florida.

Glick, Norman D. (2001).The impact of culture on sales force management. *Journal of Applied Management and Entrepreneurship,* 6(2): 116-129.

Global, 2006. Wal-Mart Stores, Inc. Sun-Sentinel, December 19, 2006, p. 3D.

Global News Wire. (2005). Human factor vital to ASIMCO'S China management retrieved July, 13 2006 from http://0-web.lexis-nexis.com.novacat.nova.edu/universe/document?

Goodman, Cindy K., "Today, it's OK to sign on the electronic line," The Miami Herald, October 1, 2000, pp. 1E, 7E.

Gonzales v. Raich, 545 U.S. 1, 125 S.Ct. 2195 (2005).

Gordon, Marcy, "SEC moves to require more exec pay disclosure," The Miami Herald, January 18, 2006, p. 3C.

Goss v. Lopez, 419 U.S. 565, 95 S.Ct. 729 (1975).

Government and Politics. 2005. Retrieved July 12, 2006 http://countrystudies.us/caribbean-islands/34.htm

Grant, John A., Jr., and Steele, Thomas T., "Restrictive Covenants: Florida Returns to the Original 'Unfair Competition' Approach for the 21st Century," The Florida Bar Journal, November 1996, pp. 53-56.

Grantz v. Bollinger, 539 U.S. 244 (2003).

Grutter v. Bollinger, 539 U.S. 306 (2003).
Greater New Orleans Broadcasting Association, Inc. v. United States, 527 U.S. 173, 119 S.Ct.1923 (1999).
Greenberger, Robert S., "Justices Back Arbitration Use In Work Arena," The Wall Street Journal, March 22, 2001, pp. A3, A10.
Greenberger, Robert S., "More Courts Are Granting Advertisers First Amendment Protection," The Wall Street Journal, July 3, 2001, pp. B1, B3.
Greenberger, Robert S., "Supreme Court Gives Workers Legal Options," The Wall Street Journal, January 16, 2002, p. B14.
Greenhouse, Linda, "Justices 5-4, Limit Use of Race for School Integration Plans," The New York Times, June 29, 2007, pp. A1, A20.
Greenhouse, Steven, "Looks aren't everything – unless you want a job," The Miami Herald, July 15, 2003, p. 21A.
Greenhouse, Linda, "Justices curb Postal Service immunity," Sun-Sentinel, February 23, 2006, p. 2A.
Greenman v. Yuba Power Products, Inc., 27 Cal. Rptr. 697, 377 P.2d. 897 (California Supreme Court 1963).
Groppi, Tania, and Scattone, Nicoletta, "Italy: The Subsidiarity Principle," 4 International Journal of Constitutional Law, pp. 131-137 (2006).
Grovis, Jaclyn, "Publix: Market leader shows shopping savvy," Sun-Sentinel, April 2, 2006, p. E1.
Grow, Brian, "A Body Blow To Illegal Labor," Business Week, March 27, 2006, pp. 86-88.
Grutter v. Bollinger, 539 U.S. 206, 123 S.Ct. 2325 (2003).
Grossman, Mark, "Confidentiality agreements have no standard form," The Miami Herald, March 3, 2003, Business Monday, pp. 27-28.
Güriz, Adnan *Constitutional Law*, in 2 INTRODUCTION TO TURKISH LAW, (Tugrul Ansay et al. eds.., 2005). Kluwer Law International.
H. Rosenblum v. Adler, 93 N.J. 324 (1983).
Guth, Robert A., "Microsoft Sues To Keep Aide from Google," The Wall Street Journal, July 20, 2005, p. B1.
Haden, Jeff (September 3, 2017). Path to promotion. *Sun Sentinel*, p. 5D.
Hennessey, Kathleen (February 2, 2014). Obama pushes to help long-term jobless. *Sun Sentinel*, p. 3D.
Henning, Peter J. (October 8-9, 2016). The Supreme Court plays Goldilocks on insider trading. *New York Times*, p. 13.
Holley, Peter, "Scooters Upend Sidewalks," *Sun-Sentinel*, January 22, 2019, p. 5b.
Hong, Nicole (August 24, 2017). Ruling Buoys Insider Prosecutions. *Wall Street Journal*, p. B1.
Herrera, Chabeli (November 3, 2016). It just got easier to volunteer while on a cruise vacation in the Dominican Republic. *Miami Herald*, p. 14A.
Higgins, Tim (January 9, 2018). Driverless Cars Pick Up Speed. *Wall Street Journal*, p. B4.
Higgins, Tim and Nicas, Jack (November 8, 2017). Waymo Hits the Road in Phoenix. *Wall Street Journal*, p. B4.
Hurley, Lawrence (June 21, 2018). Supreme court lets states force online retailers to collect sales tax. *Reuters*. Retrieved June 23, 2018 from: https://www.retuers.com/articles/us-court-taxes/supreme-court.
Hymowitz, Carol, Alpert, Lucas, I., and Vranica, Suzanne (November 11-12, 2017). *Wall Street Journal*, pp. B1, B4.
Haddad, Charles, and Pascual, Aixa M., "When You Want to Sue-But Can't," Business Week, June 10, 2002, p. 46.
Hall, Daniel, Administrative Law: Bureaucracy in a Democracy (2nd edition), Pearson Education, 2002.
Hamzah, Zain. (2005). *Legal issues on online Transactions*. Retrieved on August 3 2006 from: http://0-proquest.umi.com.novacat.nova.edu/pqdweb
Hananel, Sam, "Lay to submit papers to inquiry," Sun-Sentinel, November 8, 2003, pp. 8B, 9B.
Hanks, Douglas III, "When is a condo not a condo"? The Miami Herald, April 9, 2006, pp. 1E, 4E.
Harris v. Forklift Systems, 510 U.S. 17, 114 S.Ct. 367 (1993).
Harrison, J. Kline 1992. Individual and combined effects of behavior modeling and the cultural assimilator in cross-cultural management training. *Journal of Applied Psychology, 77*, (6), 952-962.
Hasegawa, T. (n.d.). *Investigation of Corruption in Japan*. Retrieved April 8, 2006, from http://www.unafei.or.jp/english/pdf/PDF_rms/no56/56-36.pdf
Hasnas, John, "Department of Coercion," The Wall Street Journal, March 11-12, 2006, p. A9.
Hawley, S. (2000). *Exporting Corruption: Privatisation, Multinationals and Bribery*. Retrieved April 5, 2006, from http://www.globalpolicy.org/nations/corrupt/corner.htm
Hays, Kristen, "Enron pair pay price for fraud," The Miami Herald, May 26, 2006, pp. 1A, 2A.
Hays, Kristen, "Convictions likely to be erased," Sun-Sentinel, July 27, 2006, p. 2D.
Heart of Atlanta Motel v. United States, 379 U.S. 241, 85 S.Ct. 348 (1964).
Heim, Kristi, "U.S. gives up effort to split Microsoft," The Miami Herald, September 7, 2001, pp. 1A, 2A.
Hemlock, Doreen, "Teaching linguistic nuances," Sun-Sentinel, December 13, 2004, Your Business, p. 5.
Henn, Harry G., and Alexander, John R., Laws of Corporations, West Publishing Company Hornbook Series (1983).
Henry, E. and Preston, M. (2005). *Congressman resigns after bribery plea*. Retrieved April 12, 2006, from http://www.cnn.com/2005/POLITICS/11/28/cunningham/
Herlihy, Edward D., "Eminent Domain Debate Hits the Links," The Wall Street Journal, March 28, 2006, p. D8.
Herman, Tom, and Silverman, Rachel Emma, "Telecommuters May Face New Taxes," *Wall Street Journal*, November 1, 2005, pp. D1, D2.
Hermida, Julian, "Convergence of Civil Law and Common Law in the Criminal Theory Realm," 13 University of Miami International and Comparative Law Review, pp. 163-232 (2006).
Hersey, Paul & Blanchard, Kenneth H. 1993. *Management of organizational behavior: Utilizing human resources* (6th ed.). Englewood Cliffs, NJ: Prentice-Hall.

Hiaasen, Scott, and Viglucci, Andres, "U.S. Supreme Court: Ruling on land is vital locally," The Miami Herald, June 24, 2005, pp. 1B, 10B.

Hill, John S. & Still, Richard R. & Boya, Unal O. 1991. Managing the multinational sales force. *International Marketing Review*, 8(1): 19-31.

Hodgetts, R.M., Luthans, F., & Doh, J.P. (2006). International Management: Culture, Strategy and Behavior, 6th edition. McGraw-Hill Irwin: Boston.

Hofstede, Geert 1980. *Culture's consequences: International differences in work-related values*. London, U.K.: Sage Publication Ltd.

Hofstede, Geert 1993. Cultural constraints in management theories. *Academy of Management Executives*, 7(1): 81-94.

Holmes, Stanley, "Free Speech or False Advertising," Business Week, April 28, 2003, pp. 69-70.

Holt, Michael F. (2006). The Sarbanes Oxley Act Overview and Implementation Procedures. CIMA Publishing, Oxford OX2 8.DP.

Honeycutt Jr., Earl D. and Ford, John B. 1995. Guidelines for managing an international sales force. *Industrial Marketing Management*, 24: 135-44.

Hymowitz, Carol, "Technology facilitates intellectual theft," The Miami Herald, September 12, 2005, Business Monday, p. 2.

Hymowitz, Carol, and Lublin, Joann S., "Many Companies Look the Other Way at Employee Affairs," The Wall Street Journal, March 8, 2005, pp. B1, B6.

Hynick, Jeff, "May I Borrow Your Mouse? A Note on Electronic Signatures in the United States, Argentina and Brazil," 12 Southwestern Journal of Law and Trade in the Americas, pp. 159-176 (2005).

IBM, 2006. *IBM pushes online contract mgmt.* Retrieved on August 3 2006 from: http://0-web.lexis-nexis.com.novacat.nova.edu/universe/document

Immigration, "France's Plan: Pay 'Em To Go Home," Business Week, April 24, 2006, p. 16.

Immigration Reform and Control Act of 1986, 29 United States Code Annotated, Section 1802 (Thomson/West 2006).

Import Administration: Import monitoring, licensing and compliance programs. Retrieved July 20, 2006, from http://ia.ita.doc.gov/import-monitoring.html

Inagaki, Kana, "More Japanese turning to courts," The Miami Herald, August 21, 2006, p. 14A.

Ingersoll, Bruce, "FDA Takes On 'No Cholesterol' Claims," The Wall Street Journal, May 15, 1991, p. B1.

Intel Corp. v. Hamidi, 30 Cal.4th 1342, 1 Cal.Rptr.3d 32 (California Supreme Court 2003).

Internal Revenue Code, 26 United States Code Annotated, Sections 6694, 6701, 7701, and 7206 (Thomson/West 2006).

Interpreters and Translators. Retrieved on June 22, 2006 from: http://stats.bls.gov/oco/ocos175.htm

International Shoe Company v. Washington, 326 U.S. 310, 66 S.Ct. 154 (1945).

International Trade Administration. Retrieved July 20, 2006, from http://trade.gov/index.asp

International Trade Commission. Retrieved July 20, 2006, from http://www.usitc.gov/

Islamic Network Group, 2002. *Islamic Speakers Bureau Publication*. Presenting Islam & Muslim Culture in the Content of Social Studies and Work History: School Grades 7th – 12th. Speakers Kit. Islamic Networks Group; website: www.ing.org.

Jacobs, Margaret A., "Brutal Firings Can Backfire, Ending in Court," The Wall Street Journal, October 24, 1995, pp. B1, B4.

Jacobs, Margaret A., "Red Lobster Tale: Peers Decide Fired Waitresses Fate," January 20, 1998, pp. B1, B4.

Jamaican Telecommunications Acts, 2006. *Highlights of the Jamaican Telecommunications Acts 2000*. Retrieved on August 3 2006 from: http://unpan1.un.org/intradoc/groups/public/documents/CARICAD/UNPAN009919.pdf

Jenkins, Jr., Holmes W., "The Land (and Antitrust Case) That Time Forget," The Wall Street Journal, April 26, 2006, p. A17.

J. K. Lasser Institute. (2019). *J.K. Lassers your income tax 2019*. Hoboken, NJ: John Wiley & Sons.

Johnson, Elizabeth Prior, and Burt, Frank, "English-Only Work Rules: Per Se Discriminatory or an Employer's Prerogative"? The Florida Bar Journal, November 1994, pp. 58-62.

Johnson, Tim, "Censored Search," The Miami Herald, April 13, 2006, pp. 1C, 6C.

Johnson, Tim, "Wal-Mart succumbs to state-run union," The Miami Herald, August 17, 2006, p. 2C.

Johnson, Linda, "Pfizer to sell consumer unit to J&J," Sun-Sentinel, June 27, 2006, pp. 1D, 2D.

Jordan, Miriam, "Good taste lost in ad translation," The Wall Street Journal, reprinted in the Sun-Sentinel, March 19, 2006, p. 1E.

Jordan, Miriam, "Blacks vs. Latinos at Work," The Wall Street Journal, January 24, 2006, pp. B1, B2.

Jordan, Miriam, "Testing 'English Only' Rules," The Wall Street Journal, November 8, 2005, pp. B1, B13.

Jorfinn, Sven (December 7- December 13, 2015). Poor Africans. *Bloomberg Business Week*, pp. 73-77.

Kendall, Brent (June 20, 2017). Supreme Court Rejects Curbs on Trademarks. *Wall Street Journal*, p. A2.

Kendall, Brent and Bunge, Jacob (April 10, 2018). U.S. to Allow Bayer's Monsanto Takeover. *Wall Street Journal*, pp. A1, A8.

Kendall, Brent and Fitzgerald, Drew (November 21, 2017). U.S. Sues to Block AT&T Merger. *Wall Street Journal*, pp. A1, A6.

Kendall, Brent and Fitzgerald, Drew (May 11, 2016). Judge Sinks Staples Merger. *Wall Street Journal*, pp. A1, A7.

Kendall, Brent and Gasparro, Anne (June 24, 2015). Judge Halts Merger of U.S. Food Giants. *Wall Street Journal*, pp. A1, A4.

Kendall, Brent and Matthews, Christopher M. (October 6, 2015). Top Court Rebuffs U.S. on Insider Ruling. *Wall Street Journal*, pp. C1-2.

Kendall, Brent, Kirkham, Chris, and Beaton, Andrew (May 15, 2018). *Wall Street Journal*, pp. A1, A2.

Kirkham, Chris (May 23, 2018). Shareholders Rebuke Wynn Resorts on Pay. *Wall Street Journal*, pp. B1, B2.
Kaufman, Leslie, and Underwood, Anne, "Sign or Hit the Street," Newsweek, June 30, 1997, pp. 48-49.
Kazor, Bill, "Debate heats up on eminent domain," The Miami Herald, March 16, 2006, p. 9B.
Kealey, Daniel J. & Protheroe, David R. 1996. The effectiveness of cross-cultural training for expatriates: An assessment of the literature on the issue. *International Journal of Intercultural Relations* 20(2): 141-165.
Kelo v. City of New London, Connecticut, 545 U.S 469, 125 S. Ct 2655 (2005).
Kenis, Izzettin 1977. A cross-cultural study of personality and leadership. *Group and Organization Studies*, 2(1): 49-60.
Kenya: Institutional Situation. (n.d.). Retrieved June 13, 2006, from
    http://www.etat.sciencespobordeaux.fr/_anglais/institutionnel/kenya.html
Kidwell, David, and Merzer, "A loss for Big Tobacco," The Miami Herald, July 8, 1999, pp. 1A, 6A.
Kiley, David, "A Green Flag for Booze," Business Week, March 7, 2005, p. 95.
Klass, Mary Ellen, "Tort reform bill passes house," The Miami Herald, March 17, 2006, pp. 1C, 6C.
Knight, Victoria, "Personality Tests as Hiring Tools," The Wall Street Journal, March 15, 2006, p. B3A.
Kocian, Lisa, "Dunkin' Donuts checks workers," The Miami Herald, May 31, 2006, p. 3C.
Koeppel, David, "Limit the damage ex-employees can do," The Miami Herald, May 9, 2005, Business Monday, p. 22.
Kramer, Michael, "Corruption and Fraud Stunt Third-world Growth," The White Paper, Vol. 16, No. 3, May/June 2002, p. 22f.
Kranhold, Kathryn, "Sotheby's Chief is Convicted of Price-Fixing," The Wall Street Journal, December 6, 2001, p. B1.
Kravets, David, "Court sides with doctors who advise pot use," Sun-Sentinel, October 30, 2002, p. 7A.
Kravets, David, "IBM hit with class-action suit," Sun-Sentinel, January 25, 2006, p. 3D.
Kristof, Kathy, "This Investment Vehicle is Rife with Fraud," Sun-Sentinel, March 12, 2002, p. 7D.
Labaton, Stephen, "Supreme Court to Review Antitrust Case Against Phone Companies," The New York Times, June 27, 2006, p. C3.
Labor-Management Relations Act of 1947, 29 United States Code Annotated, Sections 141 et seq. (Thomson/West 2006).
Labor-Management Reporting and Disclosure Act of 1959, 29 United States Code Annotated, Sections 401 et seq. (Thomson/West 2006).
Lanham Trademark Act of 1946, 15 United States Code Sections 1051-1128.
Larson, John W., Comiter, Richard B., and Cane, Marilyn B., "Florida's New Partnership Law," The Florida Bar Journal, November 1995, pp. 20-33.
Lavelle, Louis, "Happy Endings Not Guaranteed: Arbitration doesn't always live up to its billing," Business Week, November 20, 2000, pp. 69, 73.
LaVelle, Michael J., "A Russian Experience," 42 Arizona Attorney, pp. 30-35 (2006).
"Law on Foreign Land Ownership Passes Despite Opposition," TURKISH DAILY NEWS, Dec. 30, 2005, from
    http://www.turkishdailynews.com.tr/article.php?enewsid=32092.
Law No. 4916 Published in Article 35 the Official Gazette (*Resmi Gazete*) dated July 19, 2003 and numbered 25173.
Leicester, John, "Protesters seek status quo," The Miami Herald, March 18, 2006, p. 12A.
Leif, Carter H., and Harrington, Christine B., Administrative Law and Politics (3rd edition), Longman Publishers, 2000.
Lewis, Seth, "Protect Yourself," The Miami Herald, February 20, 2006, Business Monday, p. 4.
Leonhardt, David, and Dawley, Heidi, "A Little Booze for the Kiddies," Business Week, September 23, 1996, p. 158.
Lippman, Joanne, "FTC Is Cracking Down on Misleading Ads," The Wall Street Journal, February 1, 1991, p. B5.
Liptak, Adam, "Justices Extend Benefits to Gay Couples," The New York Times, June 27, 2013, pp. A1, A18
Liptak, Adam, "Justices Step Up Scrutiny of Race in College Entry," The New York Times, June 25, 2013, pp. A1, A12.
Lobosco v. New York Telephone Company/NYNex, 727 N.Y.S.2d 383 (New York Court of Appeals 2001).
Loci, Toni, "Employment discrimination suits get boost," The Miami Herald, June 23, 2006, p. 5A.
Lohr, Steve, "New Microsoft Browser Raises Google's Eyebrow," The Wall Street Journal, May 1, 2006, pp. A1, A16.
Lublin, Joann S., "Harassment Law in U.S. Is Strict, Foreigners Find, "The Wall Street Journal, May 15, 2006, pp. B1, B3.
Lublin, Joanne S., "Retaliation Over Harassment Claims Takes Focus," The Wall Street Journal, April 17, 2006, p. B4.
Liu, Josephine, "Two Roads Diverged in a Yellow Wood: The European Community Stays on the Path to Strict Liability," 27 Fordham International Law Journal, pp. 1940-2006 (2004).
Lazo, Alejandro and Bensinger, Greg (March 27, 2018). Arizona Pulls Uber Tests Off Roads. *Wall Street Journal*, pp. B1, B2.
Leubsdorf, Ben (January 18, 2014). Obama Tries New Tack for Long-Term Jobless, *Wall Street Journal*, p. A5.
Lie, Amy (July 13, 2018). Johnson & Johnson ordered to pay nearly $4.7B to 22 plaintiffs in talcum powder lawsuit. *Fox News*. Retrieved July 13, 2018 from: http://www.foxnews.com/health/2018/07/13/johnson-johnson.
Liptak, Adam (June 4, 2018). In Narrow Decision, Supreme Court Sides with Baker Who Turned Away Gay Couple. *New York Times*. Retrieved June 8, 2018 from: https://www.nytimes.com/2018/06/04/us/politics/supreme-court-sides-with-baker.html.
Liptak, Adam (June 20, 2016). Law Barring Disparaging Trademarks Is Rejected in a Unanimous Decision. *New York Times*, p. A14.
Liptak, Adam (May 15, 2018). Justices Nullify Law That Bans Sports Betting. *New York Times*, pp. A1, A15.
Liptak, Adam (May 22, 2018). Supreme Court upholds workplace arbitration contracts barring class actions. *Miami Herald*, p. 7A.
Mackin, Anna (May 2018). Employee Free Speech. *Texas Bar Journal*, Vol. 81, No. 5, pp. 330=34.
MacLucas, Neil (March 4, 2013). Swiss Vote 'Yes' on Executive-Pay Controls. *Wall Street Journal*, p. B3.
Maniloff, Randy (June 27, 2018). Flying Hot Dogs Make Bad Law. *Wall Street Journal*, p. A15.
McGinley, Laurie (October 3, 2018). FDA seizes documents at Juul as vaping crackdown ramps up. *Sun-Sentinel*, p. 10B.

McGinley, Laurie (October 31, 2018). Marlboro maker Altria to halt sales of flavored e-cigarettes. *Miami Herald*, pp. 13A, 14A.

McGurn, William (September 5, 2017). *Wall Street Journal*, p. A13.

Melin, Anders (February 3, 2018). In study, CEO worker pay ratio is 140-1. *Sun Sentinel*, p. 7B.

Money (November 19, 2014). Smoke pot legally? You can still get fired. Retrieved November 10, 2014 from: http://money.cnn.com/2014/11/09/news/economy/fired-for-smoking-weed/index.html.

M.C. Mirrow, "The Code Napoleon: Buried But Ruling in Latin America," 33 Denver Journal of International Law and Policy, pp. 179- 194 (Spring 2005).

Maganrini, Gary, Jurisdiction Over Foreign-Nation Manufacturers, The Florida Bar Journal, March 1994, pp. 38-45.

Maher, Kris, "Workers Are Filing More Lawsuits Against Employers Over Wages," The Wall Street Journal, June 5, 2006, p. A2.

Maher, Kris, "Lawsuits Say Hospitals Colluded To Maintain Low Pay for Nurses," The Wall Street Journal, June 21, 2006, p. B2.

Mail Fraud Act of 1990, 18 United States Code Annotated, Sections 1341-42 (Thomson/West 2006).

Marine Protection, Research, and Sanctuaries Act, 16 United States Code Annotated Sections 1401-1445, 33 United States Code Annotated Sections 1407 et seq. (Thomson/West 2006).

Martinez, Amy, "Lawsuit claims sunscreen kept us in the dark," The Miami Herald, March 31, 2006, p.p. 1C, 6C.

Mason, W. (2004). Products Liability Law in Japan. Retrieved July 20, 2006, from http://library.findlaw.com/2004/Feb/18/133288.html

Masters, Brook A., "Corporate Crime: Society's Thirst For Justice Grows," The Miami Herald, July 15, 2005, p. 3C.

Mathews, Anna Wilde, "FDA Plan Would Aid Drug Makers In Liability Suits," The Wall Street Journal, January 14, 2006, pp. A1, A4.

May, James R., "Constituting Fundamental Environmental Rights Worldwide," 23 Pace Environmental Law Review, pp. 113-82 (Winter 2005-2006).

McAdams, Terry, Neslund, Nancy, and Neslund, Kristopher, Law, Business, and Society (8th edition), Irwin-McGraw Hill, 2007.

McAdams, Tony, Neslund, Nancy, and Zucker, Kiren Dosarijh (2012). *Law, Business, and Society* (10th edition). New York: McGraw-Hill Irvin.

McCall, William, "Nike settles speech lawsuit," The Miami Herald, September 13, 2003, pp. 1C, 2C.

McCann, J. (2003). Risk *v. Reward: Contemplating the Trade-Offs of Conducting Business in the Middle East.* Retrieved July 17, 2006, from http://www.thunderbird.edu/about_us/publications/tbird_mag/vol56_no_1/index.htm

McClam, Erin, "Stewart Guilty On All Counts," The Miami Herald, March 6, 2004, pp. 1A, 11A.

McClam, Erin, "Waksal gets 87 months, $4.3M fine, The Miami Herald, June 11, 2003, pp. 1C, 4C.

McDonald v. Chicago, 130 S.Ct. 3020 (2010).

McGeehan, Patrick, "Co-creator of musical Grease files lawsuit against cruise lines," The Miami Herald, February 16, 2006, p. C2.

McMorris, Frances A., and Schmitt, Richard B., "Court Takes Broad View of Insider Trading," The Wall Street Journal, October 9, 1996, p. A7.

Mehren, Elizabeth, "Same-sex couples suffer setback," The Miami Herald, March 31, 2006, p. 6A.

Meritor Savings Bank v. Vinson, 477 U.S. 57, 106 S.Ct. 2399 (1986)

Metro-Goldwyn-Mayer Studios v. Grokster, 125 S.Ct. 2764 (2005).

Meyers, Mariyetta, "Russia and the Internet: Russia's Need to Confront and Conquer Trademark Infringement in Domain Names and Elsewhere on the Web," 9 Gonzaga Journal of International Law, pp. 200-35 (2005-2006).

Michaels, Daniel, and Wilke, John R., "U.S., EU Probe Airlines for Price-Fixing on Cargo," The Wall Street Journal, February 15, 2006, p. A3.

Miller v. California, 413 U.S. 15, 93 S.Ct. 2607 (1973).

Miller, Roger LeRoy, and Jentz, Gaylord A., Business Law Today (7th edition), Thomson/West, 2007.

Mills, Pamela J., and Morris, Duane, "Franchising Around the Globe: Relationship, Definition and Regulation." SL037 American Law Institute-American Bar Association 493-520 (2005).

Miranda v. Arizona, 384 U.S. 436, 86 S.Ct 1602 (1966).

Misawa, Mitsuru, "Shareholders' Action and Director's Responsibility in Japan," 24 Penn State International Law Review, pp. 1-57 (2005).

Misey, R. J., Goller, M., & Meldman, R. E. (2016). *Federal taxation: Practice and procedure.* Riverwoods, IL: Walters Kluwer.

Mitchell, Terence R. & Foa, Uriel G. 1969. Diffusion of the effect of cultural training of the leader in the structure of heterocultural task groups. *Australian Journal of Psychology*, 21(1): 31-43.

Mitchener, Brandon, "Germany Says Business Bribes on the Rise," The Wall Street Journal, April 14, 1997, p. A17.

Mizrahi, Rhonda 1995. The relationships between perceived leadership style and leader effectiveness when considering employee cultural diversity. Unpublished D.B.A. Dissertation, School of Business and Entrepreneurship, Nova Southeastern University, Ft. Lauderdale, Florida.

Mollers, Thomas M., "European Directives on Civil Law – Shaping a New German Civil Code," 18 Tulane European and Civil Law Forum, pp. 1-37 (2003).

Moore, S. Craig, "English-Only Rules in the Workplace," Volume 15, Labor Lawyer, pp. 295-308 (American Bar Association 1999).

Morris, Tom & Pavett, Cynthia M. 1992. Management style and productivity in two cultures. *Journal of International Business Studies*, 23(1): 169-179.

Mossberg, Walter S., and Boehret, Katherine, "Using a Fingerprint to Log On to Your PC," The Wall Street Journal, March 15, 2006, pp. D1, D14.

Mujtaba, B. G. (2014). *Capitalism and its Challenges Across Borders (edited)*. Florida: ILEAD Academy.

Mujtaba, B. G. (2014). *Managerial Skills and Practices for Global Leadership*. Florida: ILEAD Academy.

Mujtaba, B. G. (2007). *The Ethics of Management and Leadership in Afghanistan*. 2nd edition. ILEAD Academy, LLC. Davie, Florida USA.

Mujtaba. B.G. and Cavico, F.J. (May 2013). Corporate Social Responsibility and Sustainability Model for Global Firms. *Journal of Leadership, Accountability and Ethics*, Vol. 10, No. 1, pp. 58-76.

Mujtaba. B.G. and Cavico, F.J. (2014). Smoking and Vaping E-Cigarettes: Conjectures, Realities and Implications. *International Journal of Technical Research and Applications*, Vol.1, Number 1, pp. 29-33.

Mujtaba, B. G. and Cavico, F. J. (May 2013). A Review of Employee Health and Wellness Programs in the United States. *Public Policy and Administration Research*, 3(4), 01-15.

Mujtaba, B. G. and Cavico, F. J. (May 2013). Corporate Social Responsibility and Sustainability Model for Global Firms. *Journal of Leadership, Accountability and Ethics*, 10(1), 58-76.

Mujtaba, B. G. and Cavico, F. J. (February 2013). Corporate Social Responsibility and Sustainability Model for Global Firms. *Journal of Leadership, Accountability and Ethics*, 10(1), 58-76.

Mujtaba, B. G., McClelland, B., Cavico, F. J., Williamson, P. (January 2013). A Study of Bribery and Wealth in the ASEAN Community Based on the Corruption Perception Index Scores and GNP per Capita. *International Journal of Management, IT and Engineering*, 3(1), 576-597.

Mujtaba, B. G., Cavico, F. J., and Plangmarn, A. (2012). Corporate Social Responsibility and Globalization. *Proceedings of the 17th International Conference of Asia Pacific Decision Sciences Institute* (APDSI), pp. 89-109. Chaing Mai, Thailand. July 22 - 26, 2012. ISSN: 1539-1191.

Mujtaba, B. G., Tajaddini, R. and Chen, L. Y. (2011). Business Ethics Perceptions of Public and Private Sector Iranians. *Journal of Business Ethics*, 104(3), 433-447.

Mujtaba, B. G., and Cavico, F. J. (2006). *Age Discrimination in Employment: Cross Cultural Comparison and Management Strategies*. BookSurge Publishing. United States.

Muller, Joann, "Ford: The High Cost of Harassment," Business Week, November 15, 1999, pp. 94-96.

Murray, Alan, "High-Tech Titans Unite on Lifting Visa Caps," The Wall Street Journal, June 14, 2006, p. A2.

National Environmental Protection Act, 42 United States Code Annotated Sections 4321-4370 (Thomson/West 2006).

National Labor Relations Act of 1935, 20 United States Code Annotated, Section 151 (Thomson/West 2006).

National Society of Professional Engineers v. United States, 435 U.S. 679, 98 S.Ct. 1355 (1978).

Nation Briefs, "Washington State: Legislature Passes Gay Rights Bill," The Miami Herald, January 26, 2006, p. 3A.

Nevins, Buddy, "Judge says U.S. has jurisdiction over cruise lines," Sun-Sentinel, July 24, 1990, p. 3A.

Newman, Karen L. & Nollen, Stanley D. 1996. Culture and congruence: The fit between management practices and national culture. *Journal of International Business Studies*, 27(4), 753-779.

New York Times Company v. Sullivan, 376 U.S. 254, 84 S.Ct. 710 (1964).

Noise Control Act, 42 United States Code Annotated Section 4901 (Thomson/West 2006).

Norris-LaGuardia Act of 1932, 29 United States Code Annotated, Sections 101-115 (Thomson/West 2006).

Norton, Helen, "Stepping Through Grutter's Open Doors: What the University of Michigan's Affirmative Action Cases Mean for Race-Conscious Government Decision-making," 78 *Temple Law Review* 543 (Fall, 2005).

Nuclear Waste Policy Act, 42 United States Code Annotated Sections 10101 et seq. (Thomson/West 2006).

O'Brien, Gordon E., Fiedler, Fred E., & Hewett, Tom 1970. The effects of programmed culture training upon the performance of volunteer medical teams in Central America. *Human Relations*, 24(3): 209-231.

O'Boyle, Shannon, Perez, Luis, and Wallman, Britany, "Court extends property seizures," *Sun-Sentinel*, June 24, 2005, pp. 1A, 15 A.

O'Connell, Vanessa, "Massachusetts Tries to Halt Sale of 'Sweet' Cigarettes," The Wall Street Journal, May 20, 2004, pp. B1, B2.

O'Connell, Vanessa, and Lloyd, Mary Ellen, "Philip Morris Loses Appeal of Oregon Damage Award," The Wall Street Journal, February 3, 2006, p. B3.

O'Connell, Vanessa, "From the Ashes of Defeat," The Wall Street Journal, August 21, 2006, pp. B1, B4.

O'Connor, Lona, "Drawing the line on sexual harassment can be difficult," Sun-Sentinel, Your Business, April 2, 2004, p. 13.

O'Donnell, Jayne, and Woodyard, Chris, "Toyota's sex-harassment lawsuit could set standard," USA TODAY, August 8, 2006, p. 7B.

Occupational Safety and Health Act of 1970, 29 United States Code Annotated, Sections 553, 651-678 (Thomson/West 2006).

Offerman, Lynn R. & Hellman, Peta. S. 1997. Culture's consequences for leadership behavior: National values in action. *Journal of Cross-Cultural Psychology*, 28(3): 342-351.

Oil Pollution Control Act, 33 United States Code Annotated Sections 2701-2761 (Thomson/west 2006).

Oliveira, Maria Angela Jardim de Santa Cruz, "Recognition and Enforcement of United States Money Judgments in Brazil," 19 New York International Law Review, pp. 1-35 (Winter 2006).

Olkon, Sara, "Widow loses appeal in gun case," The Miami Herald, June 2, 2005, p. 9B.

Oncale v. Sundowner Offshore Services, Inc., 523 U.S. 75, 118 S.Ct. 998 (1998).

Oppenheimer, Andres, "IBM executives deny home office knew of bribes," The Miami Herald, October 1, 2000, pp. 1E, 12E.

Organized Crime Control Act, 18 United States Code Annotated, Sections 1961-1968 (Thomson/West 2006).

Organizations of ITA. Retrieved July 20, 2006, from CHART: http://www.ita.doc.gov/ooms/ITAALL.pdf

Orihuela, Sandra, and Montjoy, Abigal, "The Evolution of Latin America's Sexual Harassment Law: A Look at Mini-skirts and Multinationals in Peru," 30 California Western International Law Journal, pp. 323-344 (2000).

Orol, R. (2006). Public interest groups, government agencies spar over environmental solutions. Retrieved July 20, 2006, from http://www.cec.org/trio/stories/index.cfm?ed=18&ID=198&varlan=english

Oppenheimer, Andre (March 4, 2018), Driverless cars will save many lives – and kill many jobs. *Miami Herald*, In-Depth, The Oppenheimer Report, p. 2.

Paquette, Danielle (November 12, 2017). Firms buy coverage for bad behavior. *Sun-Sentinel*, p. 4D.

Perrone, Matthew (January 31, 2019). Study: E-cigarettes best path to quitting. *Sun-Sentinel*, p. 9a.

Pounds, Marcia Heroux (February 4, 2018), Smoke pot? You might be hired anyhow. *Sun-Sentinel*, pp. 1A, 20A.

Palsgraf v. Long Island Railroad Company, 248 N.Y. 339, 162 N.E. 99 (Court of Appeals of New York 1928).

Panztor, Andy, "Boeing, Lockheed To Gain Approval On Rocket Merger," The Wall Street Journal, March 30, 2006, p. A2.

Parents Involved in Community Schools v. Seattle School District No. 1, 127 S.Ct. 2738 (2007).

"Parliament Passes Law on Foreign Ownership of Property," TURKISH DAILY NEWS, Dec. 30, 2005, from http://www.turkishdailynews.com.tr/article.php?enewsid=32015.

Pasztor, Andy, "Boeing, Lockheed To Gain Approval On Rocket Merger," The Wall Street Journal, March 30, 2006, p. A2.

Patent and Trademark Act, 35 United States Code Section 101.

Pear, Robert, "FDA's hands are full monitoring drug ads," Sun-Sentinel, March 28, 1999, p. 14A.

Pedowitz, Arnold H., "So Long. Now Don't Compete." The New York Times, February 16, 2003, p. 10.

Pentair, Inc. (2006). *Code of Business Conduct and Ethics.* Retrieved July 17, 2006, from http://www.pentair.com/code.html

Peters, Eric, "Getting Sued for Saving Lives," The Wall Street Journal, February 25, 1999, p. A20.

Pohlman R., and Mujtaba, B. G. (2007). The Impact of Sarbanes Oxley's Act on Human Resources Management. Chapter in *The 2007 Pfeiffer Annual: Human Resource Management.* Edited by Robert C. Preziosi.

Powell, Eileen Alt, "Groups plan to oppose AT&T deal," The Miami Herald, March 17, 2006, p. C1.

Power, Stephen, "Daimler Fires Workers Following Its Bribery Probe," The Wall Street Journal, March 7, 2006, p. A3.

Prasad, S. B. 1981. Managers' attitudes in Brazil: Nationals vs. expatriates. *Management International Review,* 21(2), 78-85.

Pregnancy Discrimination Act of 1978, 42 United States Code Annotated, Section 2000e (Thomson/West 2006).

Prengamam, Peter, "Lawsuits target illegal hirings," The Miami Herald, August 23, 2006, p. 3C.

Price Waterhouse. (1996). Doing Business in India. Price Waterhouse: USA.

Price Waterhouse. (1984). Doing Business in Kenya. Price Waterhouse: Kenya.

Private Securities Litigation Reform Act of 1995, 15 United States Code Annotated Sections 77z-2, 78u-5 (Thomson/West 2006).

Professor Dr. Adnan Güriz, *Constitutional Law*, 14 Introduction To Turkish Law, Tugrul Ansay et al. eds. (2005). Kluwer Law International.

Prosser and Keeton on the Law of Torts (West Publishing Company Hornbook Series, 5th ed. 1984).

Public Company Accounting Oversight Board, Standards and Related Rules, American Institute of Certified Public Accountants, Inc., NY (2007).

Pucci, Adriana Noemi, "Arbitration in Brazil: Foreign Investment and the New Brazilian Approach to Arbitration," 60 Dispute Resolution Journal, pp. 82-87 (February-April 2005).

Putti, Joseph M. & Tong, Ang Chin 1992. Effects of leader behavior on subordinate satisfaction in a civil service-Asian context. *Public Personnel Management*, 21(1): 53-63.

Rabin, Roni Caryn (August 22, 2017). Jury Awards $417 Million in Woman's Suit Tying Baby Powder to Ovarian Cancer. *New York Times*, p. B6.

Rapoport, Michael and Michaels, Dave (March 15, 2018). Insider Trade Alleged After Equifax Breach. *Wall Street Journal*, pp. B1, B2.

Review and Outlook (October 27, 2017). A Talcum Powder Tort Blowout. *Wall Street Journal*, p. A14.

Review and Outlook (June 20, 2017). Victory for the Slants. *Wall Street Journal*, p. A16.

Rosenblatt, Joel and Bergen, Mark (September 11. 2017). A Slow-Motion Self-Driving Car Crash, *Businessweek*, pp. 22-23.

Racketeer Influenced and Corrupt Organizations Act, 15 United States Code Annotated, Sections 1961-1968 (Thomson/West 2006).

Reilly, David, and Nassauer, Sarah, "Tip-Line Bind: Follow the Law In the U.S. or EU"? The Wall Street Journal, September 6, 2005, pp. C1, C3.

Reilly, David, and Nassauer, "Tip-Line Bind: Follow the Law In the U.S. or EV"? The Wall Street Journal, September 6, 2005, pp. C1, C3.

Restatement of Contracts, American Law Institute (1932).

Restatement of the Law (Second) of Torts, Section 402A, Torts, American Law Institute Publishers, St. Paul, MN (1977).

Restatement of the Law (Third) of Torts, American Law Institutes Publishers, St. Paul, MN (1997).

Restatement (Second) of Contracts, American Law Institute (1981).
Restatement (Second) of Torts, American Law Institute Publishers, (1977).
Resource Conservation and Recovery Act, 42 United States Code Annotated Sections 6901 et seq. (Thomson/West 2006).
Reuschlein, Harold Gill, and Gregory, William A., Agency and Partnership, West Publishing Company Hornbook Series (1979).
Review and Outlook, "Antitrust Spin Cycle," The Wall Street Journal, March 13, 2006, p. A18.
Review and Outlook, Wall Street Journal, June 24, 2005, p. A12.
Review and Outlook, "Calling All Plaintiffs," The Wall Street Journal, May 2, 2006, p. A16.
Revised Model Business Corporation Act, National Conference of Commissioners on Uniform State Laws (1984).
Revised Uniform Limited Partnership Act, National Conference of Commissioners on Uniform State Laws (1976).
Richey, Warren, "Nurse sues Broward Hospital," Sun-Sentinel, September 17, 1994, p. 3B.
Riegel v. Medtronic, 552 U.S. 312, 128 S.Ct. 999 (2008).
Risk Management Institute. Retrieved June 22, 2006 from http://www.irmi.com/Expert/Articles/2004/Wagner05.aspx
Robinson-Patman Act of 1936, United States Code Annotated, Section 13 (Thomson/West 2006).
Rosen, Gary C., and Reimer, David H., "Covenants Not to Compete: Current Conflicts and Emerging Issues Affecting Enforcement," The Florida Bar Journal, November 1994,
Rosenn, K. S. (2005). *Federalism in Brazil*. Duquesne Law Review. Duquesne University: PA.
Roza, Edni, "Brazilian Banking Institution and Anti-Money Laundering Framework: Compliance with International Standards," 11 Law and Business Review of the Americas, pp. 299-318 (2005).
Rubins, Noah, "The Enforcement and Annulment of International Arbitration Awards in Indonesia," 20 American University International Law Review, pp. 359-401 (2005).
Rusch Factors, Inc. v. Levin, 284 F. Supp. 85 (RI 1968).
Rustad, Michael L., and Paulson, Sandra R., "Monitoring Employee E-mail and Internet Usage: Avoiding the Omniscient Electronic Sweatshop: Insights from Europe," 7 University of Pennsylvania Journal of Labor and Employment Law, pp. 829-904 (2005).
Salemi, Vicki (July 23, 2018). Caution: potential rip-off ahead. *New York Post*, p. 29.
Salman v. United States, U.S. Supreme Court, Slip Opinion No. 15-628 (December 6, 2016).
Savage, David G. (May 27, 2018). How old law used in new case. *Sun-Sentinel*, p. 4D.
Searcy, Dionne (December 29, 2010). U.K. bribes law has firms in a sweat. *Wall Street Journal*, Europe News, p. 6.
Senathip, T., Mujtaba, B., and Cavico, F. (2017). Policy-Making Considerations for Ethical and Sustainable Economic Development. *Economy*, Vol 4, No. 1, pp. 7-14.
Shellenbarger, Sue (September 27, 2017). How to Land a Job That's A 'Stretch." *Wall Street Journal*, p. A11.
Siddiqui, Faiz (March 20, 2018). Uber halts self-driving tests after Arizona death. *Sun-Sentinel*, p. 6A.
Smith, Michelle R. (August 28, 2018). Confidentiality agreements reviewed. *Sun-Sentinel, Money*, pp. 5-6B.
Spector, Mike (August 25, 2015). Car-Safety Debate: Is a Hacked Vehicle Also Defective? *Wall Street Journal*, pp. B1, 4.
Stein, Jeff (March 4, 2018). 'Non-poaching' agreements under scrutiny. *Sun-Sentinel*, Jobs, p. 1.
Steinberg, Matthew (February 4, 2018). Can we talk about NDAs? *Sun-Sentinel*, p. 5D.
Stohr, Greg (December 7, 2016). Court upholds insider trading prosecutions. *Sun Sentinel*, p. 12B.
Sweeeny, Dan, "Rolling Debate," *Sun-Sentinel*, January 23, 2019, p. 17A.
Safe Water Drinking Act, 21 United States Code Annotated Section 349, 42 United States Code Annotated Sections 200, 300f-300j (Thomson/West 2006).
Sanger, David E., "29 Nations Agree to a Bribery Ban," New York Times, May 24, 1997, pp. 1, 34.
Sanmaninatelli, Maria, "Vote is a test for new premier," The Miami Herald, June 26, 2006, p. 16A.
Santiago, Roberto, "Florida workers have scant job protection," The Miami Herald, September 5, 2005, p. 5B.
Sarbanes-Oxley Act of 2002, 28 United States Code Annotated Sections 1658 et seq. (Thomson/West 2006).
Sarbanes-Oxley Act of 2002, 15 United States Code Annotated Section 7201 et. seq. (Thomson/West 2006).
Sarwar, Ghulam (1995). *Islam: Beliefs and Teachings*. Dawat Offset Printers, Delhi-6.
Sasseen, Jane, "White-Collar Crime: Who Does Time"? Business Week, February 6, 2006, pp. 60-61.
Savage, David G., "For blood test, get warrant," Sun-Sentinel, April 18, 2013, p. 10A.
Savage, David G., "High court rejects suits from foreign victims of rights abuse," Sun-Sentinel, April 18, 2013, p. 10A.
Savery, Lawson K. & Swain, Pamela. A. 1985. Leadership style: Differences between expatriates and locals. *Leadership & Organization Development Journal*, 6(4): 8-11.
Scandall, Kara, "Lawsuit Charges U.S. Unite of Japanese Company With Bias," The Wall Street Journal, January 20, 2005, pp. B1, B2.
Schaffer, R., Earle, B., Agusti, F. (2005). *International Law and Its Business Environment* (6th ed.). Ohio: Thomson Corporation.
Schatz, Amy, "FCC Approves Verizon-MCI Pact and SBC's Purchase of AT&T," The Wall Street Journal, November 1, 2005, p. A2.
Schwaneberg, Robert, "Suit over loft bed falls short," The Star-Ledger, August 16, 2006, pp. 13, 16.
Schmidt, Robert, and Howley, Kathleen M., "U.S. sues Realtor trade group," The Miami Herald, September 9, 2005, pp. 1C, 4C.
Schroeder, Michael, and Fuhrmans, Vanessa, "Foreign Firms Trading in U.S. Get a Warning On Deception," The Wall Street Journal, September 3, 2000, pp. A14, A17.
Sciolino, Elaine, "Chirac to withdraw labor law," Sun-Sentinel, April 11, 2006, p. 12A.
Scott, Carole A., "Money Talks: The Influence of Economic Power on the Employment Laws and Policies of the United States and France," 7 San Diego International Law Journal, pp. 341-403 (2006).

Securities Act of 1933, 15 United States Code Annotated Sections 77a-77aa (Thomson/West 2006).

Securities Act of 1934, 15 United States Code Annotated Sections 78a-77mm (Thomson/West 2006).

Securities and Exchange Commission Rule 10b-5, 17 Code of Federal Regulations Section 240.10b-5 (Thomson/West 2006).

SEC v. W.J. Howey Co., 328 U.S. 293, 66 S.Ct.1100 (1946).

Segal, Martin E., "Beneficiaries battle over inheritances," The Miami Herald, Business Monday, May 7, 2007, p. 21.

Selim Levi, Yabancilarin Tasinmaz Mal Edinmeleri, 72, Legal Publishing (2006) (discussing the right of foreigners to purchase irremovable property in Turkey).

Selmer, Jan 1987. Swedish managers' perceptions of Singaporean work-related values. *Asia Pacific Journal of Management*, 5(1), 80-88.

Selmer, Jan 1996. What expatriate managers know about the work values of their subordinates: Swedish executives in Thailand. *Management International Review*, 36 (3): 231-242.

Shah, A. (2006). *Causes of Poverty: Corruption*. Retrieved April 8, 2006, from http://www.globalissues.org/TradeRelated/Poverty/Corruption.asp

Shellenbarger, Sue, "Employers Often Ignore Office Affairs, Leaving Co-Workers in a Difficult Spot," The Wall Street Journal, March 10, 2005, p. D1.

Shellenbarger, Sue, "Supreme Court Takes on How Employers Handle Worker Harassment Complaints," The Wall Street Journal, April 13, 2006, p. D1.

Shellhardt, Timothy D., "Jury to Consider If 'Overqualified' Signals Age Bias," The Wall Street Journal, July 27, 1998, pp. B1, B2.

Shenkar, O. and Luo, Y. (2003). *International Business*. USA: John Wiley & Sons, Inc.

Sherman Act of 1890, 15 United States Code Annotated, Section 1 and Section 2 (Thomson/West 2006).

Sherman, Mark, "Race-based school programs reined in," The Miami Herald, June 29, 2007, pp. 1A, 2A.

Shinsato, Alison Lindsay, "Increasing the Accountability of Transnational Corporations for Environmental Harms: The Petroleum Industry in Nigeria," 4 Northwestern Journal of International Human Rights, pp. 186 et seq. (2005).

Sidel, Robin, "Retailer Named Uncle Sam Claims Piece of Debit Pact," The Wall Street Journal, February 2, 2006, pp. C1, C6.

Smith, Annie Kates, "Trading in false tips exacts a price," U.S. News & World Report, February 5, 2001, p. 40.

Smith, Peter B. 1992. Organizational behavior and national cultures. *British Journal of Management*, 3: 39-51.

Smith, Craig S., "Chinese Discover Product Liability Suits," The Wall Street Journal, November 13, 1997, pp. B1, B13.

Smith, Sasha, "Spying: How Far is Too Far," Fortune Small Business, June 2001, p. 85.

Social Security Act of 1935, 42 United States Code, Sections 301-1397, as amended by the Federal Insurance Contributions Act, 26 United States Code Annotated, Sections 3101-3125 (Thomson/West 2006).

Soloman, Deborah, and Squeo, Anne Marie, "Crackdown Puts Corporations, Executives in New Legal Peril," The Wall Street Journal, June 20, 2005, pp. A1, A10.

Springen, Karen, "Smoking: Light Up and You May Be Let Go," Newsweek, February 7, 2005, p. 9.

Spencer, Jane, "Signing Away Your Right to Sue," The Wall Street Journal, October 1, 2003, pp. D1, D2.

Squeo, Anne Marie, "In Patent Disputes, A Scramble to Prove Ideas Are Old Hat," The Wall Street Journal, January 25, 2006, pp. A1, A8.

State Farm Mutual Automobile Insurance Company v. Campbell, 538 U.S. 408, 123 Sup.Ct.1513 (2003).

State Farm v. Campbell, 538 U.S. 408 (2003).

Standard Oil Company of California v. United States, 337 U.S. 293, 69 S.Ct. 1051 (1949).

Standard Oil Company of New Jersey v. United States, 221 U.S. 1, 31 S.Ct. 502 (1911).

Stop Counterfeiting in Manufactured Goods Act, 18 United States Code Sections 2318-2320, as amended by Public Law No 109-181.

State Oil Company v Khan, 522 U.S. 3, 118 S.Ct. 275 (1997).

Steighorst, Tom, "Magic Embarks on New Voyage," Sun-Sentinel, May 16, 2006, pp.1D, 2D.

Steinback, Robert L., "AT&T agrees to buy BellSouth," The Miami Herald, March 6, 2006, pp.1A, 2A.

Sullivan, Allanna, "Shell Oil, Texaco Agree To Join Units," The Wall Street Journal, March 19, 1997, pp. A3, A6.

Synder v. Phelps, 131 S.Ct. 1207 (2011).

Tamen, Joan Fleischer, "Ruling lets employers avoid court," Sun-Sentinel, March 22, 2001, pp. 1D, 8D.

Tatlow, Didi Kristen (November 7, 2015). China Bends Vow on Using Prisoner Organs for Transplants. *New York Times*, p. A4.

Taylor, Jeffrey, "New Rules Harness Power of Free Markets to Curb Air Pollution," The Wall Street Journal, April 14, 1992, pp. A1, A12.

Taylor, Jeffrey, and Kansas, Dave, "Environmentalists Vie for Right to Pollute," The Wall Street Journal, March 26, 1993, pp. C1, C19.

Telemarketing and Consumer Fraud and Abuse Prevention Act, 15 United States Code Annotated Sections 6101-6108 (Thomson-West 2006)

Telemarketing Sales Rule, 16 Code of Federal Regulations Sections 310.1-310.8 (Thomson-West 2006).

Thomas, Andrew (August 27, 2017). Straight Talk about Success. *Sun Sentinel*, p. 5D.

The Communications Decency Act of 1996, 47 United States Code Annotated Section 230 (Thomson/West 2006).

The International Court of Justice. (2006). Retrieved June 29, 2006, from http://www.icj-cij.org/icjwww/igeneralinformation/inotice.pdf

The World Trade Organization. (2006). *The Panel Process.* Retrieved June 29, 2006, from
    http://www.wto.org/english/thewto_e/whatis_e/tif_e/disp2_e.htm
Torruco-Gamas, J. (2005). *The Presence of the Federal System in Mexico.* Duquesne Law Review. Duquesne University:
    PA.
Toxic Substances Control Act, 15 United States Code Annotated Sections 2601-2692 (Thomson/West 2006).
Tracy, Ryan and Glazer, Emily (February 3, 2018). Fed Orders Wells Fargo to Change Board. *Wall Street Journal*, p. A1.
Trademark Dilution Act, 15 United States Code Annotated Section 1125 (Thomson/West 2006).
Trademark Law Revision Act of 1988 15 United States Code Annotated, 15 United States Code Annotated, Section 1121-
    27 (Thomson/West, 2006).
Triandis, Harry C. 1982. Dimensions of cultural variation as parameters of organizational theories. *International Studies of
    Management and Organization*, 12(4): 139-169.
Triandis, Harry. C. 1993. The Contingency Model in cross-cultural perspective. In M. M. Chemers & R. Ayman, editors,
    Leadership theory and research: Perspectives and direction, San Diego, CA: Academic Press.
Trotter, Greg (December 17, 2017). Corporate responsibility increasing bottom line. *Bergen Record*, p. 6B.
Truth-in-Lending Act of 1968, 15 United States Code Sections 1601-1693.
Tucker, Eric (January 6, 2016). What sets free speech hate crimes, apart? *Sun-Sentinel*, p. 14A.
Tung, Rosalie L. 1982. Selection and training procedures of U.S., European, and Japanese Multinationals. *California
    Management Review*, 25: 51-71.
Turkish Constitution, art. 70, (1924).
Ultramares v. Touche, 174 N.E. 441 (New York Appeals 1931).
U.S. Library of Congress, (2006), Turkey. Retrieved on July 30, 2006, from http://countrystudies.us/turkey/56.htm
Unfair Competition, Florida Statutes Annotated, Section 542.335 (Thomson West, 2006).
Uniform Commercial Code, National Conference of Commissioners on Uniform State Laws (1952).
Uniform Computer Information Transaction Act, National Conference of Commissioners on Uniform State Laws (1999).
Uniform Electronic Transaction Act, National Conference of Commissioners on Uniform State Laws (1999).
Uniform Limited Liability Company Act, National Conference of Commissioners on Uniform State Laws (1995).
Uniform Limited Partnership Act, National Conference of Commissioners on Uniform State Laws (1916).
Uniform Partnership Act, National Conference of Commissioners on Uniform State Laws (1914).
Uniform Trade Secrets Act, Florida Statutes Annotated, Section 688.001-688.009 (Thomson/West, 2006).
United States International Trade Commission: About us. Retrieved July 20, 2006, from
    http://www.usitc.gov/ext_relations/about_itc/index.htm
United States v. Aluminum Company of America, 148 F.2d 416 (2nd Circuit1945).
United States v. American Library Association, 539 U.S. 194, 123 SCt. 2297 (2003).
United States v. Chestman, 447 F.2d 551 (2nd Circuit Court of Appears 1991), Certiorari Denied, 503 U.S. 1004 (1992).
United States v. Colgate & Company, 250 U.S. 300, 39 S.Ct. 465 (1919).
United States v. Lopez, 514 U.S. 549, 115 S.Ct. 1624 (1995).
United States v. Microsoft, 2001 WL 721343 (D.C. Circuit 2001).
United States v. O'Hagen, 521U.S. 642, 117 S.Ct 2199 (1997).
United States v. Sacony-Vacumn Oil Co., 310 U.S. 150, 60 S.Ct. 811 (1940).
United States v. Stevens, 130 S.Ct. 1577 (2010).
UpFront, "Immigration: France's Plan" Pay 'Em To Go Home," Business Week, April 24, 2006, p. 16.
Urbina, Ian, "Ohio Supreme Court Rejects Taking of Homes for Project," The New York Times, July 27, 2006, p. A18.
Valby, Karen (August 27, 2017). For Starbucks, social impact part of success. *Sun-Sentinel.* Jobs p. 1.
Valencia, Nick and Sayers, Devon (July 21, 2017). Florida teens who recorded drowning man will not be charged in his
    death. *CNN.* Retrieved March 19, 2019 from CNN.com.
Vardi, Nathan (November 10, 2009). Founder of Dooney & Bourke Gets Jail in Bribery Case. *Forbes.* Retrieved
    November 11, 2009 from: http://www.forbes.com/2009/11/10/bourke-corrupt-foreign-business-bribery.
View (September 11, 2017). Don't Kick Neo-Nazis Off the Internet. *Bloomberg Businessweek*, p. 14.
Viswanatha, Aruna, Hong, Nicole, and Rothfeld, Michael (May 20, 2016). The Golfer, the Gambler and the Needy
    Executive, *Wall Street Journal*, pp. A1, A5.
Walker, Elaine, "Joe's lament: You can't fight the government," The Miami Herald, June 25, 2003, pp. 1C, 4C.
Walker, Elaine, "Joe's Stone Crab faces another legal setback," The Miami Herald, March 29, 2001, pp. 1C, 3C.
Wallman, Brittany, "Officials: Spring Break, scooters bad combination," *Sun-Sentinel*, January 23, 2019, pp. 1A, 17A.
Watson, C. E. (2016). *Tax procedure and tax fraud in a nutshell.* St. Paul, MN: West Academic Publishing.
Weber, Lauren (May 21, 2015). Overtime Pay for Answering Late-Night Emails? *Wall Street Journal*, pp. B1, B6.
Weaver, Jay, and Brecher, Elinor J., "Smokers' damages, class suit snuffed," The Miami Herald, July 7, 2006, pp. 1A,
    17A.
Wei,S-J. (2001).*Corruption and Globalization.* Retrieved April 2, 2006, from
    http://www.brookings.edu/comm/policybriefs/pb79.htm
Weimer, De'Ann, and Forest, Stephanie Anderson, "Forced Into Arbitration? Not Any More," Business Week, March 16,
    1998, pp. 66-68.
Whistleblower Protection Act of 1989, 5 United States Code Annotated, Section1201 (Thomson/West 2006).
White, James J., and Summers, Robert S., Uniform Commercial Code (2nd edition), West Publishing Company Hornbook
    Series, St Paul, MN (1980);
White, Michael, "GM hit with record judgment," The Miami Herald, July 10, 1999, pp. 1A, 14A.
Wikipedia Encyclopedia, (2006), Turkey. Retrieved on July 30, 2006, from http://en.wikipedia.org/wiki/Turkey

Wikipedia Encyclopedia, (2006), Economy of Turkey. Retrieved on July 30, 2006, from
    http://en.wikipedia.org/wiki/Economy_of_Turkey
Wickard v. Fillburn, 317 U.S. 111, 63 S.Ct. 82 (1942).
Wilke, John R., and Chen, Kathy, "As China's Trade Clout Grows, So Do Price-Fixing Accusations," The Wall Street
    Journal, February 10, 2006, pp. A1, A14.
Wilke, John R., and Clark, Don, "Samsung to Pay Fine for Price-Fixing," The Wall Street Journal, October 14, 2005, pp.
    A3, A6.
Wilke, John R., "Five Paint Firms Are Scrutinized For Price-Fixing," The Wall Street Journal, June 4, 2001, p. A4.
Wilke, John R., "Funeral Industry Is Hit With Casket-Pricing Suit," The Wall Street Journal, May 4, 2005, p.p. D1, D4.
Wilke, John R., "U.S. Court Rules Antitrust Laws Apply to Foreigners," The Wall Street Journal, March 19, 1997, p. A7.
Wilkinson, J. Harvie III, "The Seattle and Louisville Cases: There Is No Other Way," 121 Harvard Law Review 158
    (November, 2007).
Will, George F., "Legal Theft in Norwood," Newsweek, April 24, 2006, p. 94
Will, George, "Profit can rule the day," Sun-Sentinel, June 26, 2005, p. 5H.
Wilson, David L., "Microsoft ruled a monopoly by a federal judge," The Miami Herald, November 6, 1999, pp. 1A, 14A.
Winter, Christopher, "Price-gougers face penalties," Sun-Sentinel, September 14, 1999, pp. 1D, 9D.
Wollenberg, Skip, "Liquor makers drop old ban, will advertise over TV, radio," The Miami Herald, November 8, 1996, p.
    3A.
World Bank, Turkey Country Economic Memorandum: Promoting Sustanined Growth and convergence with the European
    Union, Volume II: Expanded Report, Report No. 33549-TR, 4, February 23, 2006.
Worchel, Stephen & Mitchell, Terence R. 1972. An evaluation of the effectiveness of the culture assimilator in Thailand
    and Greece. *Journal of Applied Psychology*, 56, (6): 472-479.
World Briefing: Europe, "Italy: Voters Reject Constitutional Challenge," The New York Times, June 27, 2006. p. A6.
Wyss, Jim, "Bill limits eminent domain," The Miami Herald, May 3, 2006, p. 3C.
Yamakawa, Ryuichi, "We've Only Just Begun: The Law of Sexual Harassment in Japan," 22 Hastings International and
    Comparative Law Review, pp. 523-558 (1999).
Yanowitz v. L'Oreal, Inc., 131 Cal. Rptr.2d 575 (California Appeals 2003).
Yeh, Rhy-Song 1988. Values of American, Japanese and Taiwanese managers in Taiwan: A test of Hofstede's framework.
    Proceedings, Academy of Management, Anaheim, CAL.
Yeh, Quey-Jen 1995. Leadership, personal traits and job characteristics in R&D organizations: A Taiwanese case.
    Leadership and Organizational Development Journal, 16(6): 16-28.
Yuen, Rachel A., "Beyond the School Yard: Workplace Bullying and Moral Harassment Law in France and Quebec," 38
    Cornell International Law Journal, pp. 625-649 (2005).
Zakah Guide. *IslamiQ Zakah Payment Gateway: Unlocking the Potential of your Charitable Donations.* London.
    IslamiQ.com
Zamora, Stephen, and Cossio, Jose Ramon, "Mexican Constitutionalism After Presidencialismo," 4 International Journal
    of Constitutional Law, pp. 411-437 (2006).
Zeira, Yoram, Harari, Ehud & Nundi, Dafna I. 1975. Some structural and cultural factors in ethnocentric multinational
    corporations and employee morale. *The Journal of Management Studies*, 66-82.
Zoldan, Ari (October 8, 2017). What to look for when hiring college grads. *Sun Sentinel*, Jobs, p. 1.

Appendices

Appendix I - Success

To conclude the 4th edition of their text the authors now wish to offer a few thoughts and suggestions as to how one can be a successful person. First, to be successful, you must set worthy and attainable goals. To be successful, you must set worthy and attainable goals. A person can naturally "aim high" and "think big," yet nevertheless one should start out modestly considering the "facts on the ground" and one's conditions, knowledge-base, and capabilities. If you set smaller and more modest and thus more readily achievable objectives, and then attain them; and next set more achievable goals and attain them too, you will be "on the road" to a very positive, "onwards and upwards" journey to success and fulfillment and sustainable success. Of course, make sure your short-term objectives fit into your long-term goals, and naturally be committed to achieving both short-term objectives and long-term goals. Be persistent in fulfilling your goals; actually be passionate about it; but be patient too.

A critical factor will be to develop and enhance your skills, knowledge, and expertise by a variety of methods, to wit: training, education, continuing education, workshops; seminars, and conferences as well as learning from traditional and online sources of knowledge and information. Of course, and the next point is obvious, make sure you have basic competencies in the "3-Rs": reading, writing, and arithmetic. You should strive to accelerate, expand, and improve your scope and rate of learning and knowledge acquisition beyond the basics.

You should also be prepared to "re-tool" yourself, if necessary, in order to develop a new field of endeavor. Be adaptable. In addition to acquiring and develop "hard skills" you should develop the "soft skills," such as speaking in public and communicating on a personal level with people. Yet what if a person is shy or diffident? Well, then, one should look for opportunities to speak publicly and to communicate and then force oneself to become active and engages. It is important to be a good communicator (ideally in more than one language). You have and be able to demonstrate strong collaboration skills and thus be able and willing to collaborate to achieve organizational strategies and goals.

One should always be polite and have a positive attitude as well as a good work ethic; and you must always act in an honest and ethical manner. Having a reputation for integrity is a critical factor to one's success.

You must be prepared to challenge conventional beliefs and perceived "truths" and be prepared to engage in critical thinking and analysis. Yet you should possess common sense as well as a "healthy dose" of realism. For example, find out what you like to do and do well. Yet note that you do not have to be good in everything; as such, realize that others will be able to assist you in weak areas. Conversely, it is also important to find out what you do *not* like to do and do *not* do well. And do not worry if you are not sure what direction to take; be persistent and you will figure it out. Recall the old maxim: "There is a person for every job, and a job for every person." So, if necessary, start part-time, be a temporary or entry-level employee, but all the time you will acquire knowledge, skills, and experience, and thus will be able to advance to full-time as well as to expand your knowledge and skills base.

Learn by doing and learn from your mistakes; and be able and willing to admit your mistakes. Admit that you may need to be educated and trained. Consequently, "own" your errors and then be willing and able to move forward from those miscues. The idea is to take responsibility for your actions, which is what trustworthy people and leaders do.

Naturally, look for role models; learn from successful people; seek their counsel; and learn from mentors and coaches. Accordingly, seek out the counsel and advice of these people (and do not be shy about it, yet don't be a "pain" either). Look for a leader who nurtures talent, who is willing to spend time with you, take an interest in you, and answer the questions you ask in an honest fashion. Look for someone who will "take a chance on you."

The object is for you to achieve excellence; to become very good, and to be recognized as being very good, at something; and to be recognized as a high-achiever. You also want to be regarded as a "go-to" person in your firm and organization; that is, you can solve problems, even if they technically are not in your job description, or you know the person who can solve someone's problems. Strive to reduce the boss' workload as well as stress.

You must develop your leadership skills. As such, strive to be the leader of a team, department, division, and ultimately an organization. And in your role as a leader you should provide people with education, training, and skills for them (and concomitantly you) to be successful. Be a teacher of others; empower competent people; and as they rise you and the company or organization shall rise too. Look for hidden and untapped potential in employees and others and seek to draw them out into jobs or tasks you feel they would be good. Yet note that at times it can be a "hard sell" to push people into jobs or tasks they feel they are not qualified for or able to do. Consequently, you may have to encourage and motivate people and provide them with a sense of safety and security. Always be fair-minded and impartial in your dealings with people. The objective is to create and develop relationships where both parties receive value. Overall, you must create a culture of respect, mutual support, openness, and success; and as such you should strive to establish a nurturing and caring culture and one of fun too. Value diversity among people and the fresh ideas, opinions, and perspectives that diversity brings, particularly in the workplace.

Please note that there is nothing wrong with self-interest, making money, and being successful financially, even very successful. There is, the authors emphasize, no substitute for the traditional "work ethic and "hard work," which will pay off in long-run. One should always attempt to save money; and for a young person starting the authors suggest 10% of one's earnings in case of a "rainy day. It is best to prepare a budget; keep track of expenses; and keenly know difference between mere "wants" and "needs."

Yet in addition to all the hard work you also should have a "family life," which will bring the proper balance to your life. The idea is to achieve a "work-life" balance and allow yourself time to relax, reenergize, reset, and have quality time with your family and friends. This balance will afford you the opportunity to build relationships with people, get counsel and "feedback" – from family, friends, co-workers, clients, and customers. And listen carefully to different points of view and weigh and measure opposing opinions.

It is critical for you to be successful, and ultimately at a high level, to be responsible, reliable, and dependable. It is also critical for you to develop a well-deserved reputation for integrity, ethics, honesty, and trust. You must demonstrate respect for people. The idea is for you to respect all and to be respected by all. Moreover, you should get engaged in the community and charitable and civic affairs; be socially and environmentally responsibility (that is be "sustainable"; be a volunteer; and help others financially and with your time and effort. Remember the old adage: "You can do well by doing good."

Look and act in a professional manner; and be very careful of social media usage, especially for young people. Employers will not take a chance on someone with a poor, embarrassing, or incriminating reputation.

Have a positive attitude; be optimistic; have a "pleasant personality." Also, be forgiving and compassionate. Be modest and humble and avoid arrogance and self-righteousness. As such, be willing to share credit for successes. Similarly, avoid negativity and negative people; associate yourself with positive people; and do not be negative with yourself; do not admonish yourself; do not upbraid yourself; and do not dwell on the past. Overcome any rejection, which is inevitable in life; do not take rejection personally. Therefore, learn from the past and move on – onwards and upwards. And, and this point seems very basic, but today it must be emphasized especially for young people: Do not do drugs! No one is going to hire you or keep you for long if you do drugs!

To be successful at some point you will have to take some chances and risks; and do so but make intelligent choices. Look for opportunities; take advantage of opportunities; and if need be you can try to create opportunities where you can apply and demonstrate your knowledge, skills, and capabilities. As such, be entrepreneurial, innovative, nimble, and adaptable; have a strategy for success and the tactics to achieve that strategy. Execute your strategy for success; have "to-do" lists (short-term and long-); have goals (again short-term and long-) and objectives; then achieve them, and, as pointed out previously, set more goals and objectives and achieve them, and so-forth-and-so-on. To be a successful person you need to take a long-term perspective as well as to be willing to undergo some short-term sacrifice and expense to maximize your own greater, long-term good. You also in today's interrelated economy and global society for you to be aware of globalization and to be culturally mature and competent.

The idea is for you to be a "shaper" and not a mere "reactor"; and thus for you to be willing and able to spot and to respond to new circumstances. Also, be aware of your "blind-spots," that is, weak areas that you need to develop; but also be cognizant of "hidden-strengths," that is, the knowledge, talents, skills, and capabilities that you are not using or perhaps using but not adequately publicizing.

Naturally, it helps to have "good luck" and good fortune, for as Machiavelli said: "For the Goddess Fortuna to smile on you." Yet, the authors submit you can "make your own luck" by persistence and perseverance, empowering yourself, being competitive, taking advantage of opportunities, and making opportunities. As Machiavelli also said: "Fortune favors the young for the young are bold." That is, the "young" (including the "young at heart") will take more risks (perhaps because they have less or little to lose). Moreover, the authors also submit that the harder you work the luckier you will be. Moreover, remember that a talented person is a lucky person. It also helps to be in U.S., which despite all its problems and challenges is still the "land of opportunity"! So, to conclude this discussion of your personal success the authors emphatically state that if you take heed of the authors' advice there is a great future for you out there! Your success will be one of greatest reasons for our satisfaction and happiness.

-   *Frank and Bahaudin*

Appendix II – Sample Text-Based Term Paper Assignment

Paper Format Suggestions

Legal, Ethical, Social Responsibility, and Sustainability Analysis
Format, Requirements, and Grading Criteria

Title to Paper – A Legal, Ethical, Social Responsibility, and Sustainability Analysis
of _____

Official Cover Page with Honor Code and Author Certification Statements

I. *Introduction*

- Statement of purposes of paper and major analytical sections
- State topic to be examined and why important
- Topic must be a current controversy involving business directly or indirectly
- Provide adequate background information about topic

II. *Legal Analysis*

A. Introduction
- Purpose of this section of the paper
- Statement of laws to be used
- Laws can be constitutional laws, statutes, case law, administrative rules and regulations, executive orders, and/or international treaties
- Laws can be U.S. laws (federal, state, and/or local) or laws from foreign jurisdictions

B. Statement of Legal Principles
- State the legal principles that will be governing your topic

C. Application of Legal Principles to Topic
- Apply the legal principles to your topic to determine in a well-reasoned manner the legality or illegality of topic

D. Legal Conclusion
- Statement of legal conclusion
- Note: If there already is a legal conclusion by a court or other government tribunal, state whether you agree or disagree with the government's legal conclusion based on the law.
- Transition sentence to ethics section.

III. Ethical Analysis

A. Introduction
   - Purpose of this section of paper
   - Statement of ethical theory to be used
   - Ethical theory can come from text, professor's videos, or other academic sources

B. Statement of Ethical Principles from an Ethical Theory
   - State the ethical principles to be used to determine the morality of your topic

C. Application of Ethical Principles to Topic
   - Apply the ethical principles to your topic to determine in a well-reasoned manner the morality or immorality of the topic

D. Moral Conclusion
   - Statement of moral conclusion
   - Transition sentence to social responsibility and sustainability section

IV. Social Responsibility and Sustainability Analysis

A. Introduction
   - Purposes of this section of the paper

B. Definitions of "Social Responsibility" and "Sustainability"
   - Definition of social responsibility
   - Definition of sustainability
   - Definitions can come from text, other academic sources, or company websites

C. Application of Definitions to Topic
   - Is company, firm, or organization acting in a socially responsible manner? Why or why not?
   - Is company, firm, or organization acting in a "sustainable" manner? Why or why not?
   - Note: Even if company, firm, or organization is acting in a socially responsible and sustainable manner provide at least two suggestions of what else the entity could be doing in these areas.

V. Conclusion

- Restatement of major conclusions
- Make any predictions you deem appropriate as to possible legal as well as practical consequences.
- State any personal feelings or beliefs in the matter.
- Provide what you believe is a just solution.

Bibliography

Requirements

- Paper topic must be approved by professor
- Groups (optional), up to three students, must be approved by professor
- Suggested length of paper is approximately 10-20 pages depending on topic or if group effort
- Paper must be double-spaced and in Word processing format
- APA style required for sources, citations, quotes

Grading Criteria

- Conformity of paper to required format
- Clarity of writing style
- Conformity to APA
- Grammar, spelling, and punctuation
- Ability to discern issues
- Depth of knowledge, that is, degree of substance to statements of principles, definition of terms, and recommendations
- Critical thinking and level of reasoning, that is, the ability to reason from principles to logical conclusions
- Integration of paper, especially if group effort

Biographies

Frank J. Cavico is a Professor Emeritus of Business Law and Ethics at the H. Wayne Huizenga College of Business and Entrepreneurship of Nova Southeastern University. He was the principal creator of the school's required MBA law and ethics course: "The Values of Legality, Morality, and Social Responsibility in Business"; and he presently serves as Key Professor for that course. In 2000, he was awarded the Excellence in Teaching Award by the Huizenga School. In 2006, he was honored as Professor of the Year by the Huizenga School; and in 2012 he received the Faculty Member of the Year Award from the Huizenga School. His fine record is manifested by numerous research and writing endeavors, principally law review and management journal articles in the broad sectors of business law and ethics as well as a business ethics textbook, *Business Ethics: Transcending Requirements through Moral Leadership*, co-authored with Dr. Bahaudin G. Mujtaba. He also is co-author, along with Dr. Mujtaba, of the books *Age Discrimination in Employment* and *Legal Challenges for the Global Manager and Entrepreneur*. Professor Cavico holds a J.D. degree from St. Mary's University School of Law and a B.A. from Gettysburg College. He also possesses a Master of Laws degree from the University of San Diego School of Law and a Master's degree in Political Science from Drew University. Professor Cavico is licensed to practice law in the states of Florida and Texas. He has worked as a federal government regulatory attorney and as counsel for a labor union; and has practiced general civil law and immigration law in South Florida.

Bahaudin G. Mujtaba is a full Professor of Management with the H. Wayne Huizenga College of Business and Entrepreneurship at Nova Southeastern University (NSU). Bahaudin has worked as an internal consultant, trainer, and teacher in retail management as well as in the human resources aspect of the corporate arena. Dr. Mujtaba also worked in retail management for 16 years. He was awarded the prestigious Faculty of the Year Award for the 2011 and 2005 Academic Years at the School of Business and Entrepreneurship of NSU. He attended Habibia High School in Afghanistan, Fort Myers High School in the USA, Edison Community College, University of Central Florida, Nova University, and Nova Southeastern University in the United States. His doctorate degree is in Management, and he has two post-doctorate specialties: Human Resource Management and International Management. Bahaudin is author and co-author of twenty books and three hundred academic as well as professional journal articles. During the past thirty years he has had the pleasure of working in the United States, Brazil, Bahamas, China, Vietnam, India, Pakistan, Afghanistan, St. Lucia, Grenada, Myanmar, Thailand, and Jamaica. He was born in Khoshie of Logar province, and raised in Kabul, Afghanistan. Currently, he lives in Fort Lauderdale, Florida. He can be reached at: mujtaba@nova.edu.

Contributor Biographies

1. *Dr. Donald L. Ariail*, a Certified Public Accountant, is Assistant Professor of Accounting at Texas A&M University - Kingsville, System Center San Antonio. He has published numerous articles on taxation and has presented papers at both national and international conferences. He also was recipient of the 2006 KPMG Outstanding dissertation Award presented by the Gender Issues and Worklife Balance Section of the American Accounting Association. Prior to entering academia in 2005, he was the owner of a successful local CPA practice in Atlanta, Georgia, and had worked in the Public Accounting profession since 1972. He is the holder of a doctorate degree in accounting from the H. Wayne Huizenga School of Business and Entrepreneurship of Nova Southeastern University.

2. *Dr. John Wayne Falbey* is a faculty member and Program Chair for Real Estate Development at the H. Wayne Huizenga School of Business and Entrepreneurship, Nova Southeastern University; He is a member of the Florida and Colorado Bar Associations. Dr. Falbey also is Managing Member and President of The Falbey Group, LLC, a real estate development firm in Florida. He has been actively engaged in real estate development for more than thirty years.

3. *Stephanie C. Ferrari*, *MBA*, is a Web Developer at the H. Wayne Huizenga School of Business and Entrepreneurship of Nova Southeastern University. She received her Bachelor of Science degree in Computer Science and completed her Master of Business Administration degree at Nova Southeastern University. Stephanie currently teaches Online Communications and Internet Competency for the

Huizenga School's doctoral programs. She and her husband, Silvano Ferrari, also own and manage a Precision Tune Auto Care franchise in Lauderhill, Florida.

4. ***Dr. Stephen C. Muffler*** is a full-time attorney in private practice handling corporate civil litigation and business transactions in the tri-county area of South Florida. He has been a member of the Florida Bar for over 13 years. He graduated with a Juris Doctorate and was conferred a second law degree in international law (LL.M.-Master of International Laws). He is a member of the Florida Bar's International Law Section. Dr. Muffler is the Chairman of the Fort Lauderdale Citizens Police Review Board which investigates complaints against Fort Lauderdale Police Officers and reviews the Fort Lauderdale Police's Internal Affairs Department Findings and Reports. Dr. Muffler is an adjunct professor teaching MBA students their required basic corporate law and ethics class for Nova Southeastern University. Dr. Muffler's publications include articles published in legal journals concerning the Foreign Corrupt Practices Act and the influences of the Russian Mafia on international business.

5. ***Dr. Miguel A. Orta***, a native of Cuba, has been teaching Import/Export Management, Comparative Management and International Negotiations, International Legal Environment, and Law, Ethics, and Society for Nova Southeastern University. Miguel has a BA in Political Science and Mass Communications from Florida State University, A Juris Doctor from Duke University and a Masters in International Business from Nova Southeastern University. As founder of American Strategic Consultants, he has conducted market research, feasibility studies, and business planning for the development of international enterprises in Venezuela, Colombia, Argentina, Brazil, Ecuador, Mexico, and Panama. He is presently involved in strategic planning for Chinese, Indian, Malaysian, and Thai companies entering the United States and Latin American markets. During the 1990's, he served as a special business and trade consultant to Fernando Color de Mello, the first democratically elected president in Brazil after the fall of the military dictatorship.

6. ***Nicolas-Michel Polito***, MSA, MBA, is a graduate of Fairleigh Dickinson University's MS in accounting program. In addition, he holds an MBA in finance from Nova Southeastern University in Florida, a Bachelor's degree from Rutgers University, and also a degree from the Culinary Institute of America in Hyde Park, New York. Nicolas completed and passed all four parts of the CPA exam and is working at Bederson LLP, a local accounting firm. Nicolas began teaching accounting as an adjunct professor at Fairleigh Dickinson University's in 2019. Nicolas provided research assistance for many professors for their peer review articles, as well as for the AACSB accreditation review. Over his academic career, Nicolas has been recognized by several academic honor societies and co-authored two publications.

7. ***Dr. Marissa Samuel*** teaches business law and ethics courses at the H. Wayne Huizenga School of Business and Entrepreneurship of Nova Southeastern University. In addition to teaching, Marissa practices law with a focus on small business clients. Marissa possesses a J.D. degree from Columbia University School of Law, an M.B.A from Columbia Business School, and a B.S. in Industrial & Labor Relations from Cornell University. Prior to teaching, Marissa practiced corporate law at McDermott, Will & Emery. Marissa's research interests include labor and employment law, human resource management, and the economic improvement of developing countries.

8. ***Dr. Belay Seyoum*** is professor of International Business at the H. Wayne Huizenga School of Business, Nova Southeastern University, Fort Lauderdale, Florida, where he teaches a variety of courses in international business. He is a recipient of the Fulbright Scholar Award for 2007.

Index Table

CPSIA information can be obtained
at www.ICGtesting.com
Printed in the USA
BVHW041352140121
597858BV00004B/272